FRAMEWORK HOUSES

BERND & HILLA BECHER

FRAMEWORK HOUSES
OF THE SIEGEN INDUSTRIAL REGION

THE MIT PRESS
CAMBRIDGE, MASSACHUSETTS
LONDON, ENGLAND

Library of Congress Cataloging-in-Publication Data

Becher, Bernd, 1931–
Framework houses; of the Siegen industrial region / Bernd and Hilla Becher.
p. cm.
Includes index.
ISBN 0-262-02499-3 (hc: alk. paper)
1. Wooden-frame houses—Germany—Siegen Region—Pictorial works. I. Becher, Hilla.
II. Title.

TH4809.G3 B43 2001
728'.37'0943551—dc21

00-064599

Printed in Germany by Passavia, Passau
A Schirmer/Mosel Production

CONTENTS

PREFACE

The Siegen industrial region is located some sixty miles east of Cologne, between Sauerland and Westerwald. It is one of the oldest iron-producing regions of Europe, since iron ore was already being extracted and smelted there in prehistoric times.

During the middle ages Siegen iron products were sold throughout Europe because of their high quality and also because guilds regulated production and distribution.

In the seventeenth and eighteenth century the Siegen district was one of the last iron ore areas that, owing to self imposed restrictions, still had enough forest preserves to continue production charcoal for iron smelting. The constantly rising demand for charcoal had led to a peculiar form of economy unique to this area: the *Haubergswirtschaft* (mountain lumbering); the wood was communally rationed. The forest was divided into eighteen equal parts of which only the oldest was cut each year, an eighteen-year-old trunk being the proper size for charcoal-making. For this reason there was never any acute lack, but the quantity of iron production was strictly limited. To smelt one ton of iron ore, four tons of charcoal were necessary; only as much iron could be smelted as there was charcoal. By this limitation the semi-agricultural structure of the region was preserved until the late nineteenth century.

Efficient use of the forest took various forms: treetrunks became charcoal; a tanning substance was extracted from the bark and provided the basis for a prosperous leather industry; branches were used for heating and bread-baking. Root stocks were left to continue growing. During the first two years of new growth, rye and buckwheat were planted in the spaces between the shoots. Later, when the young trees were strong enough, cattle were driven into the forest to graze. By this exceptional form of husbandry the Siegen area maintained its monopoly for a long period of time, while other iron regions depleted their forests.

This advantageous situation finally disintegrated when, after long experiments in England, a method was found to transform coal into coke, which was used instead of charcoal for iron smelting. The possibility of producing almost unlimited quantities of iron provoked a chain reaction of inventions and improvements. These primarily served new mining and steel-making methods, but they also influenced other sectors of industry. As soon as iron was available in large quantities, new and existing ideas could be implemented.

In Siegen the transition from charcoal to coke was made comparatively late. It depended on the completion of the railroad in 1861, which supplied coke from the Ruhr district. The precondition for quick development already existed, however: a skilled population, high quality iron ore deposits, and deep mines capable of expansion. The economy no longer remained constant and a boom took place. Many immigrants, primarily from the surrounding farming areas of Westerwald, Wittgenstein, and Hessen came to work in the mines or in the blastfurnace plants. Most of them became permanent settlers. All aspects of life in the district showed increasing energy. Demand for housing led to a booming construction and necessitated a new type of functional framework house that could be erected quickly and inexpensively.

The ideal framework structure had developed from a law passed in 1790, one hundred years earlier, intended to save wood for iron production by preventing its excessive use for house-building. The law prescribed the amount of lumber structurally required and forbade construction elements serving only ornamental purposes. It also specified the maximum strength for beams, sills, cornerposts, and studs. Horizontal braces between the studs were to be dispensed with and diagonal braces were no longer allowed to join the vertical posts and thus weaken them. Over the centuries the traditional framework house was elaborated by rich ornamental additions, but once this law took effect, the use of timber was reduced to basic structural elements. A functional framework, combined with neo-classical proportions, determined the new type of house, but was also applied to other buildings: barns, churches, shops, inns, schools, factories, and mine buildings.

At the turn of the century, a single family dwelling cost about 3500 marks (833 dollars). Scaffolding was erected in one or two days, a two-floor dwelling took three days.

The timbers were prepared by the carpenters in their workshops. The parts were laid out on the floor, fitted to one another and numbered. Often, the carpenters cut the lumber during the winter for the homes to be erected in the summer. Apart from the services of carpenters, cabinetmakers and roofers, the owner did much of the work himself. Thus most miners and iron workers could afford their own homes – an unusual circumstance at that time in Europe.

To fill in the sustaining walls, builders used pumice blocks transported from the volcanic region of the Neuwieder Becken near Koblenz.

Slating the outside walls was desirable because it provides insulation against humidity and eliminated periodic painting. But since it was expensive, slating was often restricted to the waterside or just the gable, which was difficult to paint because of its height. Slating the street facade was more for show – it gave the house an urban appearance and emphasized the neoclassical proportions.

Also important for the neo-classical look of the streetside was the *Kniestock* (half a story under the roof) built in most houses after 1870, which produced a wider angle of the roof and a higher space above the upper windows. An additional advantage was that the *Kniestock* provided a habitable room, the lowest part of which could accommodate a bid. For this reason, in many of the older houses the roof was lifted.

Most of the houses shown in this book were built between 1870 and 1914, primarily in highly industrialized communities such as Kreuztal, Geisweid, Dahlbruch, Weidenau, Siegen, Eiserfeld, Eisern, Niederscheldern, Niederschelderhütte, Gosenbach, Wehbach, Herdorf, Neunkirchen, and Salchendorf.

INDEX

The following facts were gathered by questioning the inhabitants.

Street	Nr.	Year	Name of Owner	Profession	Plate Nr.
ACHENBACH					
Achenbacher Str.	298	1892	Heinrich Klinkert	joiner	148, 257
ALLENBACH					
Sieben Eichen	1	1890	Gemeinde Allenbach		167
ALLENDORF					
Haigerer Str.	2	ca. 1910			4, 309
Hauptstr.	11	ca. 1850			59
Holzhäuser Str.	25	1906	Emil Müll	miner	1
BIRKEN					
Hauptstr.	3	1905	Robert Utsch	turner	105, 255, 279
Löhrstr.	14	ca. 1890	Hermann Schneider	bookbinder	18
BIRLENBACH					
Abendröthe	3	1900	Friedrich Eckhardt	model-maker	30, 122, 217, 276
BRACHBACH					
Siegstr.	11	1914	Ferdinand Utsch	miner	136
BÜRBACH					
Obere Dorfstr.	21	ca. 1820	Hof	baker	82, 301
BURBACH					
Haiger Weg	3	1906	Hermann Brücher	miner	109
Haiger Weg	7	1905	Gustav Pusch	painter	100

Street	Nr.	Year	Name of Owner	Profession	Plate Nr.
BÜSCHERGRUND					
Büscherstr.	2	1902	Jacob Irle	farmer	207
Büscherstr.	9	ca. 1800			77
Mühlenbergstr.	1	ca. 1890	August Klein	blacksmith	2
Olper Str.	15	ca. 1900	Hermann F. Irle	joiner	47, 293
Olper Str.	19	1865	Hermann Waffenschmied	blacksmith	5, 305
Siegener Str.	155	1878	Heinrich Seidel	miller	67
Siegener Str.	167	1899	Heinrich Bäumer	tanner	24, 284
Triftstr.	19	1898	Wwe. Friedrich Bäumer		25
Triftstr.	48	1901	Friedrich Achenbach	waggoner	200, 273
Triftstr.	58	1880	Leimfabrik Karl Reppel		64, 65, 290
Wendinger Str.	3	ca. 1865	Eberhard Ising	tanner	71
Wendinger Str.	4	1912	Ev. Glaubensvereinigung Michel & Co.		143
Wendinger Str.	8	1911	Heinrich Quast	farmer	106
DAHLBRUCH					
Bahnhofstr.	8	1905	Wilhelm Spies	metal worker	132
Hillnhütter Str.	61	1904	Wilhelm Feldmann	metal-worker	121
Hillnhütter Str.	62	1906	Robert Setzer	assembler	153, 170, 254, 278
DEUTZ					
Marburger Str.	27	1905	Friedrich Dietermann	blacksmith	133
DREIS-TIEFENBACH					
Setzer Weg	19	1906	Karl Hellmann		131
Siegstr.	150	1876	Martin Flender	shoemaker	87
EISERFELD					
Bahnhofstr.	21	ca. 1870	Friedrich Münker	baker	86
Bahnhofstr.	90	ca. 1880	Grube Gilberg		120
Bahnhofstr.	155	ca. 1900			212, 233, 296
Eisernstr.	70	ca. 1850	Friedrich Cronrath	baker	68
Eisernstr.	114	1873	Leonhard Boller	miner	55
Eisernstr.	117	1873	Johannes Hoffmann	steelworker	177
Eisernstr.	119	1874	Carl Scholl	steelworker	185
Eisernstr.	120	ca. 1875			184
Eisernstr.	121	ca. 1875			183
Eisernstr.	122	1874			156, 188
Eisernstr.	130	1900			174
Eisernstr.	158	1897	Joh. Heinrich Kretzer	miner	201, 262
Freiengründerstr.	4	1910	Otto Ohrendorf	carrier	190
Freiengründerstr.	21	1896	Friedrich Steffe	mining ingeneer	95, 194, 263, 312

Street	Nr.	Year	Name of Owner	Profession	Plate Nr.
Freiengründerstr.	104	1898	Heinrich Giesler	building contractor	151
Freiengründerstr.	112	1898	Friedrich Höfer	blacksmith	96
Grabettstr.	87	1911	Wilhelm Gerhards	machinist	58
Hüttenstr.	6	1885	Wilhelm Schneider	miner	186
Hüttenstr.	43	1913	Wilhelm Maas	miner	221
Lindenstr.	69	1903	Otto Hees	miner	204, 271, 272
Querstr.	2	1901	Simon Steiner	miner	99, 163, 240
Siegtalstr.	10	1872	Louis Thomas		119
Siegtalstr.	36	1898	Friedrich Vetter	steelworker	179, 225, 244, 286
Siegtalstr.	40	1883	Walzwerk Steinseifer		117, 211, 313
Talsbachstr.	11	ca. 1880	Friedrich Meyer		44
EISERN					
Eiserntalstr.	65	ca. 1910	Gustav Neef	miner	169
Eiserntalstr.	83	1869	Gebr. Schmidt		32
Eiserntalstr.	116	1912	Tillman Panthöfer	miner	223
Eiserntalstr.	120	1878	Tillman Stolz	post-office manager	46
Eiserntalstr.	138	1902	Alfred Krämer	machinist	197, 222, 247
Eiserntalstr.	142	1908	Friedrich Hofmann	miner	50, 124
Eiserntalstr.	150	1872	Heinrich Schneider	steelworker	281
In der Bitze	3	ca. 1900	Engelhard Panthöfer	steelworker	48, 294
Schulstr.	24	1906/07	Albert Roth	miner	134, 251
Wiesenstr.	2	1907	Christian Schwier	school headmaster	157
FLAMMERSBACH					
Feldstr.	5	ca. 1890	Ferdinand Scheld	saw-mill worker	149, 232
Hauptstr.	36	ca. 1600	Adolf Wehn	miner	80, 303
FREUDENBERG					
Am Silberstern	4	1902	Friedrich Ohrendorf	locksmith	113, 250
Bahnhofstr.	54	1896	Julius Strüder	clockmaker	115
Friedenshortstr.	9	1901	Heinrich Haak	mine-master	238
Kölner Str.	4	ca. 1860			22
Kölner Str.	4A	ca. 1880			23
Krottorfer Str.	43	1896	Friedrich Wirth	brick-layer	16
Krottorfer Str.	48	1911	Robert Meyer	baker	114
Krottorfer Str.	53	1906	Karl Reppel	merchant	203
Krottorfer Str.	57	1890	Karl Steinseifer	railway employee	126
Oststr.	10	1887	Albert R. Siebel	communal treasurer	61, 299
Oststr.	16	ca. 1880	Gemeinde Freudenberg		54, 56, 147, 274
FREUSBURG					
Bogenstr.	8	ca. 1680	Wilhelm Zöller	miner	83, 302

Street	Nr.	Year	Name of Owner	Profession	Plate Nr.
GEISWEID					
Birlenbacherstr.	92	1909	Jos. Hamacher	assembler	187
Geisweiderstr.	127	1883	Wwe. Henriette Weigel		220
Marktstr.	32	1904	Friedrich Speck	merchant	189, 226
Philipstr.	2	1905	August Fick	carpenter	224
GILSBACH					
Hambachwaldstr.	9	1905	Martin Wissenbach	miner	41, 292
Wilnsdorferstr.	26	1905	Reinhard Scholl	miner	35, 300
Wilnsdorferstr.	65	1926	Friedrich Türk	miner	6, 298
GOSENBACH					
Auf der Hütte	45	1878	Bänfer	steelworker	19, 116, 146, 245, 304
Maiweg	23	1903	Hermann Fries	miner	28, 140, 285
Kampenstr.	42	1897	Friedrich Bäumer	baker	27
Kampenstr.	44	1898	Jakob Falk	miner	45
Siegener Str.	6	1908	Karl Künkler	blacksmith	249
Siegener Str.	10	1900	Eduard Hartmann	miner	248
Siegener Str.	67	1880	E. Neumann	miner	162, 236, 288
Siegener Str.	104	1901	Leopold Georg	miner	191
GRISSENBACH					
Siegtalstr.	50	1903	Friedrich Schöler	turner	49
HAIGER					
Obertor	38	ca. 1900			158
HAIGER-DILLBRECHT					
Schwarzbachstr.	57B	ca. 1830	Wilhelm Fuhr	miner	74
HAIGER-SEELBACH					
Tränkestr.	3	1914			7, 26, 141, 275
HARBACH					
Haus Nr.	3	ca. 1750	Wilhelm Buchen	miner	78
HERDORF					
Schneiderstr.	56	1901	Heinrich Schneider	slater	130
HILCHENBACH					
Bruchstr.	70	ca. 1890	Friedrich Dreisbach	tanner	123
Ferndorfstr.	7	1897	Schwarz	tailor	91
Kirchplatz	3	1886	Ev. Kirchengemeinde		142

Street	Nr.	Year	Name of Owner	Profession	Plate Nr.
KAAN MARIENBORN					
Hauptstr.	25	1899	Wilhelm Buch	metal worker	196, 265
Schloßblick	17	1914	August Meinhardt	tanner	51, 90, 178, 252, 267, 277
KREDENBACH					
Dr.-Stelbrink-Str.	3	1906	Völkel	locksmith	202
KREUZTAL					
Heesstr.	31	1875			20
MAUSBACH					
Mausbacher Str.	60	1901	Wilhelm Ohrendorf	farmer	33
MUDERSBACH					
Hohlweg	5	1880	Ferdinand Utsch	farmer	208
MÜSEN					
Baume Ecke	4	ca. 1850	Arnold Zimmer	turner	69
Hauptstr.	77	1894	Gemeinde Müsen		92
NETPHEN					
Bahnhofstr.	71	1910	Clemens Schneider	tailor	62
Kronprinzenstr.	25	1911	Adam Klöckner	farmer	63
NEUNKIRCHEN					
Bahnhofstr.	28	1896	Wilhelm Klein	innkeeper	53, 137, 193
Hofgarten	10	ca. 1880	Emil Henrichs	miner	10
In der Trift	8	ca. 1910	Richard Klaas	miner	88, 182
Löhrstr.	38	1907	Gustav Ginsberg	mine-master	102
NIEDERDIELFEN					
Rödgerstr.	7	1906	Karl Hartmann	miner	108, 198
Siegener Str.	54	ca. 1900	Grübener	miner	206
			Ernst Lersch	miner	
NIEDERDRESSELNDORF					
Brunnenstr.	2	ca. 1860	Familie Mülln		3
Brunnenstr.	14	ca. 1818	Johann Heinrich	farmworker	79
Zur Hirzgabel	11	ca. 1850			70
NIEDERFISCHBACH					
Bachstr.	5	1910	Josef Mockenhaupt	merchant	94, 199
Bergstr.	11	ca. 1900			307
Konrad Adenauer Str.	1	1910	August Günther	shoemaker	15, 112, 264, 297

Street	Nr.	Year	Name of Owner	Profession	Plate Nr.
NIEDERNDORF					
Dirlenbacherstr.	68	1906	Wilhelm Wagener	miner	213
Schulplatz	6	1888	Gemeinde Niederndorf		57, 260, 261, 311
NIEDERSCHELDEN					
Bühlstr.	152	1881	Johann L. Donges	saw miller	239
Friedhofstr.	11	ca. 1900	Charlottenhütte		29, 145, 306
Johannesstr.	5	1900	Georg Koch		152, 241
Körnerstr.	6	1899	Karl Pfeifer		165
Siegtalstr.	164	1911	Hugo Junker	bookbinder	234, 295
Ziegeleistr.	7	1901	Heinrich Sturm	storage worker	160
NIEDERSCHELDERHÜTTE					
Adolfstr.	36	1907	Karl Elzner	miner	138
Am Gosenbach	3	1877	Wilhelm Hoffmann	miner	85, 139, 289
Am Gosenbach	15	1902	Gustaf Sänger	building contractor (?)	154, 237
Am Gosenbach	17	1902	Georg Krötz	mason	125
Karlstr.	4	1899	Josef Sehr	miner	39, 127, 218, 243, 253
Kirchberg	3	1890	Friedrich Bottenberg	carrier	258
Waldstr.	119	1903	Wilhelm Bender	miller	228
OBERDIELFEN					
Oberdielfer Str.	14	ca. 1830			73
Oberdielfer Str.	18	1832	Ewald Heimann	miner	72, 308
OBERHEUSLINGEN					
Heuslingstr.	342	1898	Friedrich Hein	farmer	12
Heuslingstr.	348	1913	Robert Schmolz	miner	209
Zum Rimberg	6	ca. 1900	Tillmann Klappert	cart-wright	21
OBERSDORF					
Rödgener Str.	60	1900	Gustav Schütz	miner	66
Rödgener Str.	62	1904	Anton Heide	miner	164
PLITTERSHAGEN					
Löcherbacher Weg	6	1900			31
RINSDORF					
Eiserfelderstr.	13	1908	Hermann Traut	road supervisor	111
Eiserfelderstr.	37	1639			75
Im Dudenbach	27	1905	Gustav Hopp	mailguard	205

Street	Nr.	Year	Name of Owner	Profession	Plate Nr.
SALCHENDORF					
Arbachstr.	5	1925	Robert Dietrich	merchant	135
Fritz Schäfer Str.	22	1906	Fritz Dietrich	miner	52, 310
Fritz Schäfer Str.	24	ca. 1900			17, 235, 256, 280
Kölner Str.	318	1904	Gustav Wiltraud	miner	104
Kölner Str.	336	1914	Friedr. Wilh. Weidt	miner	159
Kölner Str.	351	1906	Friedrich Schreiber	miner	37
Rensdorfstr.	1	1901	Friedrich Hassel	miner	40
Rensdorfstr.	5	1900	Familie Gerhard		9, 131
Rensdorfstr.	13	1905	Wilhelm Böcking	miner	14, 150, 172, 245, 287
Wildener Str.	7	1906	Heinrich Roth	farmer	36, 84, 259, 283
Wildener Str.	11	ca. 1875			8, 101, 282
Wildener Str.	25	1904	Hermann v. d. Heyden	miner	171, 246
Wildener Str.	46	1899	Heinrich Schneider	miner	38
Wildener Str.	64	1904	Heinrich Friedrich	miner	43
Wildener Str.	78	1910	Fritz Heinrich	miner	42
SIEGEN					
Arndtstr.	6	ca. 1870			93, 175, 227
Eintrachtstr.	4	1872			161
Fischbacherbergstr.	9	1892			176
Frankfurter Str.	78	1899	Karl Schneider	building contractor	192
Friedrich Wilhelm Str.	30	ca. 1880			168
Hohler Weg	45	ca. 1875			180
Kampenstr.	44	ca. 1890			118
Kirchweg	5	1886	Adam Freyling	blacksmith	268
Kirchweg	52	ca. 1900	Göbel	joiner	110
Koblenzer Str.	186	ca. 1880			195
Marienborner Str.	237	1883	Heinrich Reichel	tanner	173
Siegbergstr.	34	1901	Familie Weber		270
Sieghütter Hauptweg	61	ca. 1890			219
Wiesenstr.	35	ca. 1875			11
STRUTHÜTTEN					
Kölner Str.	26	1891	Ewald Ginsberg	blacksmith	107
TRUPBACH					
Trupbacher Str.	9	1903	Emil Nöll	joiner	89
Wickersbacher Weg	7	ca. 1900	Hermann Reuter	miner	60, 144, 291

Street	Nr.	Year	Name of Owner	Profession	Plate Nr.
WAHLBACH					
Freier Grund Str.	20	1913	Fritz Krumm	merchant	214
Freier Grund Str.	28	1903	Ludwig Zahn	miner	103
WEHBACH					
Steinstr.	11	1898	Friedrichshütte		129
Wehbacher Str.	15	1898	Friedrichshütte		128, 155
WEIDENAU					
Försterstr.	12	1912	Karl Beier	boilermaker	98, 266
Untere Rolandstr.	3	ca. 1890	Familie Hering		269
Weidenauerstr.	115	1890			181
Weidenauerstr.	119	1910	Grube Neue Haardt		97, 229
WIEDERSTEIN					
Mischenbachstr.	7	ca. 1800			76
WILDEN					
Eiserner Weg	9	1721	Julius Böcking	miner	210
Freier Grunder Str.	25	1908	Heinrich Zöllner	miner	166
WILNSDORF					
Albert Schweitzer Str.	2	ca. 1850	Josef Büdenbender	miner	215
Hagener Str.	19	1901	Karl A. Schneider	miner	34
Hagener Str.	26	1903	Dr. Schneider	physician	230
Hagener Str.	37	1927	Dr. Emil Gräf	physician	13
Weißtalstr.	1	ca. 1913	Heinrich Kleikamp	miner	216
ZEPPENFELD					
Auf der Forth	2	ca. 1820	Robert Lorenz	miner	81

PLATES

I.
GIEBELSEITEN
GABLE SIDES

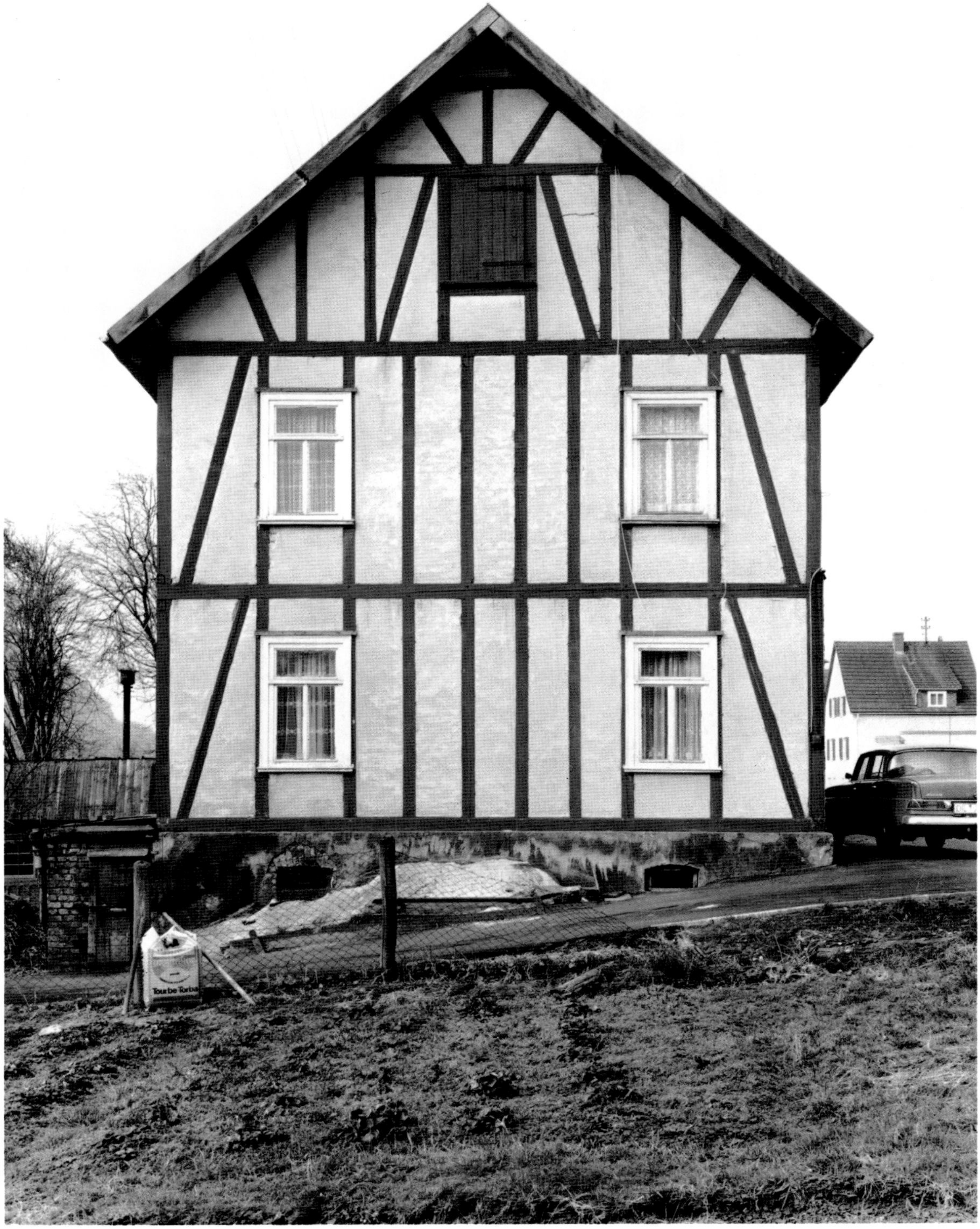

1

Holzhäuser Straße 25, Allendorf, 1973.

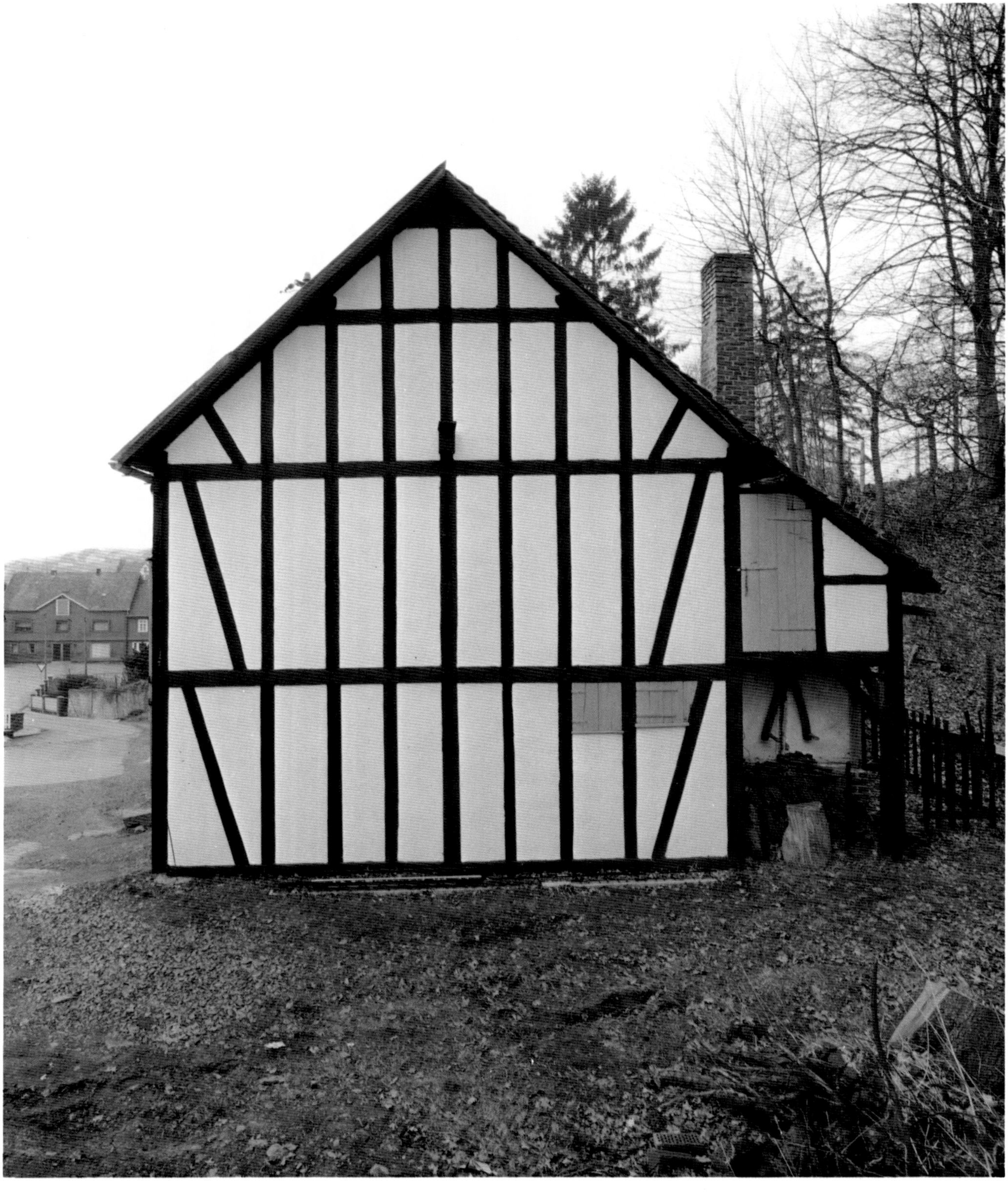

2
Mühlenbergstraße 1, Büschergrund, 1971.

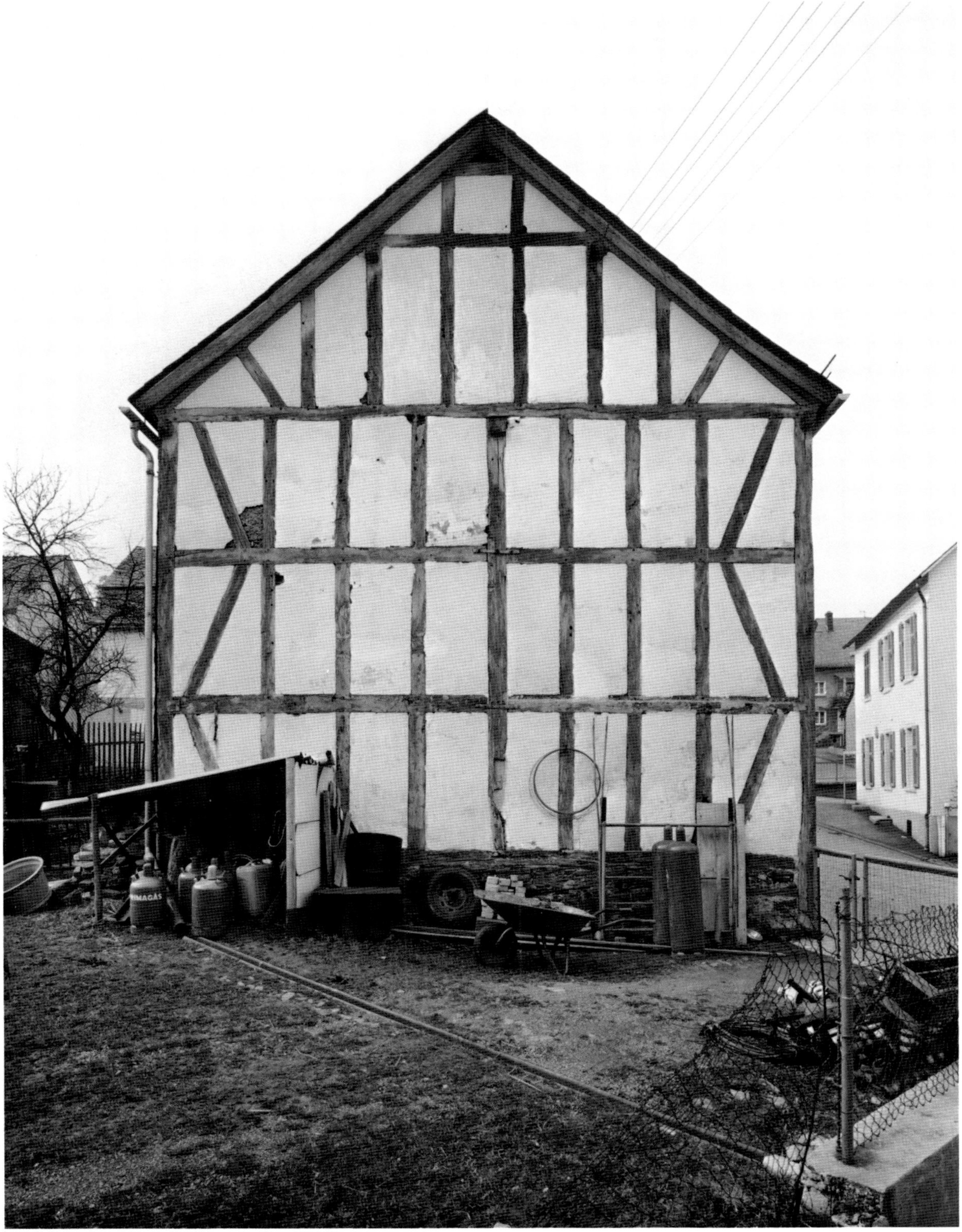

3
Brunnenstraße 2, Niederdresselndorf, 1973.

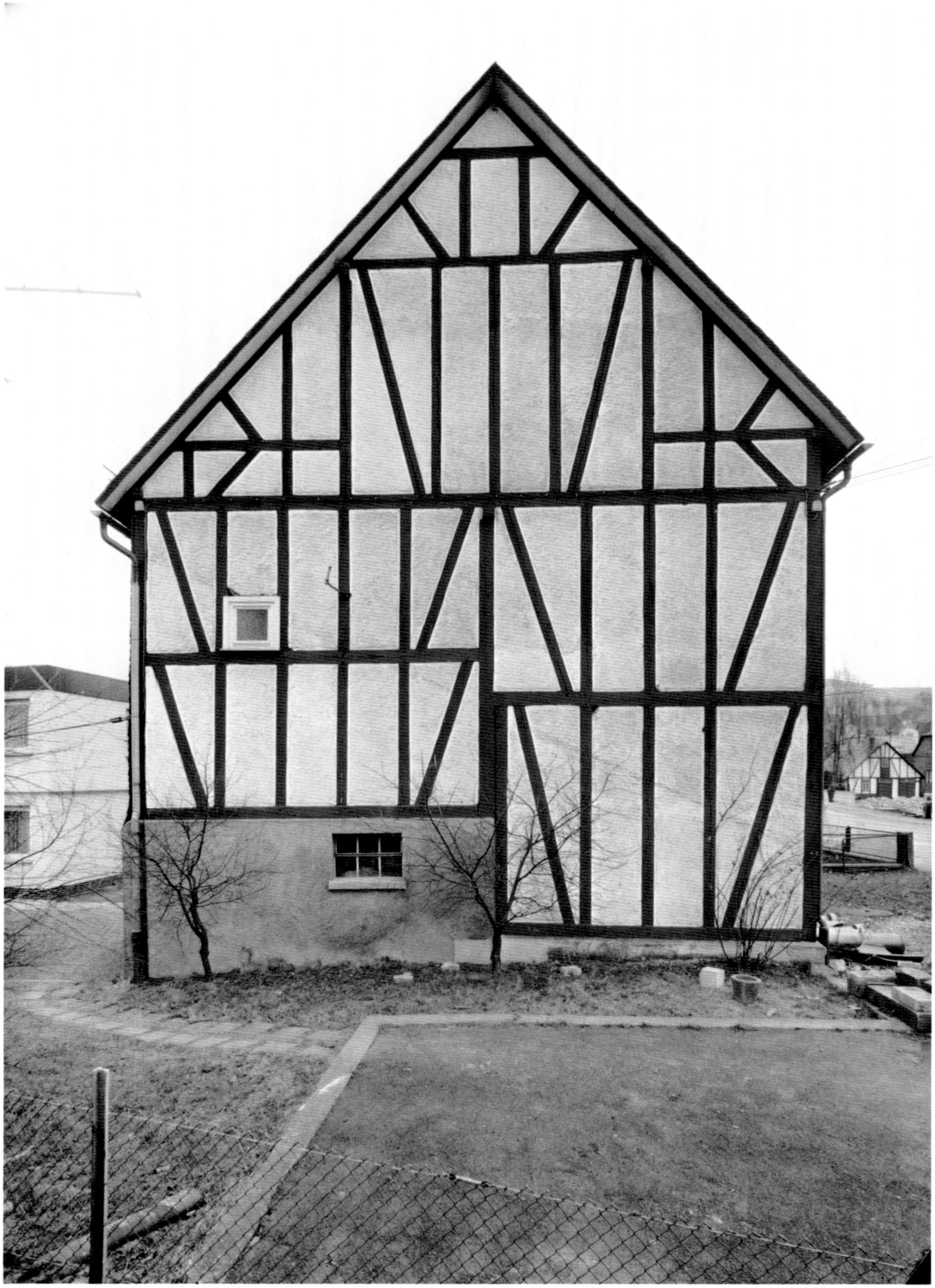

4

Haigerer Straße 2, Allendorf, 1972.

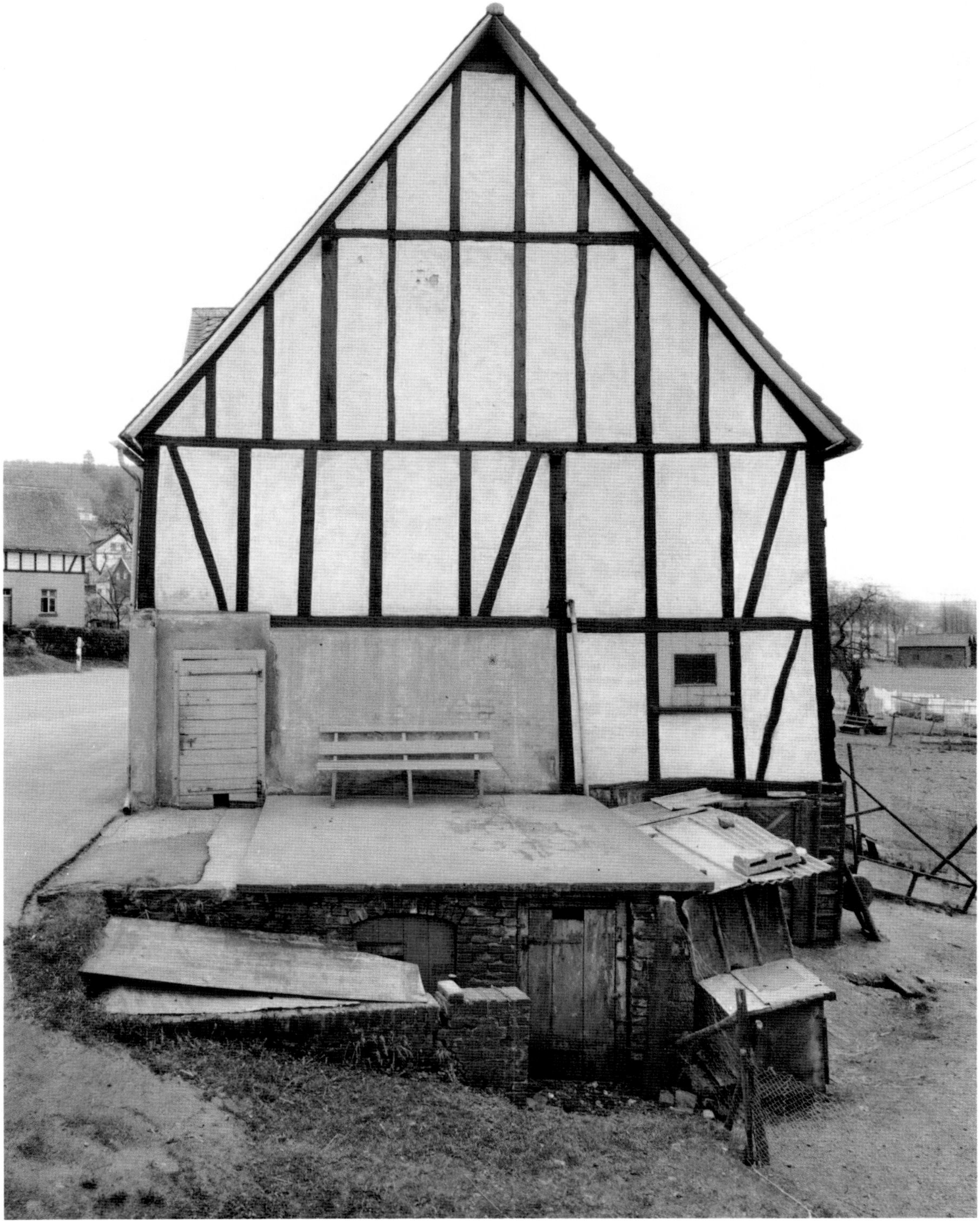

5
Olper Straße 19, Büschergrund, 1970.

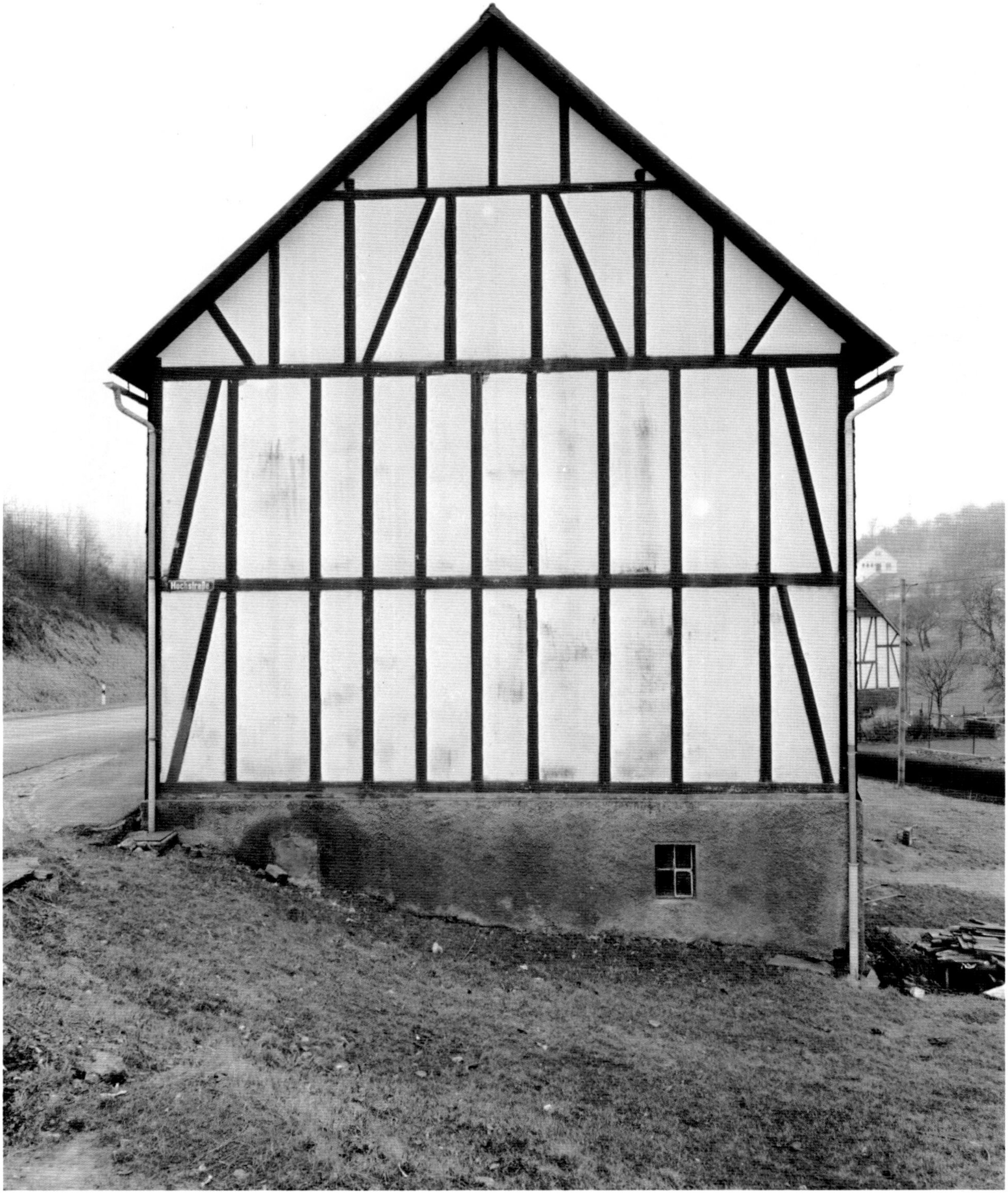

6
Wilnsdorfer Straße 65, Gilsbach, 1970.

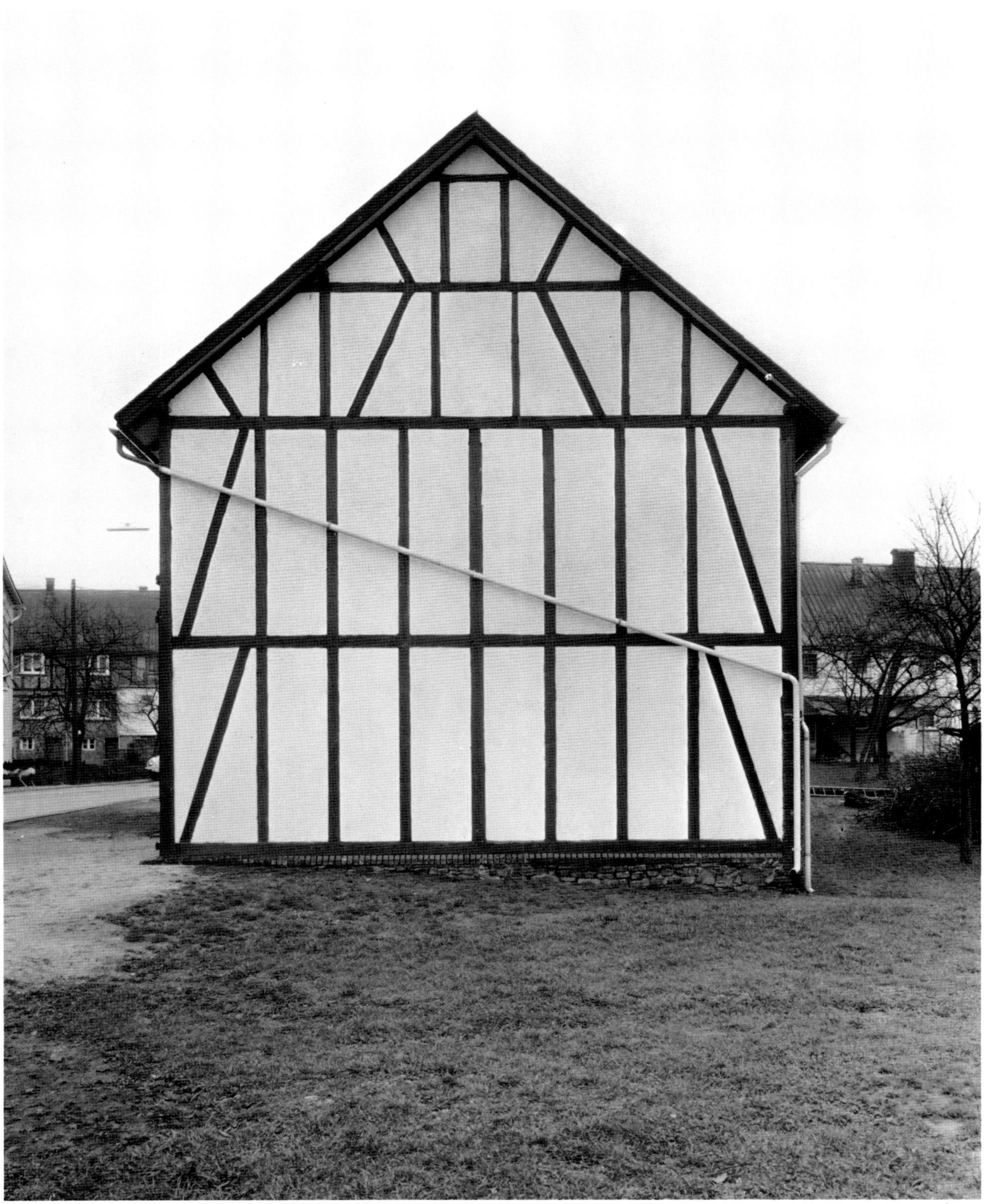

7

Tränkestraße 3, Haiger-Seelbach, 1972.

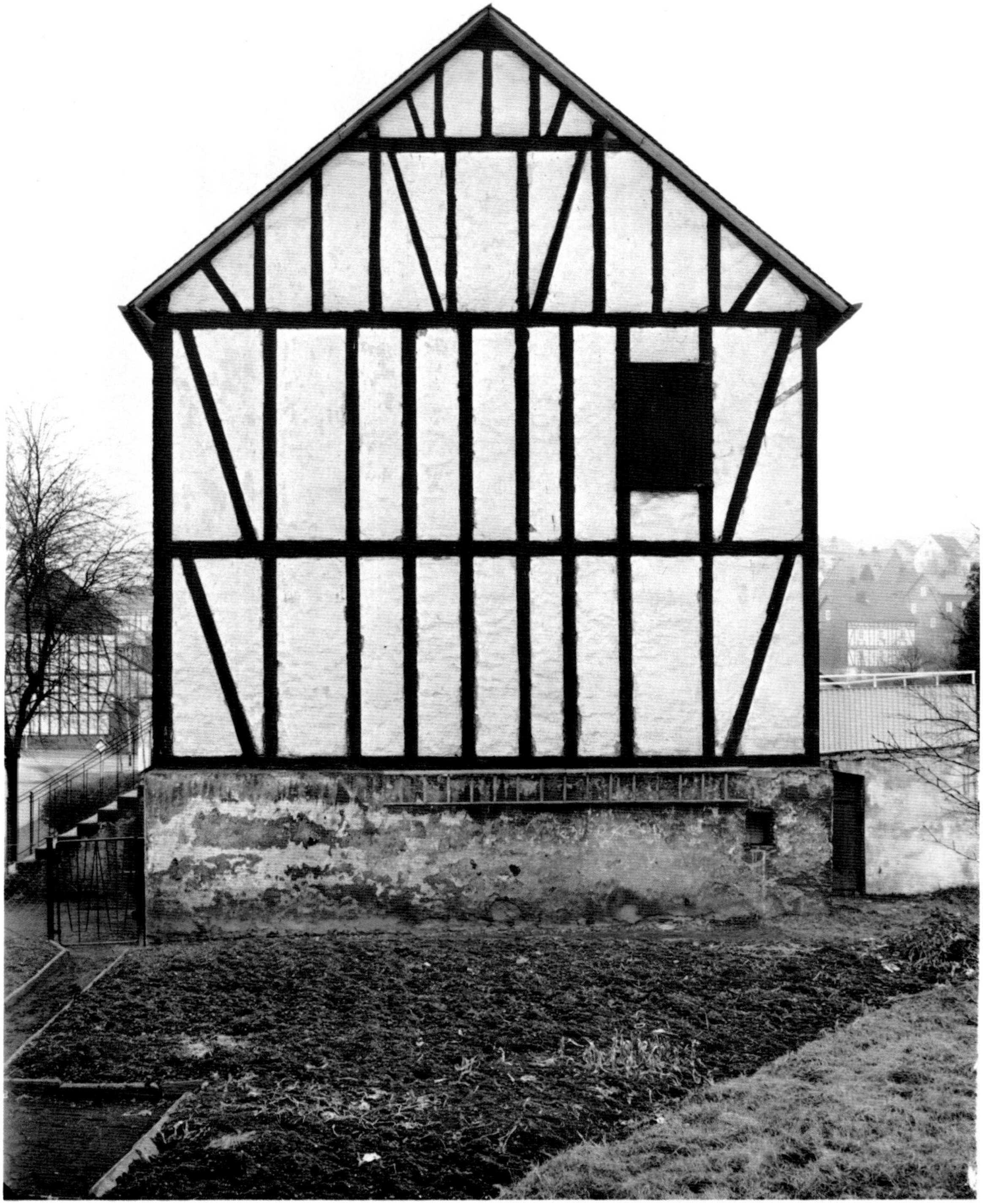

8

Wildener Straße 11, Salchendorf, 1961.

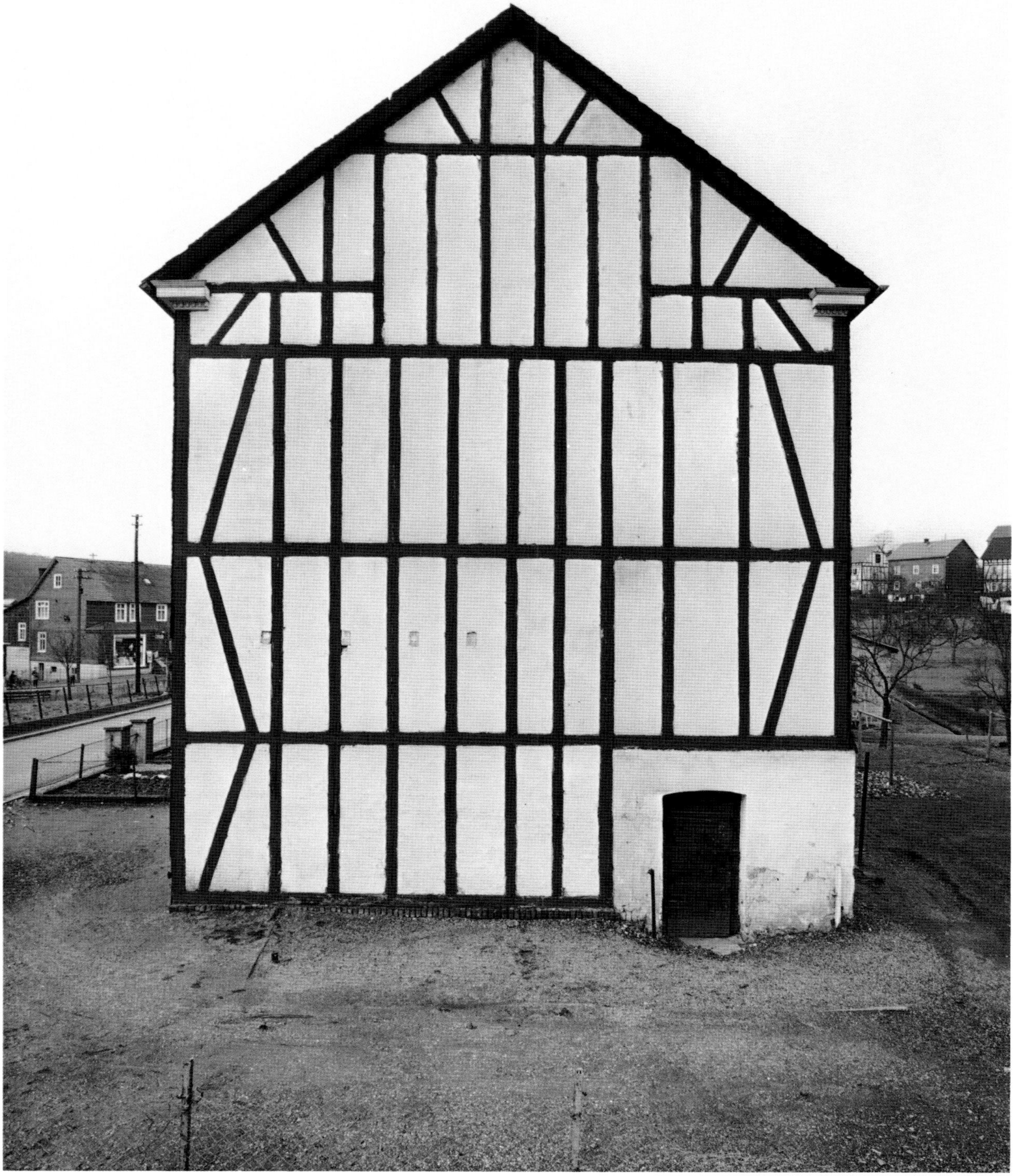

9
Rensdorfstraße 5, Salchendorf, 1959.

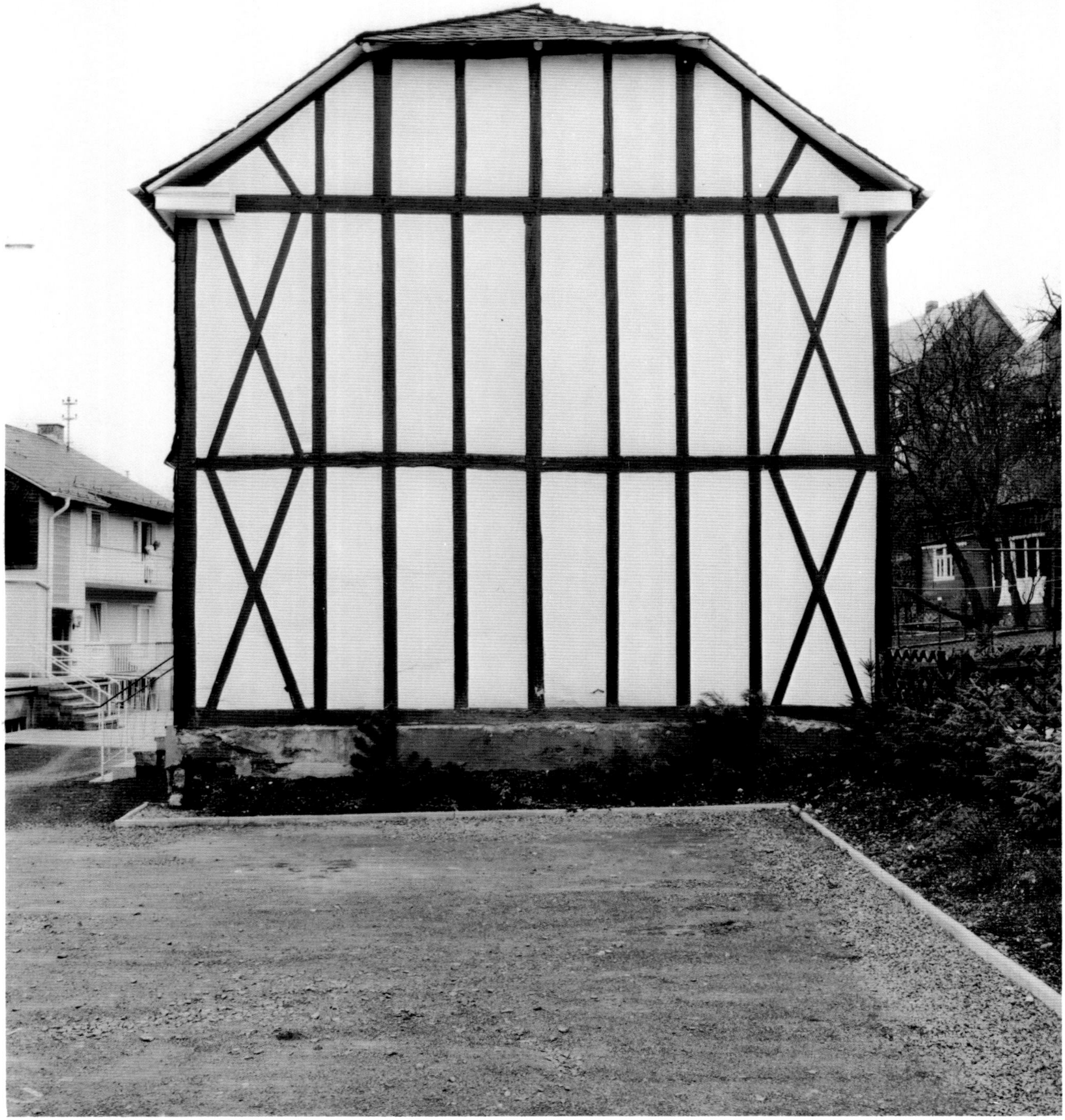

10
Hofgarten 10, Neunkirchen, 1970.

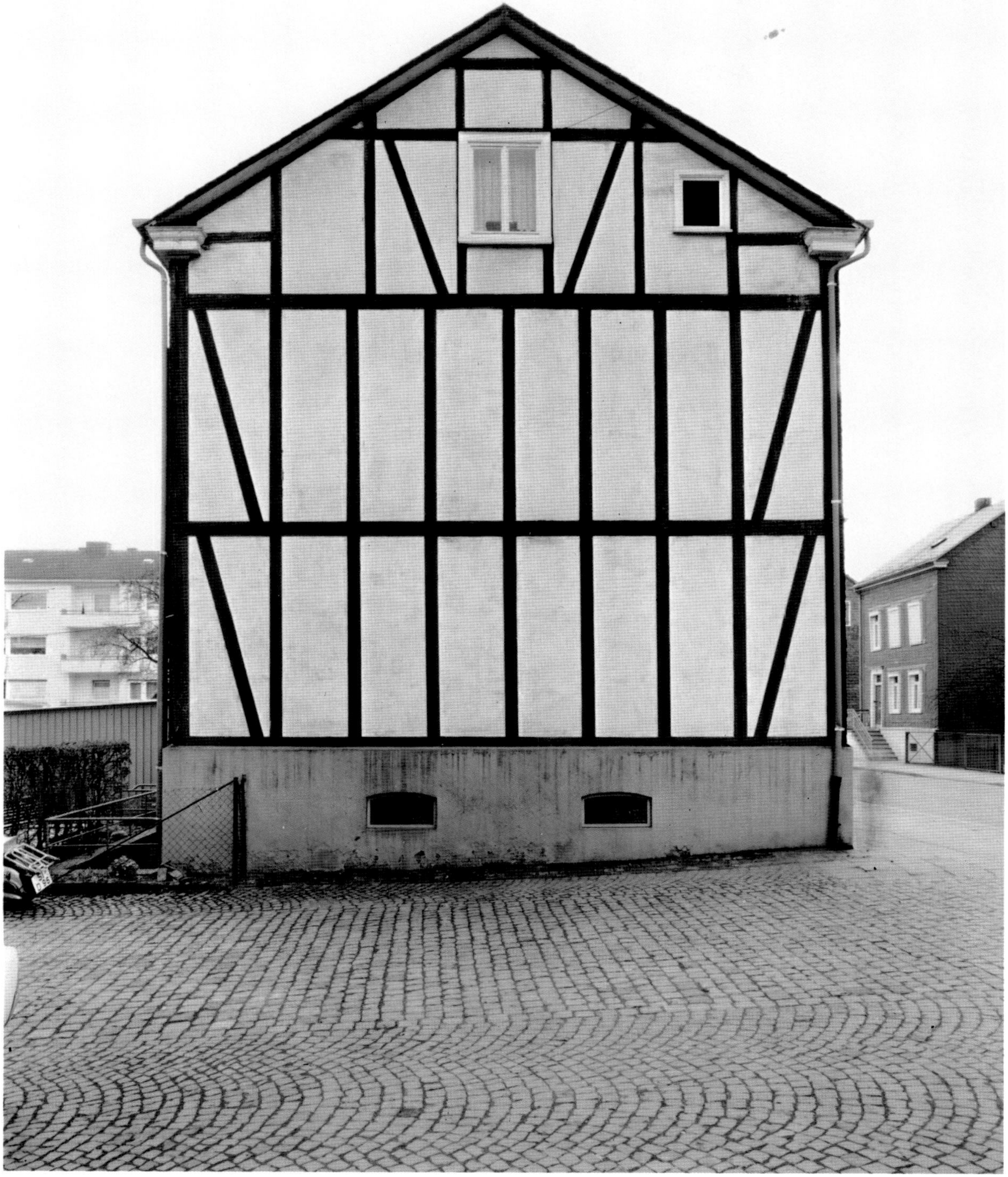

11
Wiesenstraße 35, Siegen, 1970.

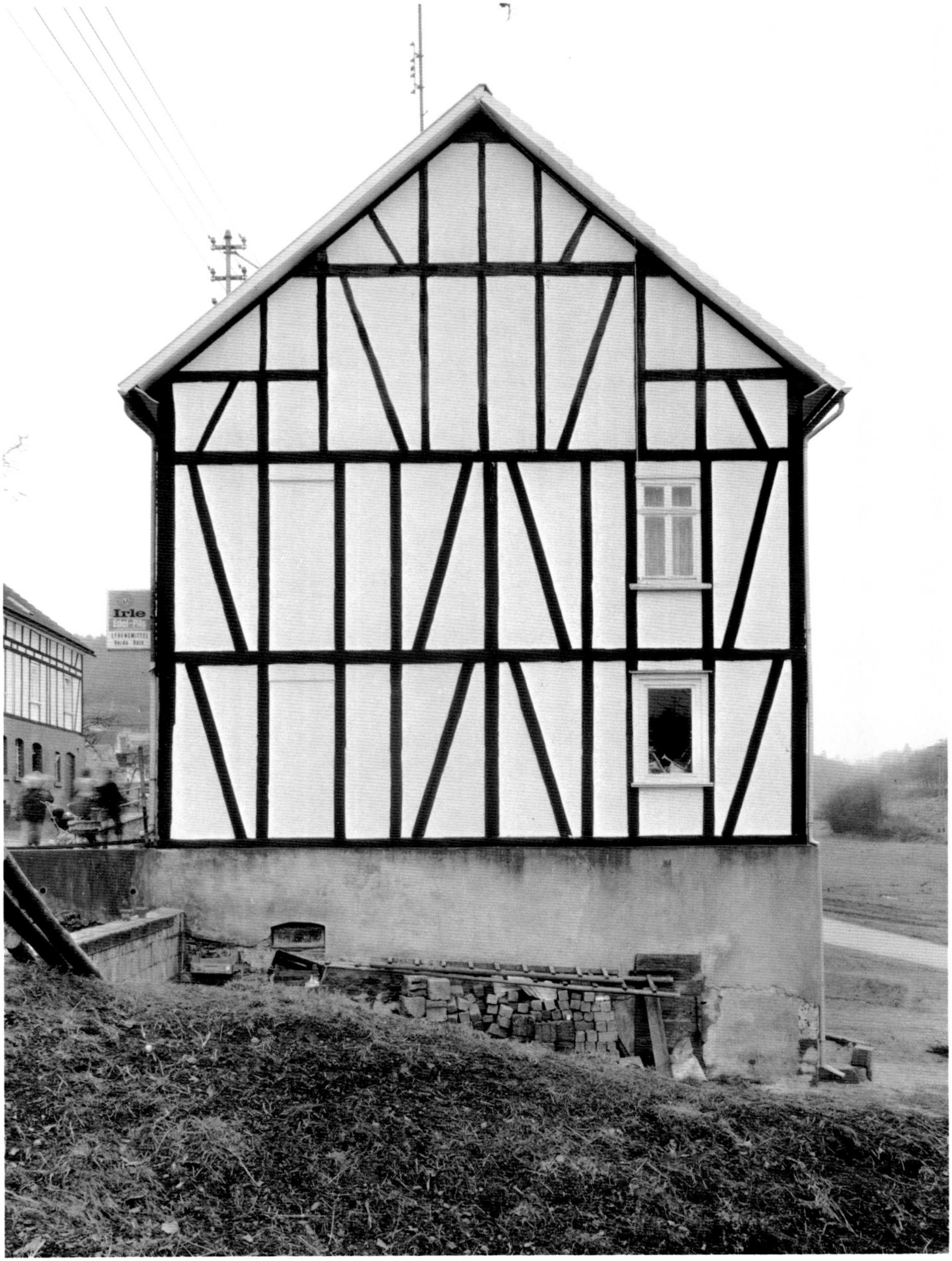

12
Heuslingstraße 342, Oberheuslingen, 1970.

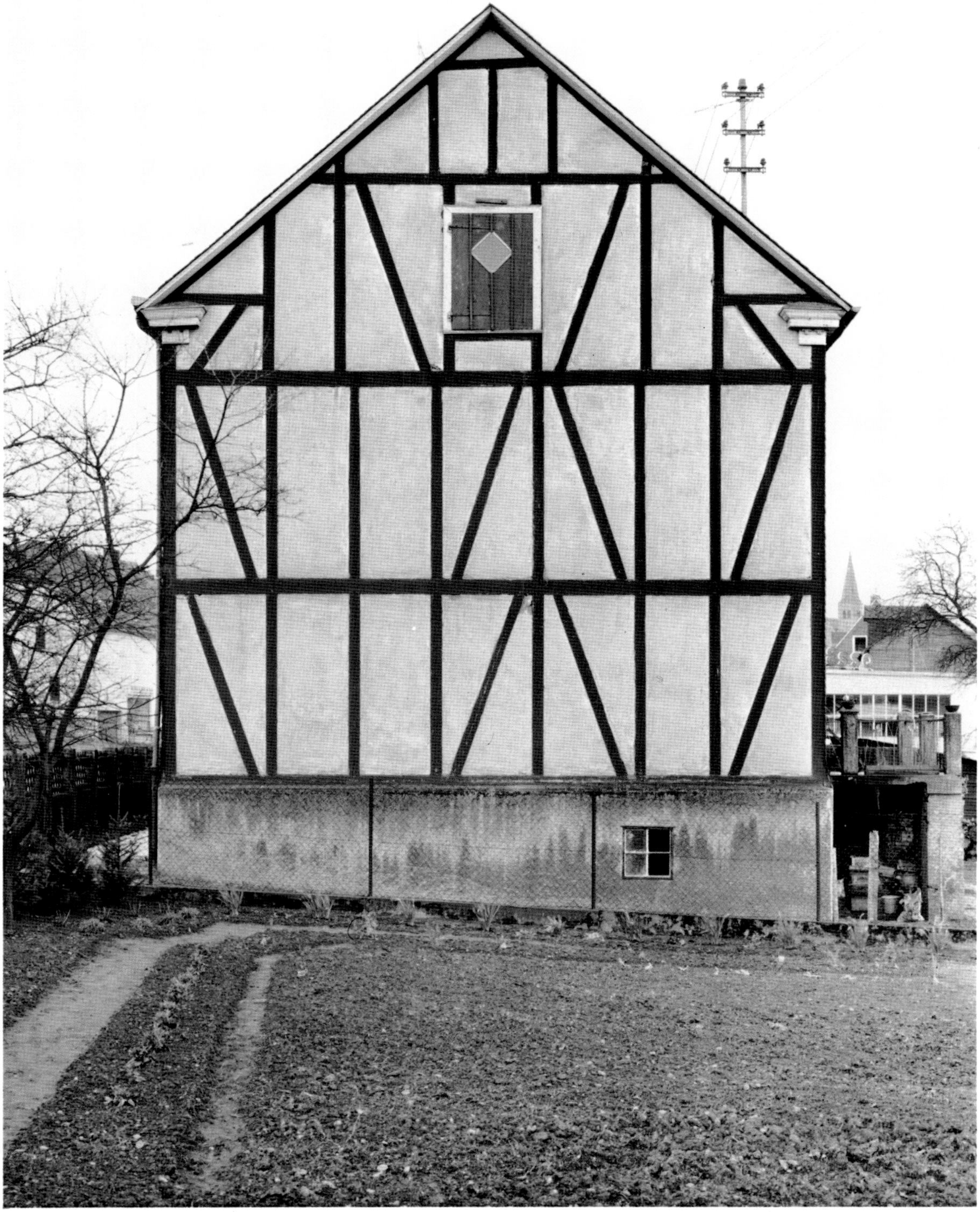

13
Hagener Straße 37, Wilnsdorf, 1970.

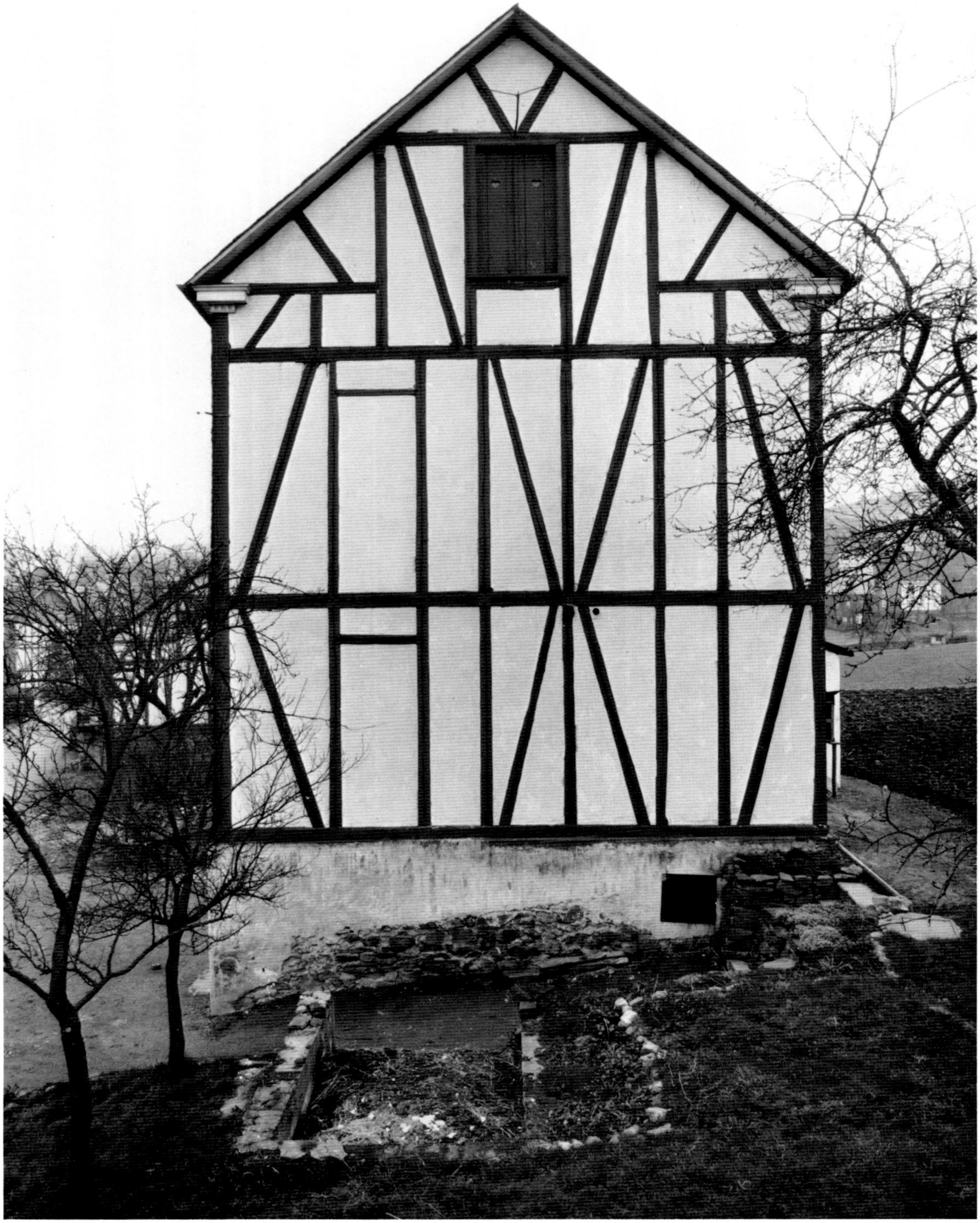

14
Rensdorfstraße 13, Salchendorf, 1960.

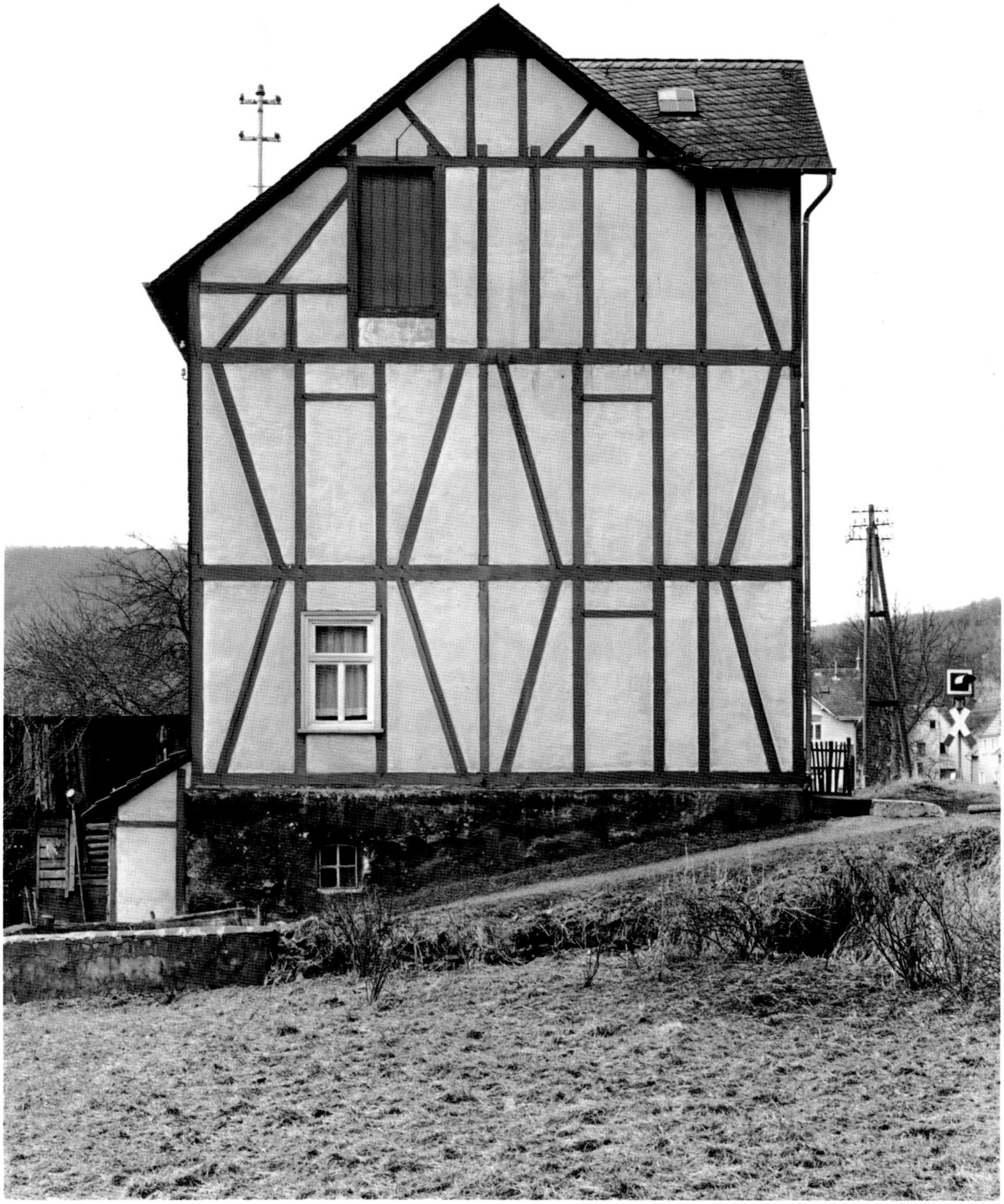

15
Konrad-Adenauer-Straße 1, Niederfischbach, 1962.

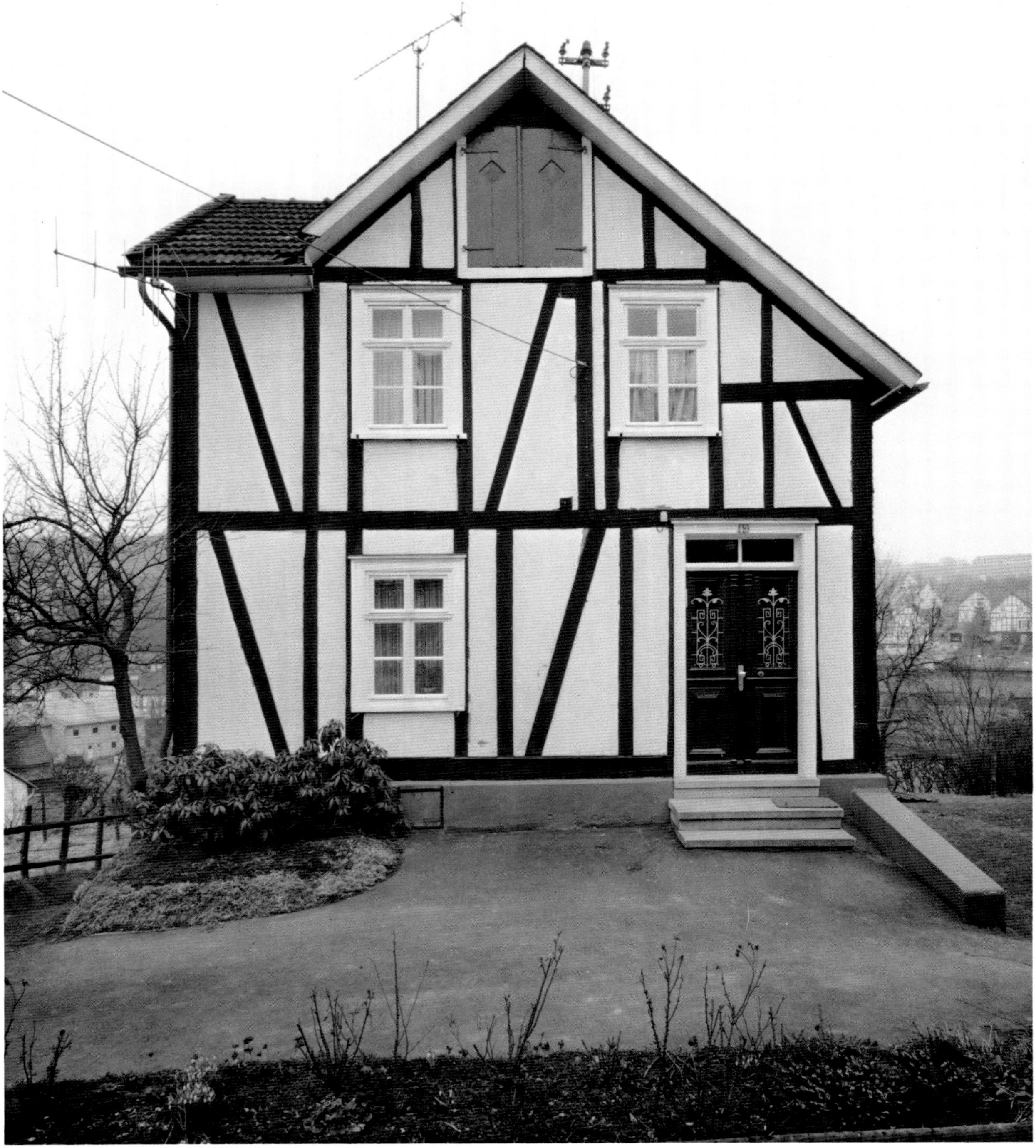

16
Krottorfer Straße 43, Freudenberg, 1970.

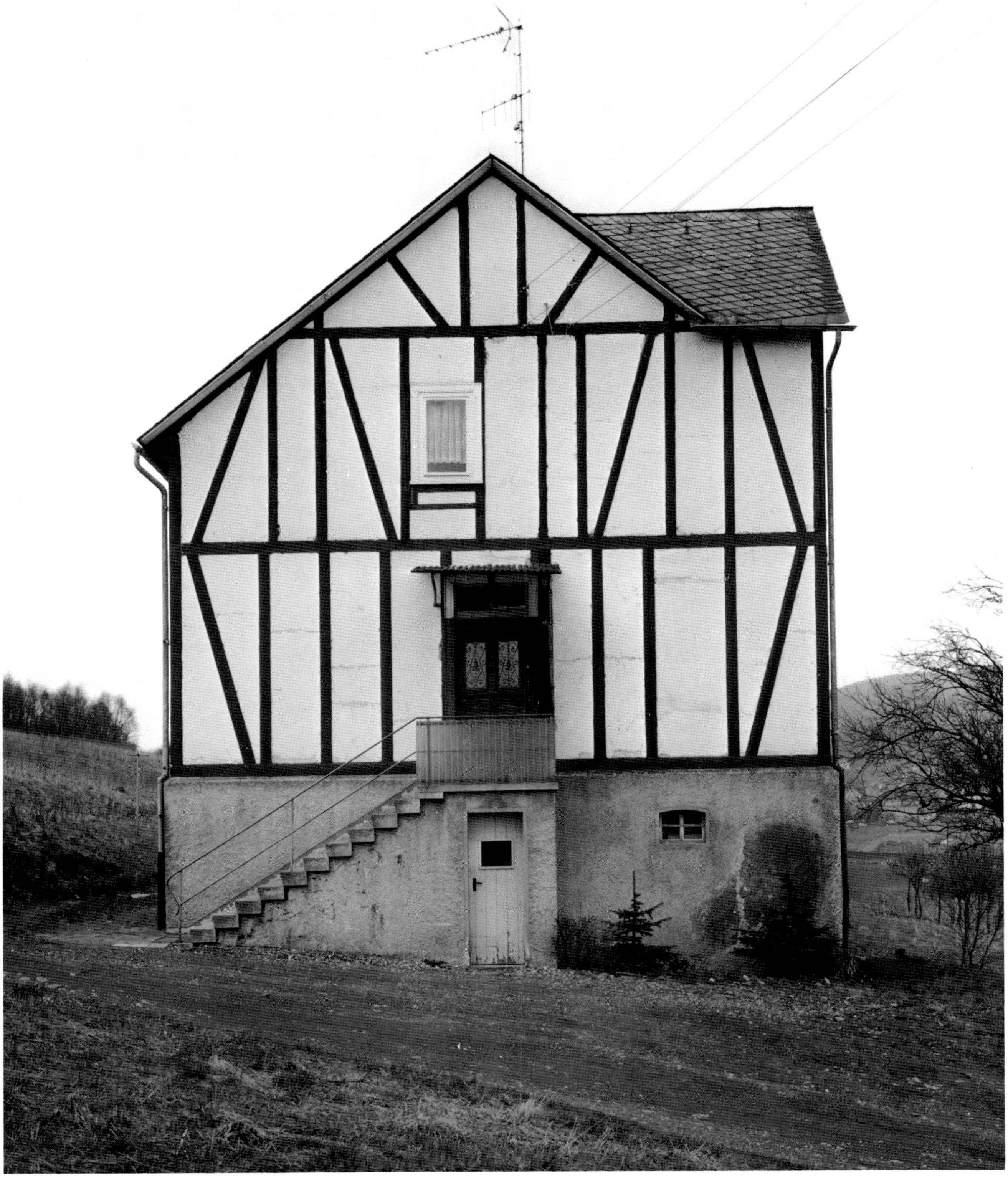

17
Fritz-Schäfer-Straße 24, Salchendorf, 1971.

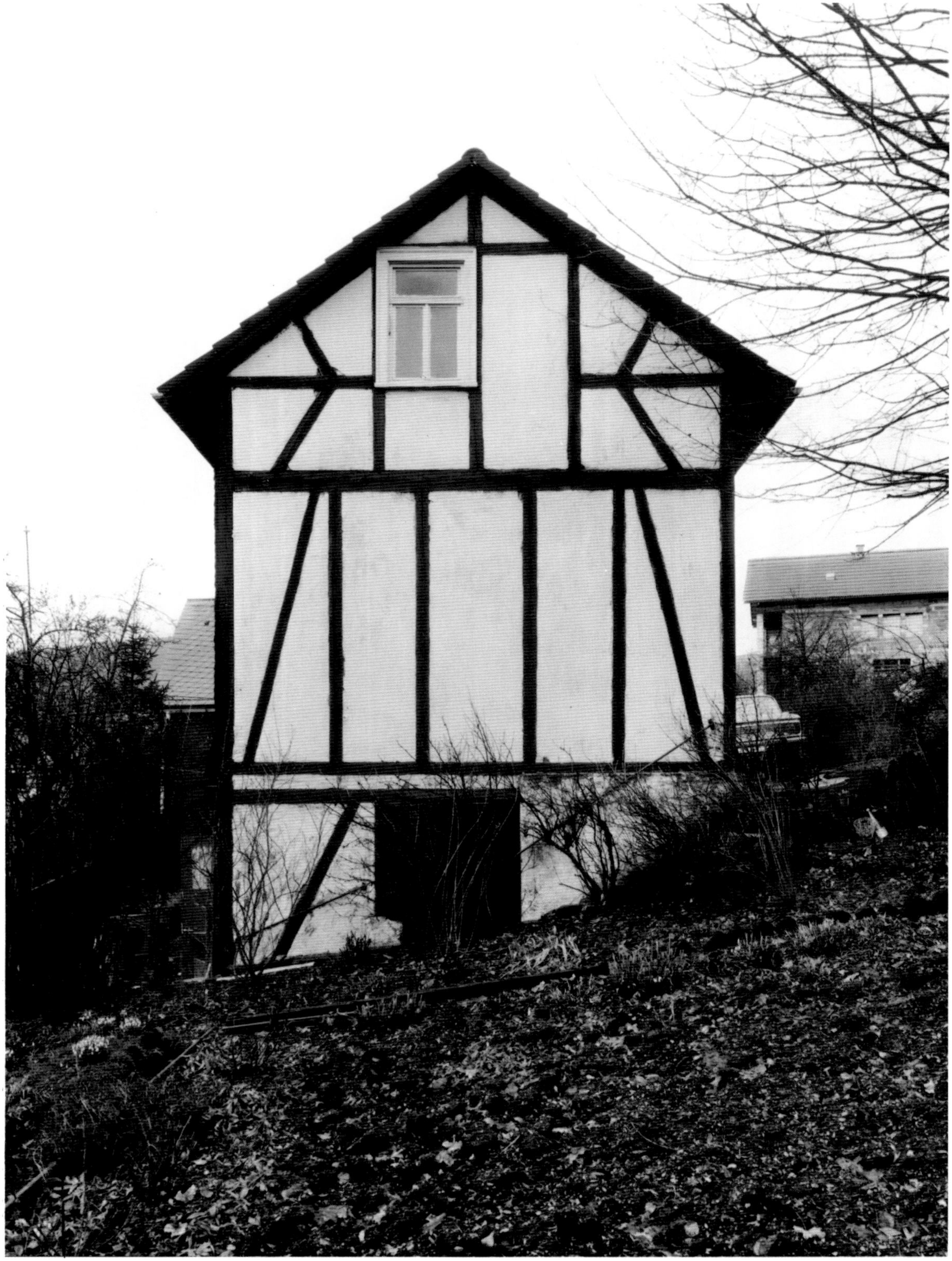

18
Löhrstraße 14, Birken, 1973.

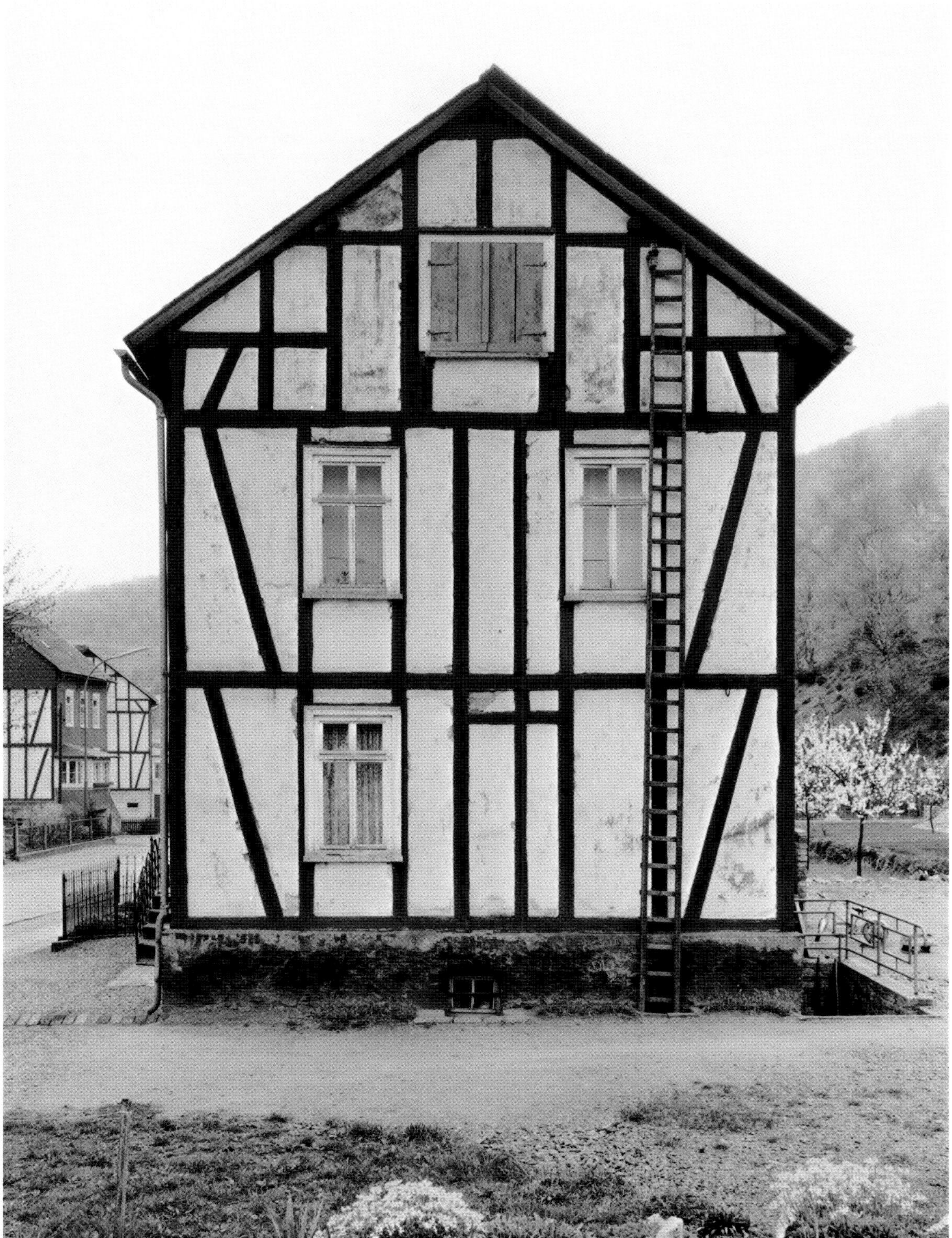

19
Auf der Hütte 45, Gosenbach, 1961.

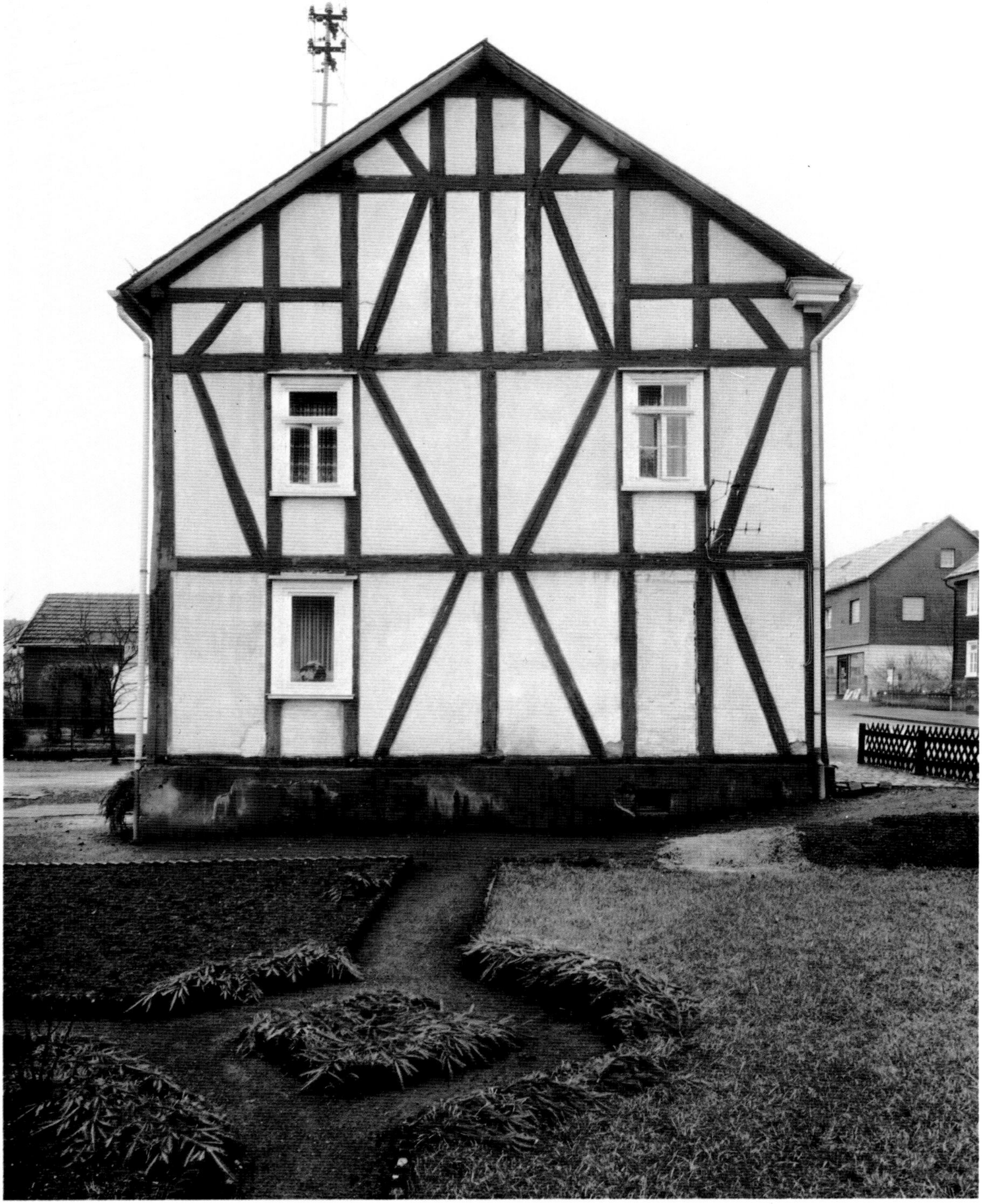

20
Heesstraße 31, Kreuztal, 1972.

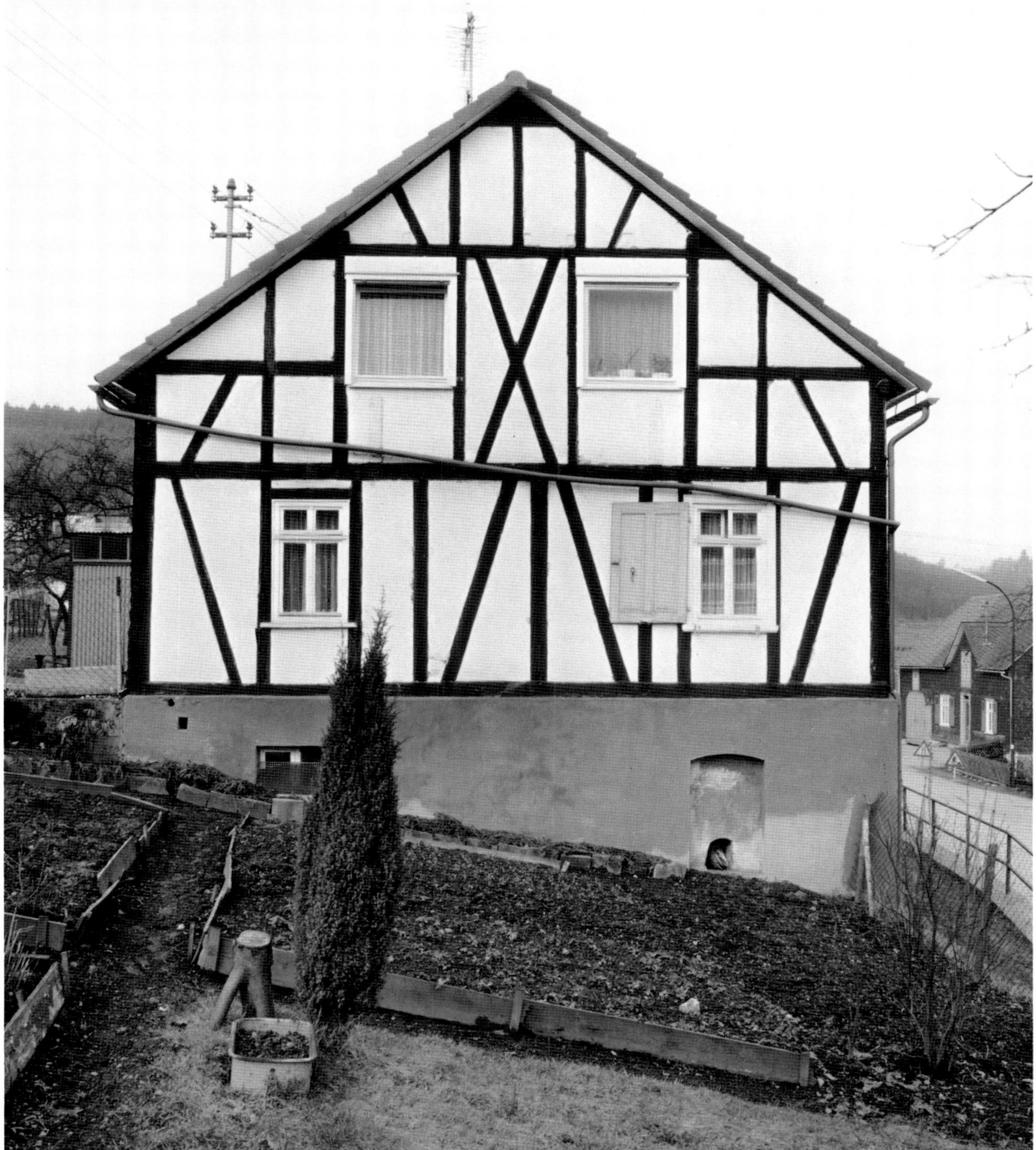

21
Zum Rimberg 6, Oberheuslingen, 1972.

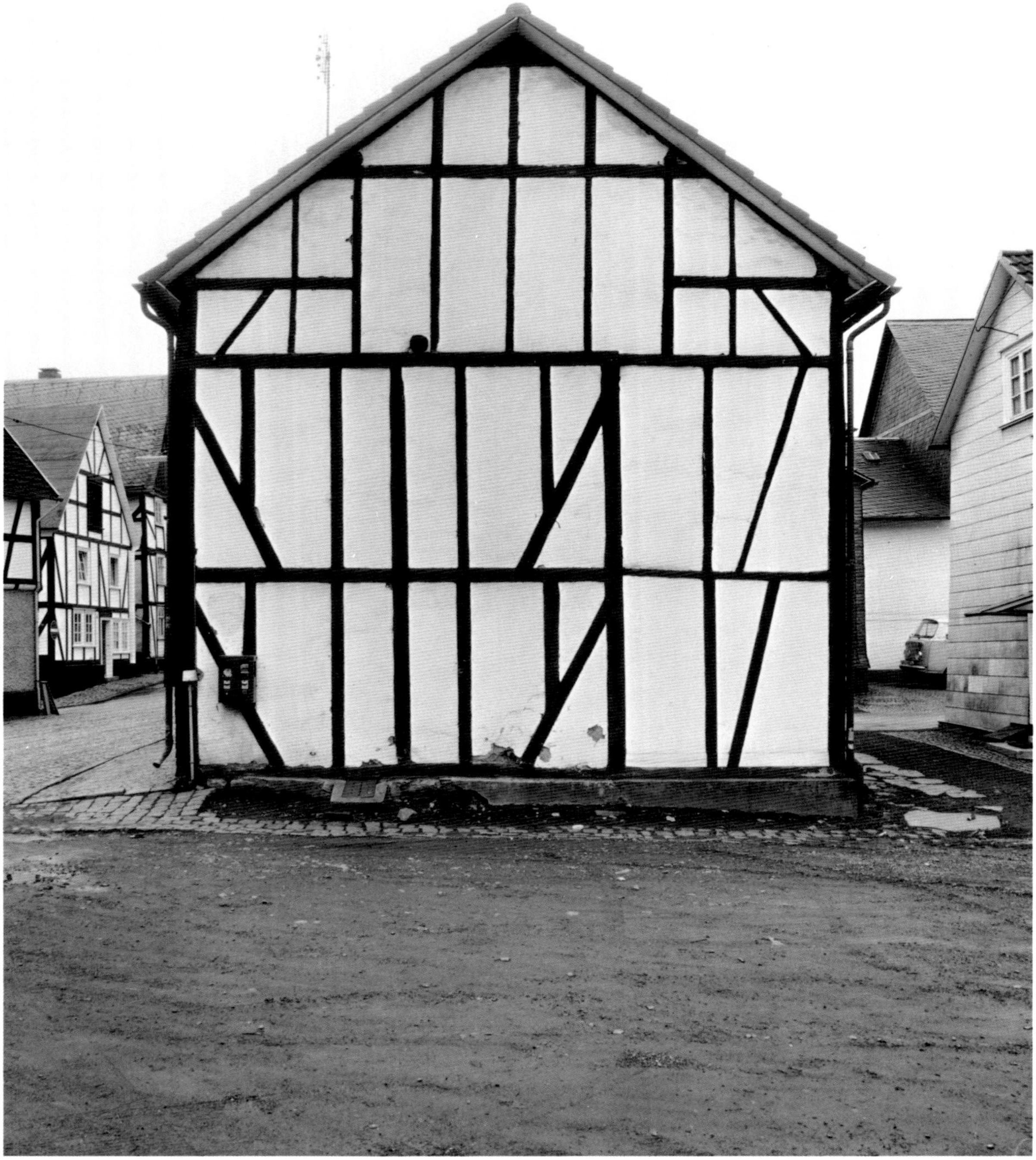

22

Kölner Straße 4, Freudenberg, 1969.

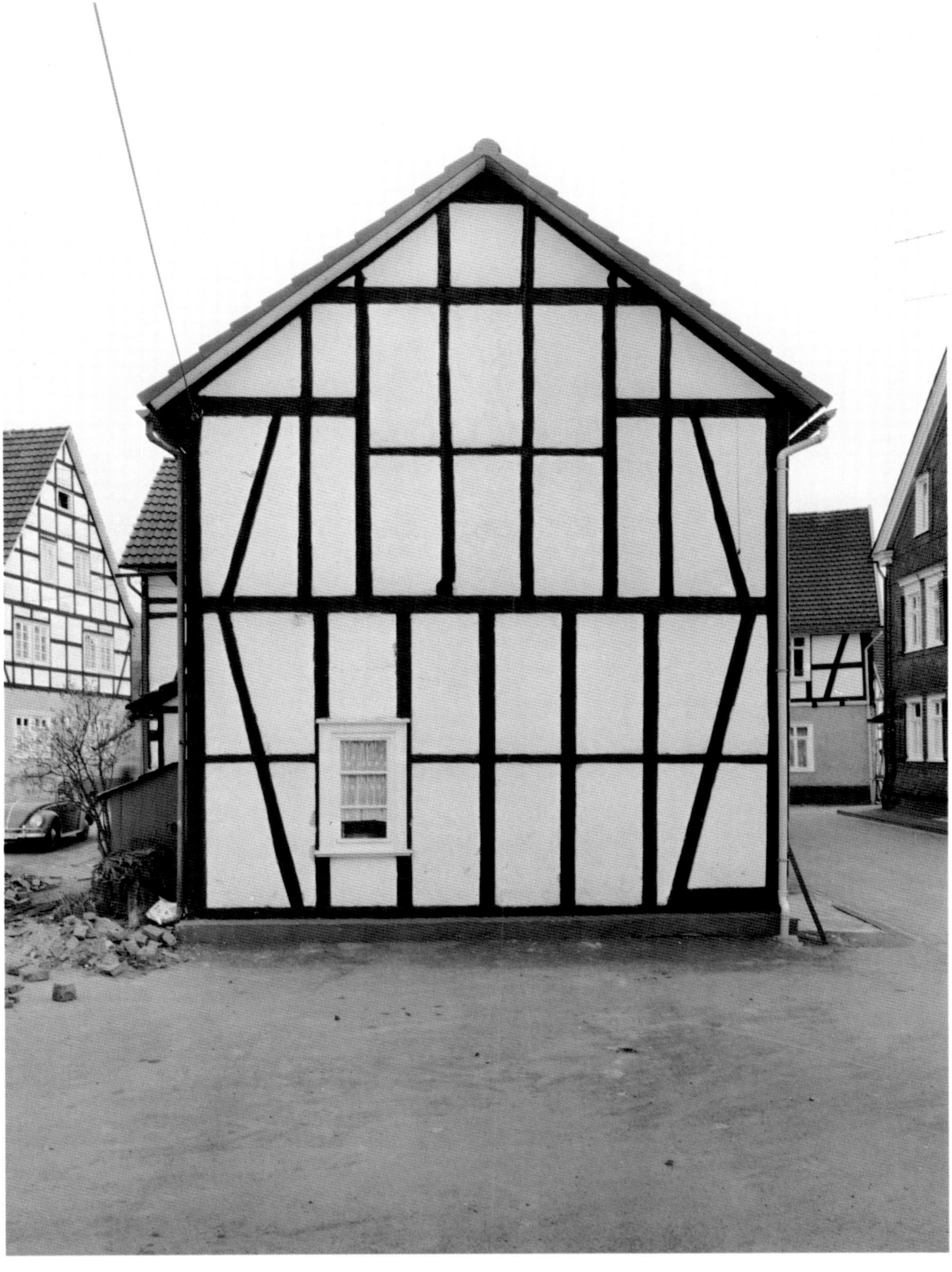

23
Kölner Straße 4a, Freudenberg, 1972.

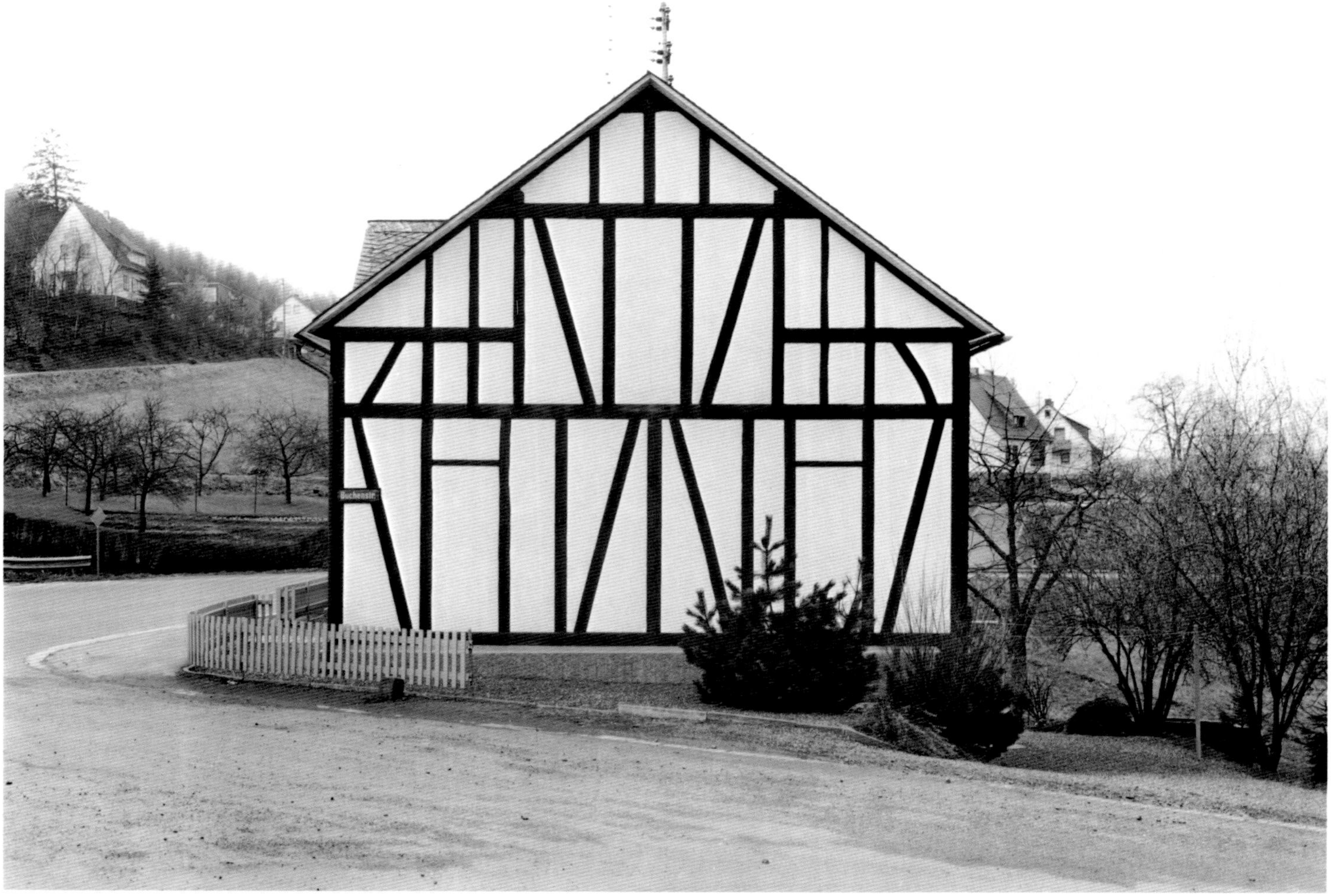

24
Siegener Straße 167, Büschergrund, 1966.

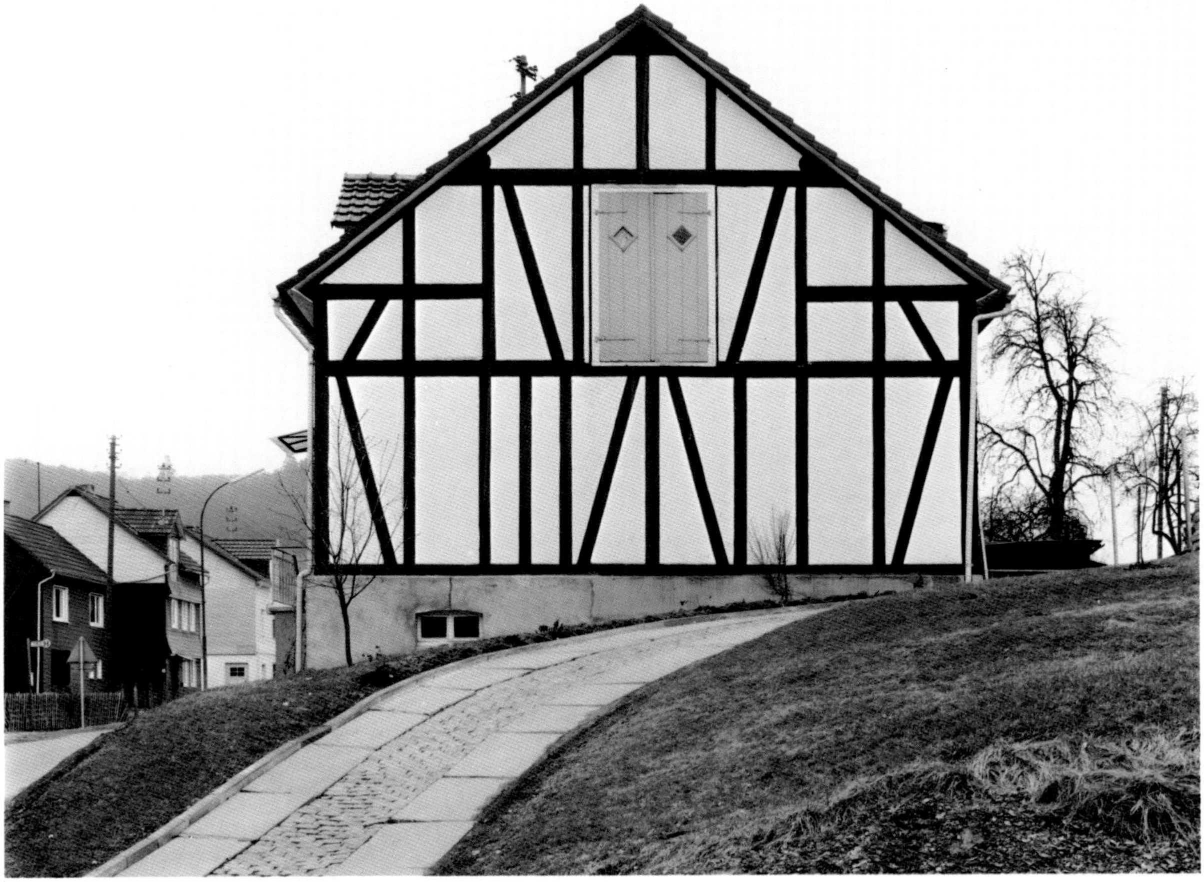

25
Triftstraße 19, Büschergrund, 1971.

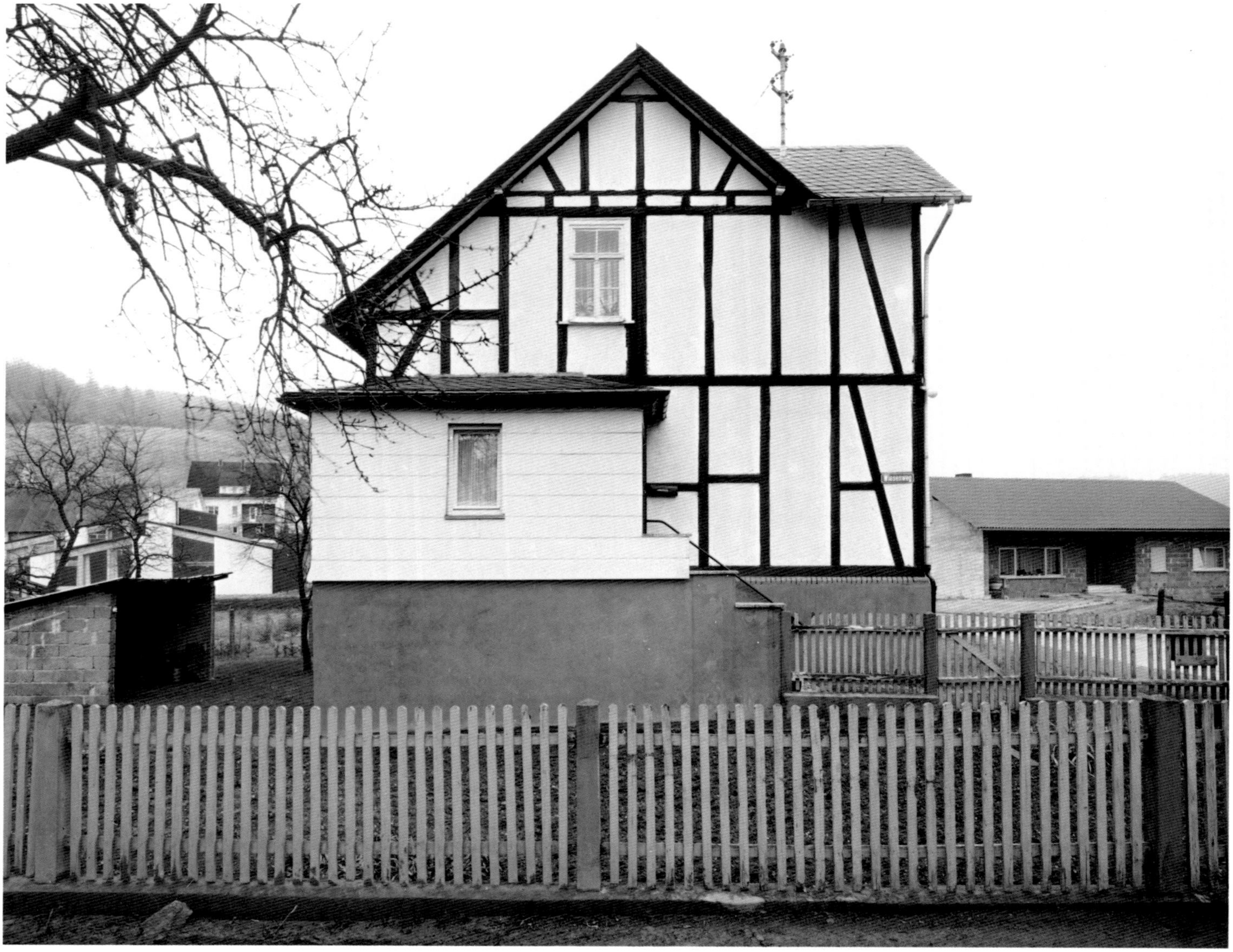

26
Tränkestraße 3, Haiger-Seelbach, 1972.

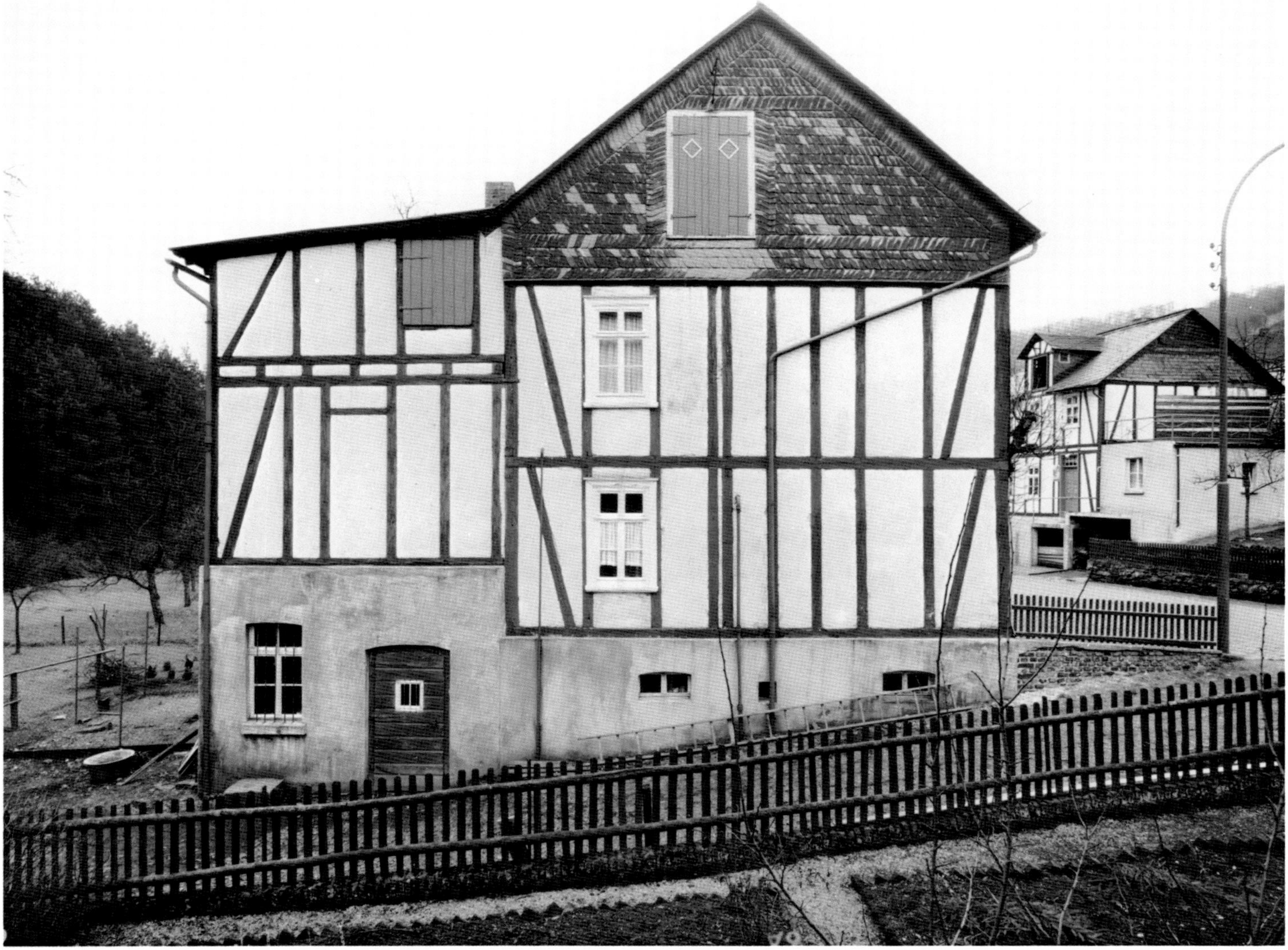

27
Kampenstraße 42, Gosenbach, 1958.

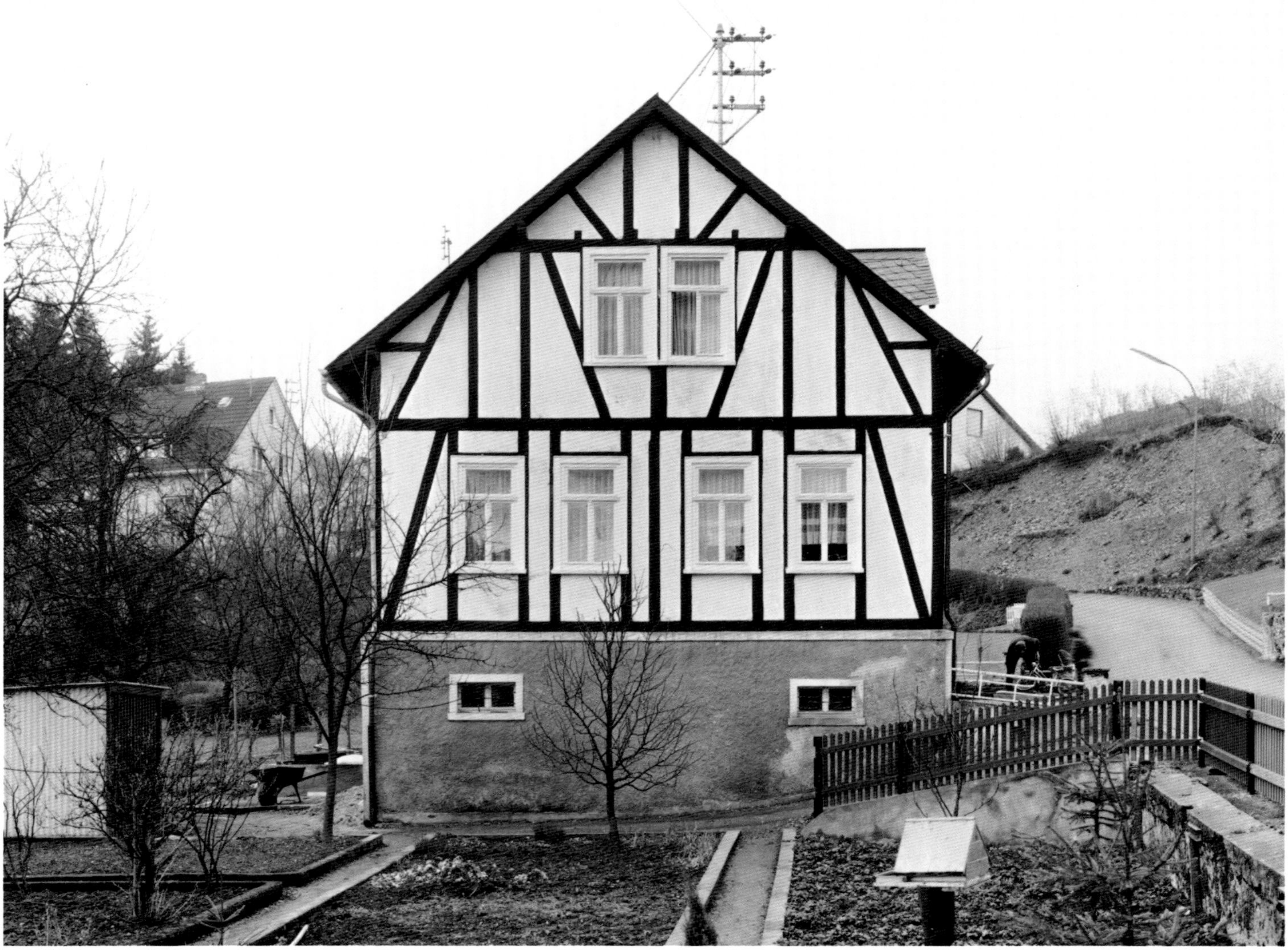

28
Maiweg 23, Gosenbach, 1967.

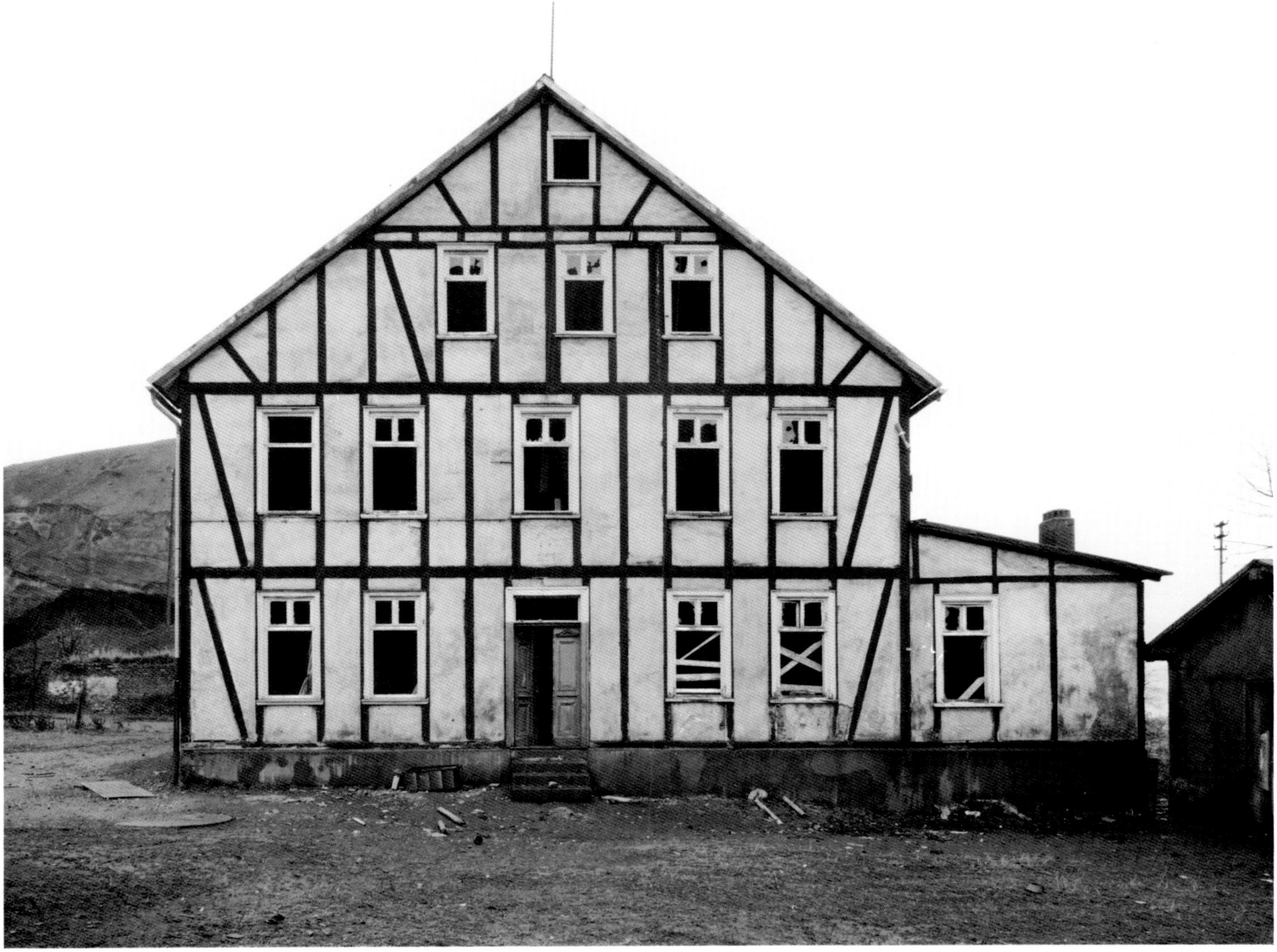

29
Friedhofstraße 11, Niederschelden, 1970.

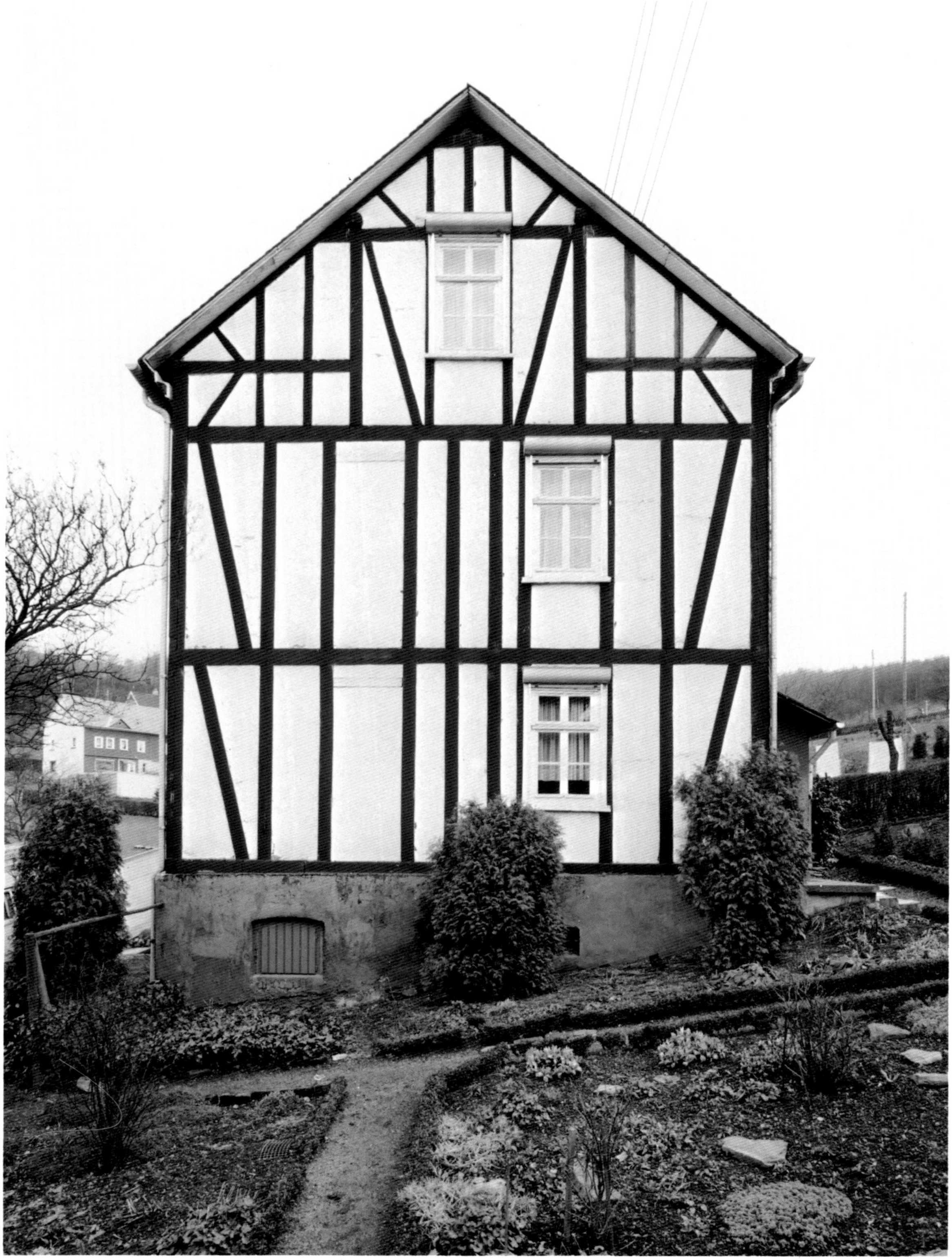

30

Abendröthe 3, Birlenbach, 1972.

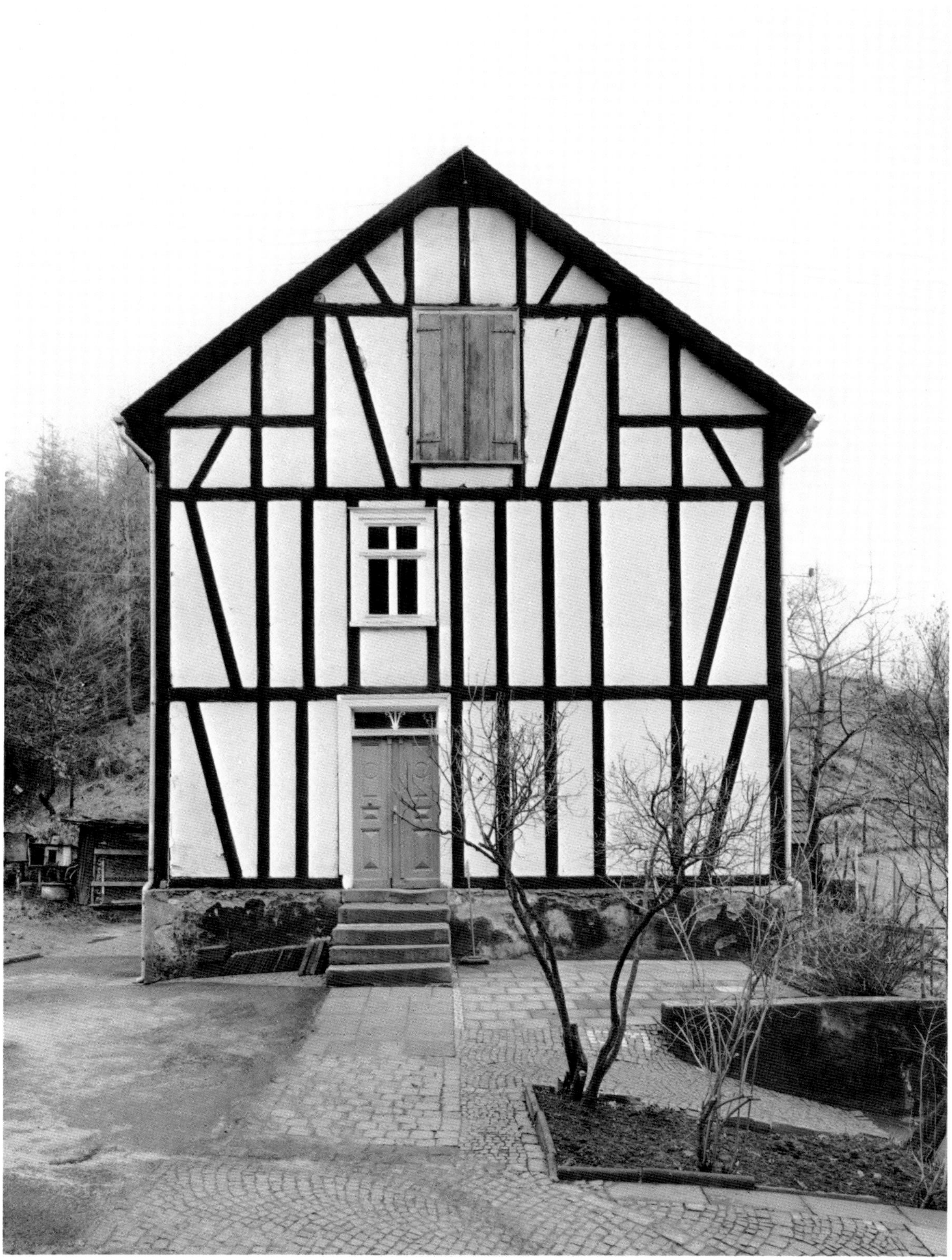

31
Löcherbacherweg 6, Plittershagen, 1970.

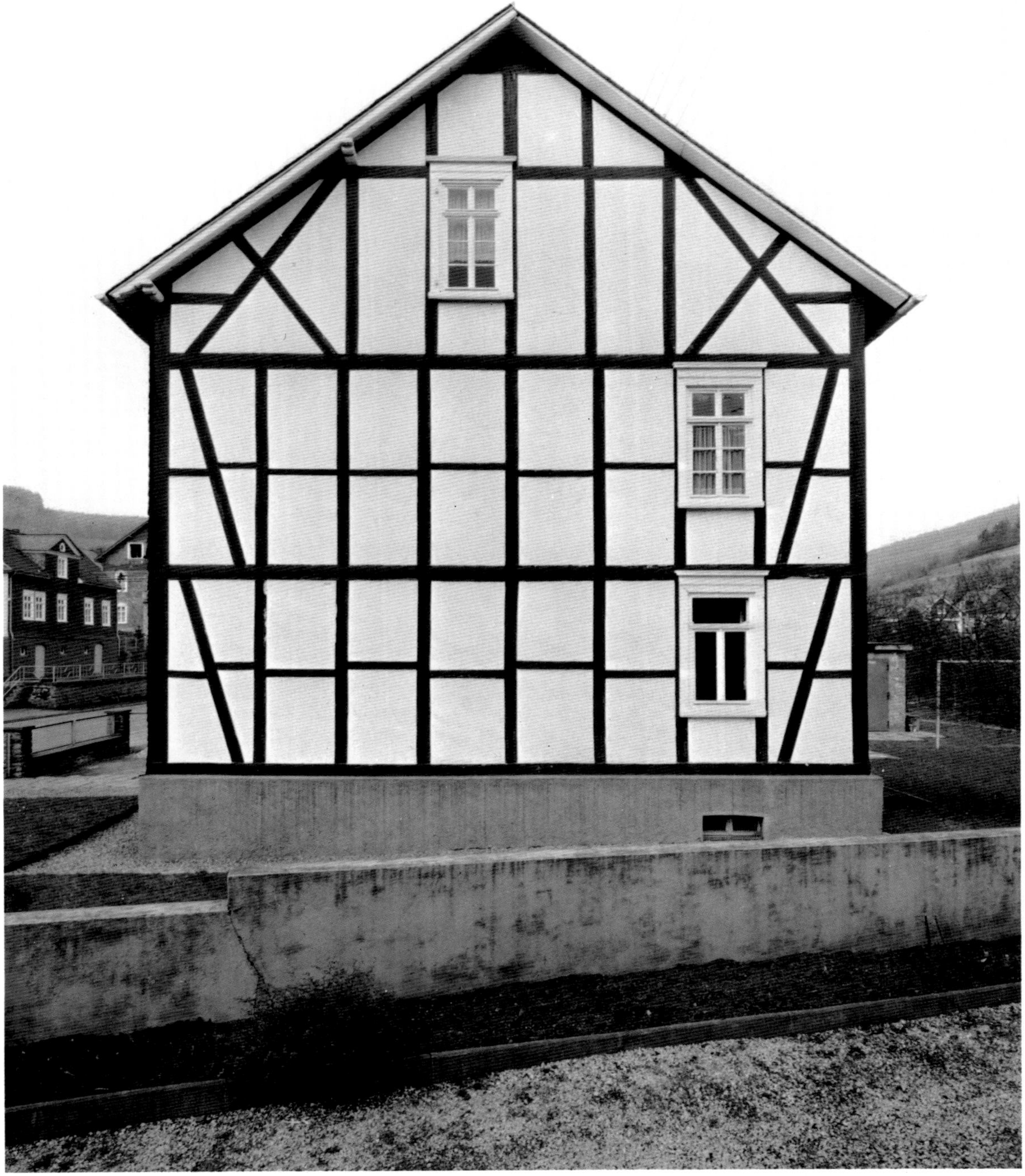

32
Eiserntalstraße 83, Eisern, 1968.

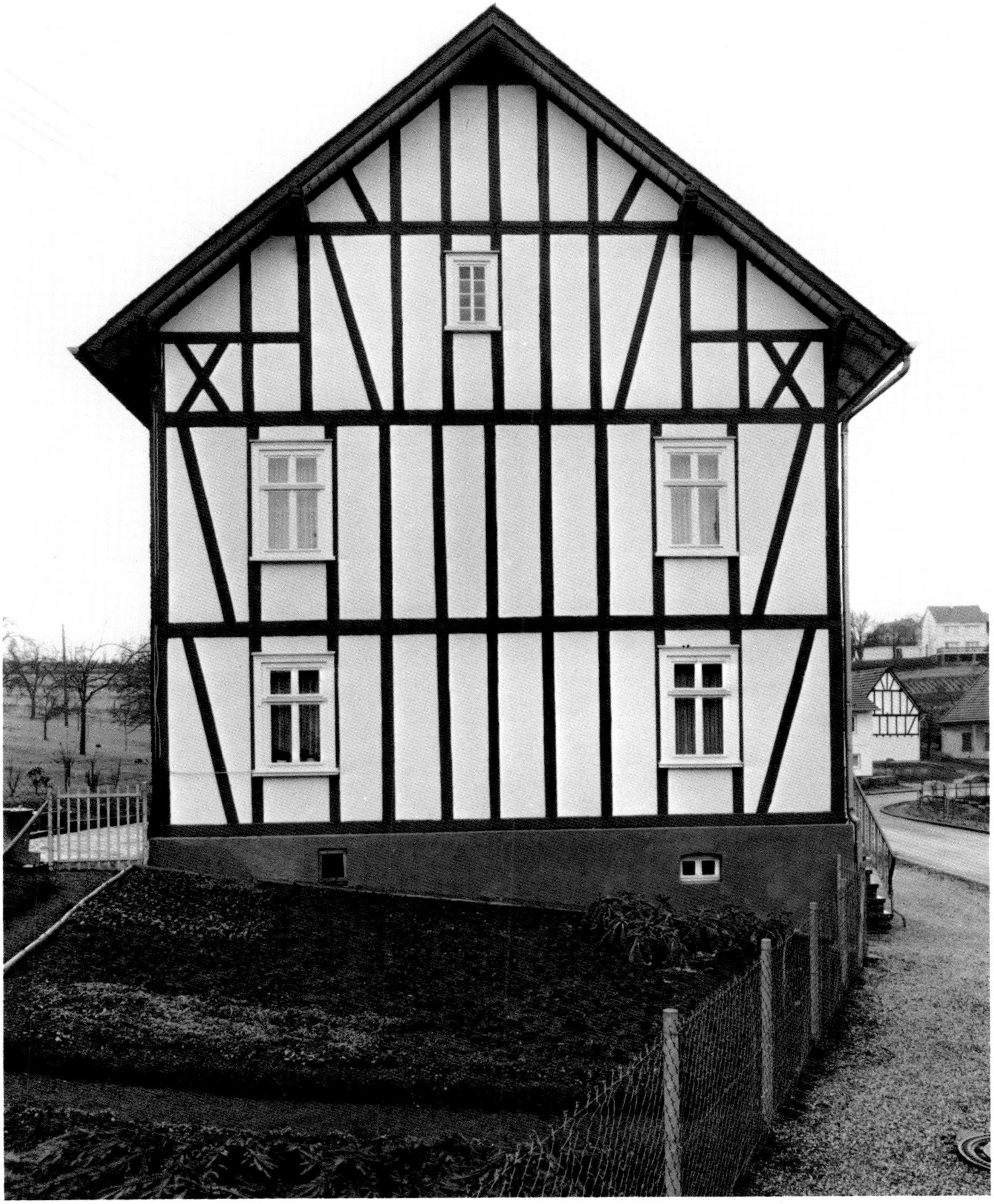

33
Mausbachstraße 60, Mausbach, 1967.

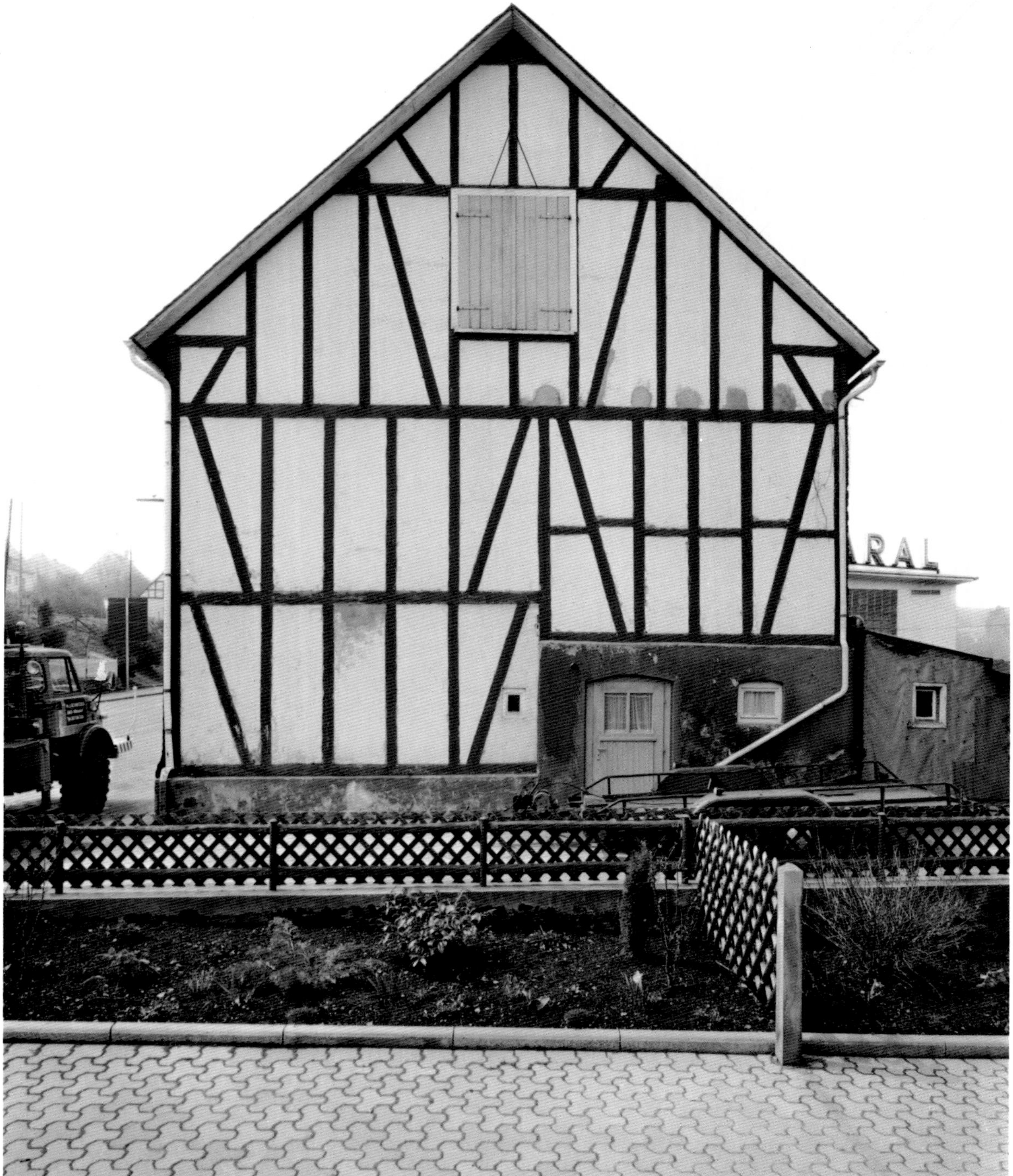

34

Hagener Straße 19, Wilnsdorf, 1972.

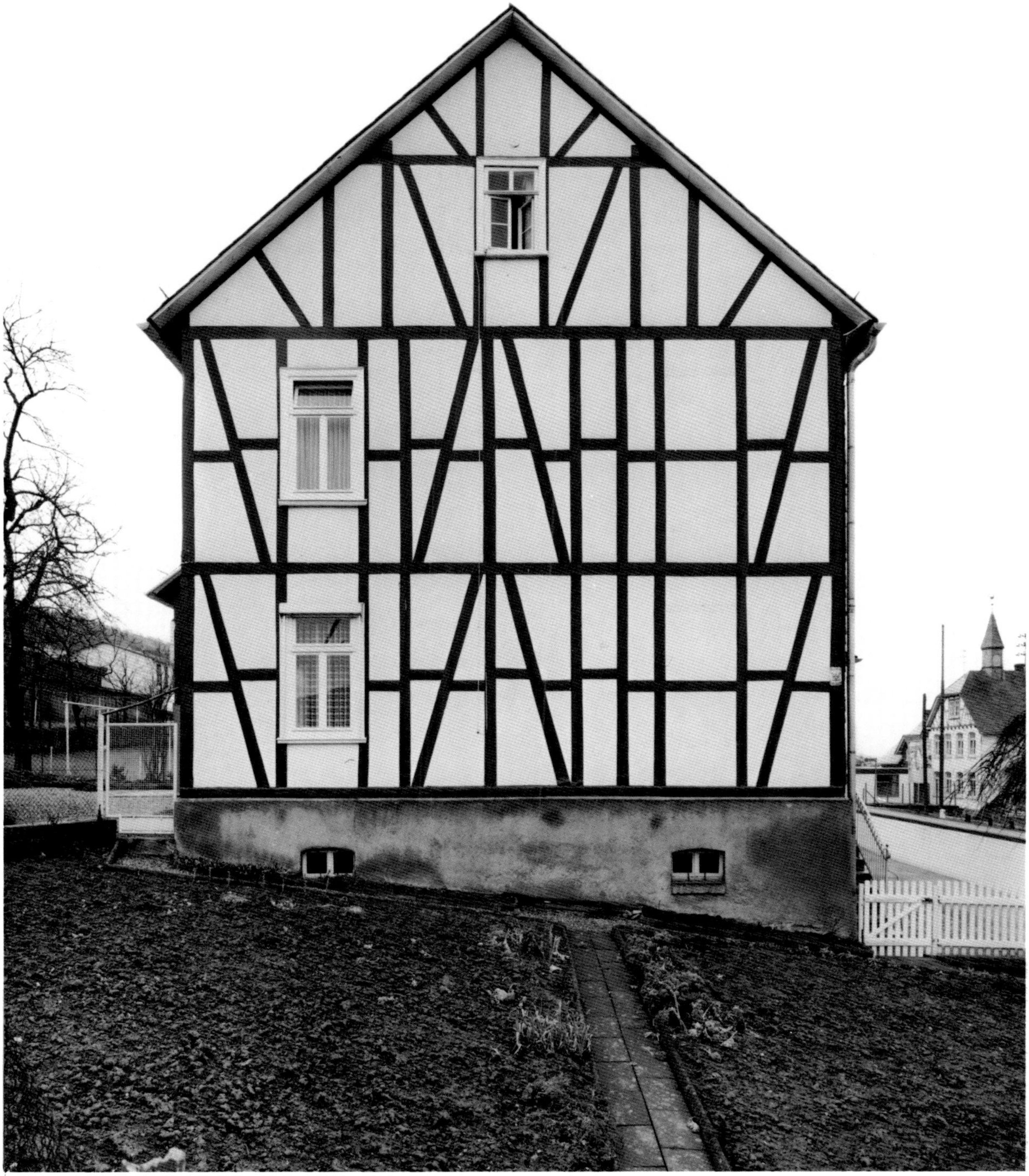

35
Wilnsdorfer Straße 26, Gilsbach, 1972.

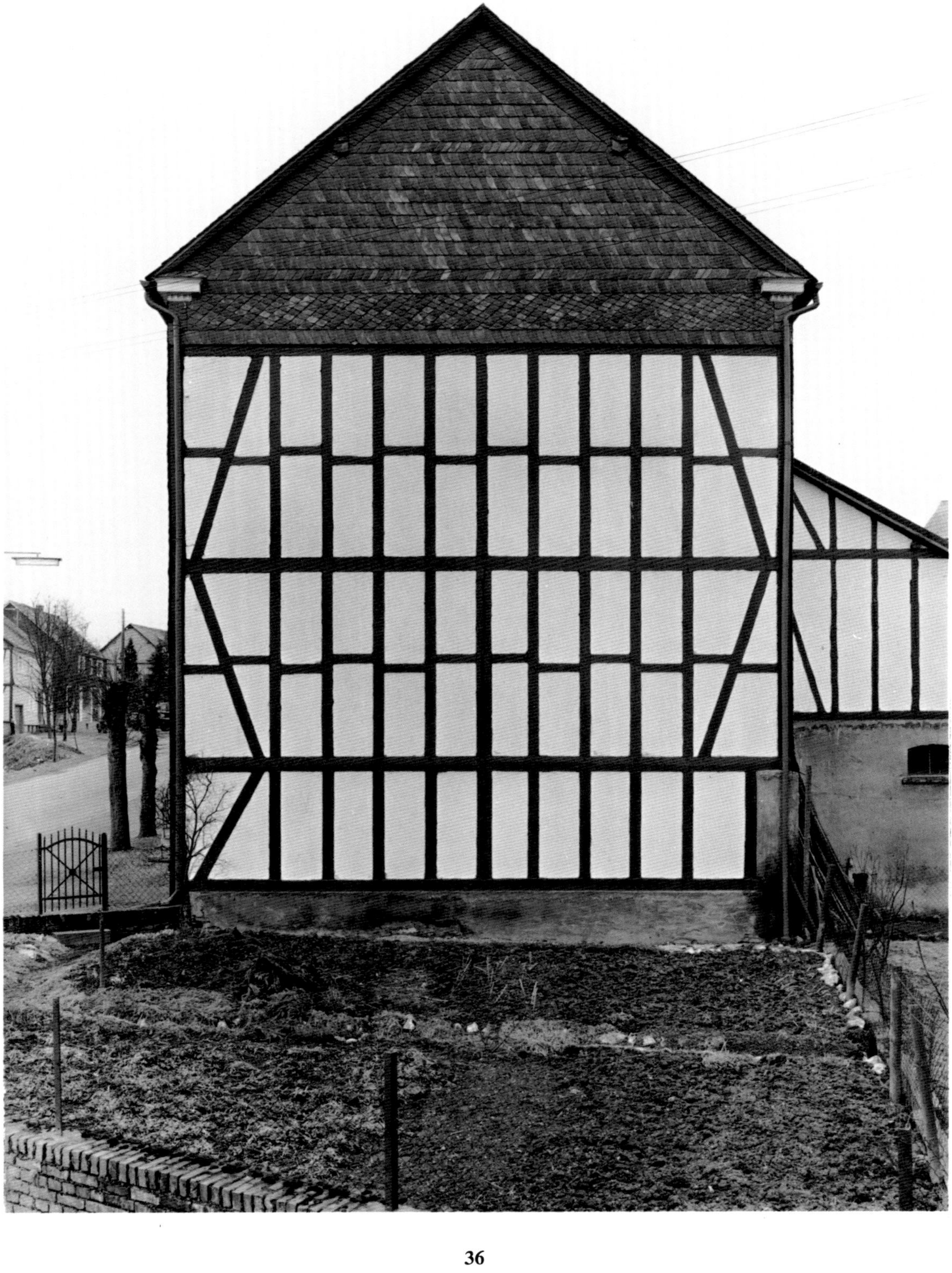

36
Wildener Straße 7, Salchendorf, 1961.

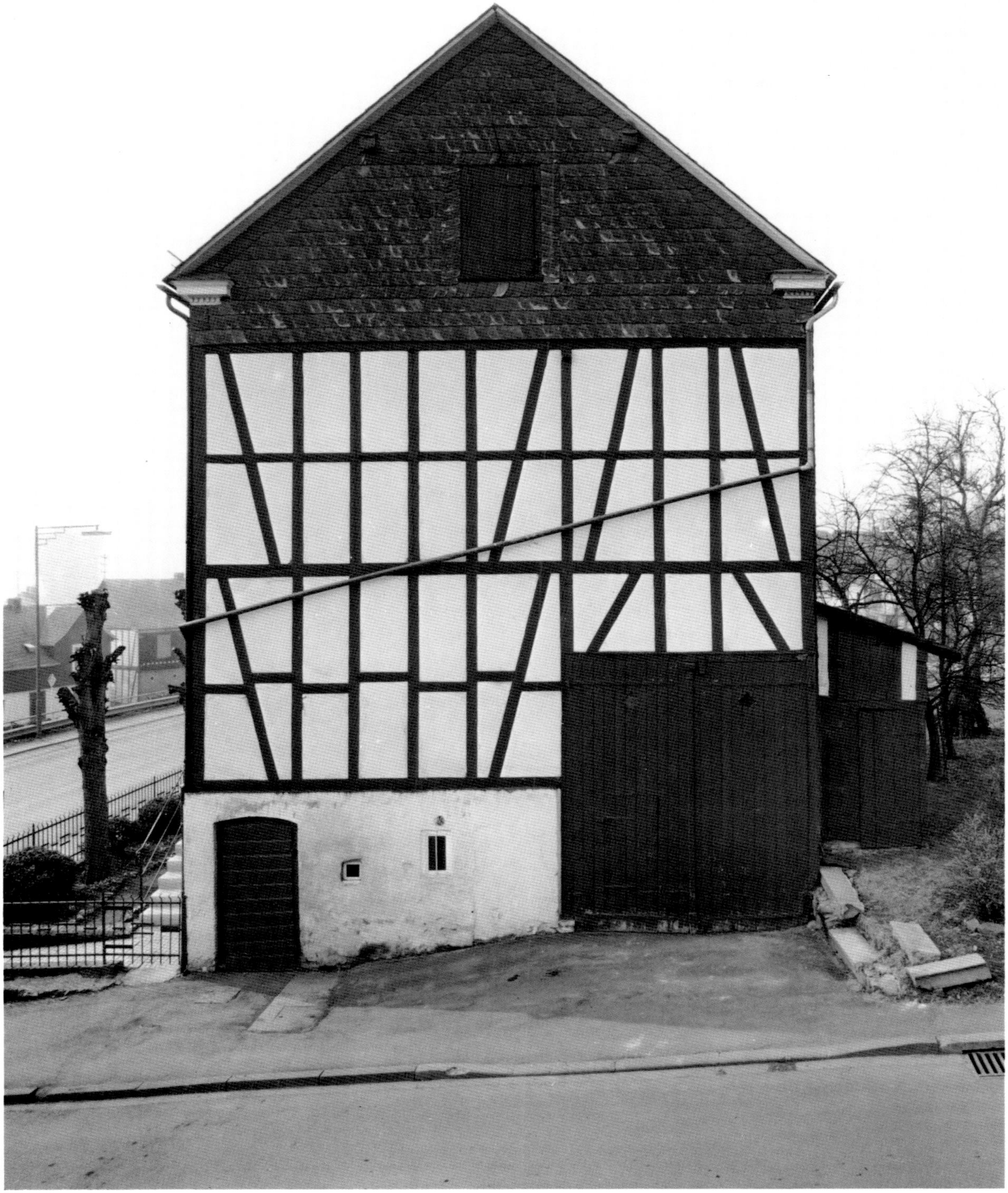

37
Kölner Straße 351, Salchendorf, 1969.

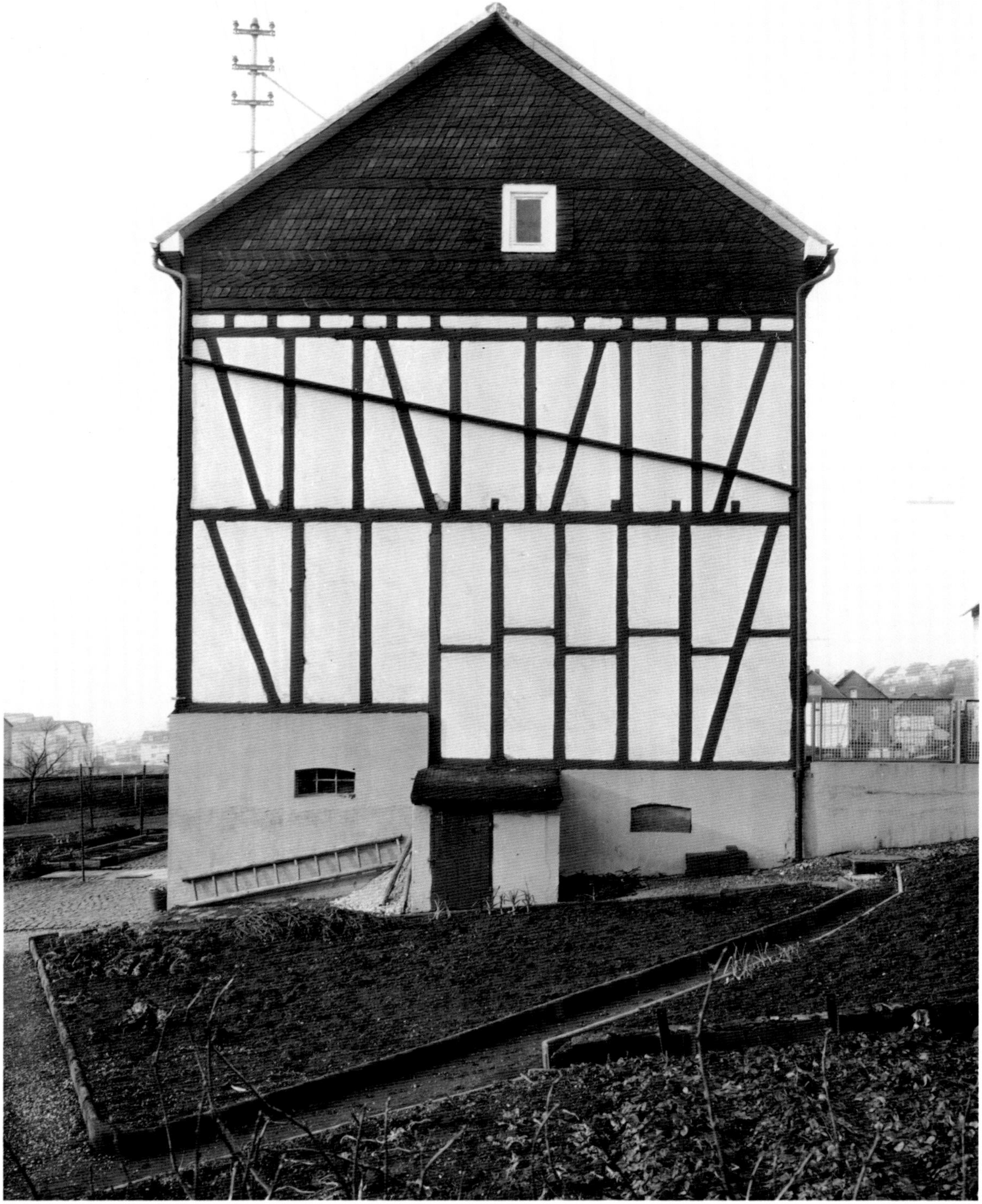

38
Wildener Straße 46, Salchendorf, 1973.

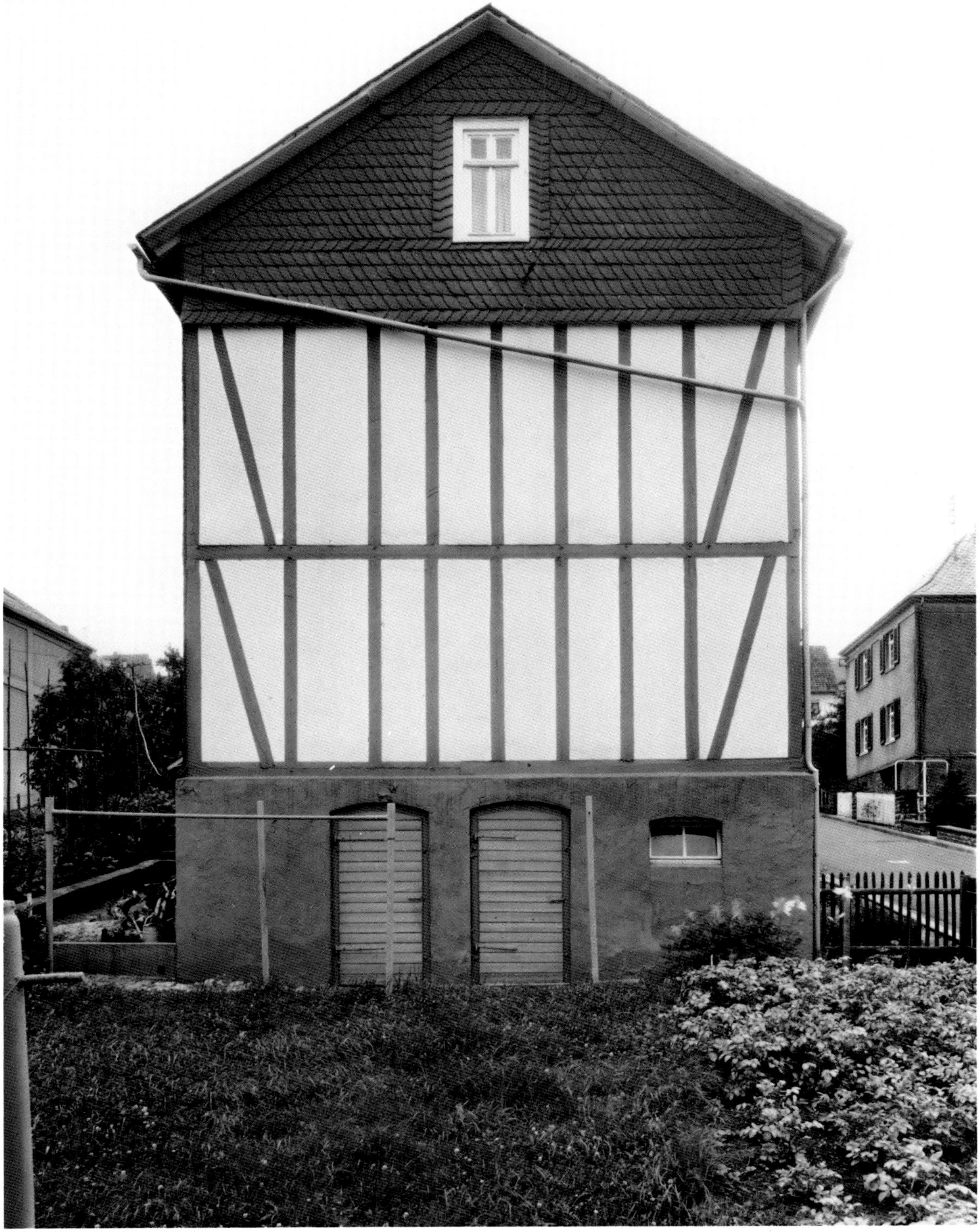

39
Karlstraße 4, Niederschelderhütte, 1973.

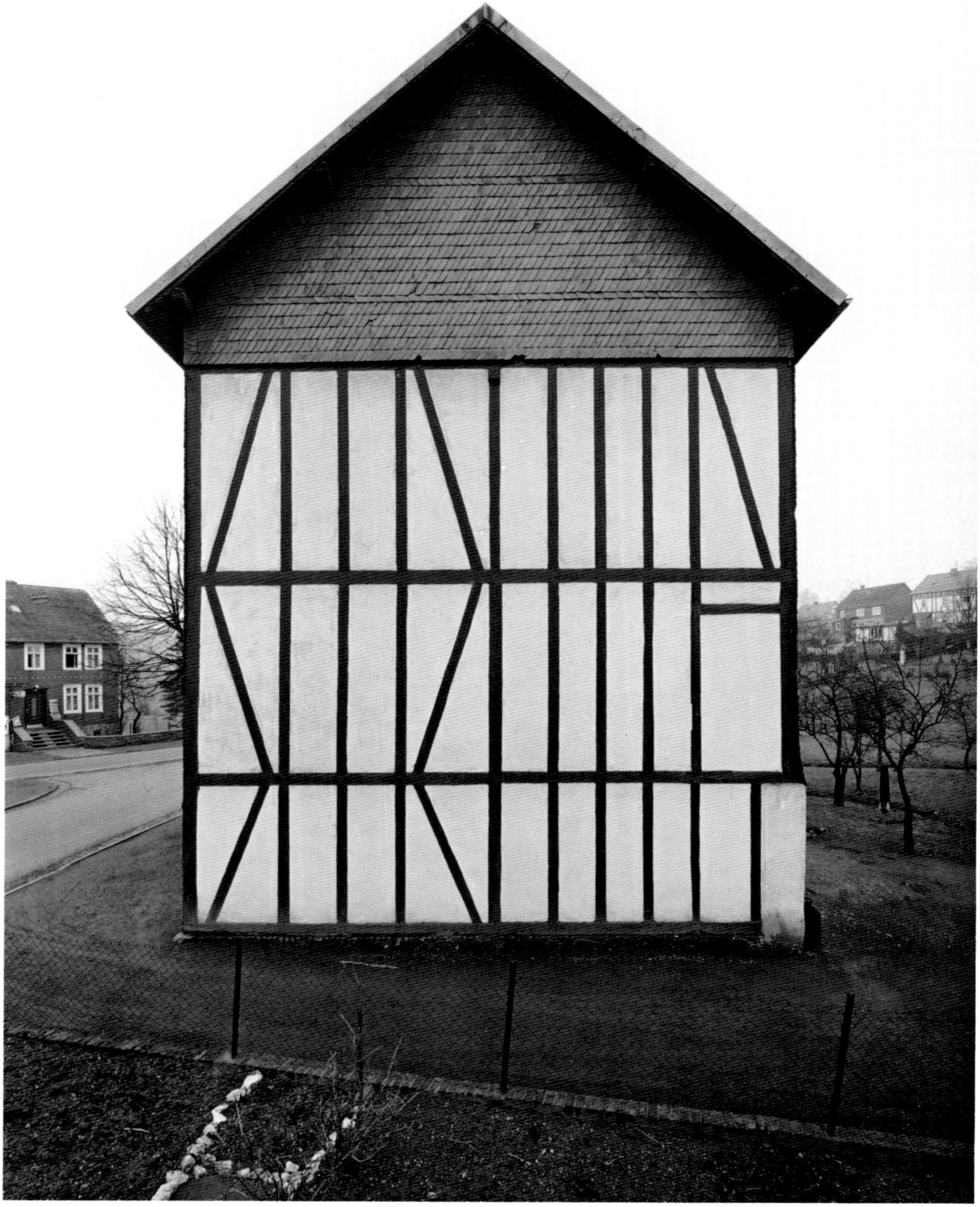

40
Rensdorfstraße 1, Salchendorf, 1961.

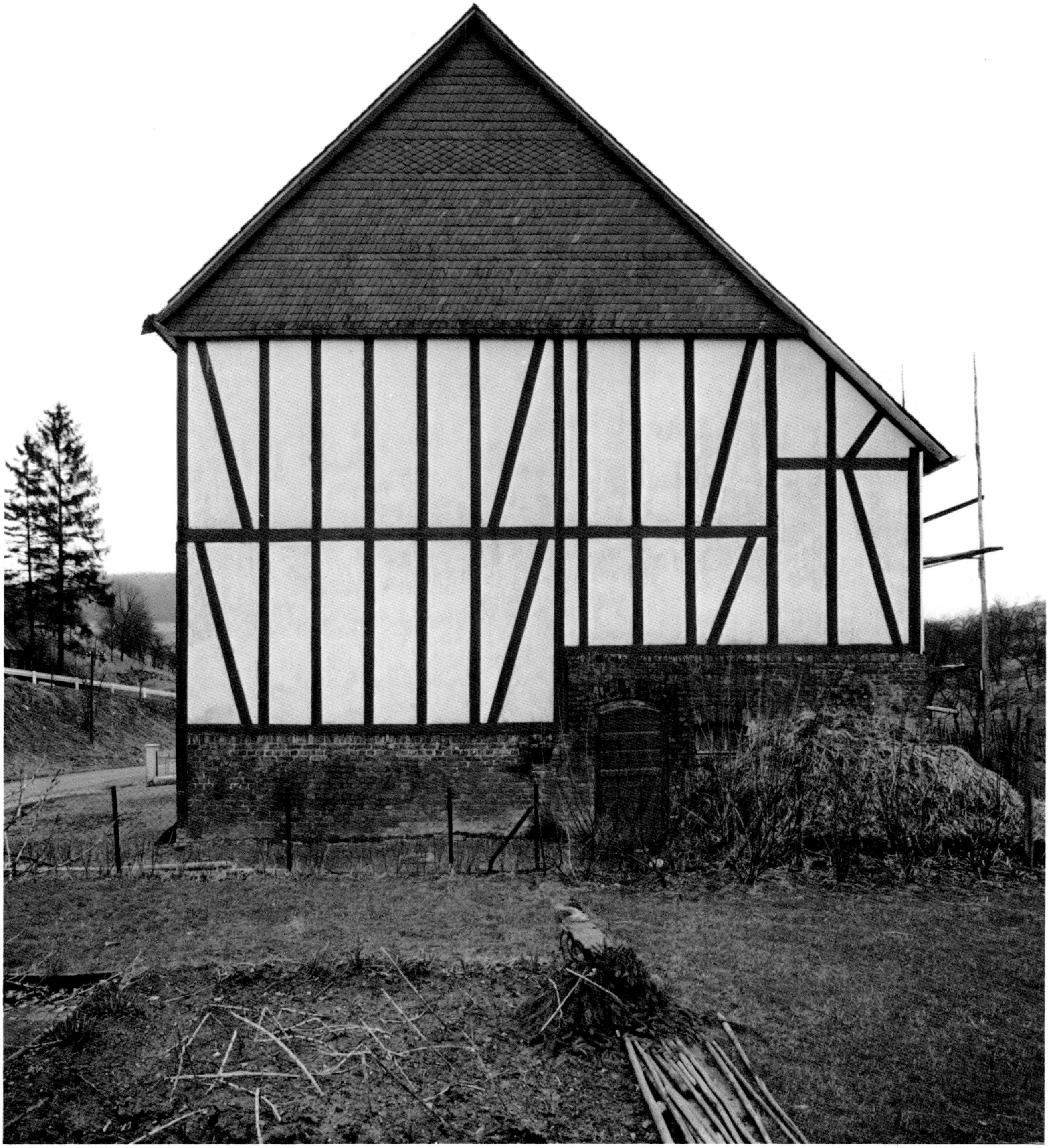

41
Hambachwaldstraße 9, Gilsbach, 1962.

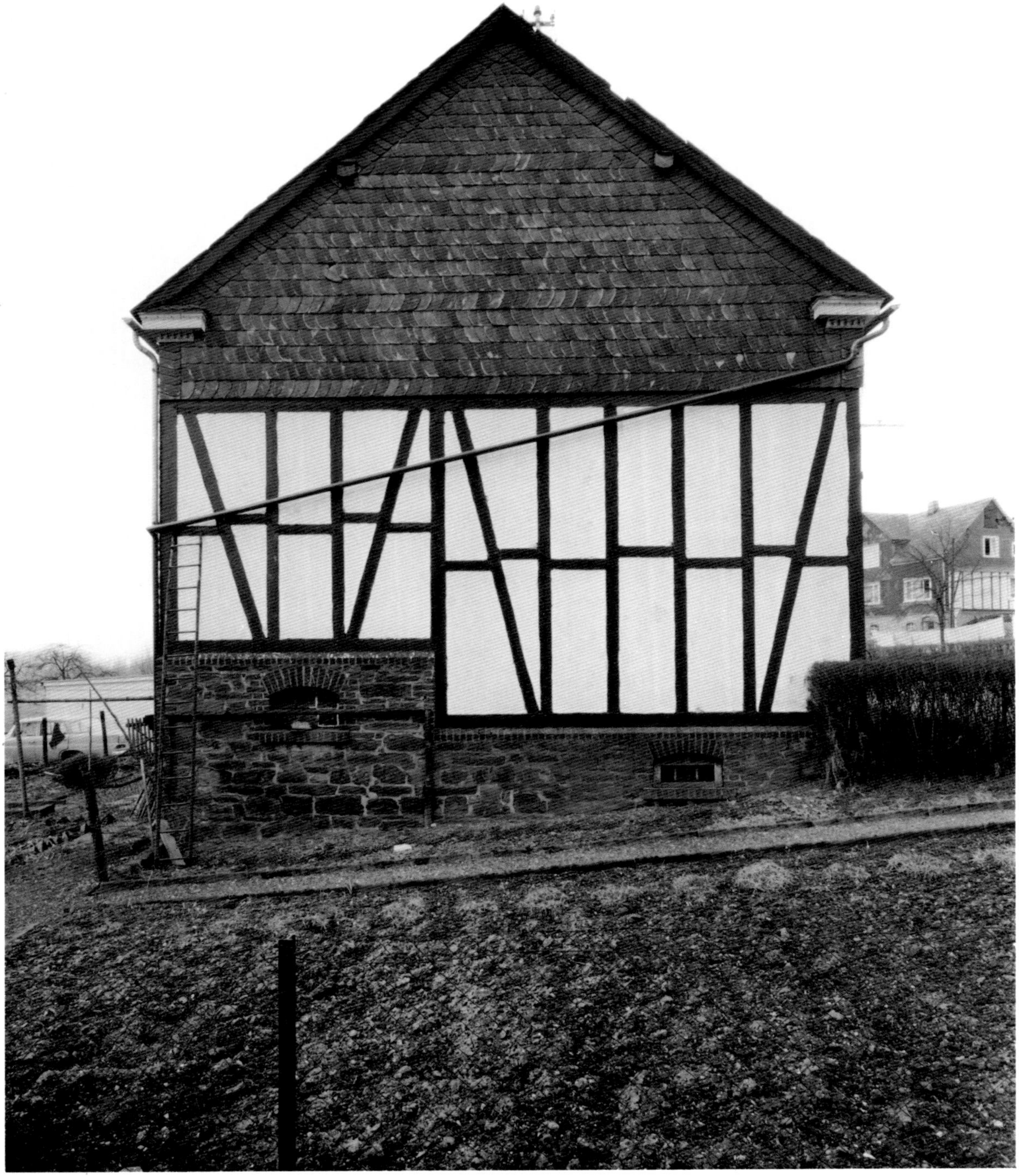

42

Wildener Straße 78, Salchendorf, 1968.

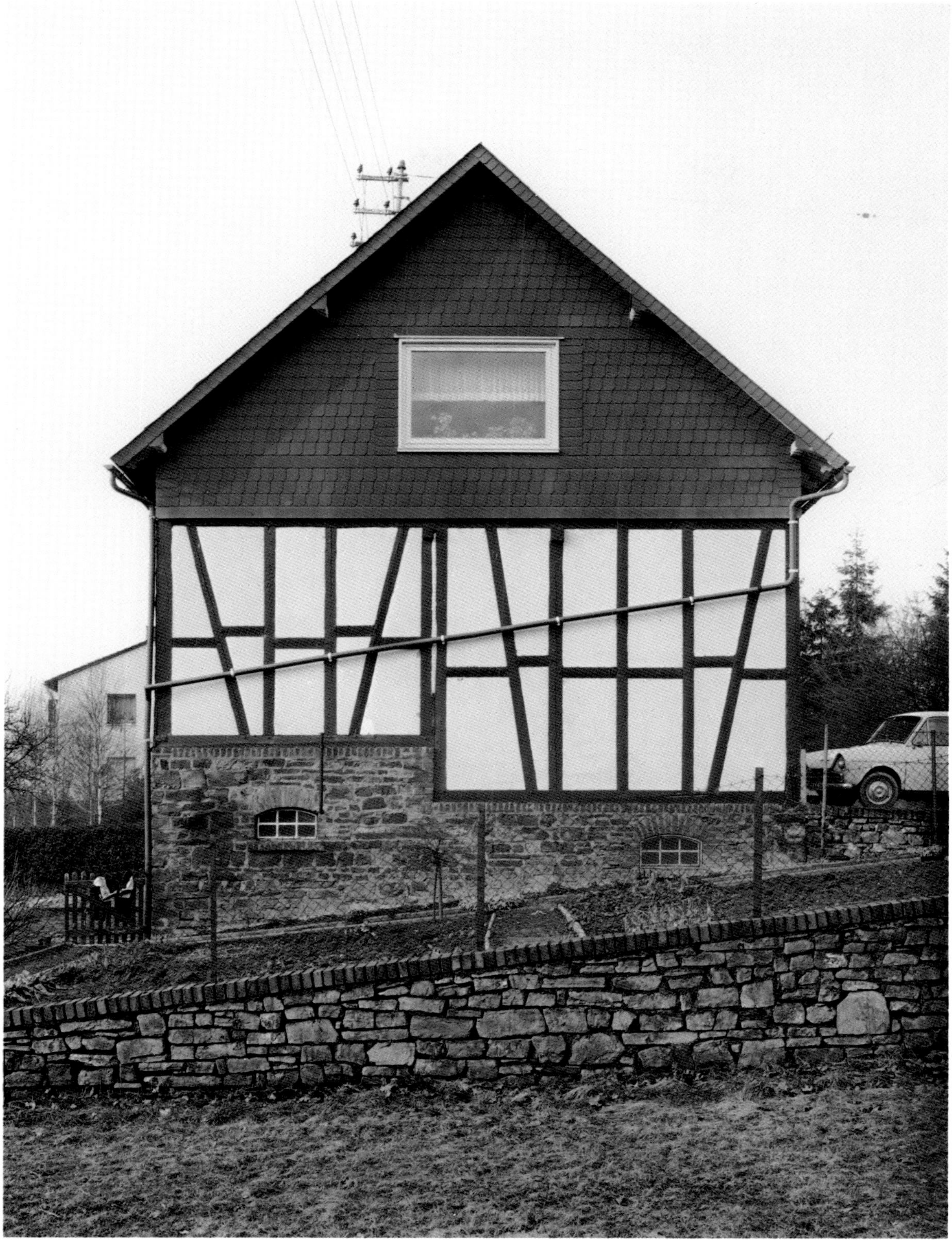

43
Wildener Straße 64, Salchendorf, 1973.

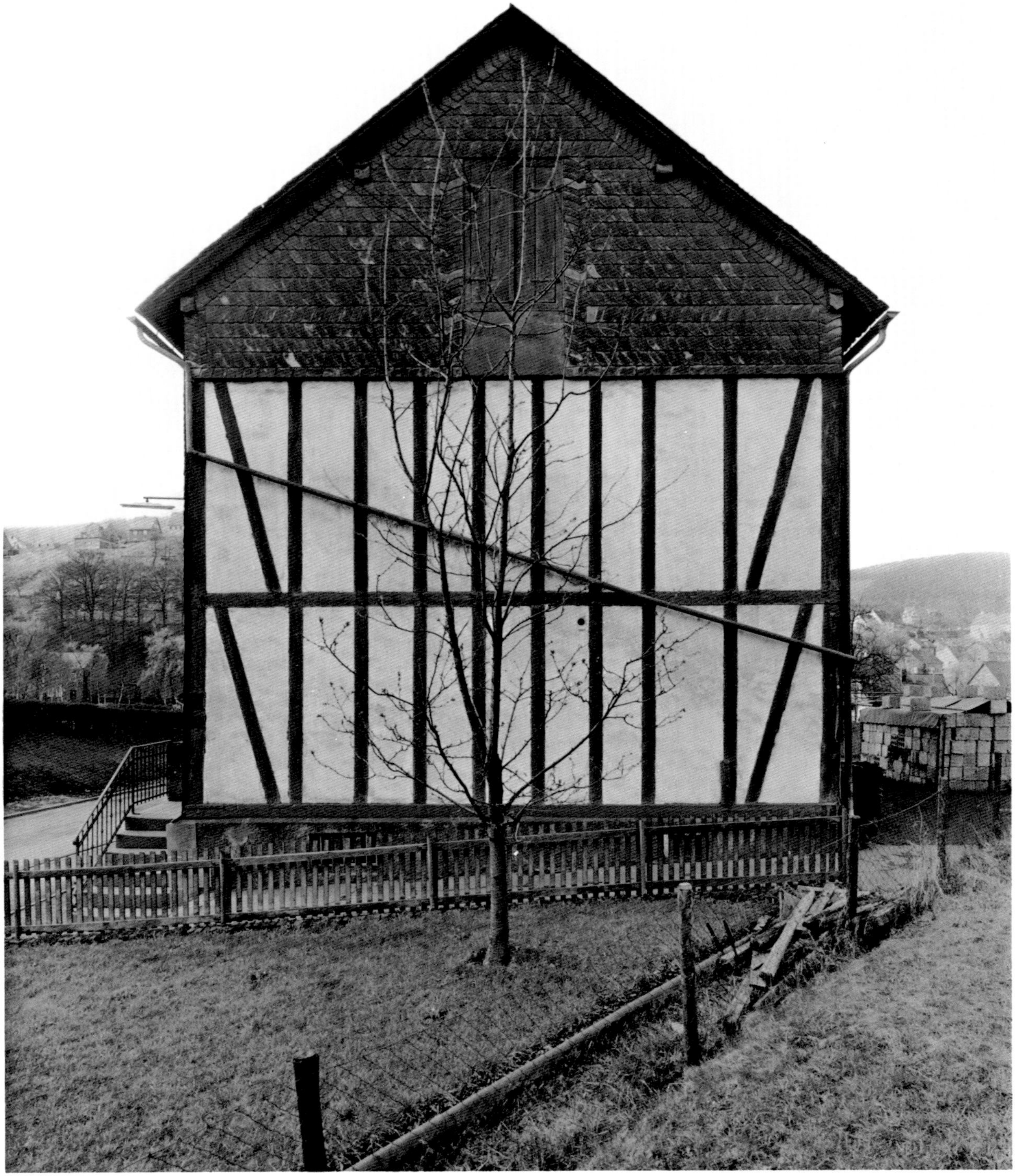

44
Talsbachstraße 11, Eiserfeld, 1960.

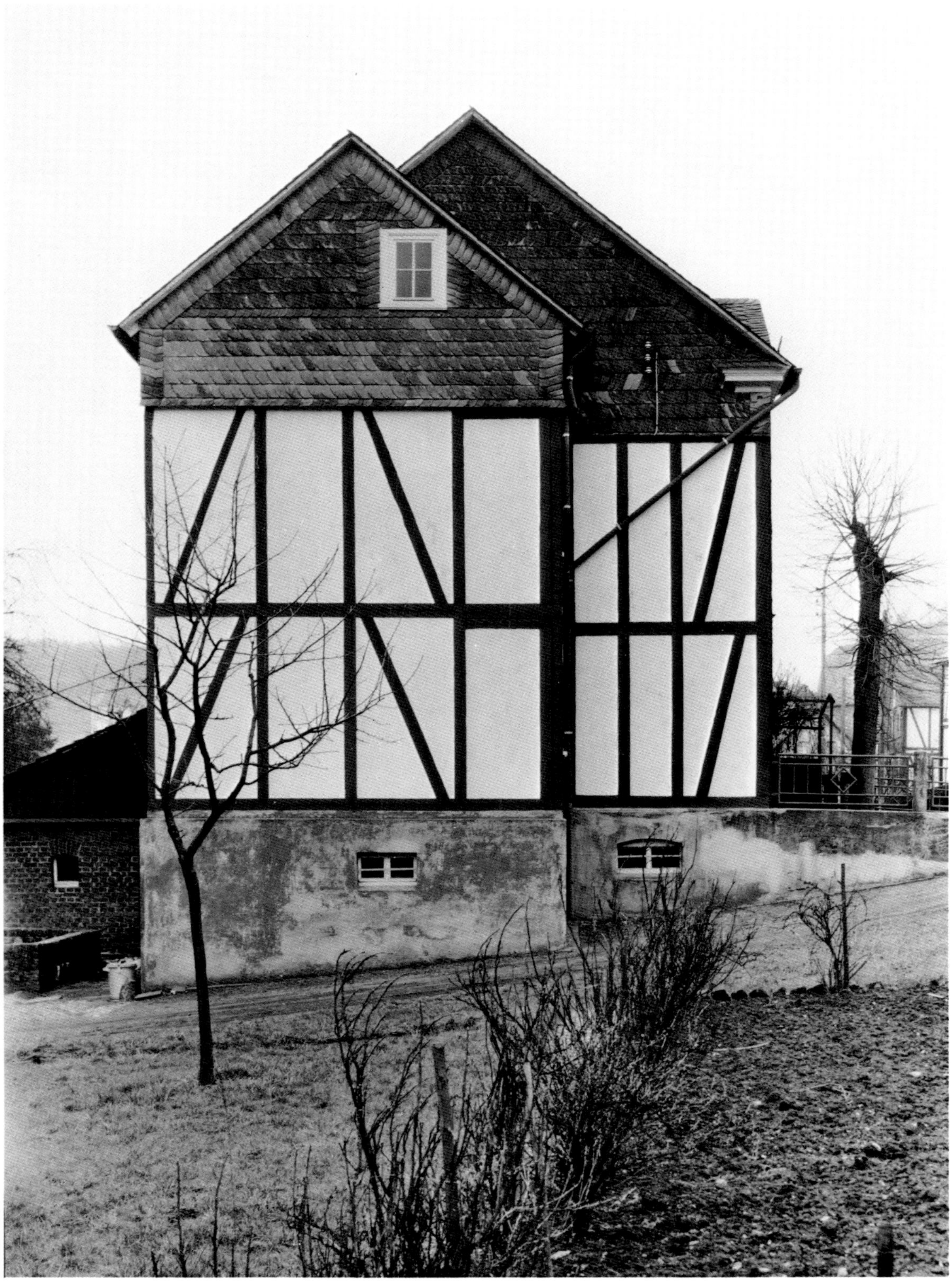

45
Kampenstraße 44, Gosenbach, 1959.

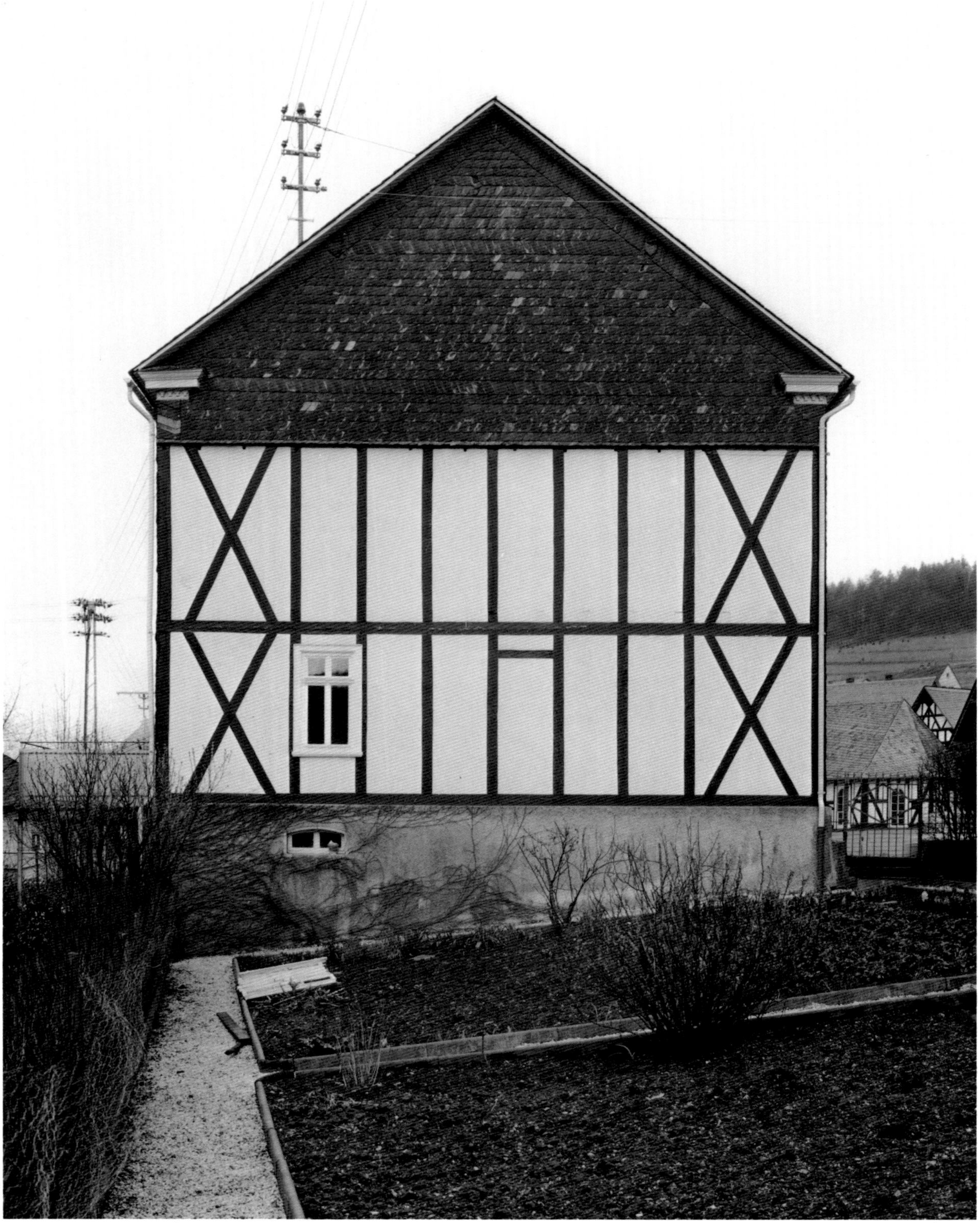

46
Eiserntalstraße 120, Eisern, 1972.

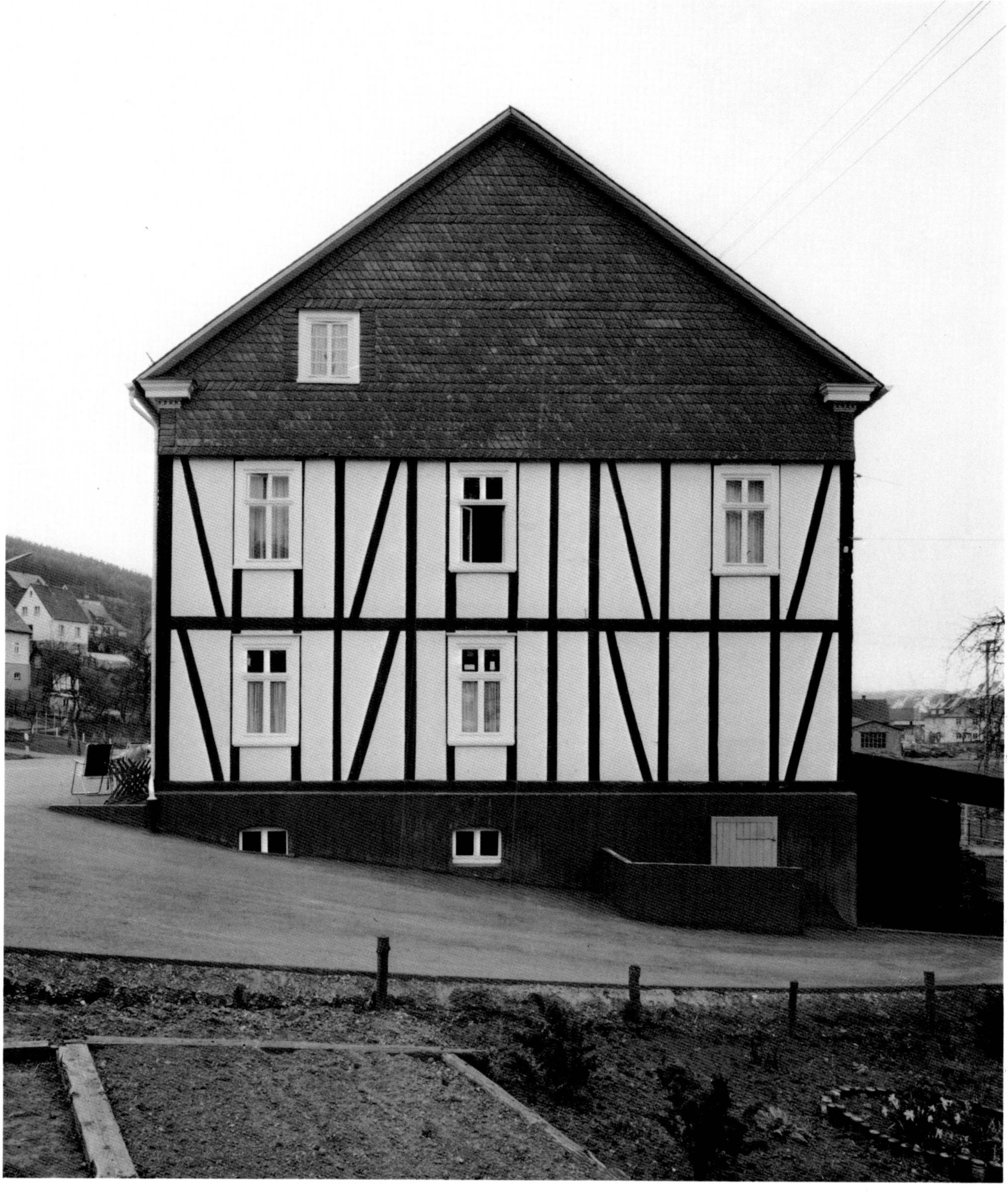

47
Olper Straße 15, Büschergrund, 1970.

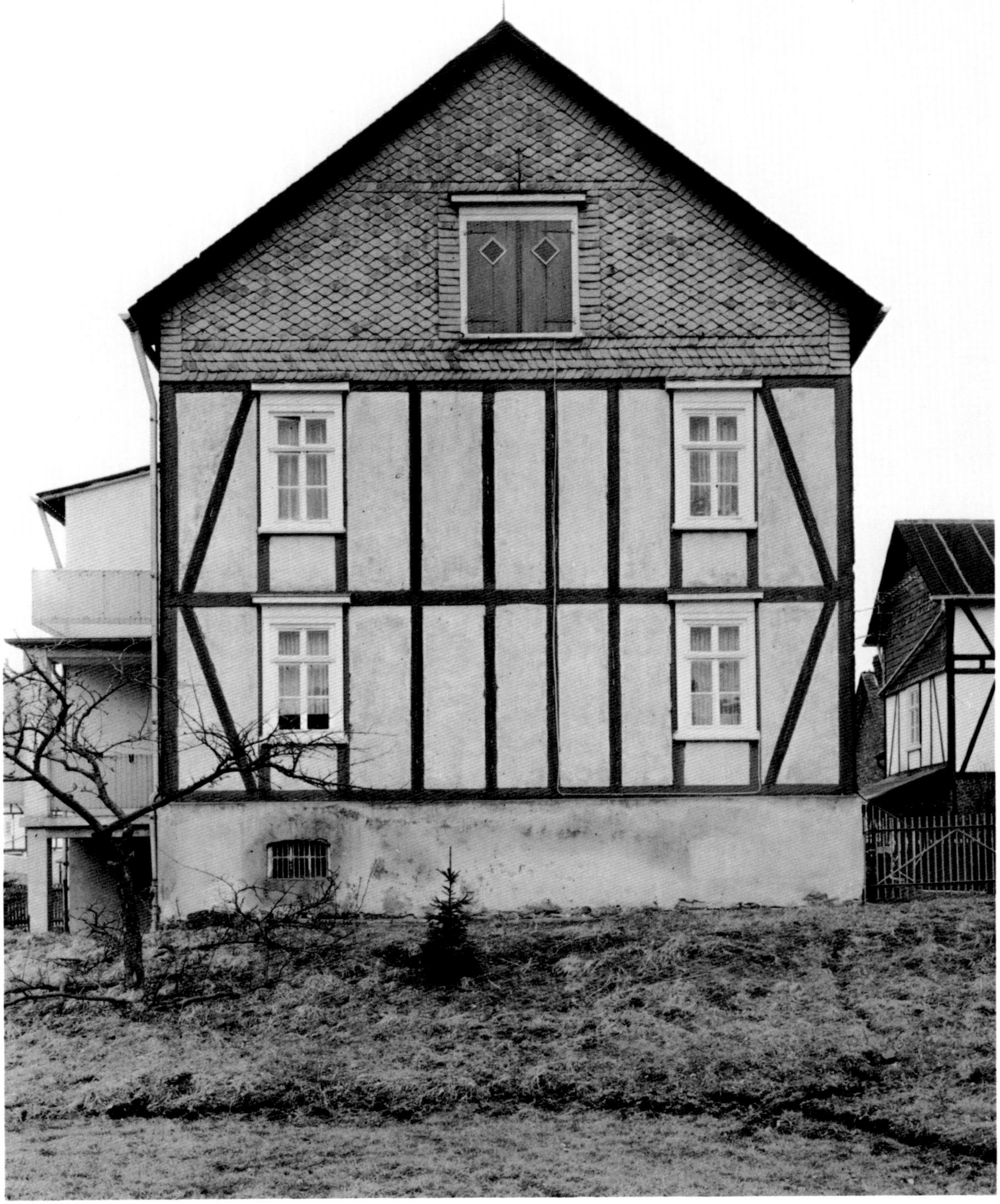

48
In der Bitze 3, Eisern, 1972.

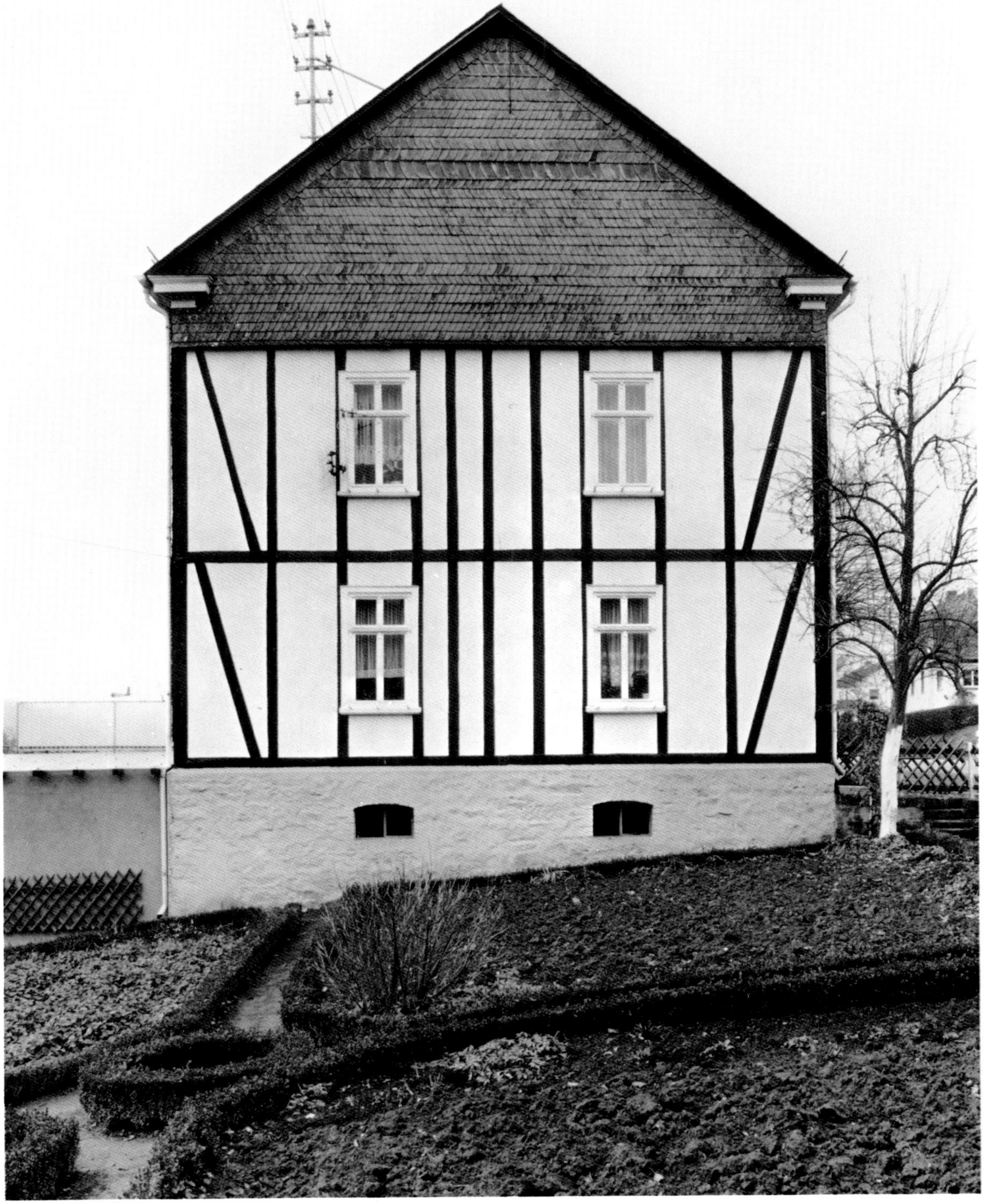

49
Siegtalstraße 50, Grissenbach, 1972.

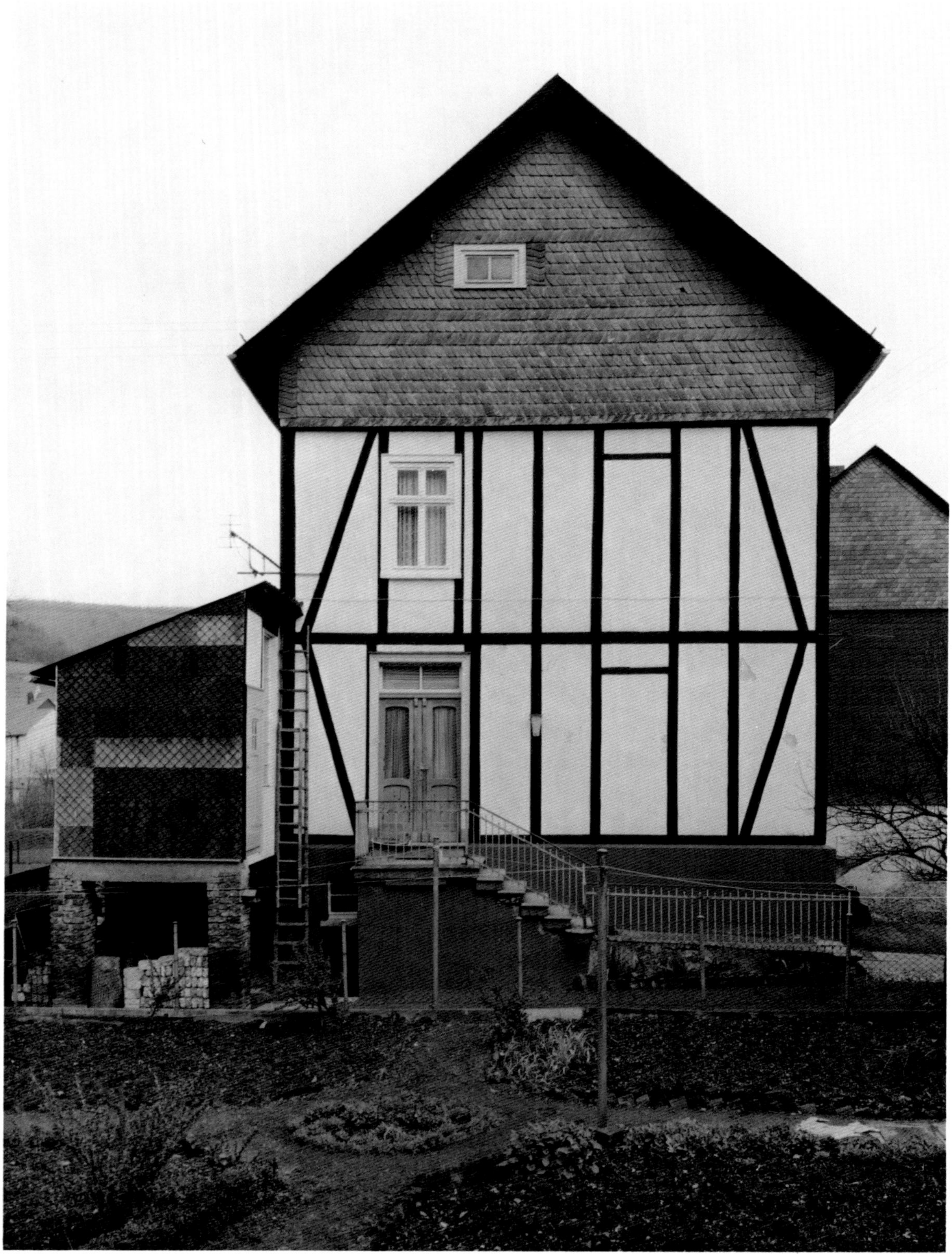

50
Eiserntalstraße 142, Eisern, 1970.

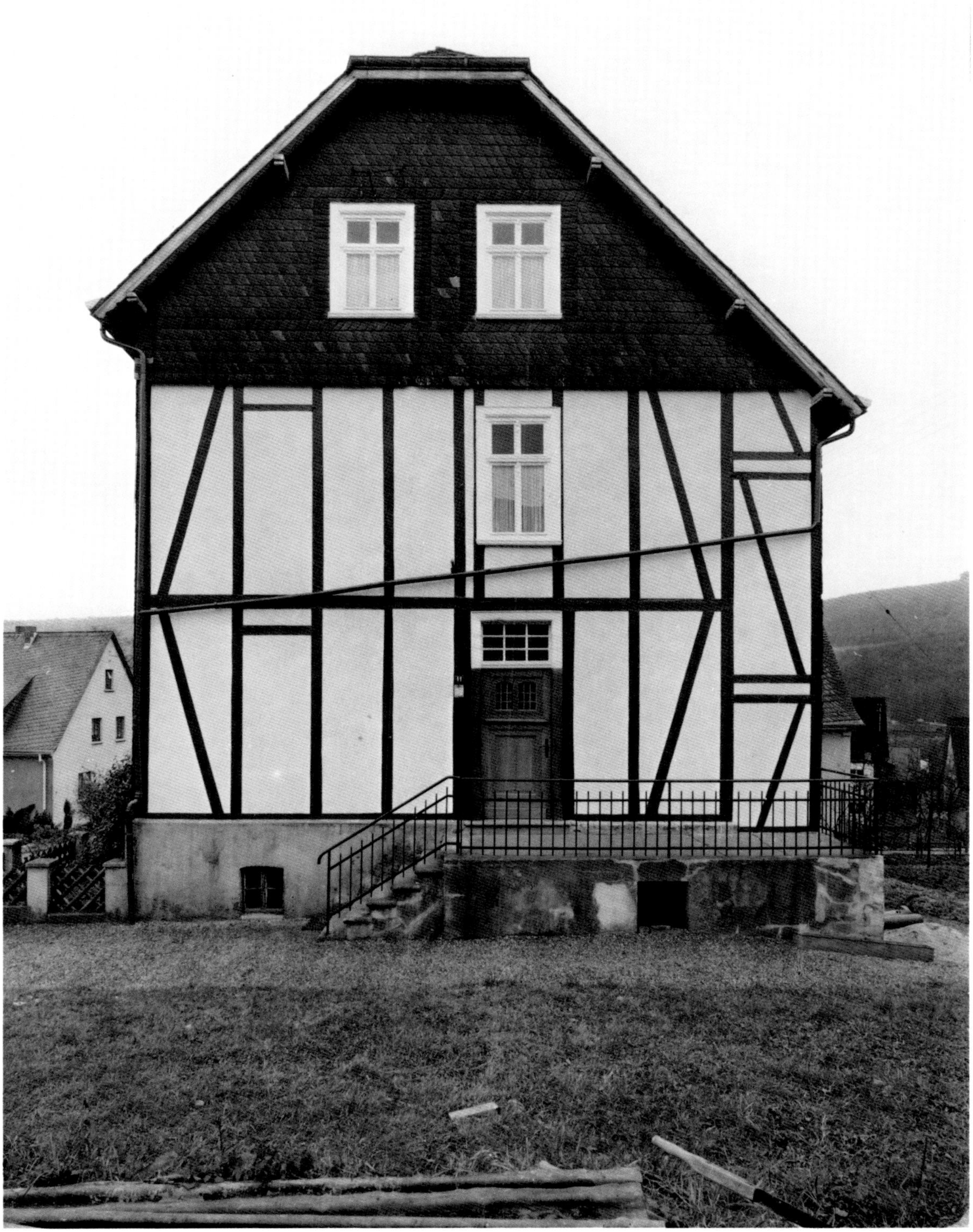

51
Schloßblick 17, Kaan-Marienborn, 1962.

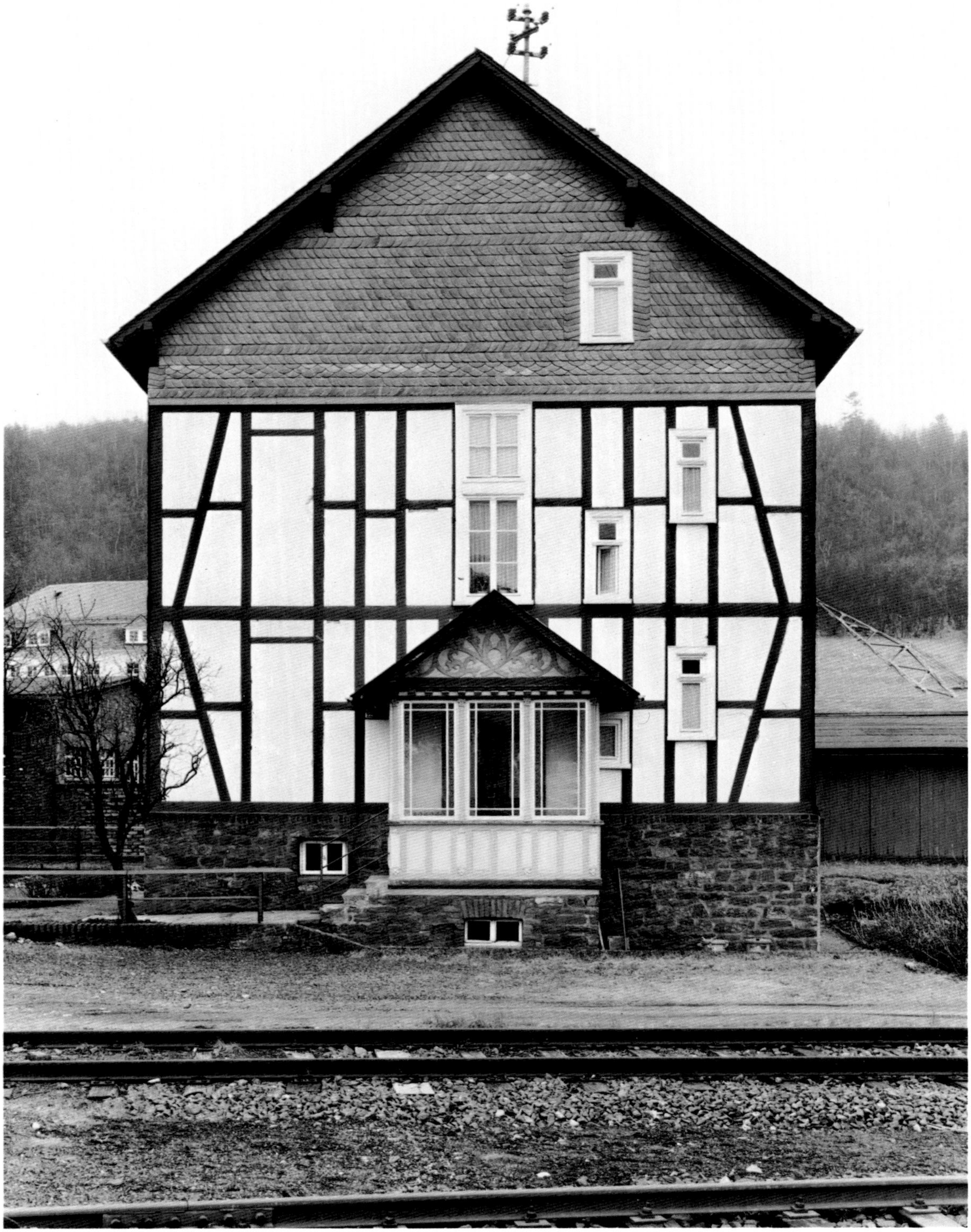

52
Fritz-Schäfer-Straße 22, Salchendorf, 1964.

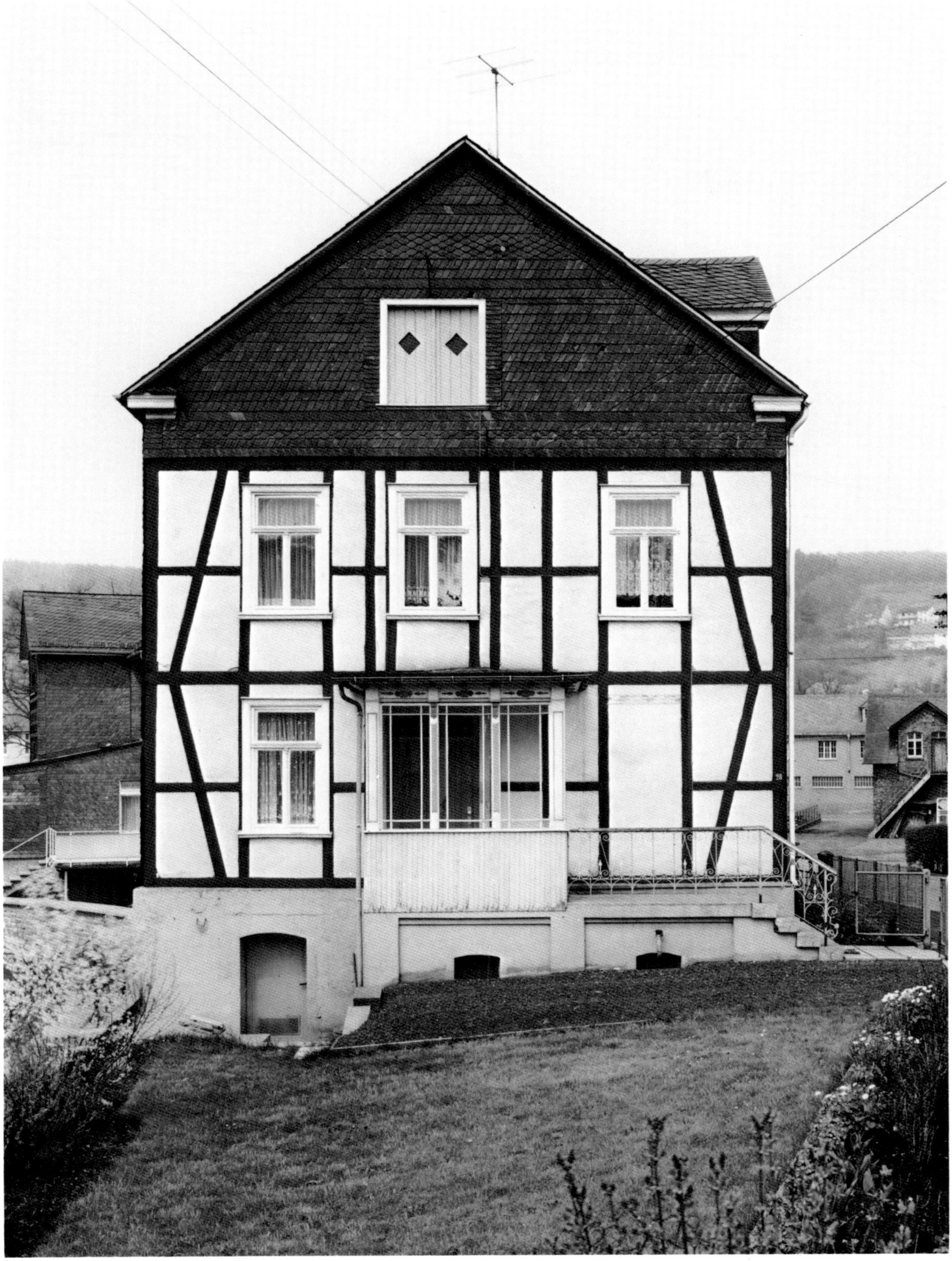

53

Bahnhofstraße 28, Neunkirchen, 1969.

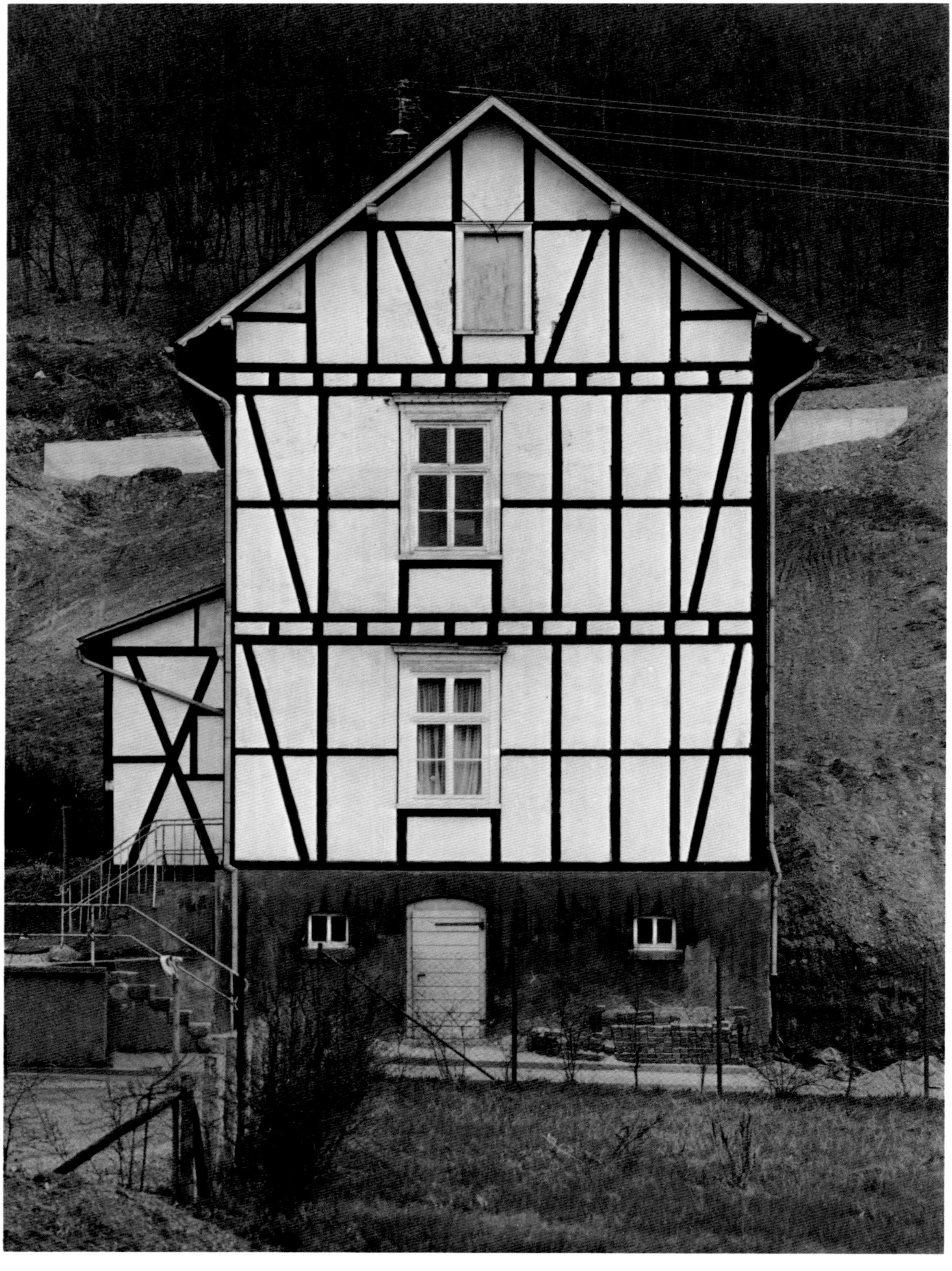

54
Oststraße 16, Freudenberg, 1971.

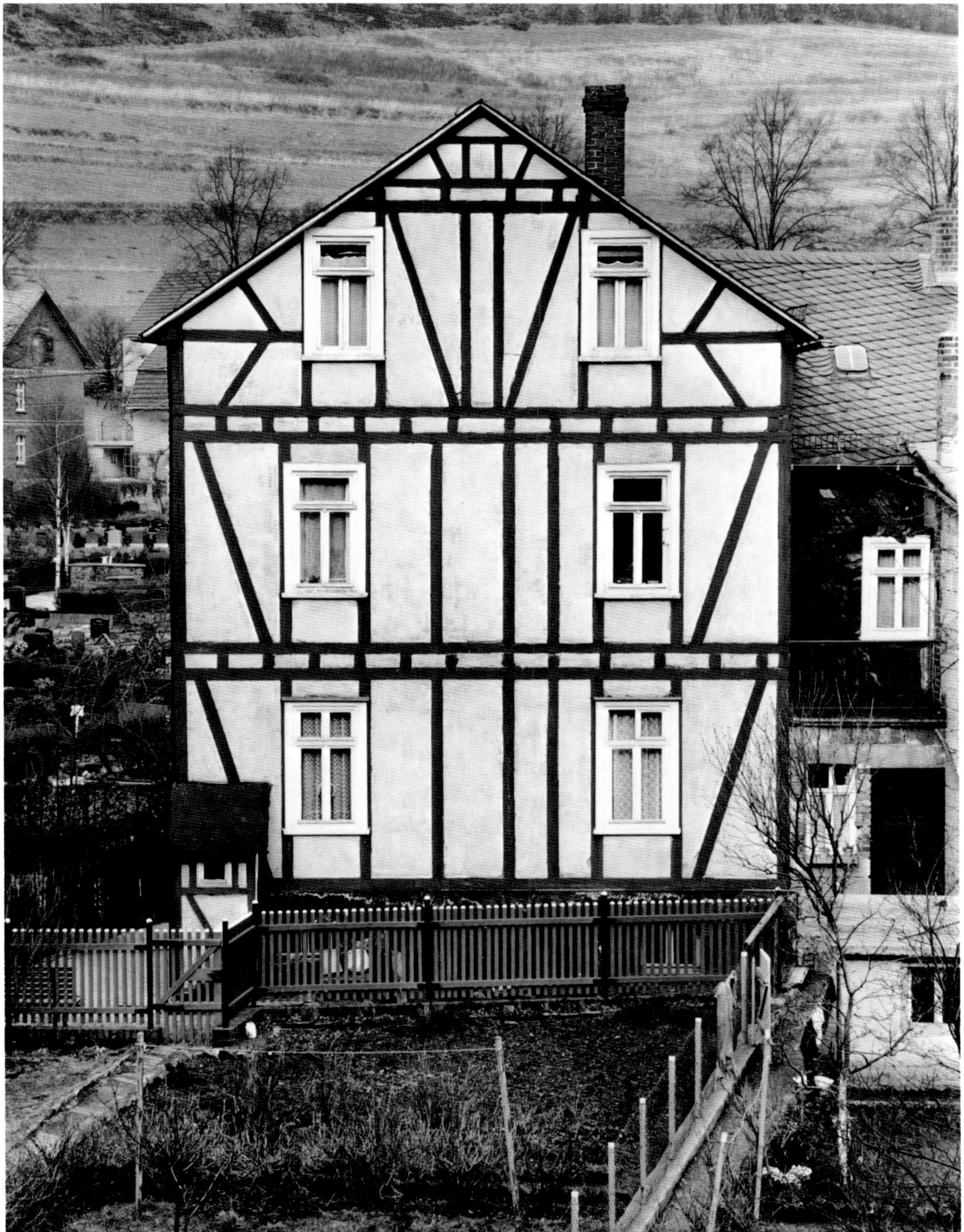

55
Eisernstraße 114, Eiserfeld, 1961.

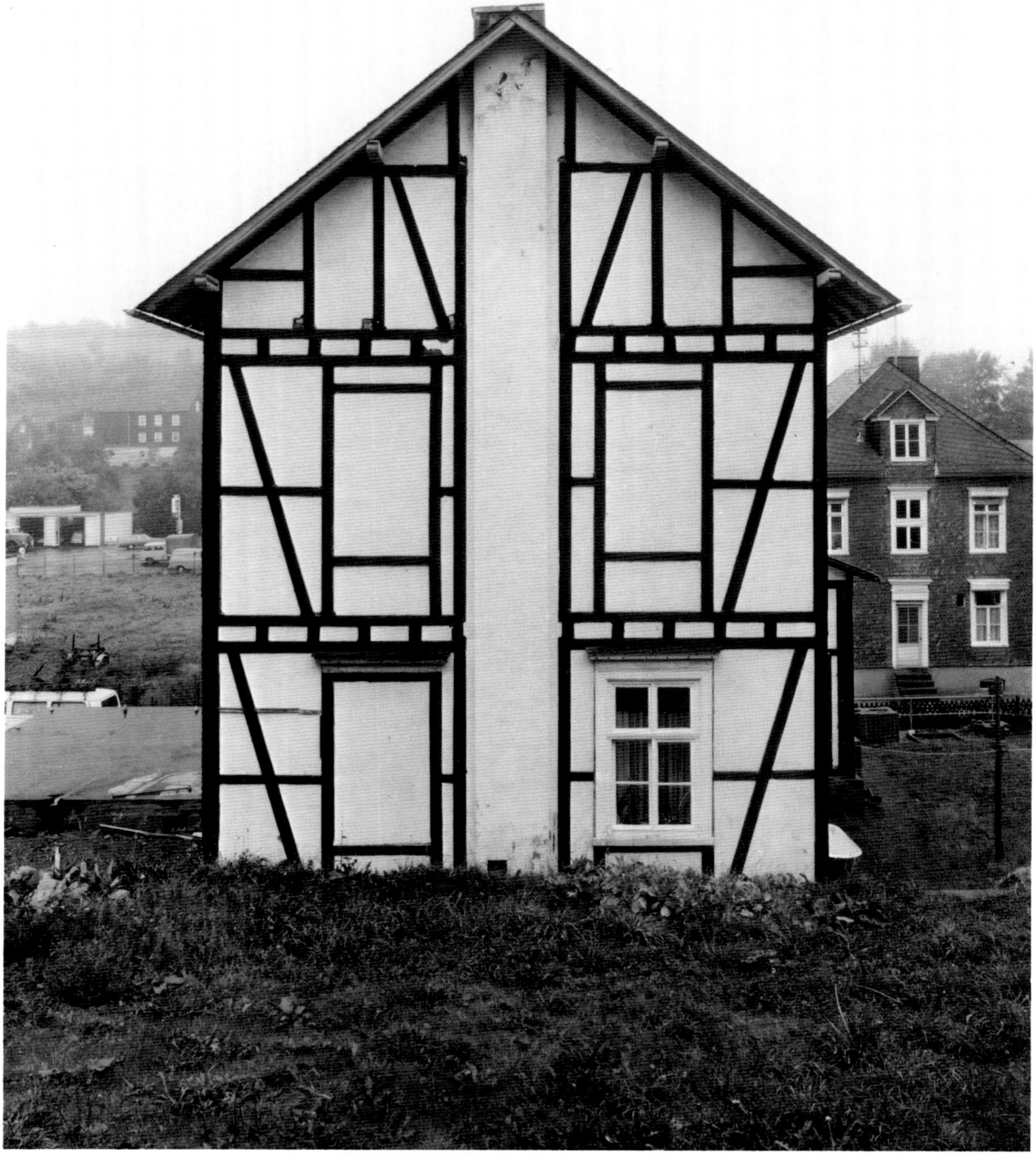

56
Oststraße 16, Freudenberg, 1971.

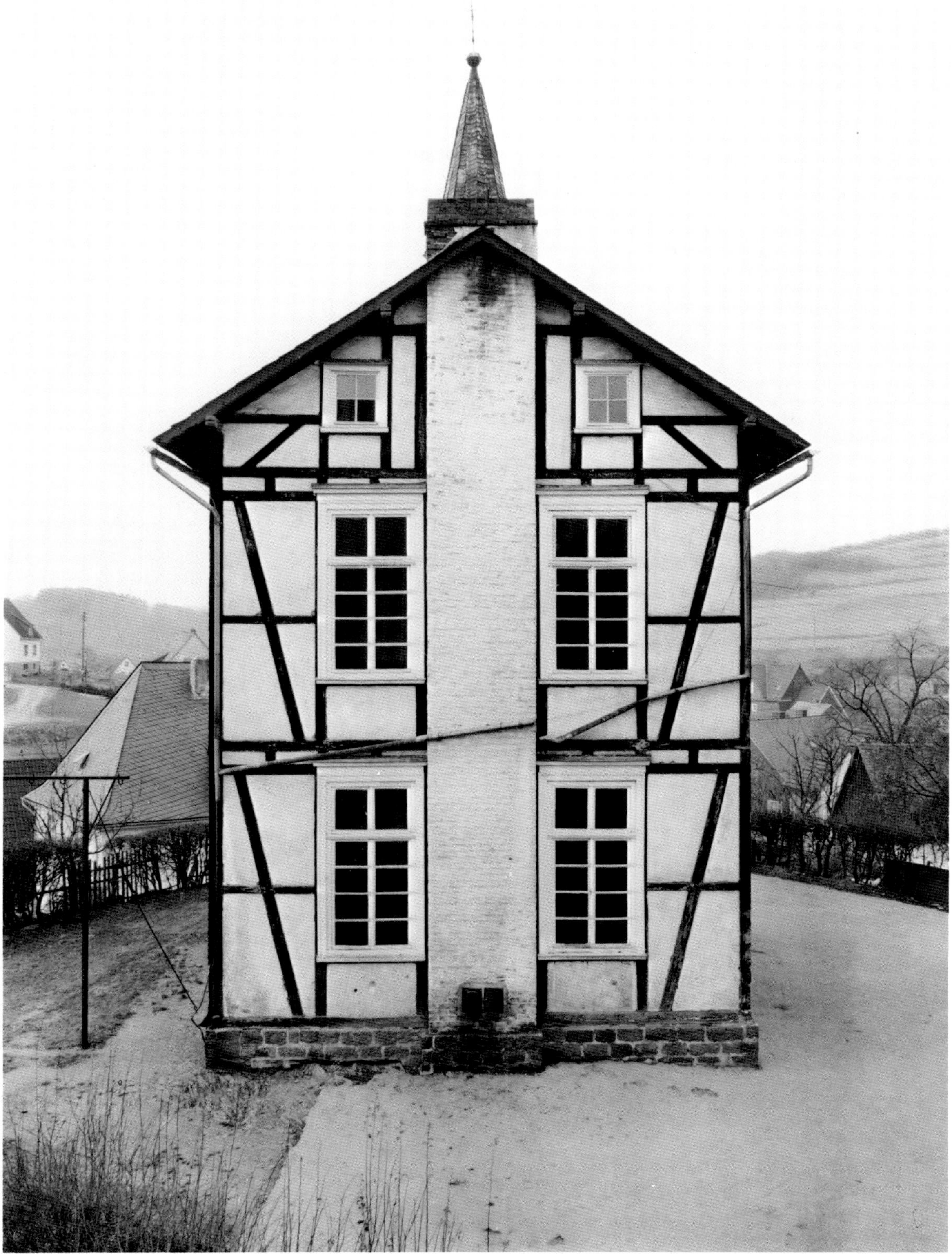

57
Schulplatz 6, Niederndorf, 1964.

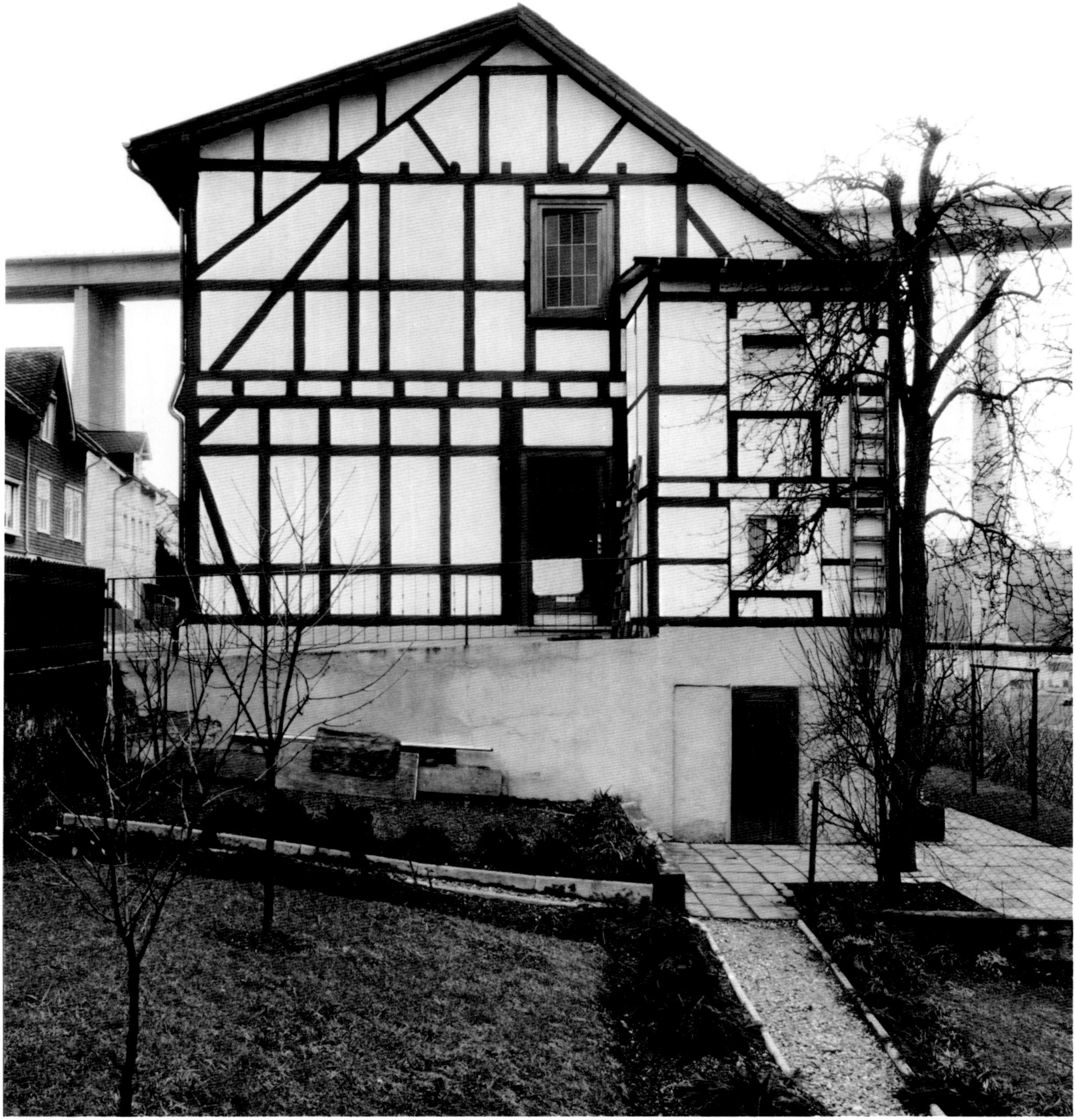

58
Grabettstraße 87, Eiserfeld, 1973.

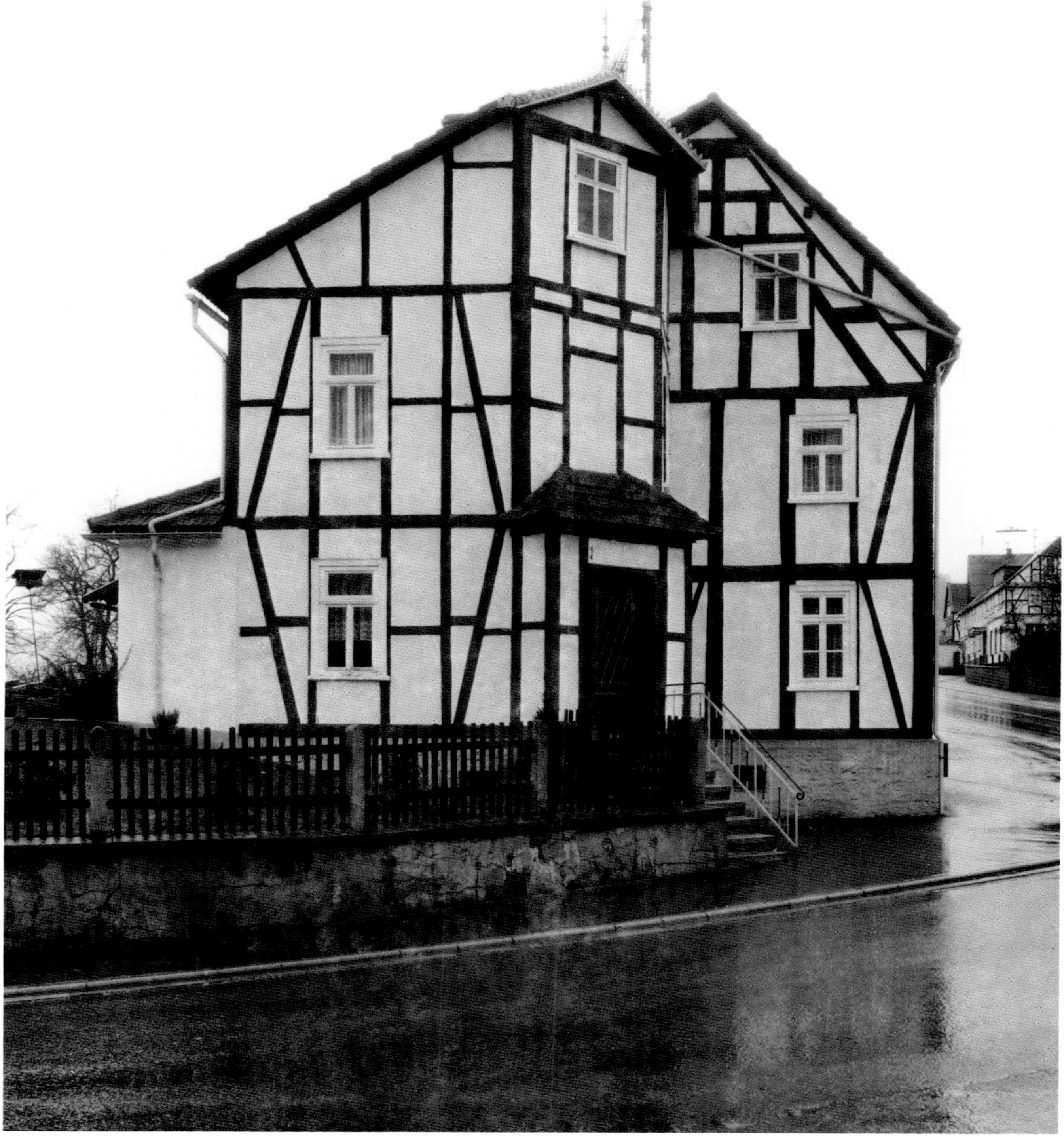

59
Hauptstraße 11, Allendorf, 1973.

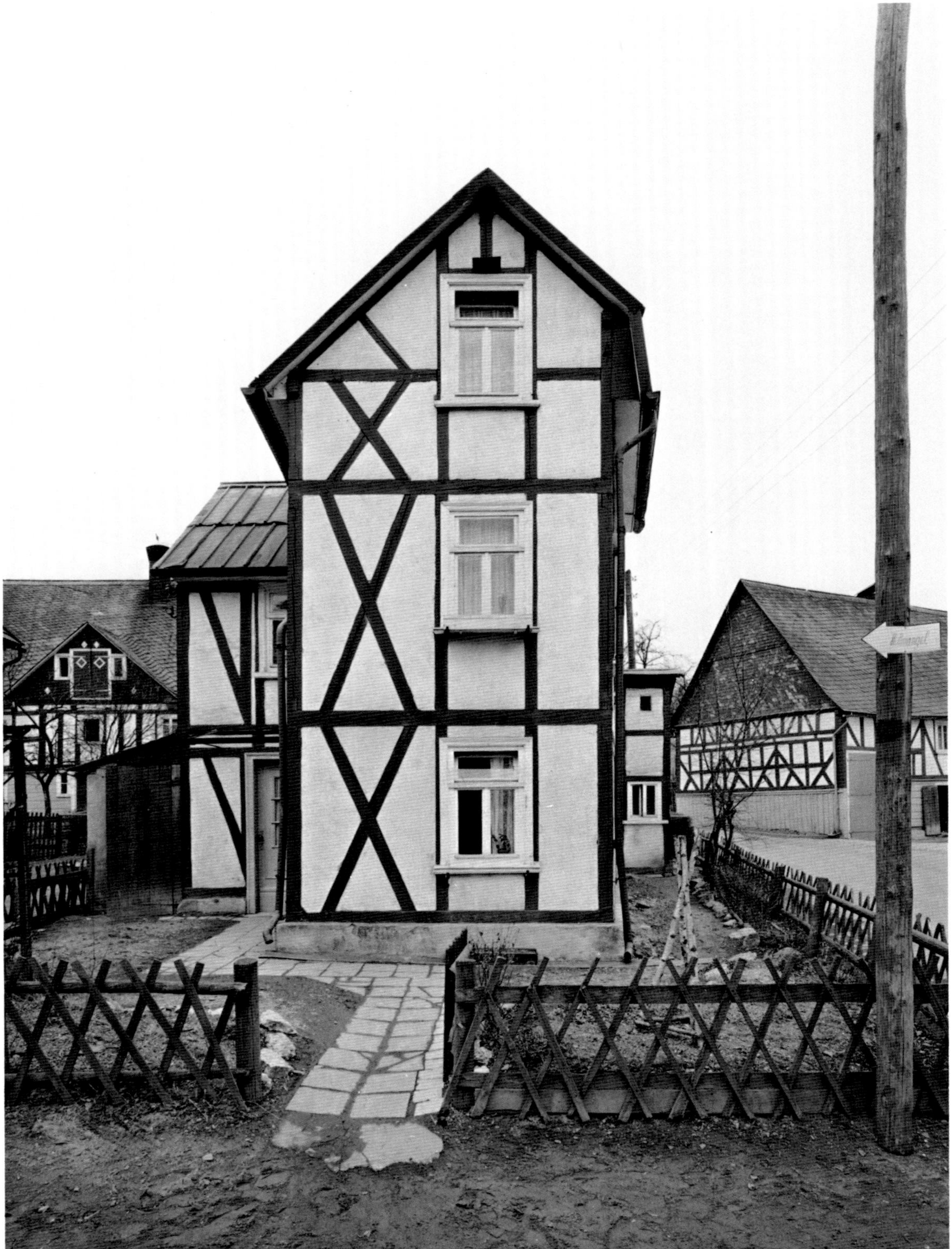

60
Wickersbacher Weg 7, Trupbach, 1961.

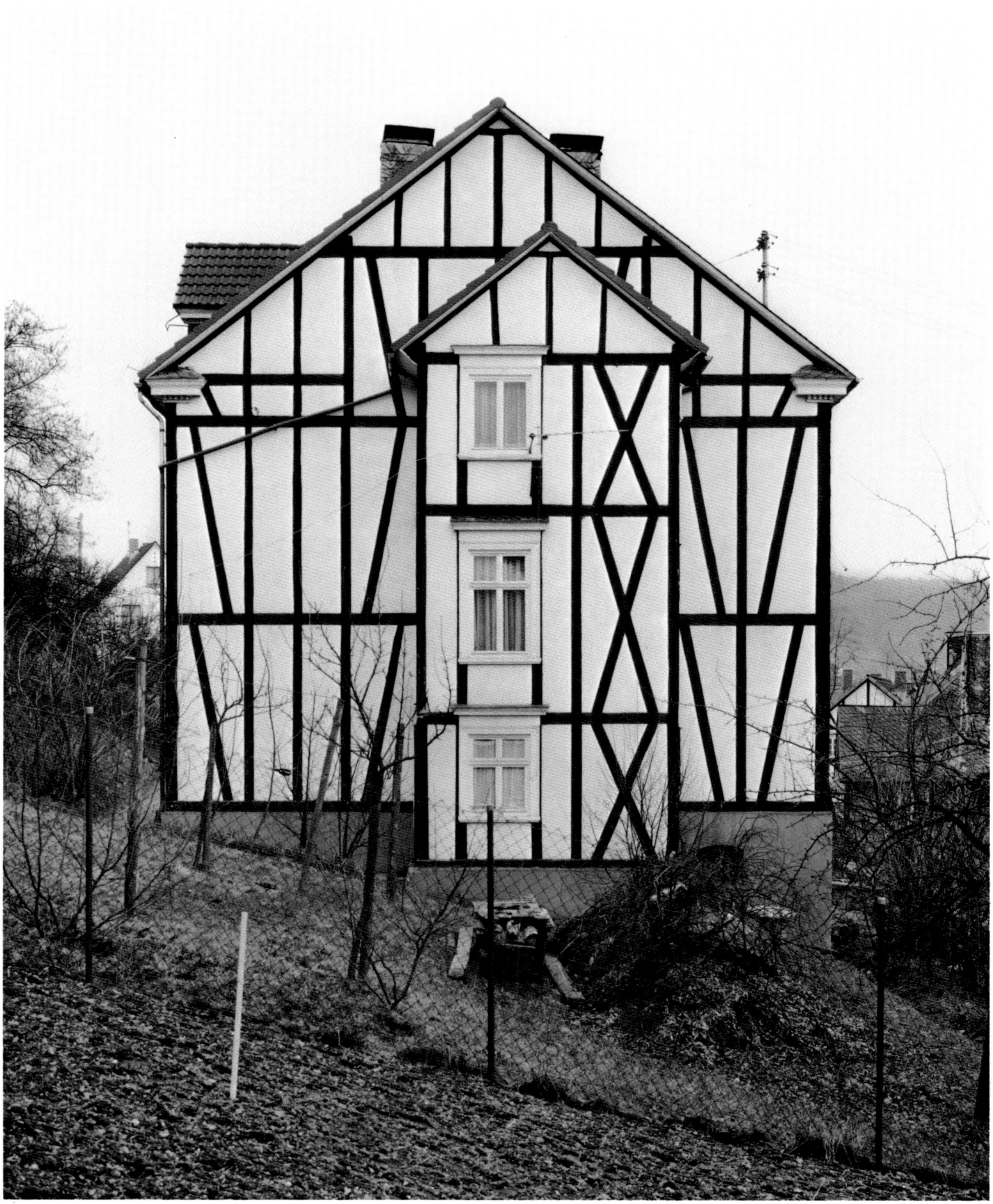

61
Oststraße 10, Freudenberg, 1968.

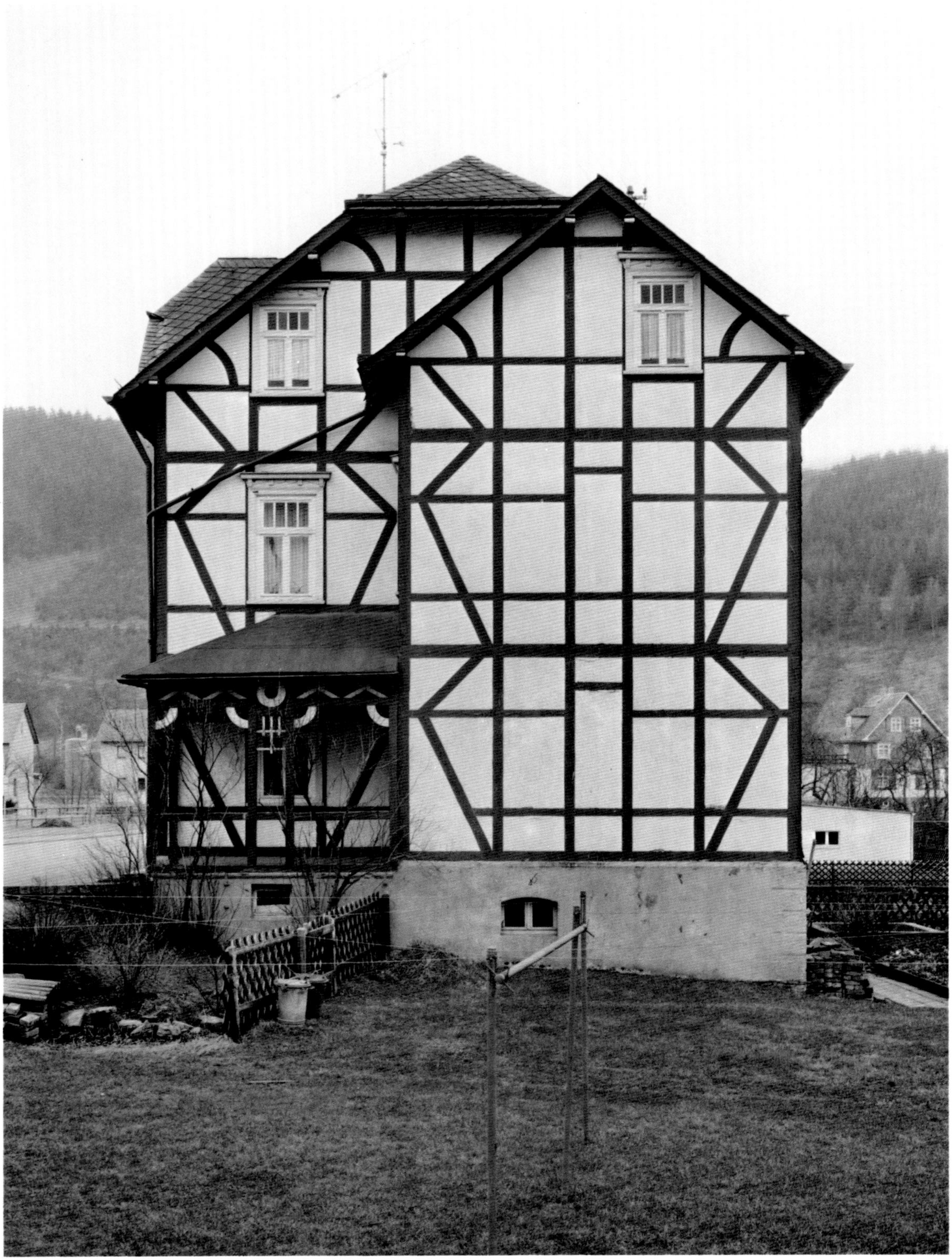

62
Bahnhofstraße 71, Netphen, 1974.

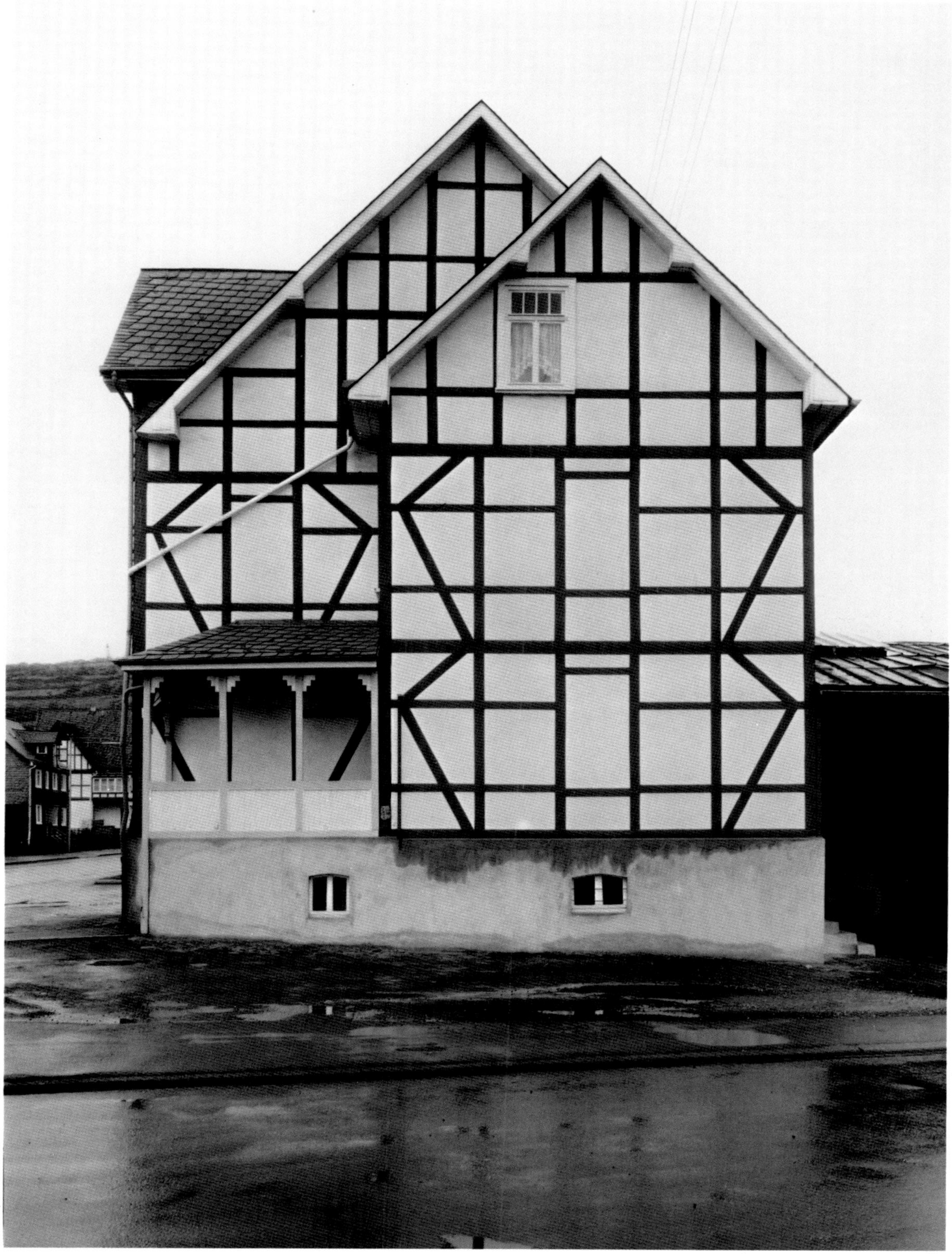

63
Kronprinzenstraße 25, Netphen, 1974.

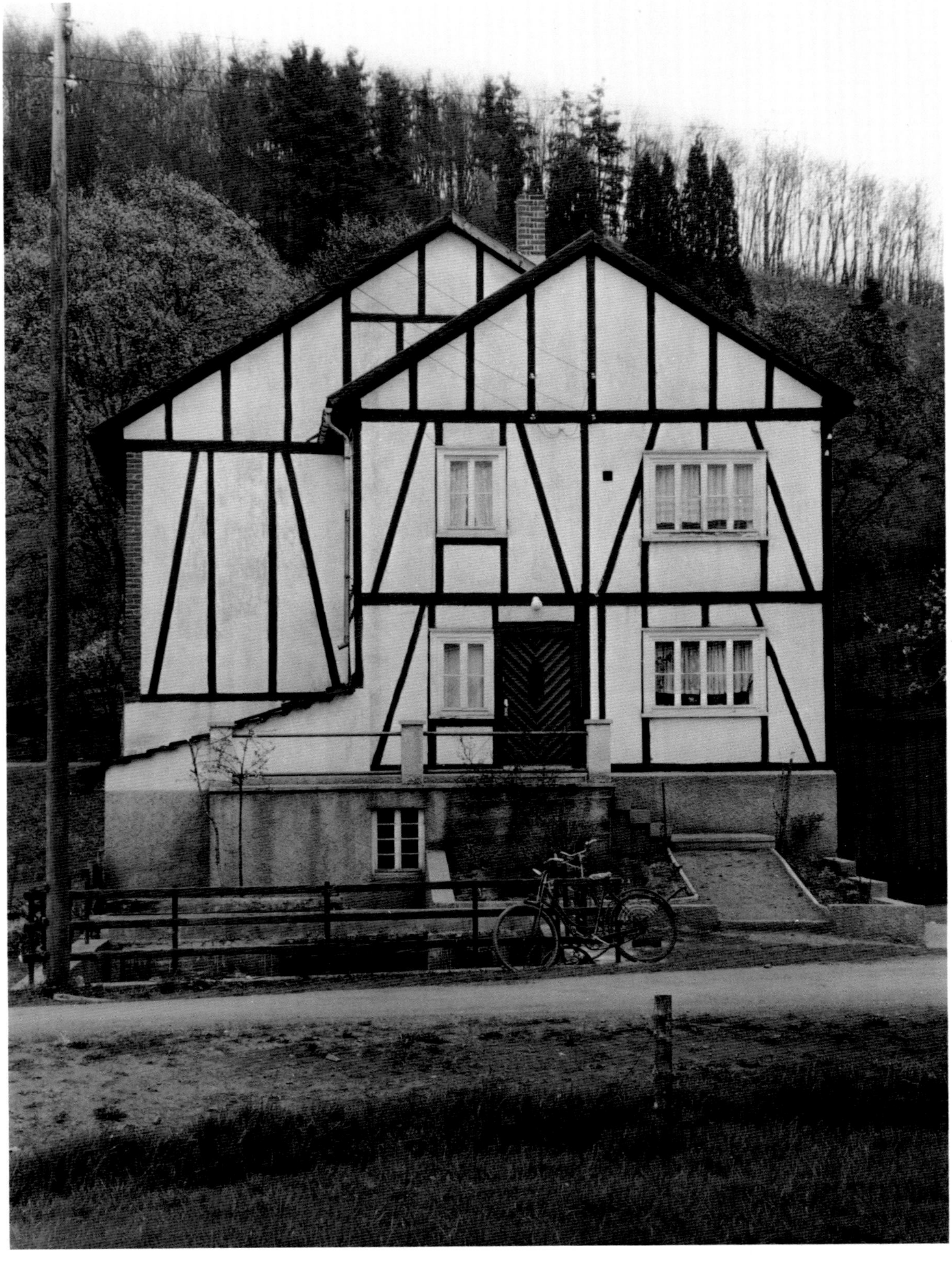

64

Triftstraße 58, Büschergrund, 1959.

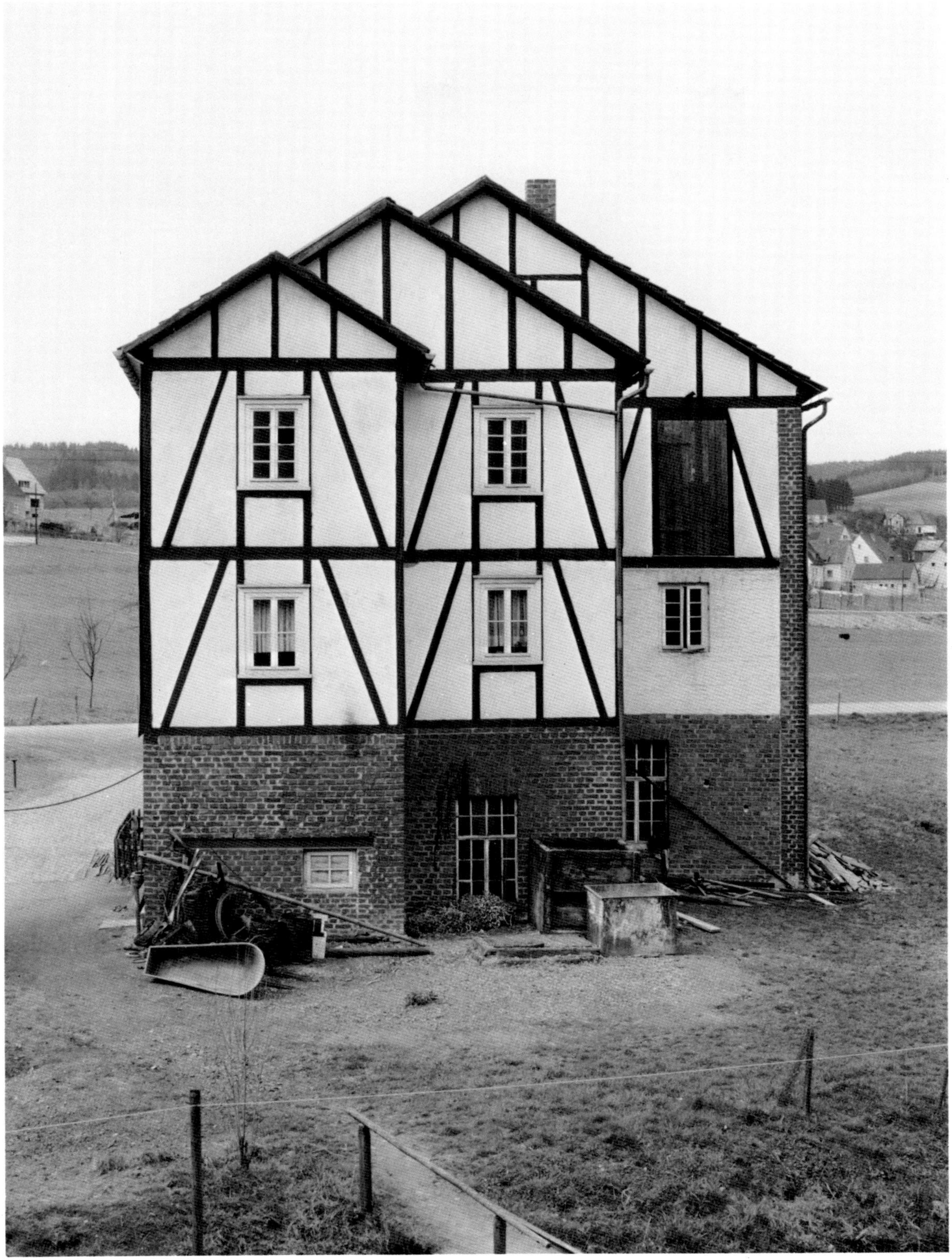

65

Triftstraße 58, Büschergrund, 1959.

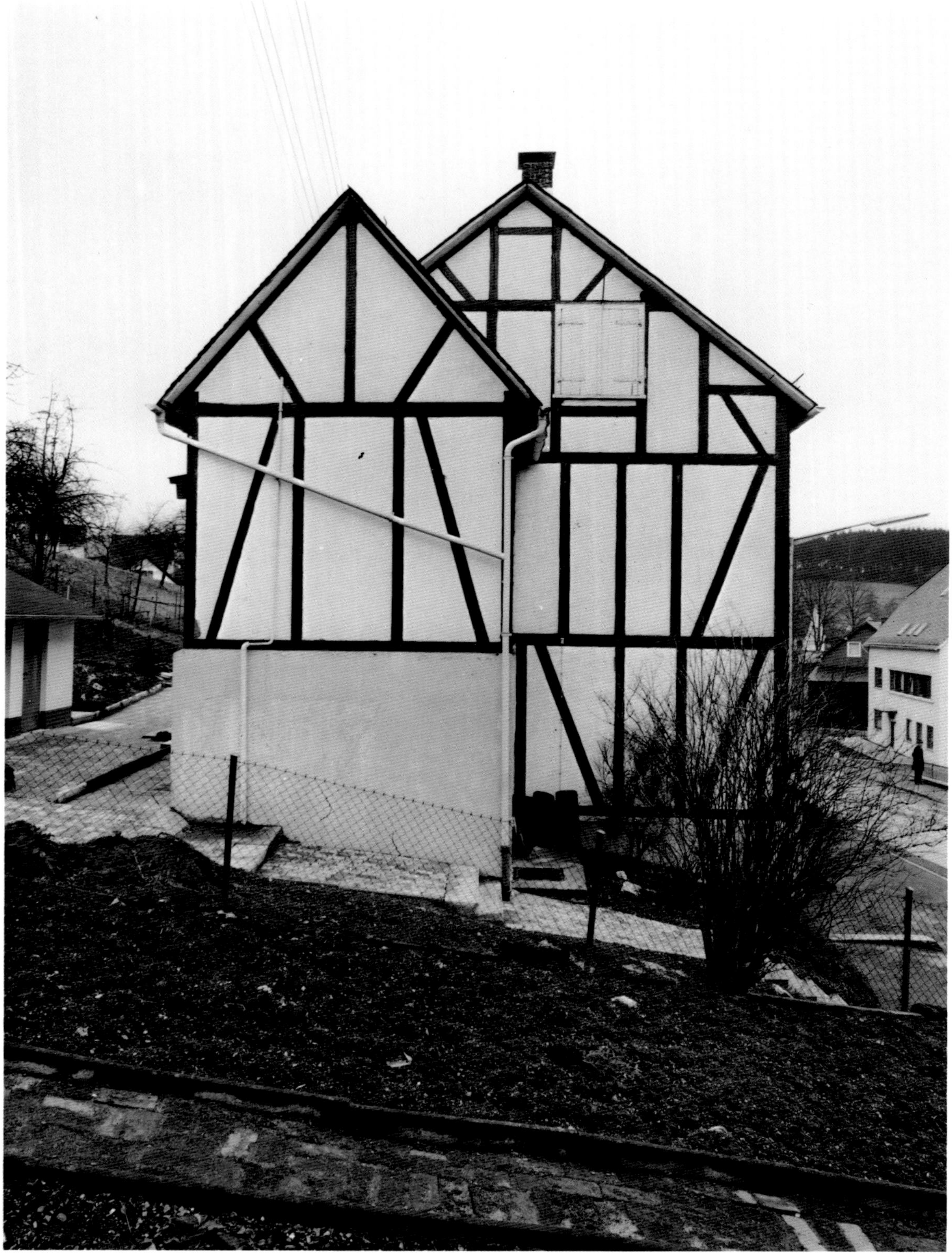

66
Rödgener Straße 60, Obersdorf, 1973.

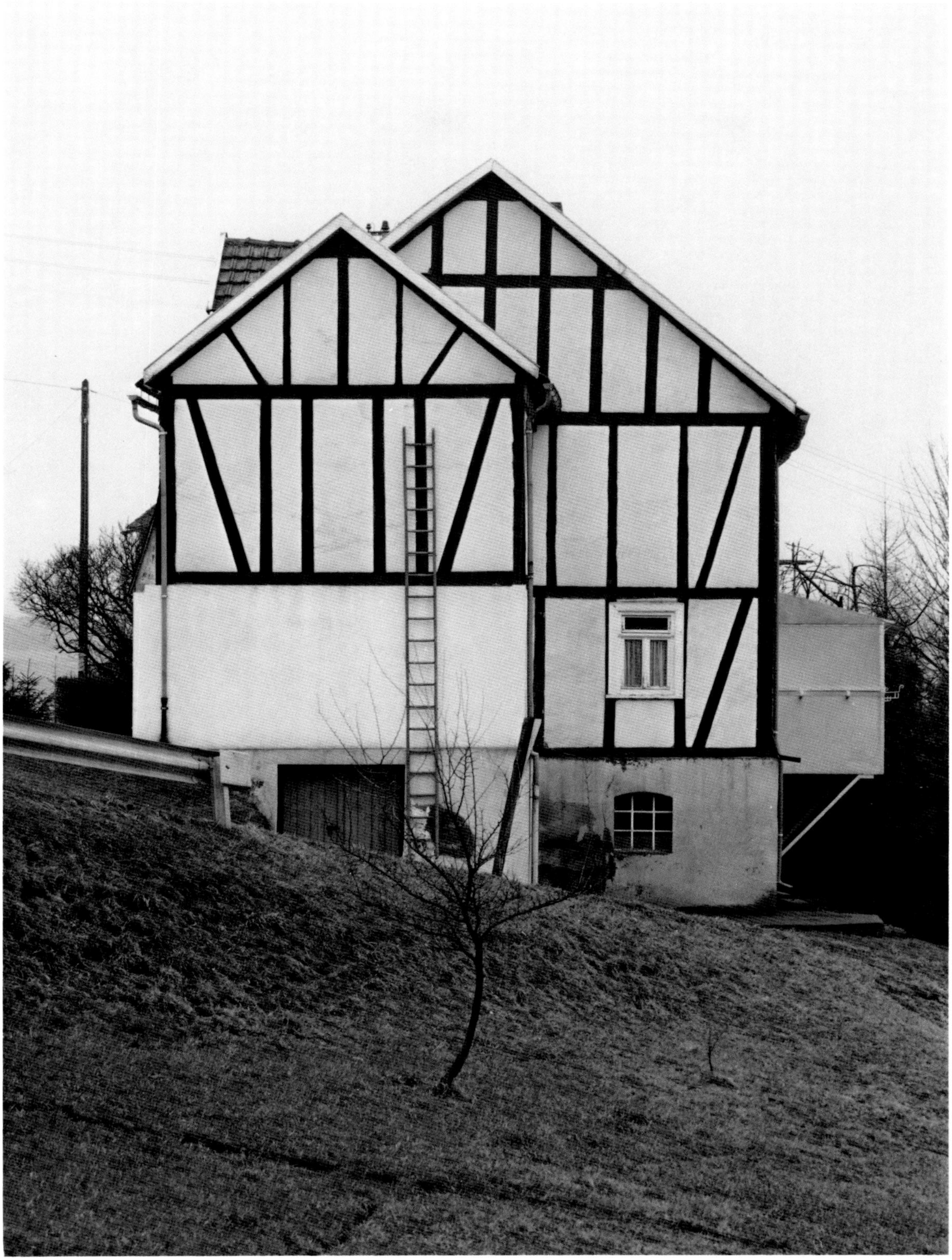

67
Siegener Straße 155, Büschergrund, 1972.

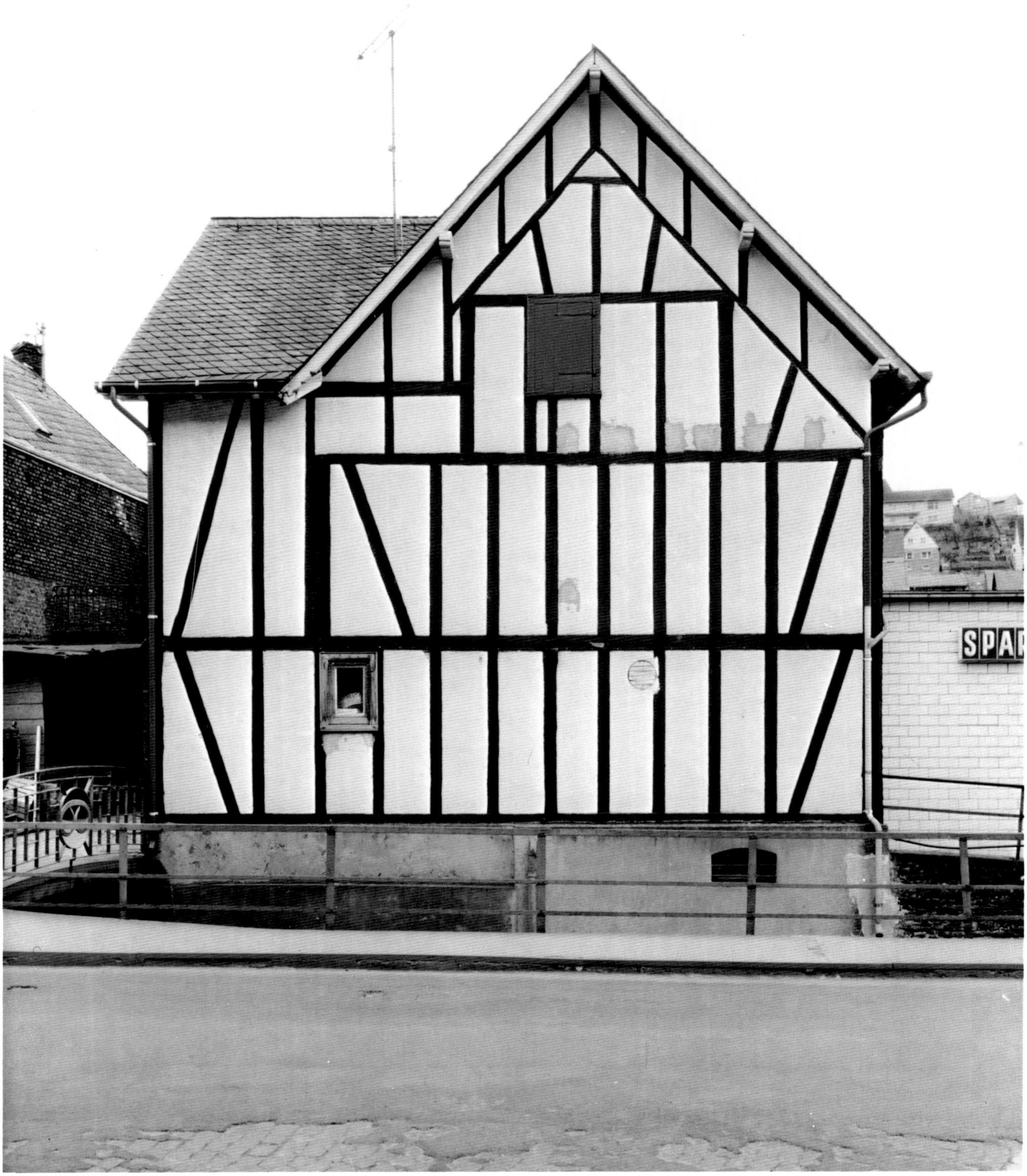

68
Eisernstraße 70, Eiserfeld, 1969.

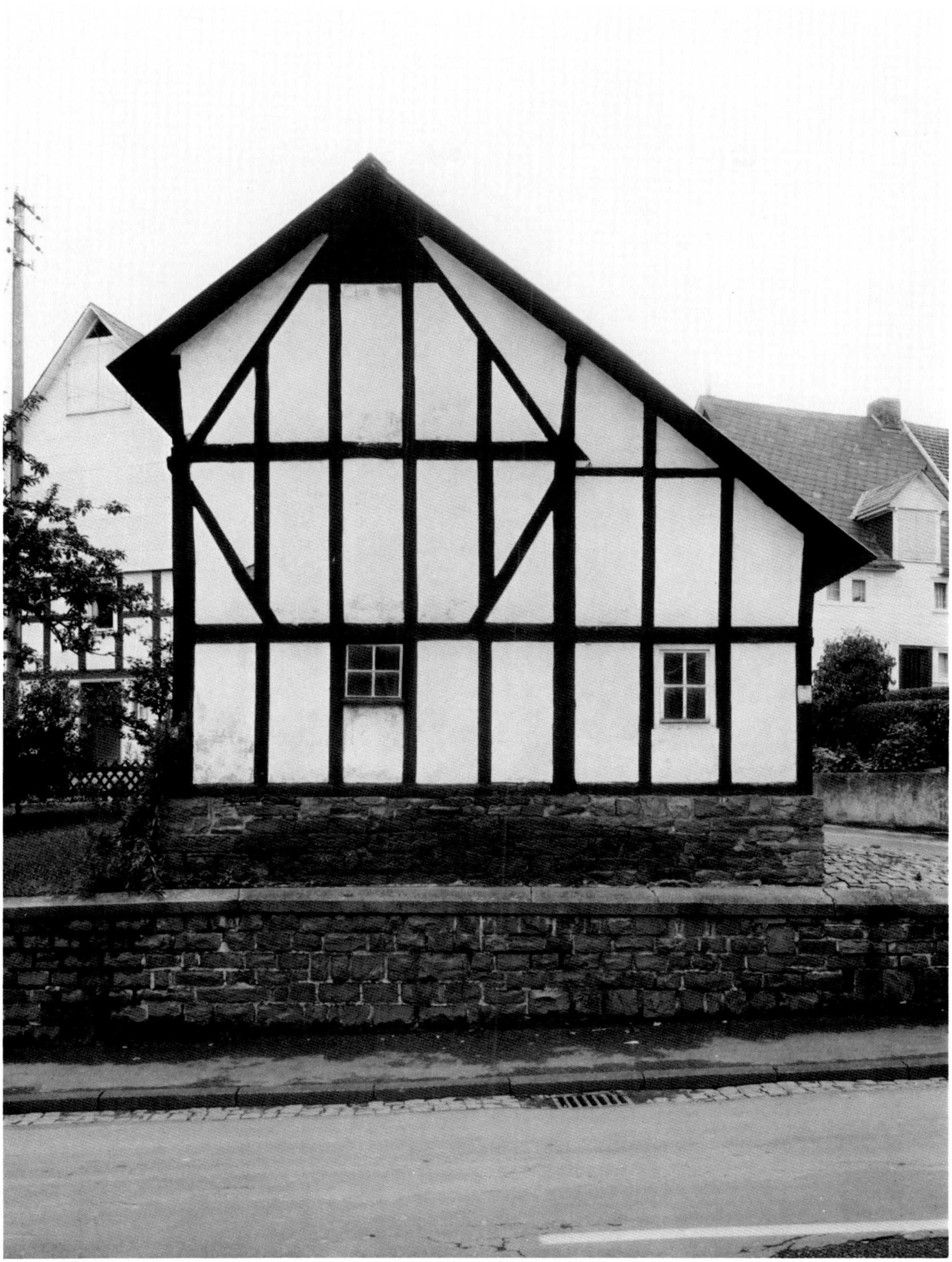

69
Baume Ecke 4, Müsen, 1968.

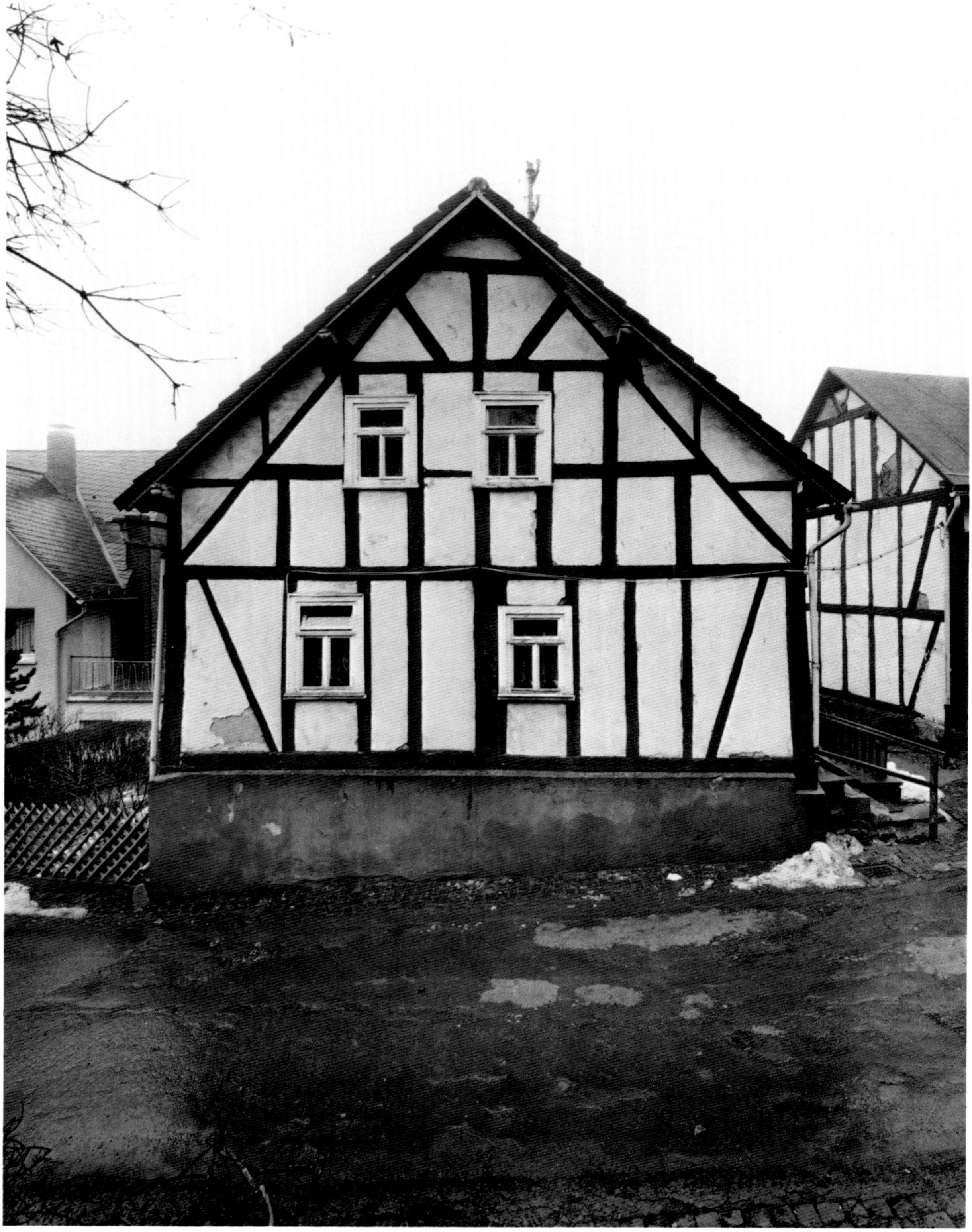

70
Zur Hirzgabel 11, Niederdresselndorf, 1967.

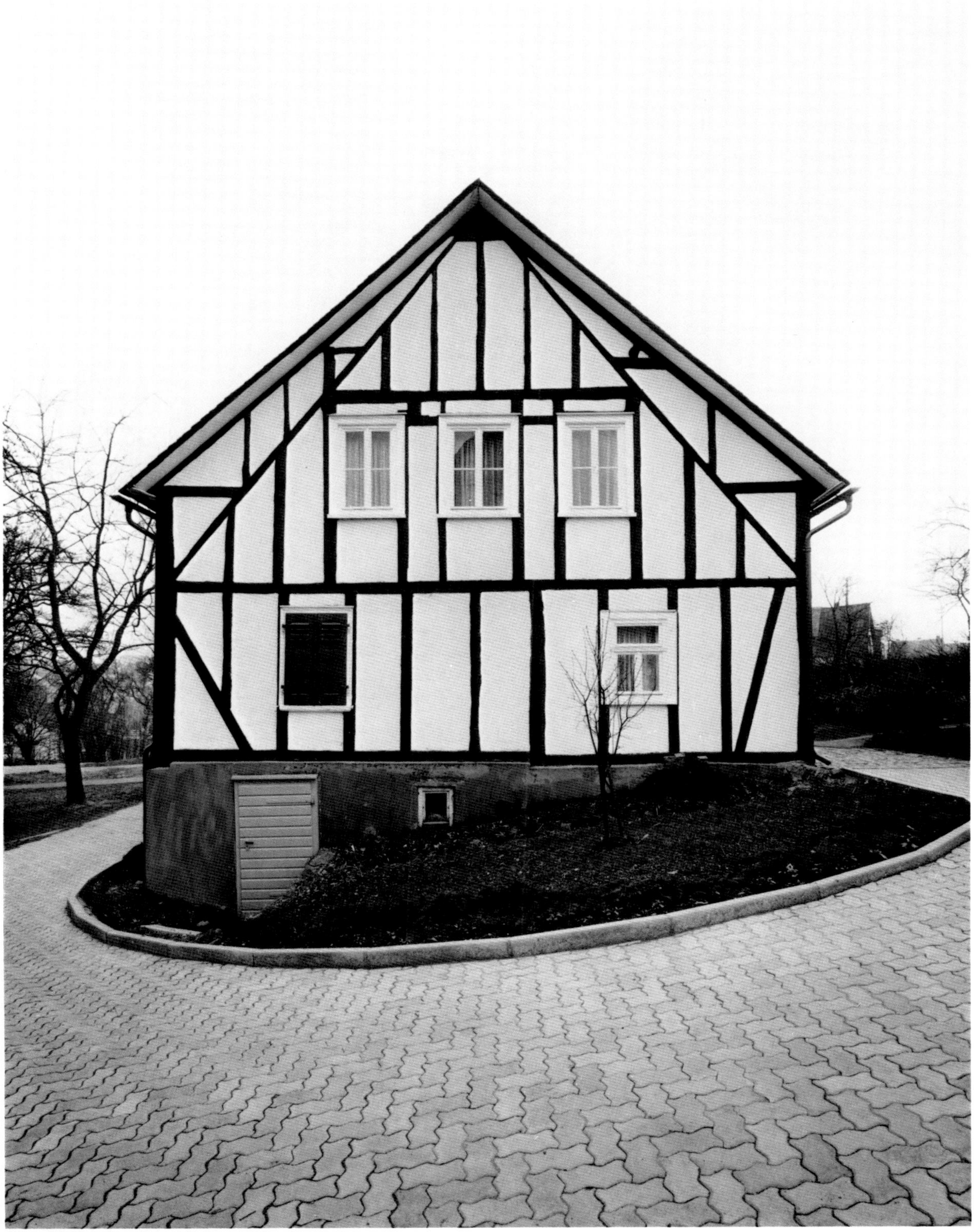

71
Wendiger Straße 3, Büschergrund, 1972.

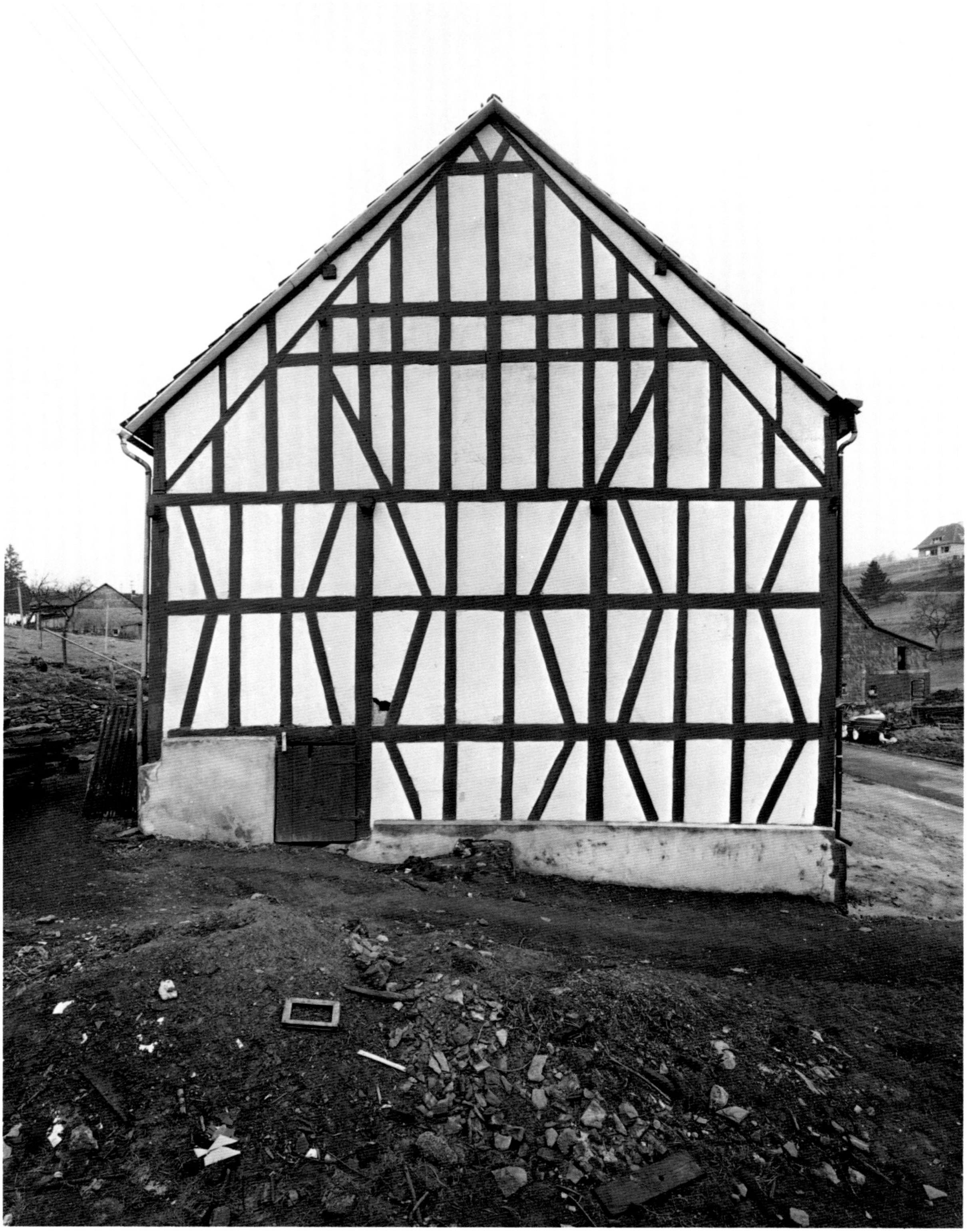

72
Oberdielfer Straße 18, Oberdielfen, 1962.

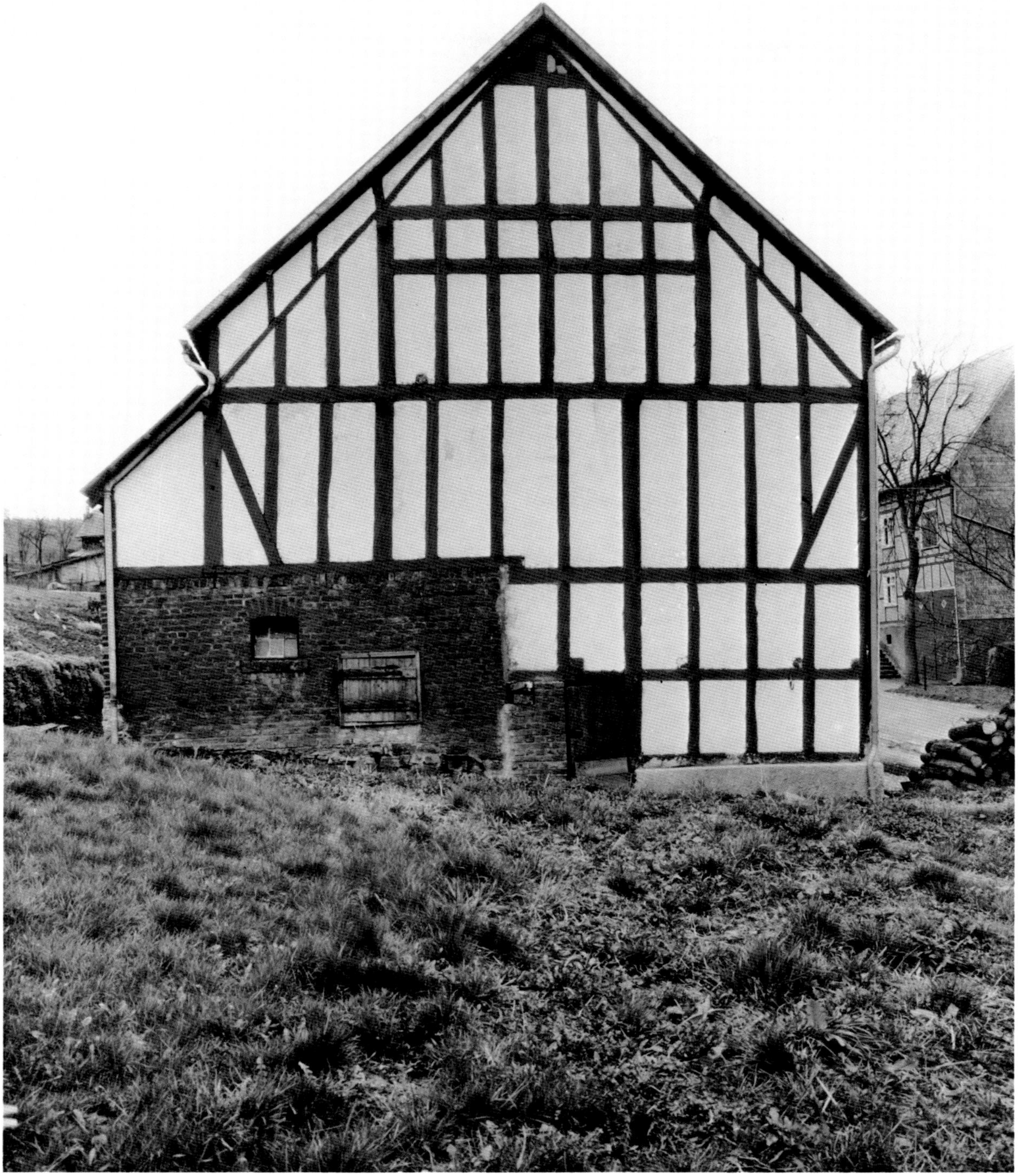

73
Oberdielfer Straße 14, Oberdielfen, 1960.

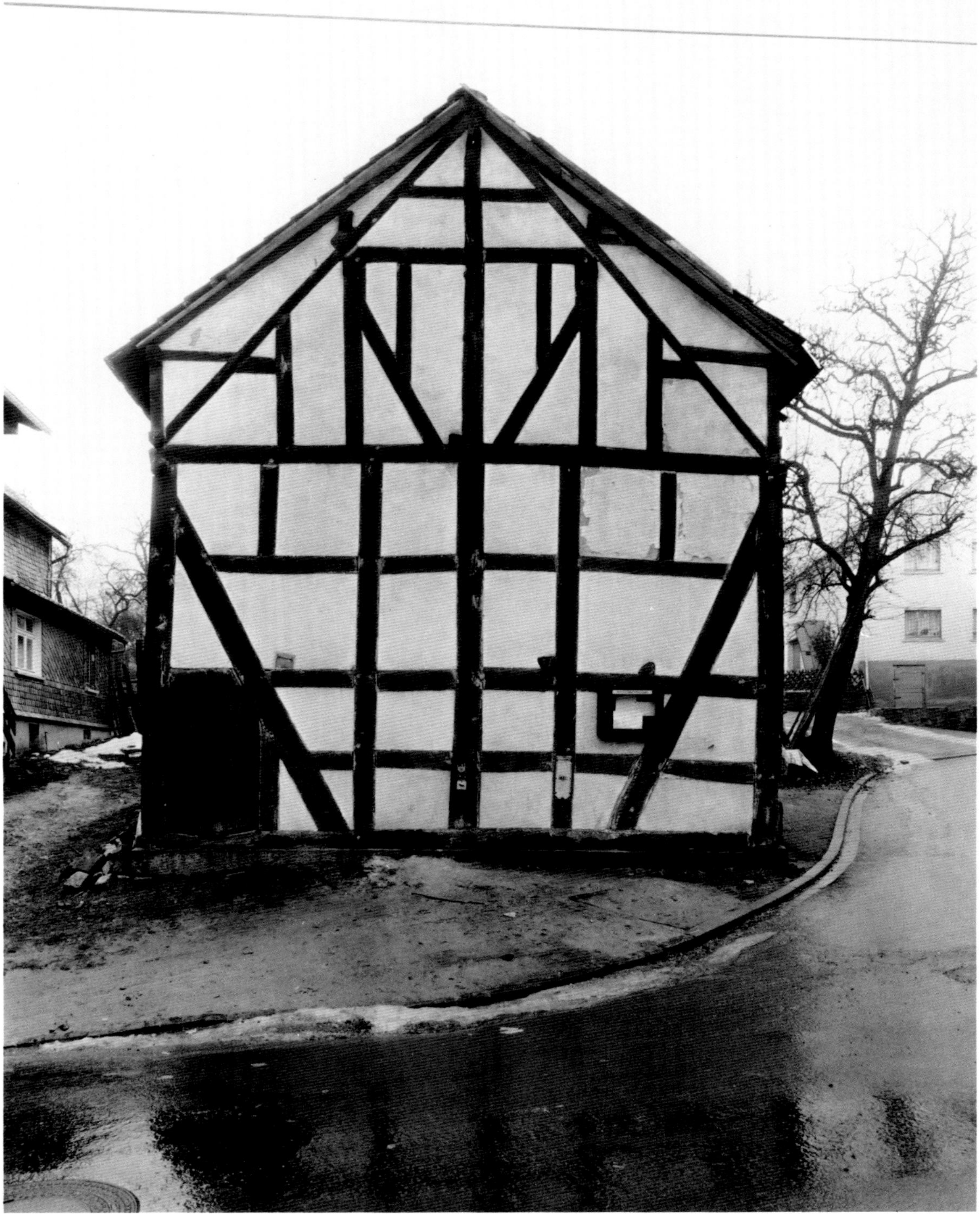

74
Schwarzbachstraße 57b, Haiger-Dillbrecht, 1972.

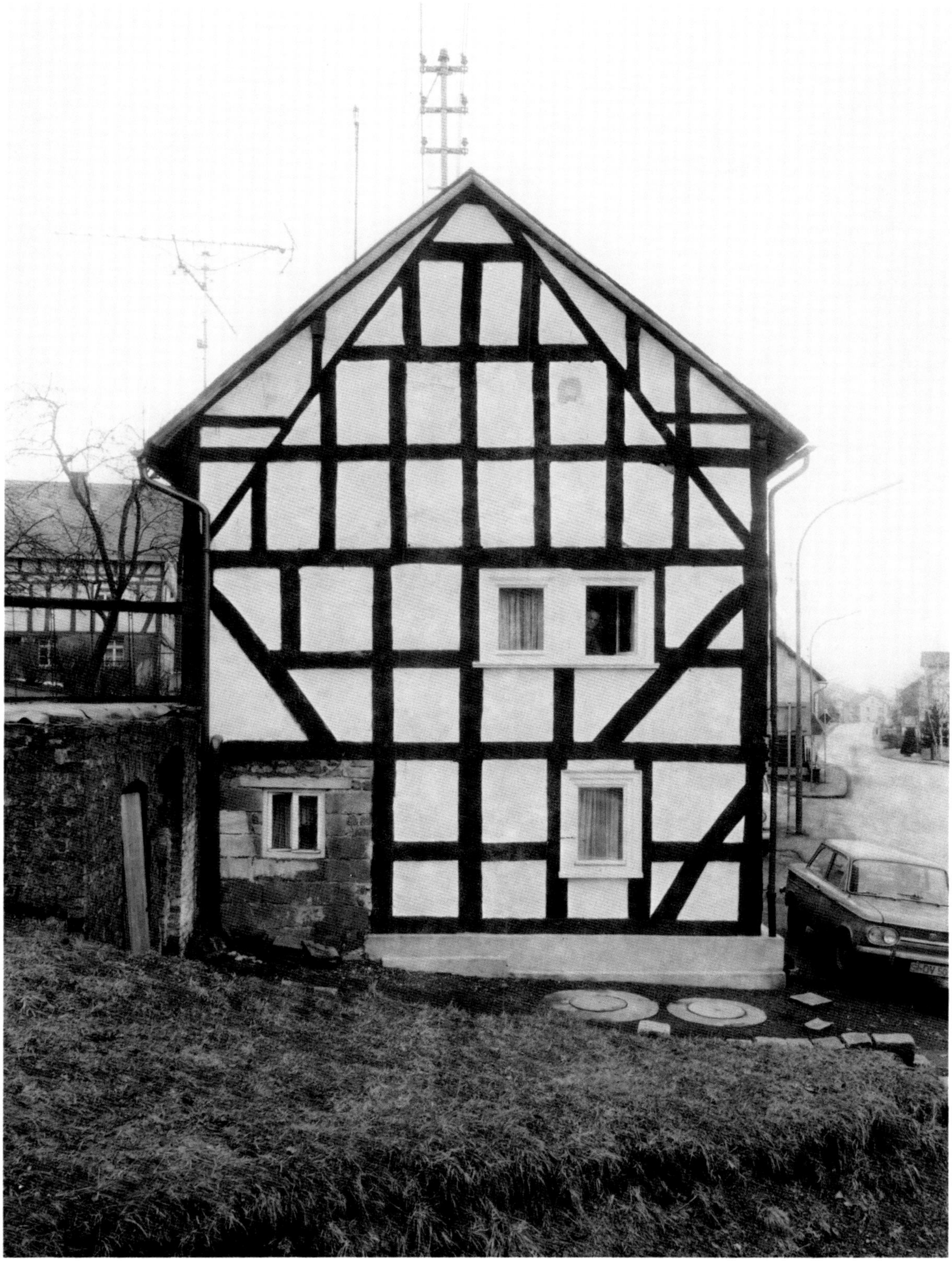

75
Eiserfelder Straße 37, Rinsdorf, 1973.

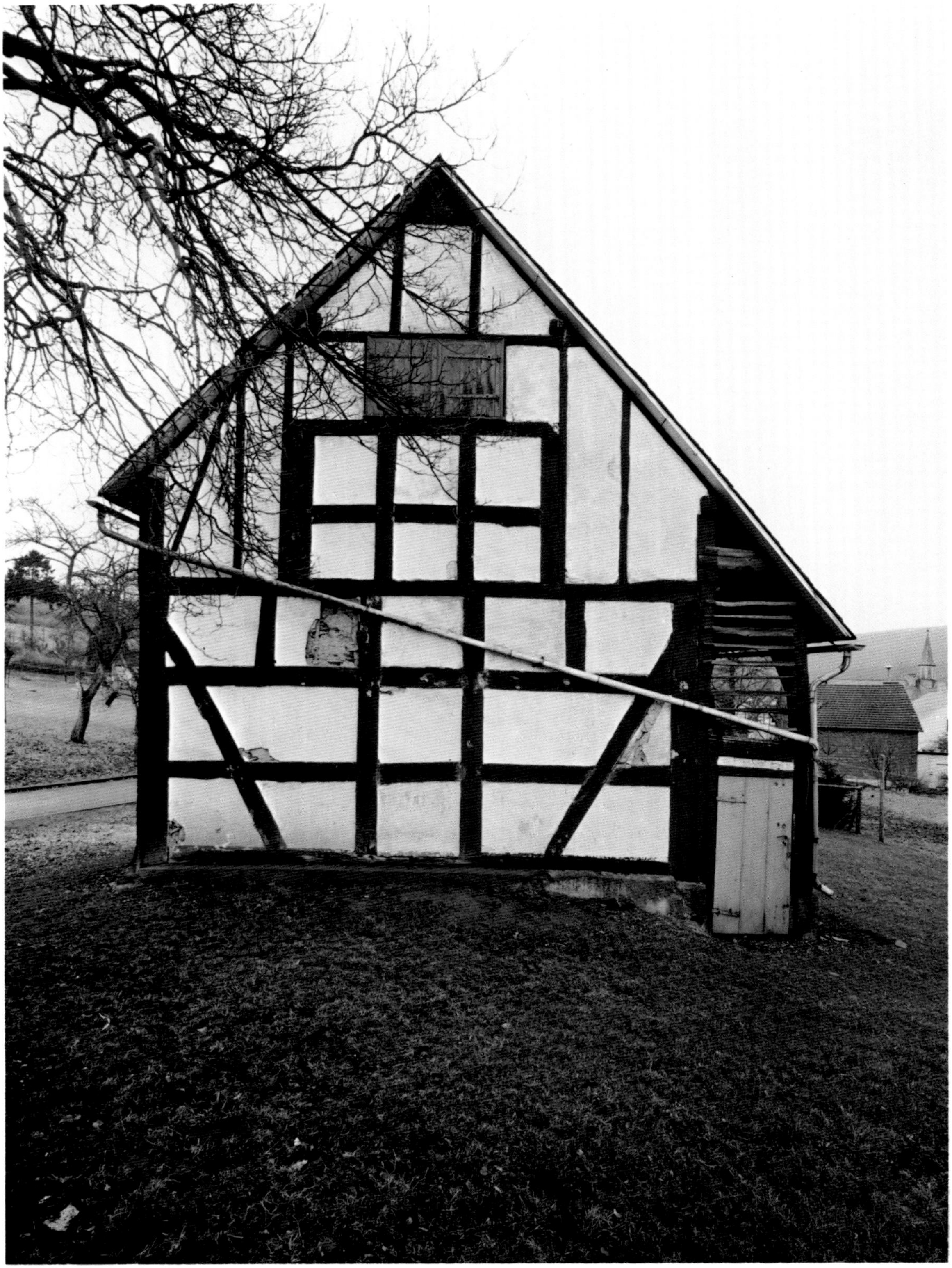

76
Mischenbachstraße 7, Wiederstein, 1966.

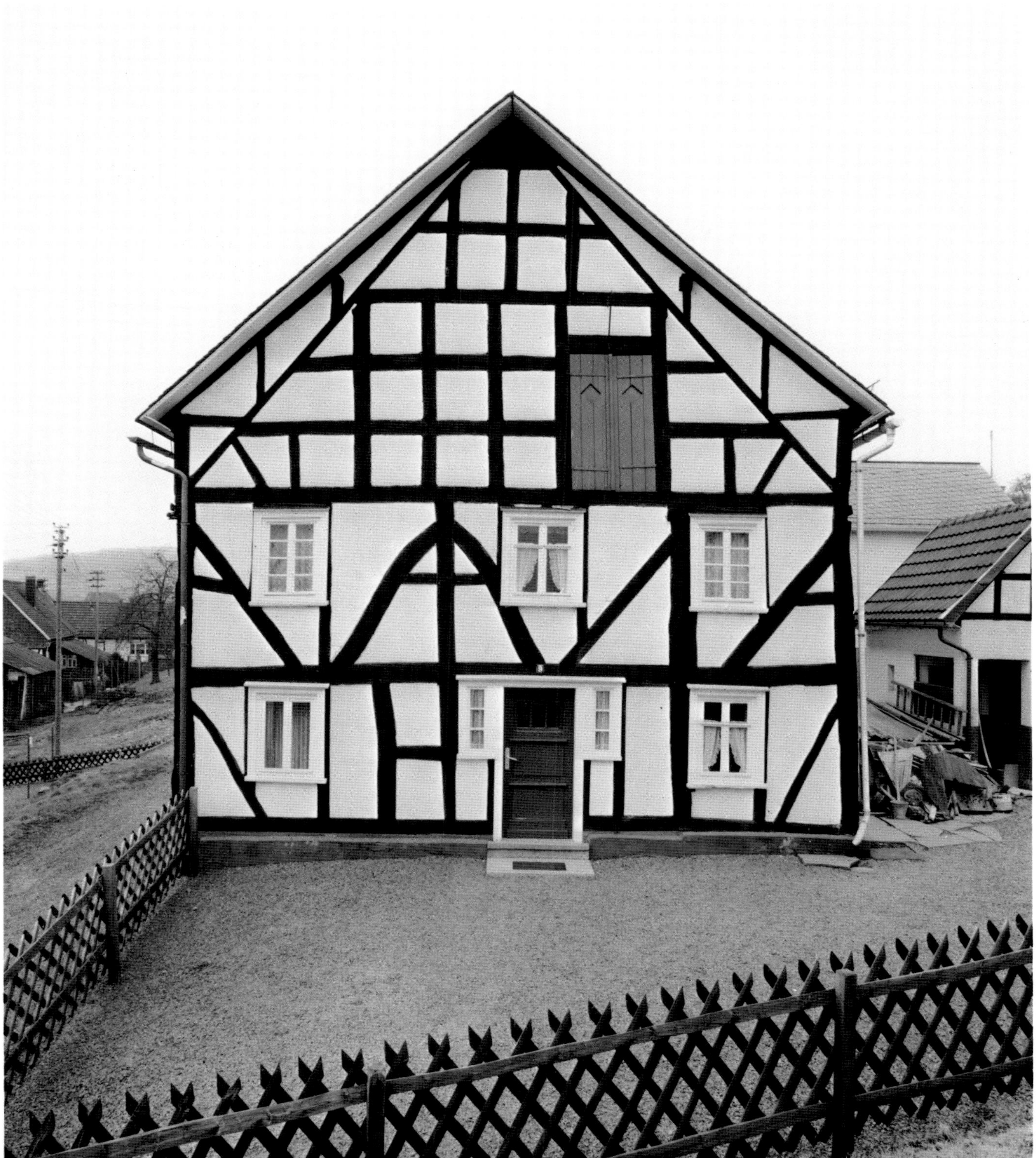

77
Büscherstraße 9, Büschergrund, 1972.

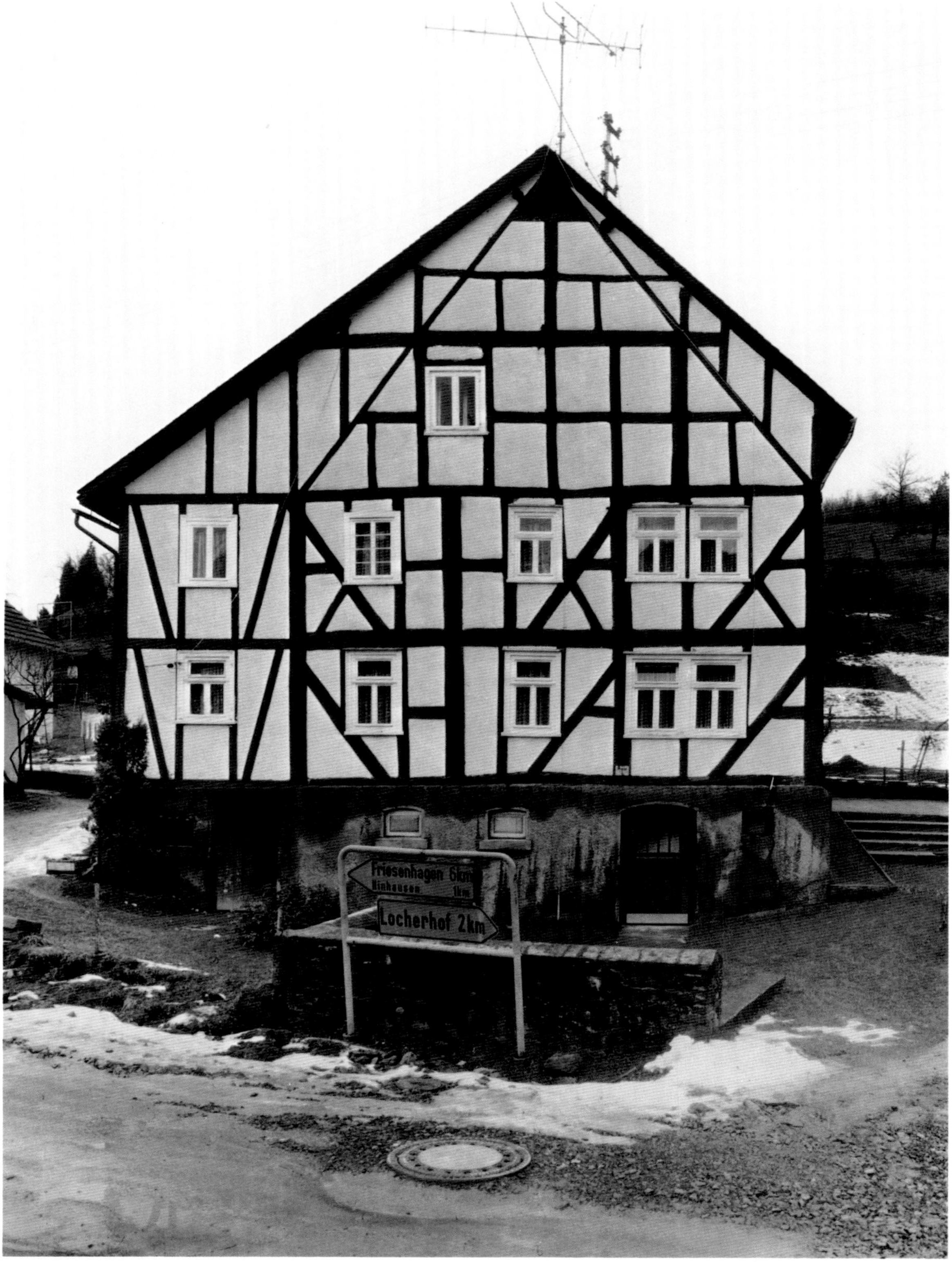

78
Harbach Nr. 3, 1972.

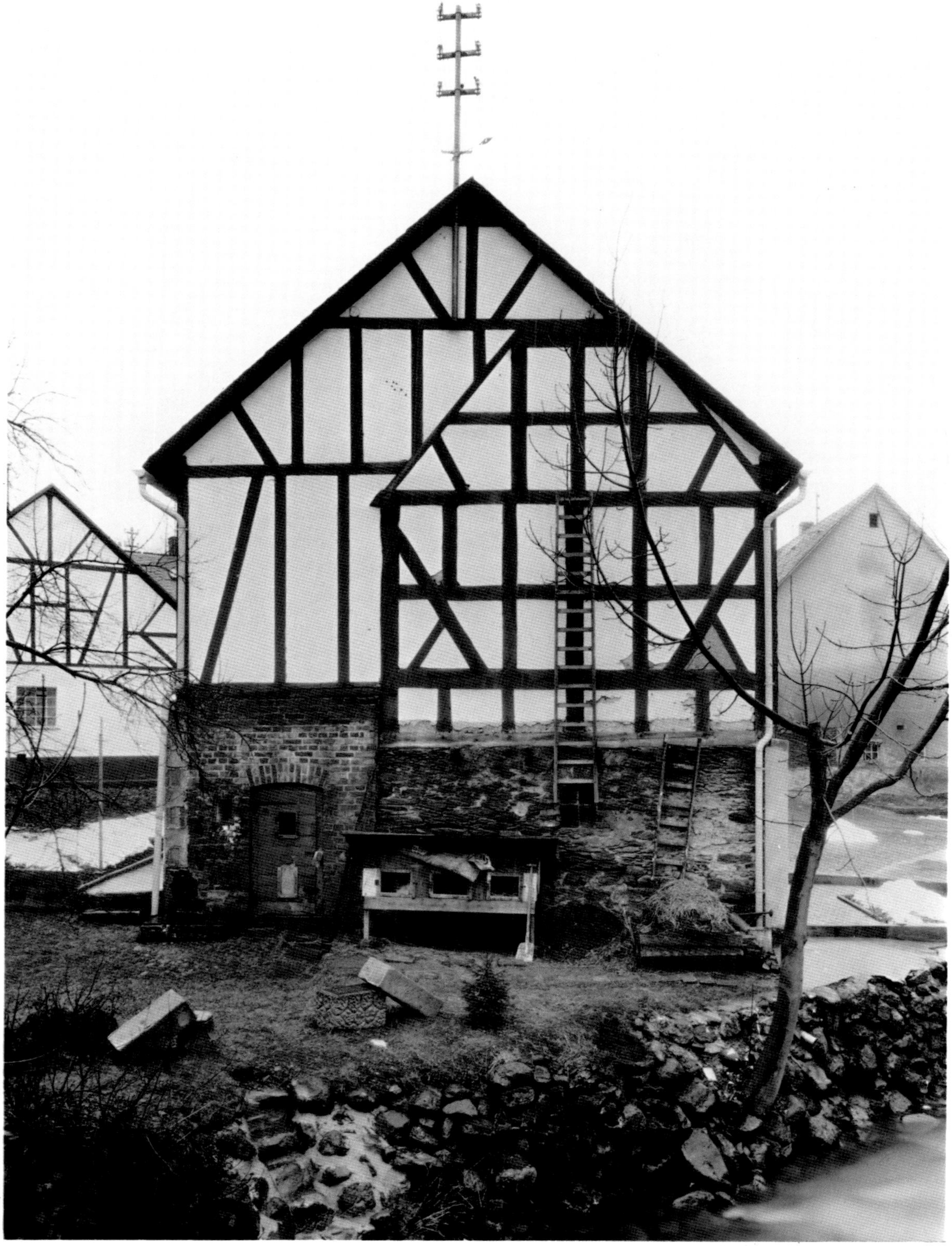

79
Brunnenstraße 14, Niederdresselndorf, 1972.

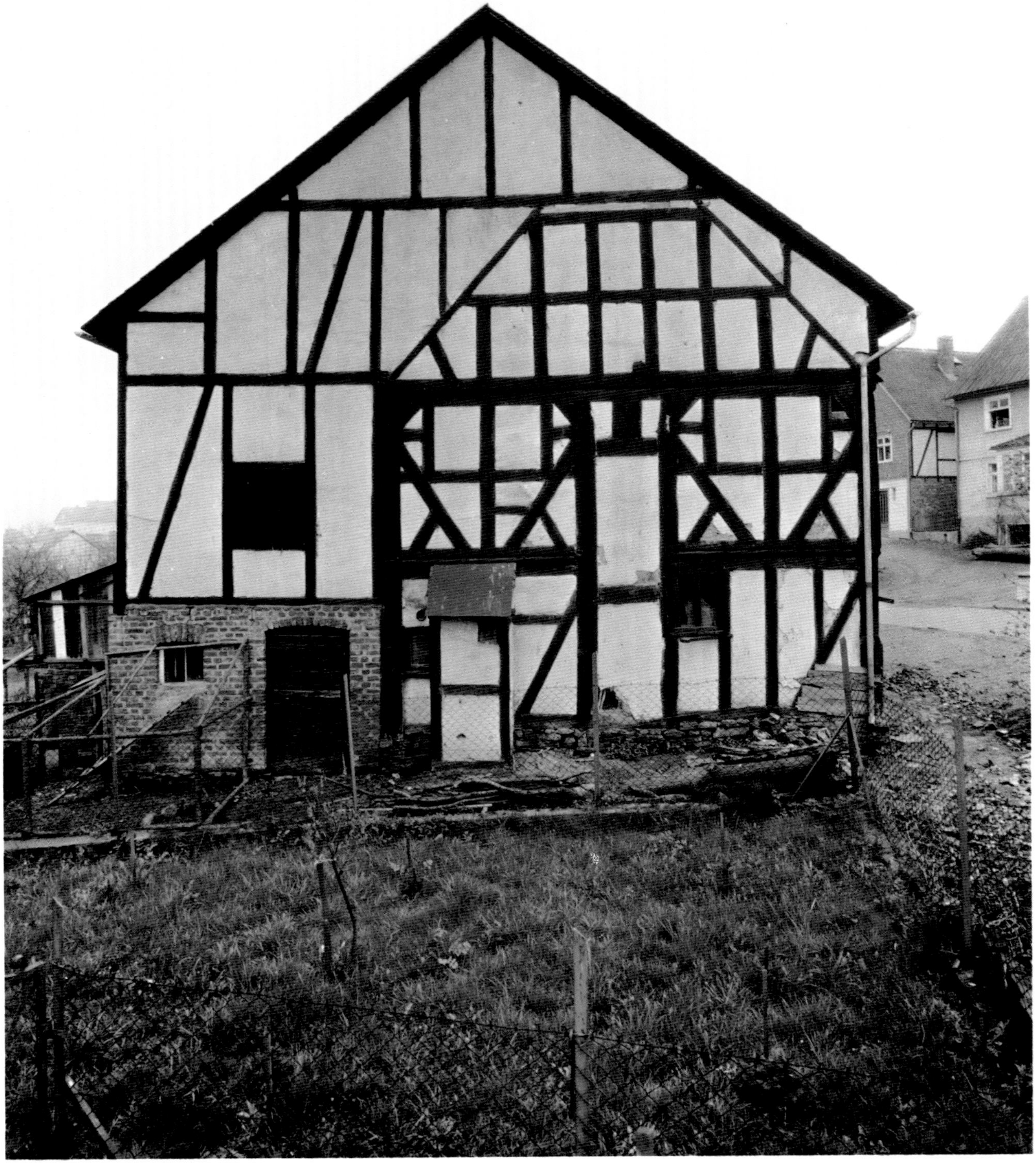

80
Hauptstraße 36, Flammersbach, 1960.

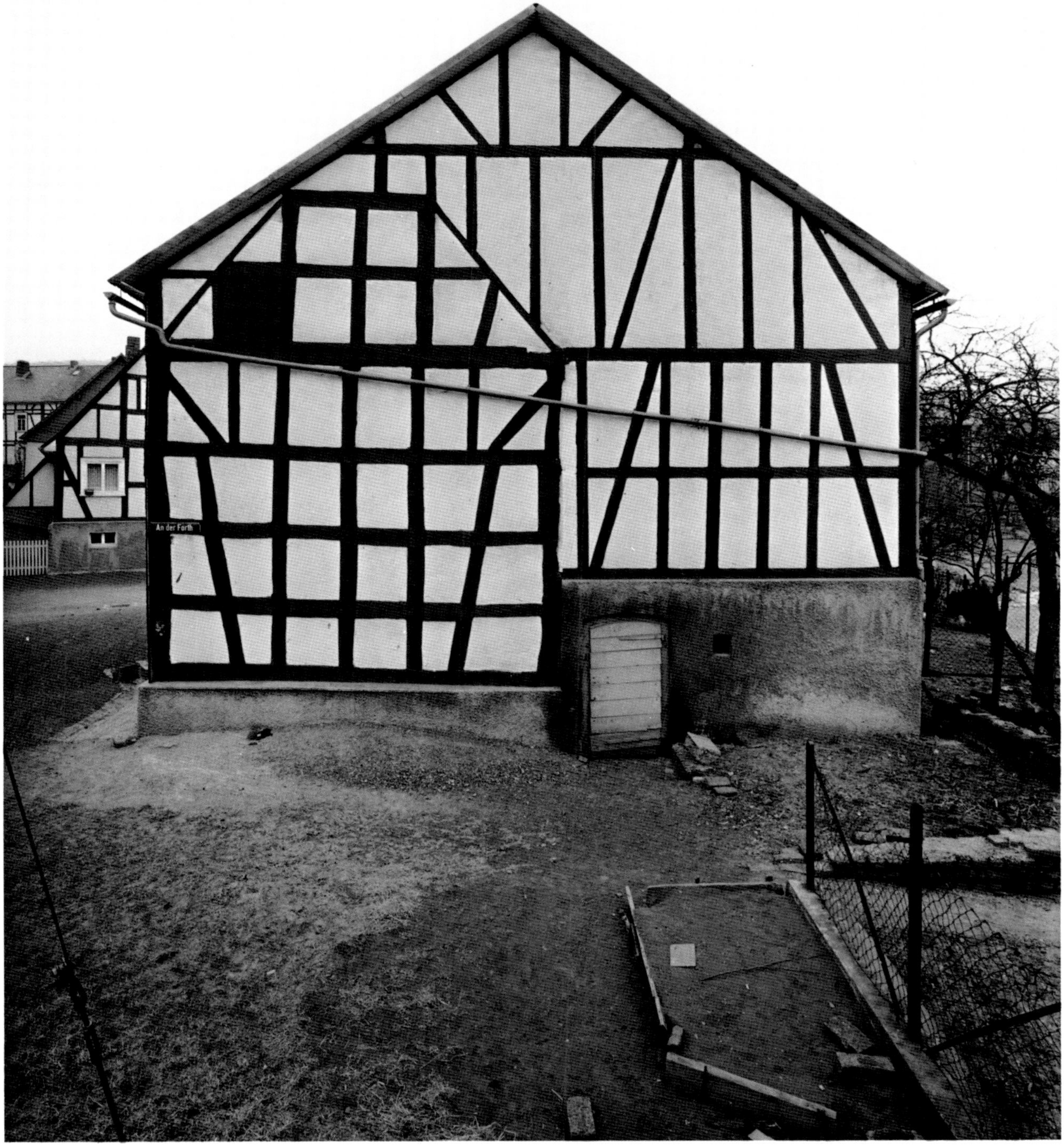

81
Auf der Forth 2, Zeppenfeld, 1961.

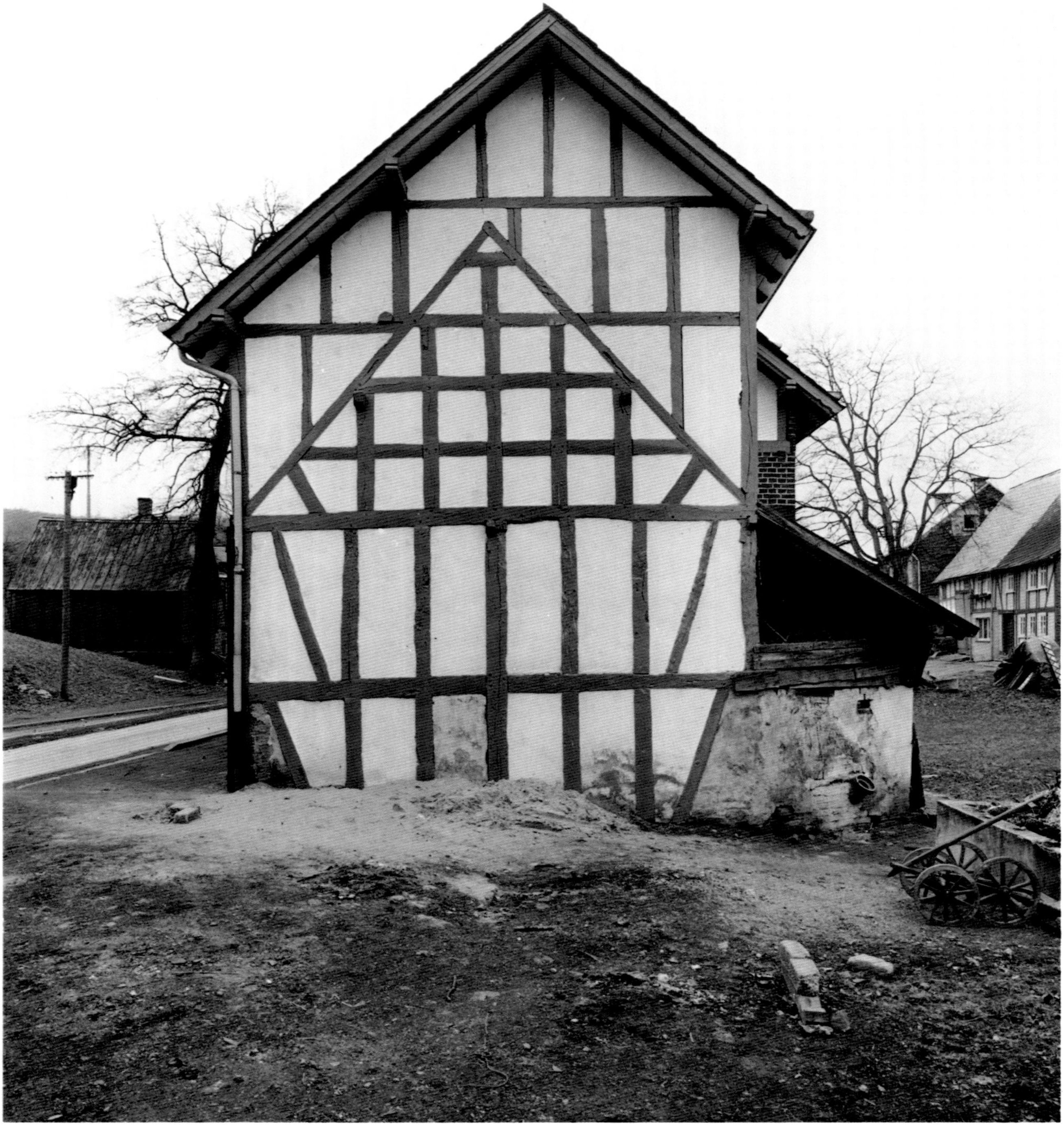

82
Obere Dorfstraße 21, Bürbach, 1962.

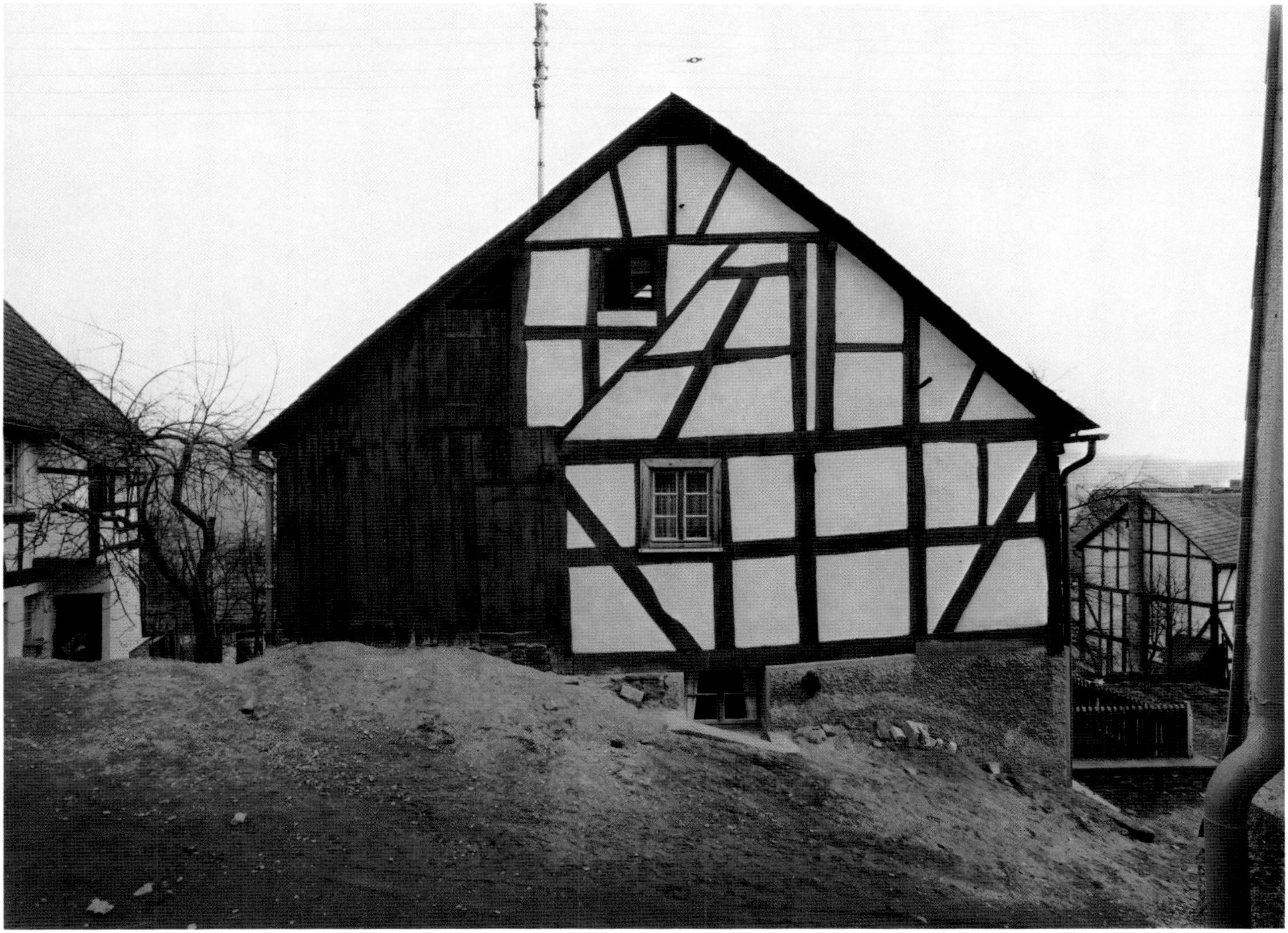

83
Bogenstraße 8, Freusburg, 1963.

II.
VERSCHIEFERTE GIEBELSEITEN
SLATED GABLE SIDES

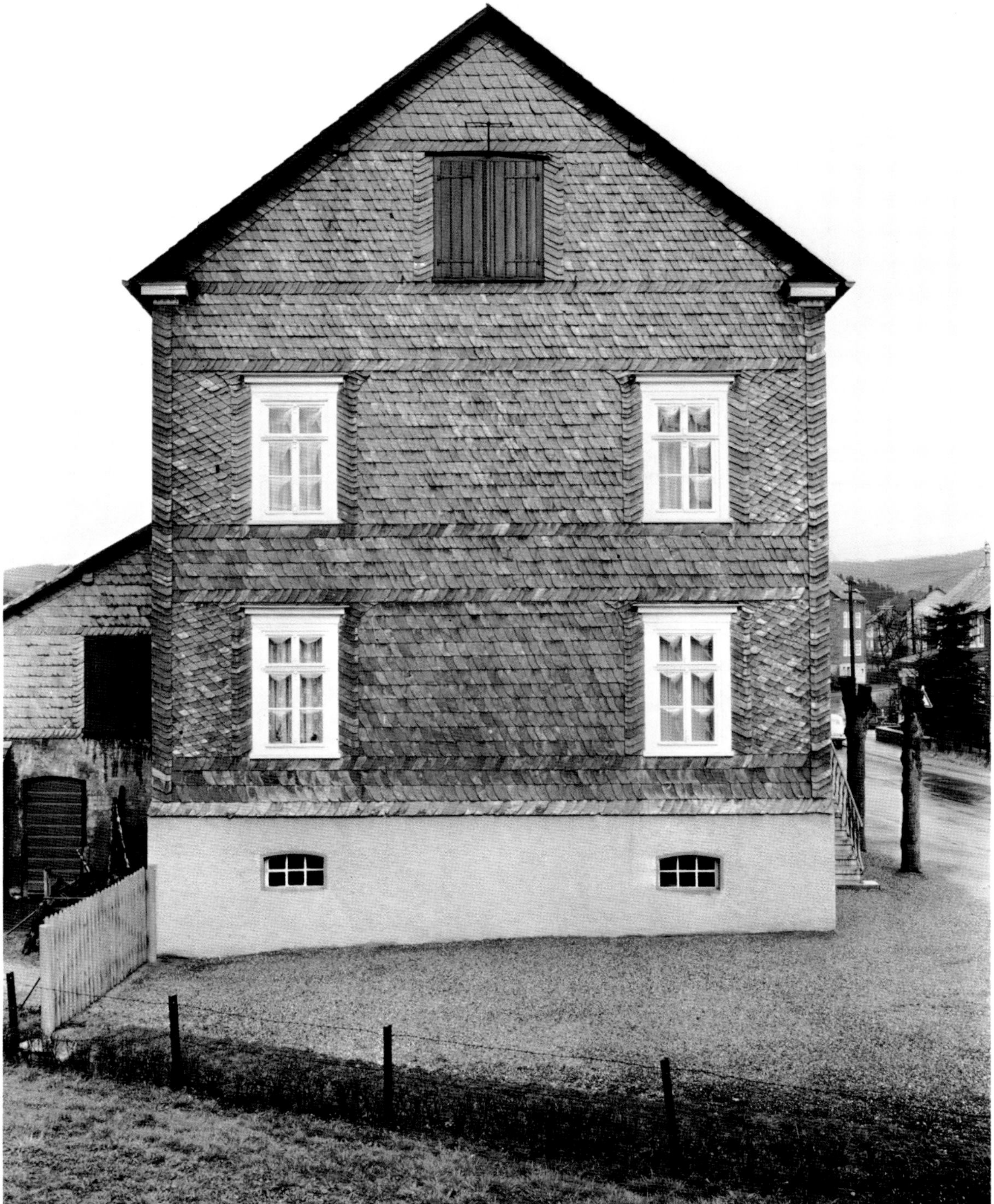

84
Wildener Straße 7, Salchendorf, 1961.

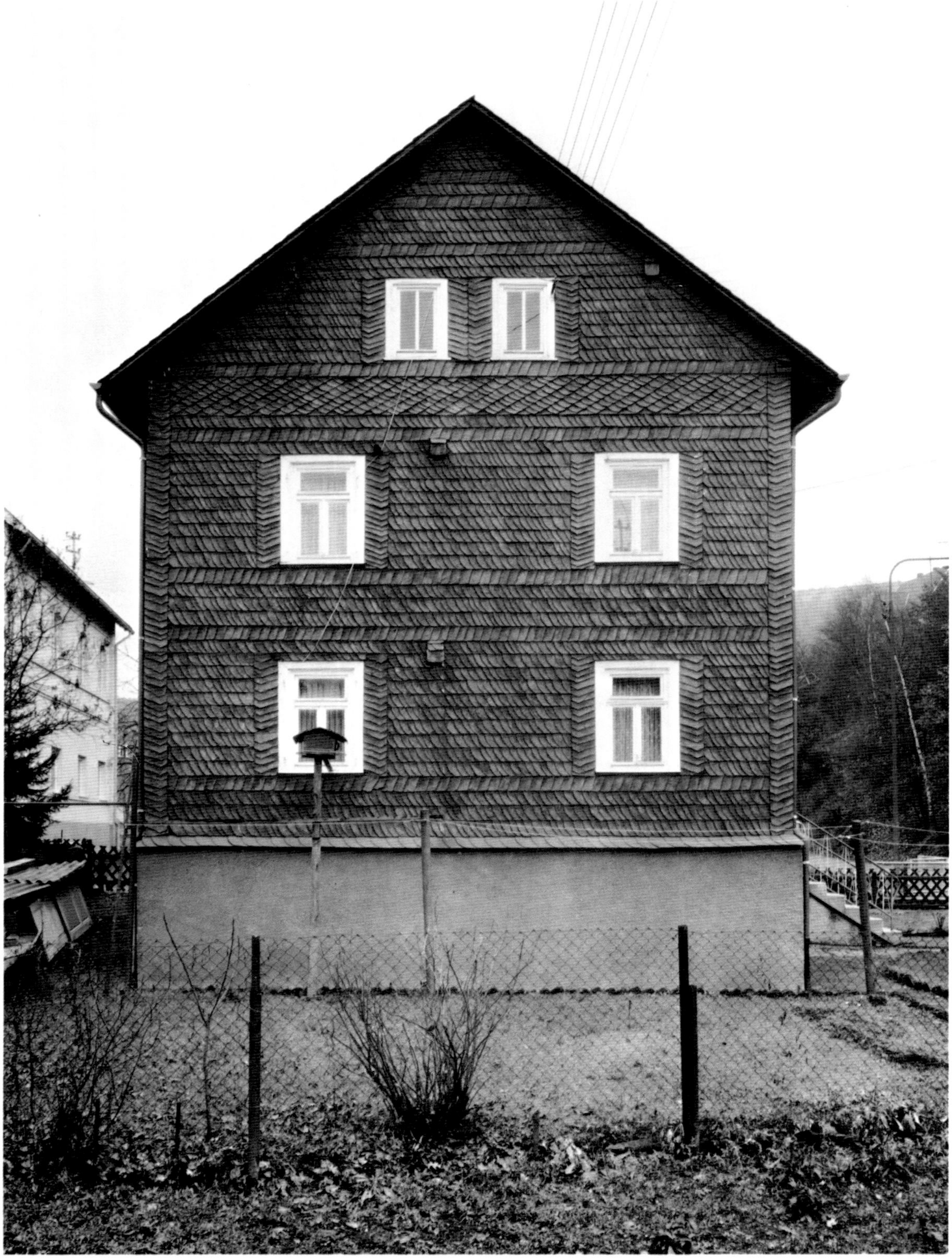

85
Am Gosenbach 3, Niederschelderhütte, 1962.

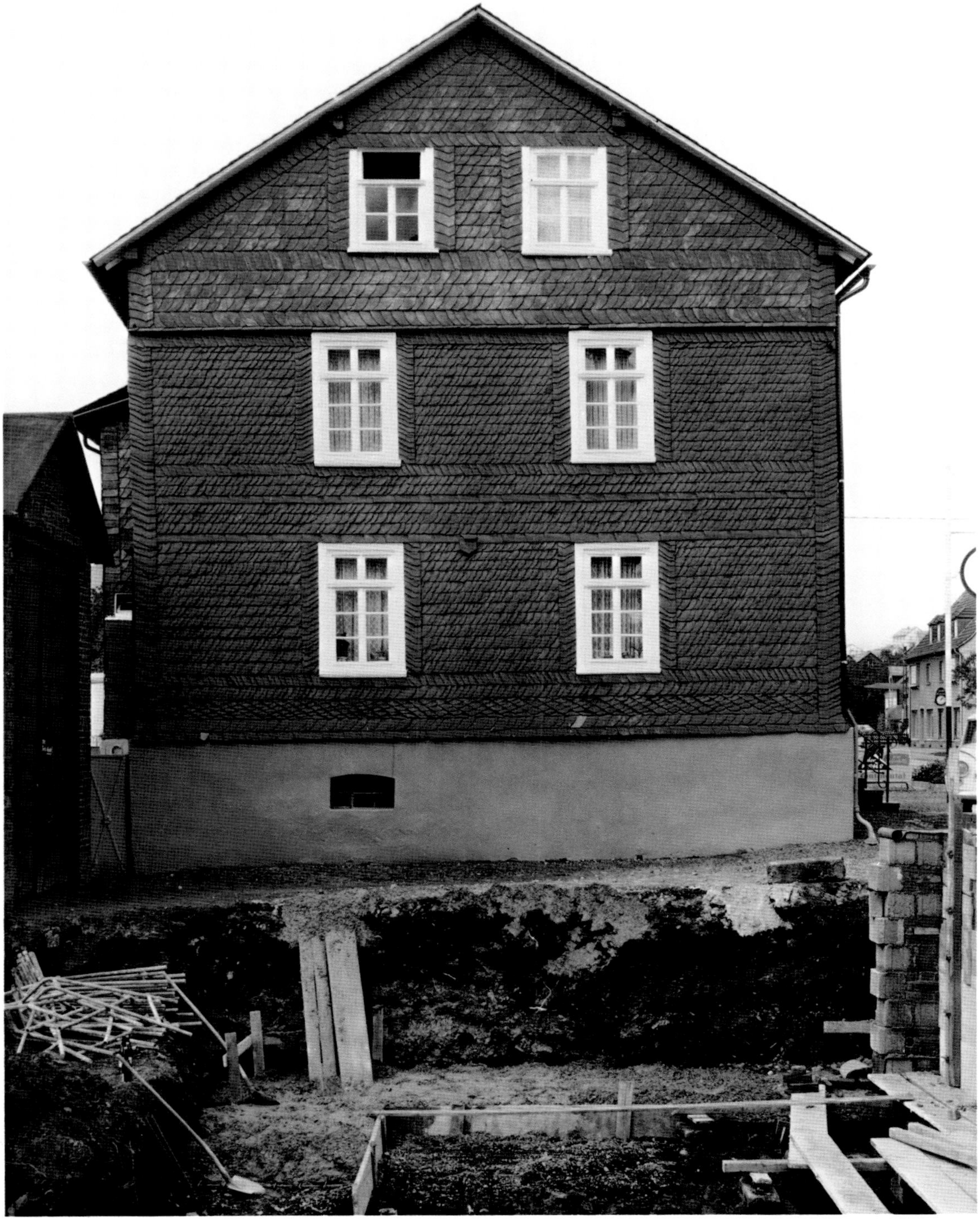

86
Bahnhofstraße 21, Eiserfeld, 1964.

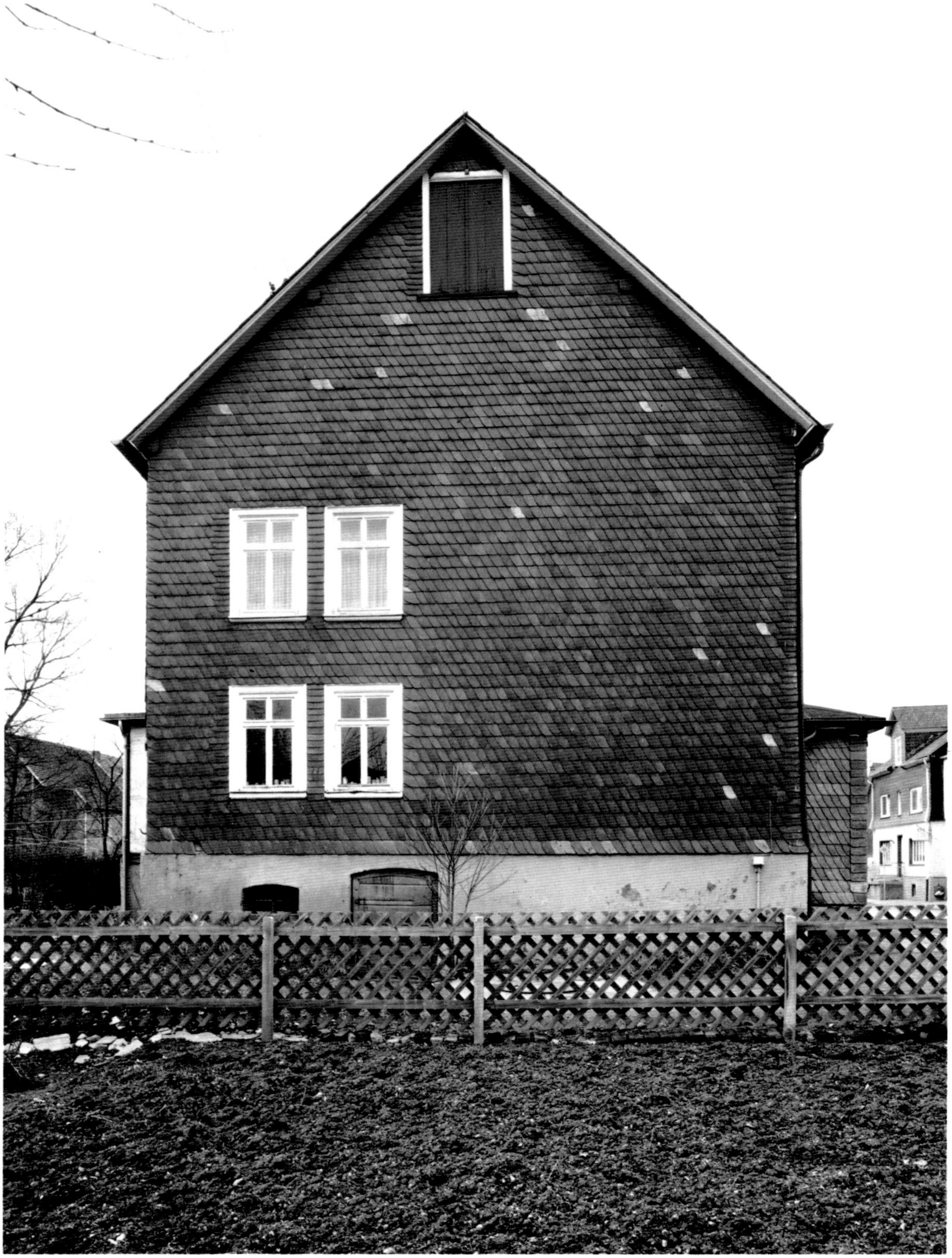

87
Siegstraße 150, Dreis-Tiefenbach, 1970.

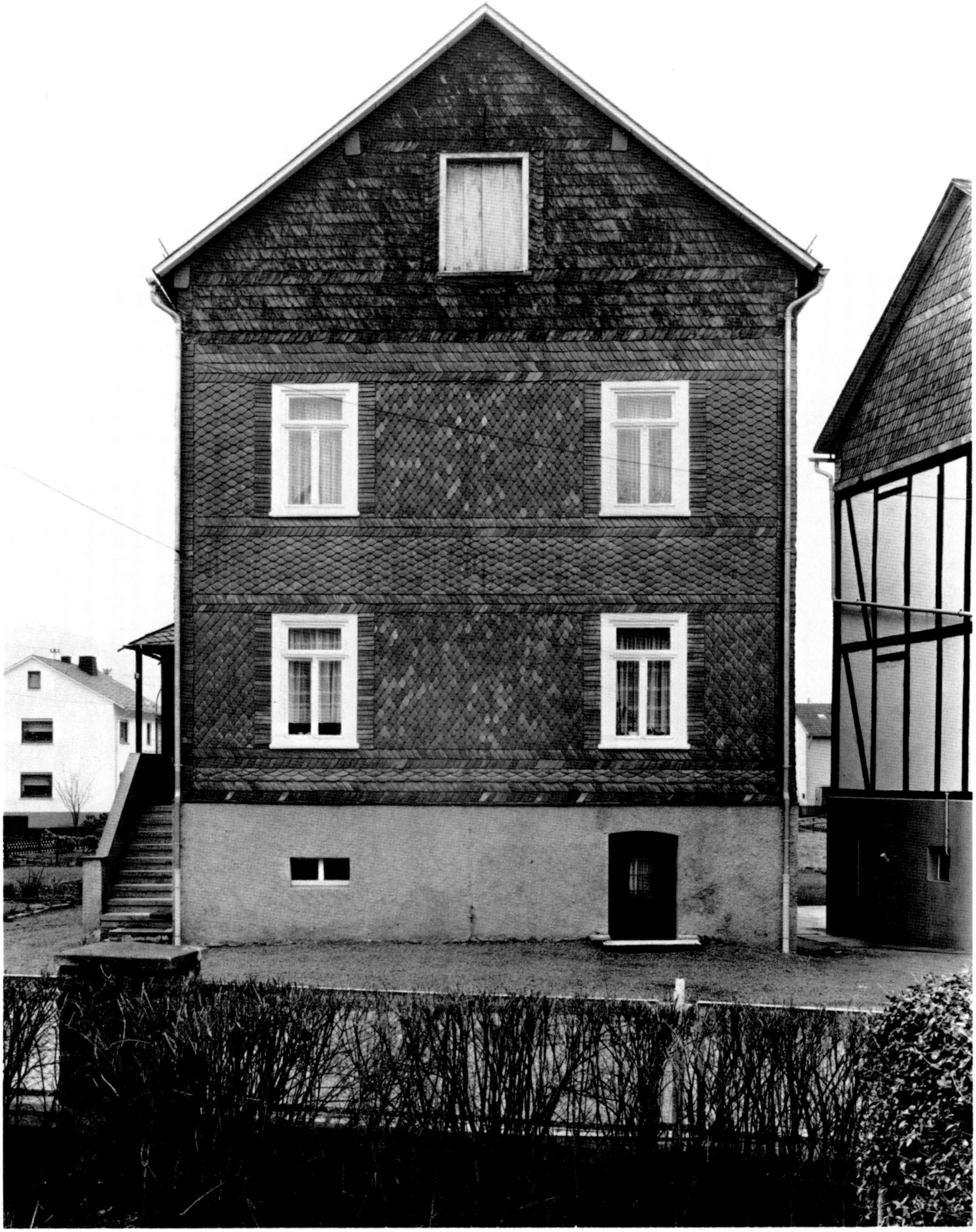

88
In der Trift 8, Neunkirchen, 1972.

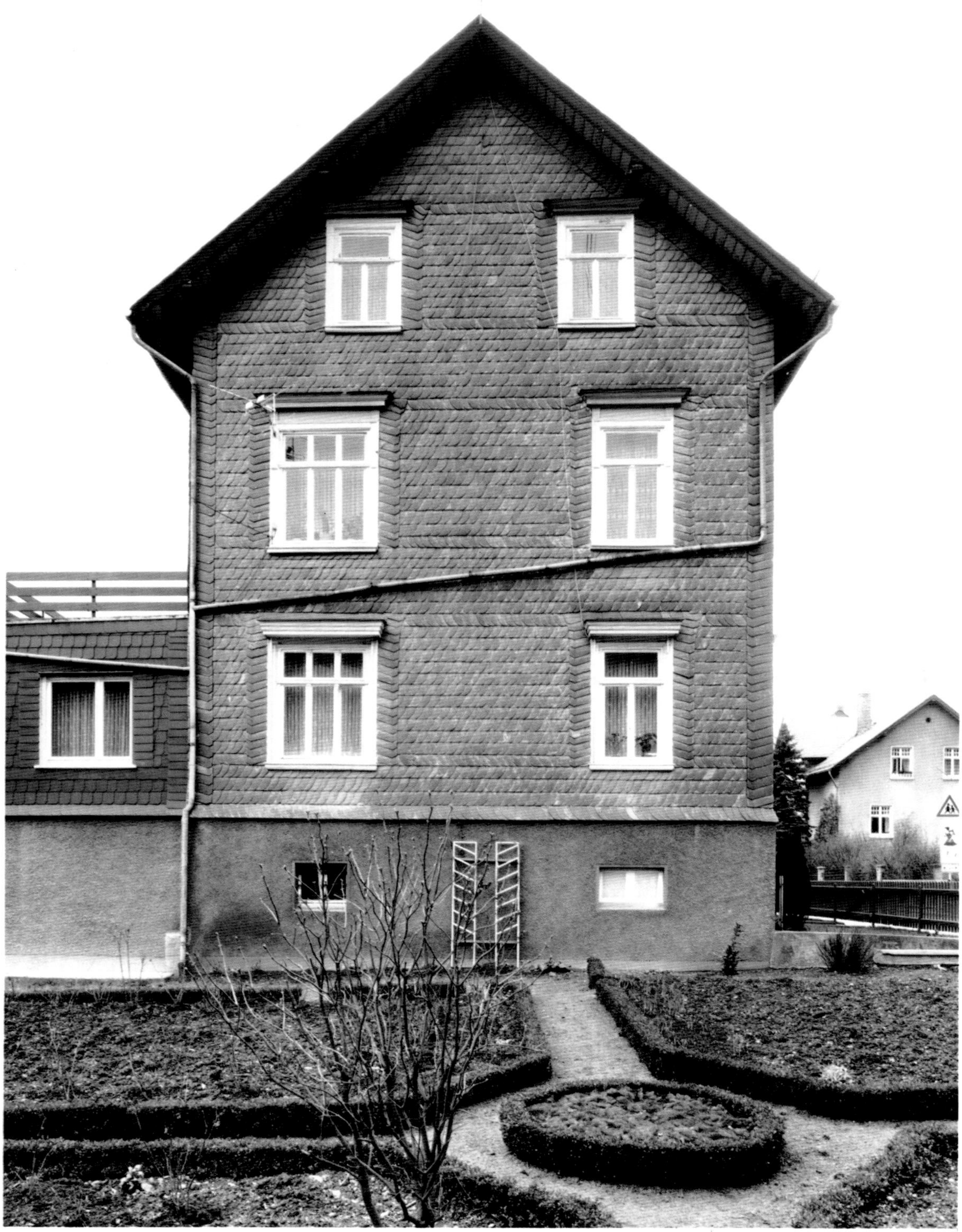

89
Trupbacher Straße 9, Trupbach, 1972.

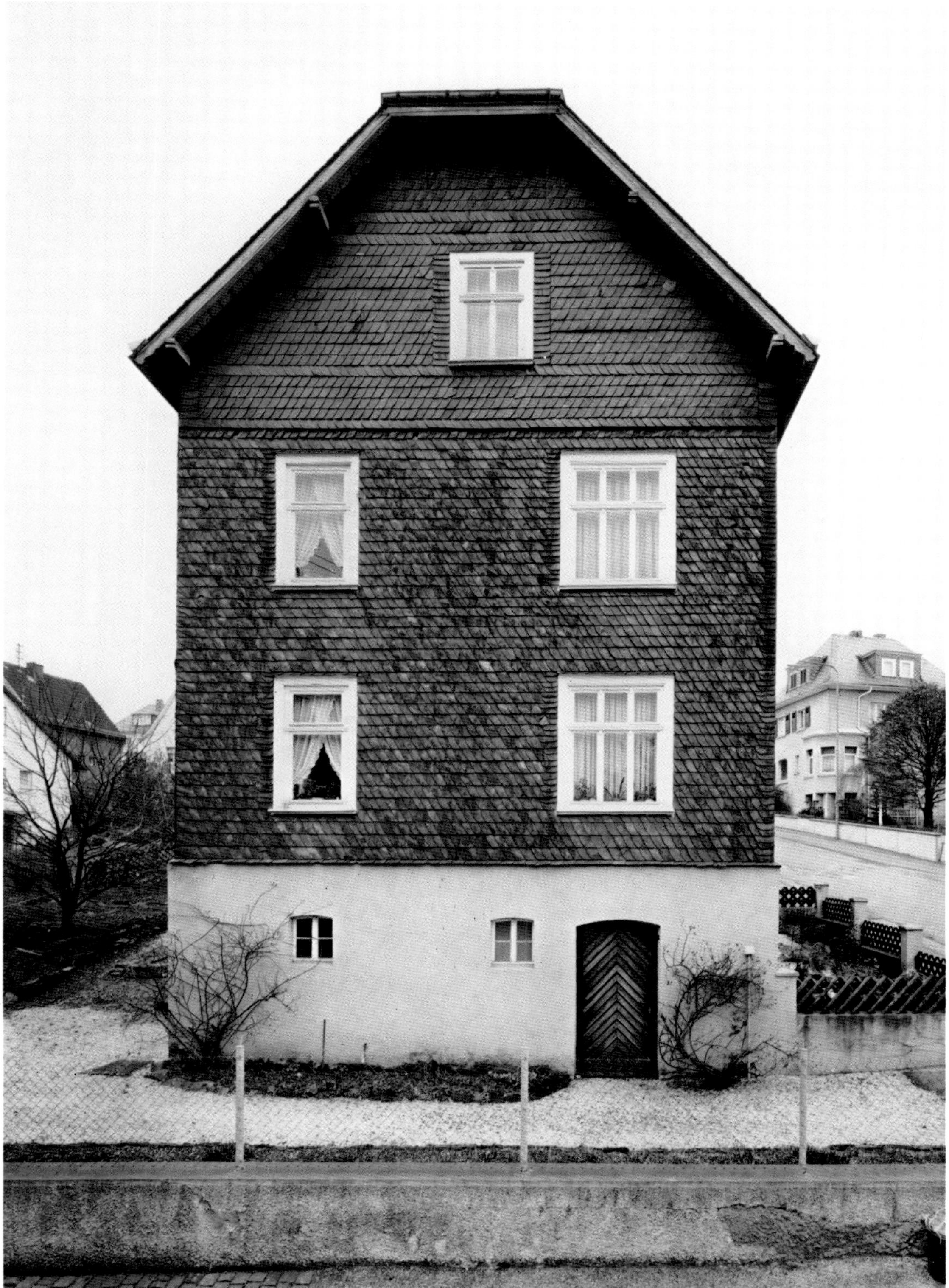

90
Schloßblick 17, Kaan-Marienborn, 1972.

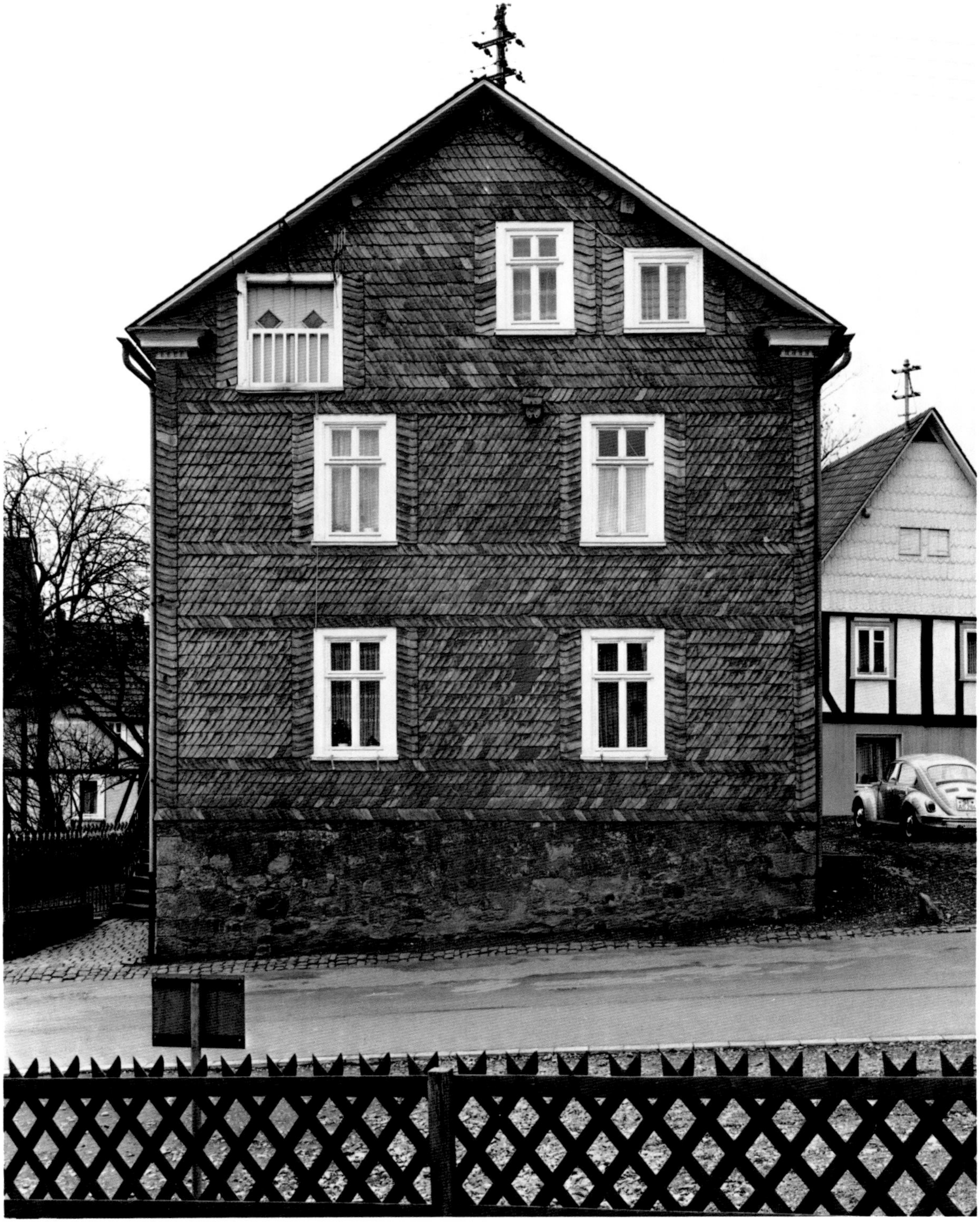

91

Ferndorfstraße 7, Hilchenbach, 1972.

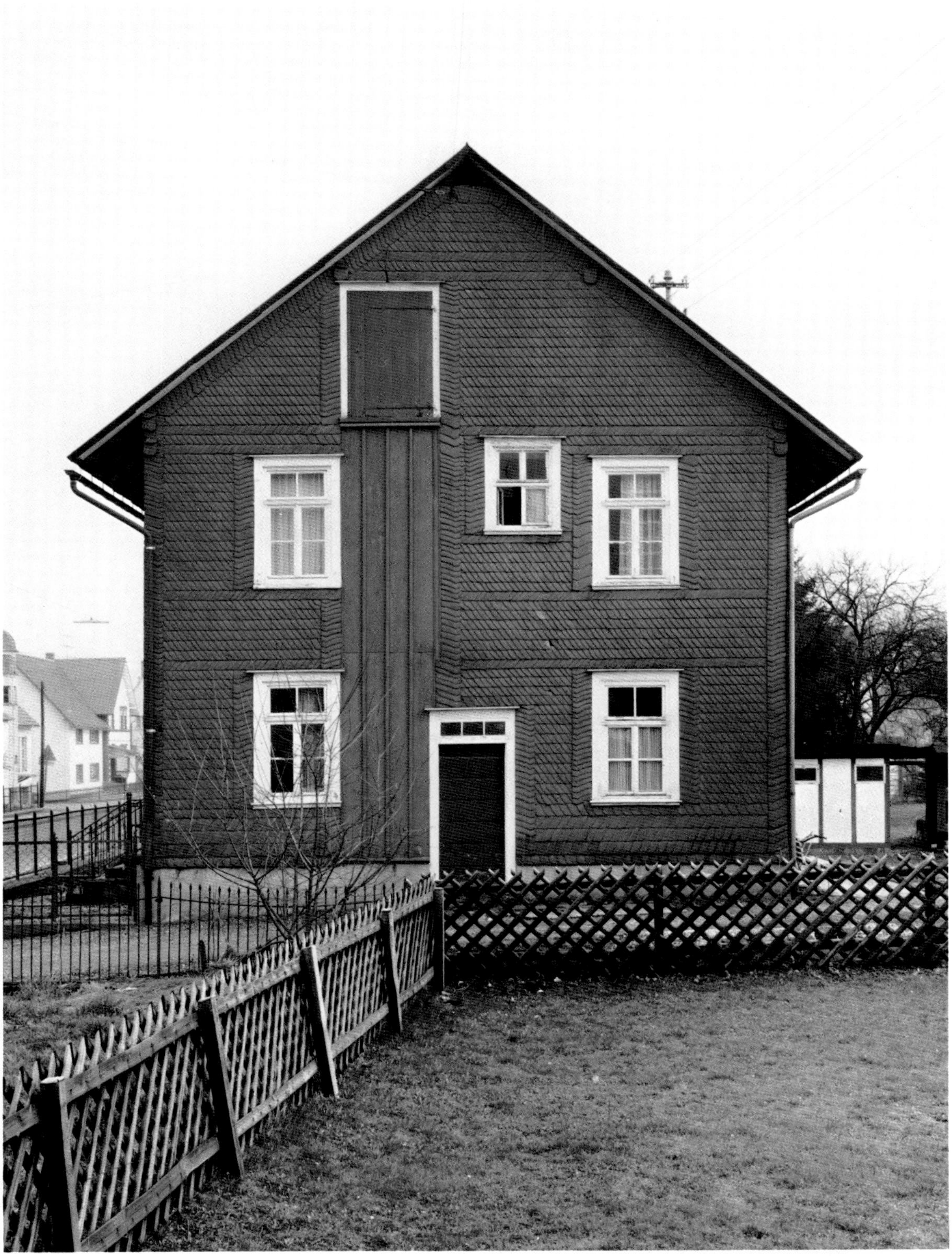

92
Hauptstraße 77, Müsen, 1970.

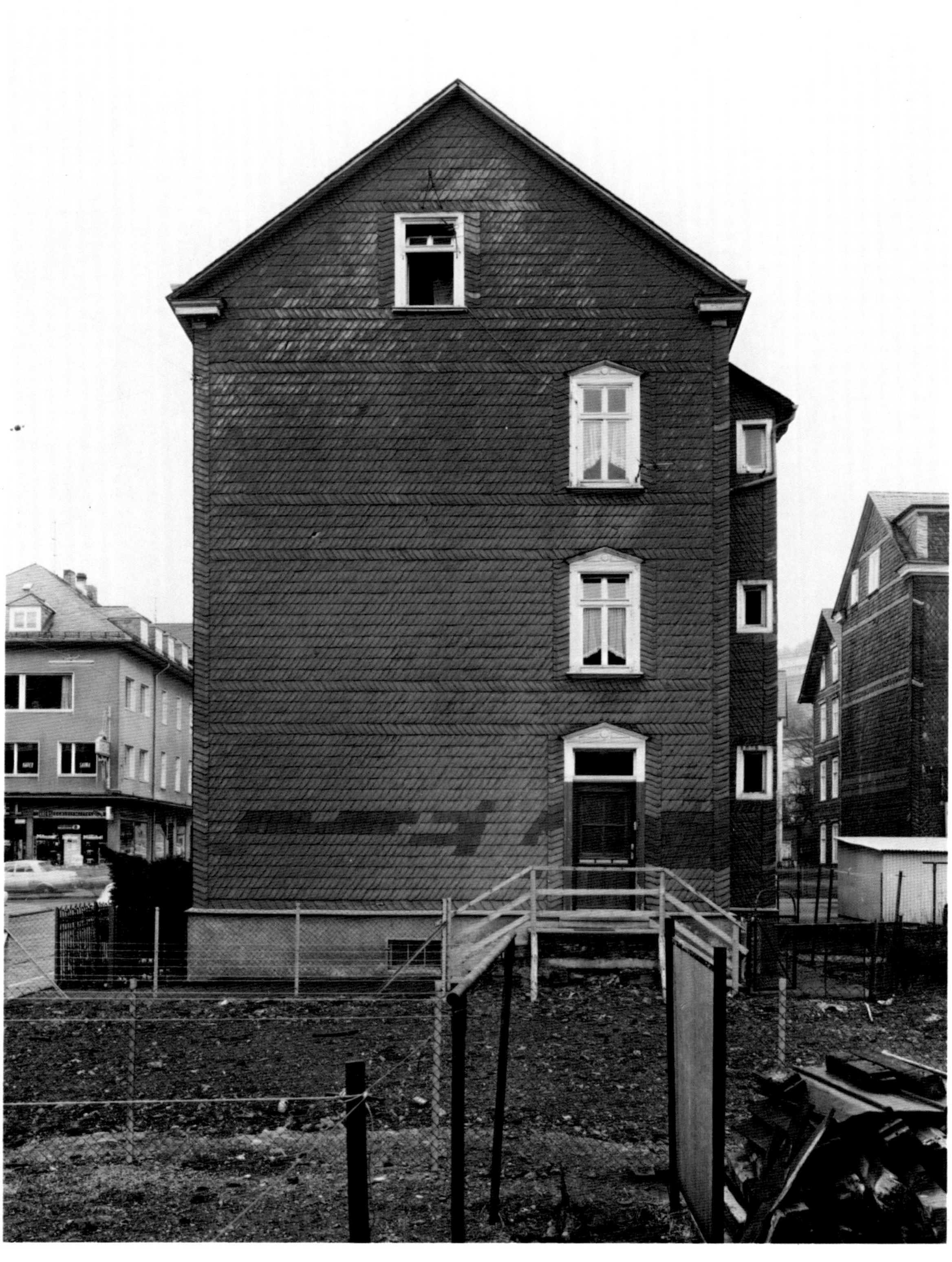

93

Arndtstraße 6, Siegen, 1974.

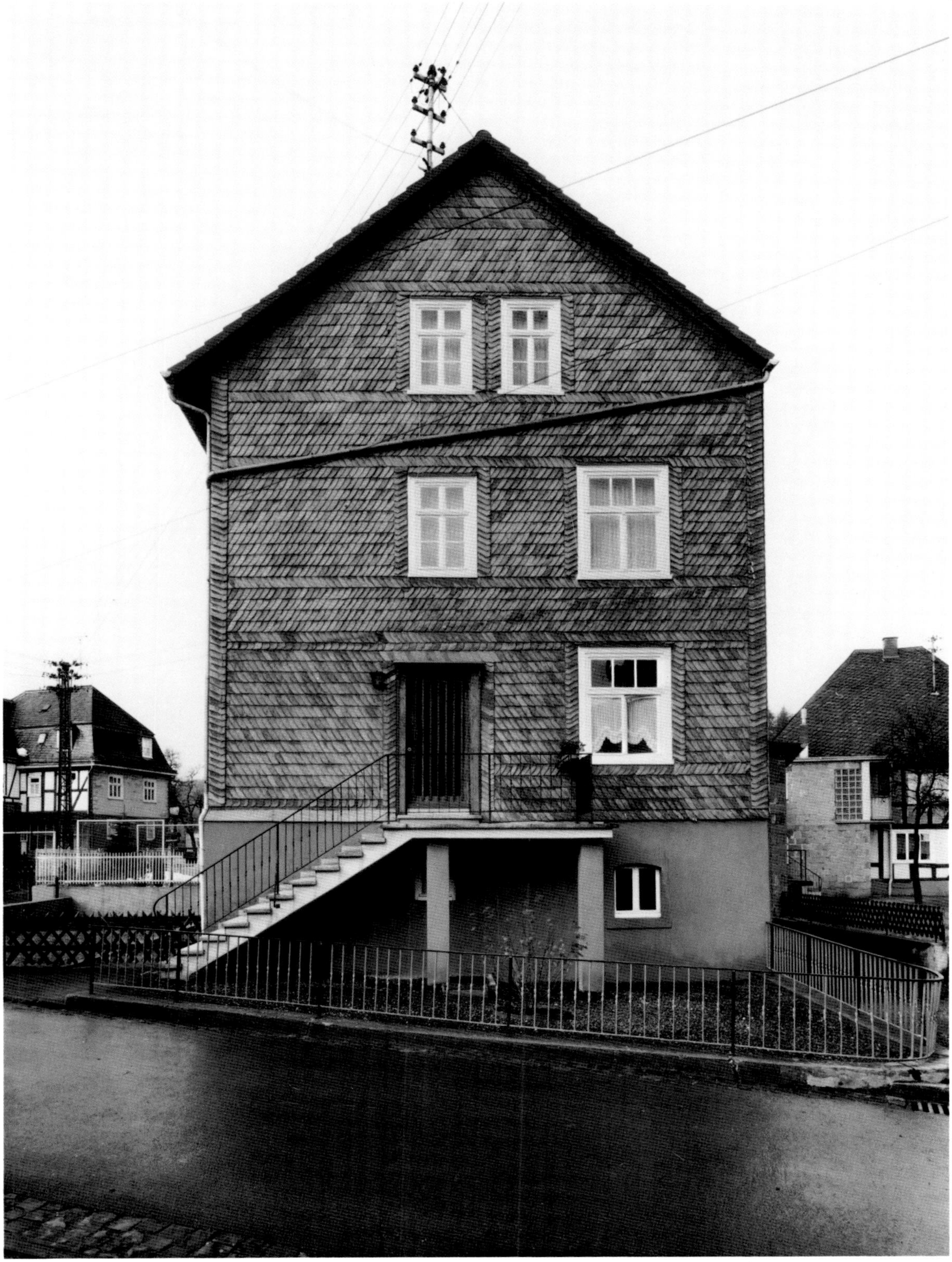

94
Bachstraße 5, Niederfischbach, 1973.

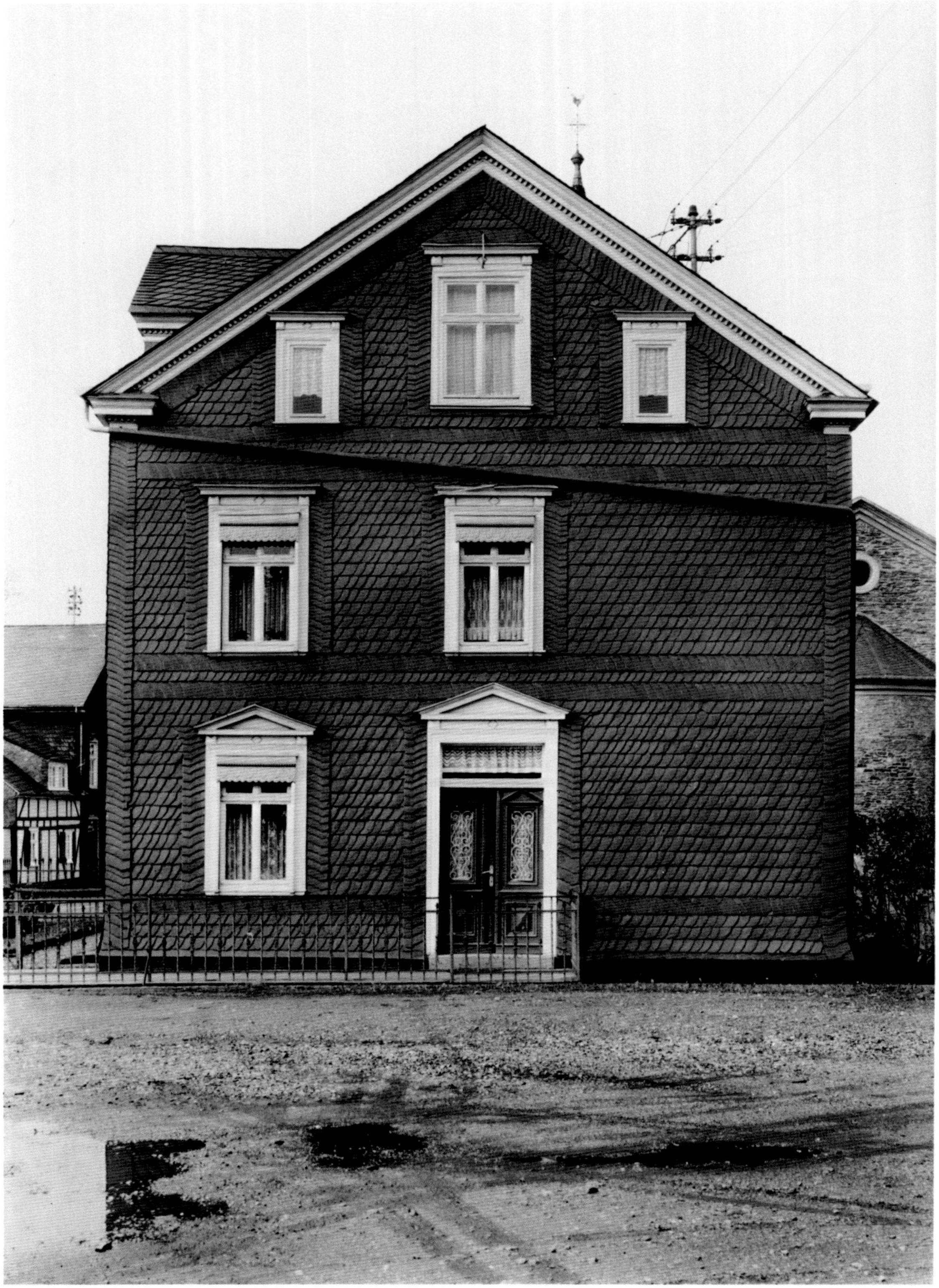

95
Freiengründerstraße 21, Eiserfeld, 1960.

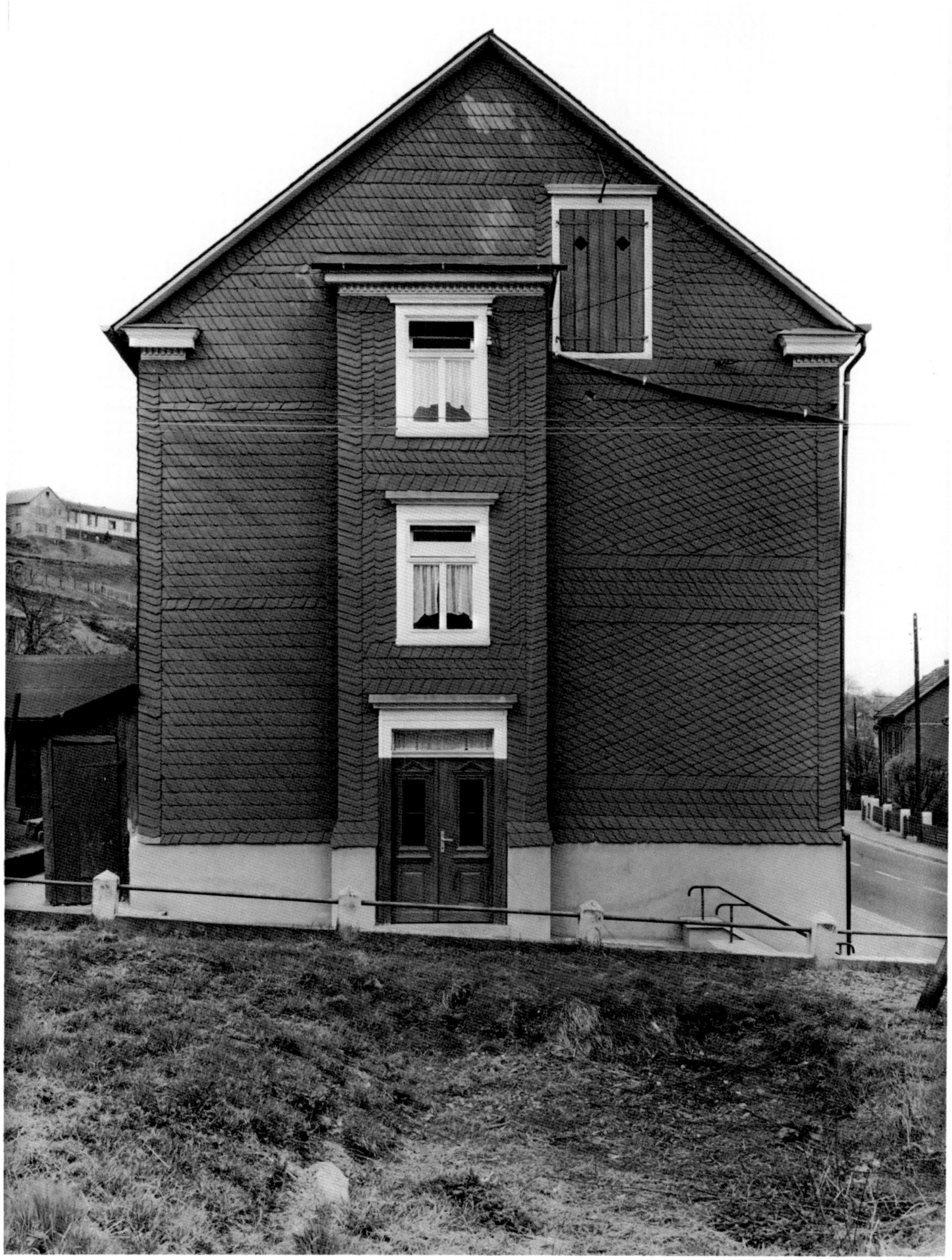

96
Freiengründerstraße 112, Eiserfeld, 1961.

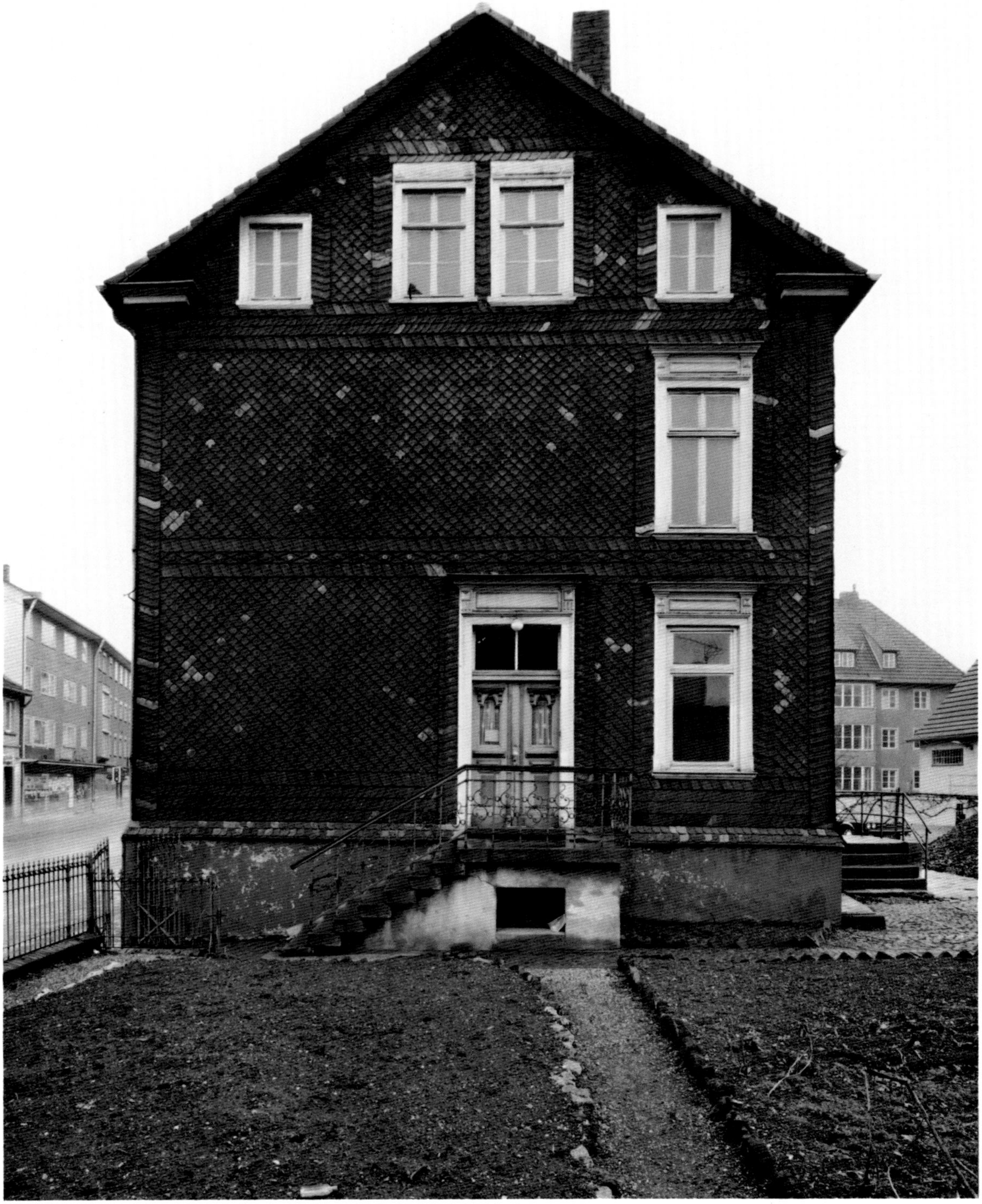

97
Weidenauer Straße 119, Weidenau, 1970.

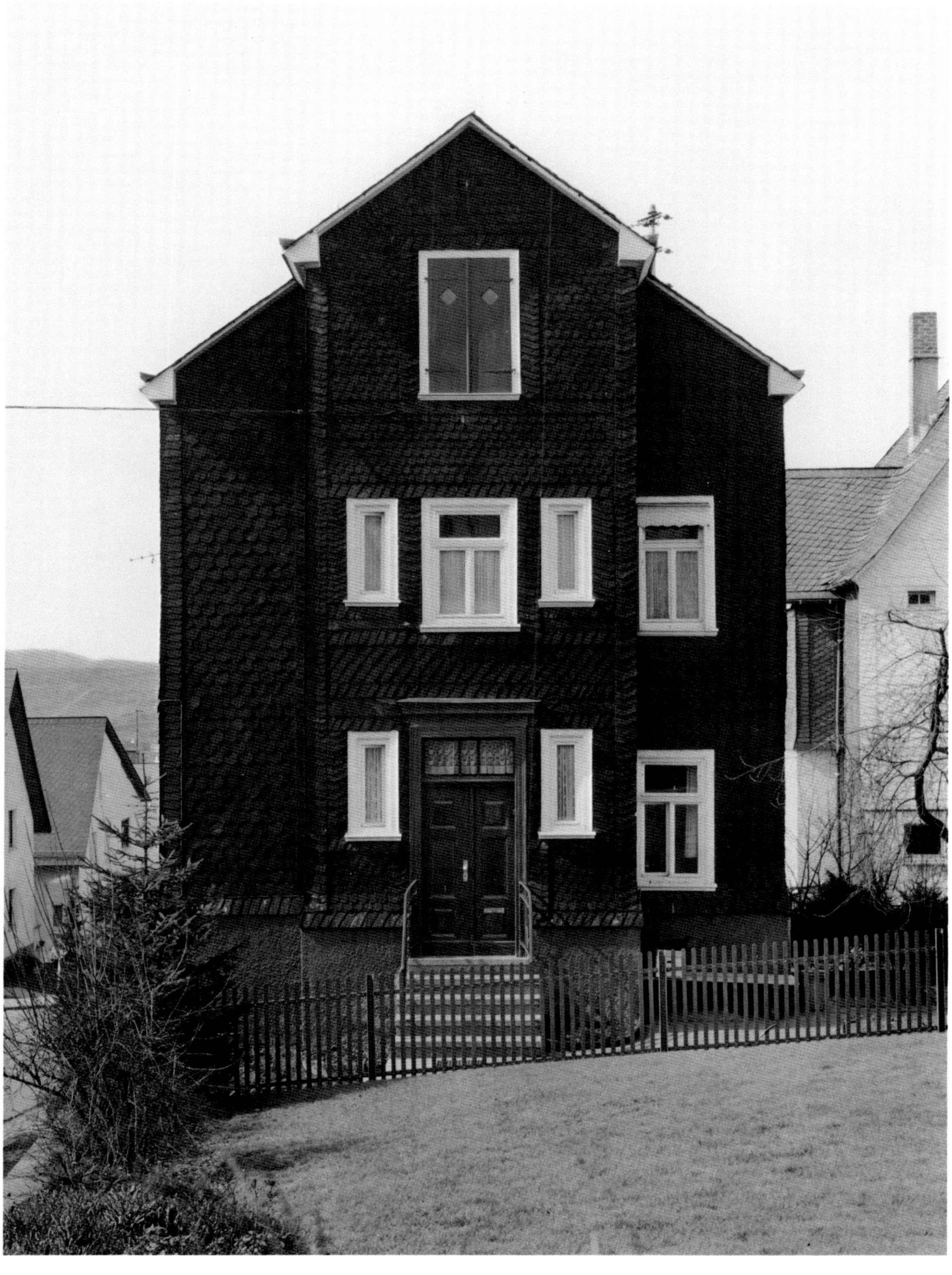

98
Försterstraße 12, Weidenau, 1965.

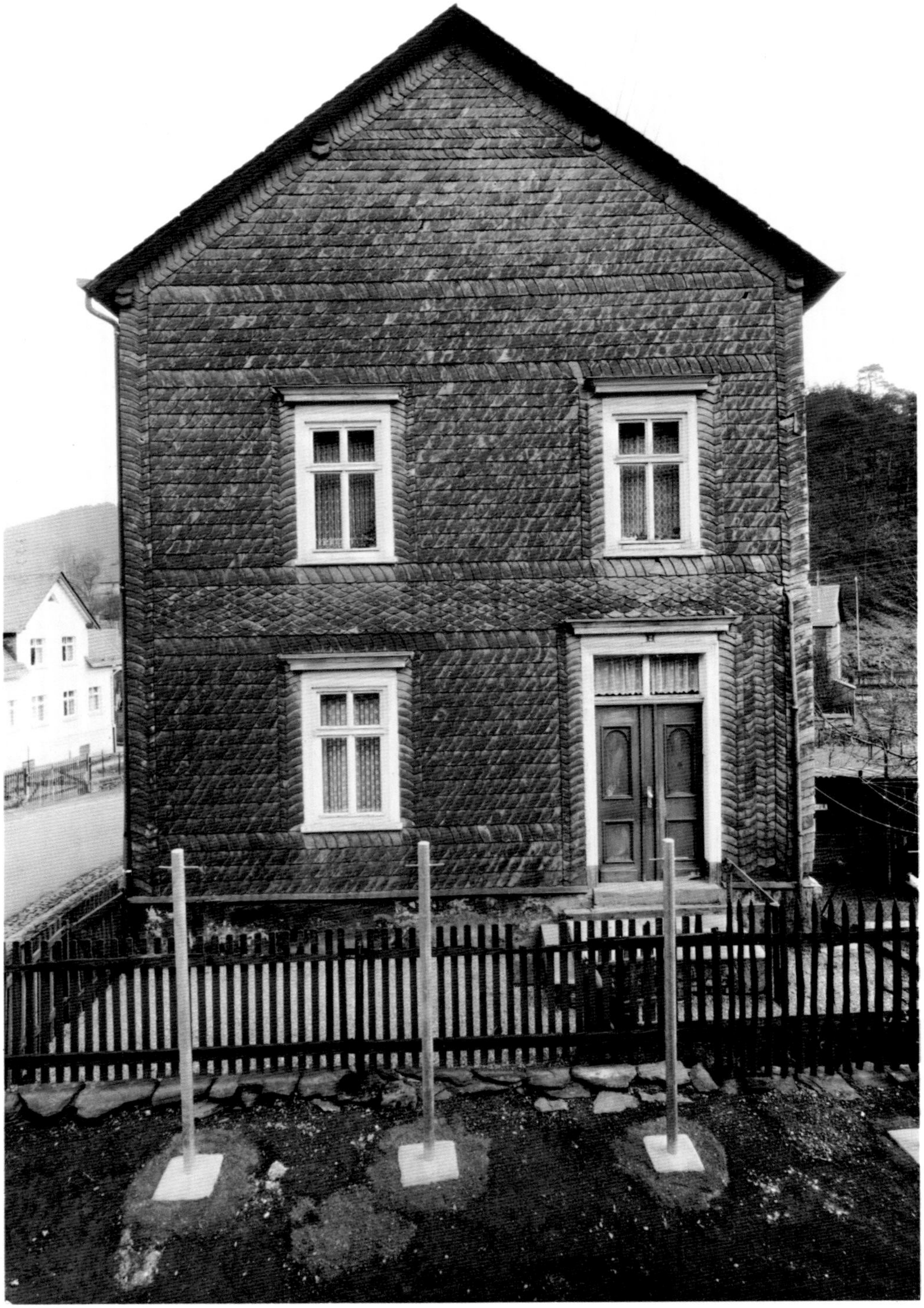

99

Querstraße 2, Eiserfeld, 1961.

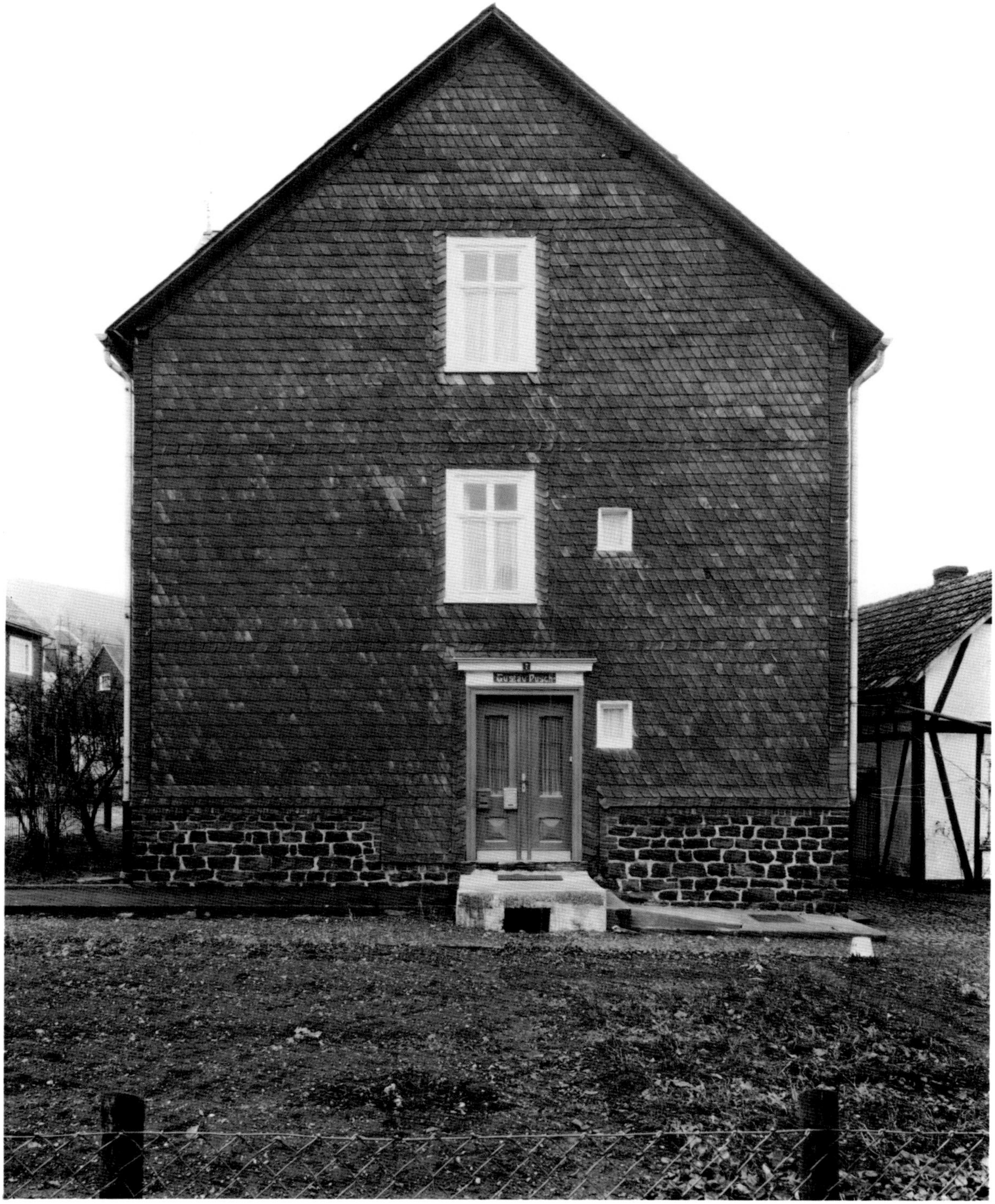

100
Haiger Weg 7, Burbach, 1964.

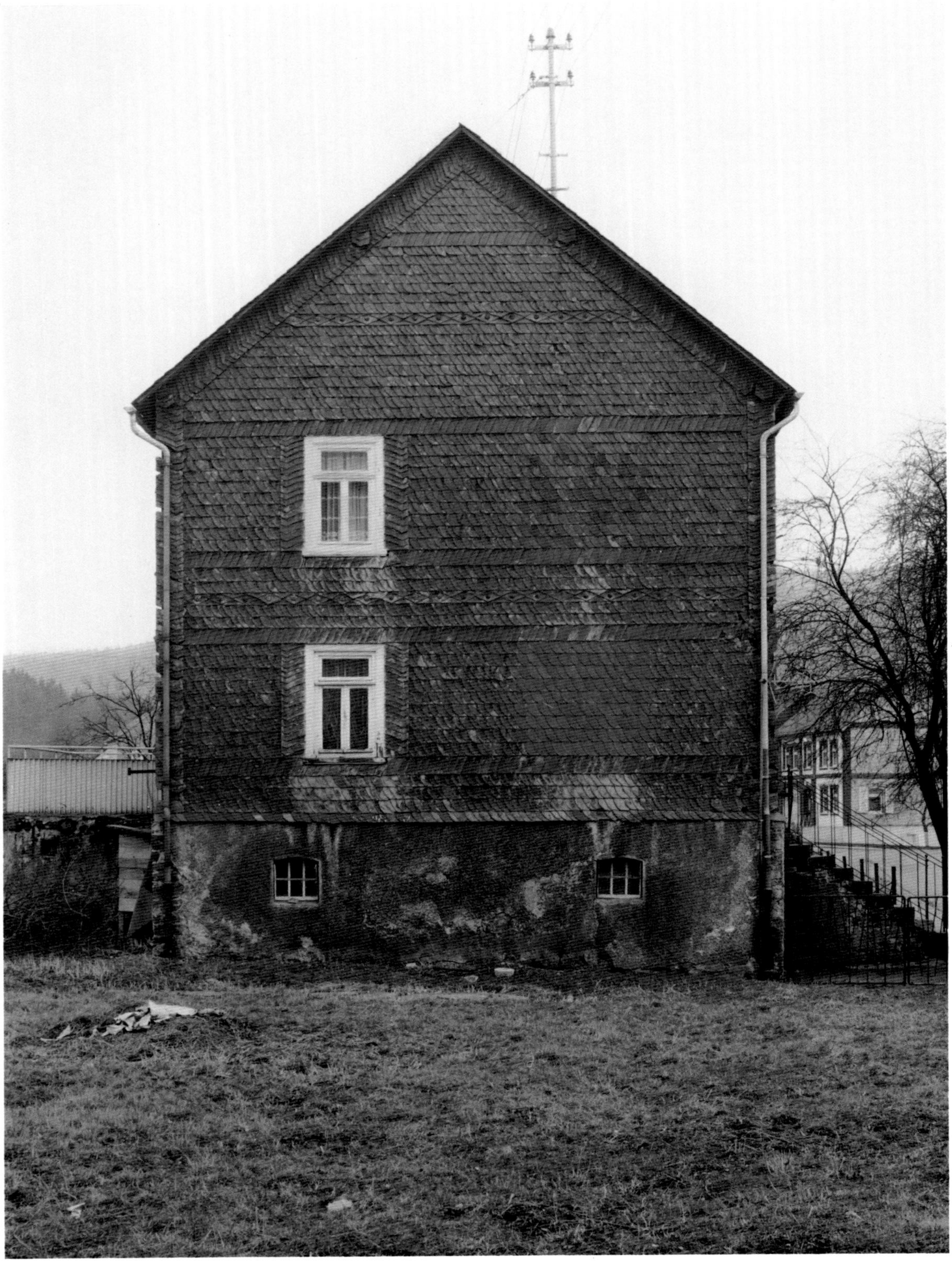

101
Wildener Straße 11, Salchendorf, 1961.

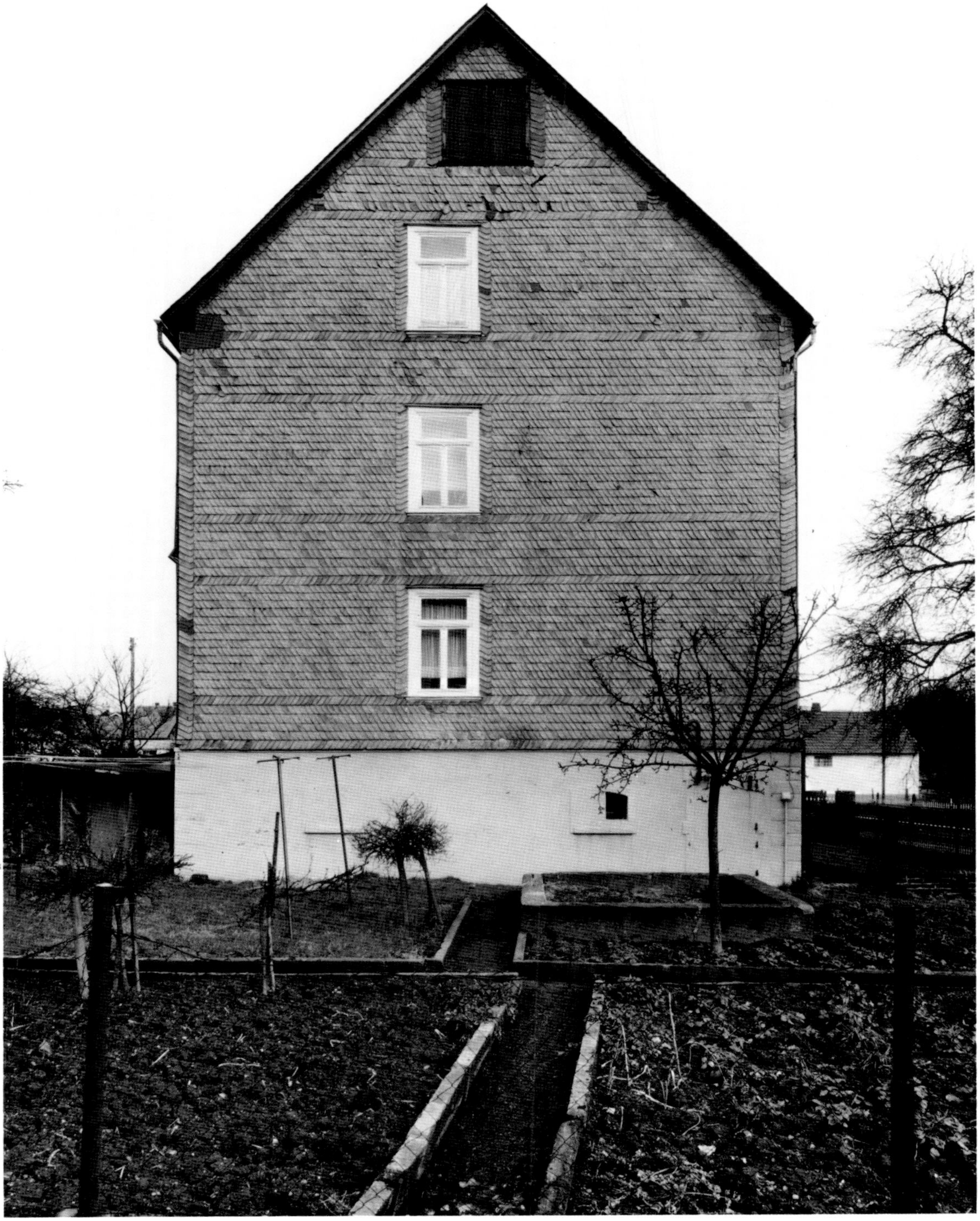

102
Löhrstraße 38, Neunkirchen, 1962.

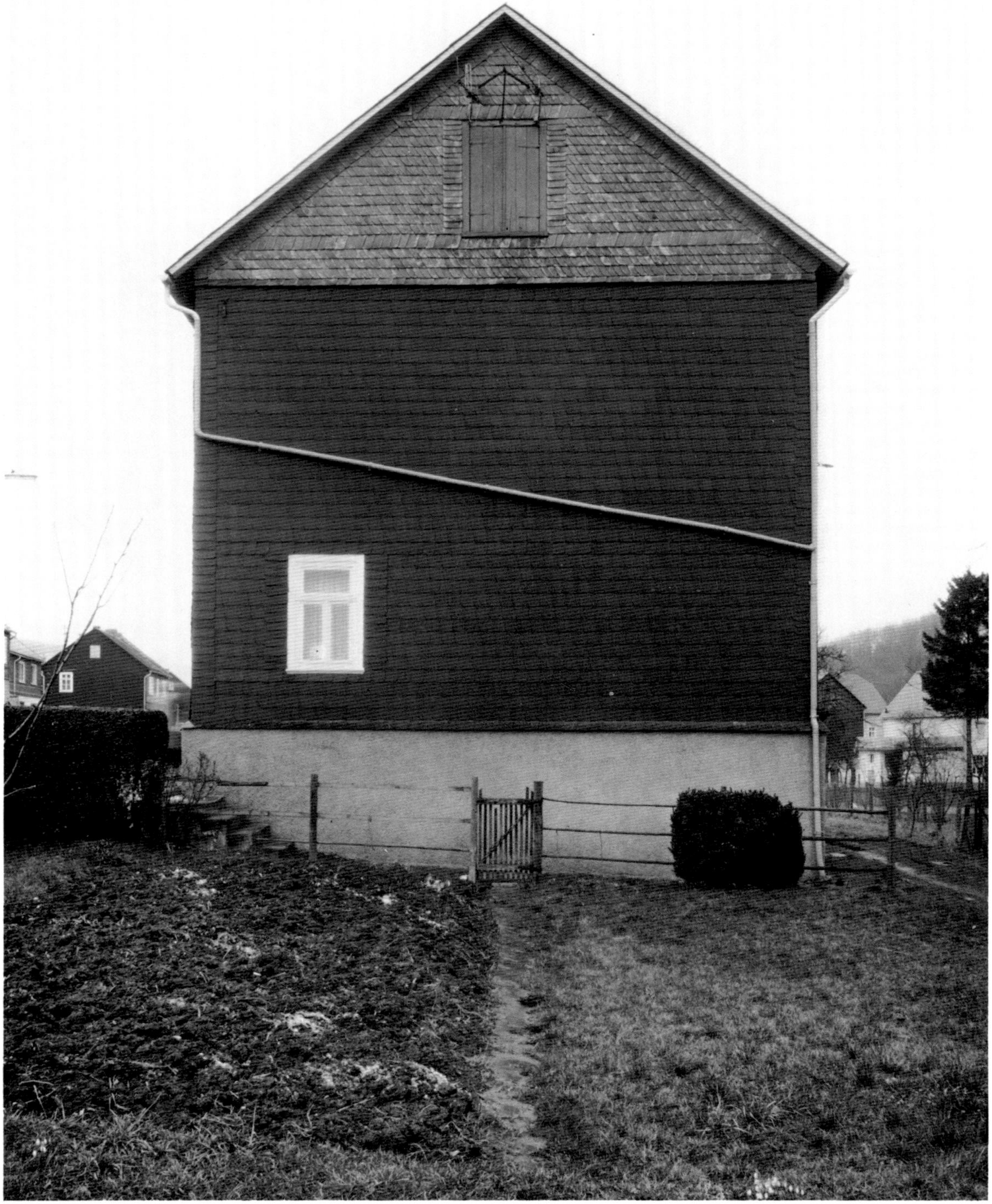

103
Freier Grund Straße 28, Wahlbach, 1972.

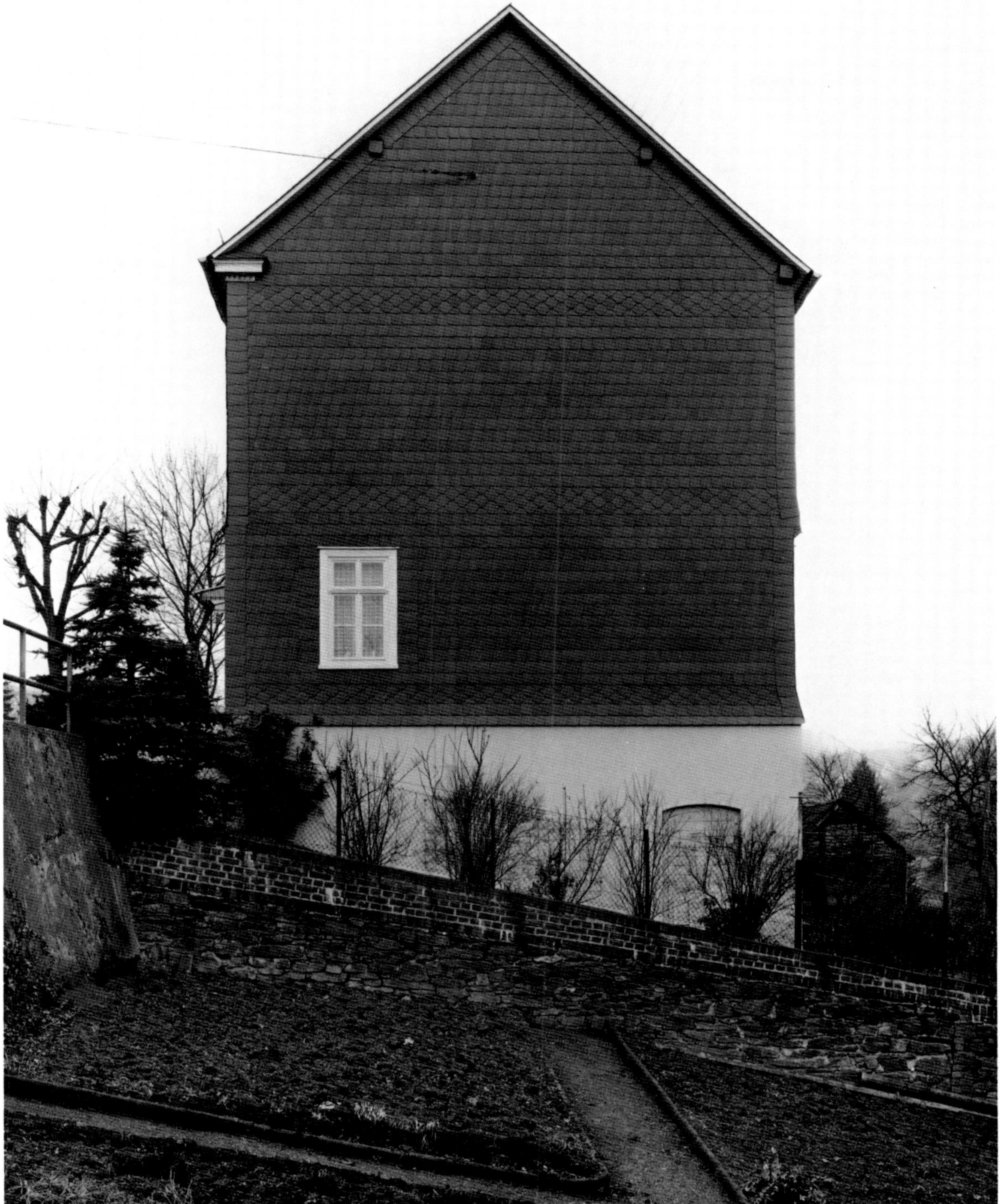

104
Kölner Straße 318, Salchendorf, 1972.

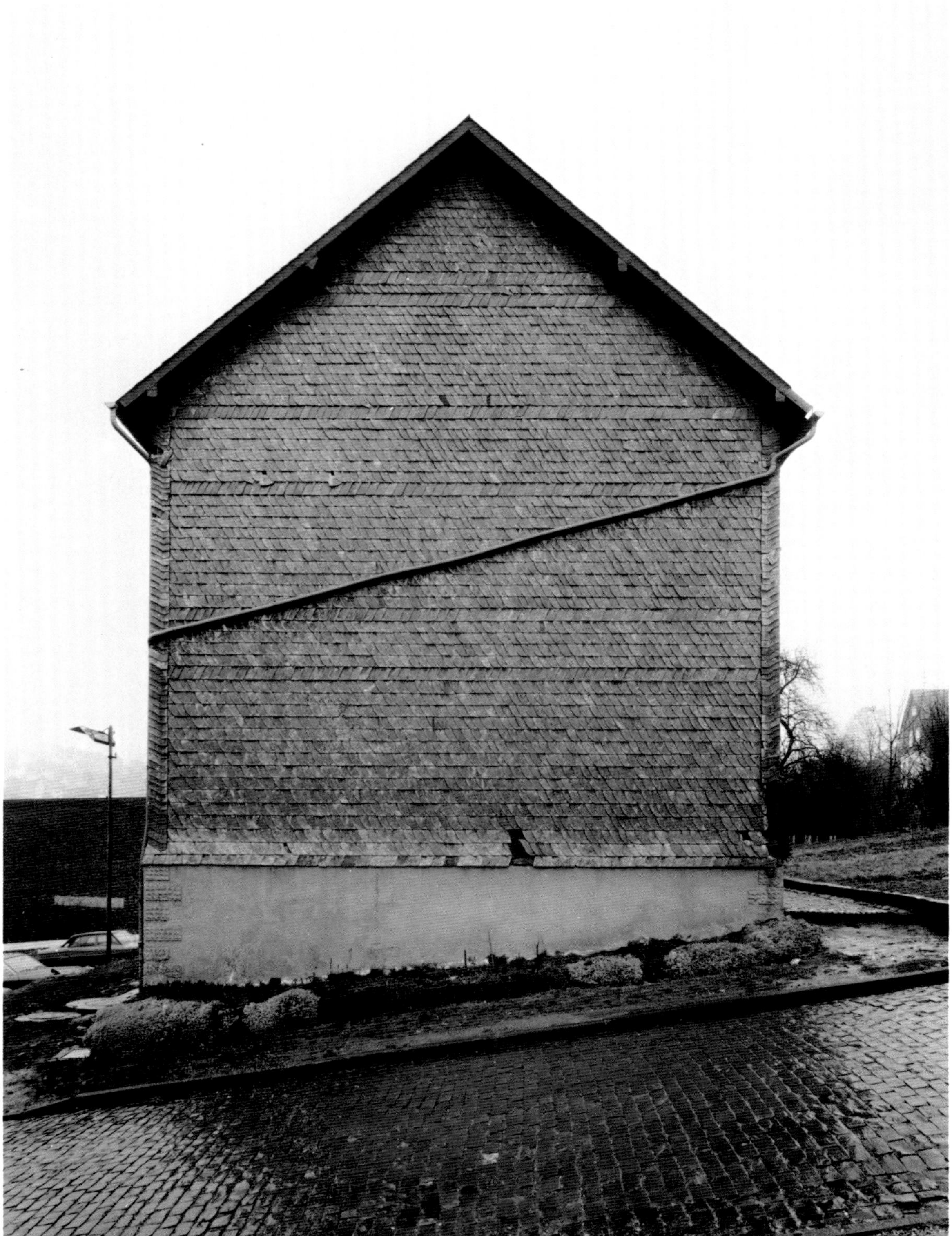

105
Hauptstraße 3, Birken, 1971.

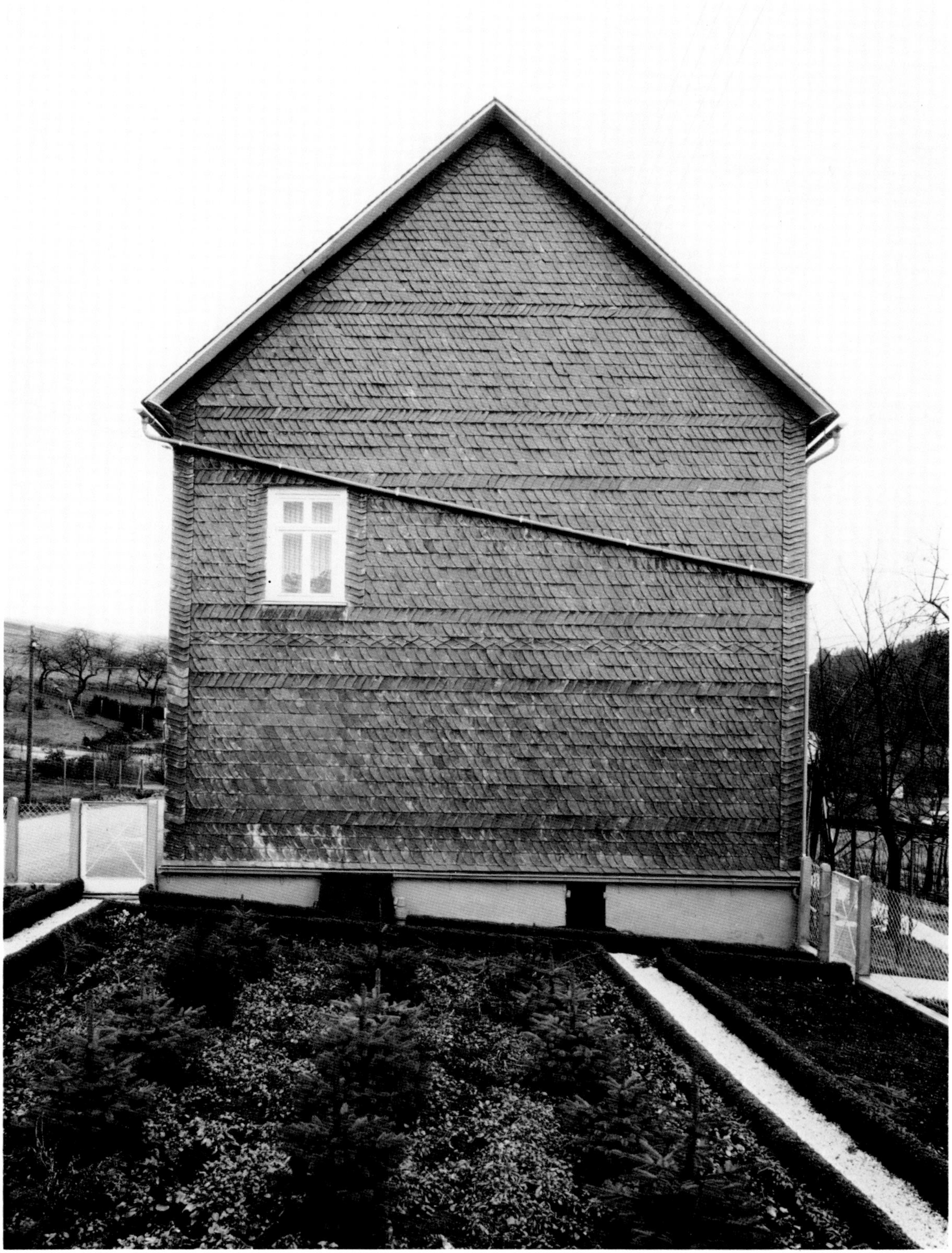

106
Wendinger Straße 8, Büschergrund, 1973.

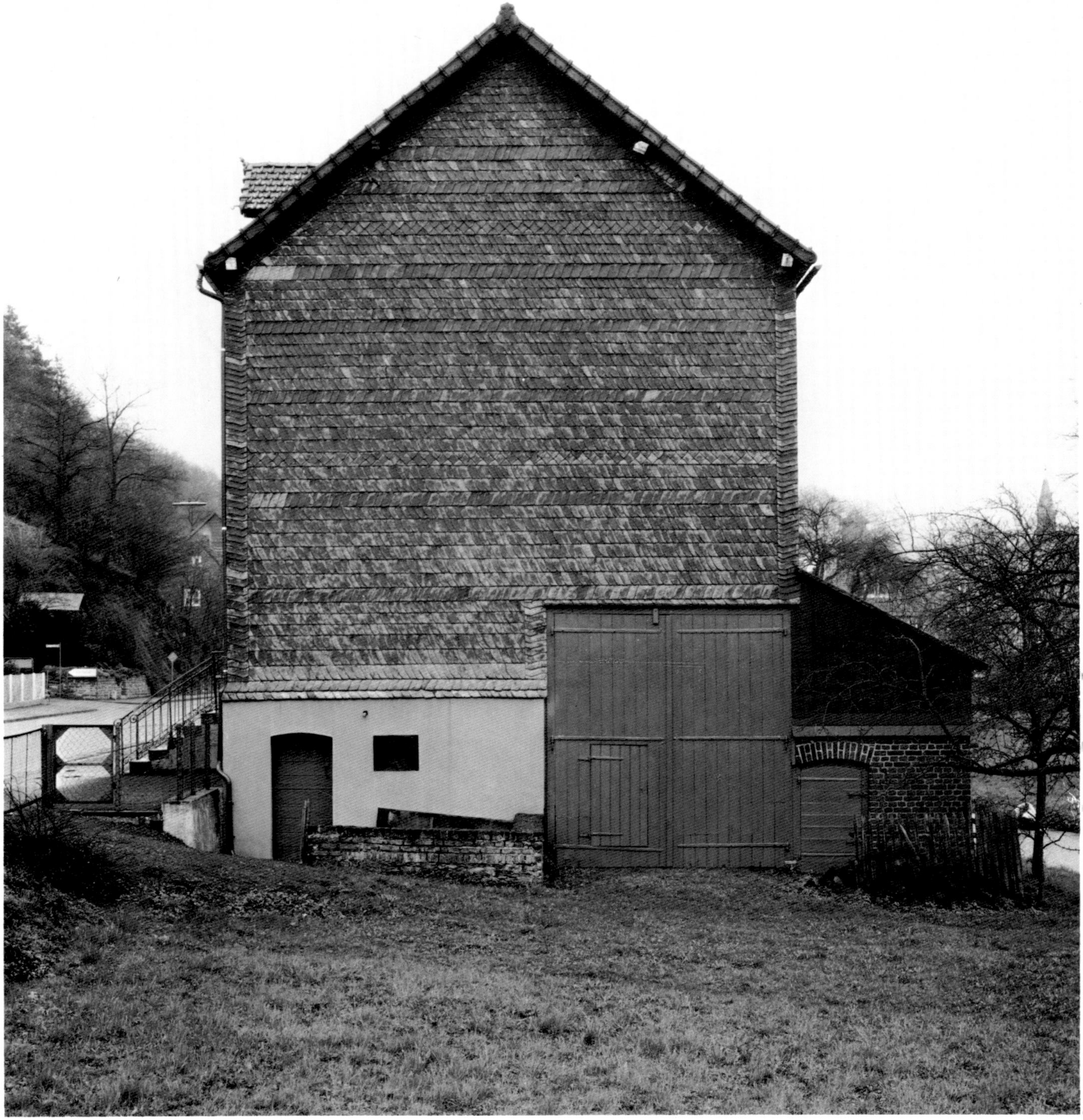

107
Kölner Straße 26, Struthhütten, 1964.

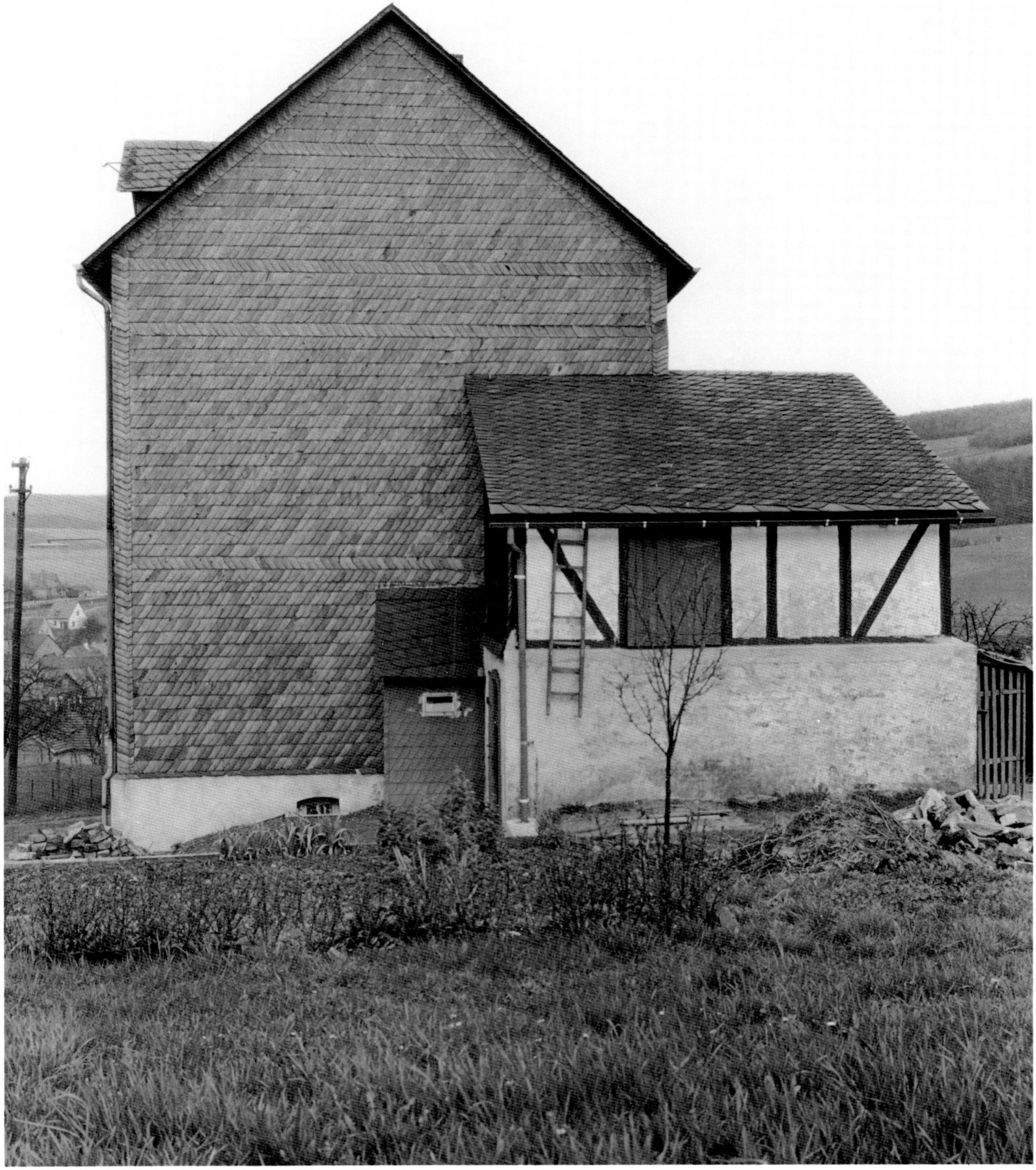

108
Rödgerstraße 7, Niederdielfen, 1960.

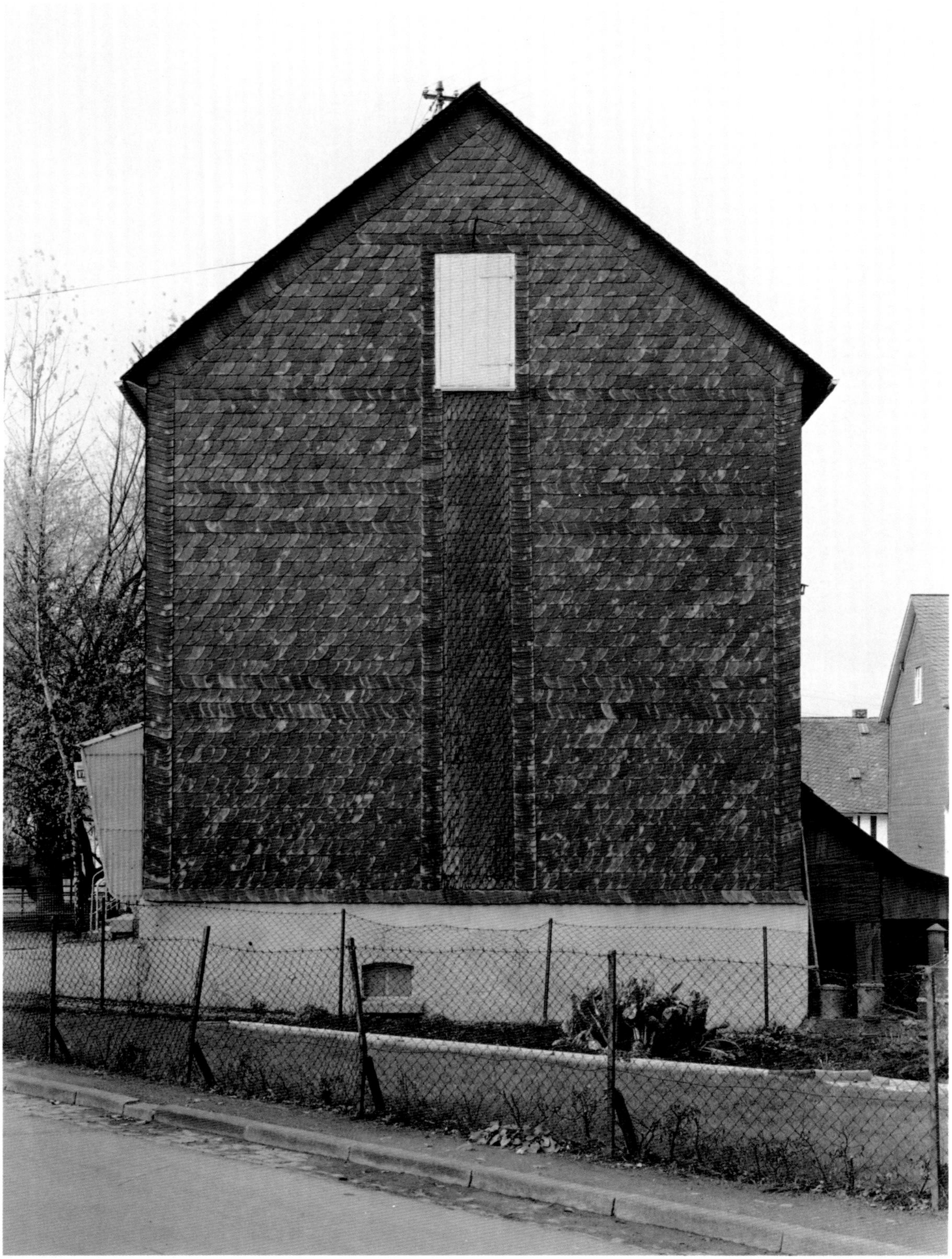

109

Haiger Weg 3, Burbach, 1964.

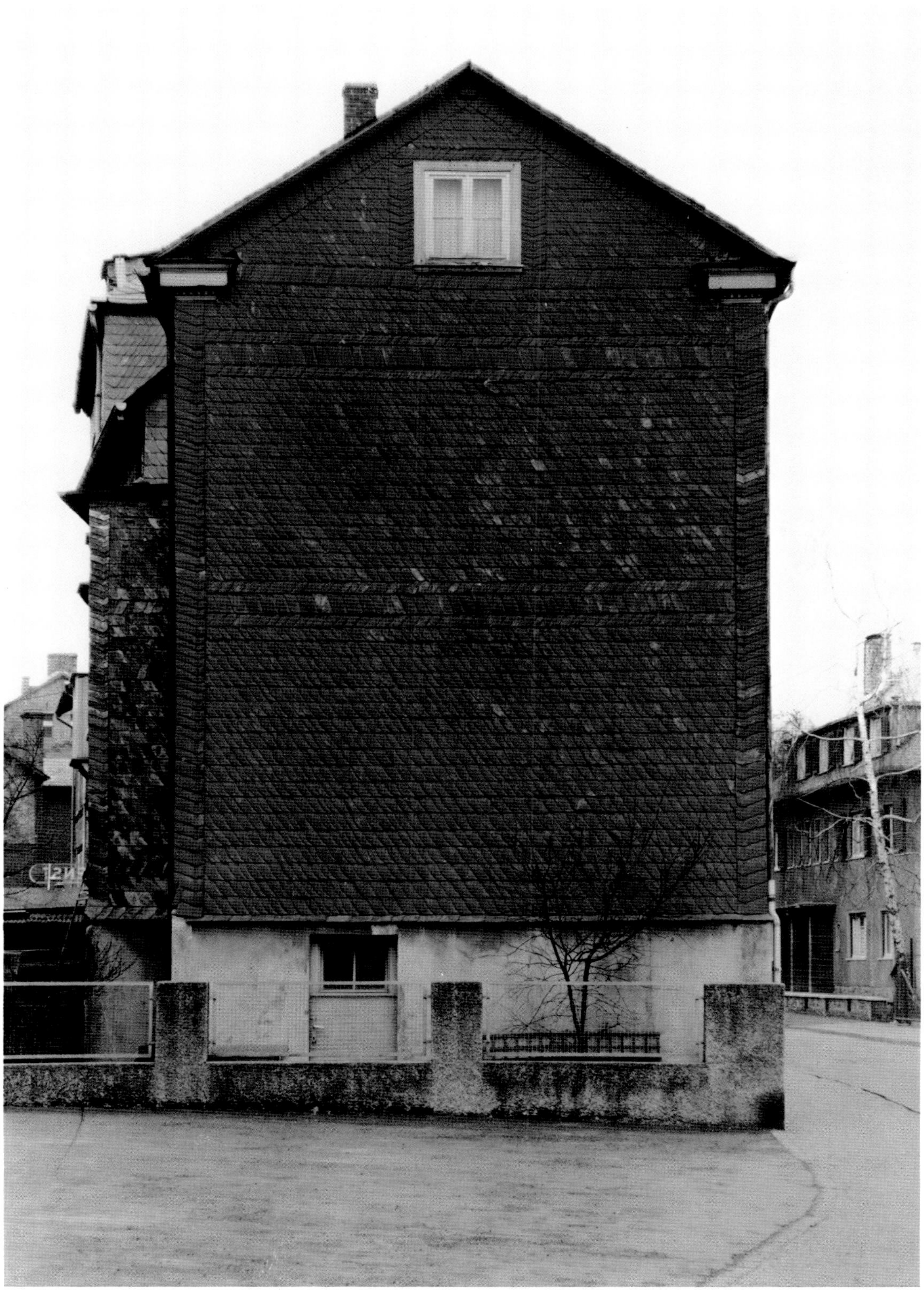

110
Kirchweg 52, Siegen, 1959.

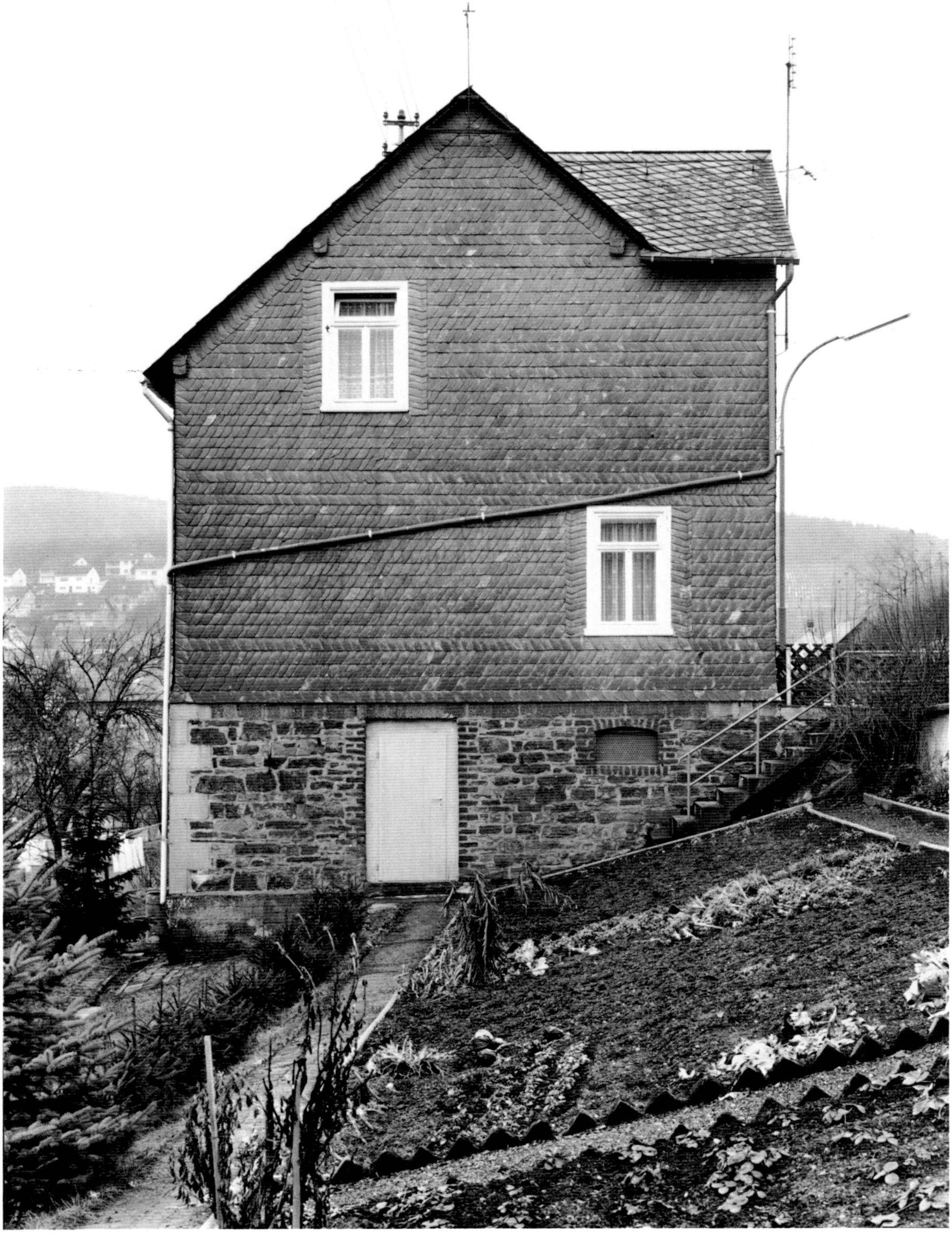

111

Eiserfelder Straße 13, Rinsdorf, 1967.

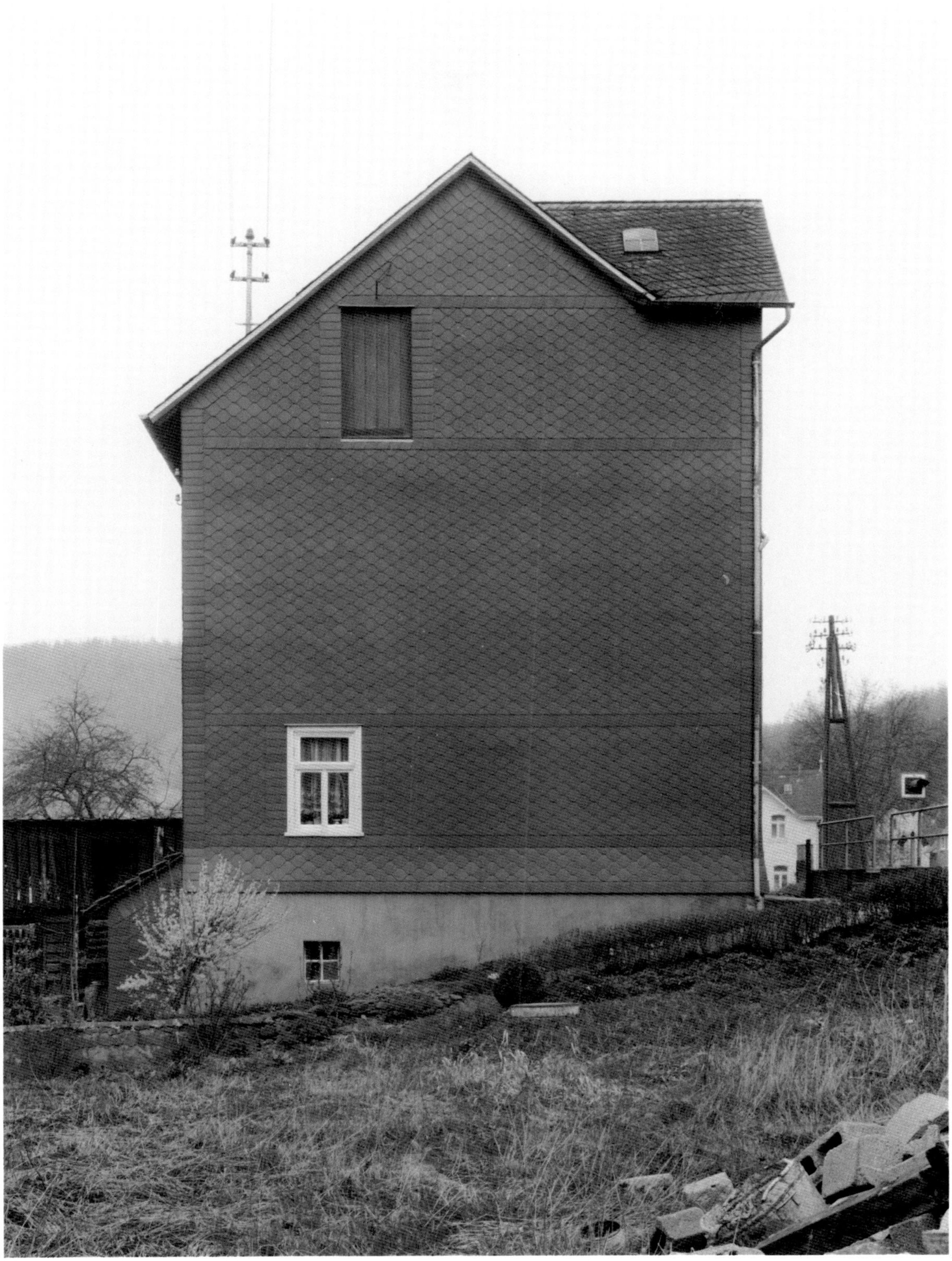

112

Konrad-Adenauer-Straße 1, Niederfischbach, 1971.

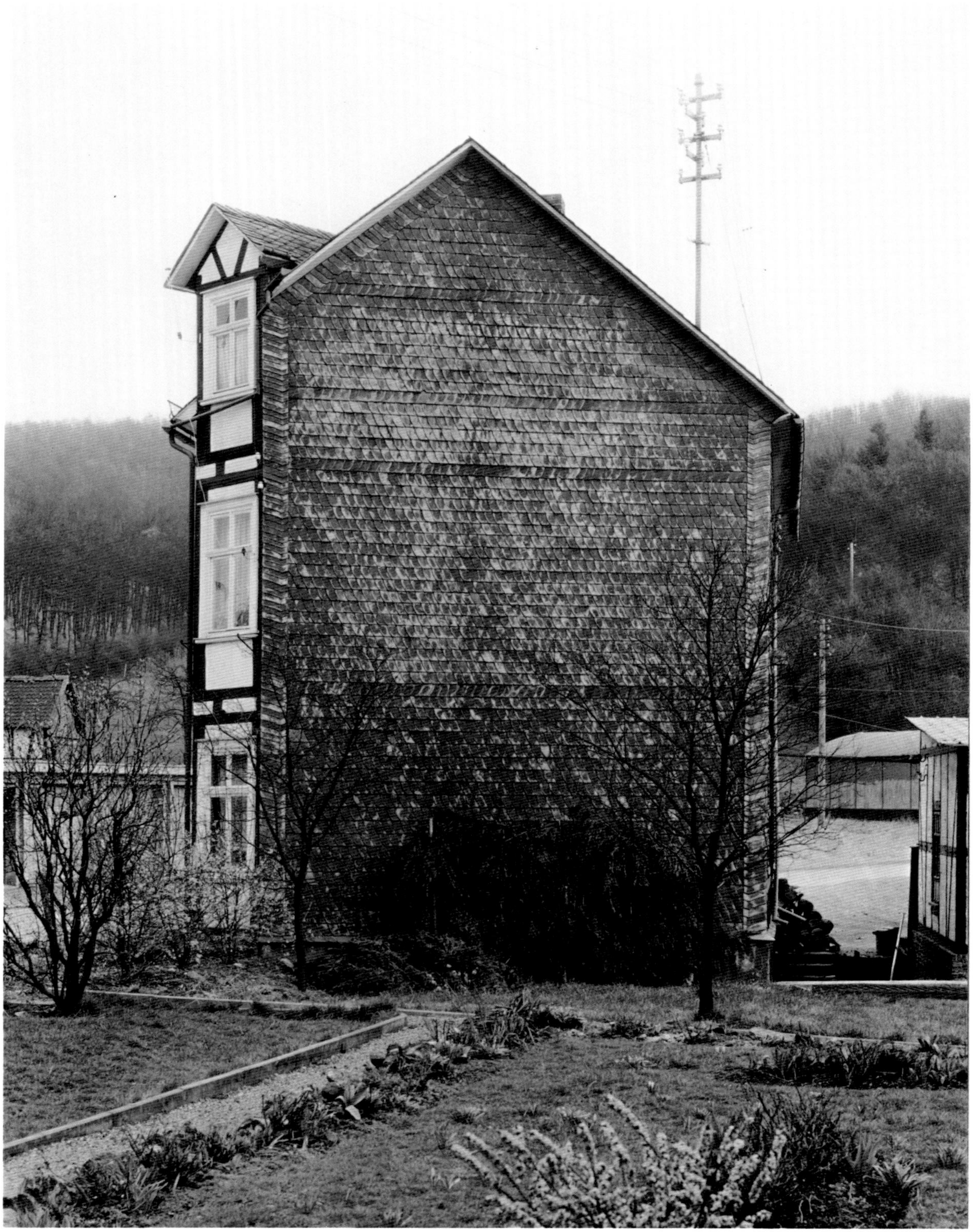

113
Am Silberstern 4, Freudenberg, 1960.

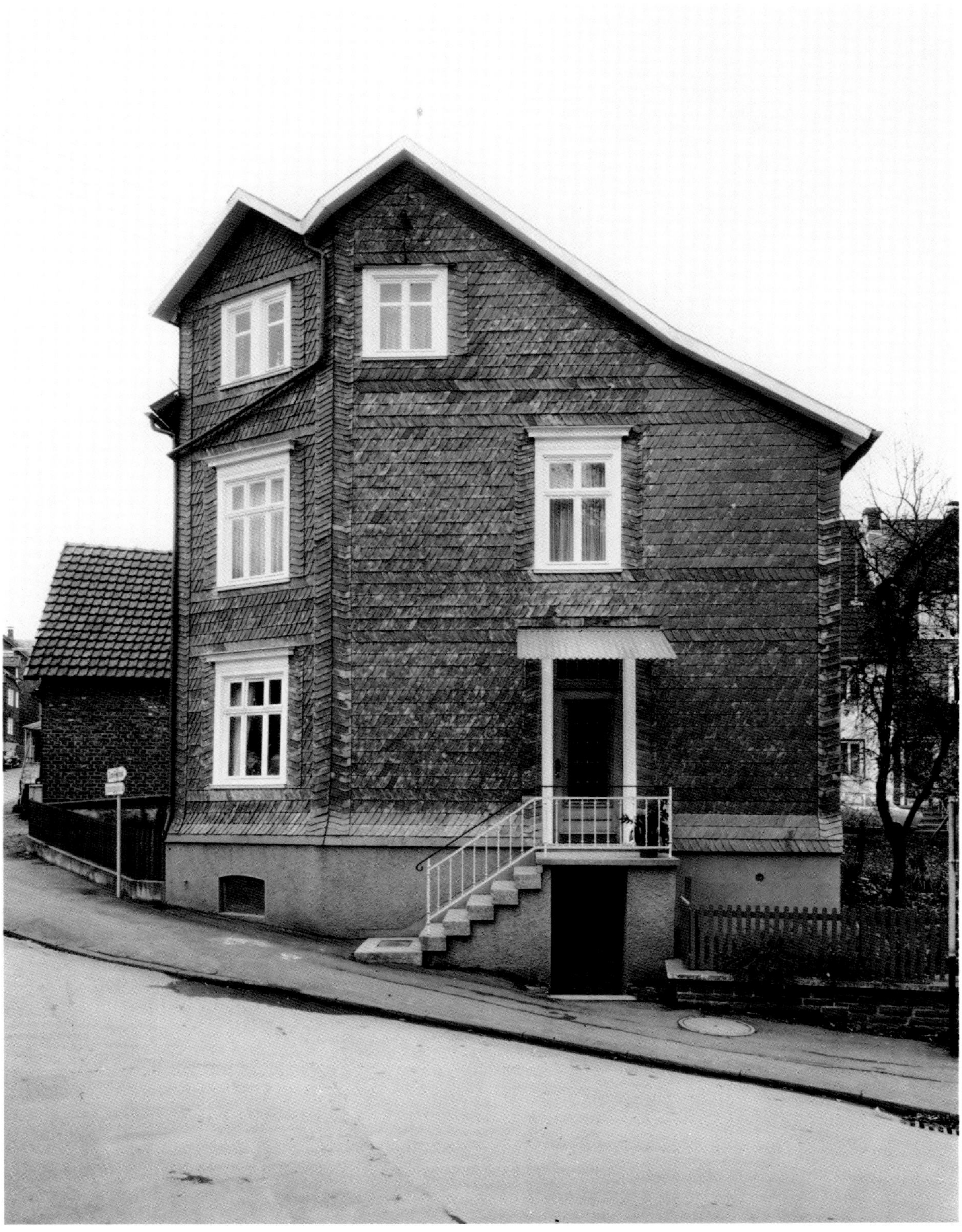

114

Krottorfer Straße 48, Freudenberg, 1965.

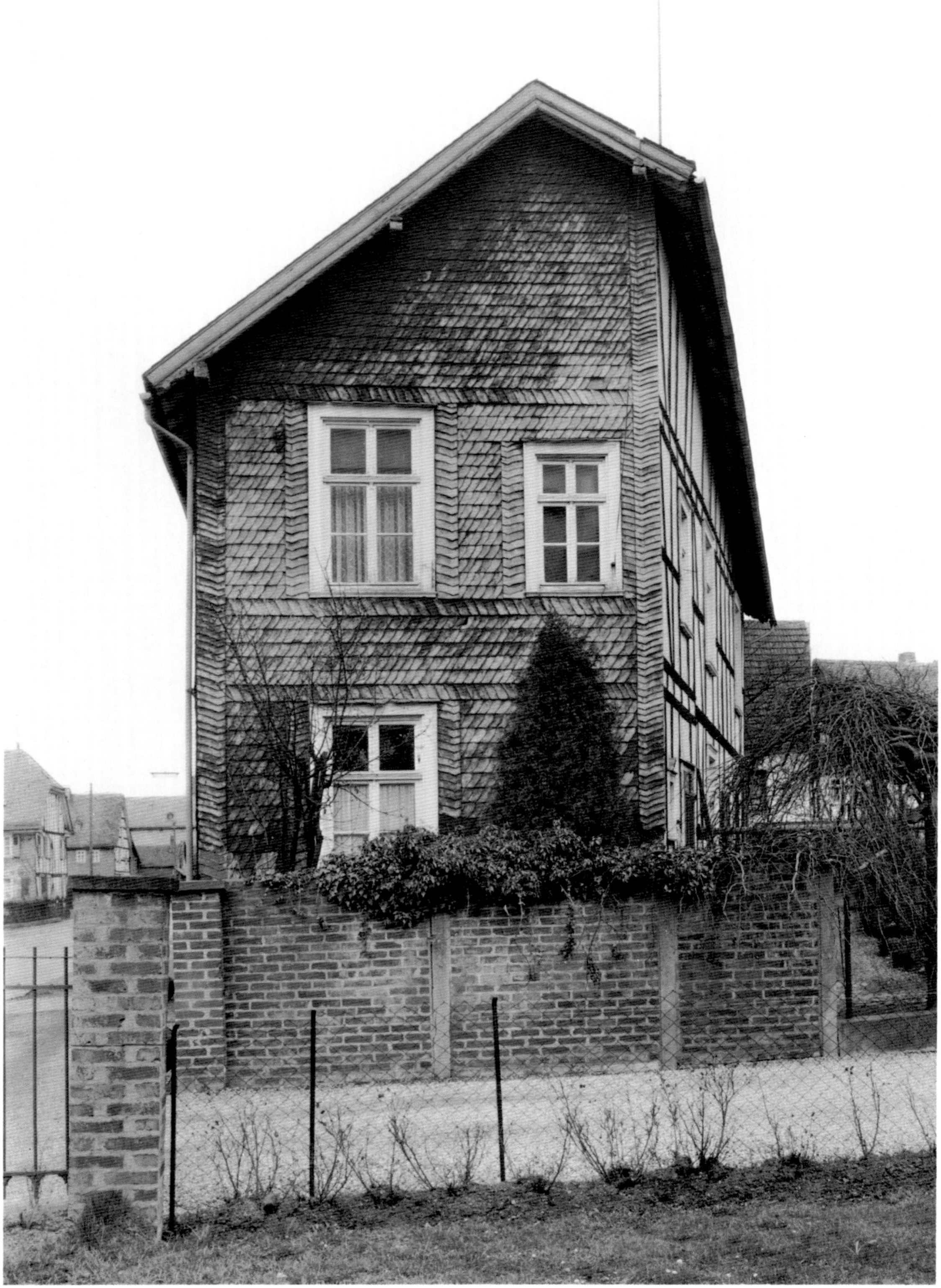

115
Bahnhofstraße 54, Freudenberg, 1960.

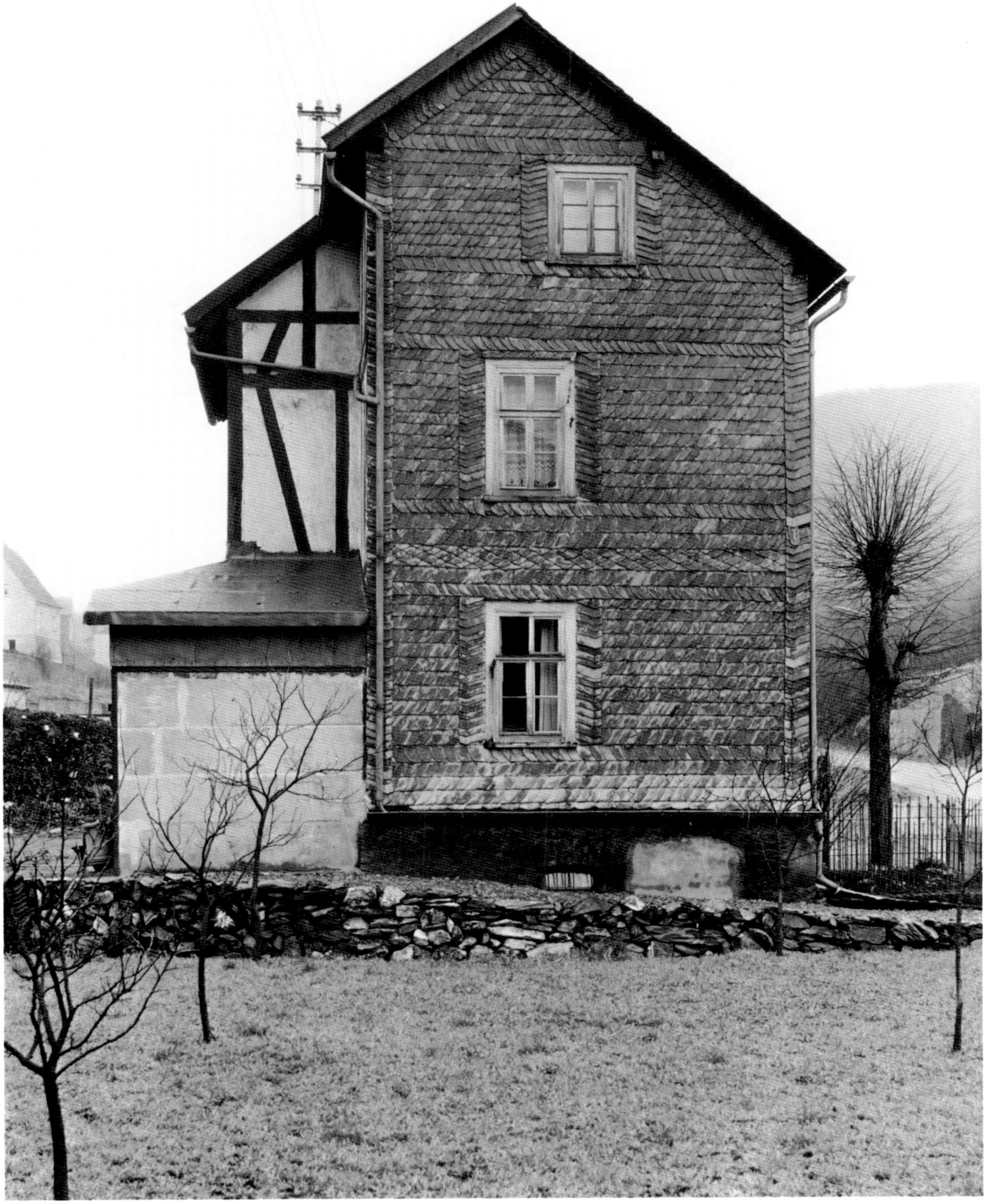

116
Auf der Hütte 45, Gosenbach, 1961.

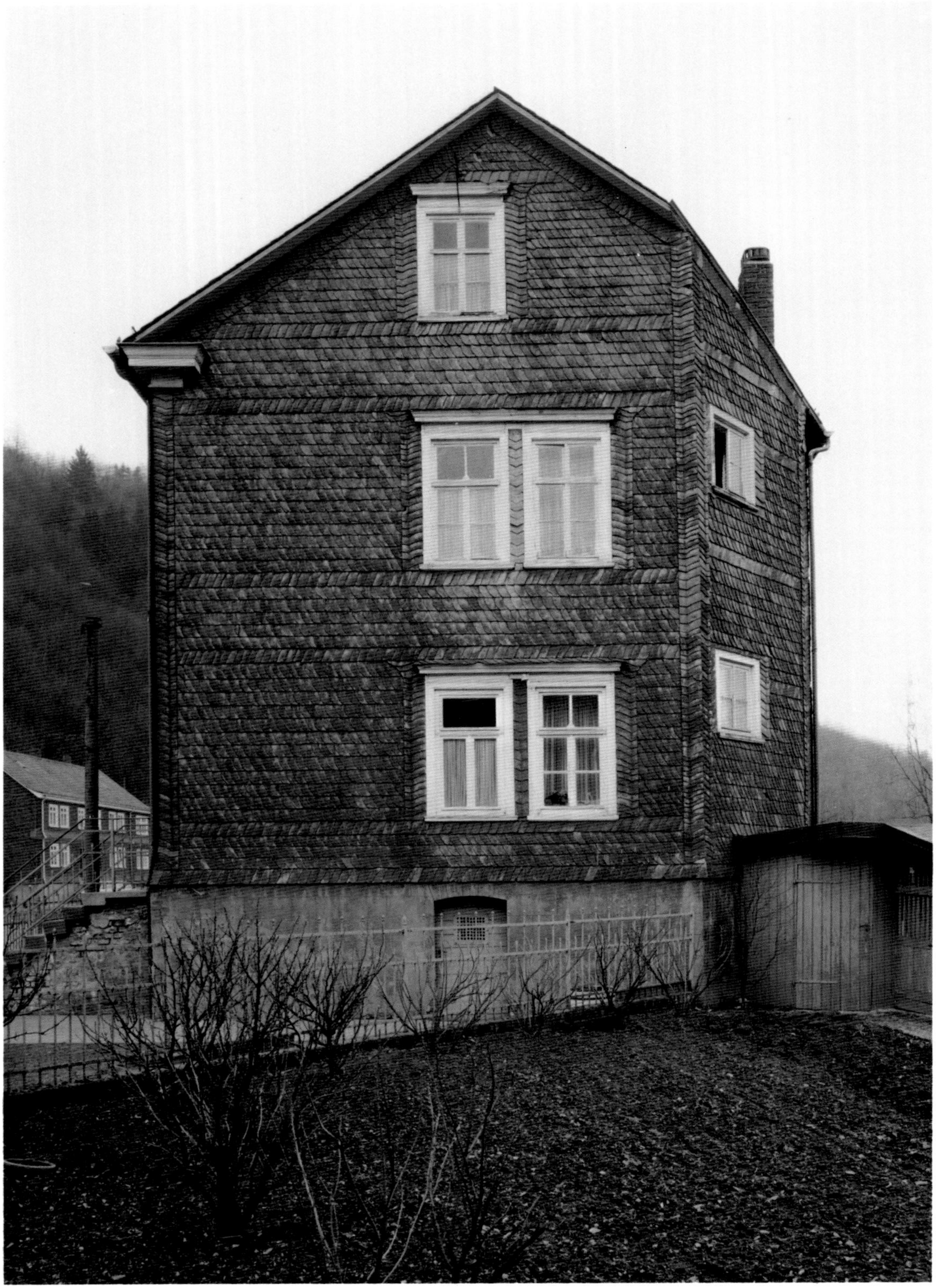

117
Siegtalstraße 40, Eiserfeld, 1971.

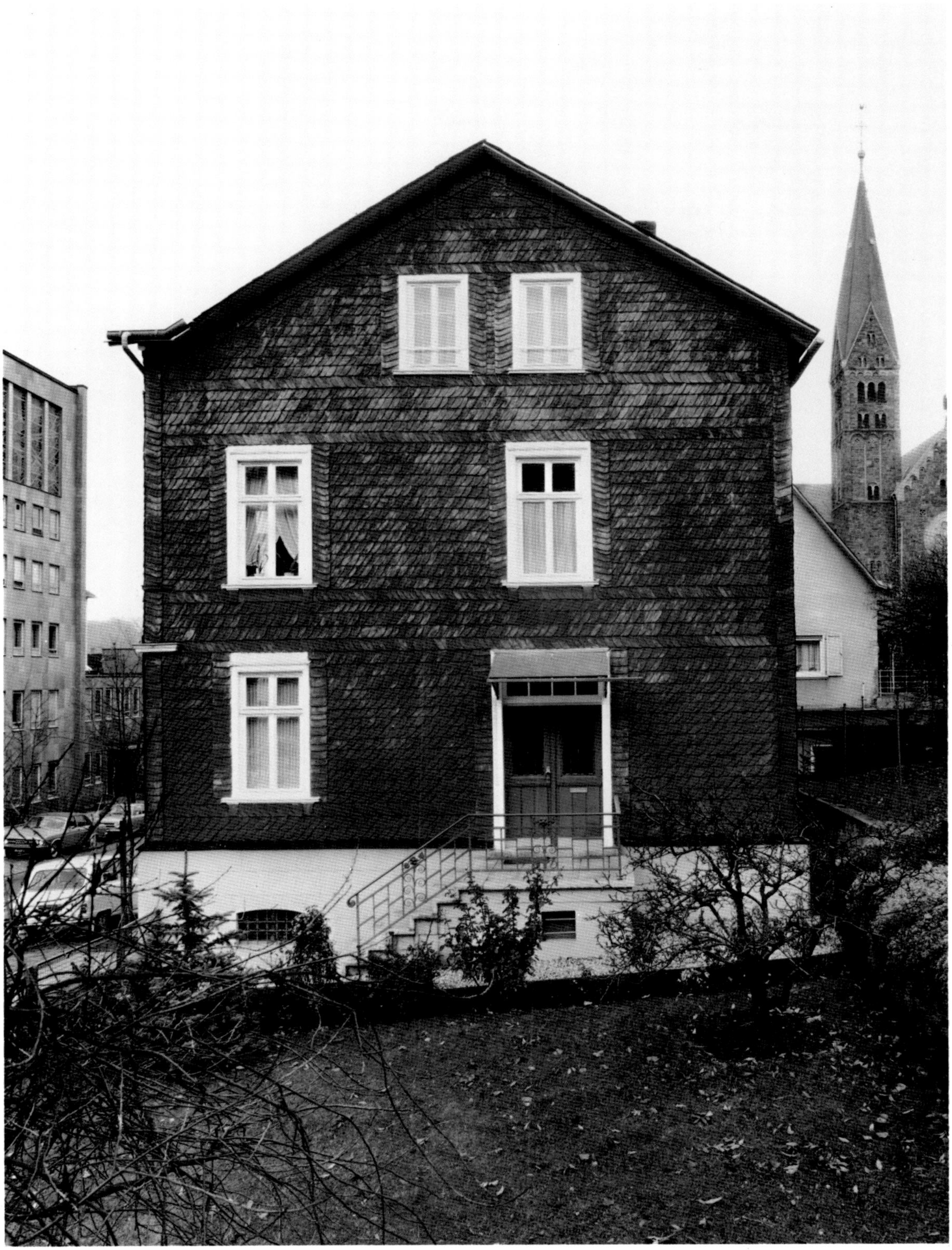

118
Kampenstraße 44, Siegen, 1974.

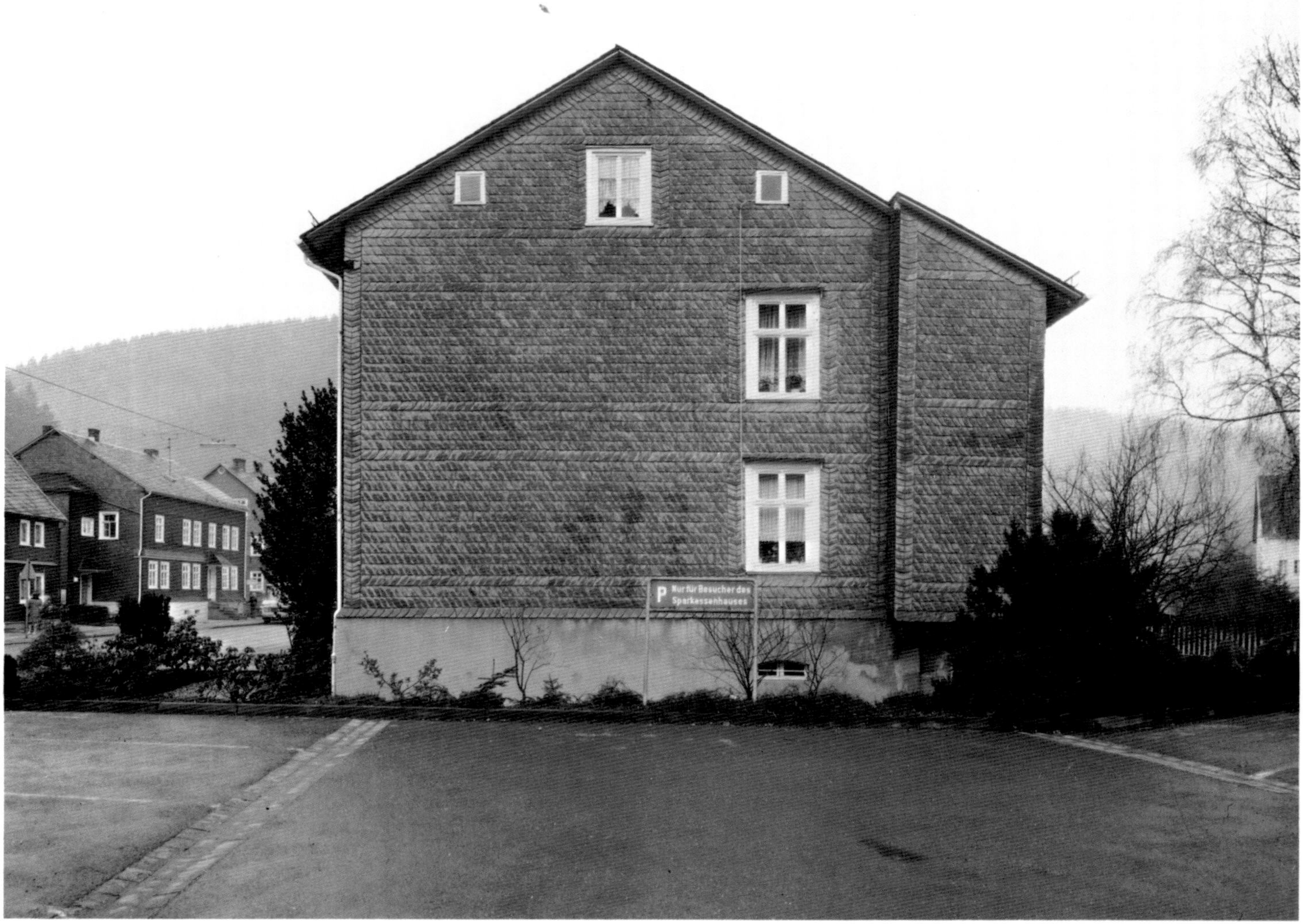

119
Siegtalstraße 10, Eiserfeld, 1970.

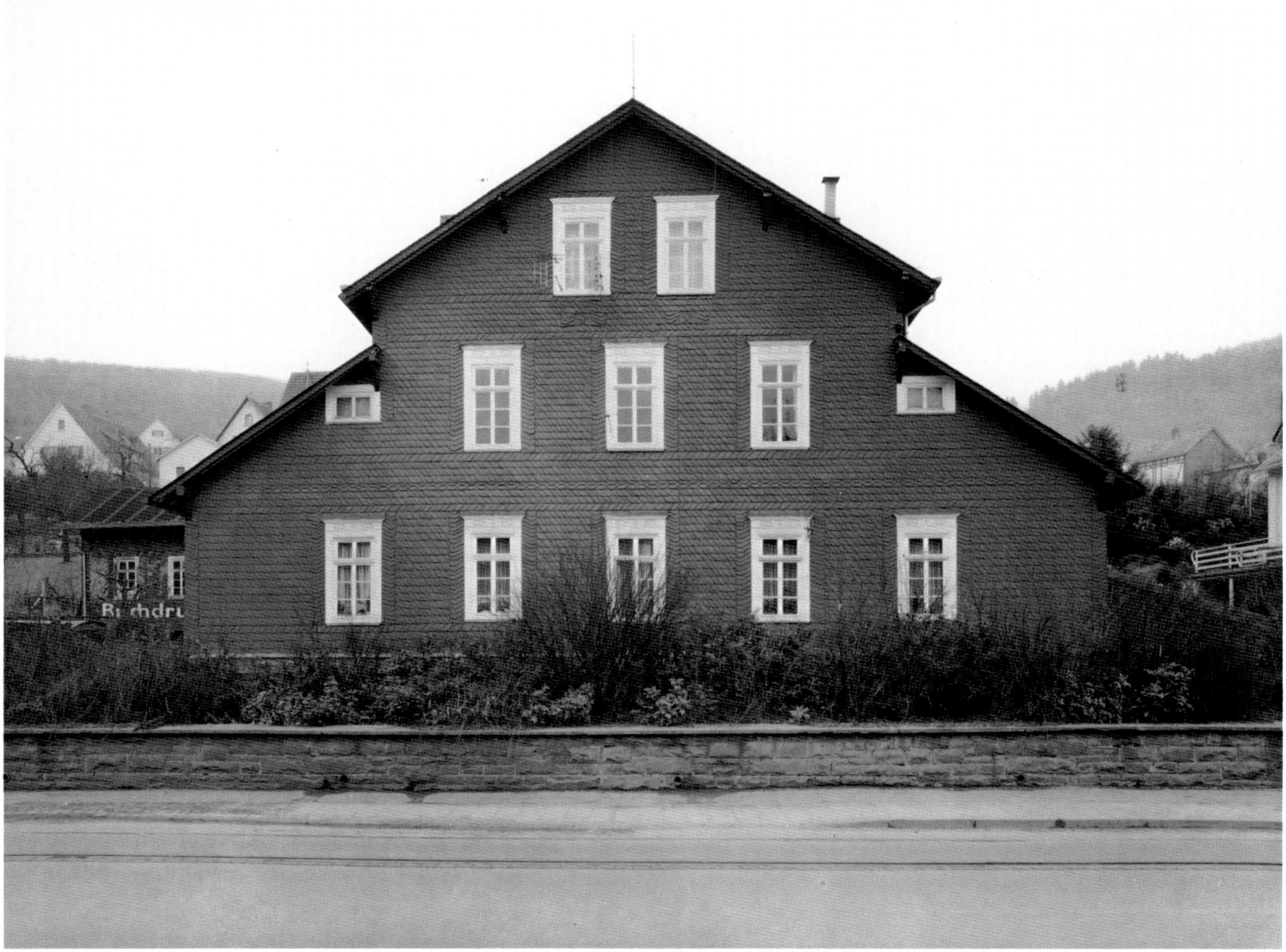

120
Bahnhofstraße 90, Eiserfeld, 1970.

III.
STRASSEN- UND RÜCKSEITEN
STREET AND REAR SIDES

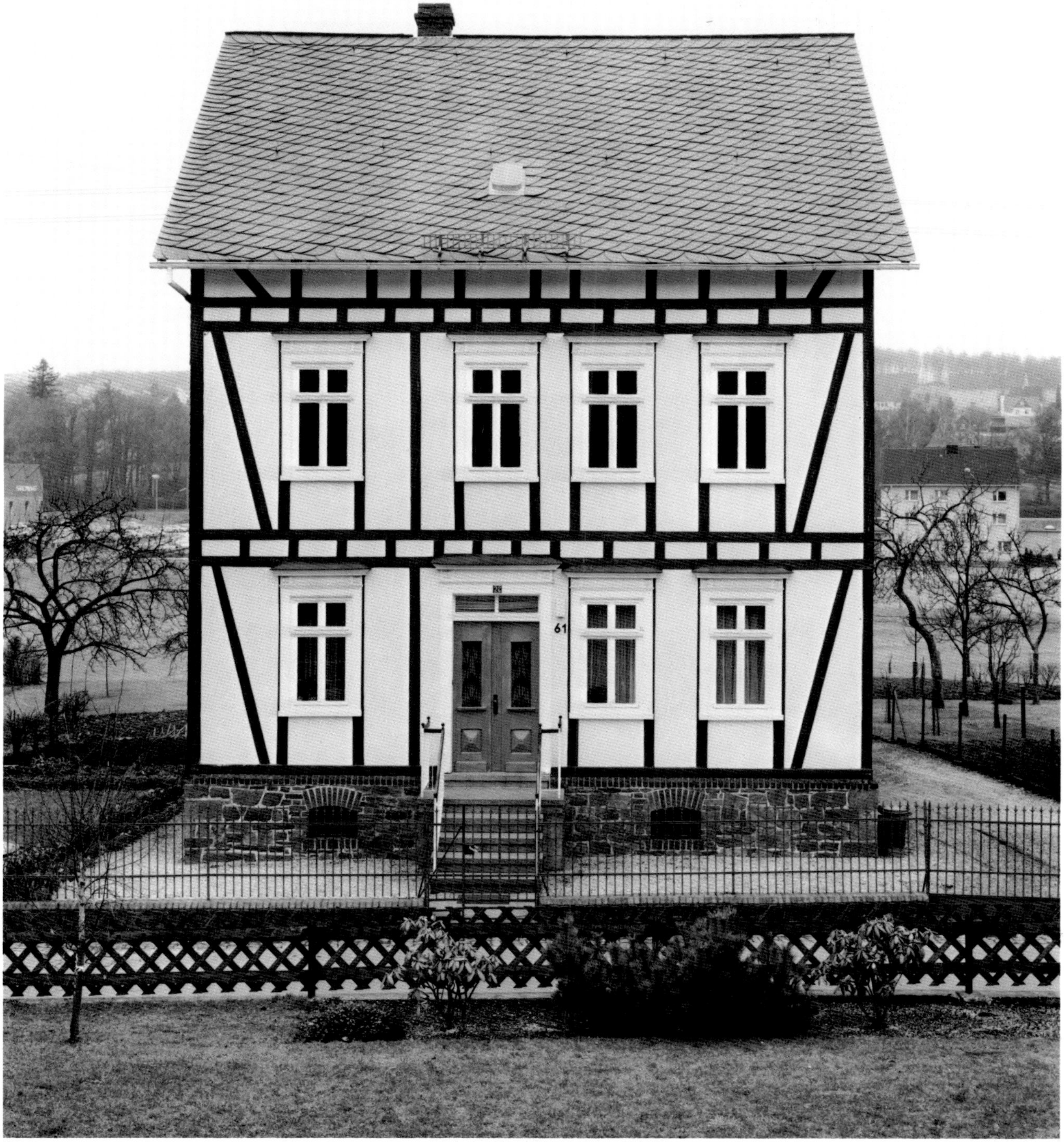

121
Hillnhütter Straße 61, Dahlbruch, 1971.

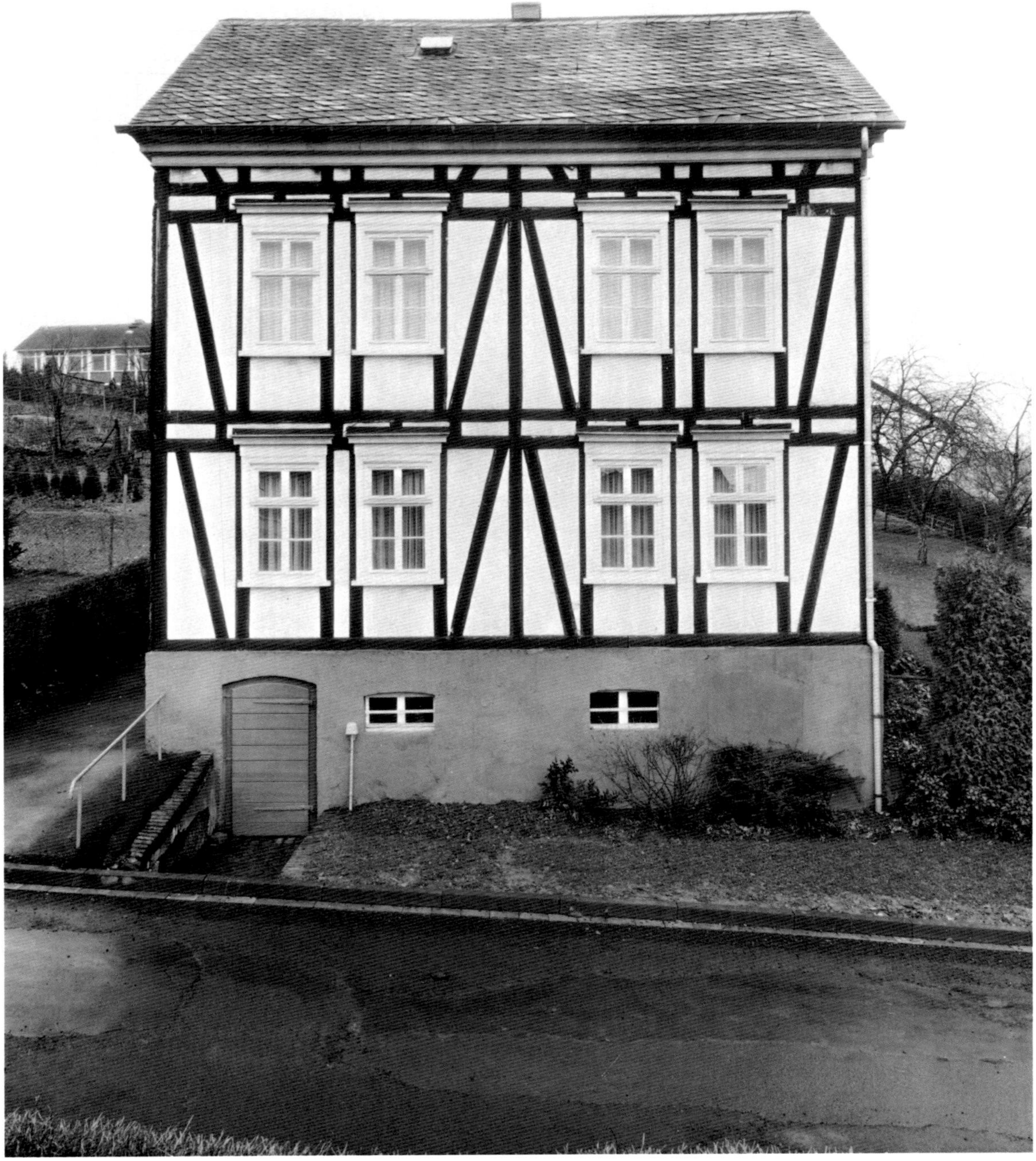

122
Abendröthe 3, Birlenbach, 1972.

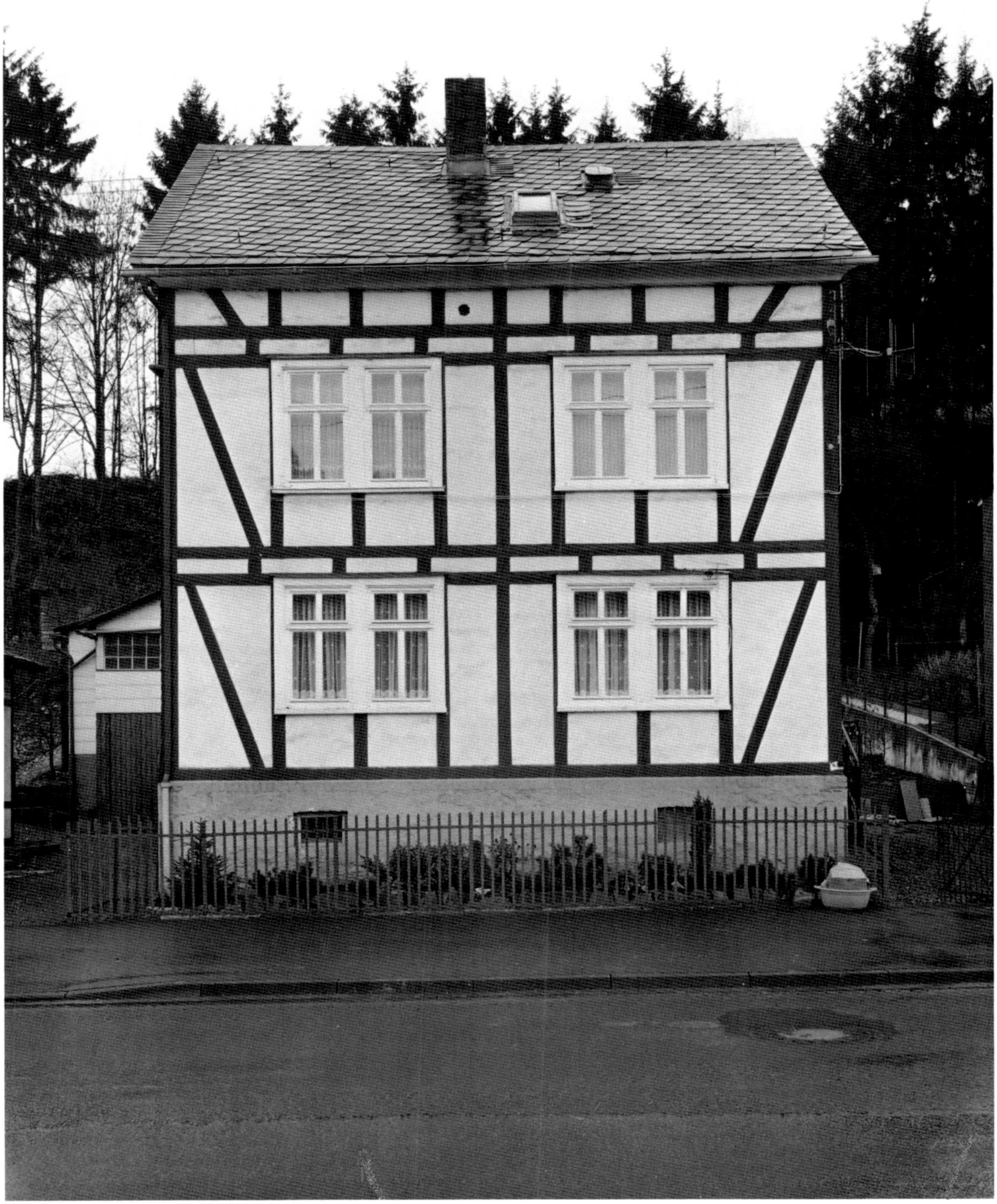

123
Bruchstraße 70, Hilchenbach, 1972.

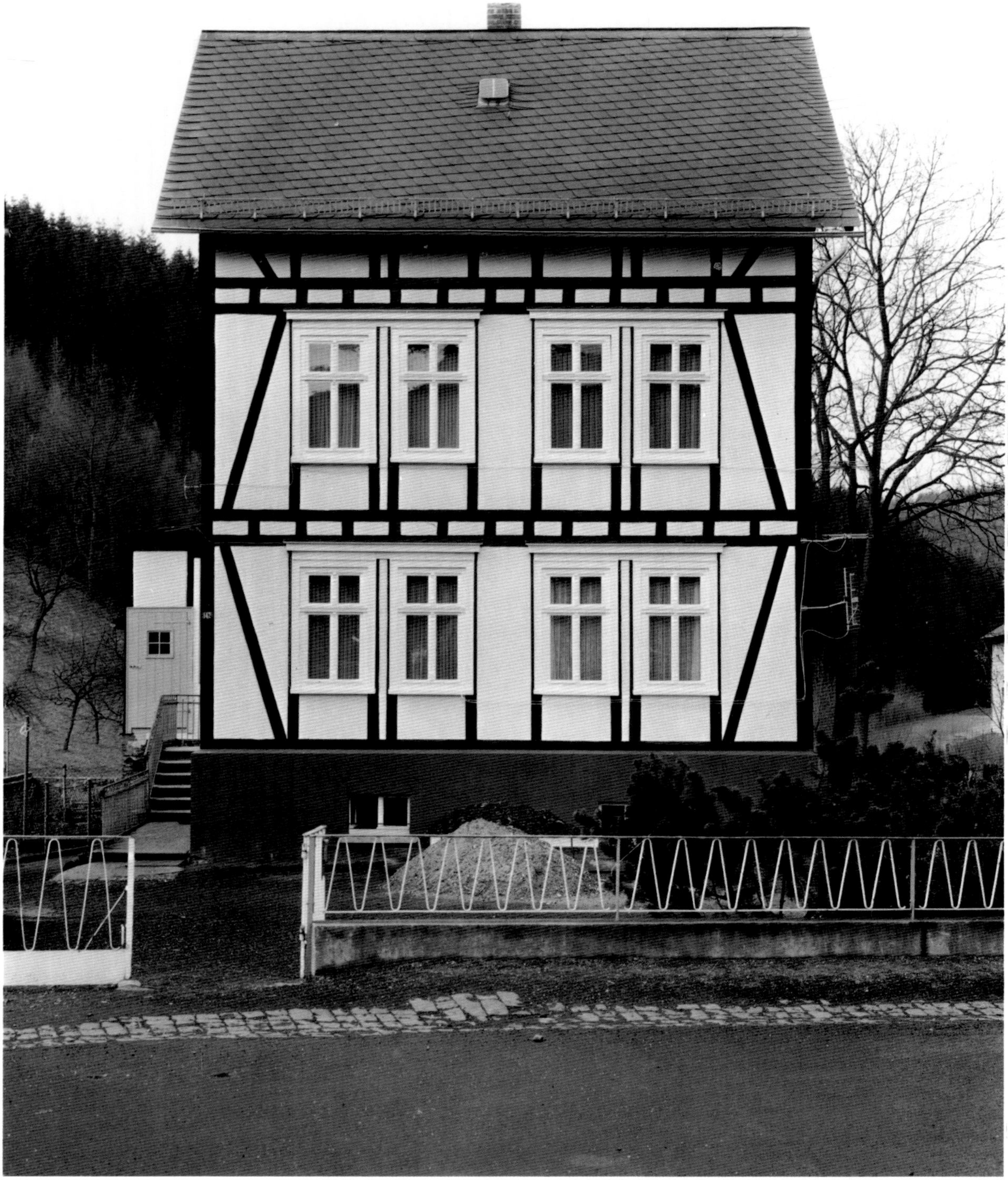

124
Eiserntalstraße 142, Eisern, 1971.

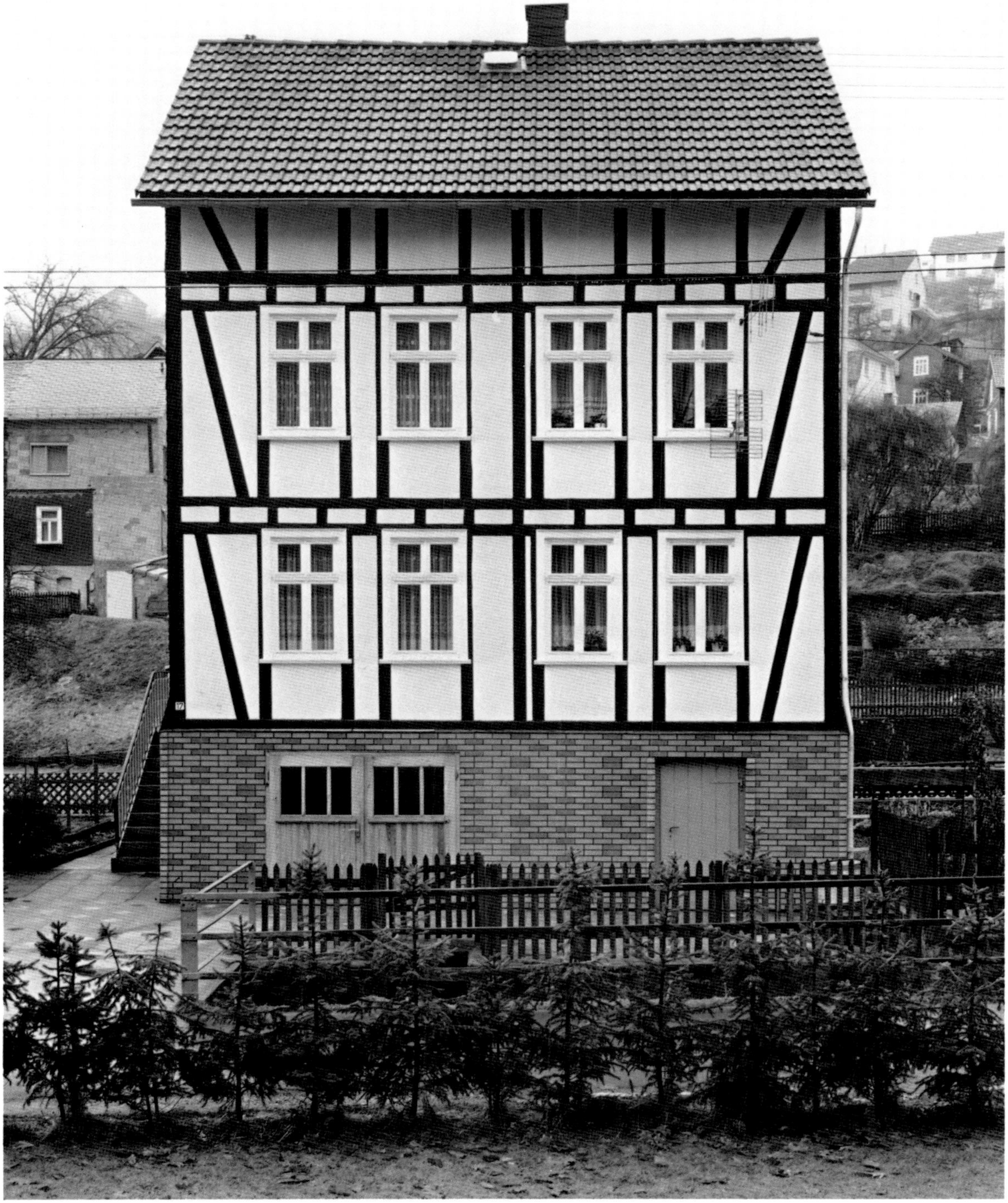

125
Am Gosenbach 17, Niederschelderhütte, 1972.

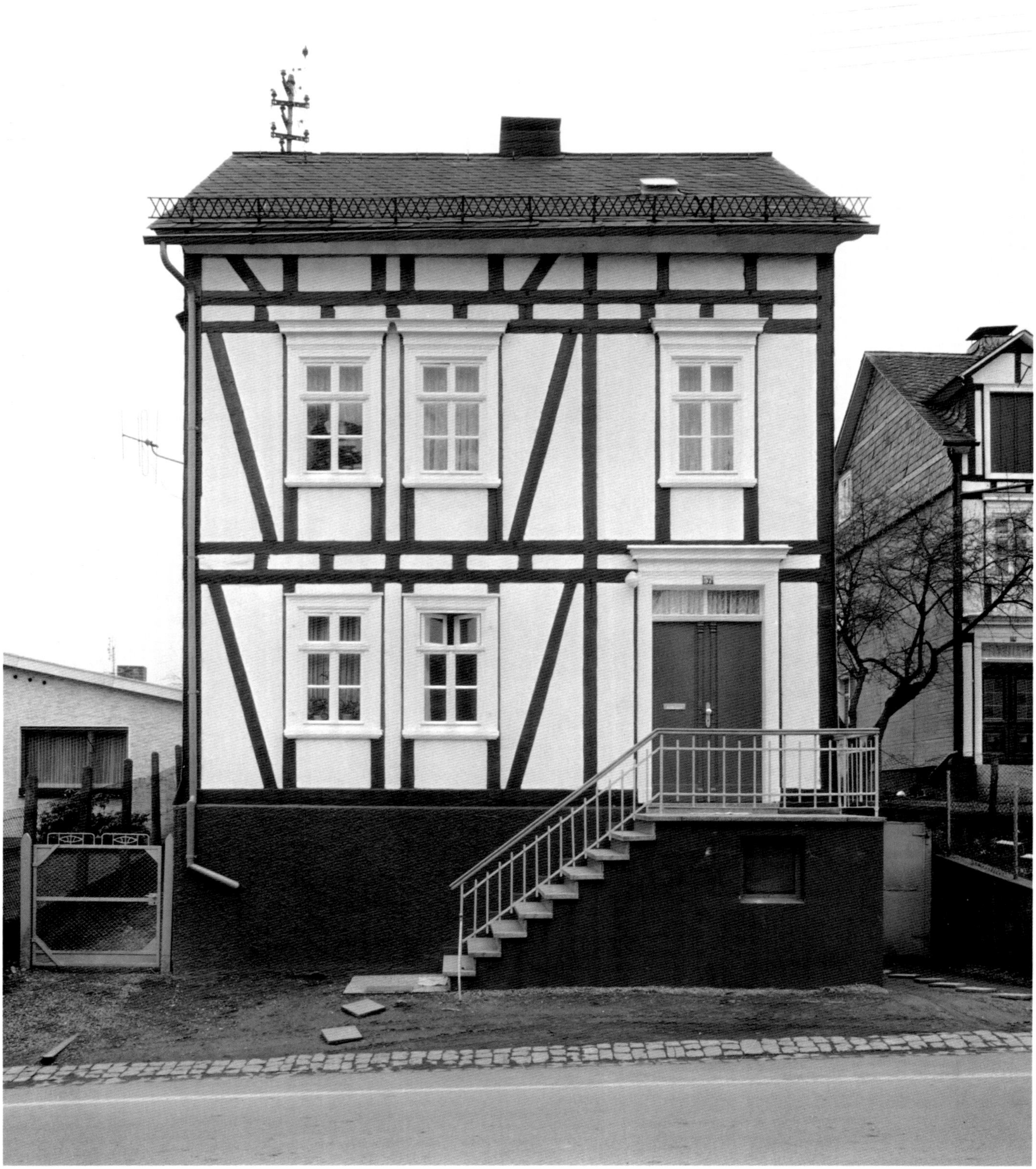

126
Krottorfer Straße 57, Freudenberg, 1972.

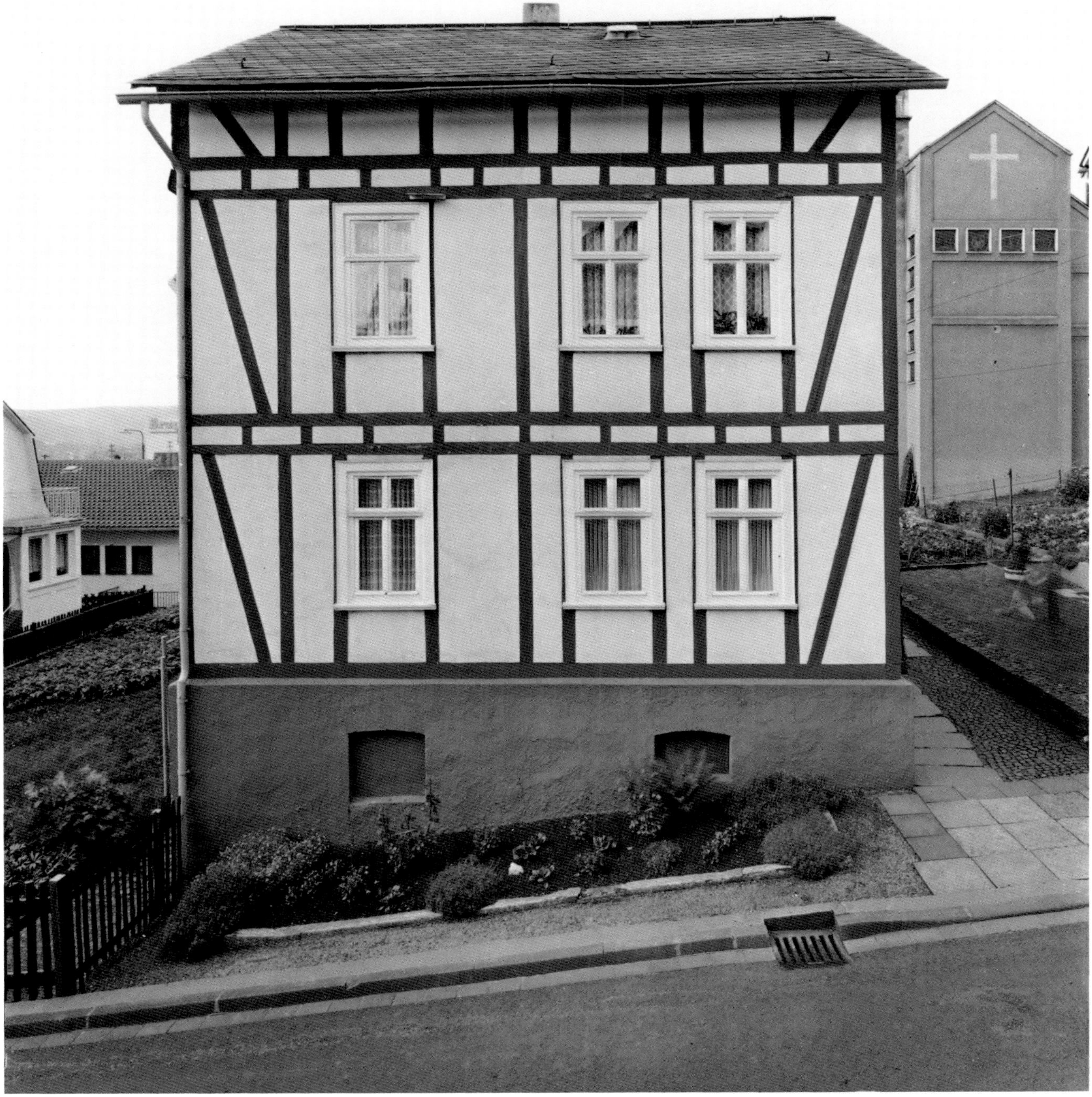

127
Karlstraße 4, Niederschelderhütte, 1973.

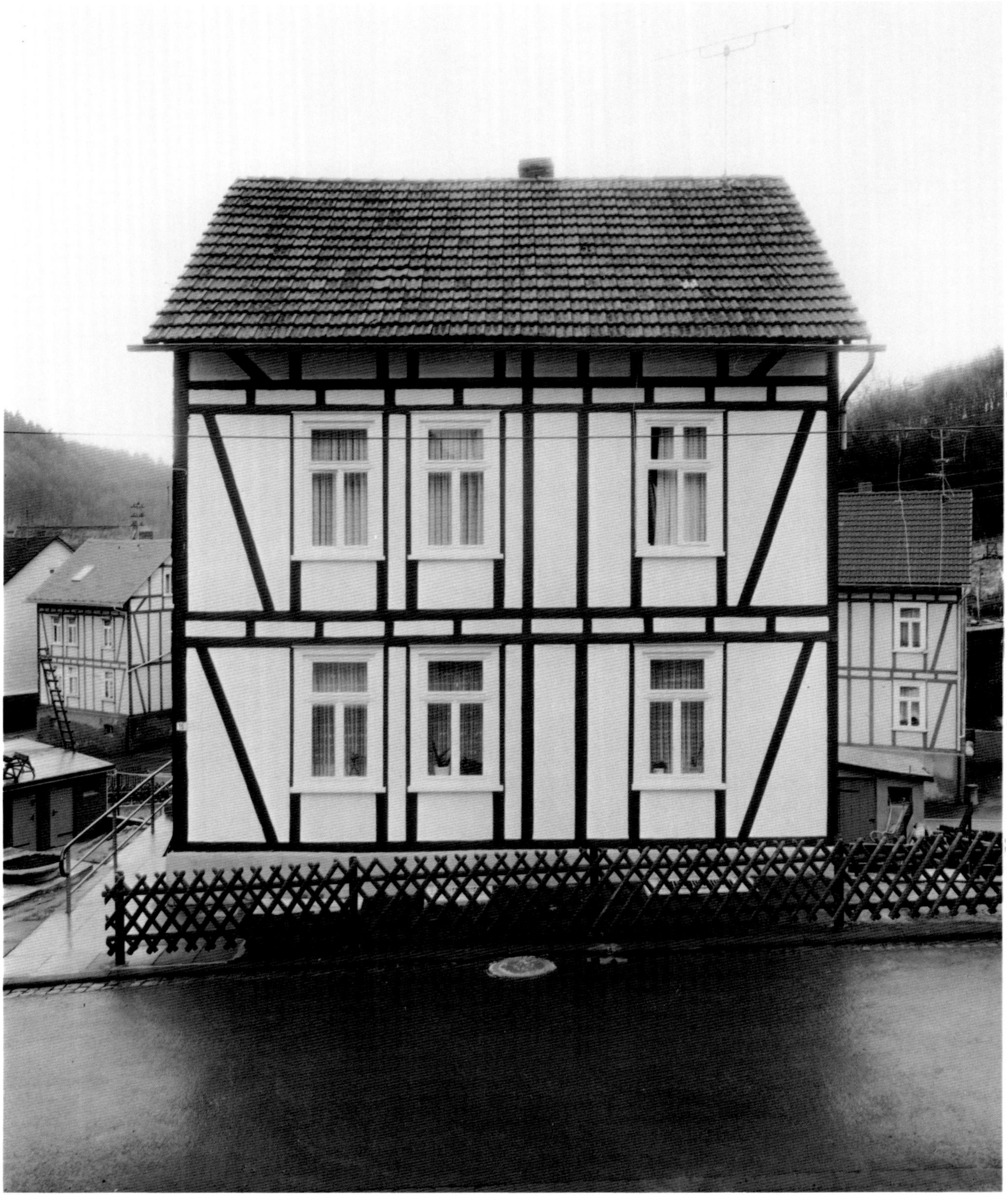

128
Wehbacher Straße 15, Wehbach, 1973.

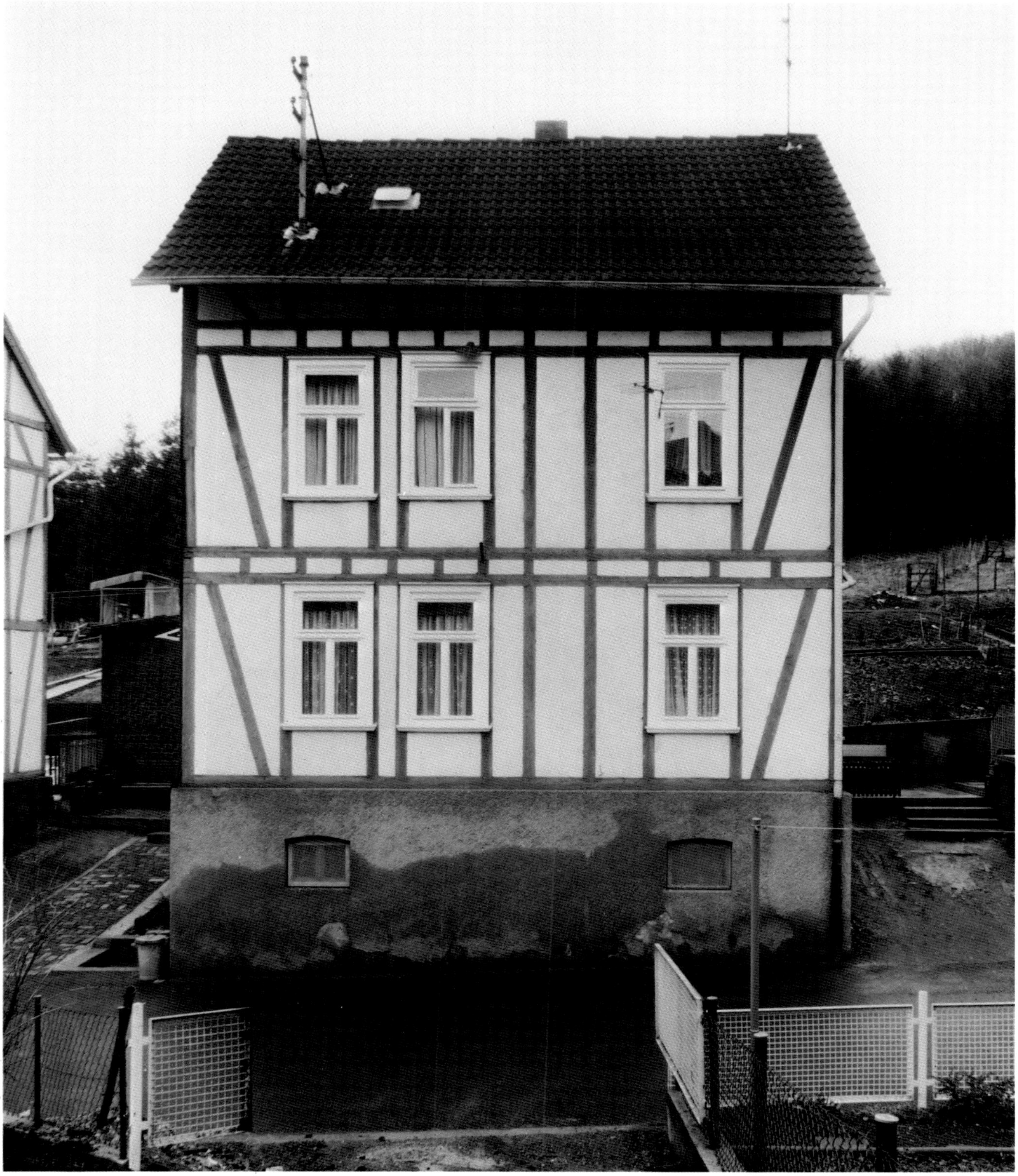

129
Steinstraße 11, Wehbach, 1973.

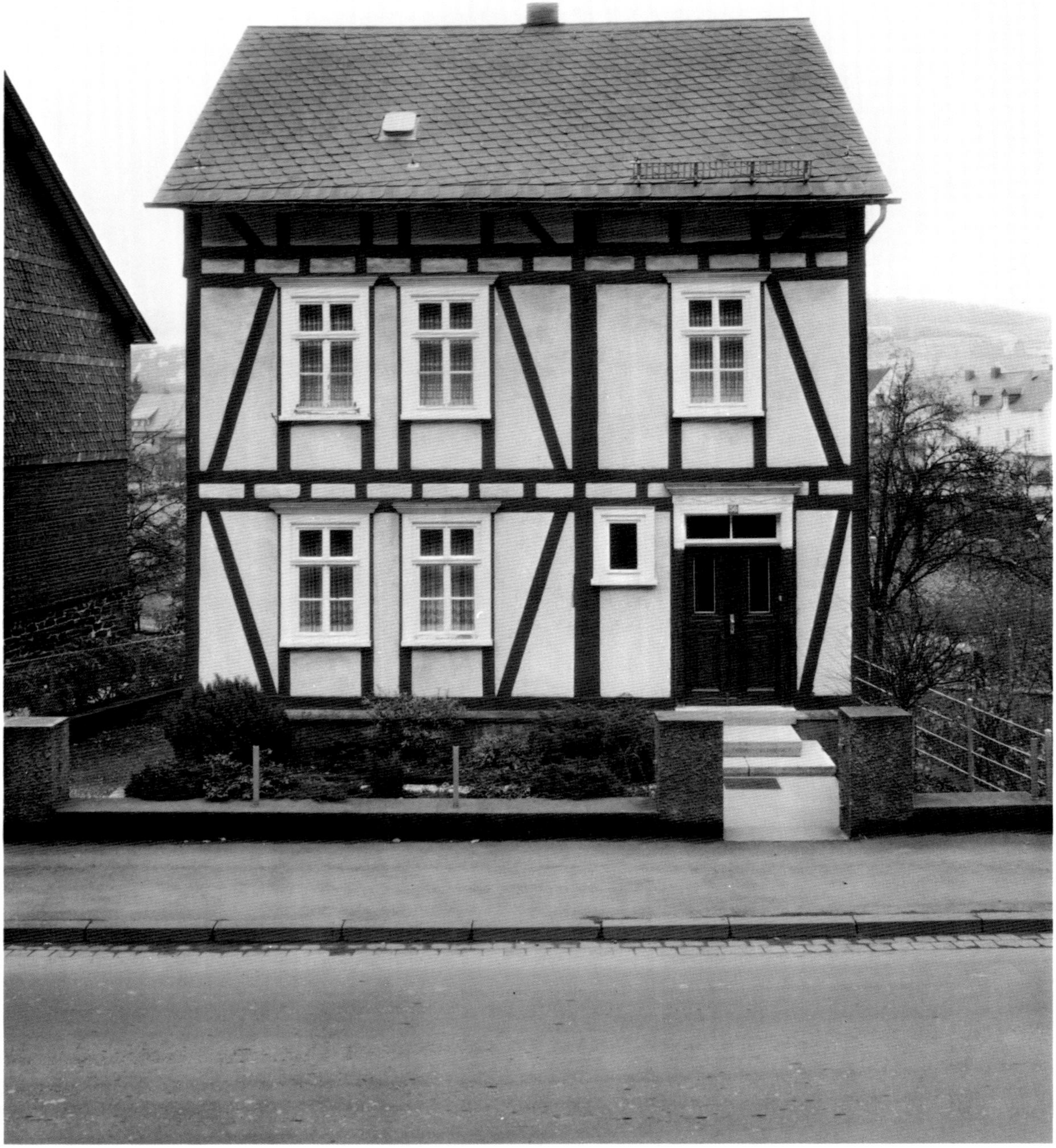

130
Schneiderstraße 56, Herdorf, 1970.

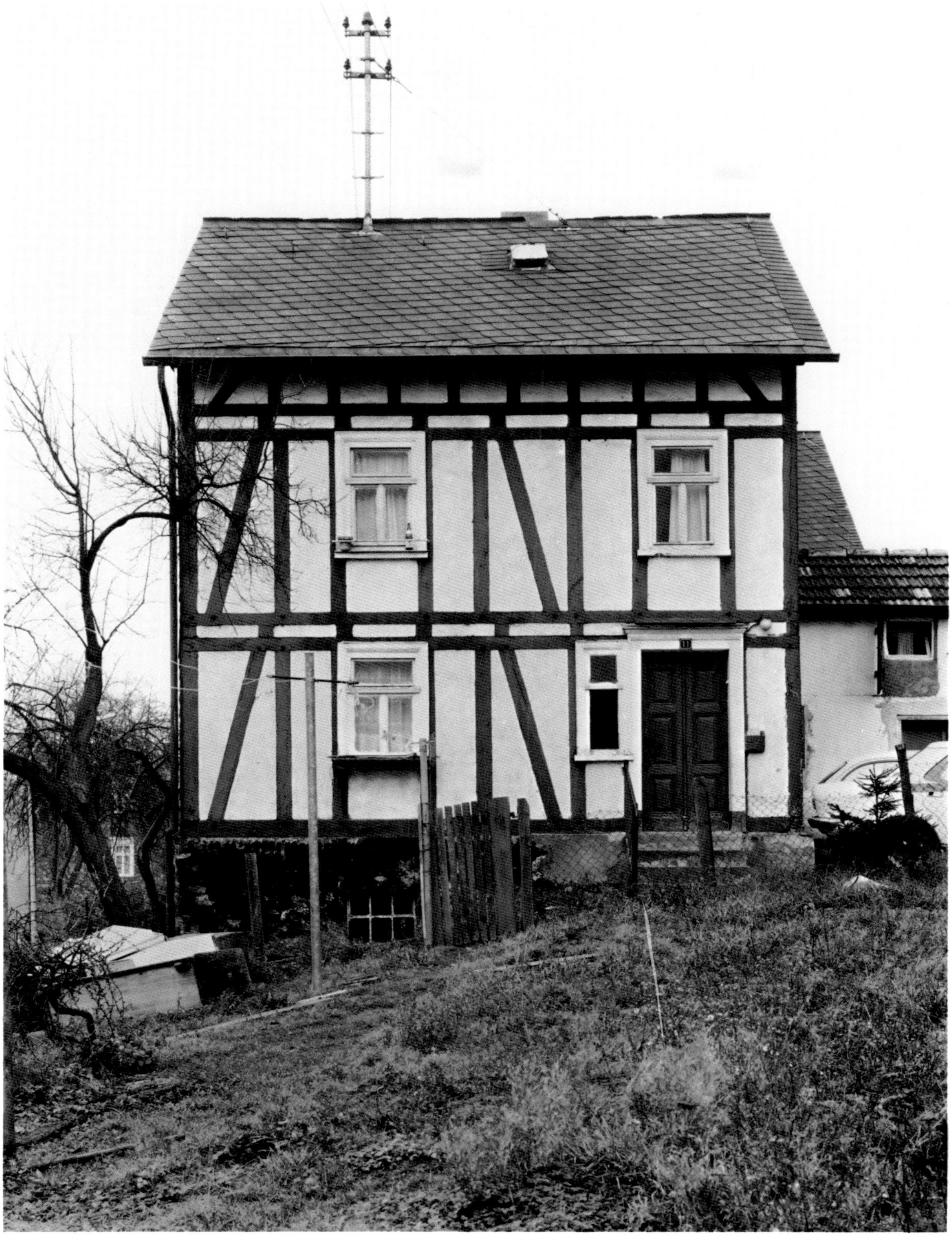

131

Setzer Weg 19, Dreis-Tiefenbach, 1973.

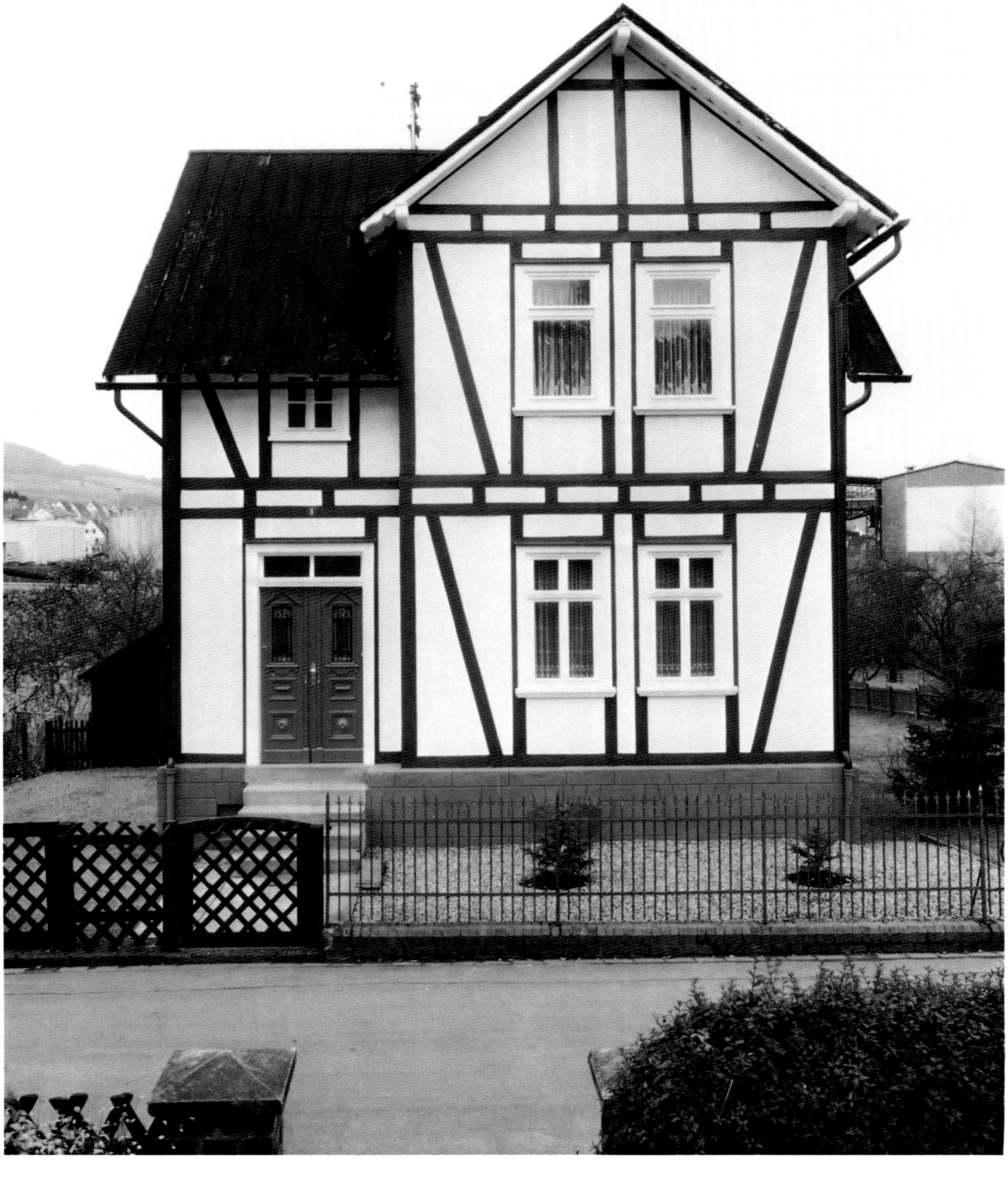

132
Bahnhofstraße 8, Dahlbruch, 1972.

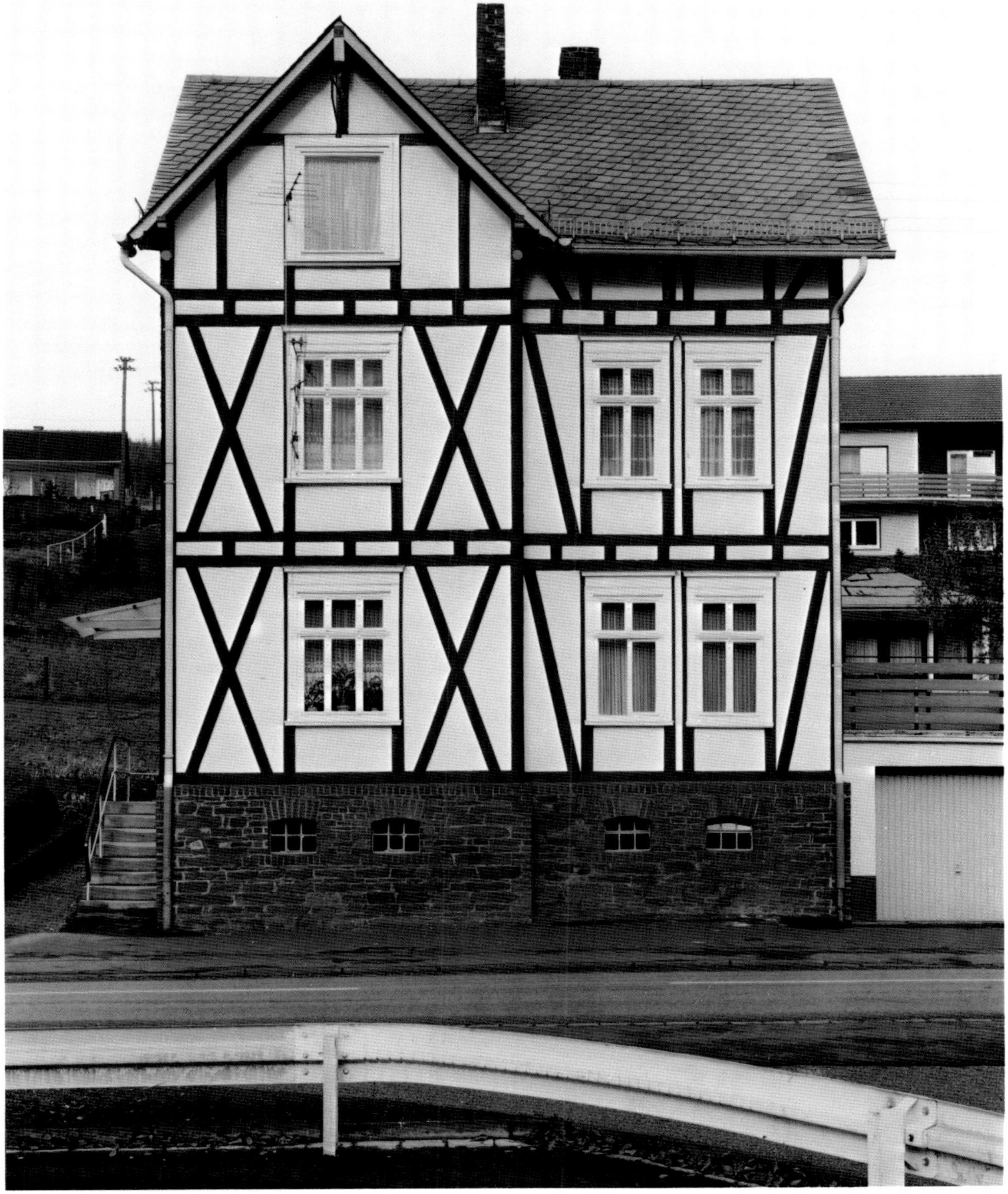

133
Marburger Straße 27, Deutz, 1973.

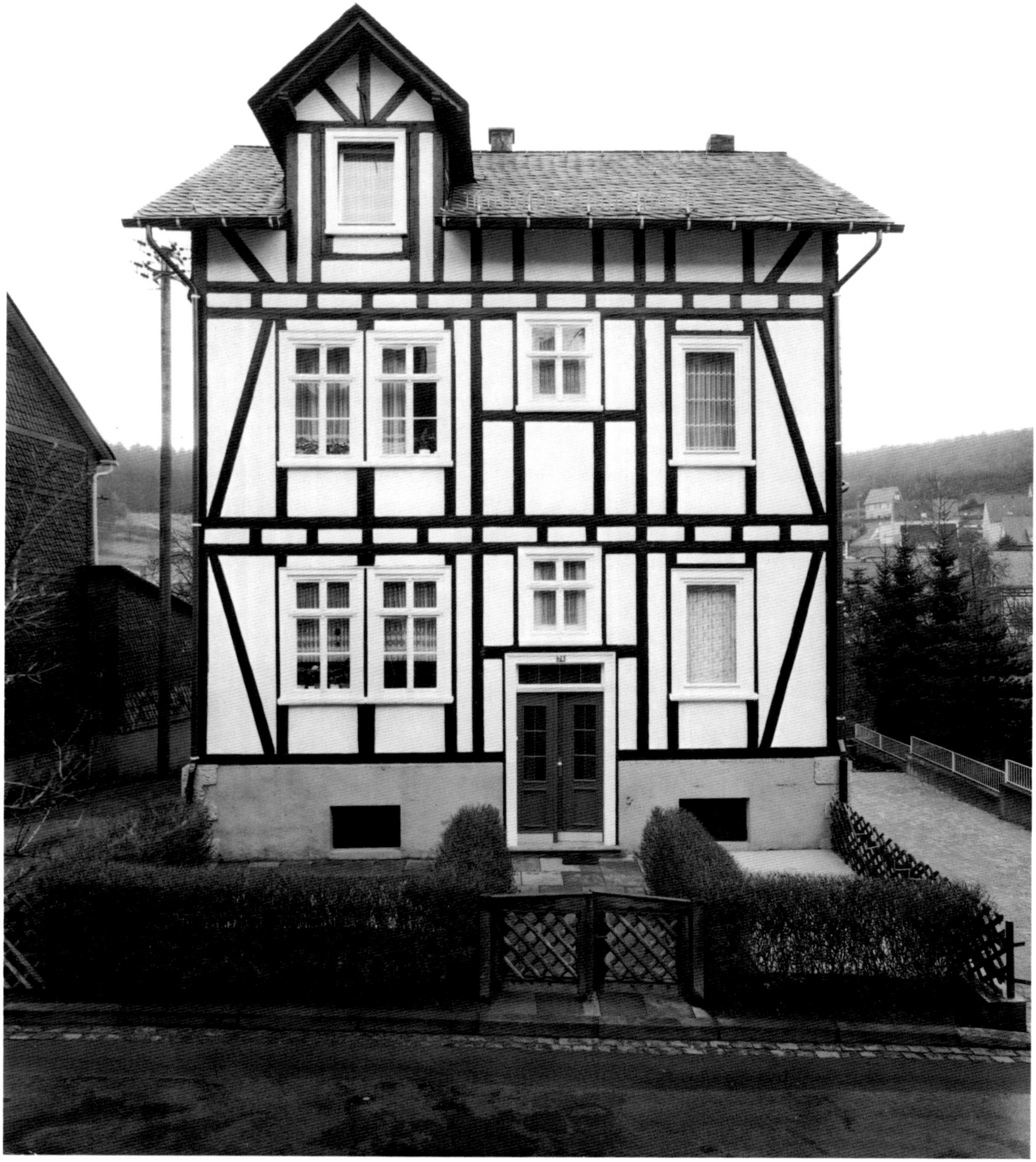

134
Schulstraße 24, Eisern, 1971.

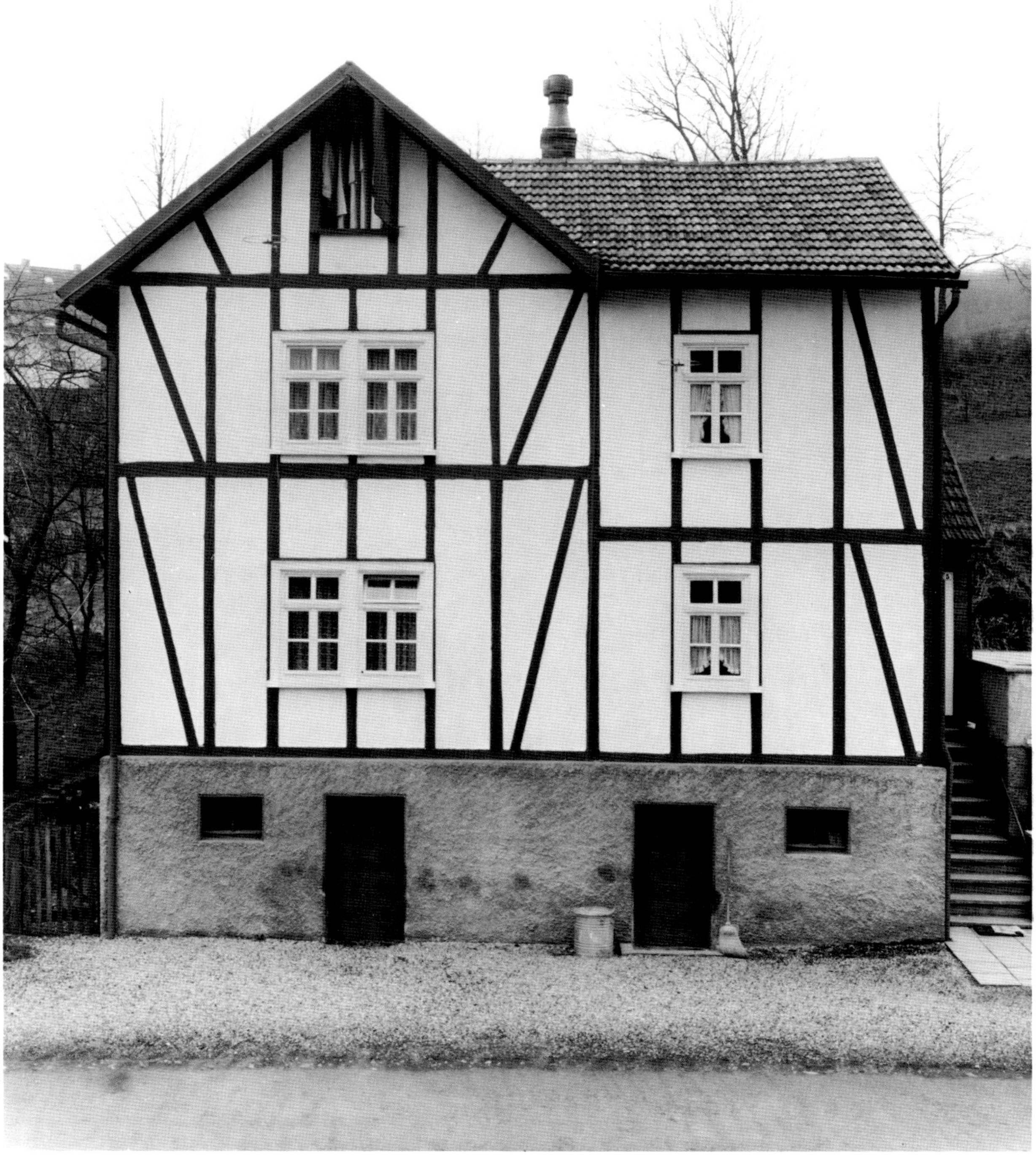

135
Arbachstraße 5, Salchendorf, 1960.

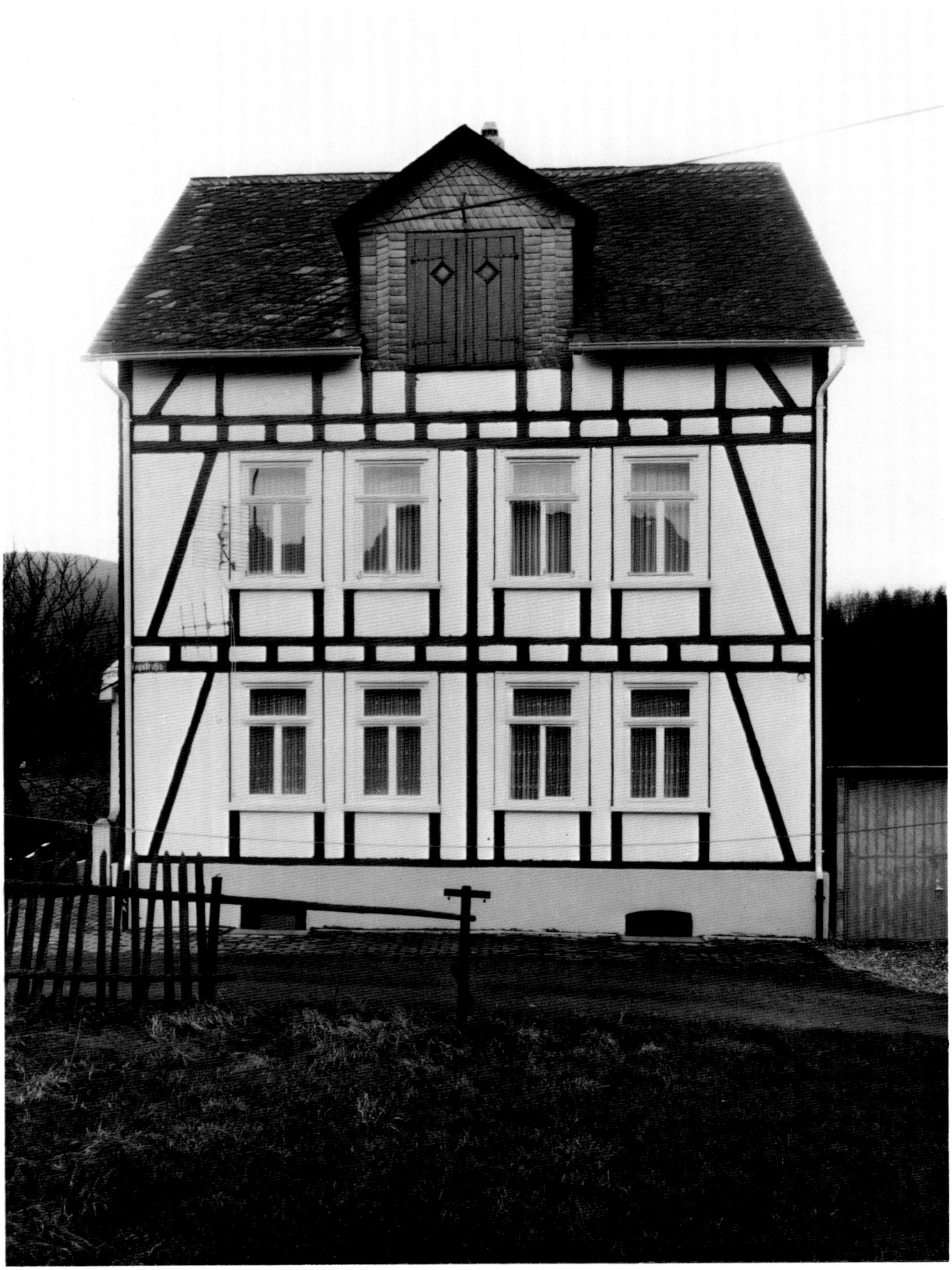

136
Siegstraße 11, Brachbach, 1972.

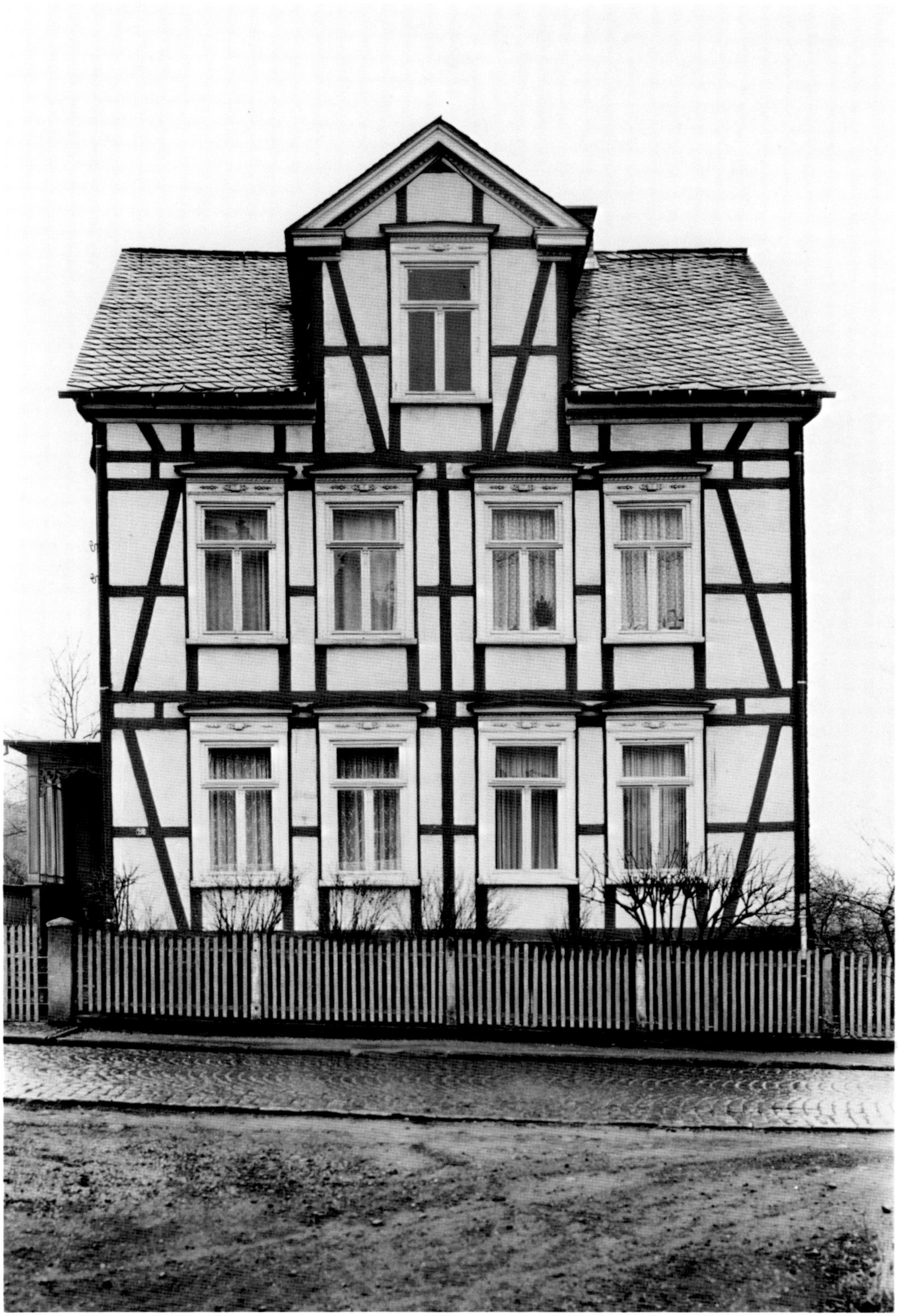

137
Bahnhofstraße 28, Neunkirchen, 1958.

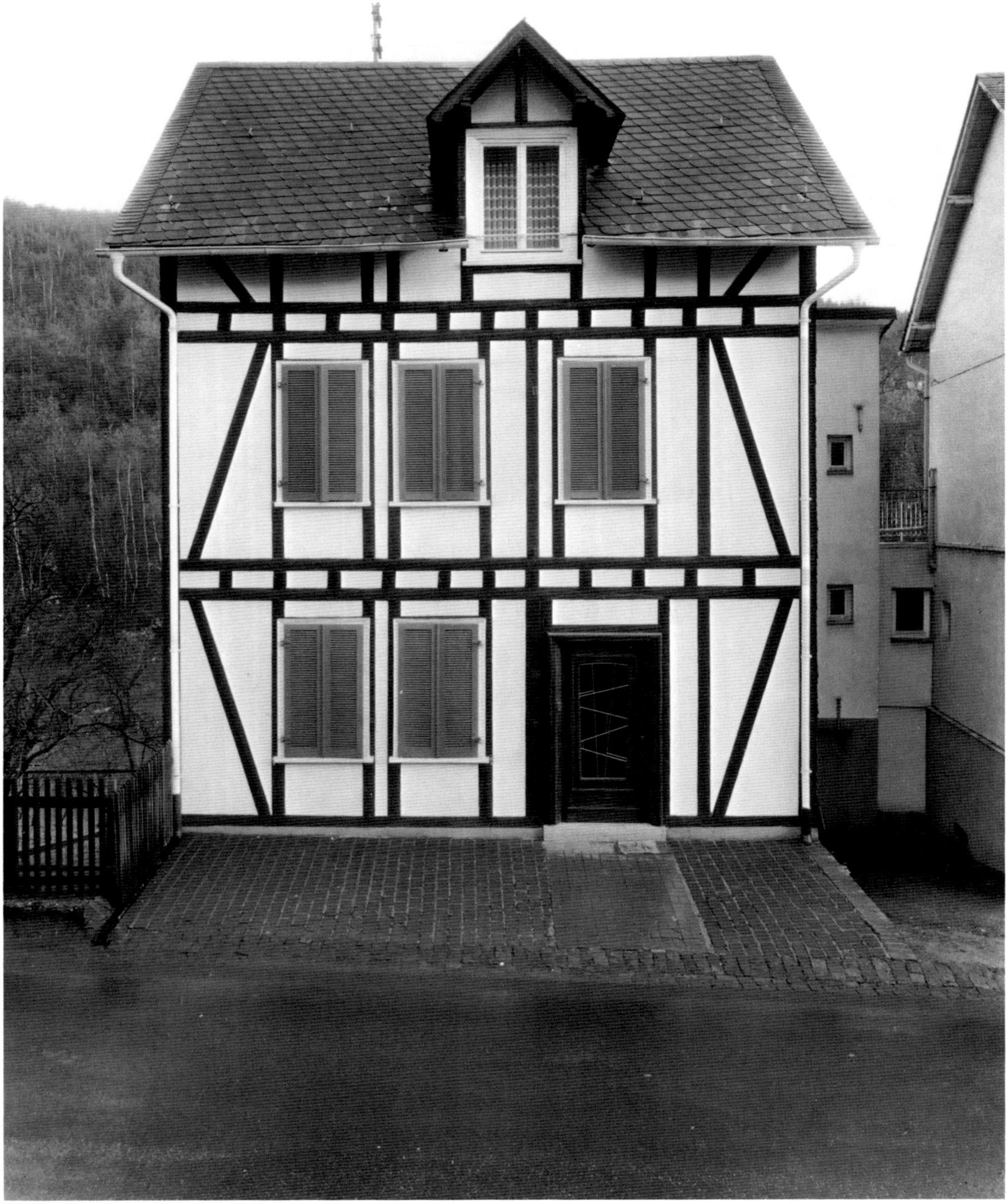

138
Adolfstraße 36, Niederschelderhütte, 1973.

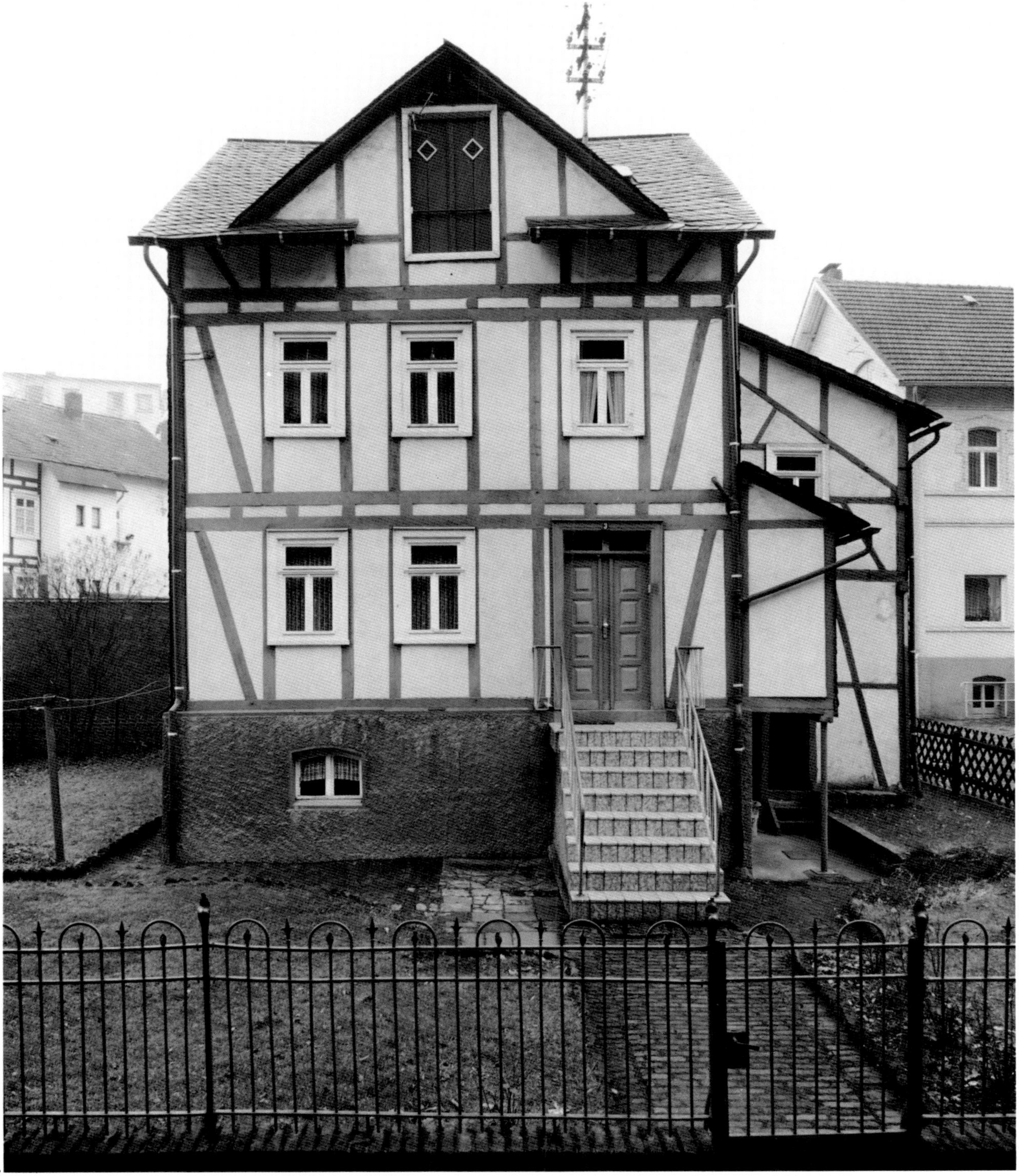

139

Am Gosenbach 3, Niederschelderhütte, 1972.

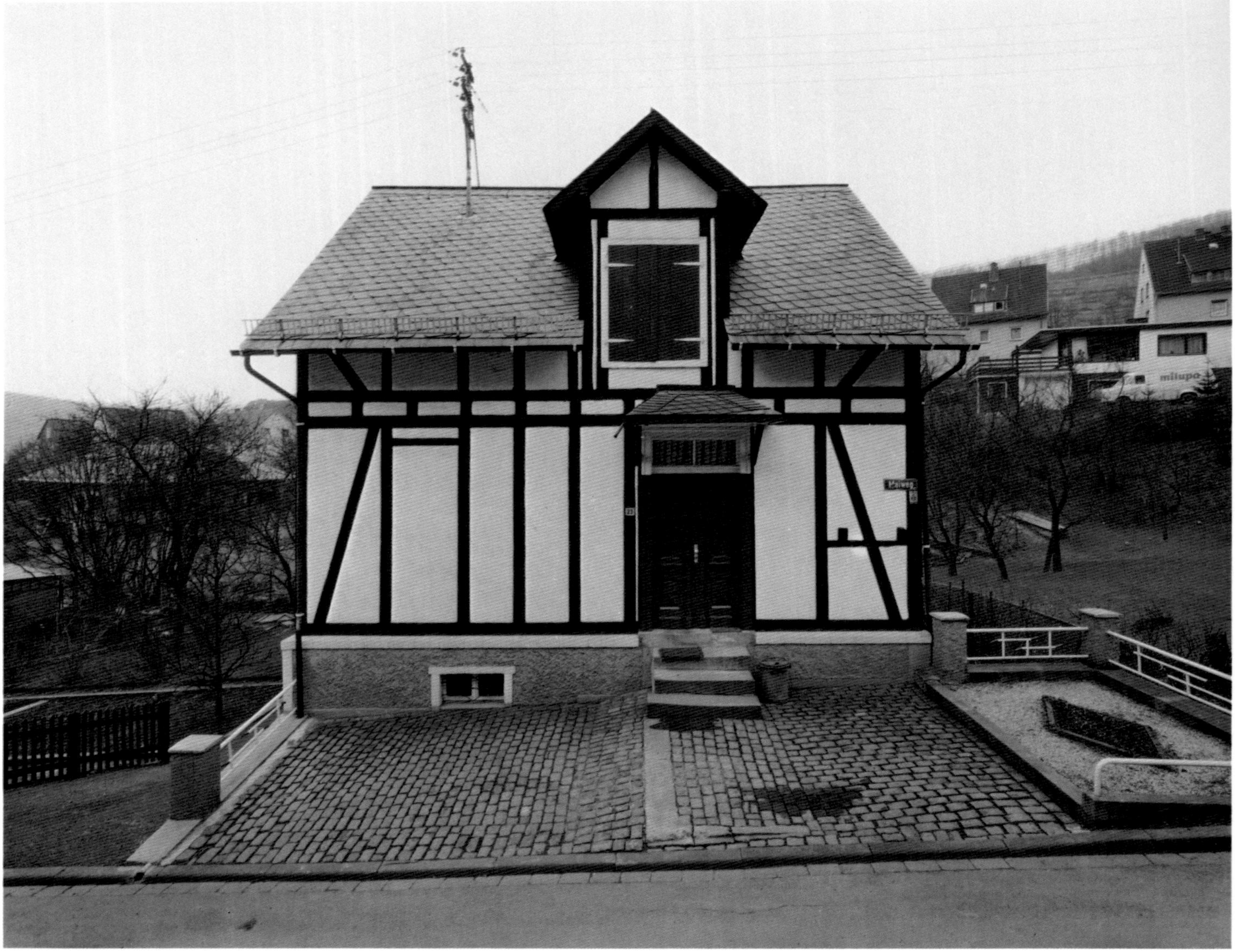

140
Maiweg 23, Gosenbach, 1970.

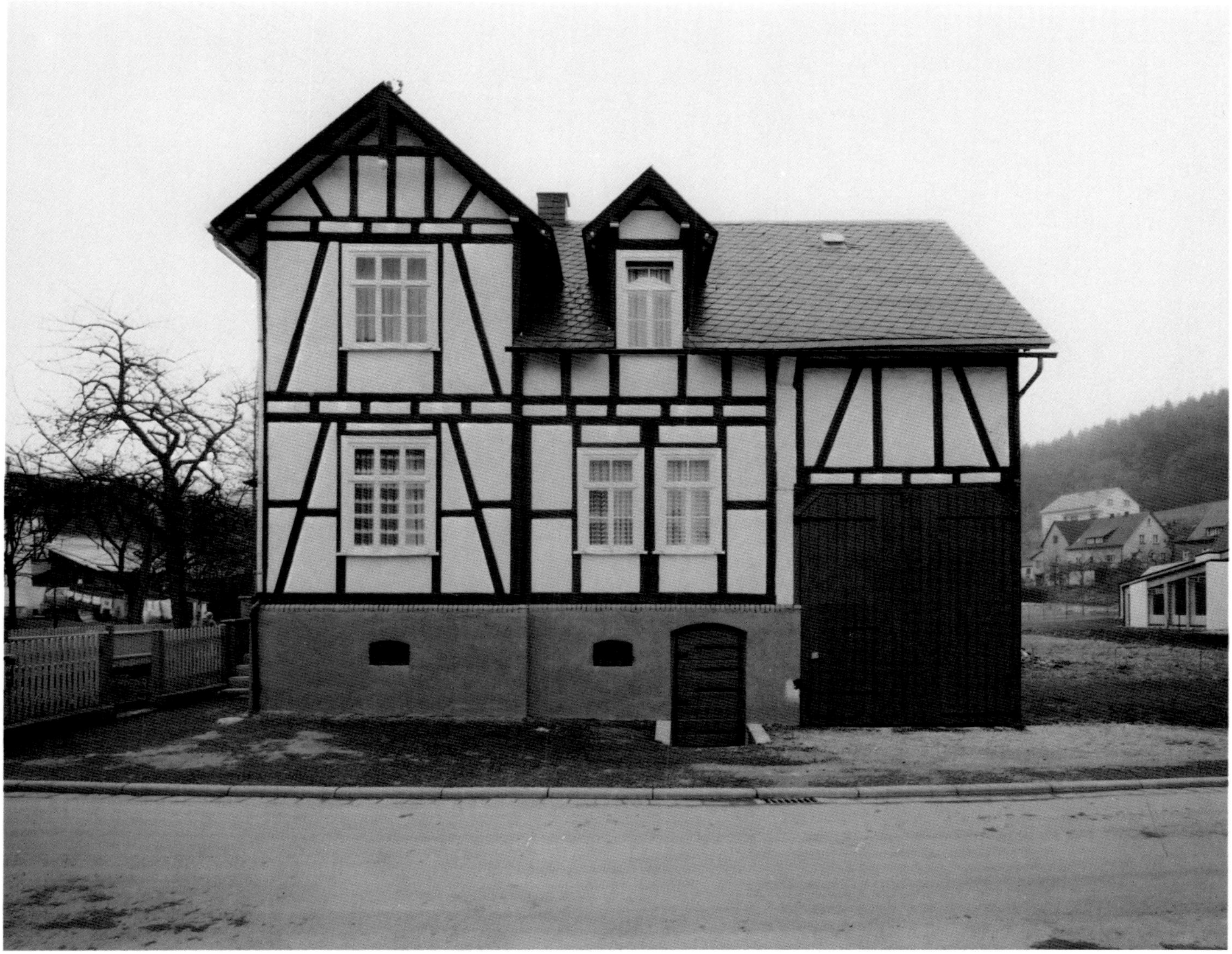

141
Tränkestraße 3, Haiger-Seelbach, 1972.

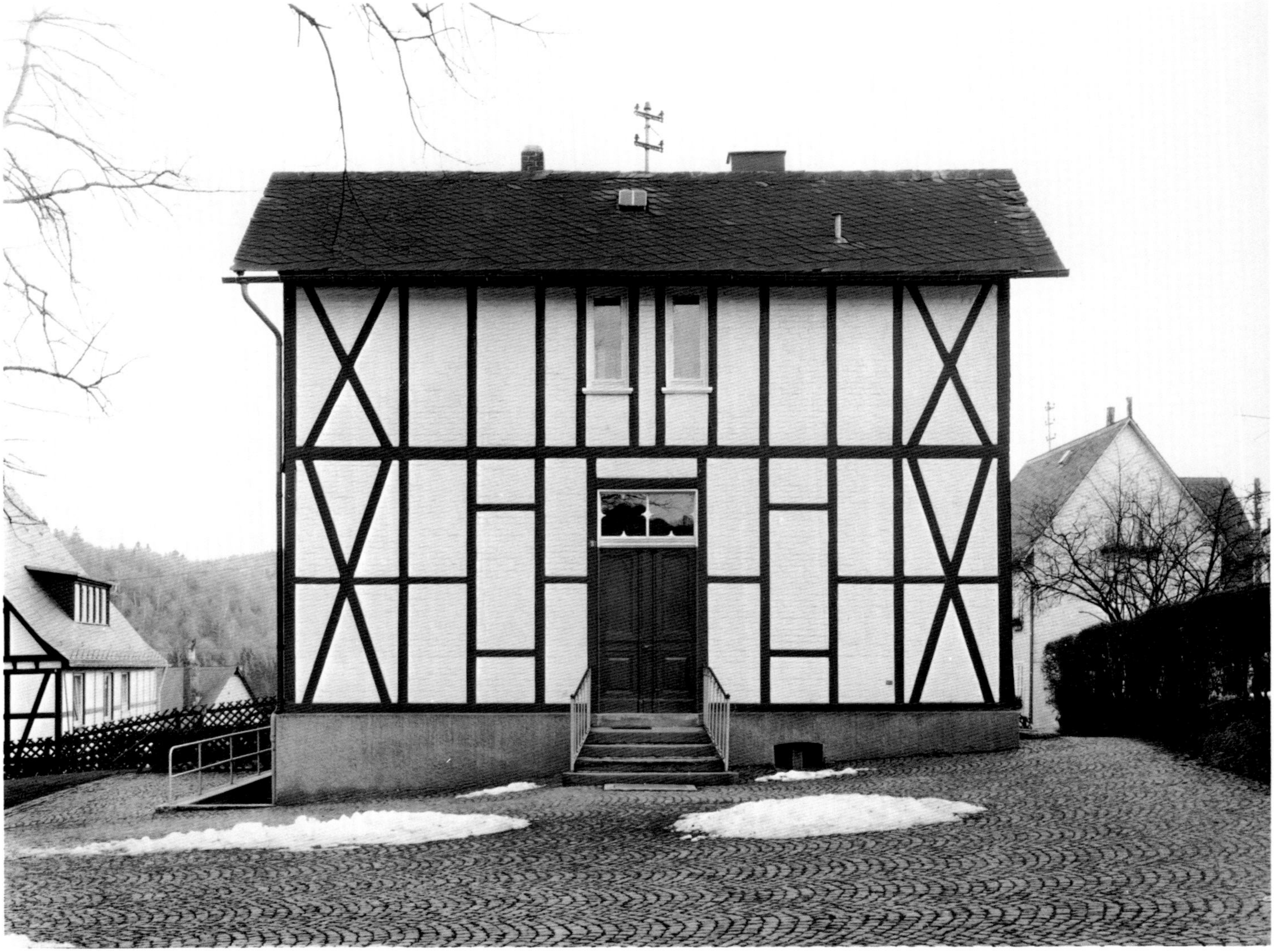

142
Kirchplatz 3, Hilchenbach, 1967.

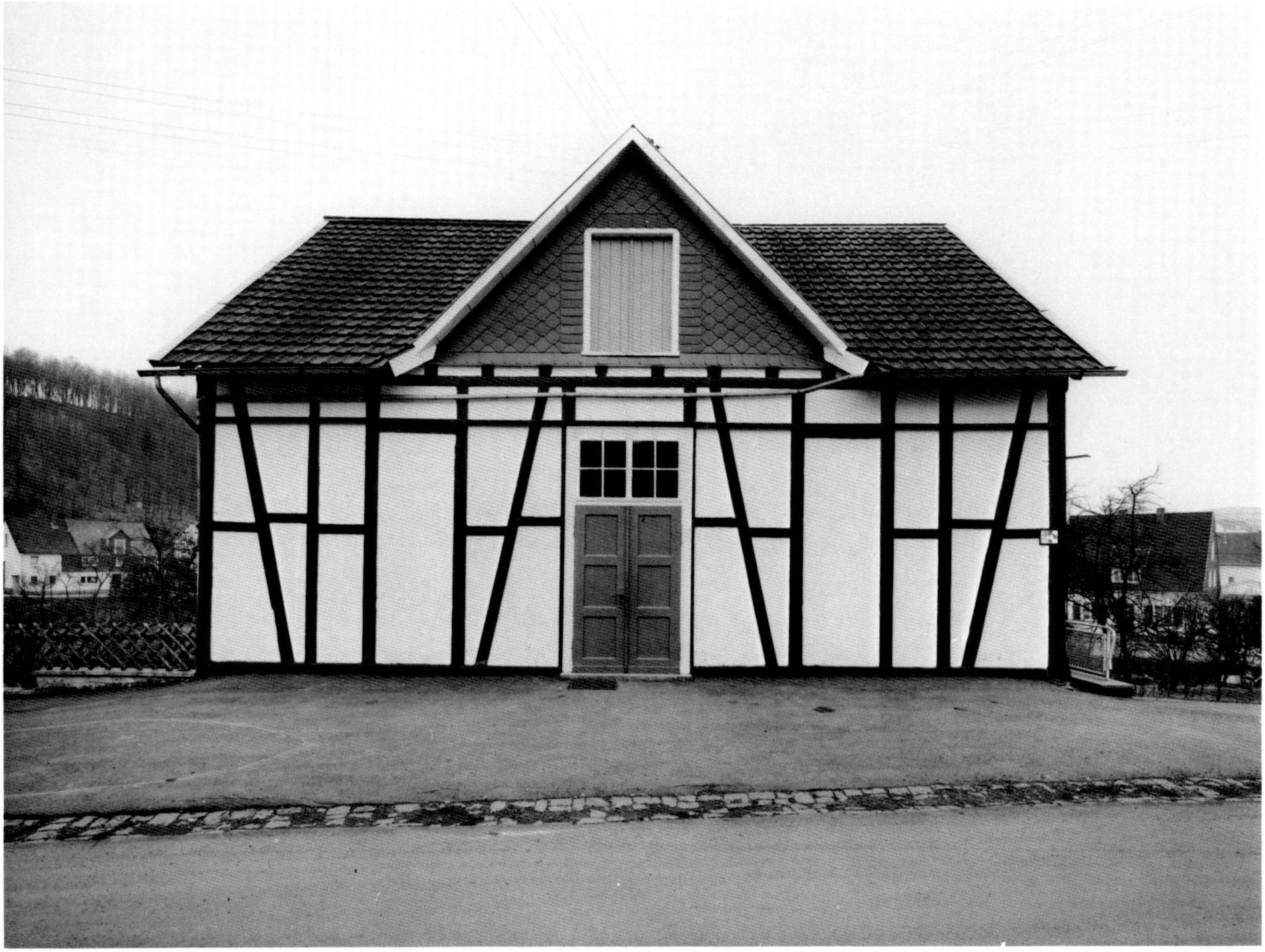

143
Wendiger Straße 4, Büschergrund, 1972.

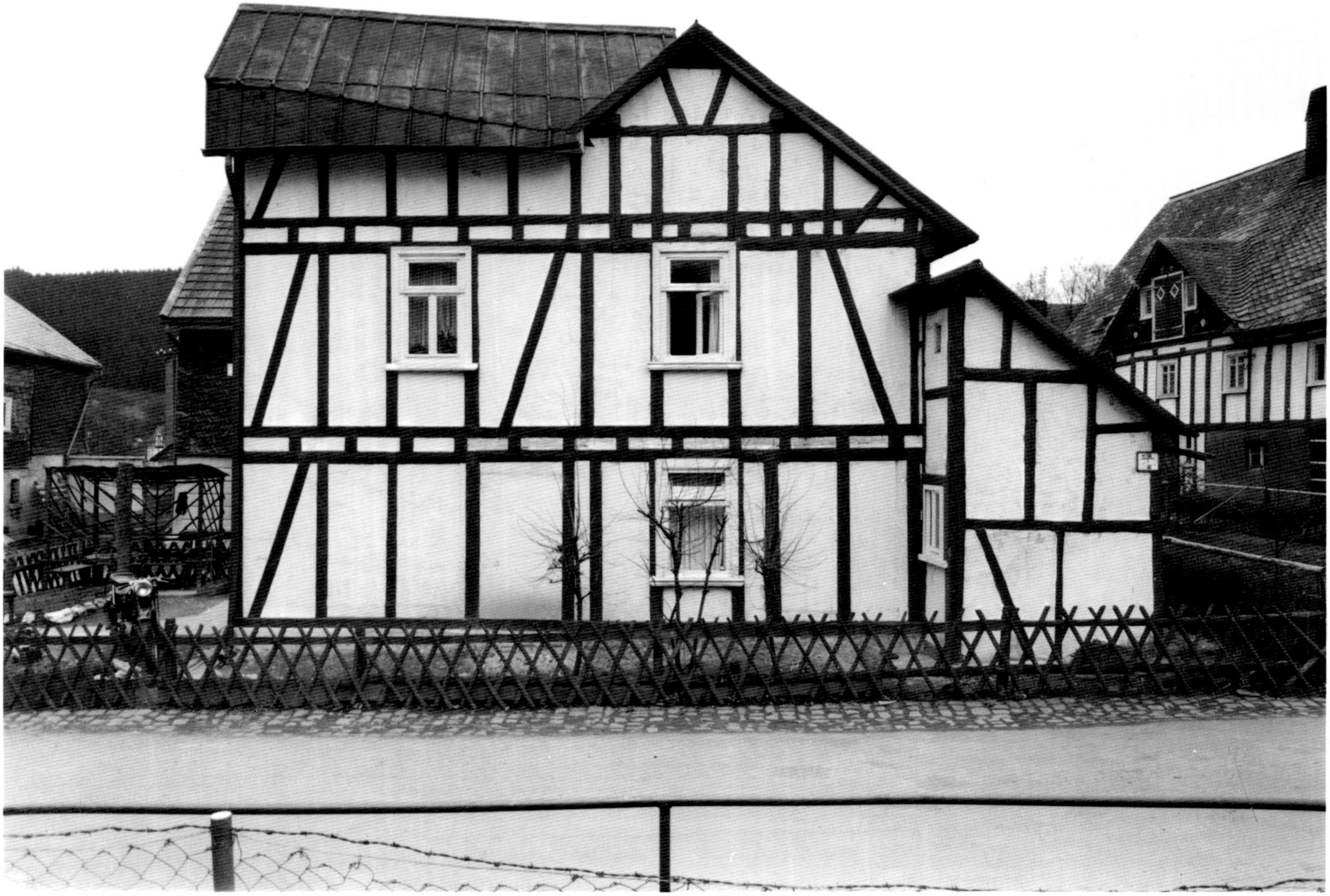

144
Wickersbacher Weg 7, Trupbach, 1960.

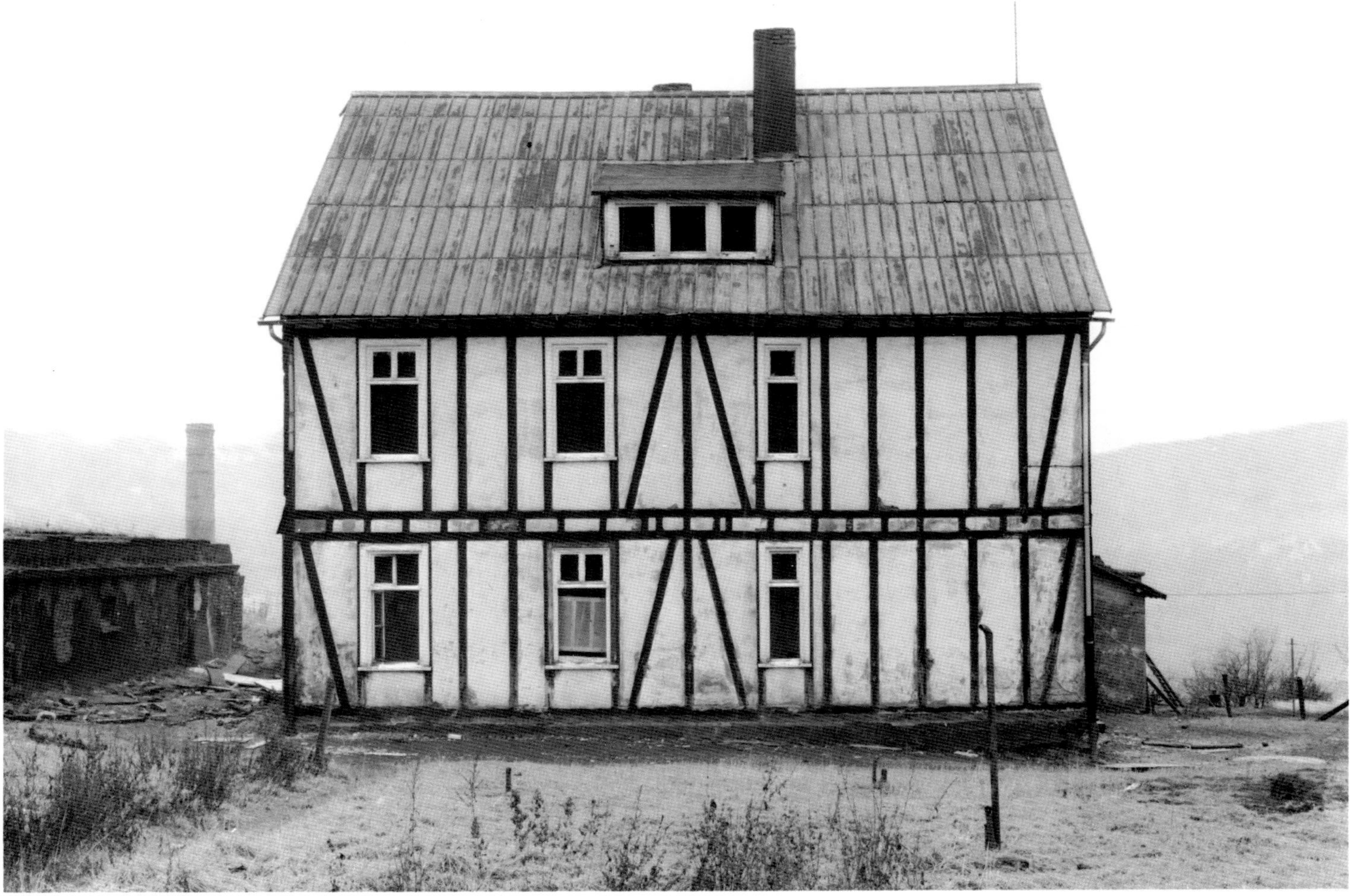

145

Friedhofstraße 11, Niederschelden, 1970.

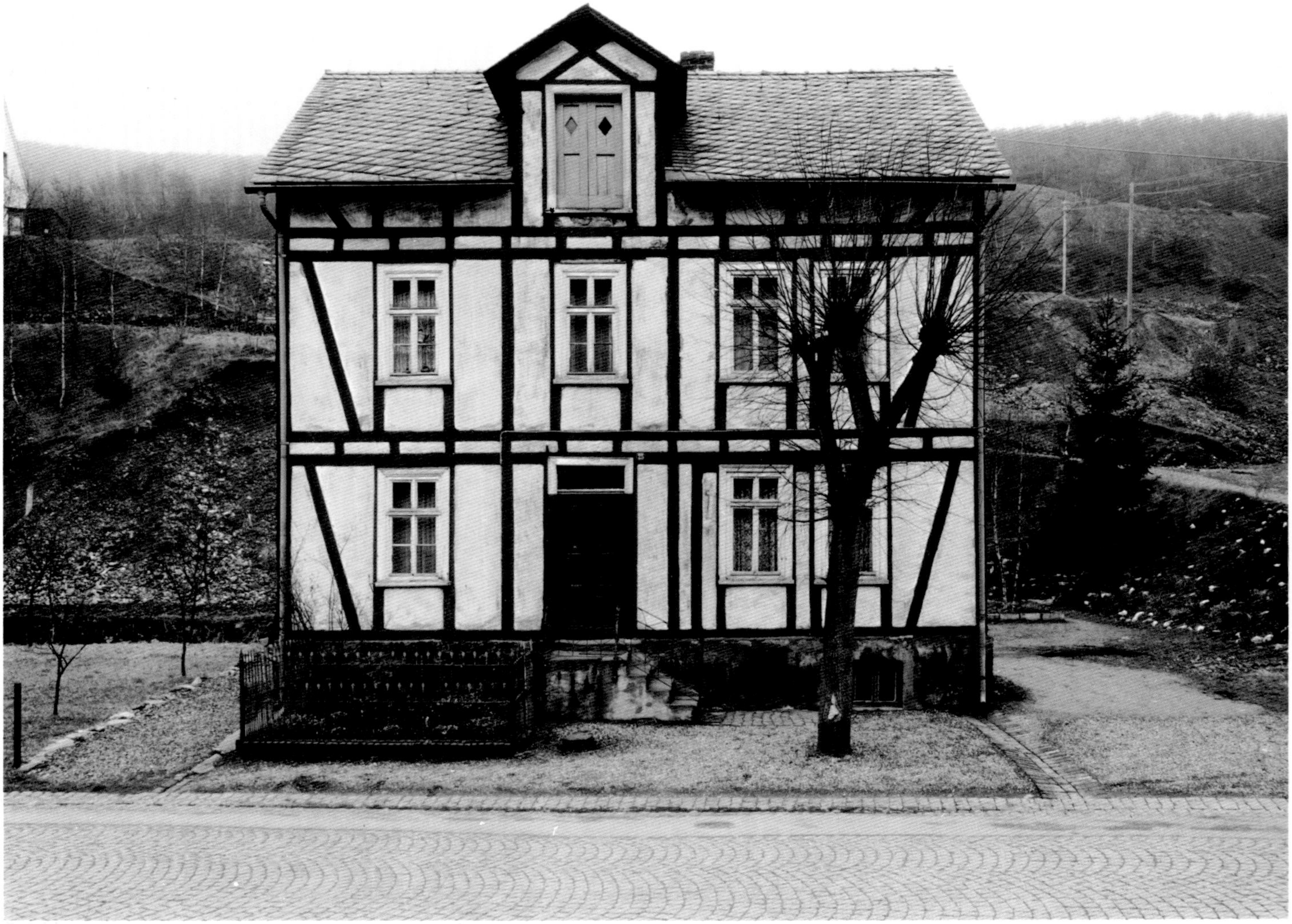

146
Auf der Hütte 45, Gosenbach, 1961.

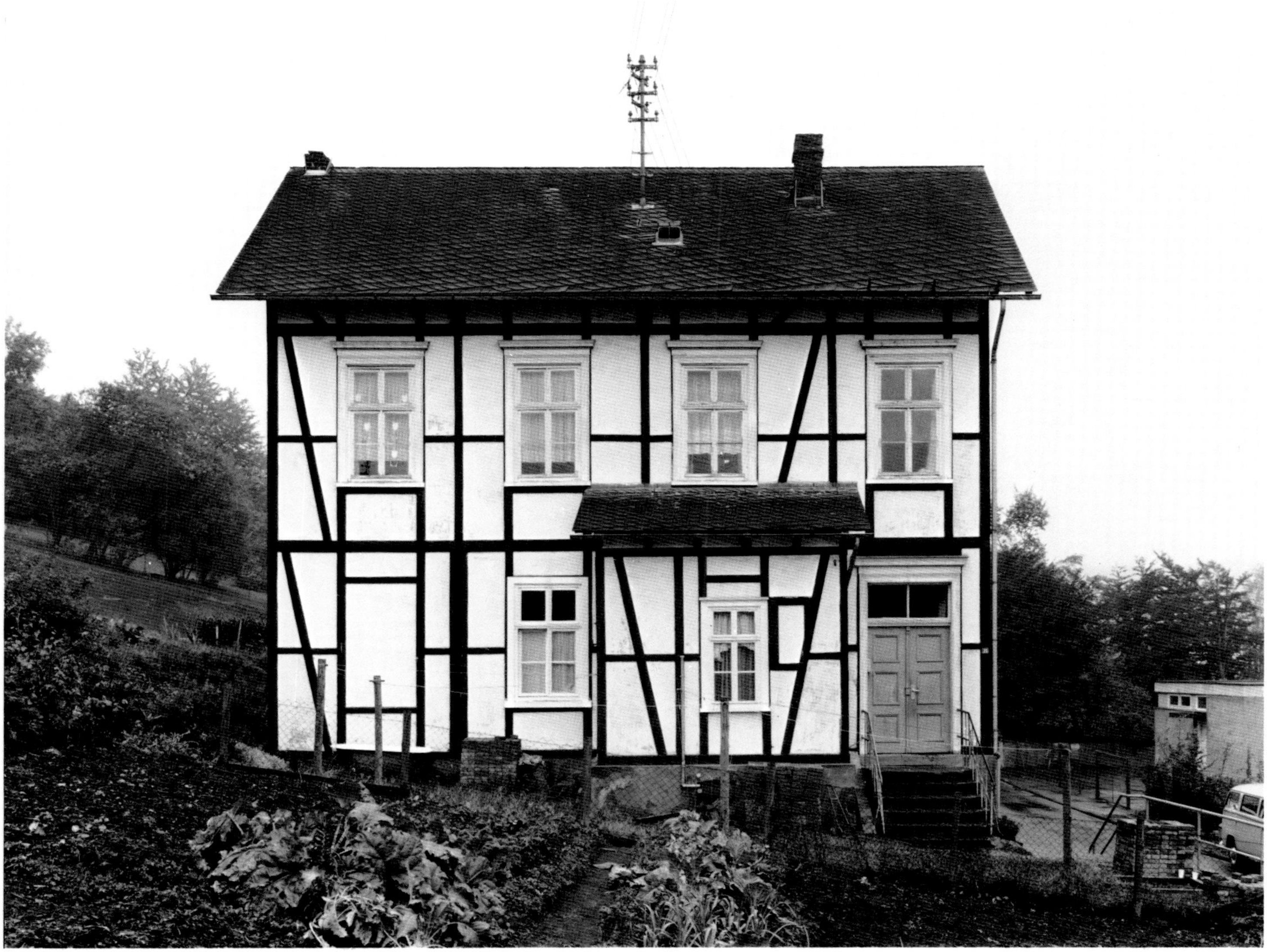

147
Oststraße 16, Freudenberg, 1971.

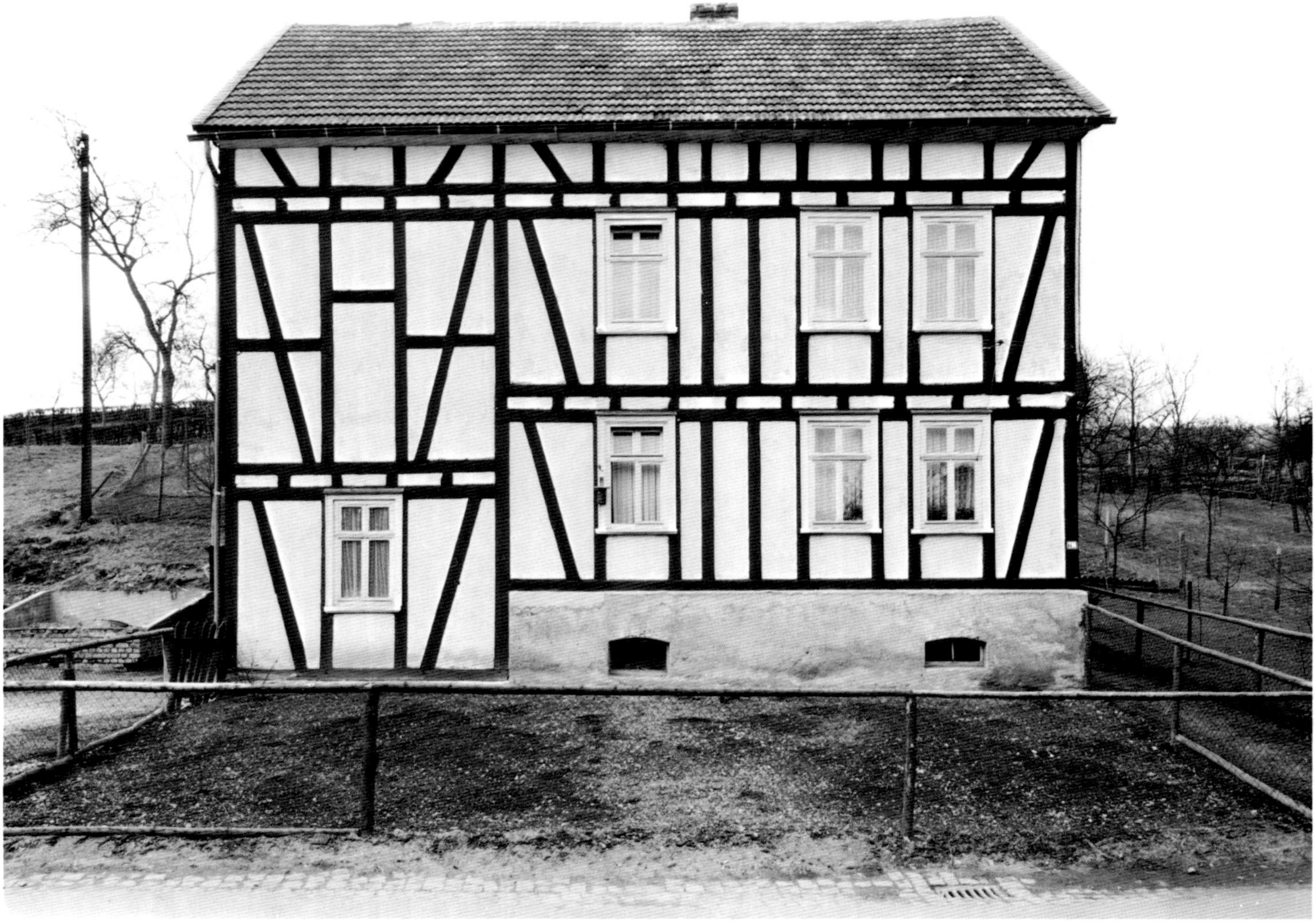

148
Achenbacher Straße 298, Achenbach, 1960.

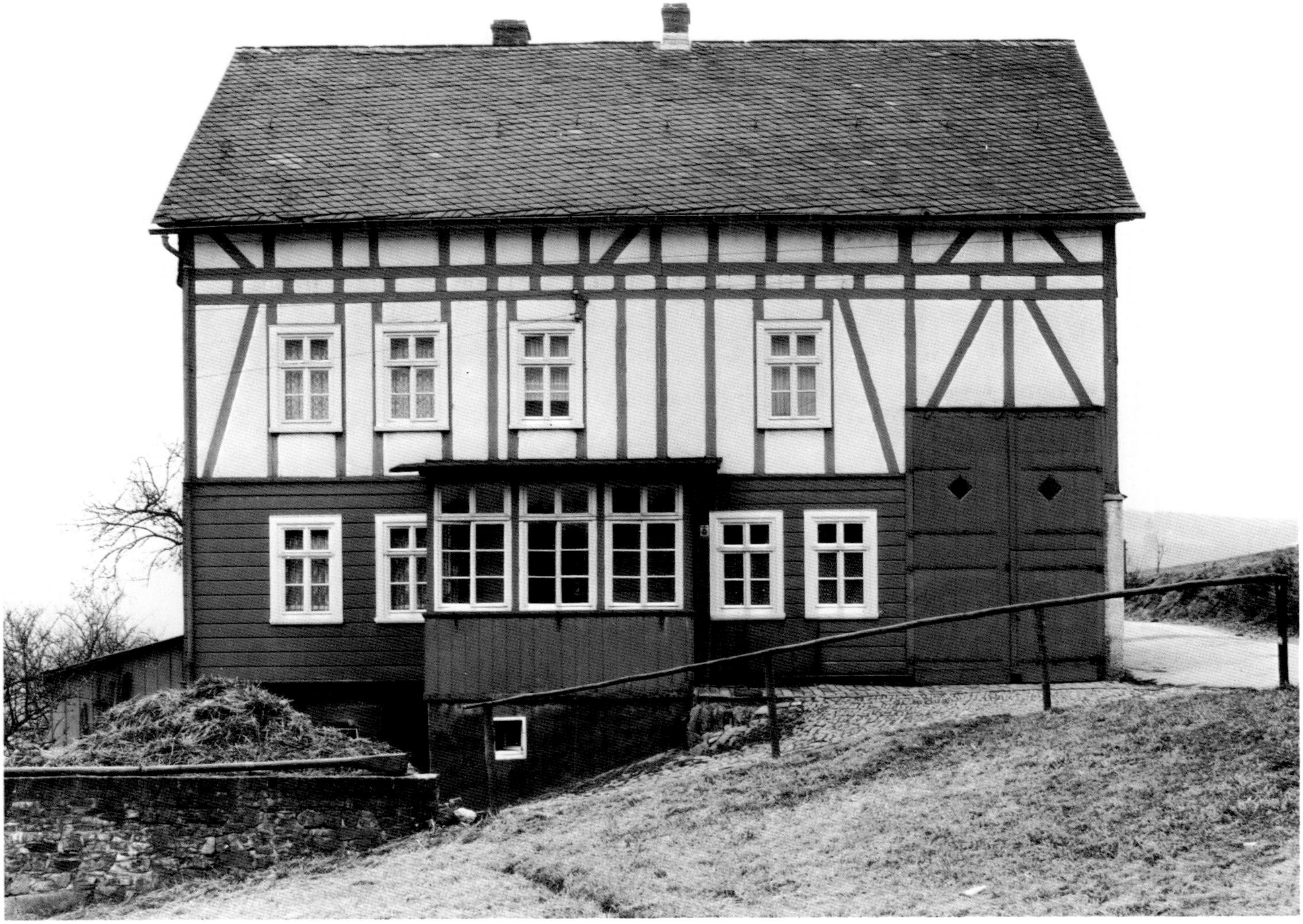

149
Feldstraße 5, Flammersbach, 1960.

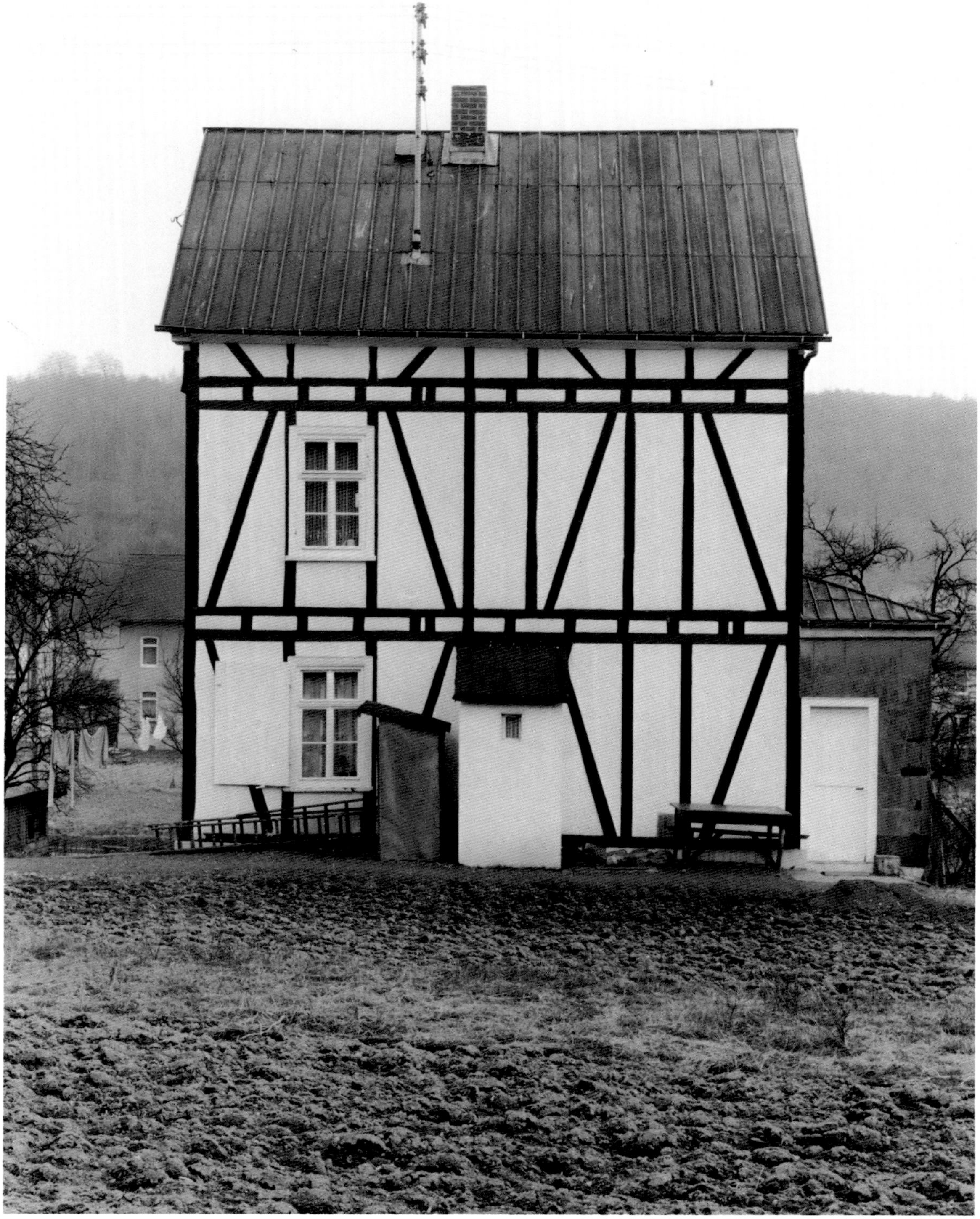

150
Rensdorfstraße 13, Salchendorf, 1969.

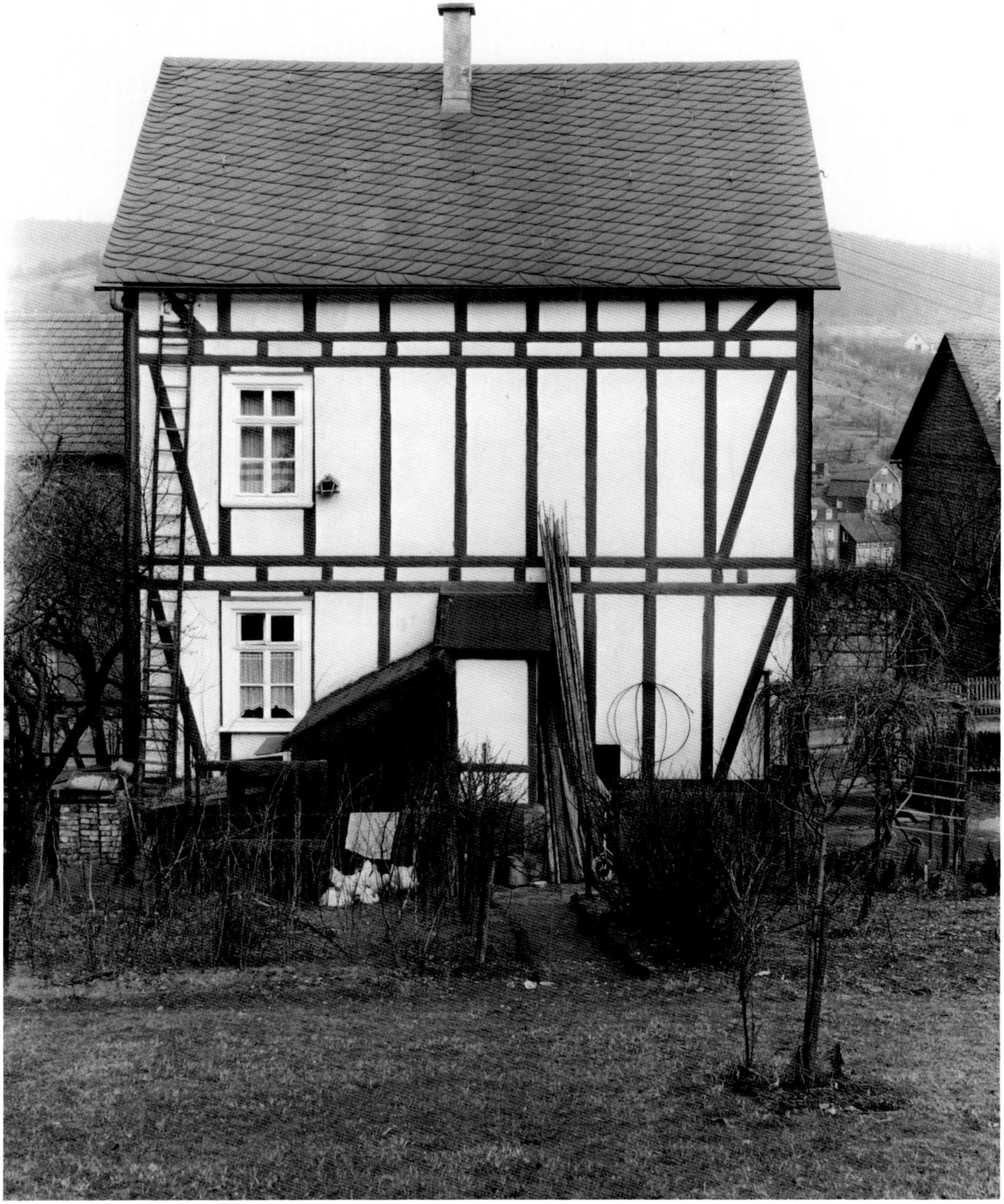

151
Freiengründerstraße 104, Eiserfeld, 1960.

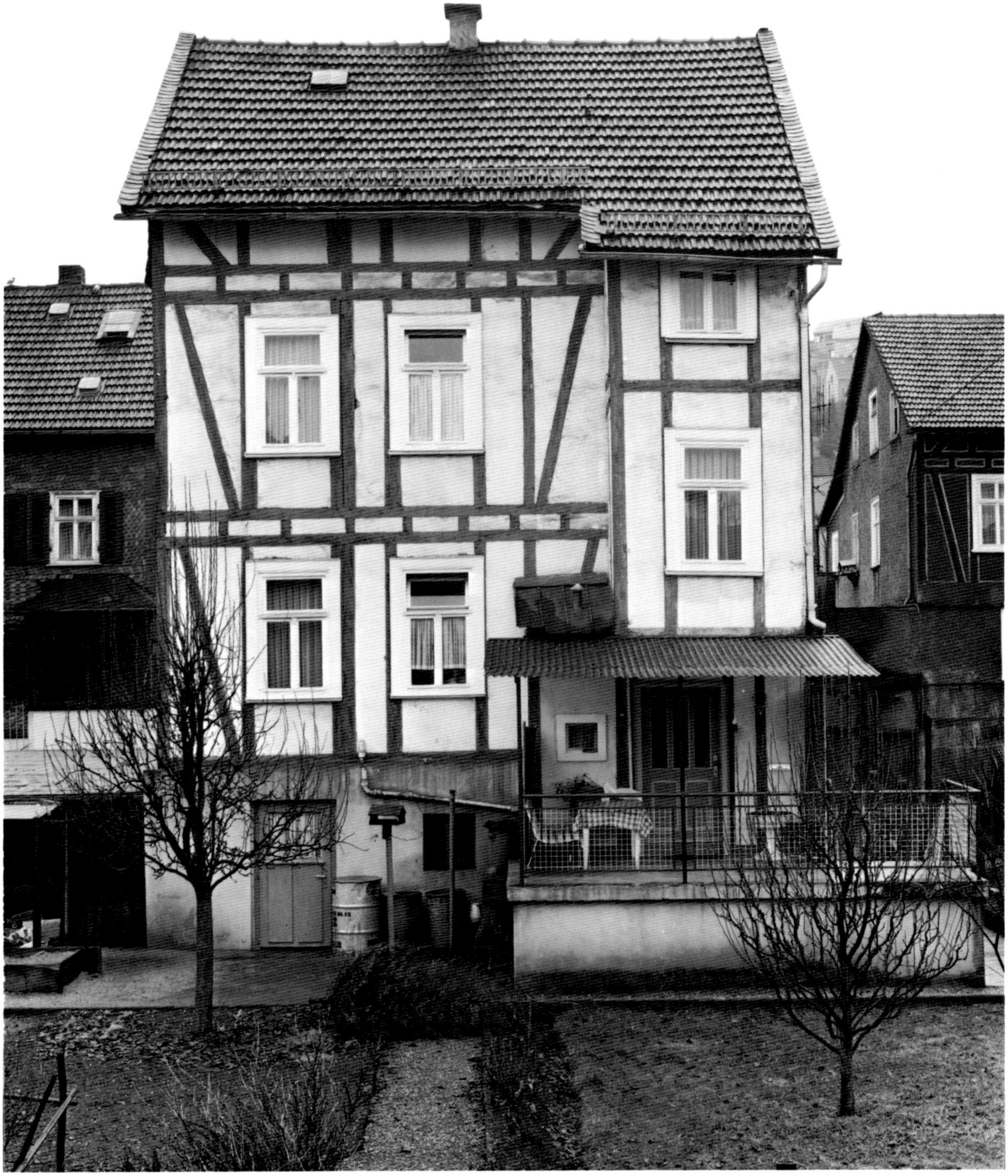

152
Johannesstraße 5, Niederschelden, 1970.

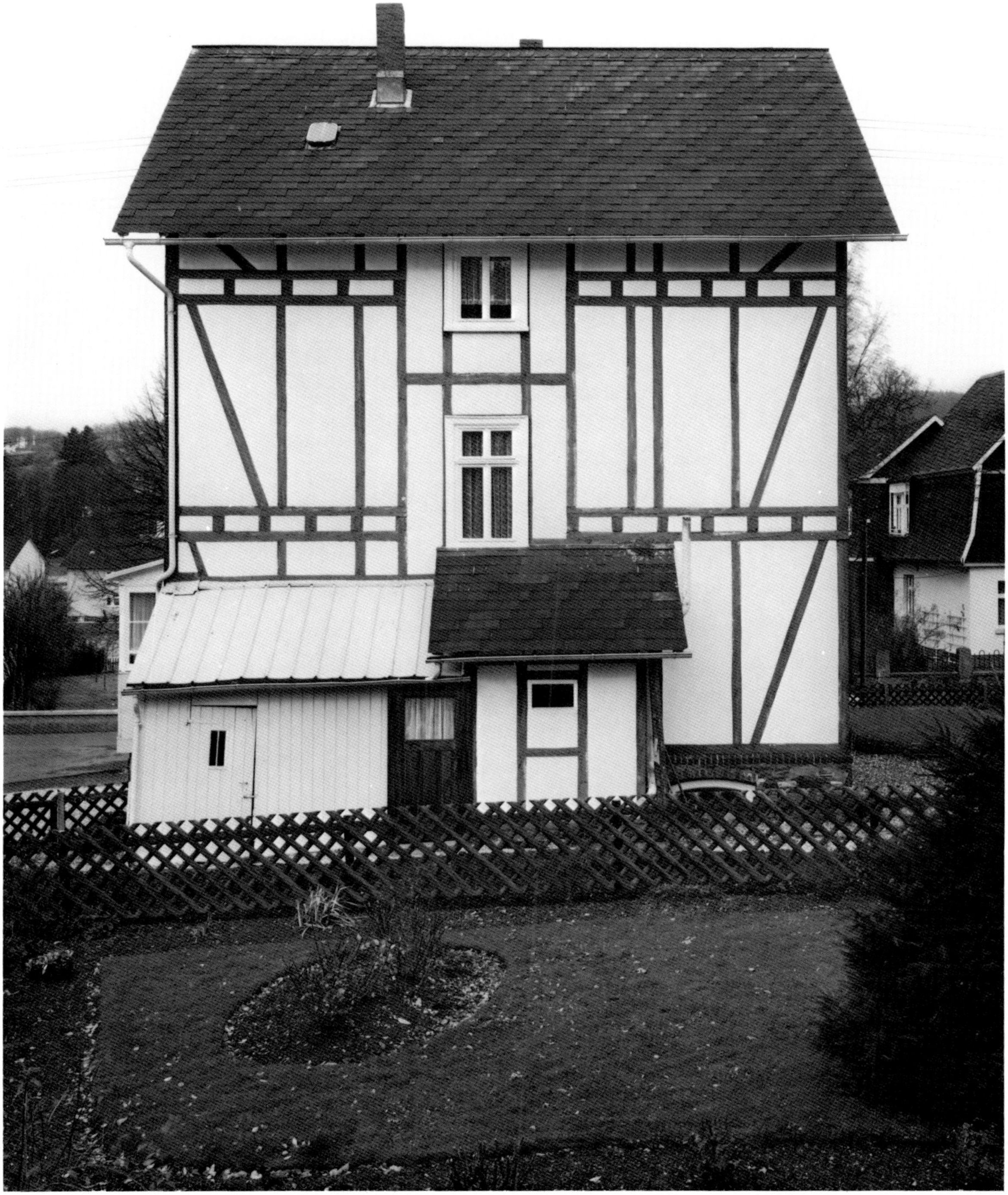

153
Hillnhütter Straße 62, Dahlbruch, 1971.

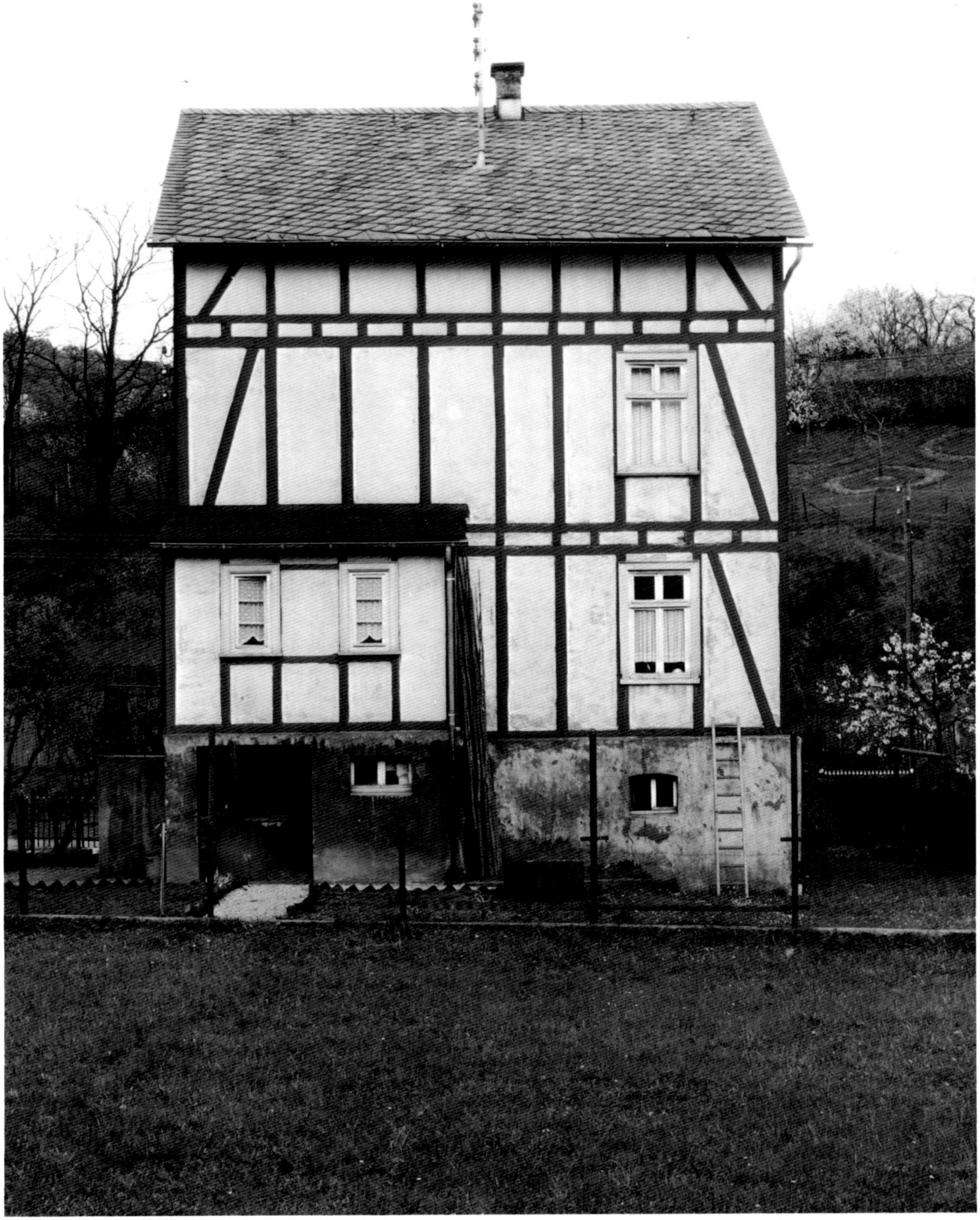

154

Am Gosenbach 15, Niederschelderhütte, 1960.

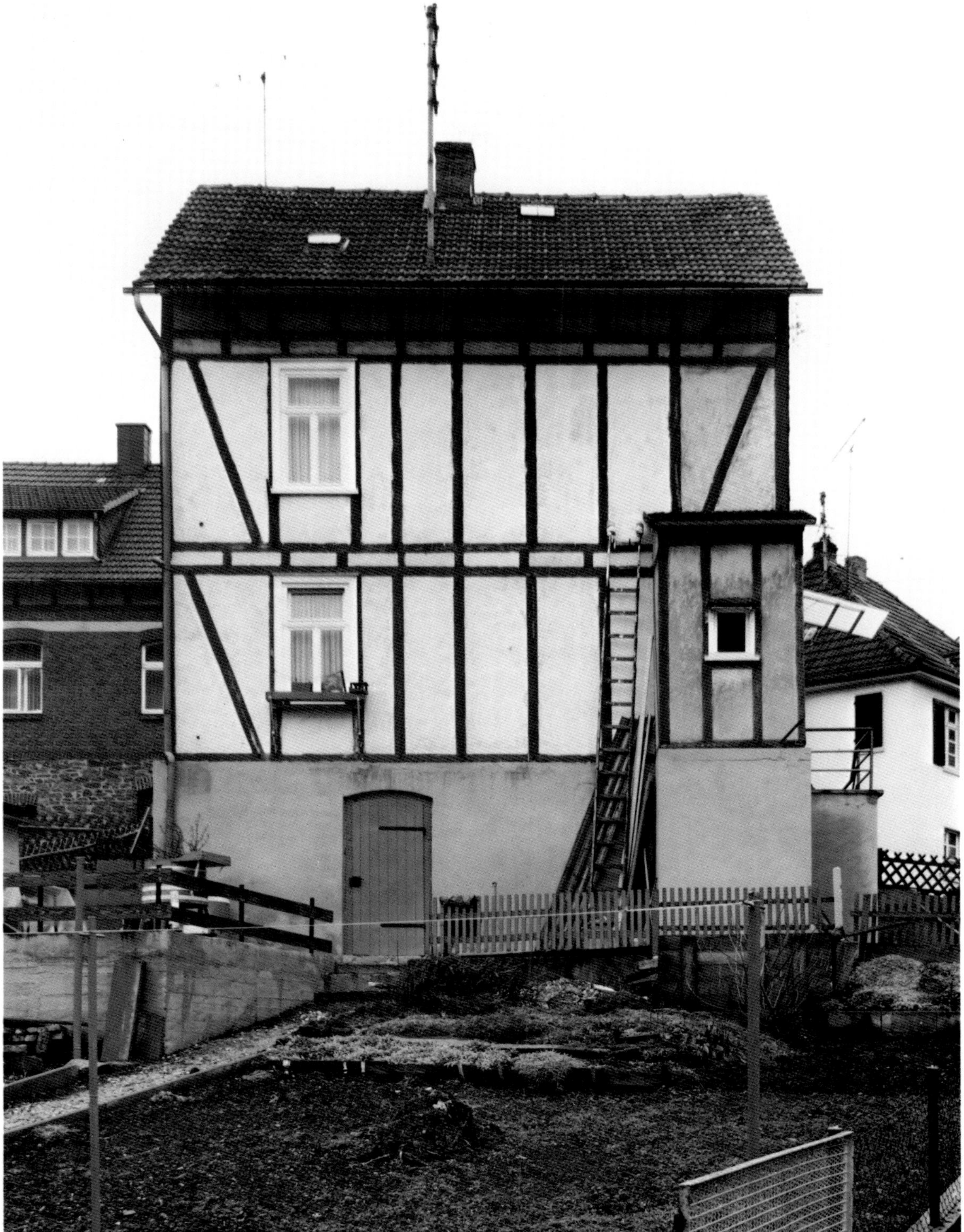

155
Wehbacher Straße 15, Wehbach, 1970.

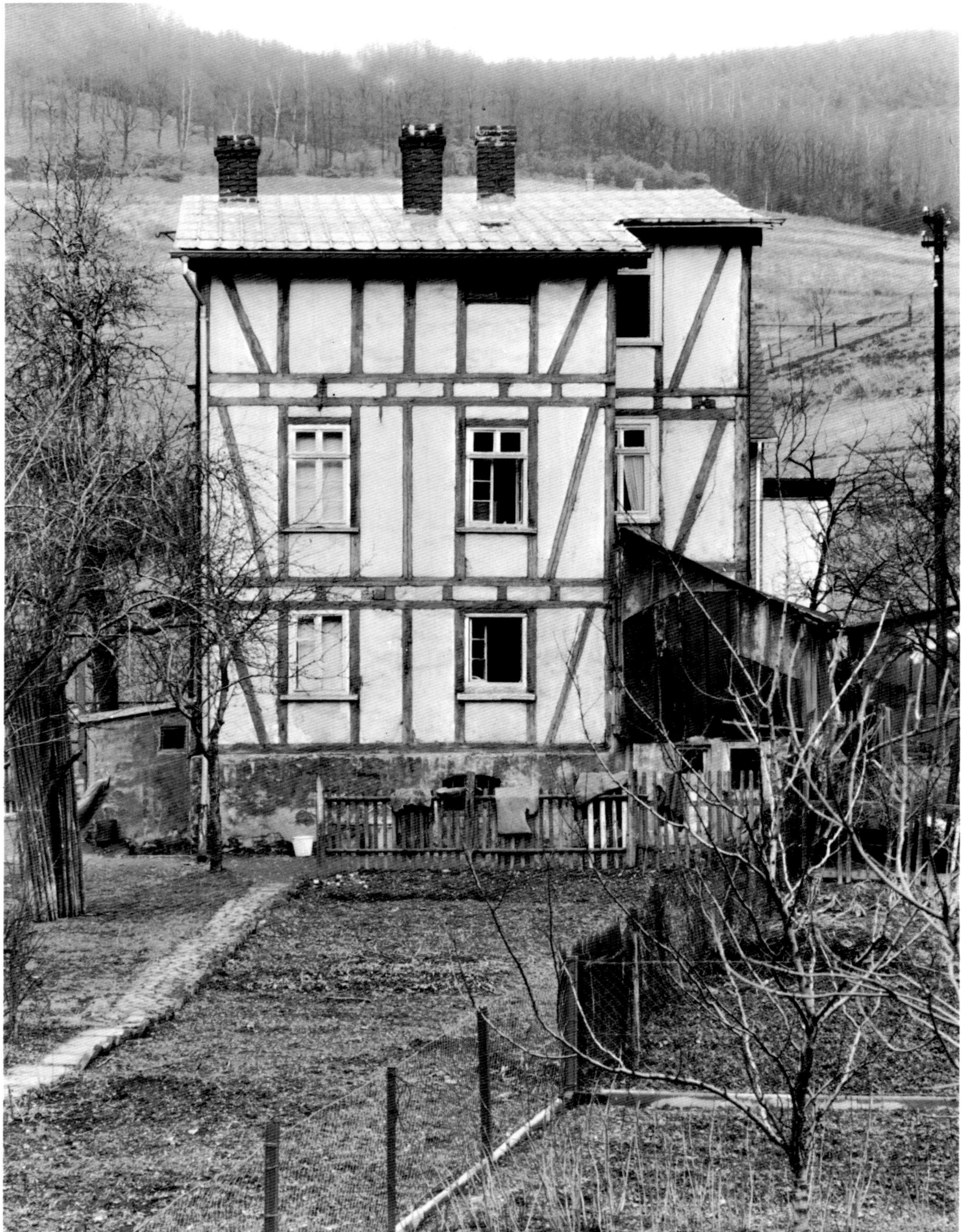

156
Eisernstraße 122, Eiserfeld, 1959.

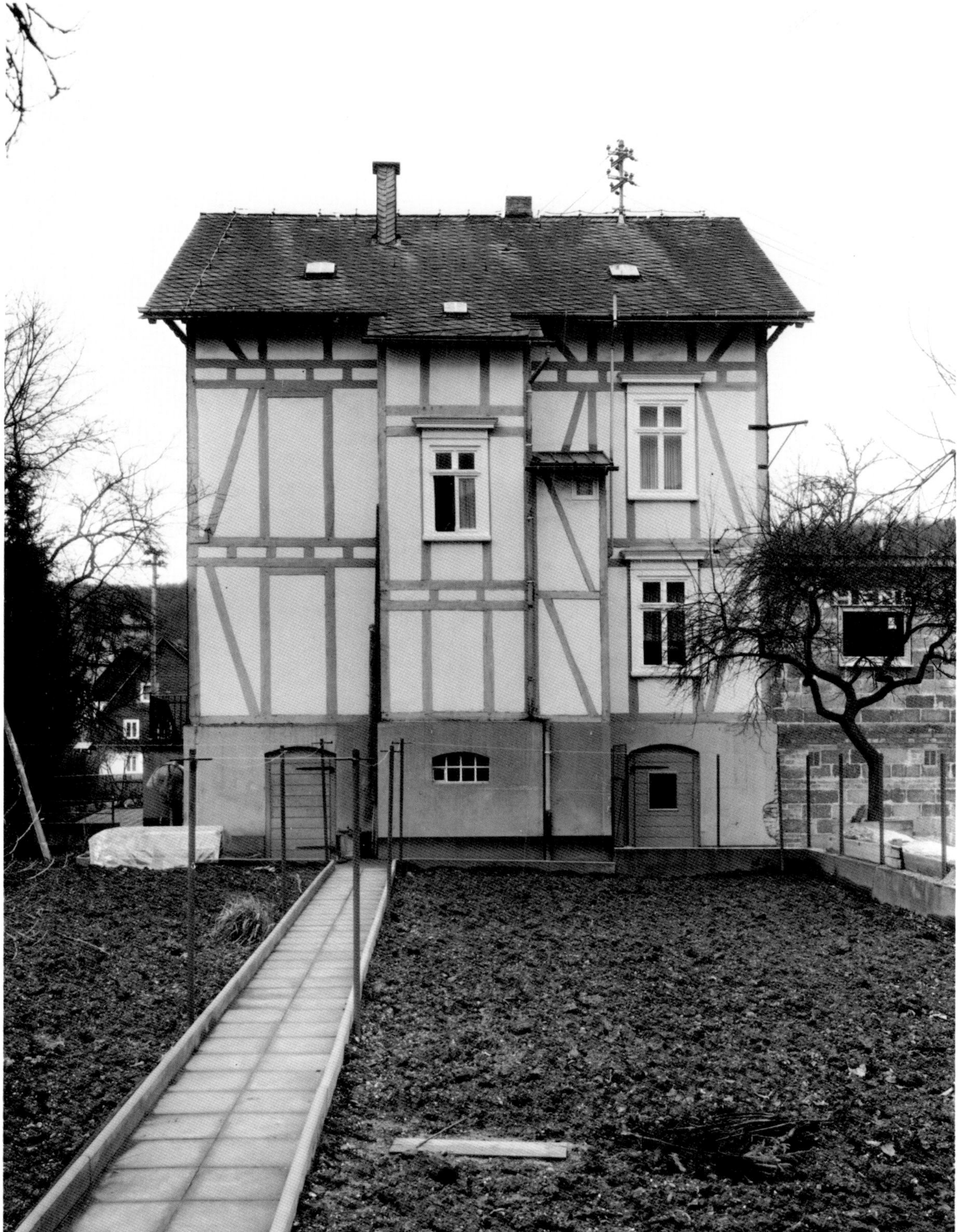

157
Wiesenstraße 2, Eisern, 1973.

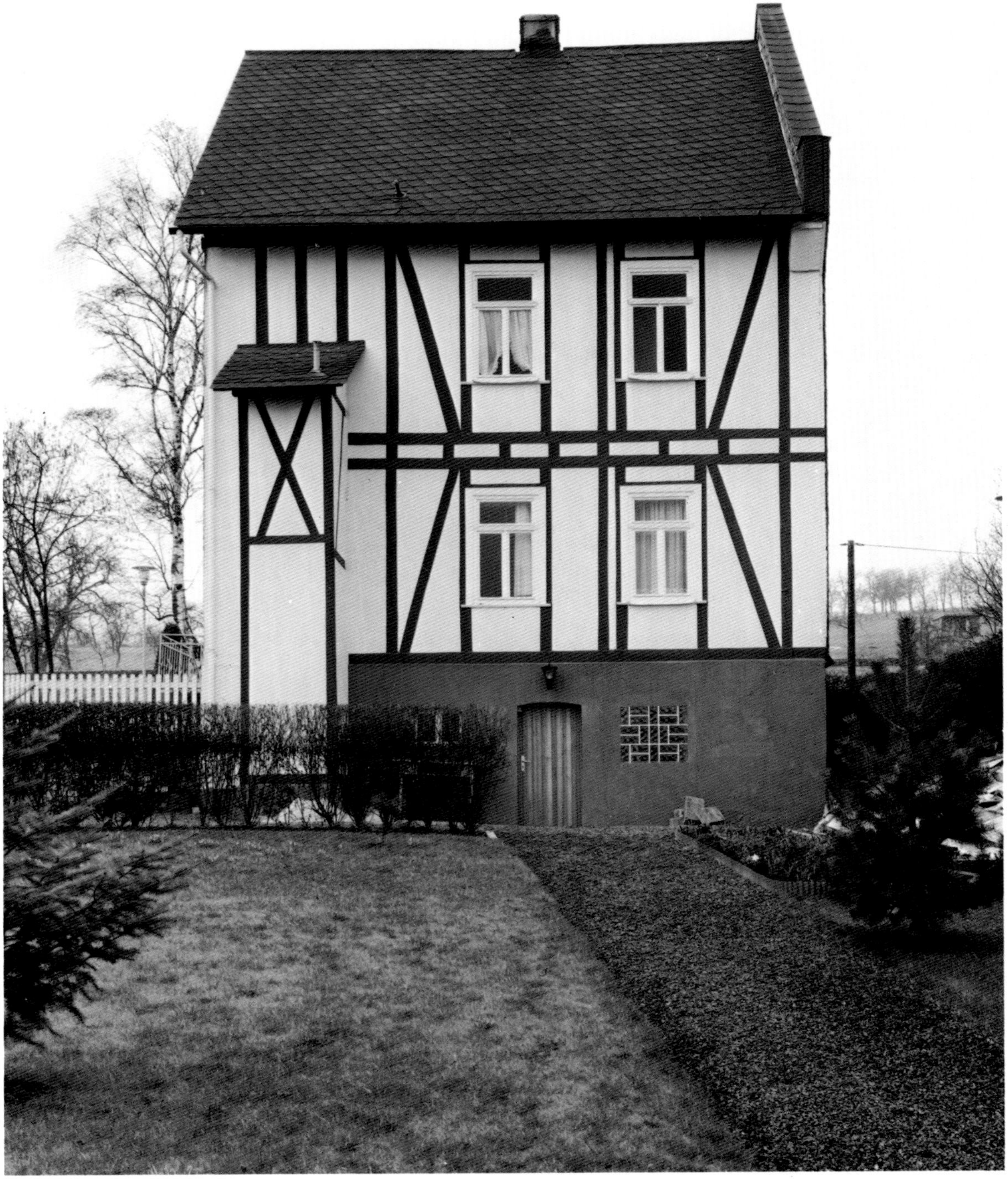

158
Obertor 38, Haiger, 1972.

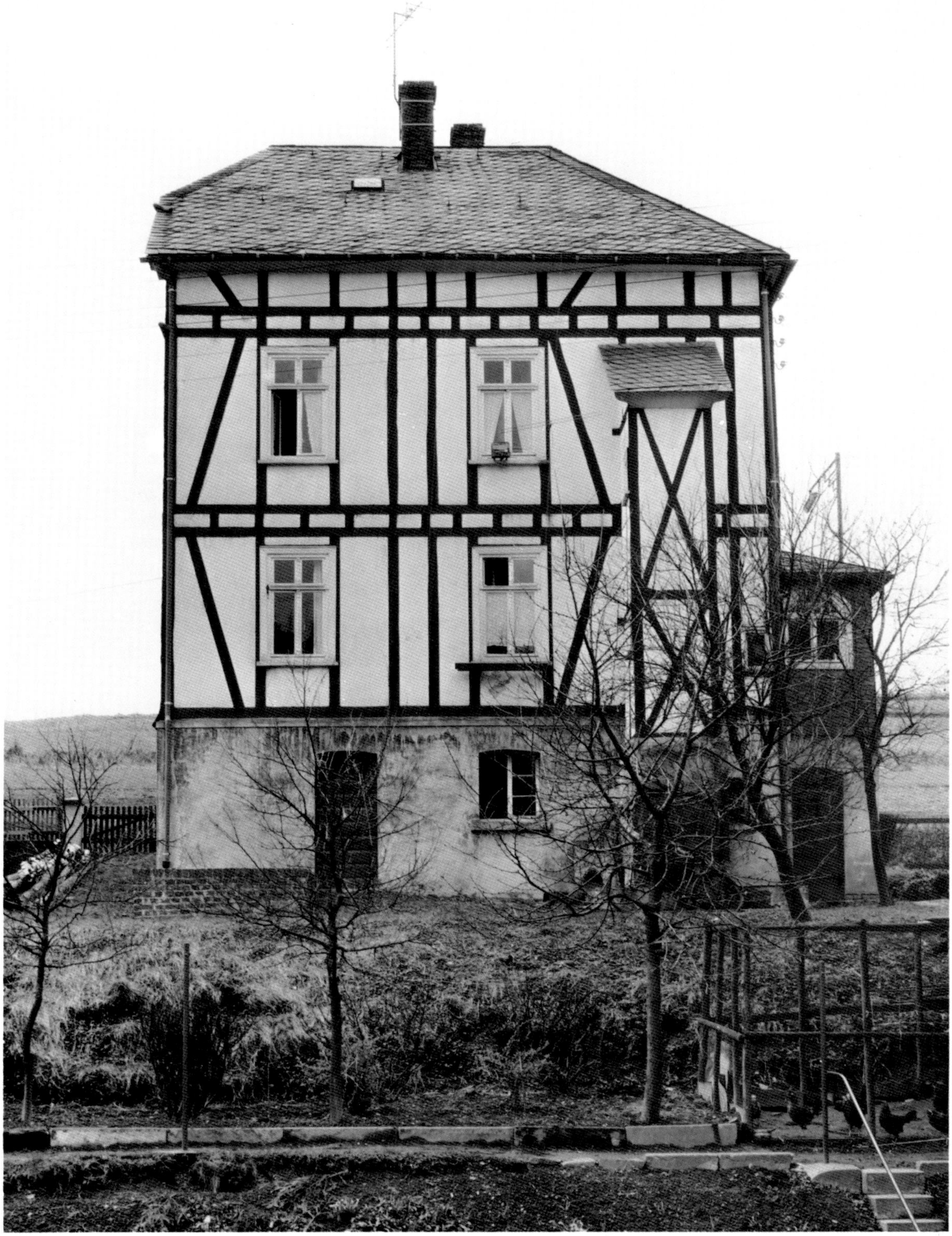

159
Kölner Straße 336, Salchendorf, 1960.

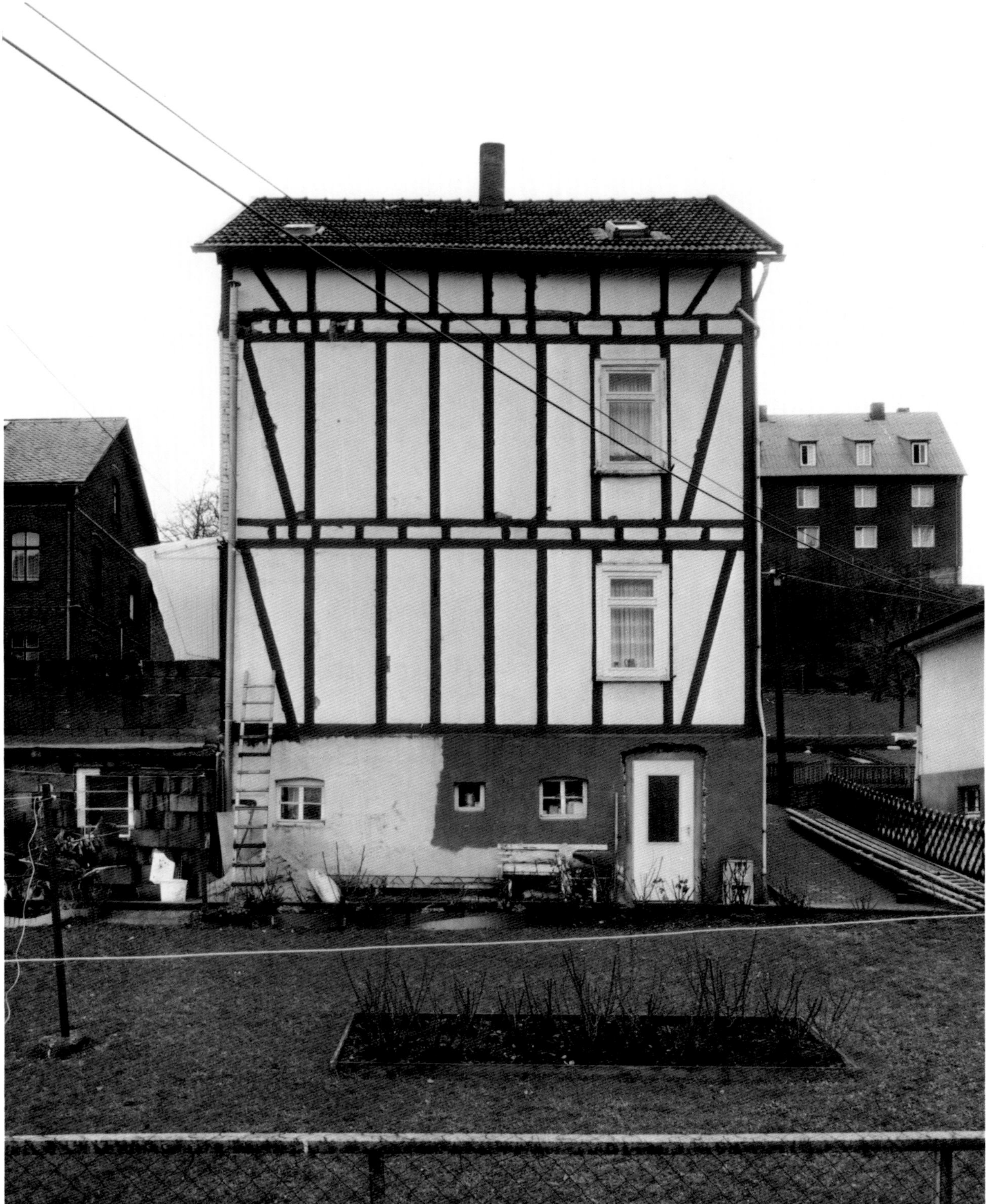

160
Ziegelstraße 7, Niederschelden, 1973.

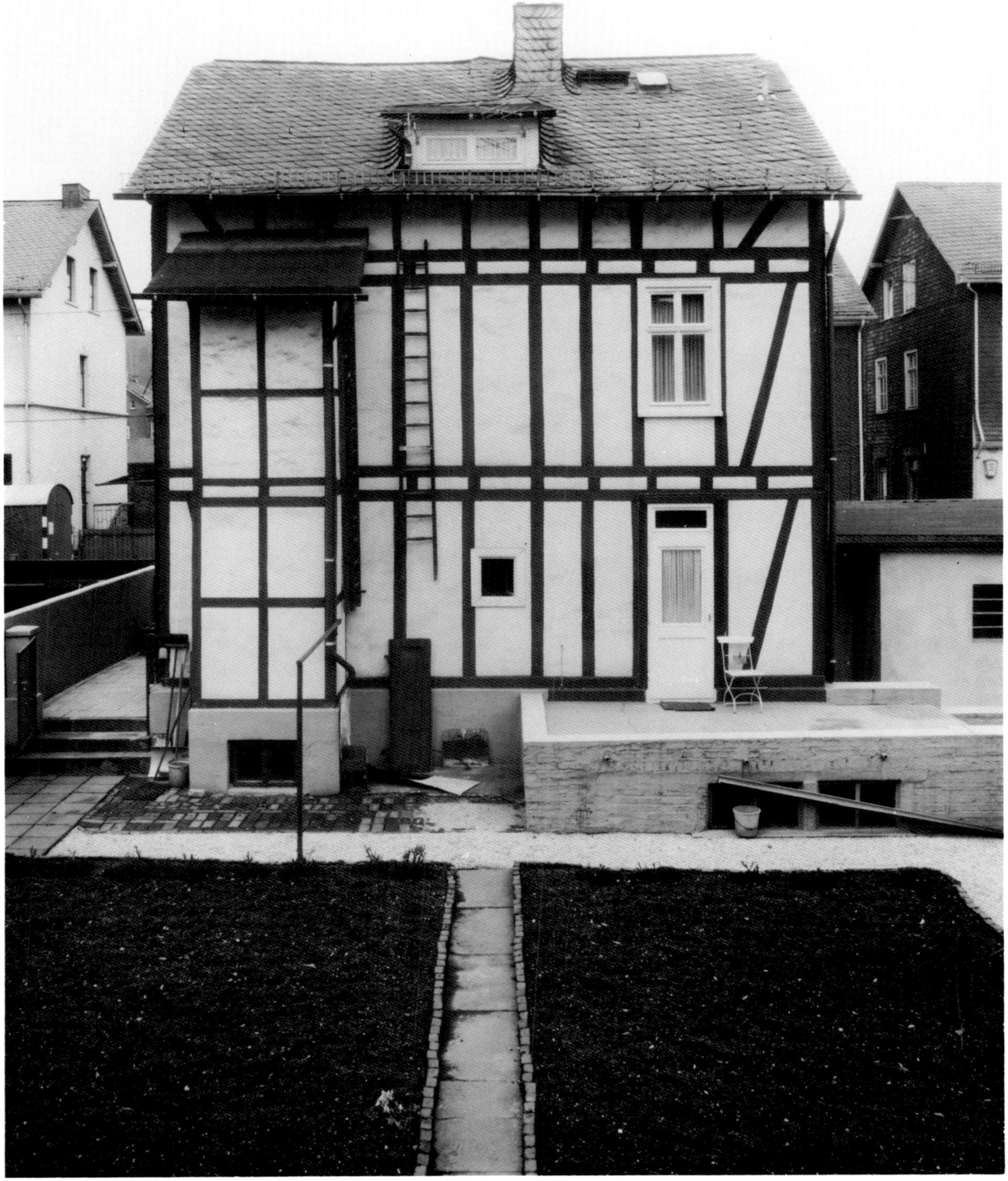

161

Eintrachtstraße 4, Siegen, 1973.

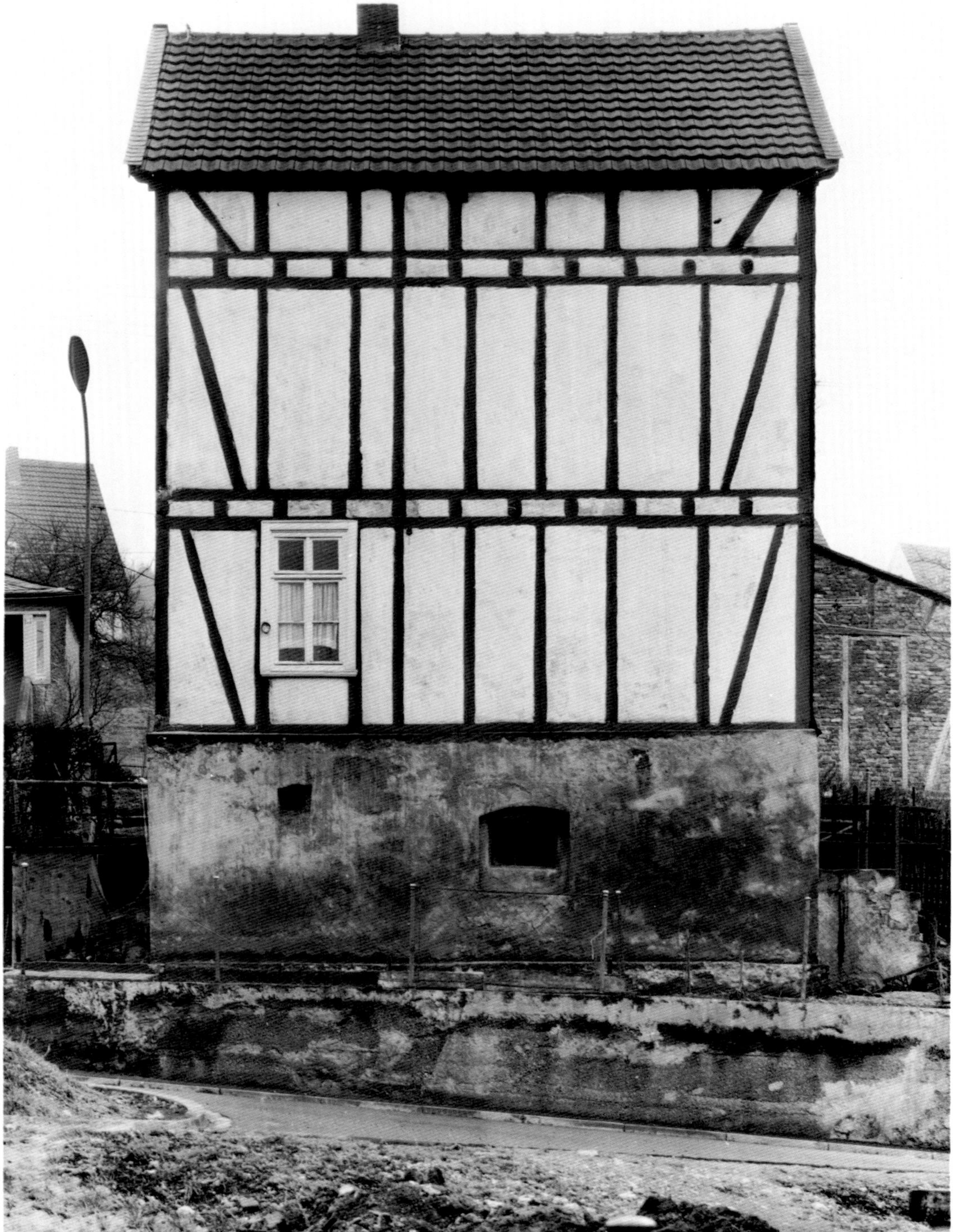

162

Siegener Straße 67, Gosenbach, 1960.

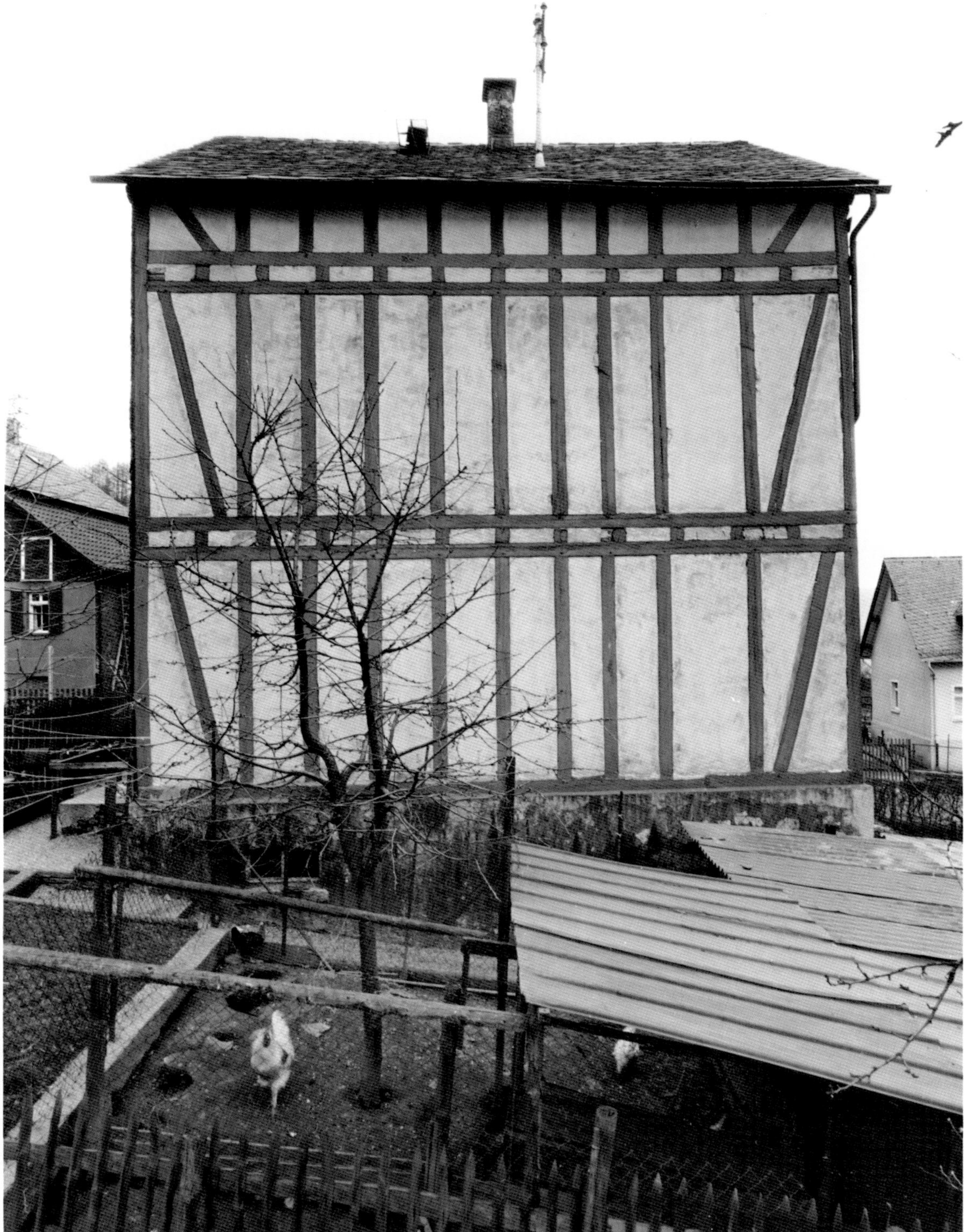

163
Querstraße 2, Eiserfeld, 1961.

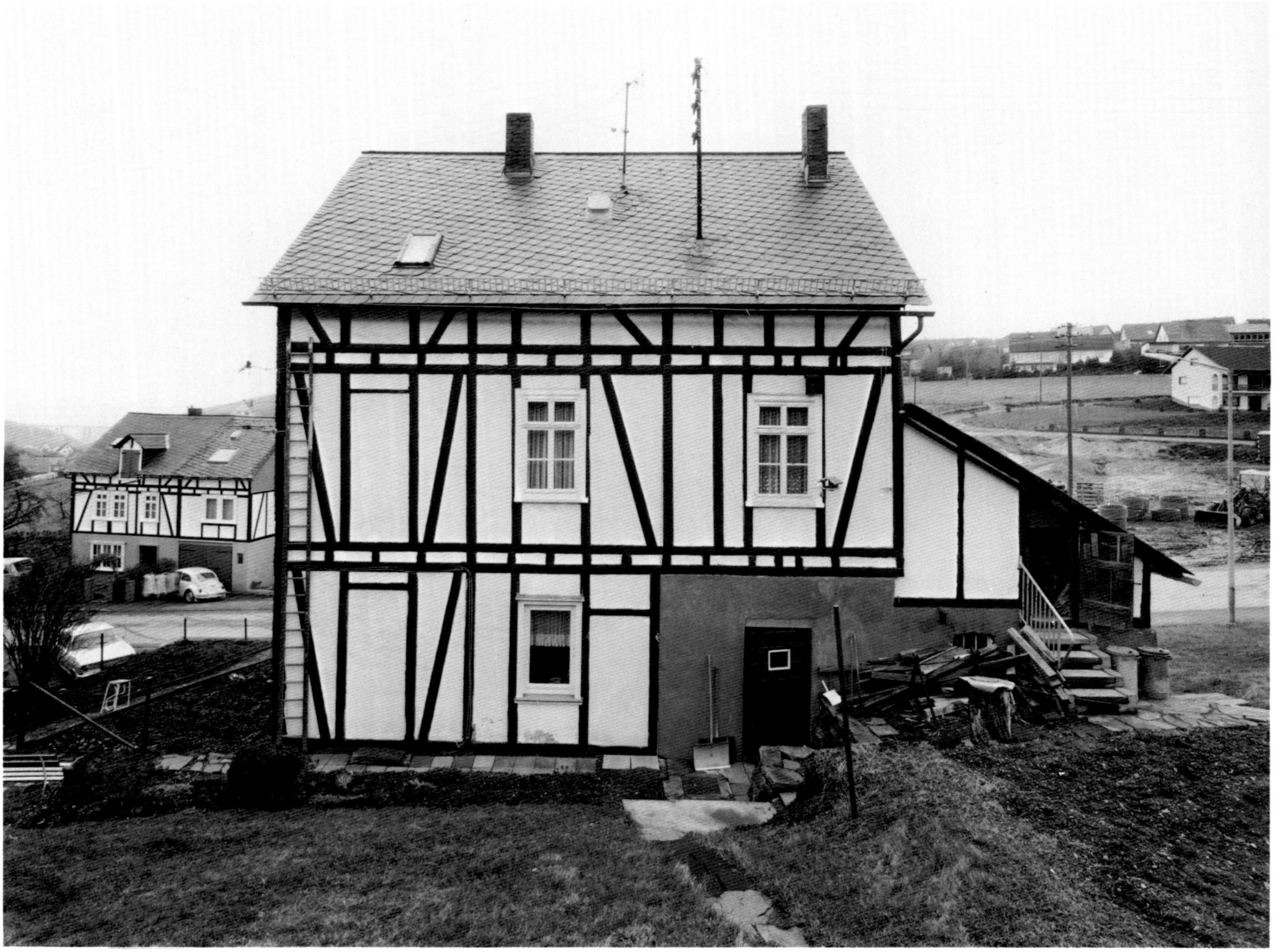

164
Rödgener Straße 62, Obersdorf, 1972.

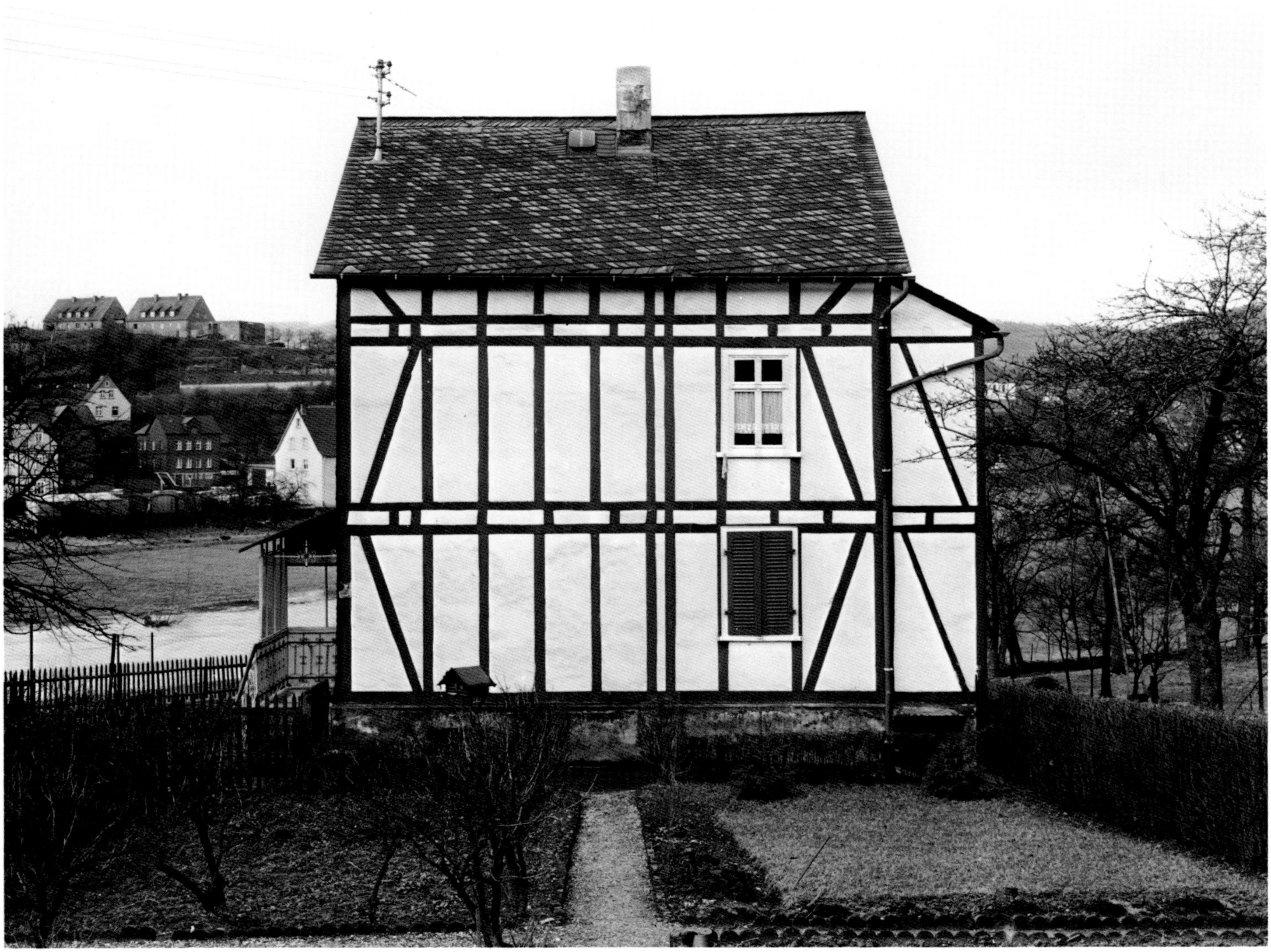

165
Körnerstraße 6, Niederschelden, 1962.

IV.
VERSCHIEFERTE STRASSEN- UND RÜCKSEITEN
SLATED STREET AND REAR SIDES

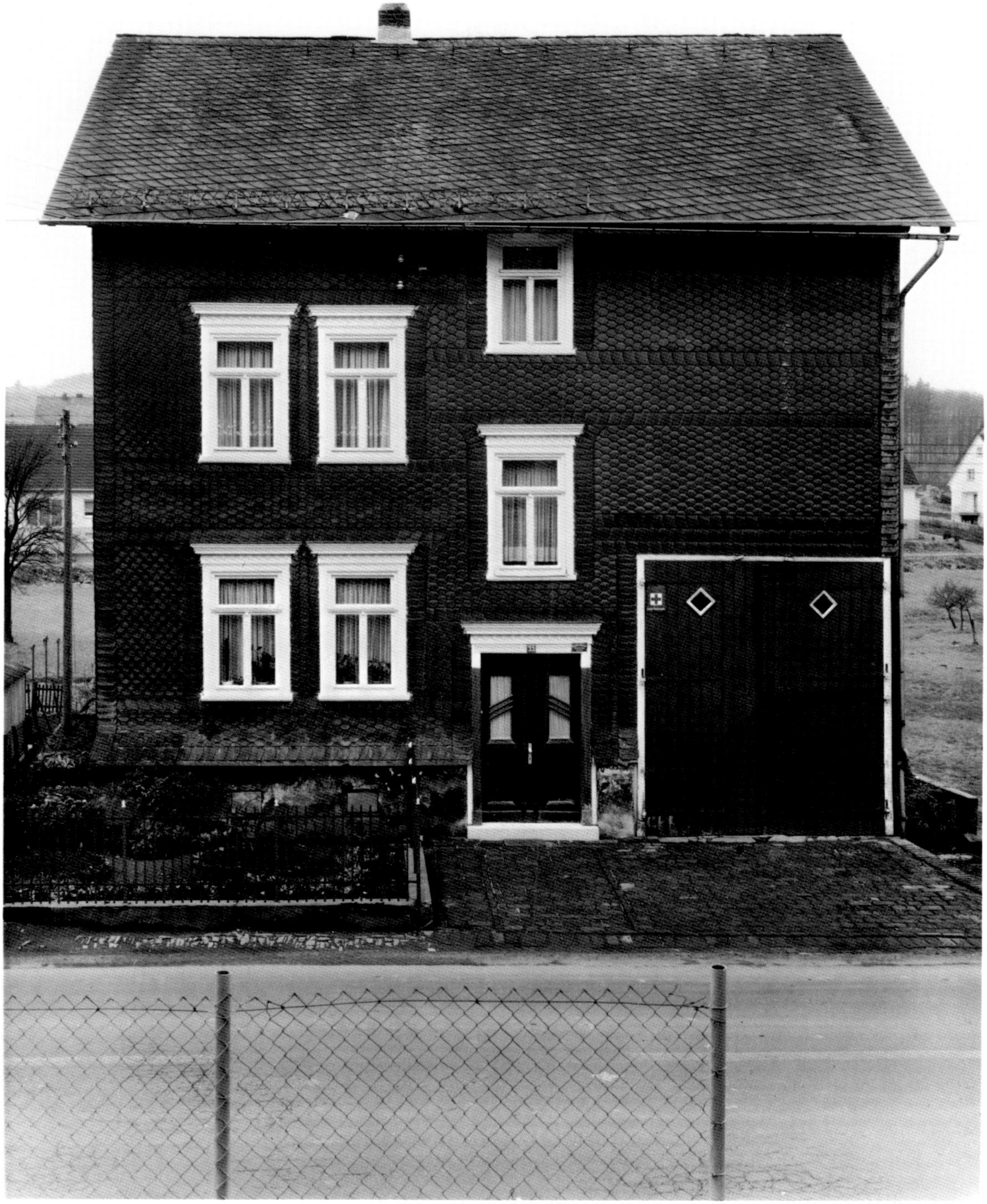

166
Freier Grunder Straße 25, Wilden, 1965.

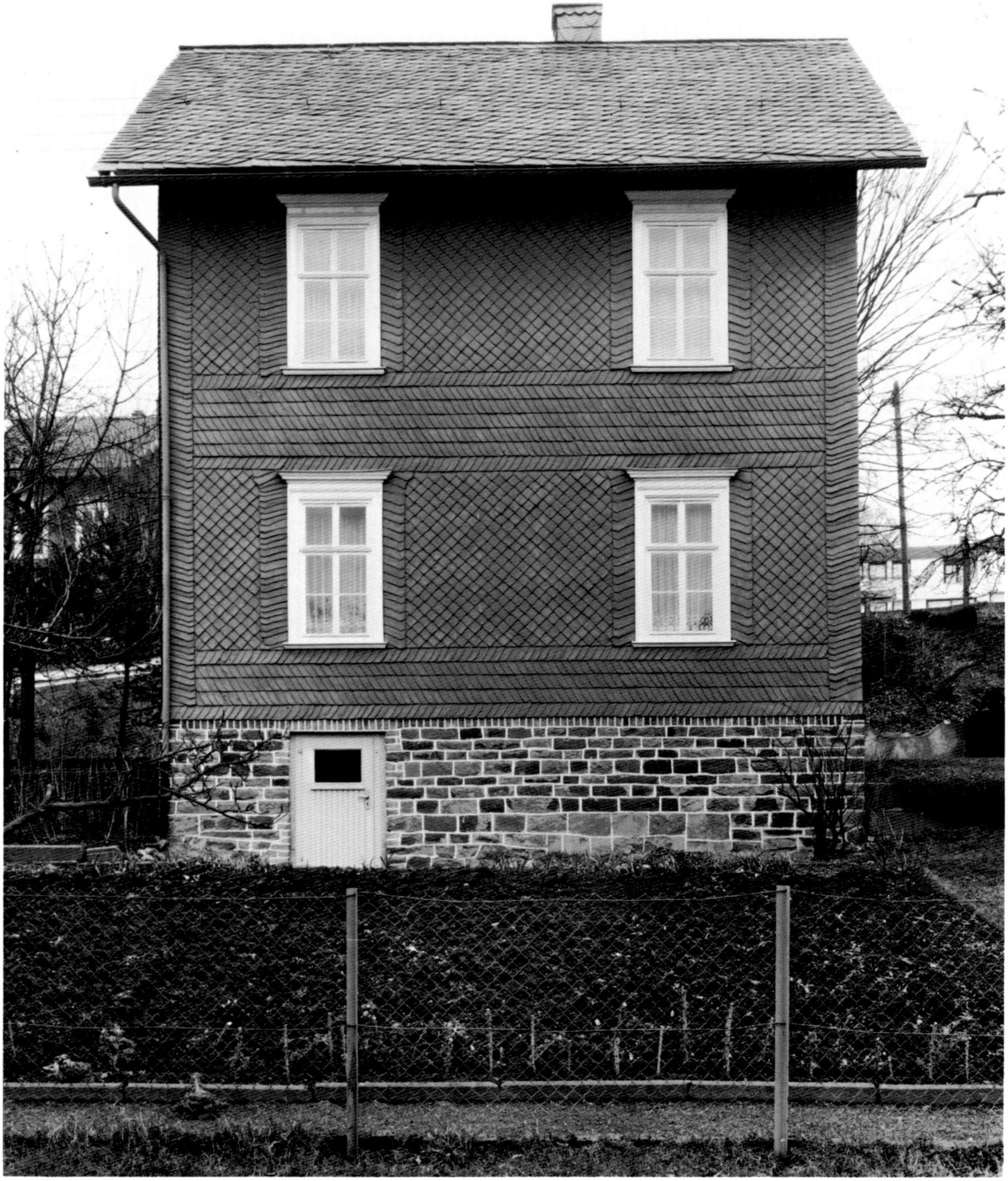

167
Sieben Eichen 1, Allenbach, 1970.

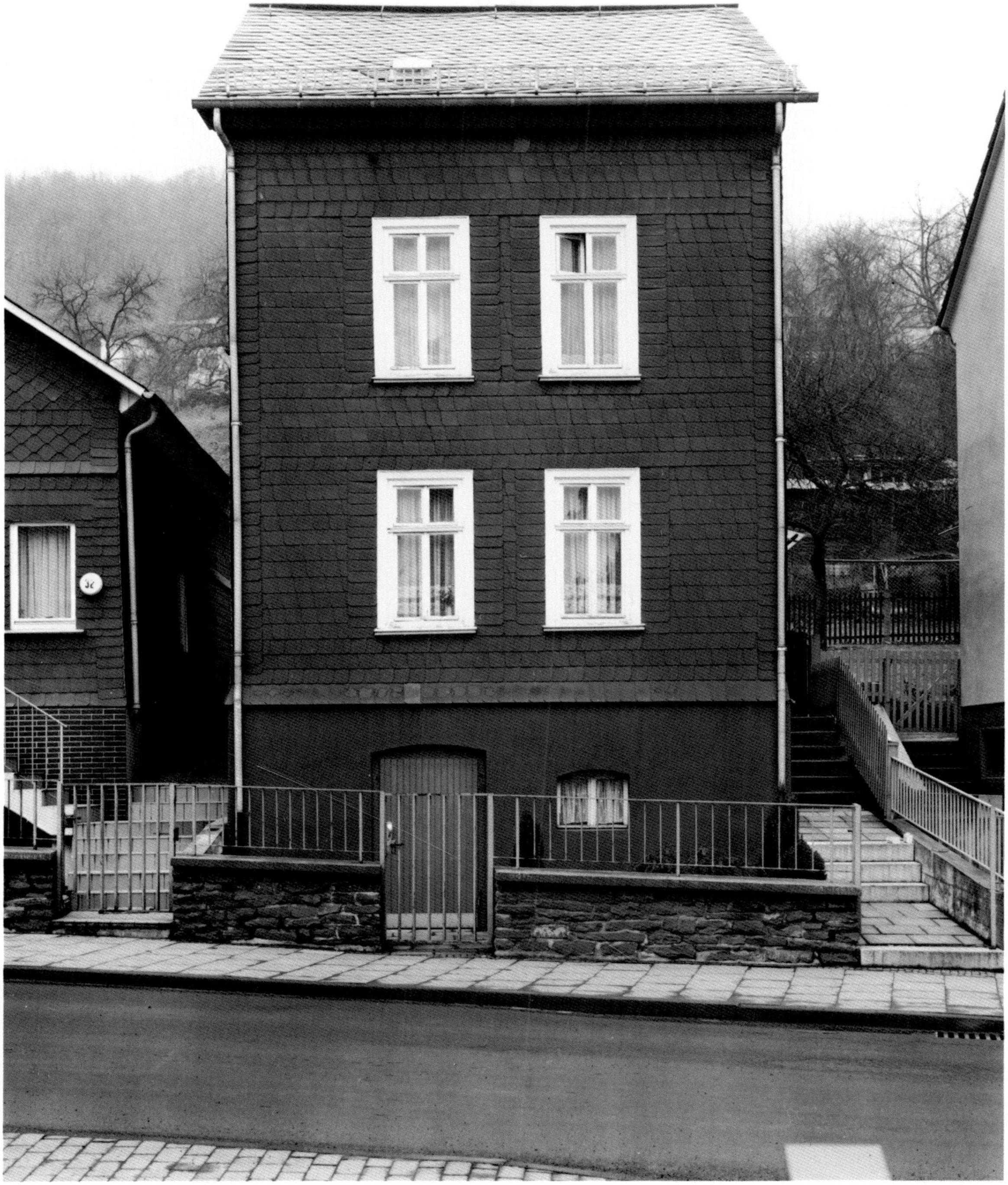

168
Friedrich-Wilhelm-Straße 30, Siegen, 1972.

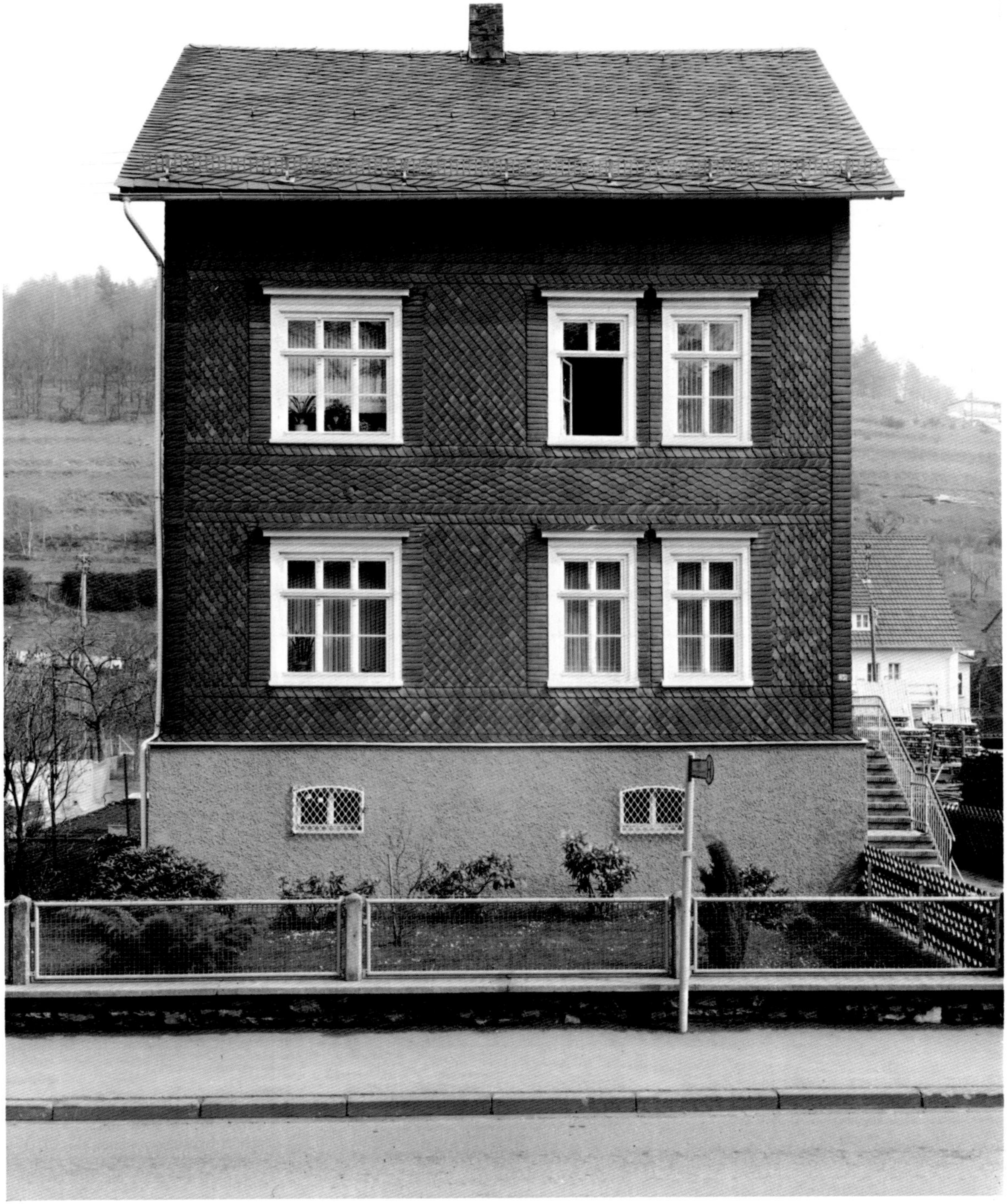

169
Eiserntalstraße 65, Eisern, 1969.

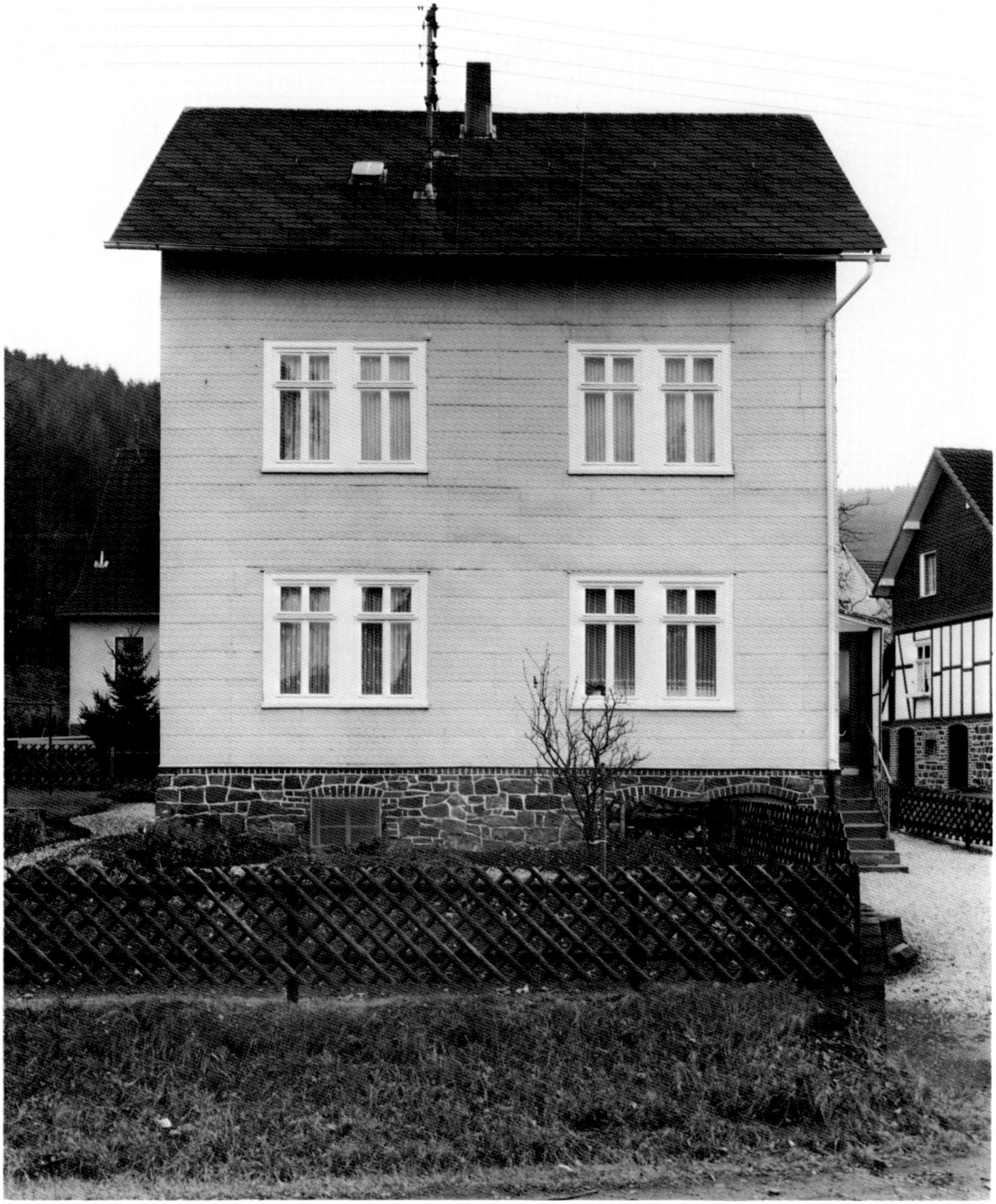

170
Hillnhütter Straße 62, Dahlbruch, 1971.

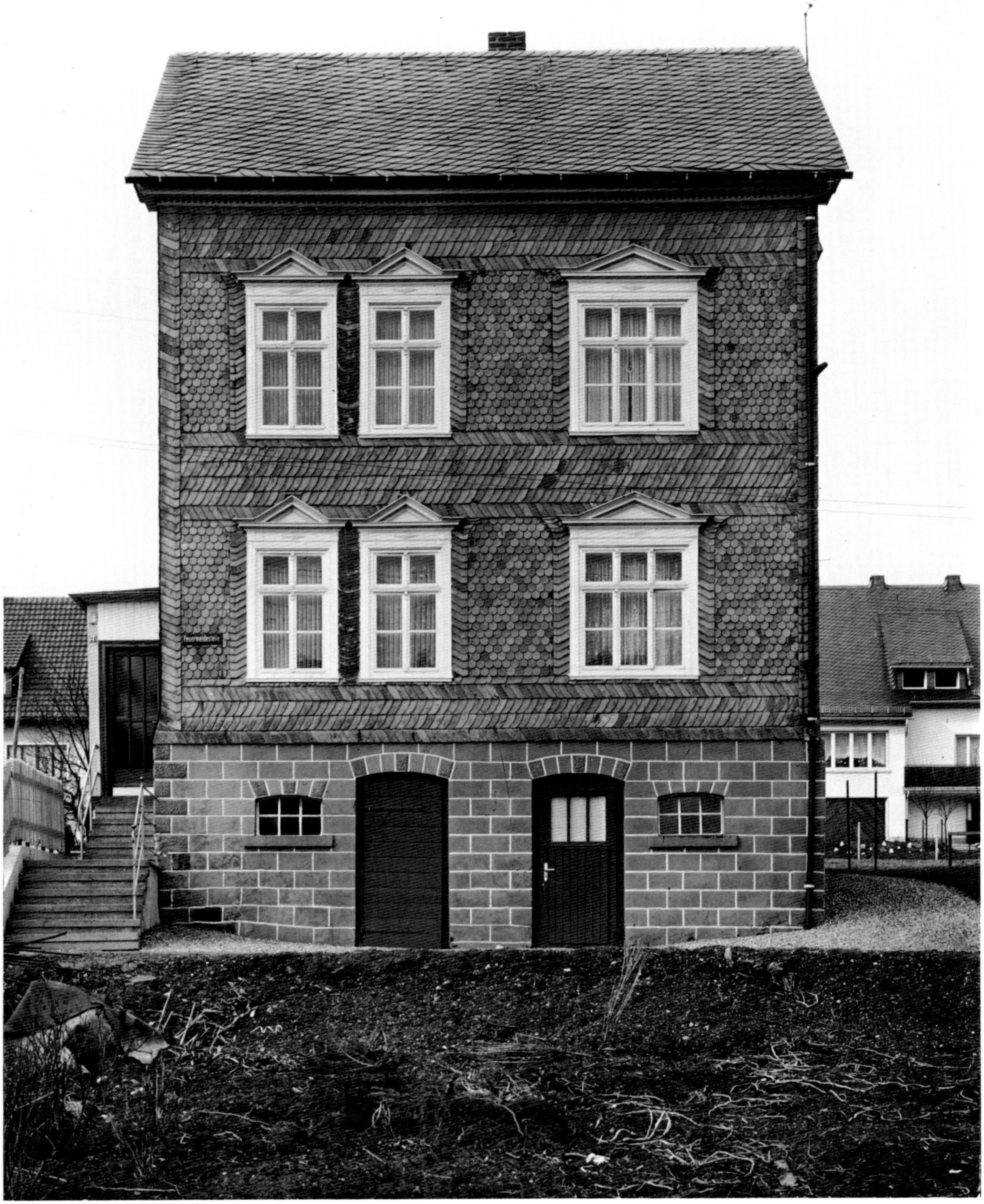

171
Wildener Straße 25, Salchendorf, 1962.

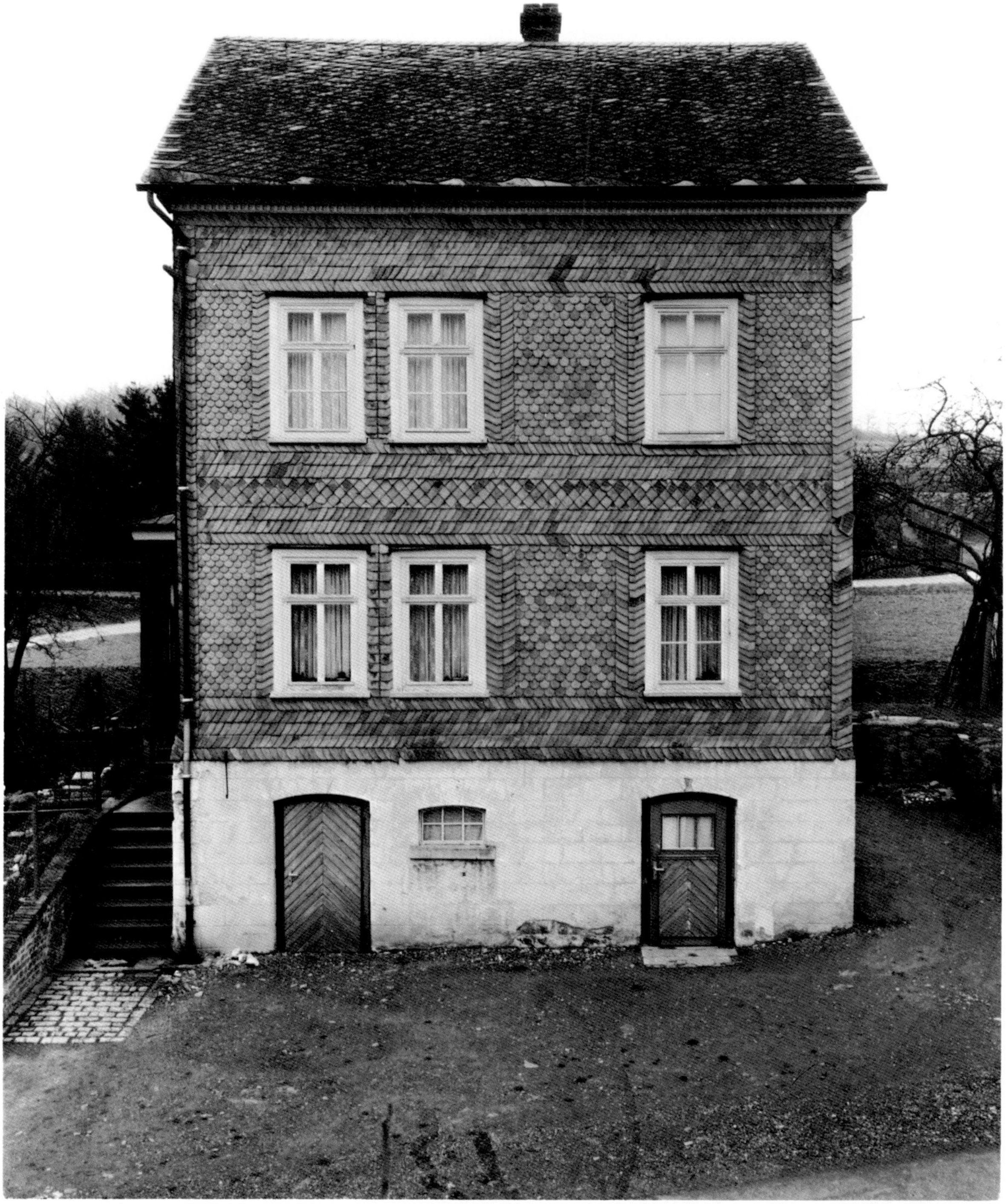

172
Rensdorfstraße 13, Salchendorf, 1960.

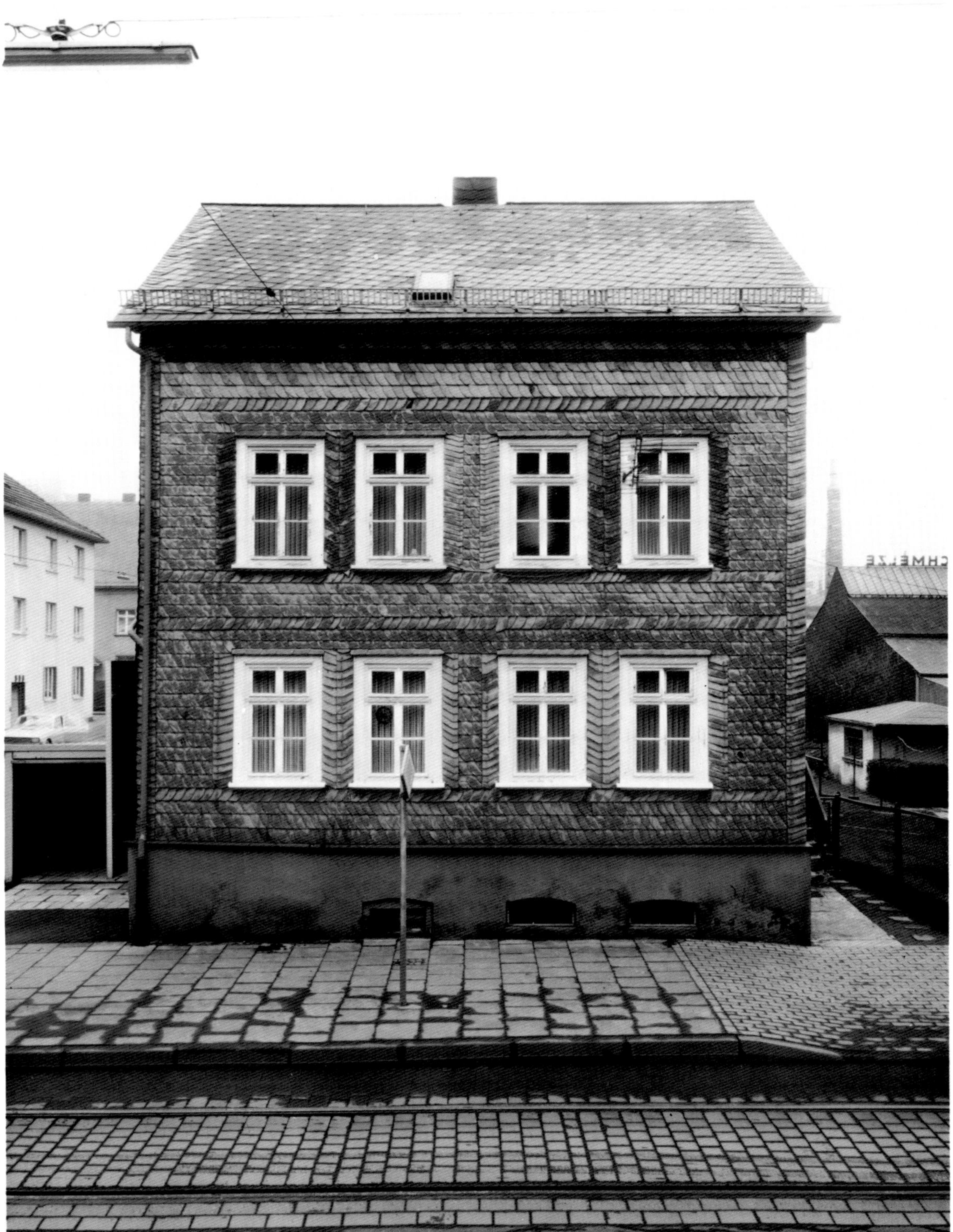

173
Marienborner Straße 237, Siegen, 1968.

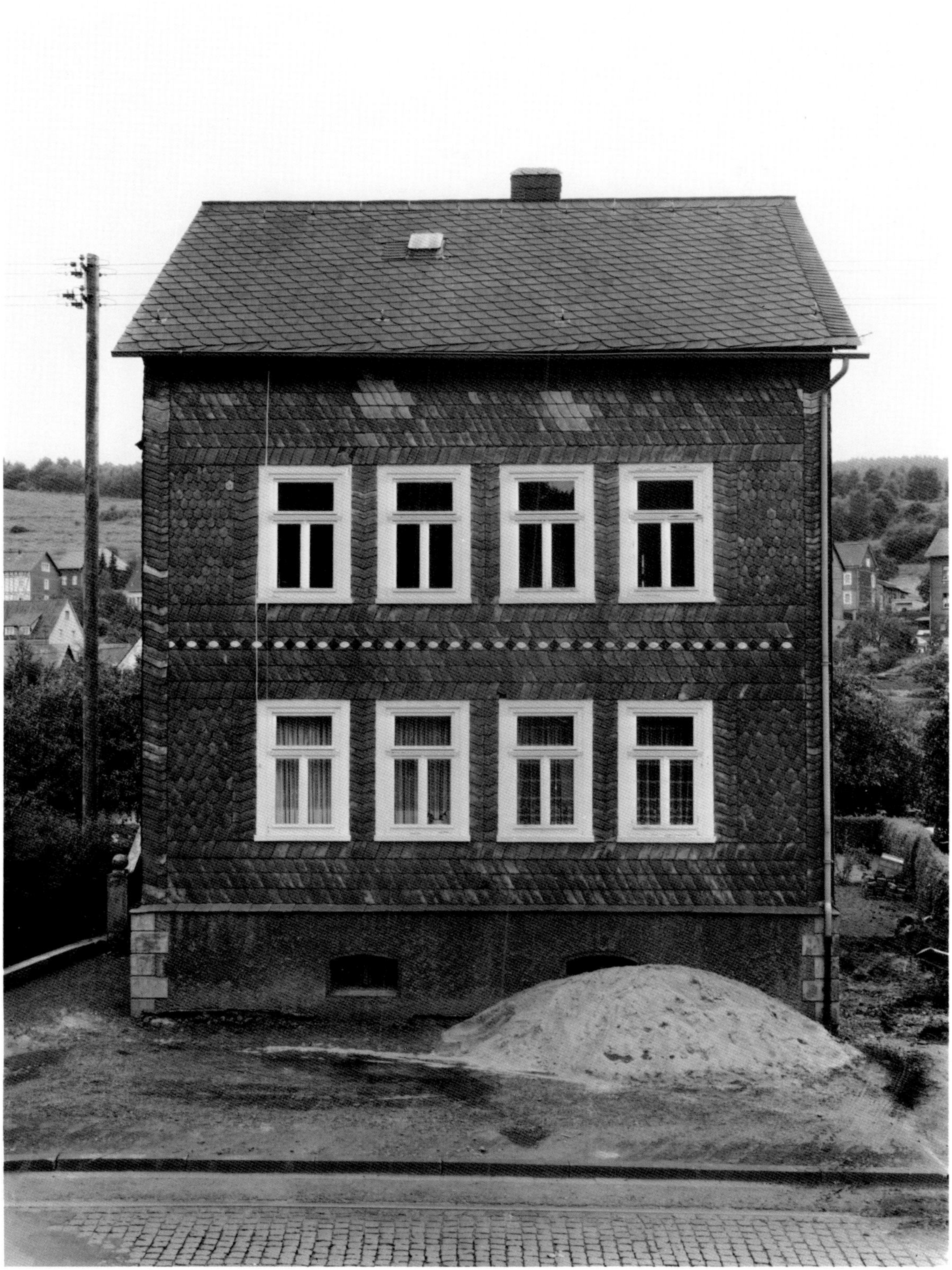

174
Eisernstraße 130, Eiserfeld, 1964.

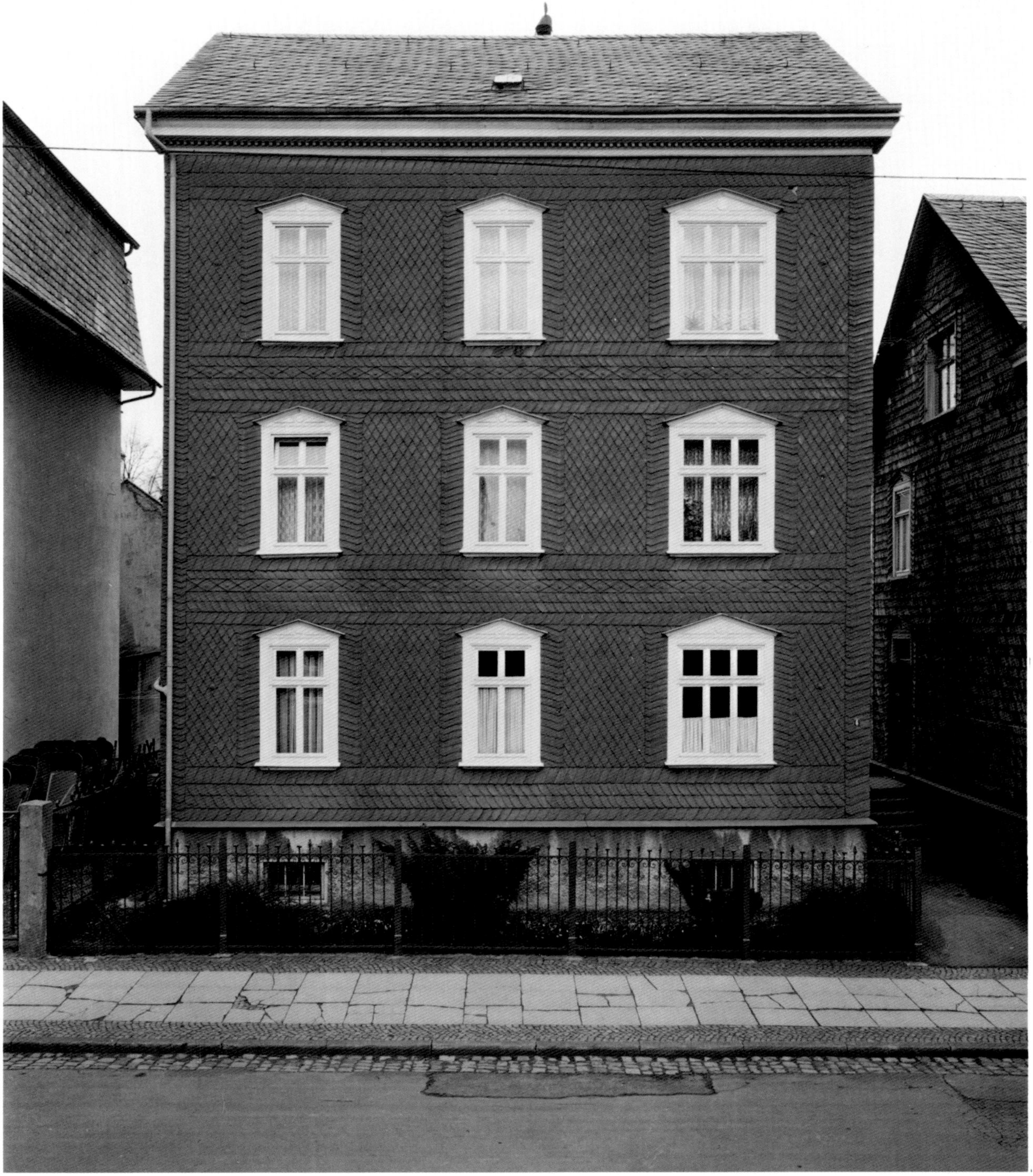

175
Arndtstraße 6, Siegen, 1962.

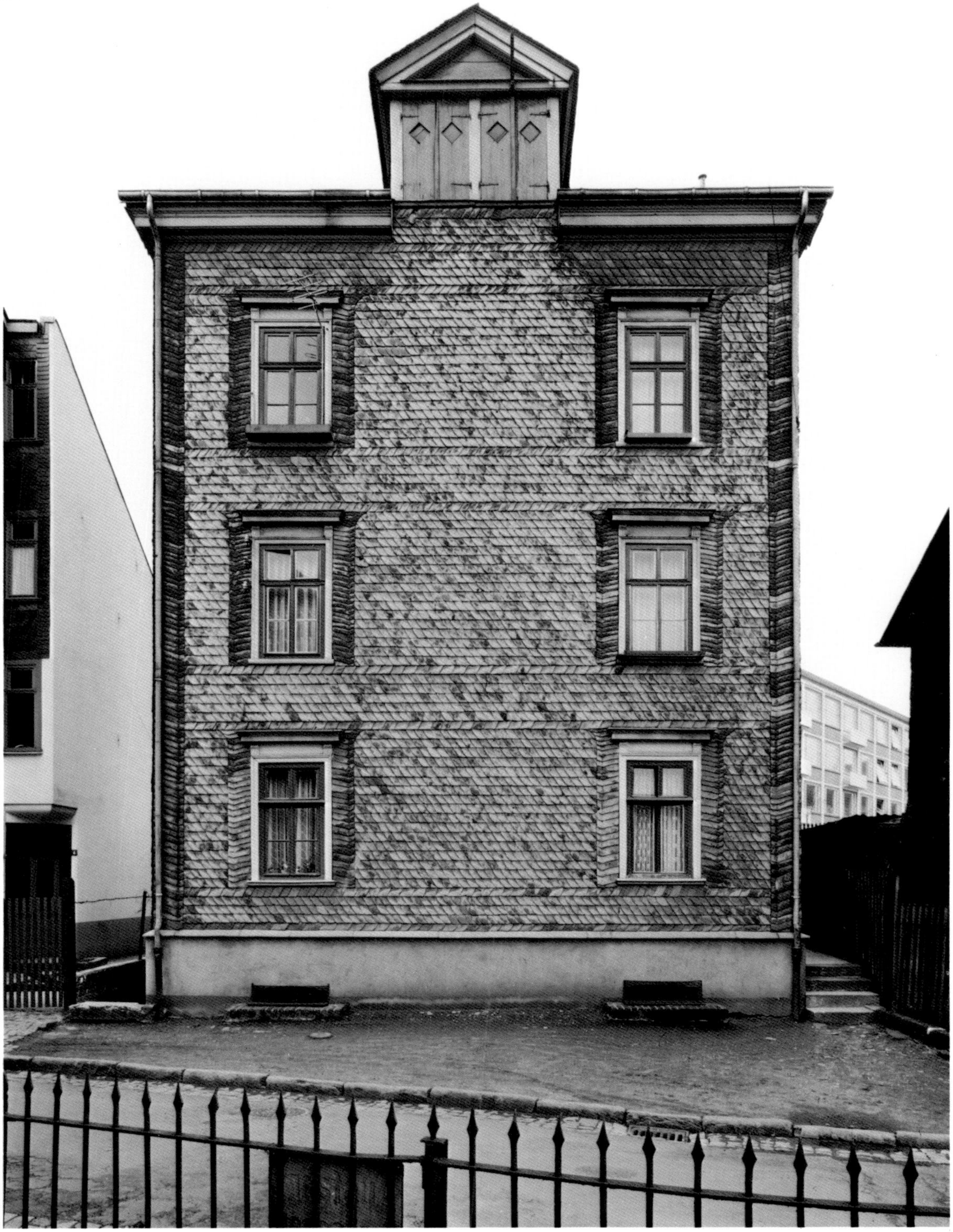

176
Fischbacherbergstraße 9, Siegen, 1962.

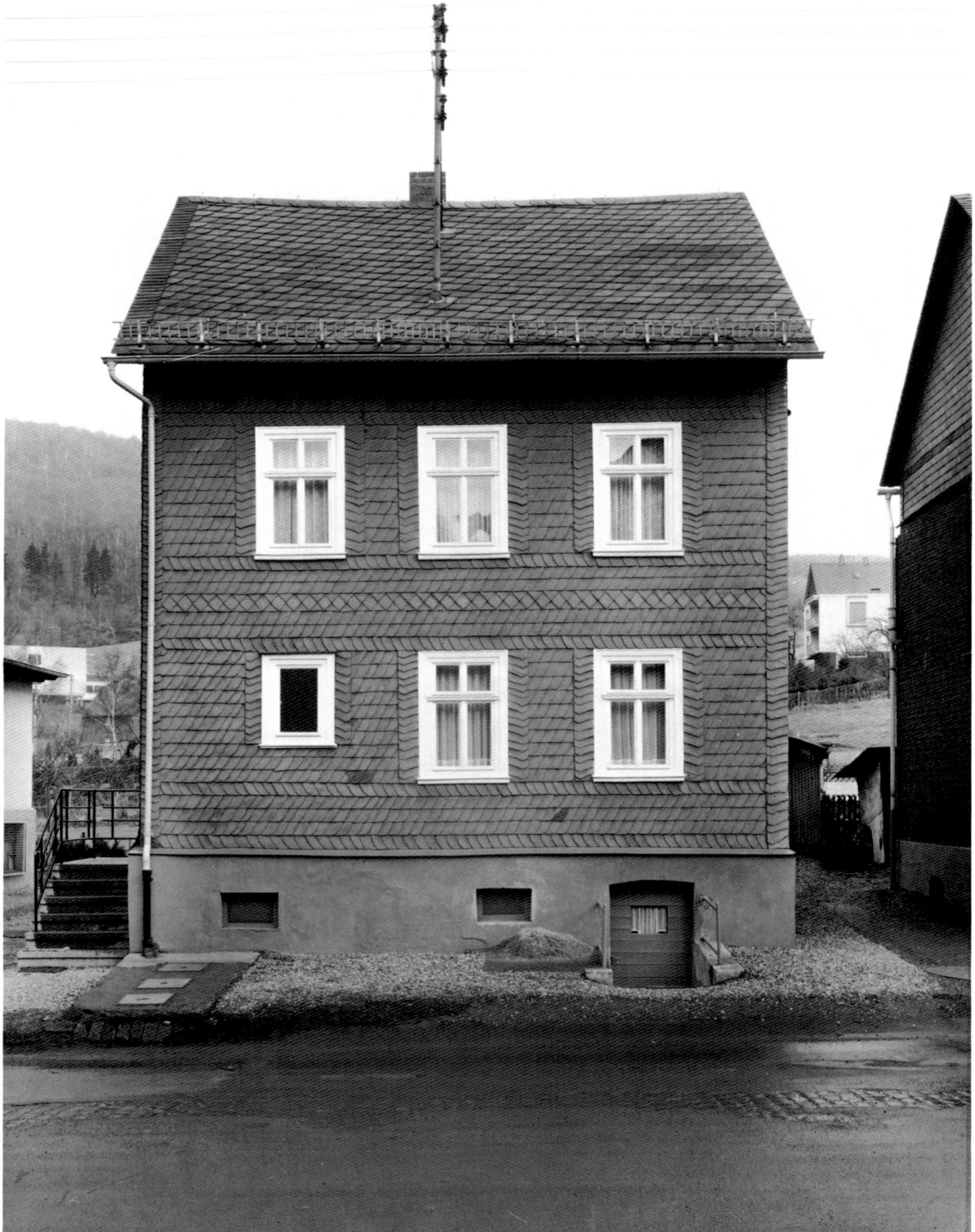

177
Eisernstraße 117, Eiserfeld, 1971.

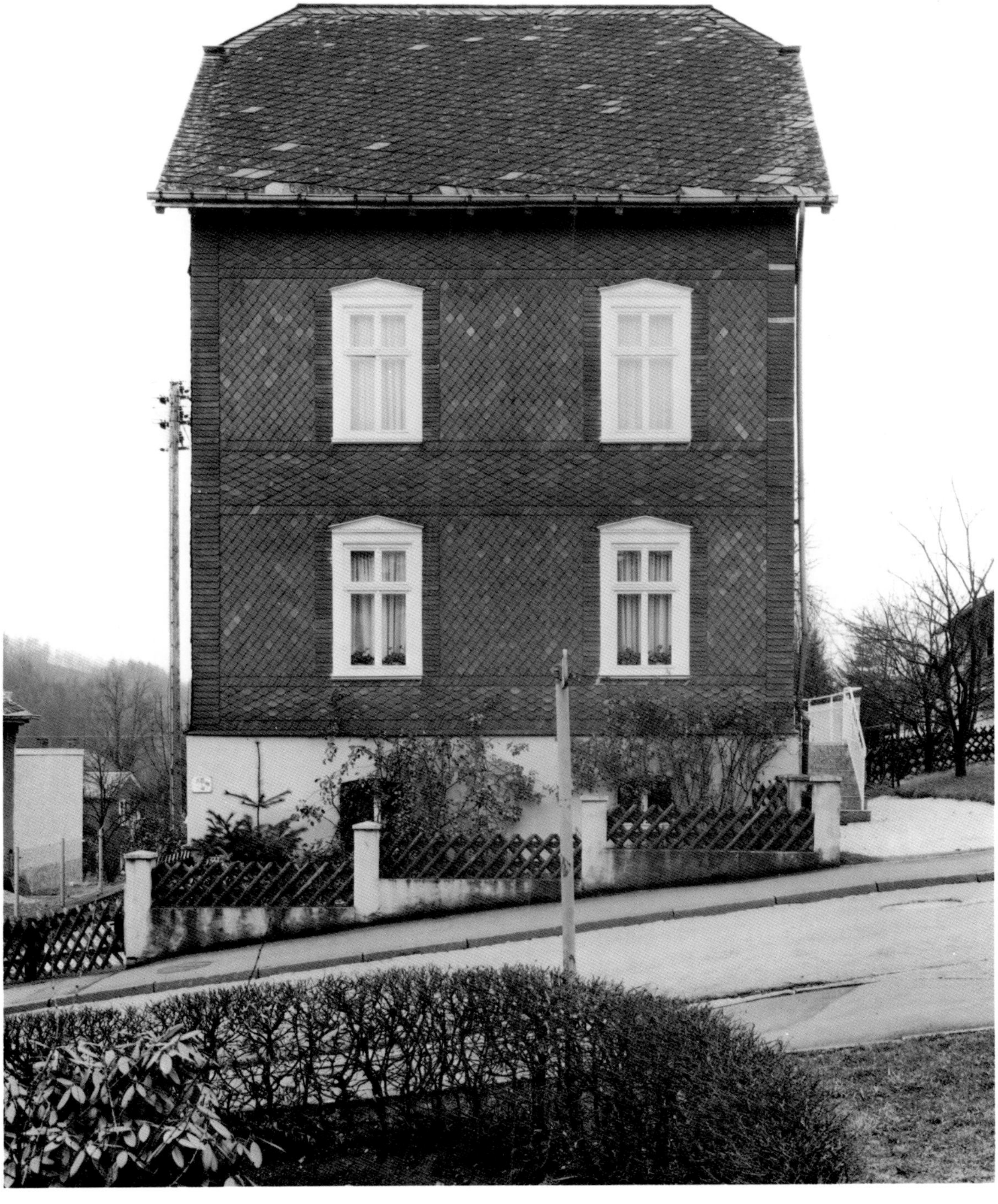

178
Schloßblick 17, Kaan-Marienborn, 1972.

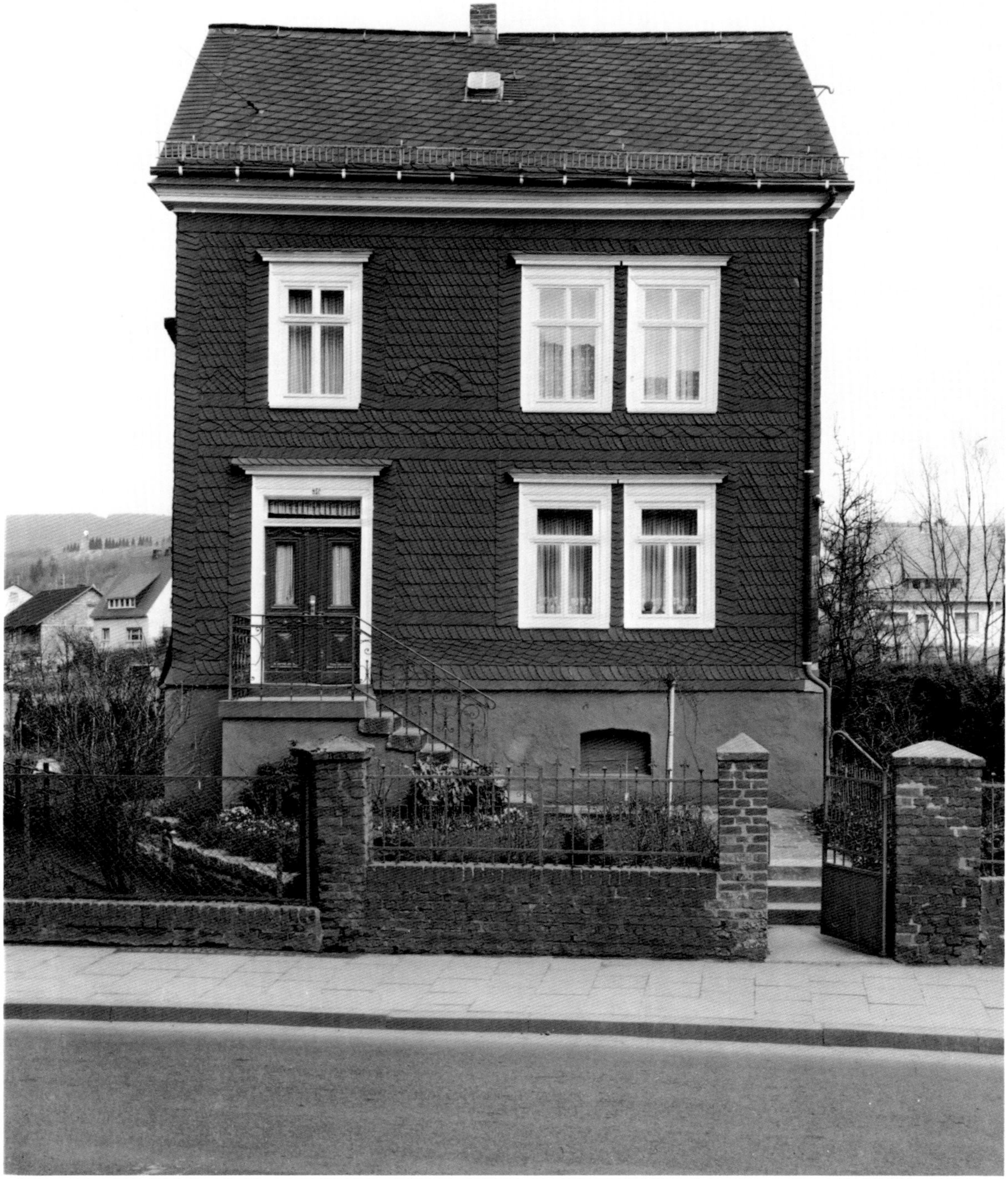

179
Siegtalstraße 36, Eiserfeld, 1971.

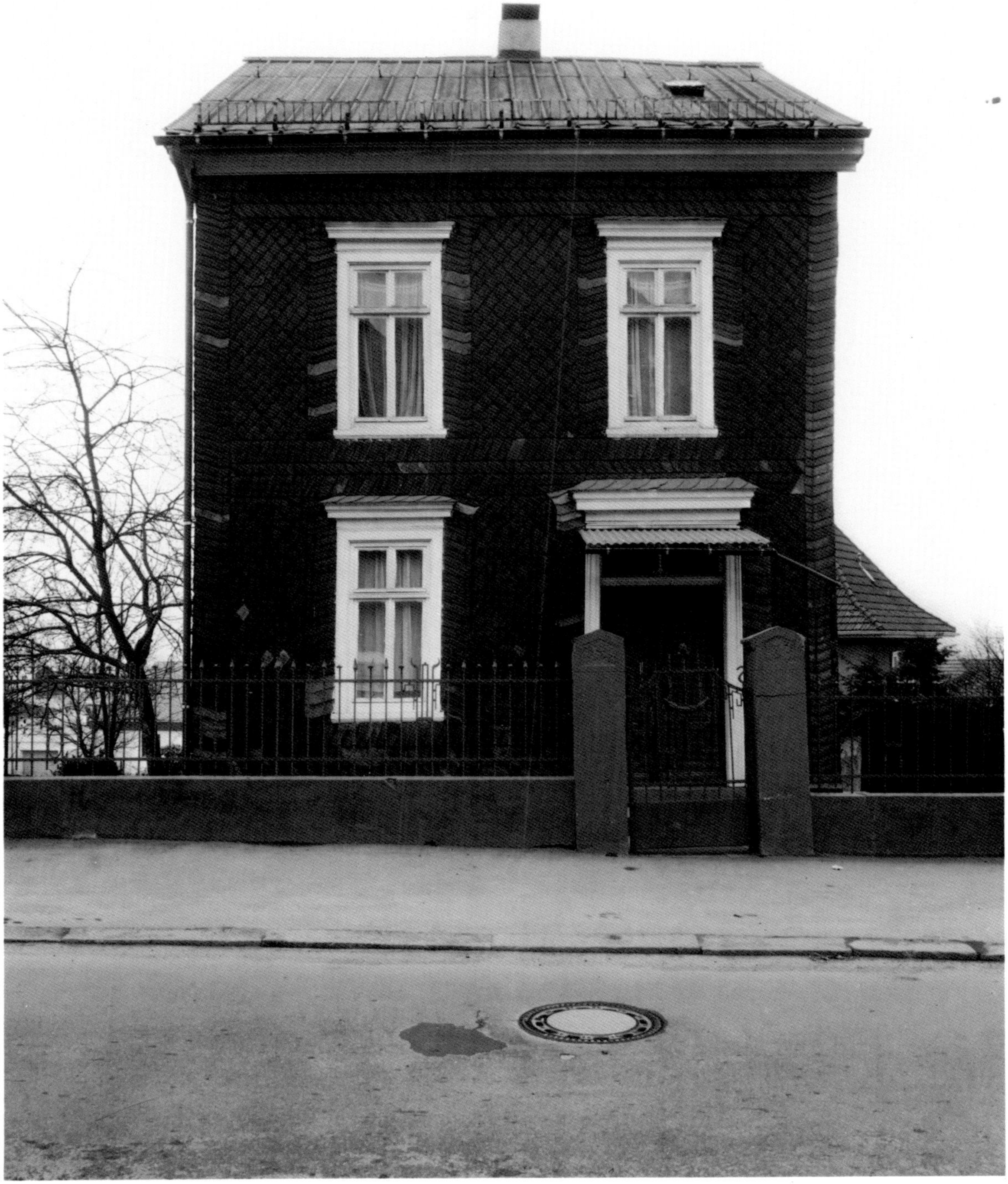

180
Hohler Weg 45, Siegen, 1970.

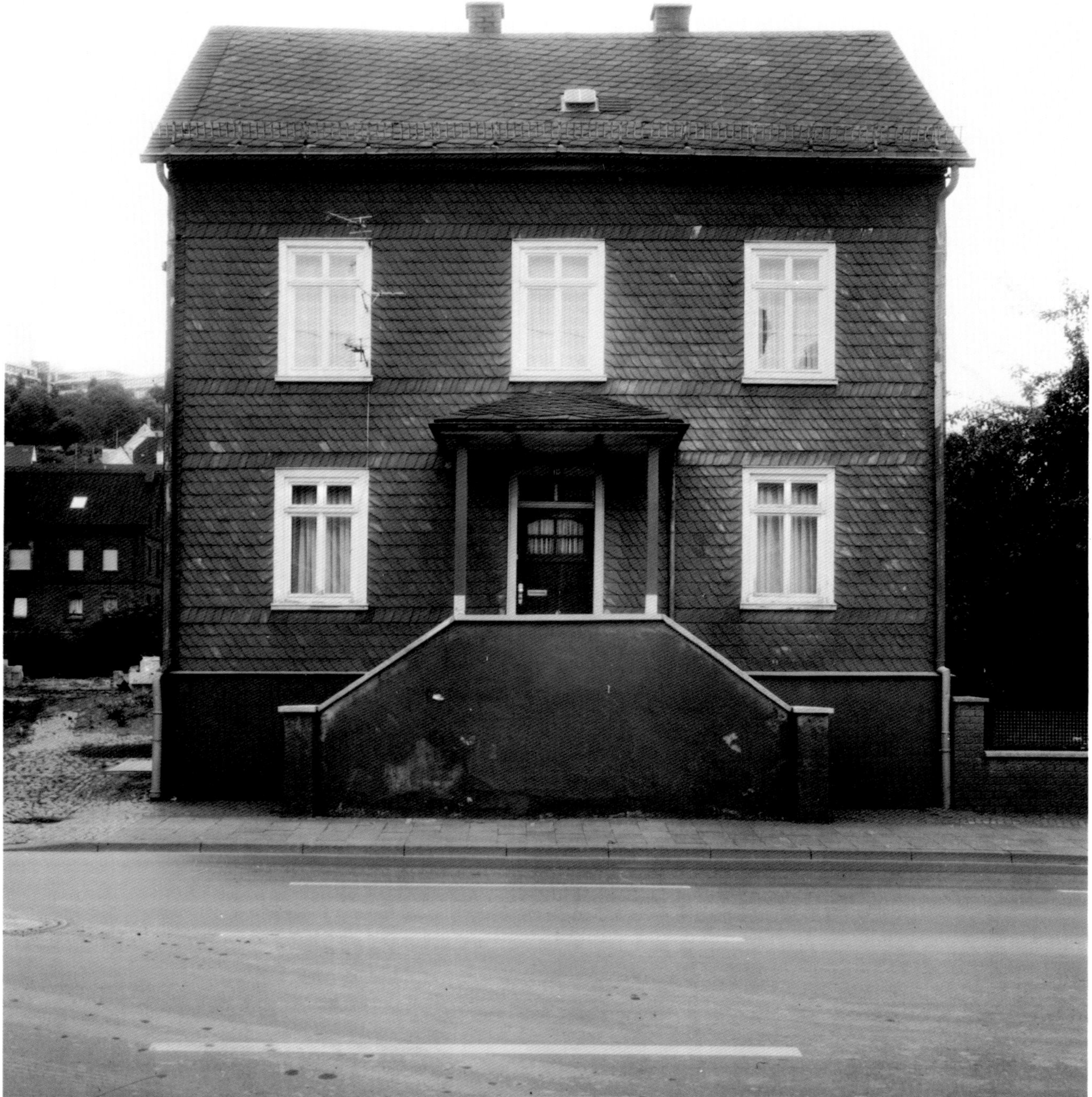

181
Weidenauer Straße 115, Weidenau, 1971.

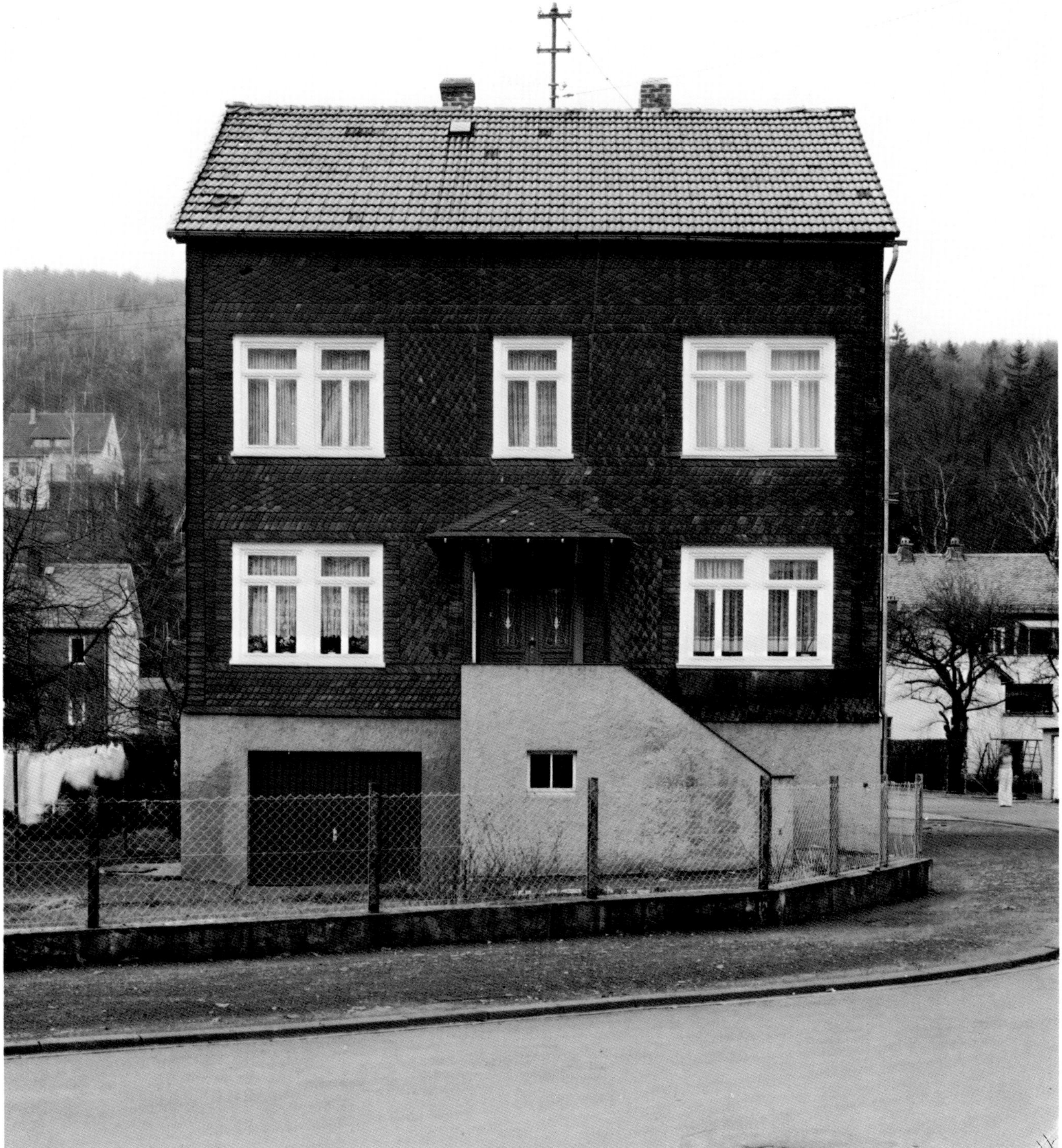

182

In der Trift 8, Neunkirchen, 1959.

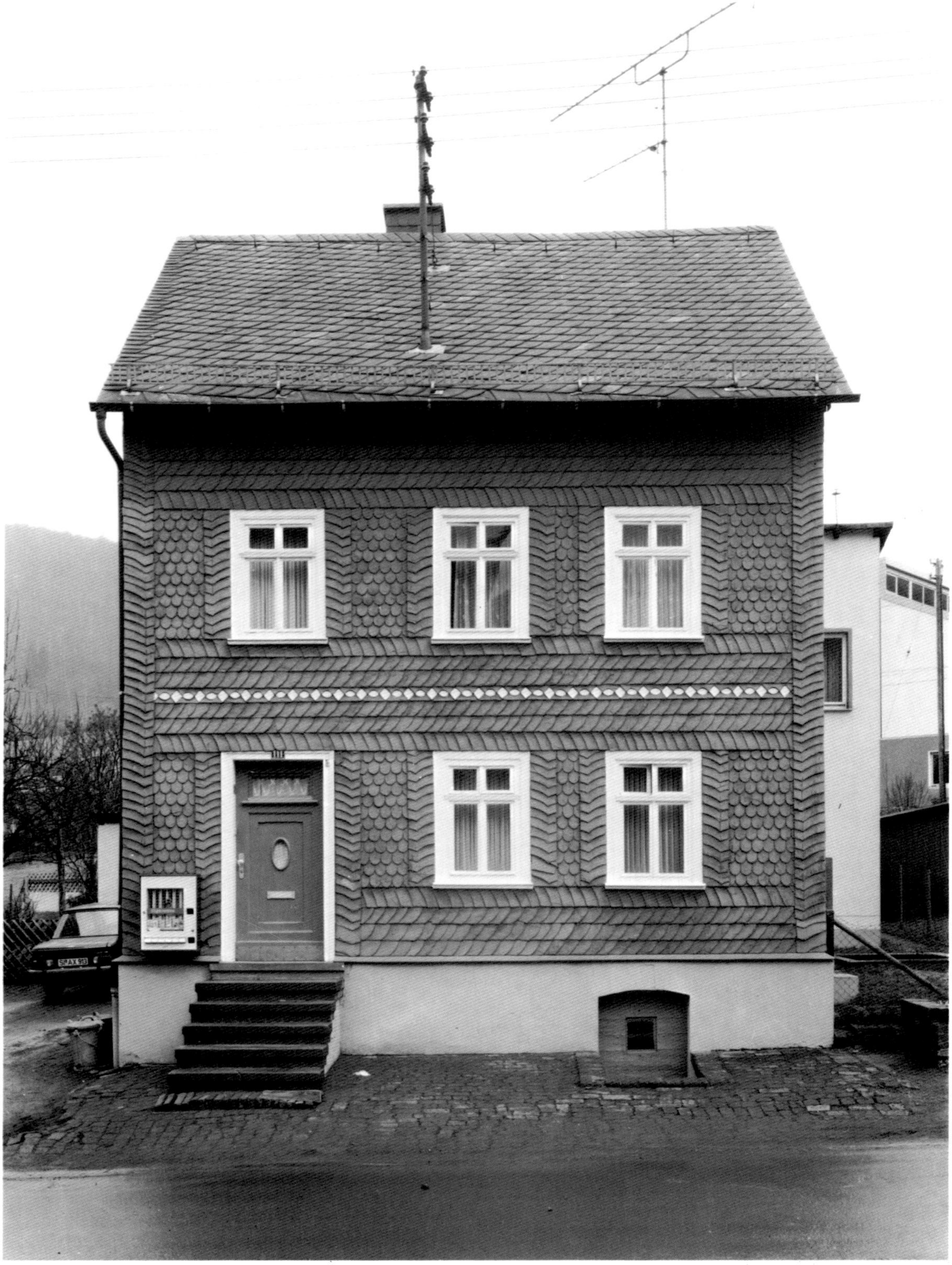

183
Eisernstraße 121, Eiserfeld, 1971.

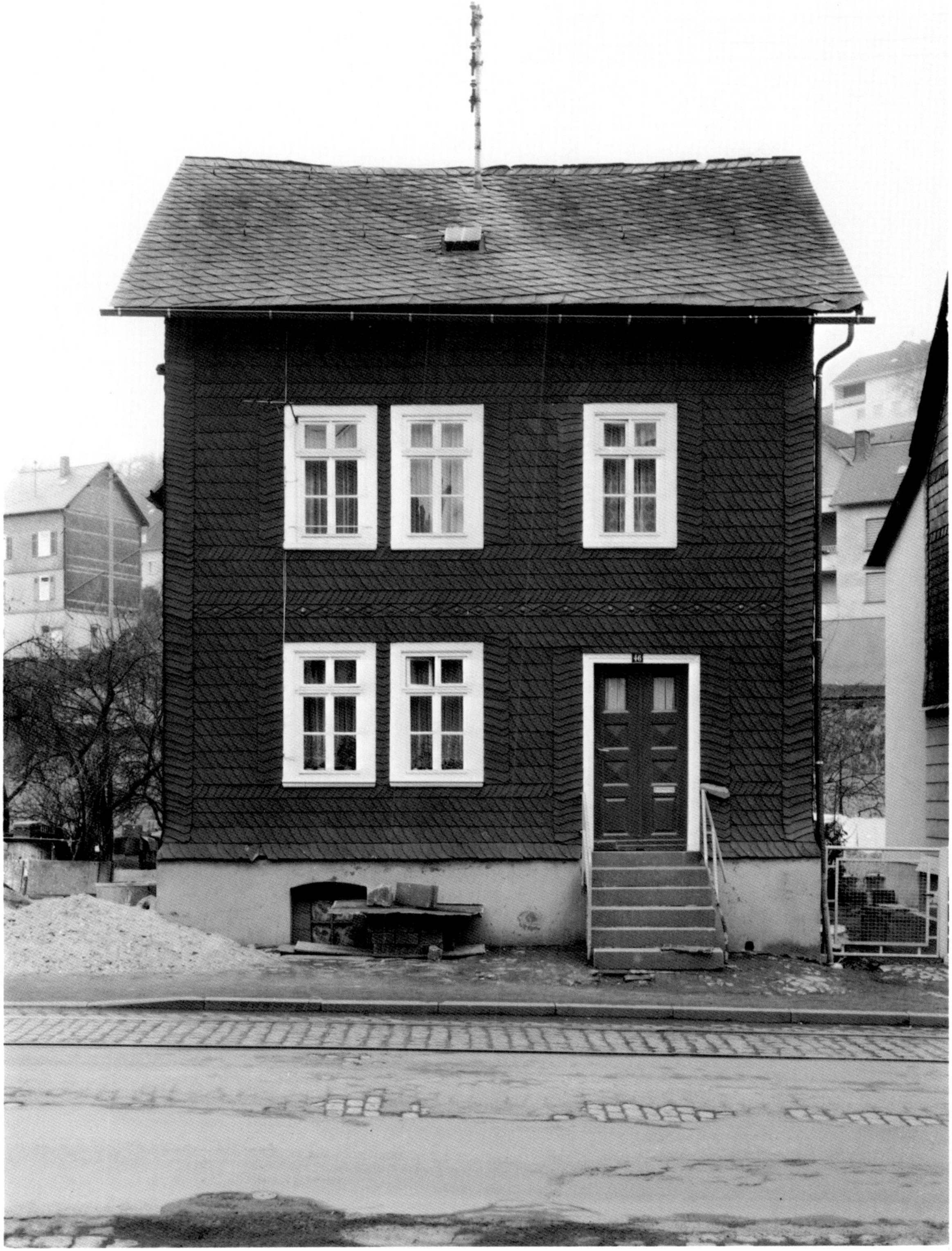

184
Eisernstraße 120, Eiserfeld, 1961.

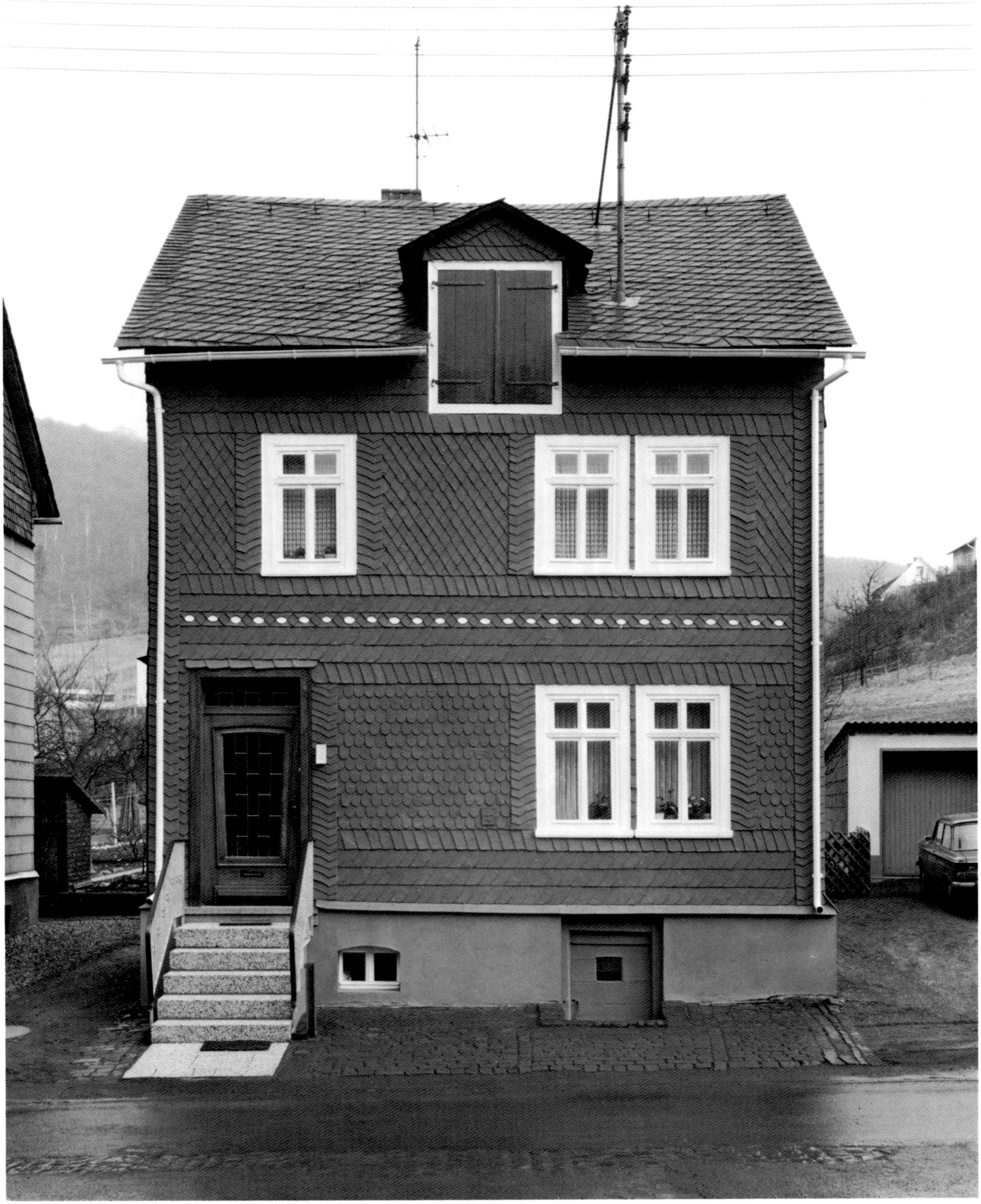

185
Eisernstraße 119, Eiserfeld, 1970.

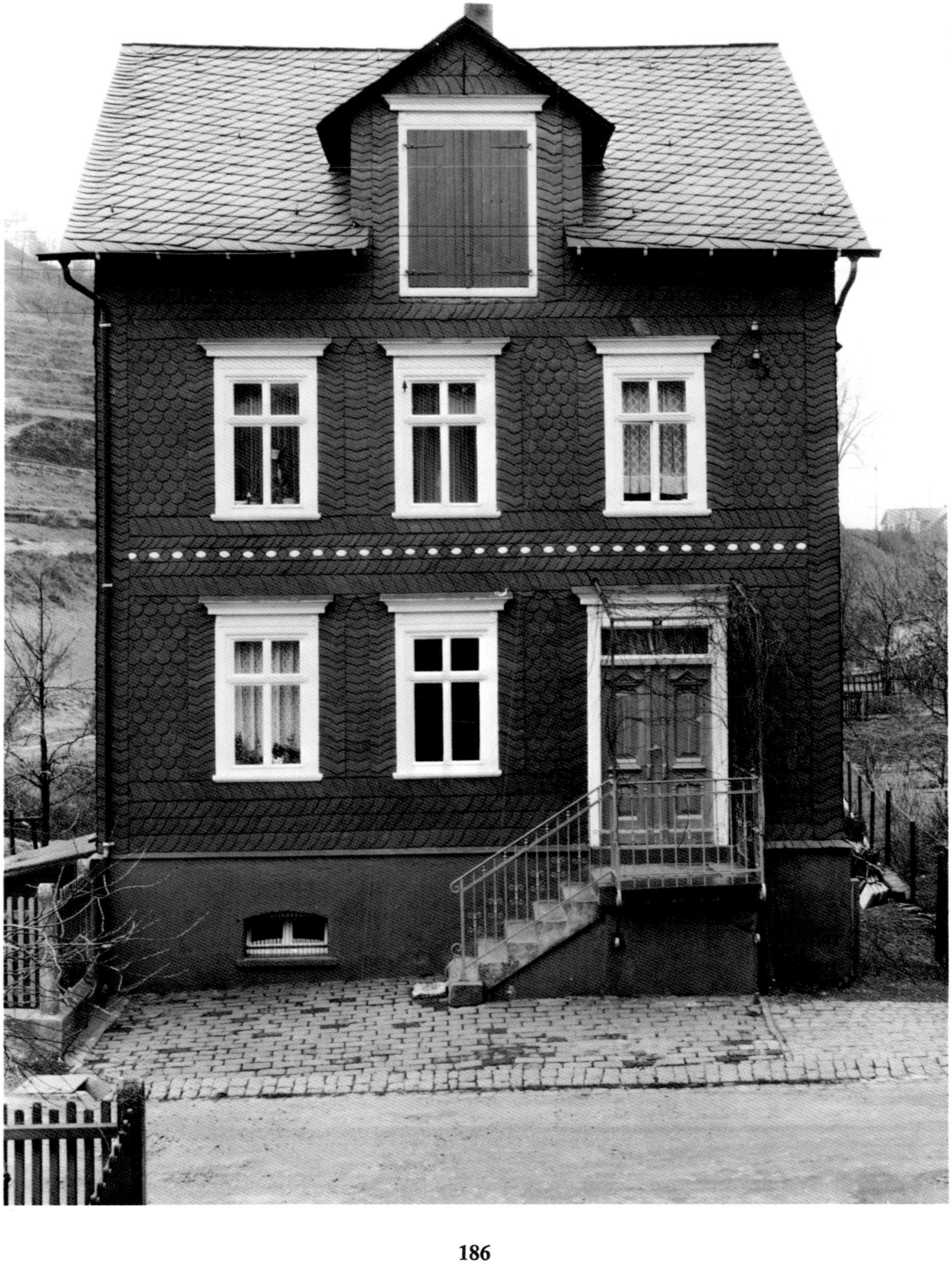

186
Hüttenstraße 6, Eiserfeld, 1960.

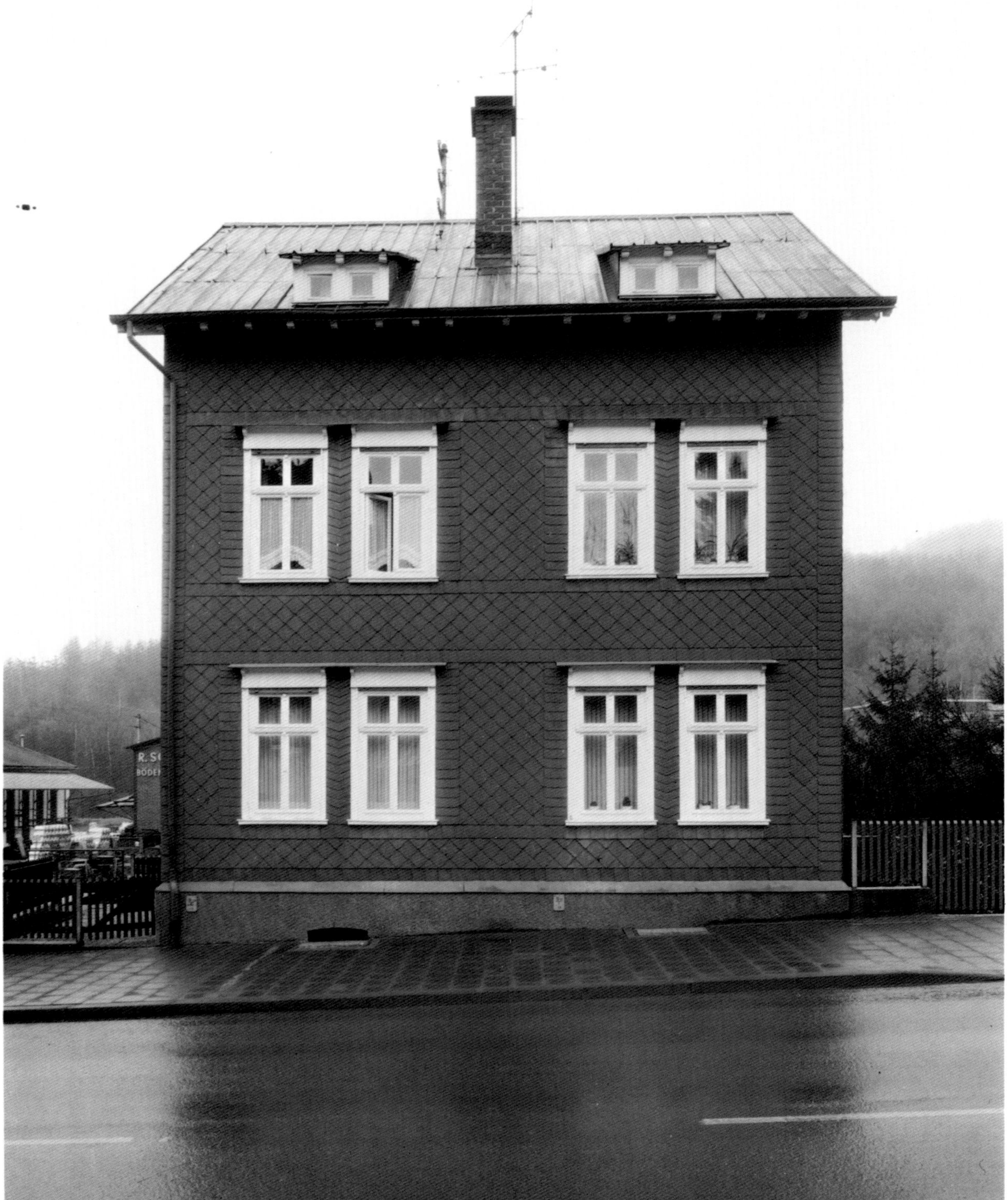

187

Birlenbacher Straße 92, Geisweid, 1969.

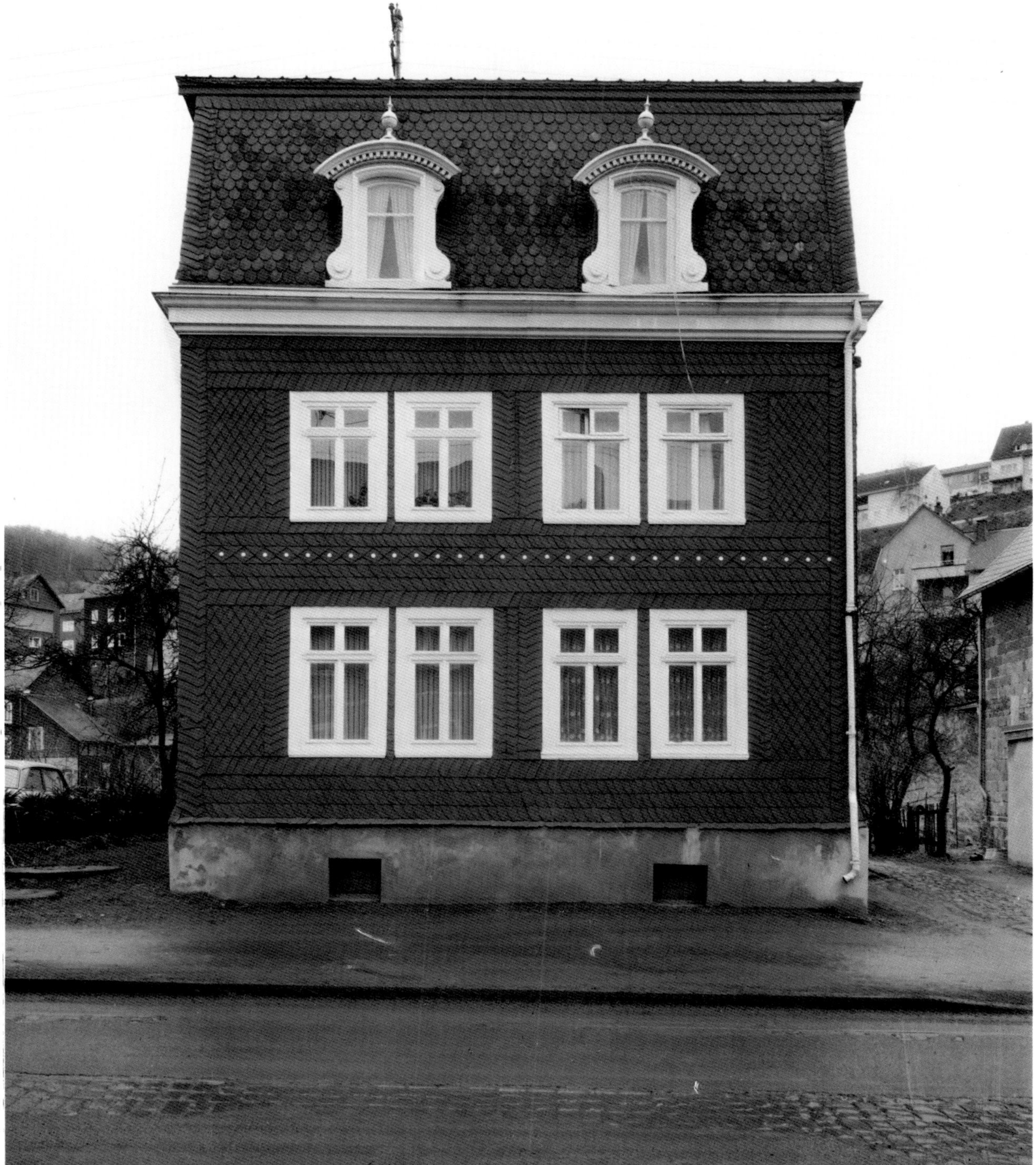

188
Eisernstraße 122, Eiserfeld, 1968.

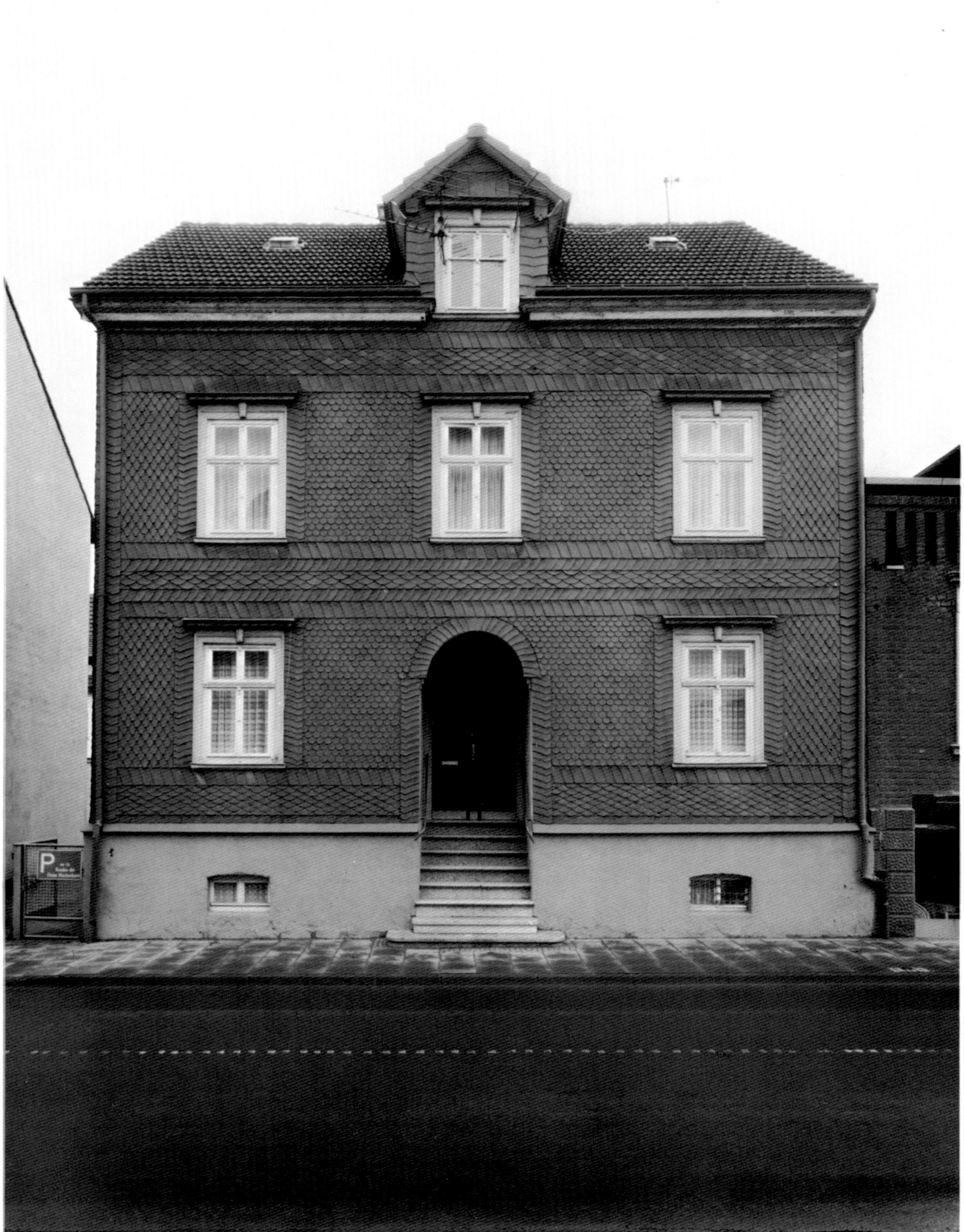

189

Marktstraße 32, Geisweid, 1969.

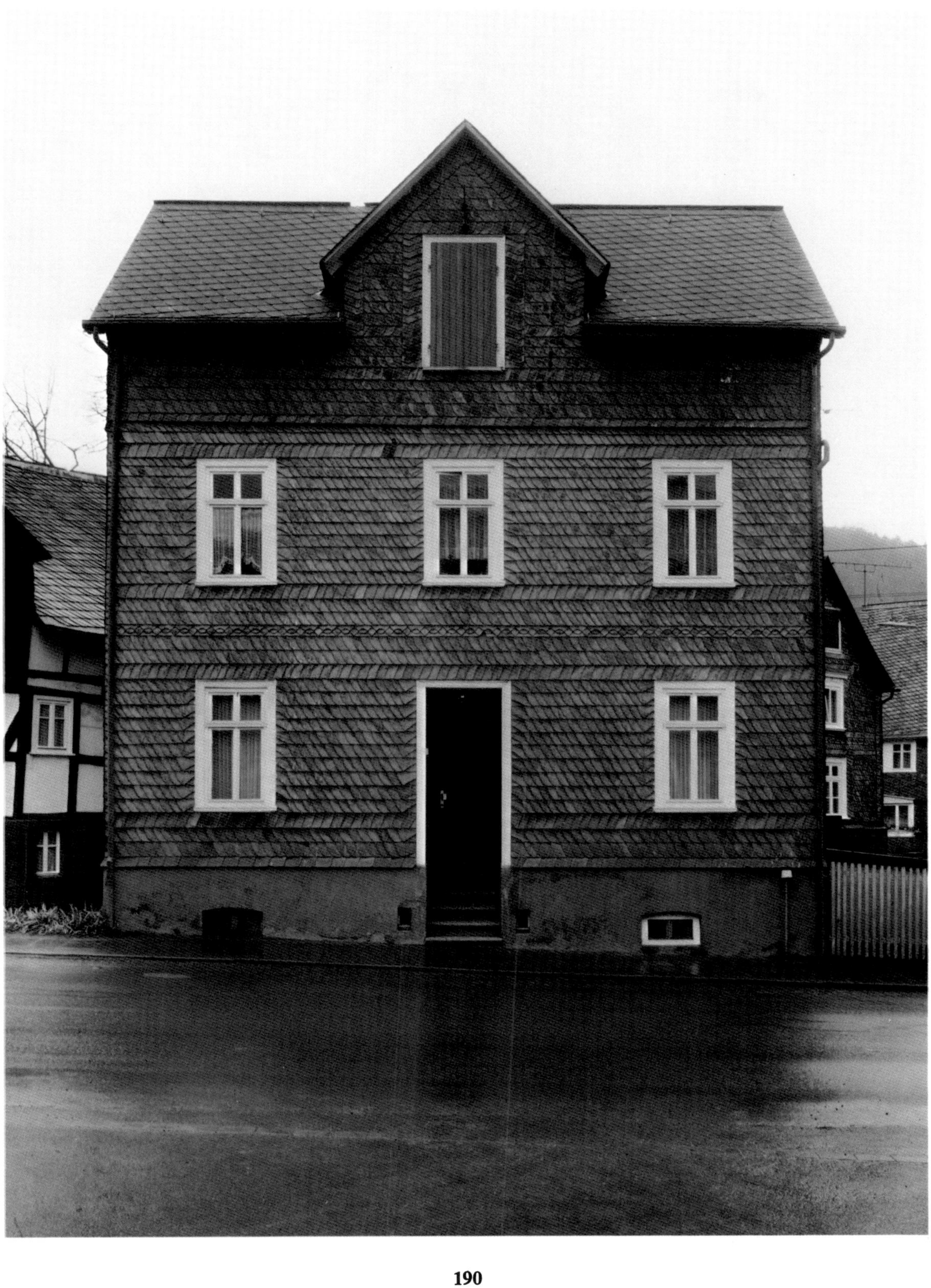

190
Freiengründerstraße 4, Eiserfeld, 1962.

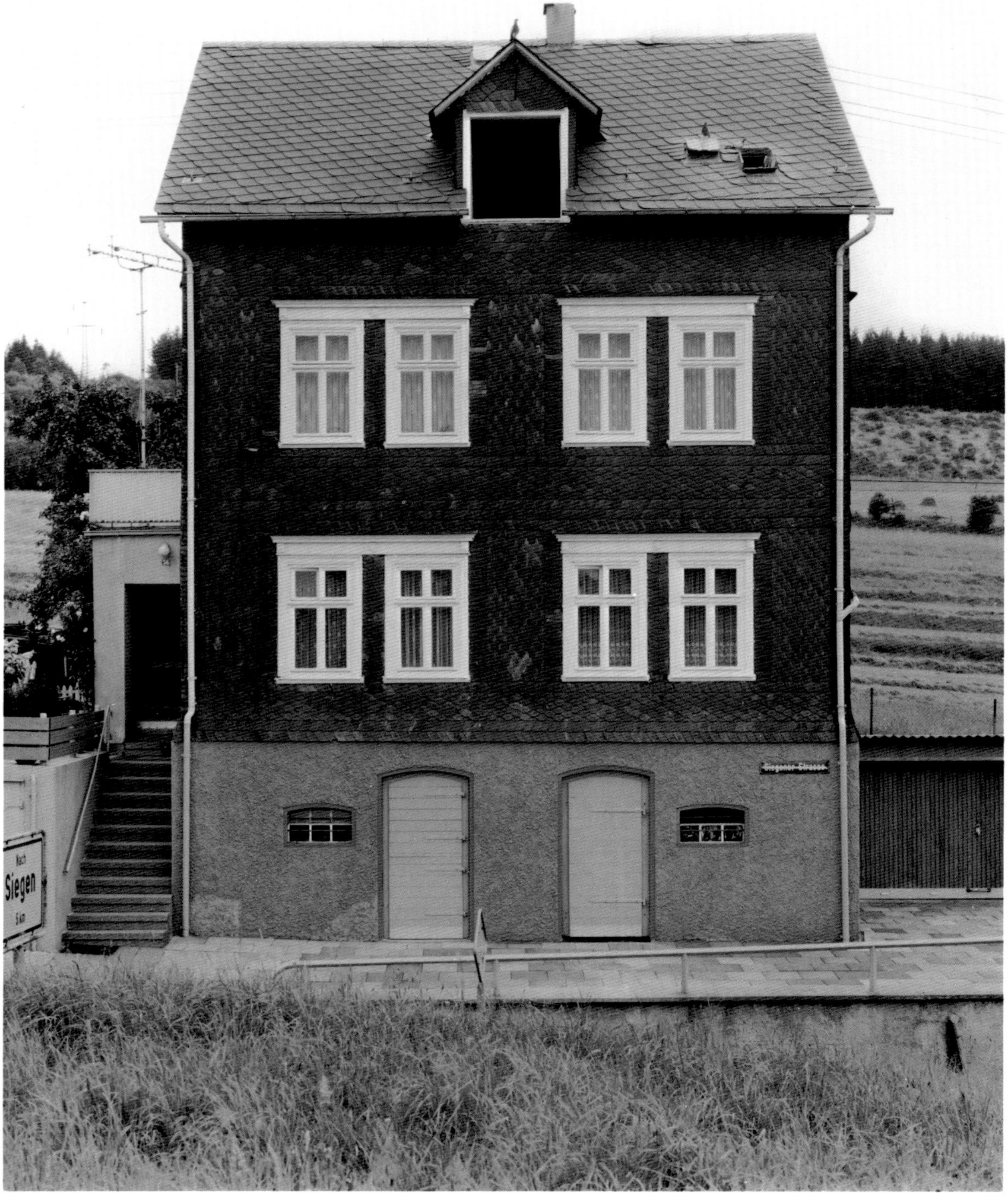

191

Siegener Straße 104, Gosenbach, 1968.

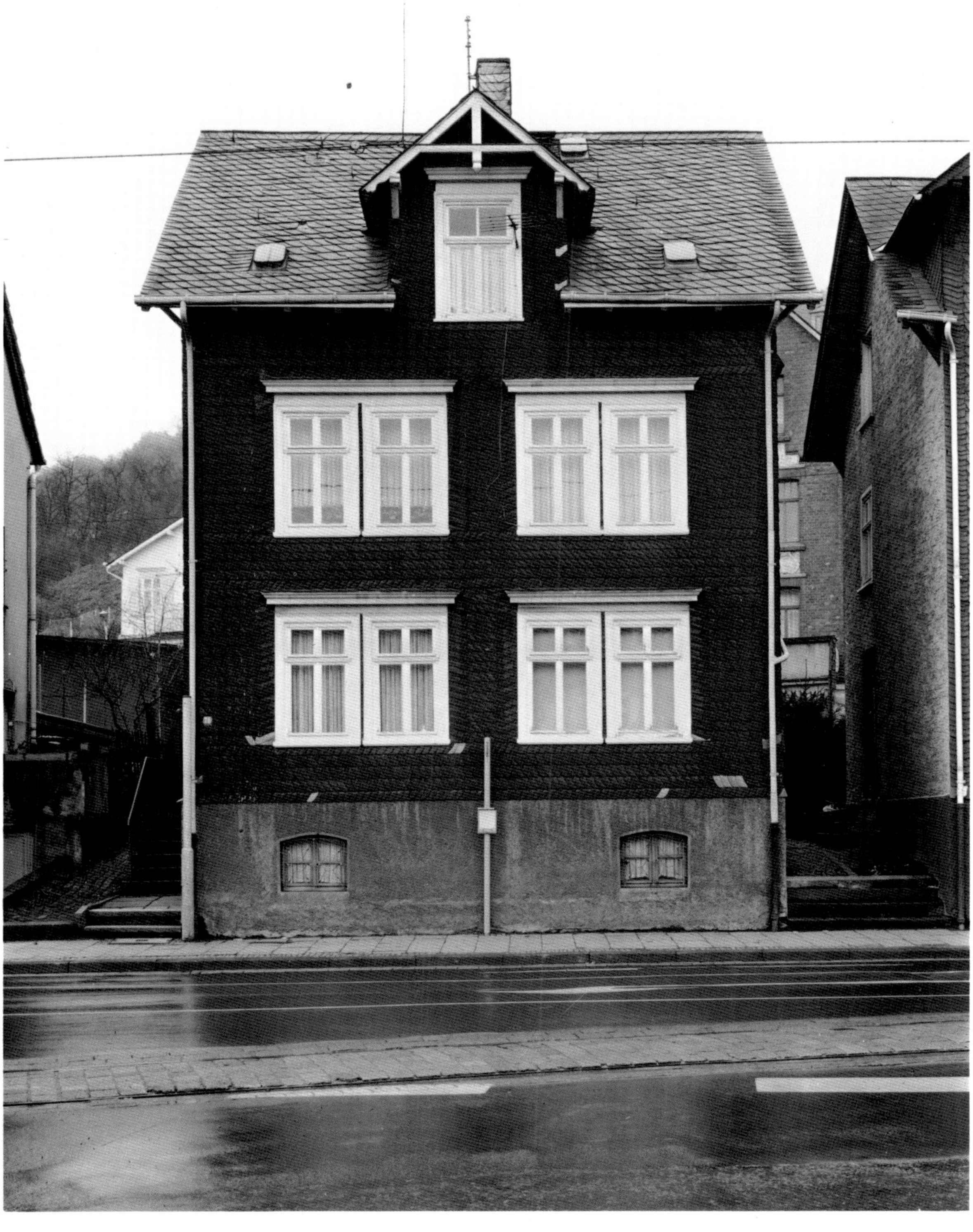

192

Frankfurter Straße 78, Siegen, 1971.

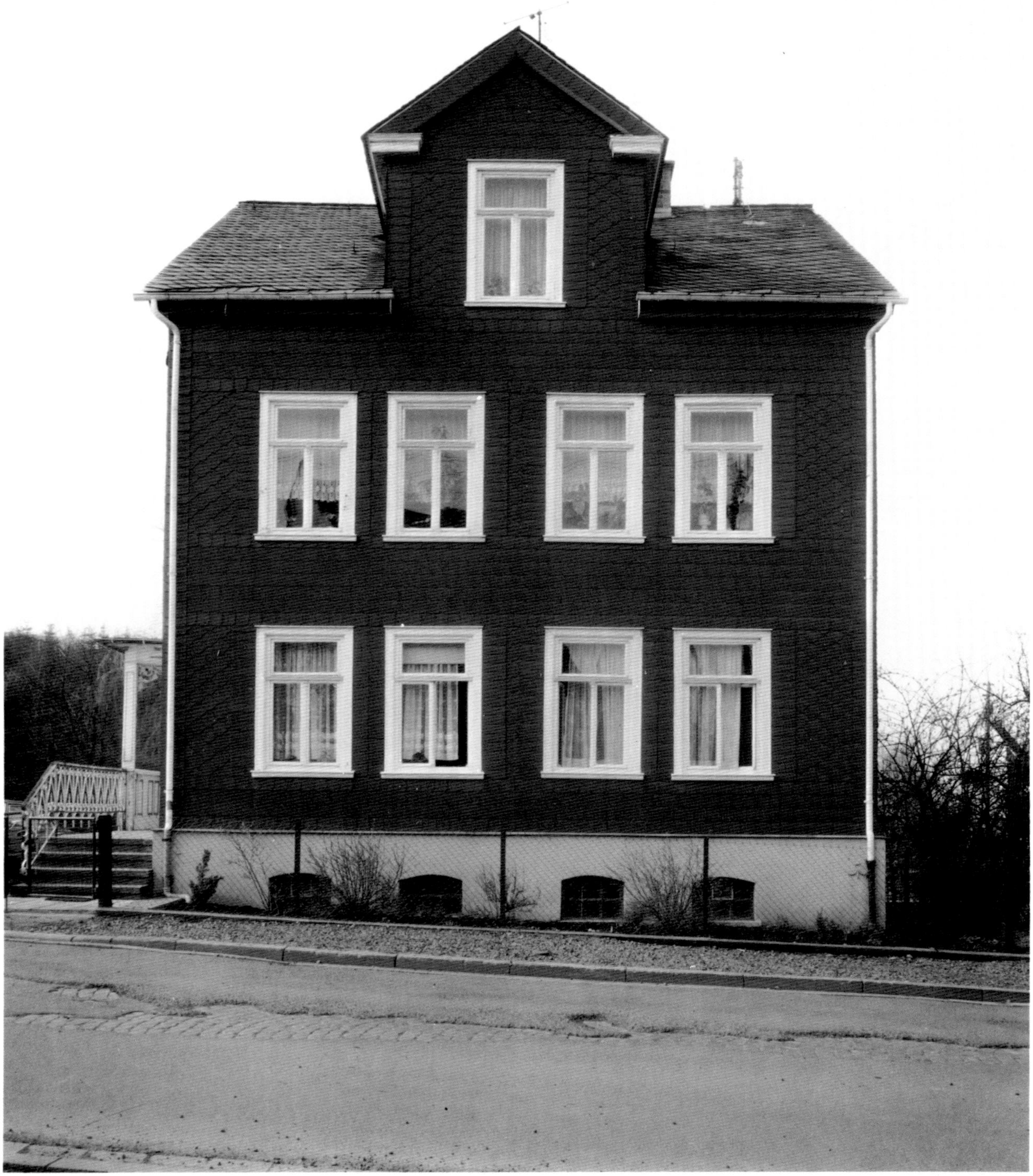

193
Bahnhofstraße 28, Neunkirchen, 1972.

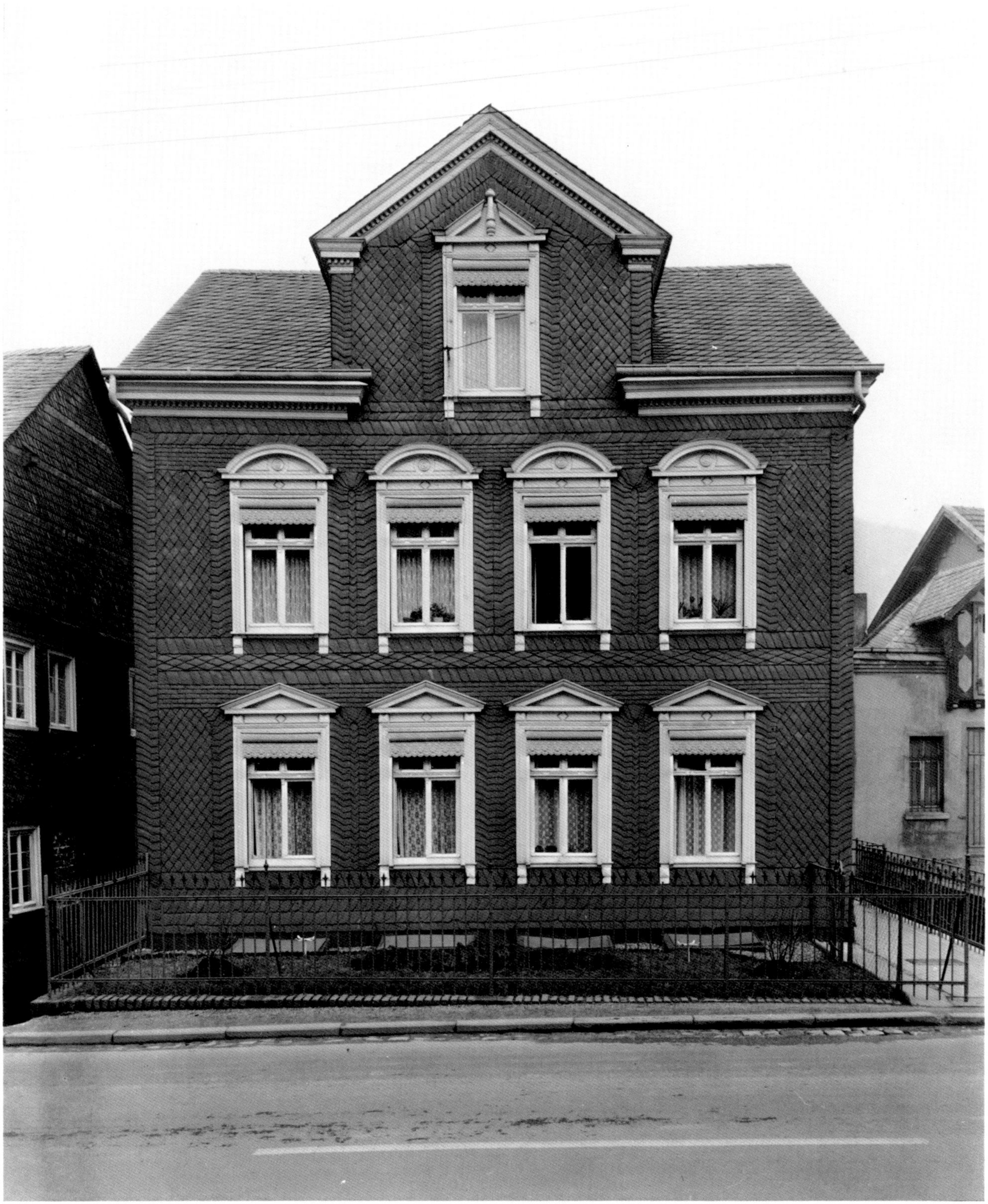

194
Freiengründerstraße 21, Eiserfeld, 1960.

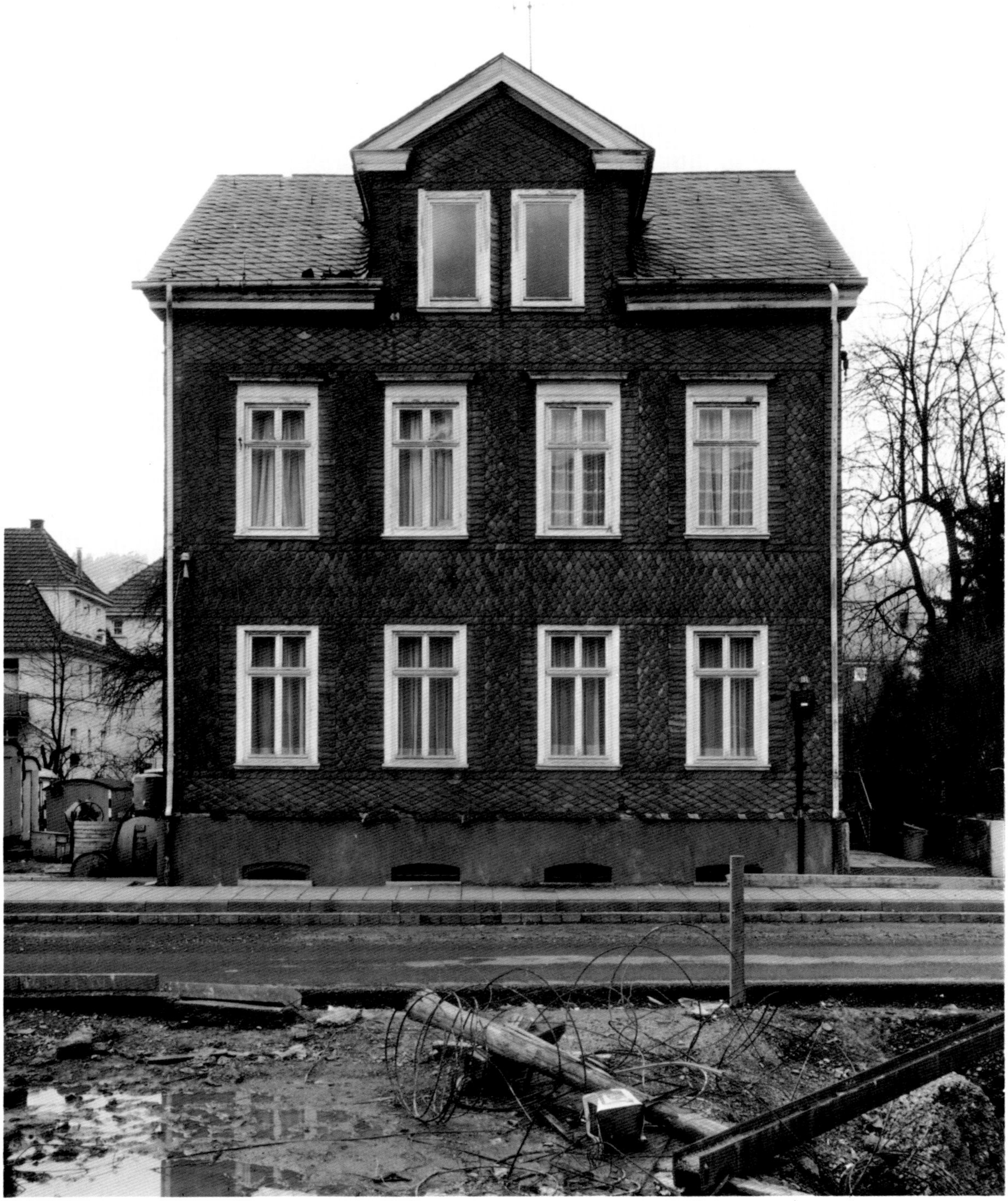

195
Koblenzer Straße 186, Siegen, 1964.

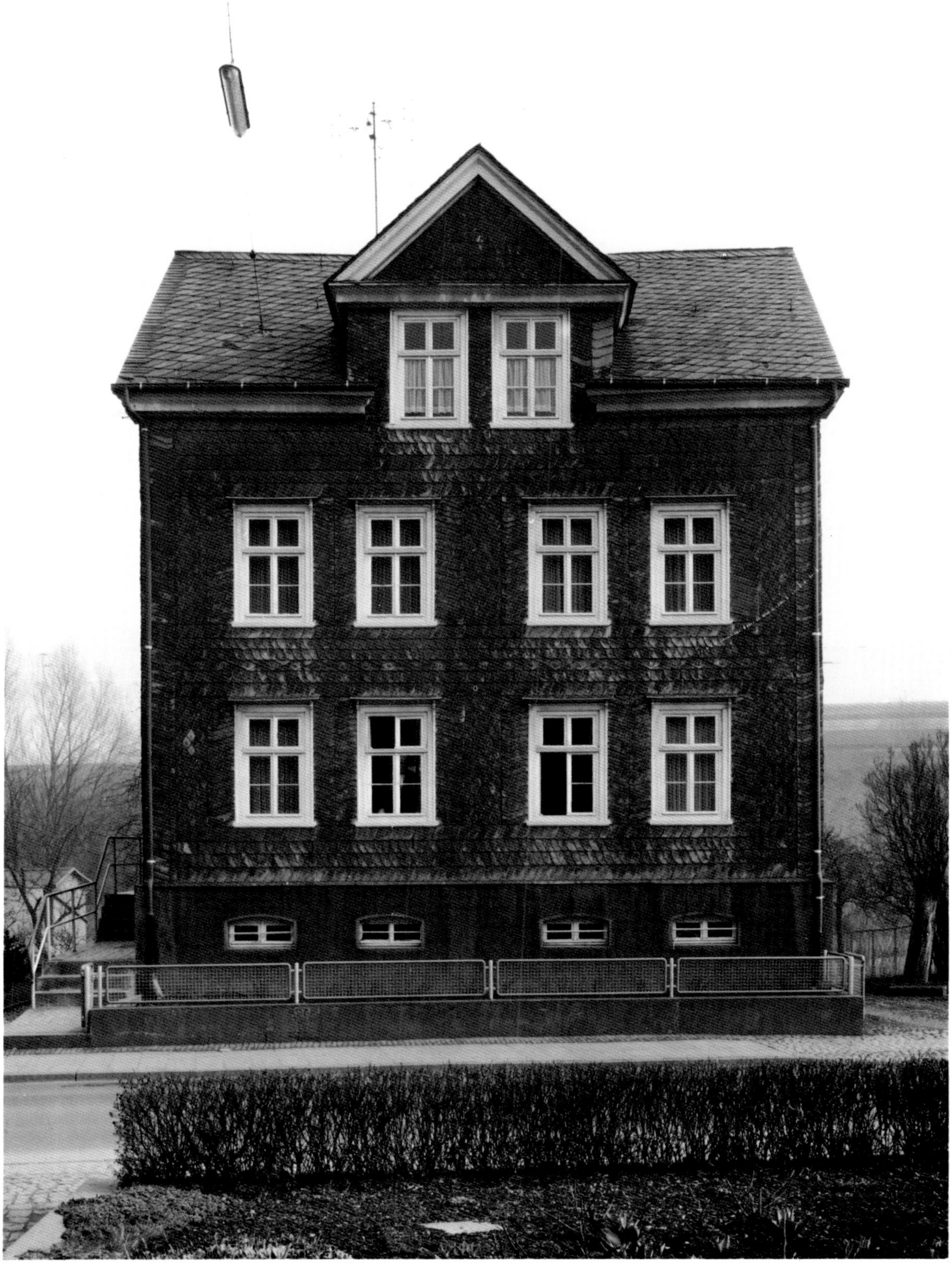

196
Hauptstraße 25, Kaan-Marienborn, 1971.

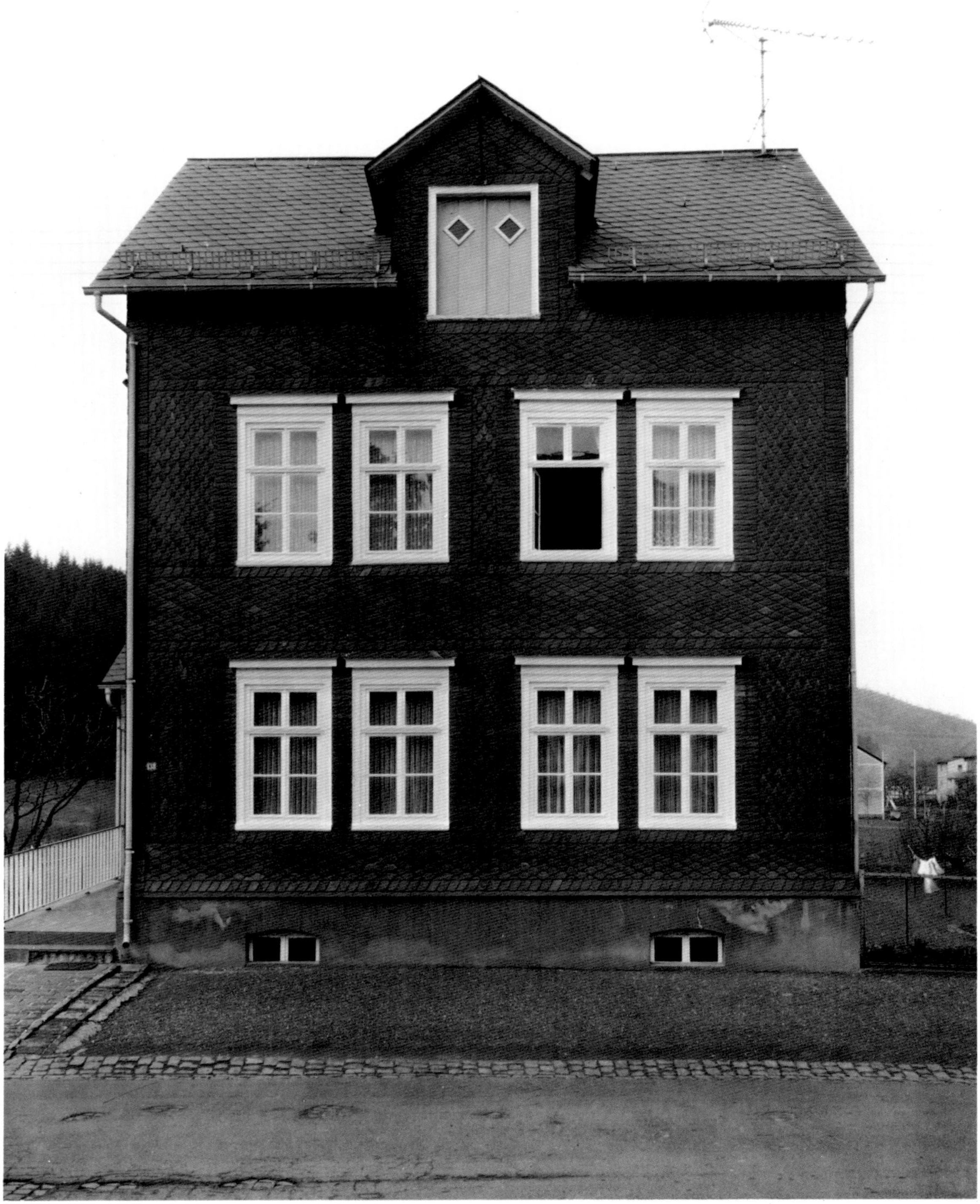

197
Eiserntalstraße 138, Eisern, 1970.

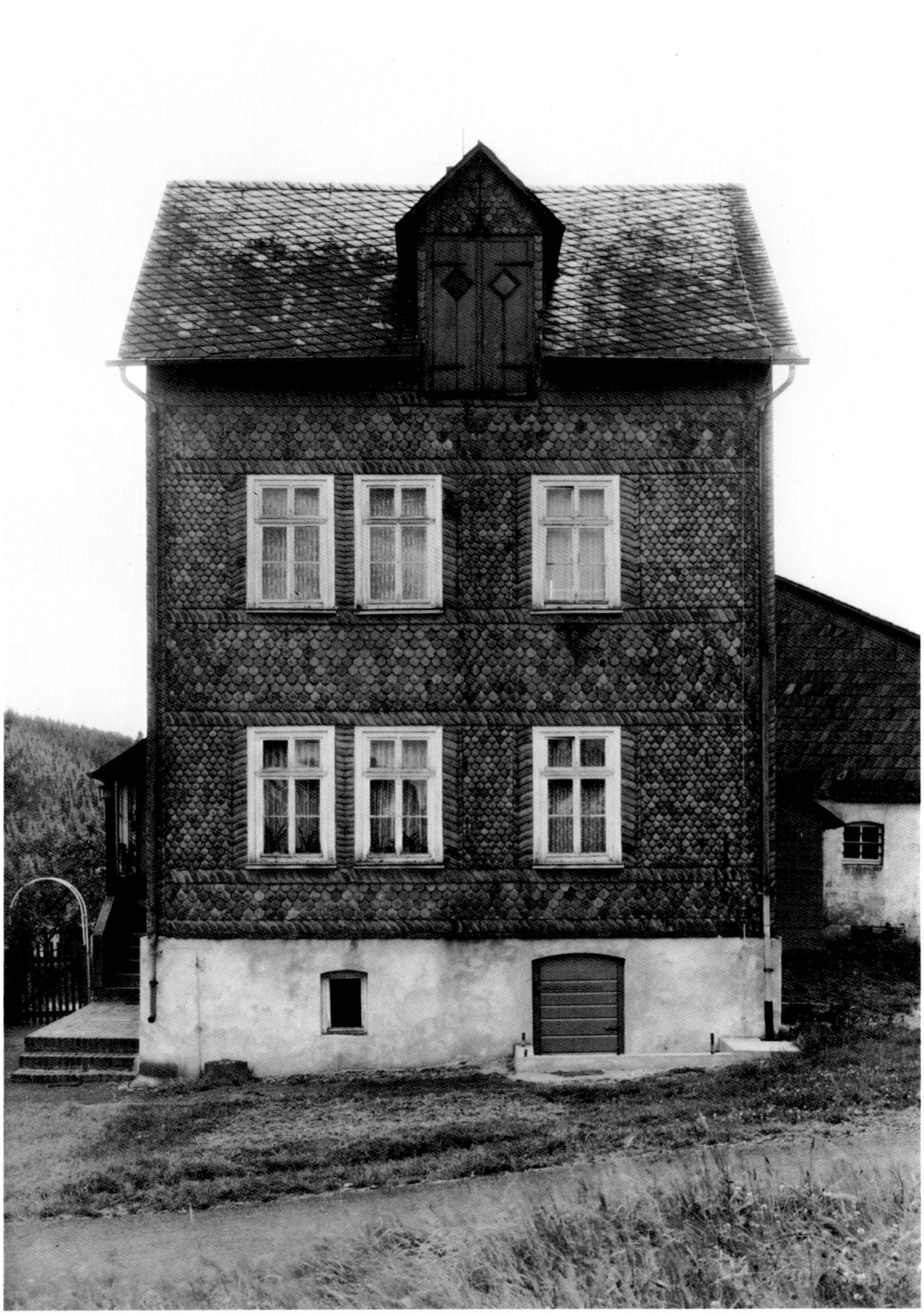

198
Rödgerstraße 7, Niederdielfen, 1960.

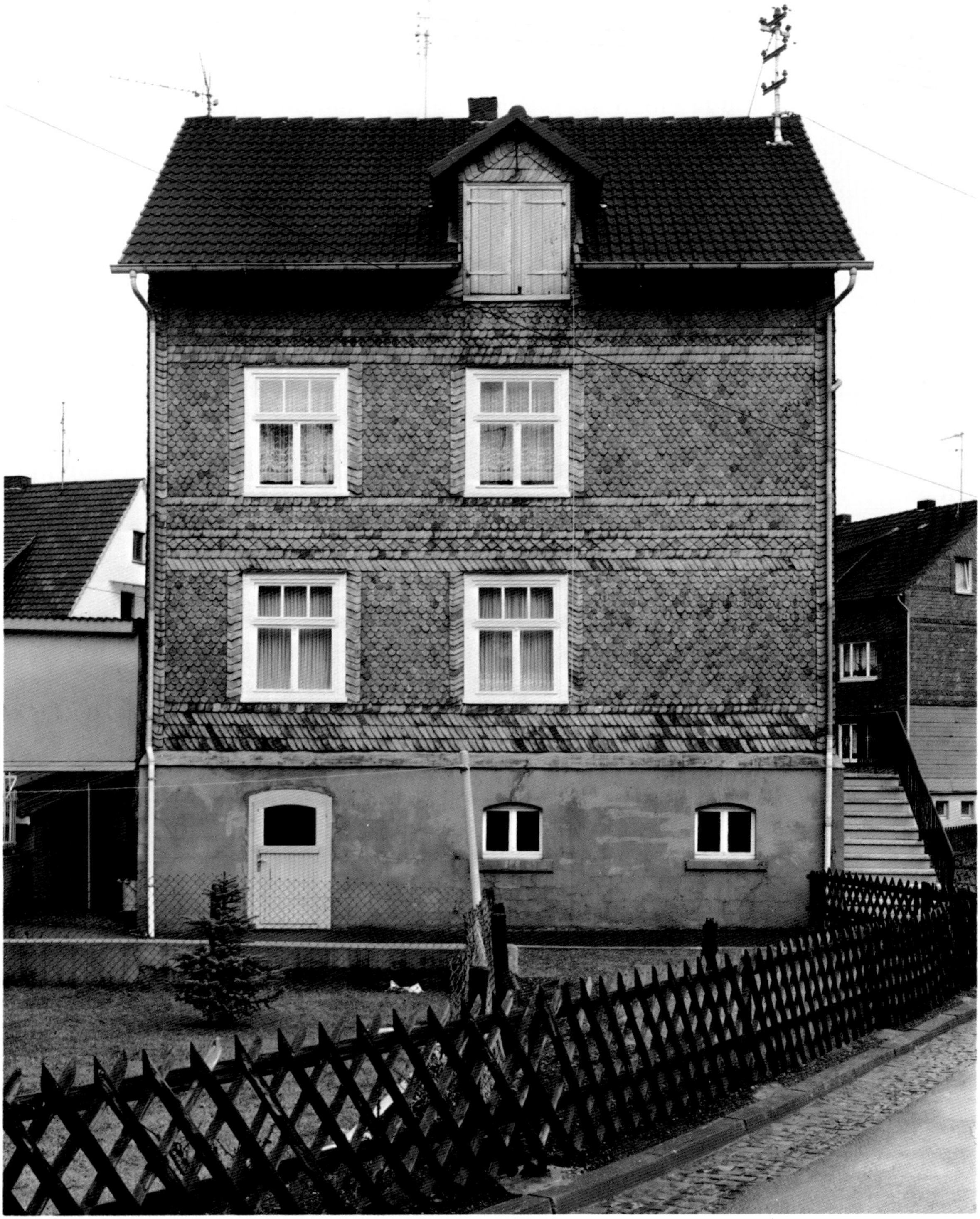

199

Bachstraße 5, Niederfischbach, 1969.

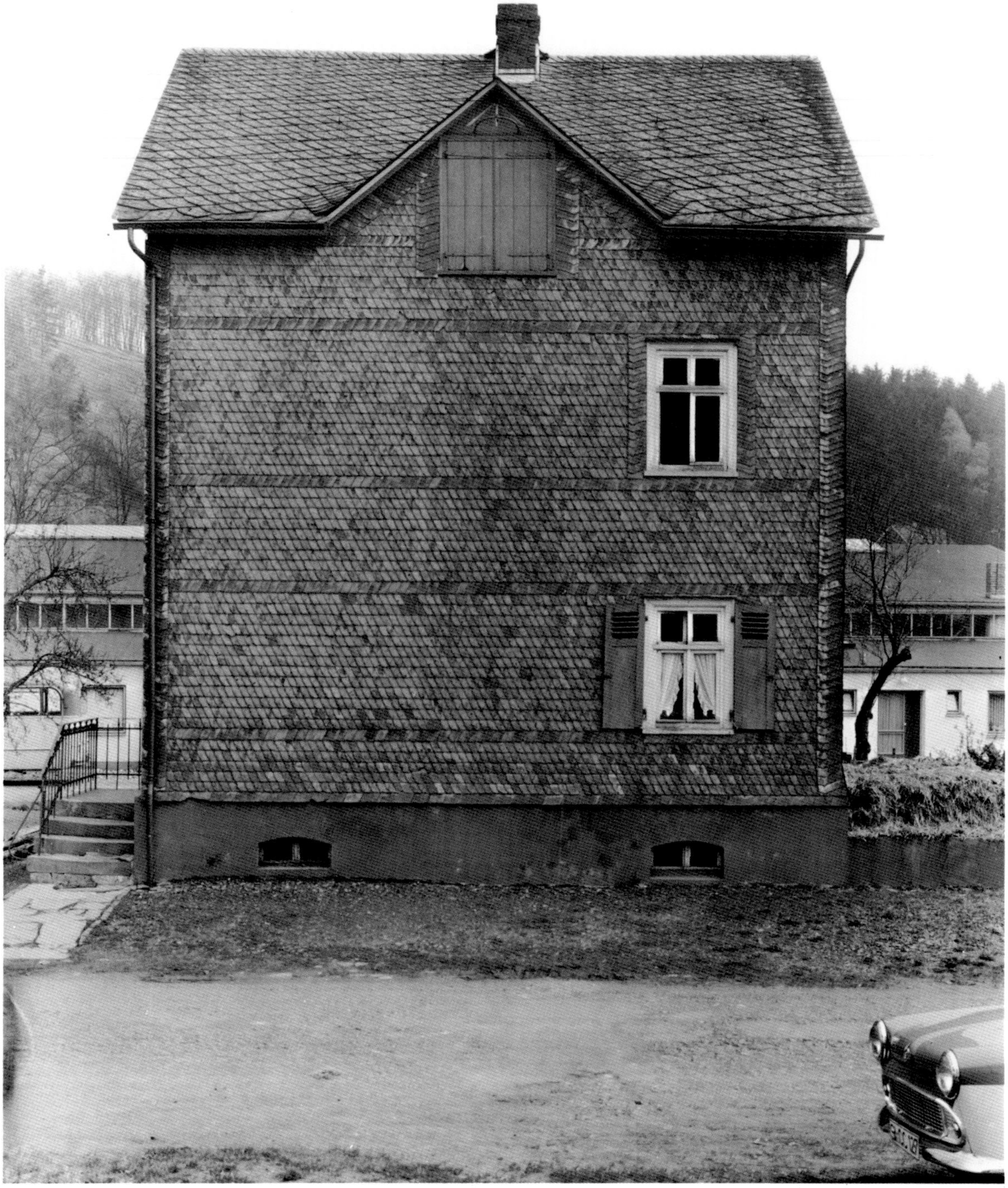

200

Triftstraße 48, Büschergrund, 1960.

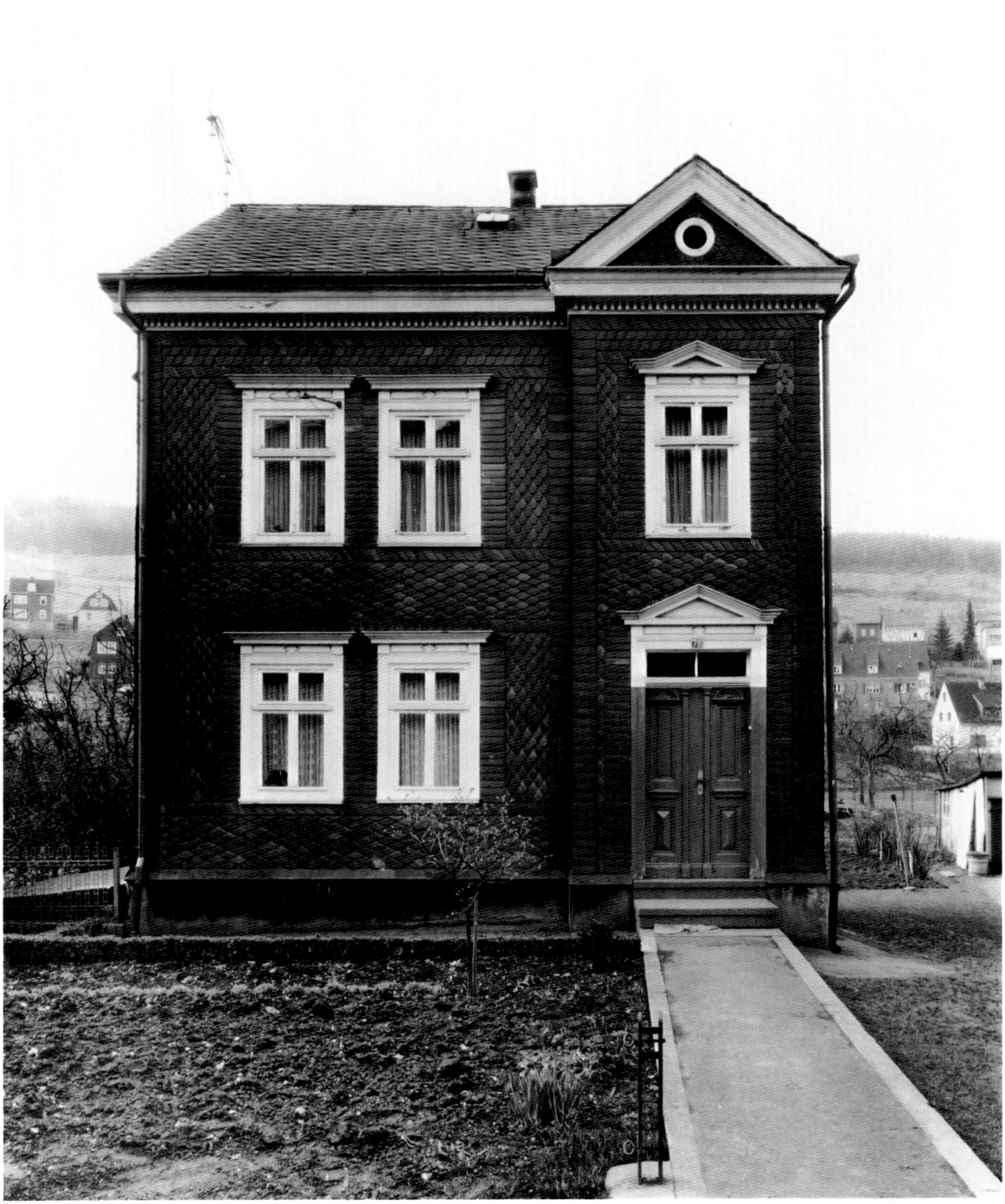

201

Eisernstraße 158, Eiserfeld, 1970.

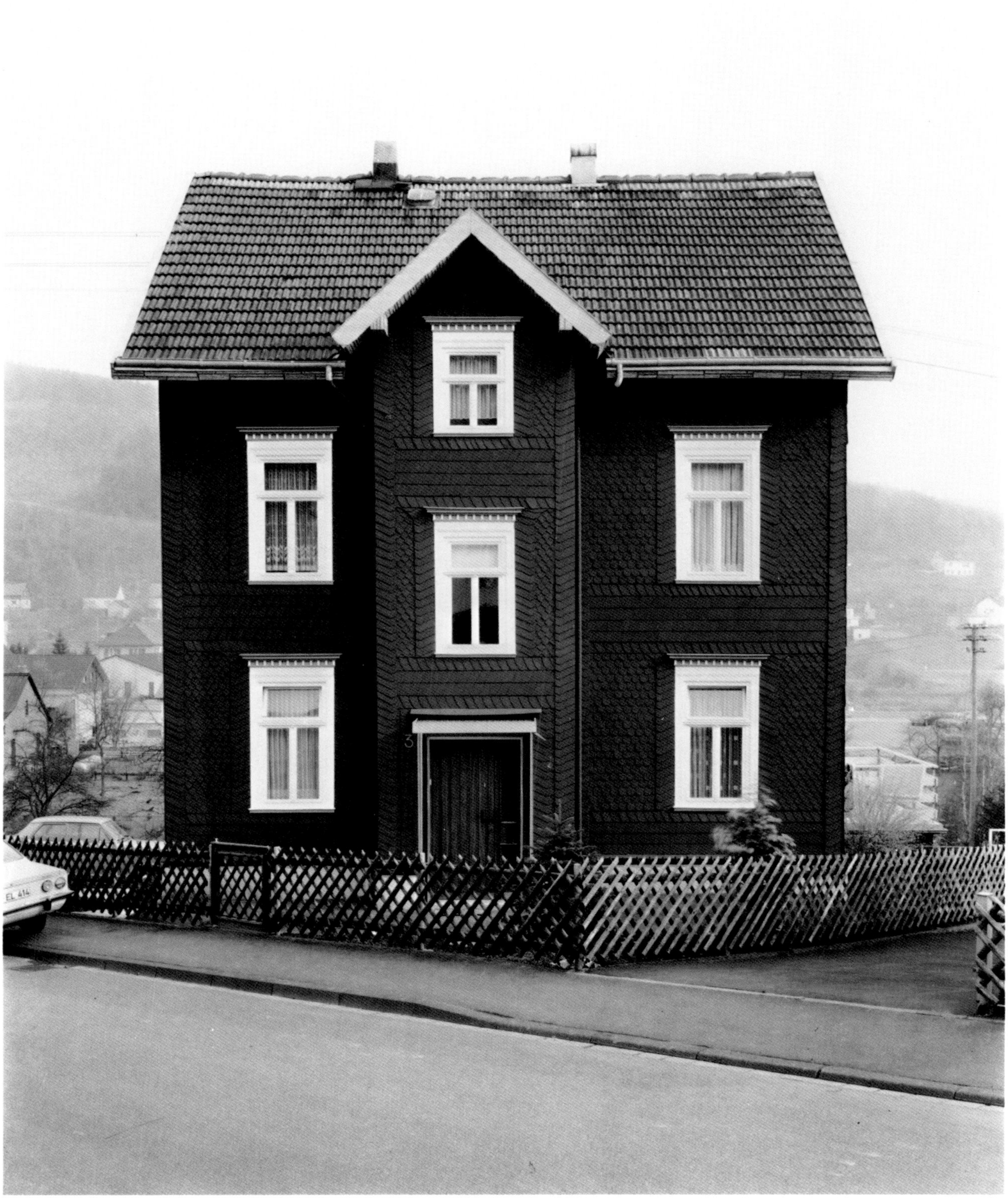

202
Dr.-Stelbring-Straße 3, Kredenbach, 1972.

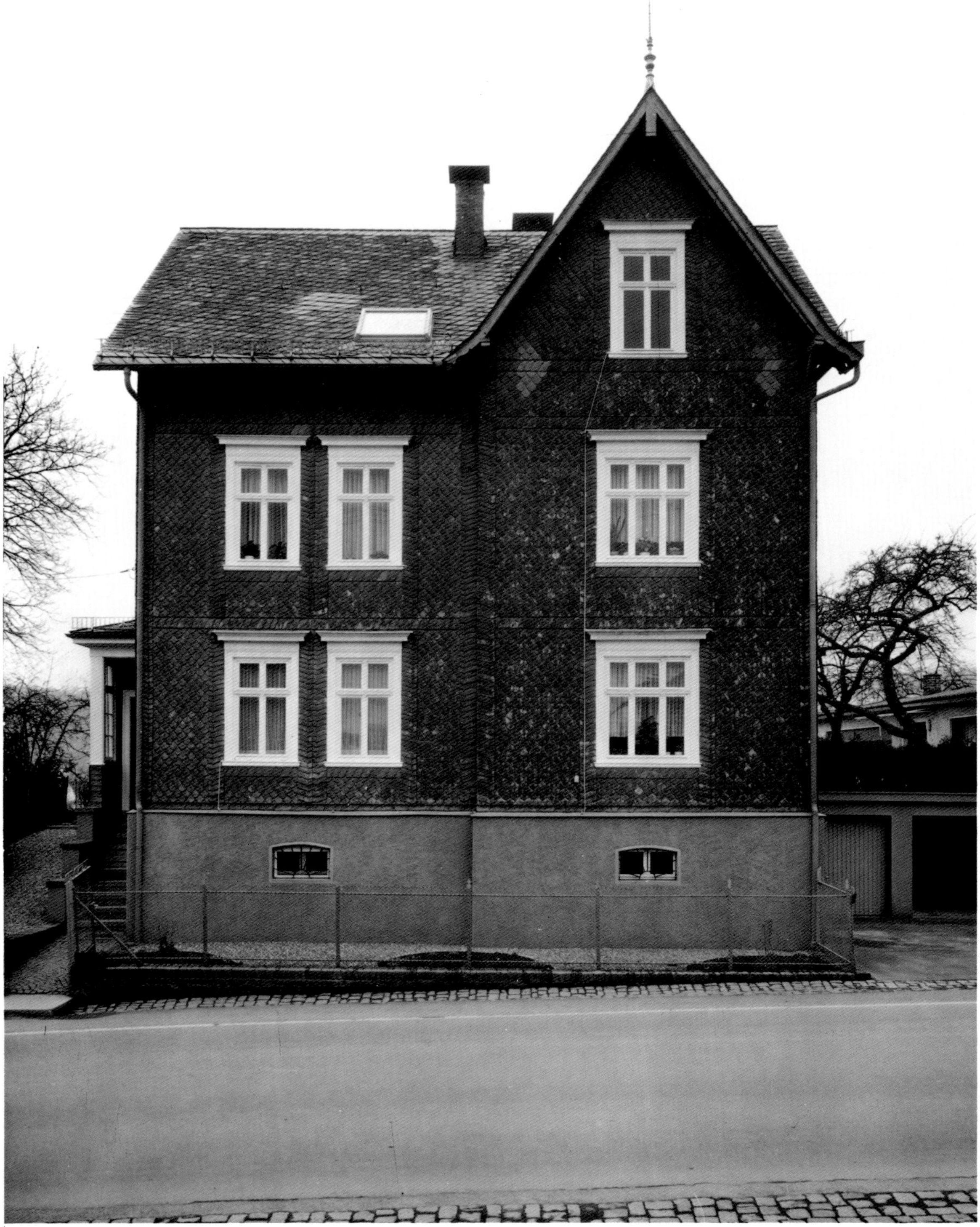

203

Krottorfer Straße 53, Freudenberg, 1971.

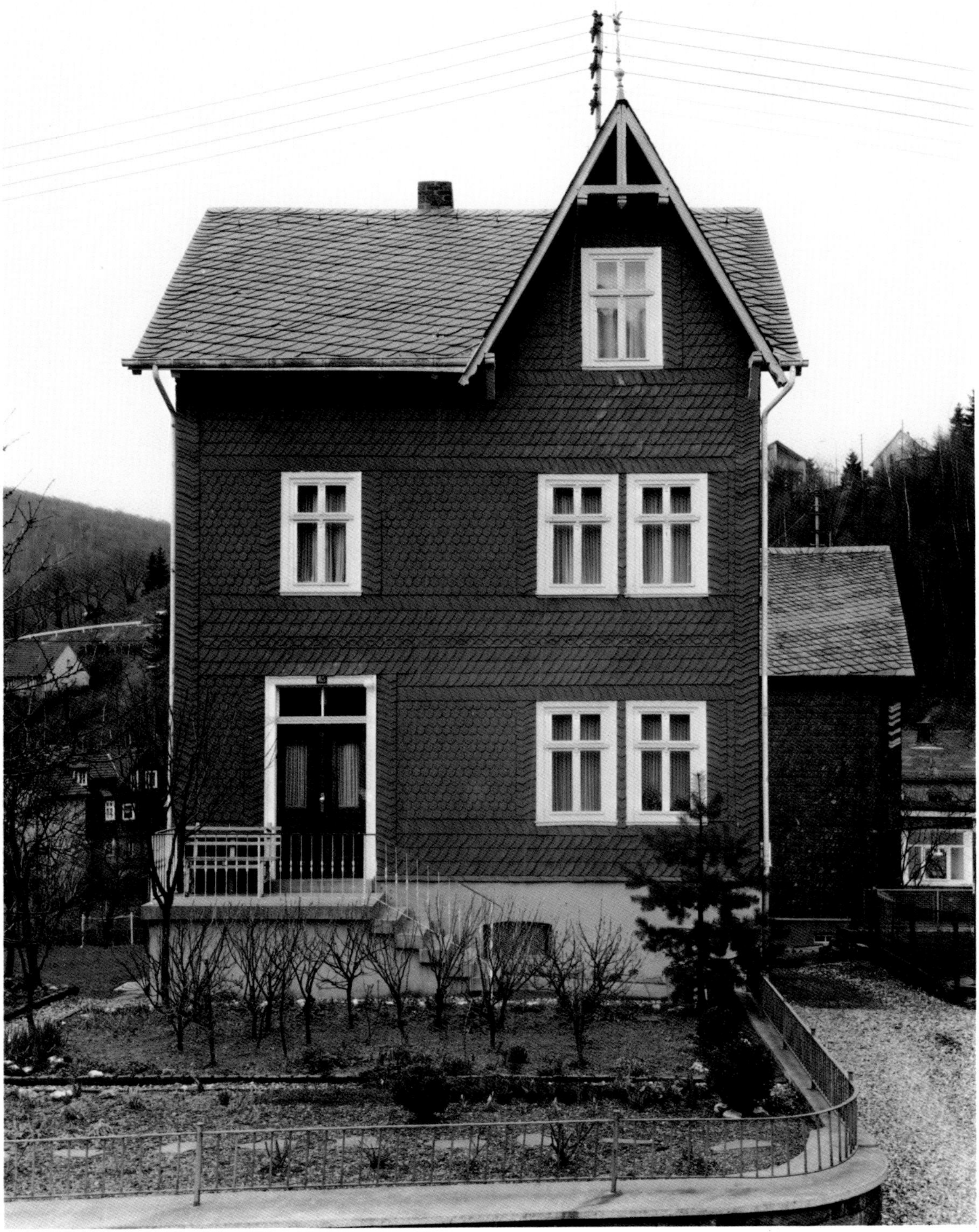

204

Lindenstraße 69, Eiserfeld, 1970.

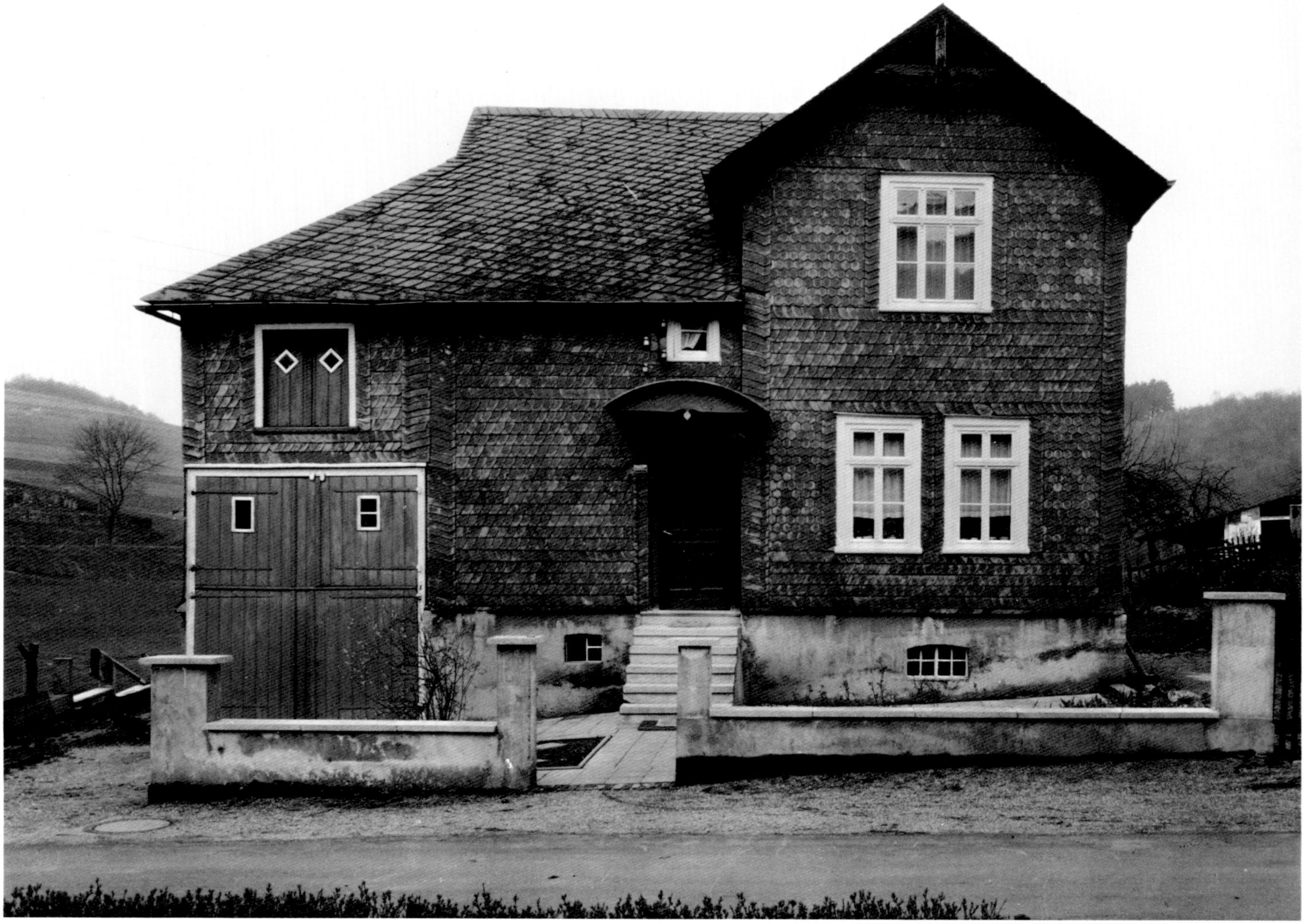

205
Im Dudenbach 27, Rinsdorf, 1961.

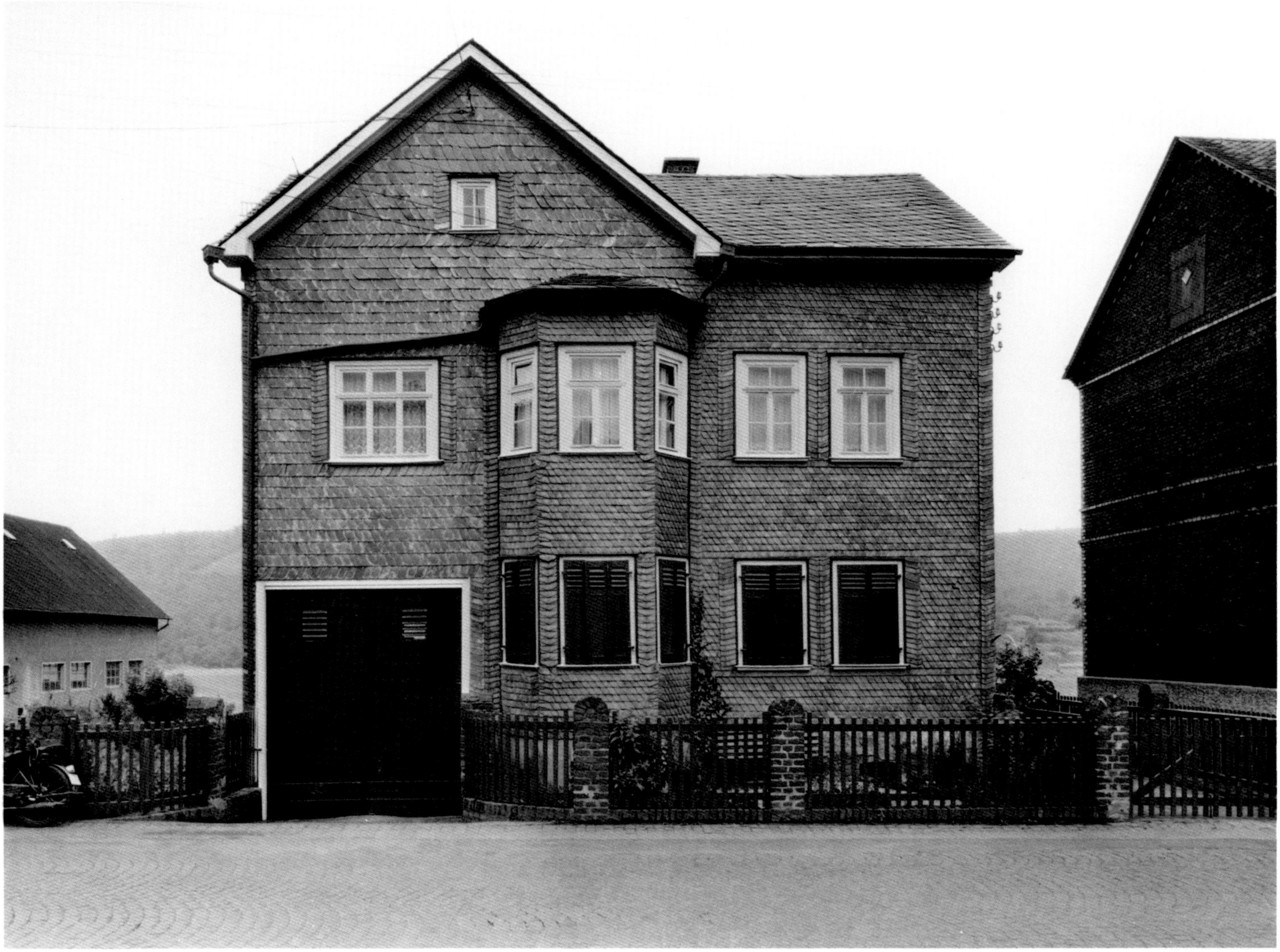

206
Siegener Straße 54, Niederdielfen, 1961.

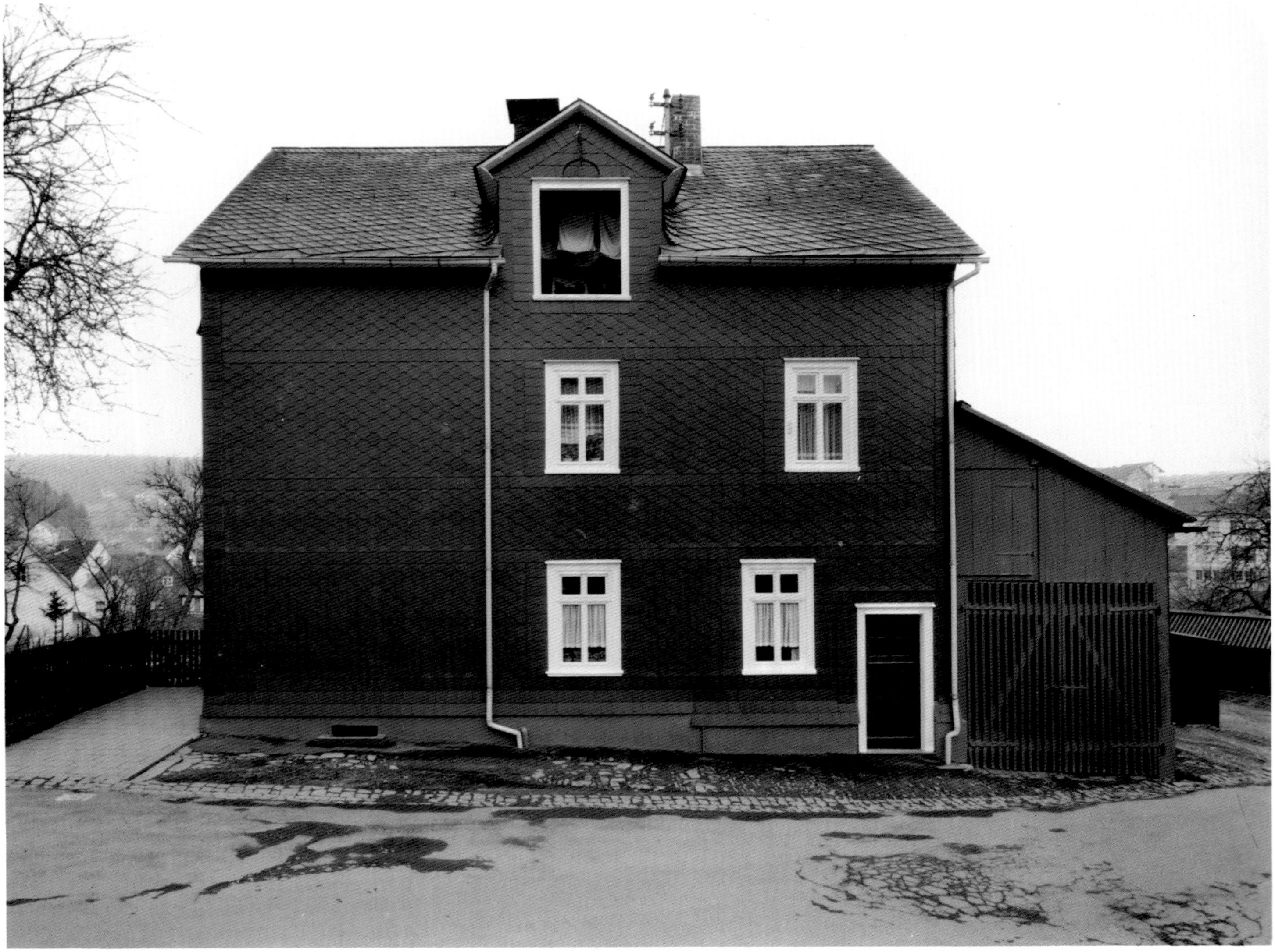

207
Büscher Straße 2, Büschergrund, 1969.

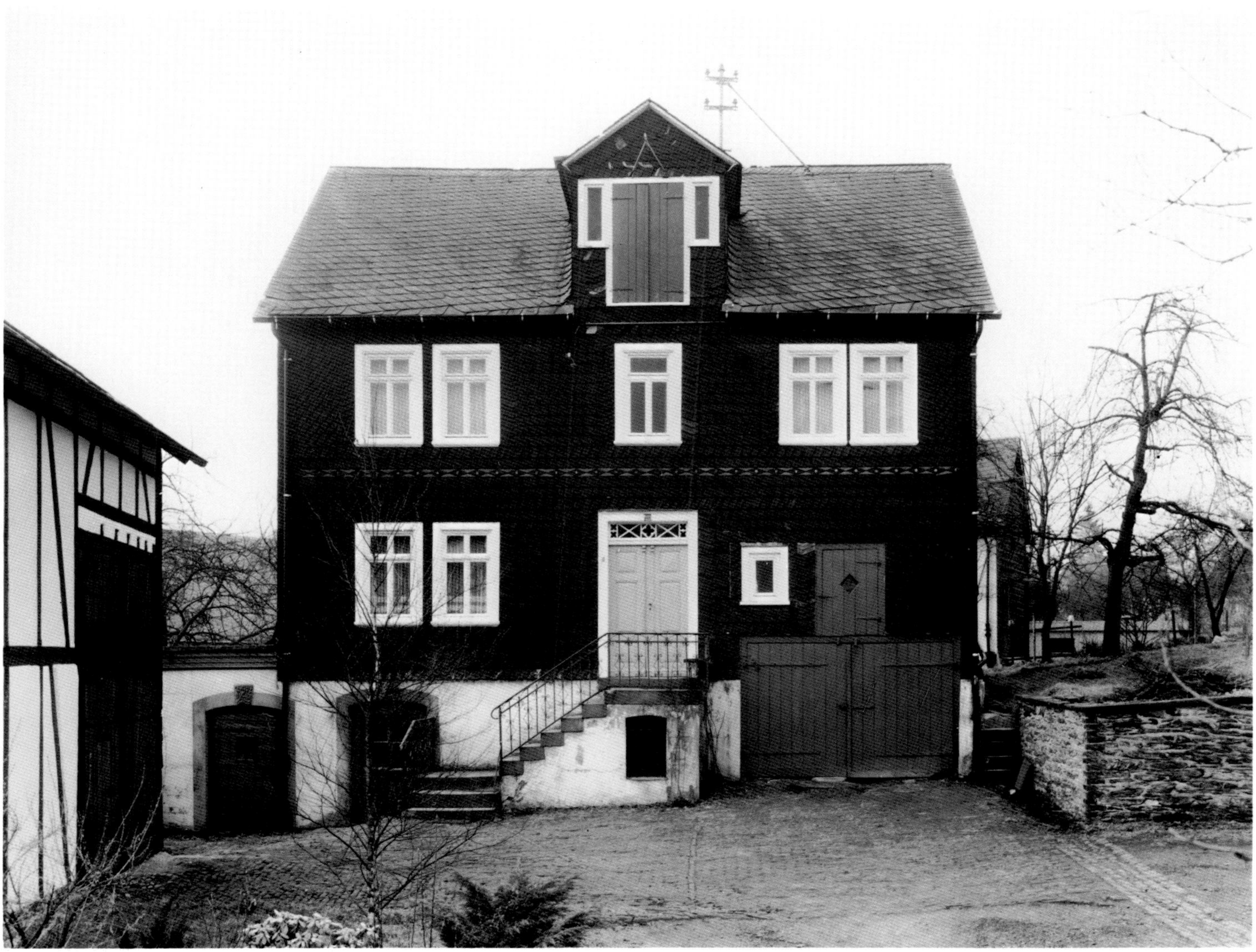

208
Hohlweg 5, Mudersbach, 1968.

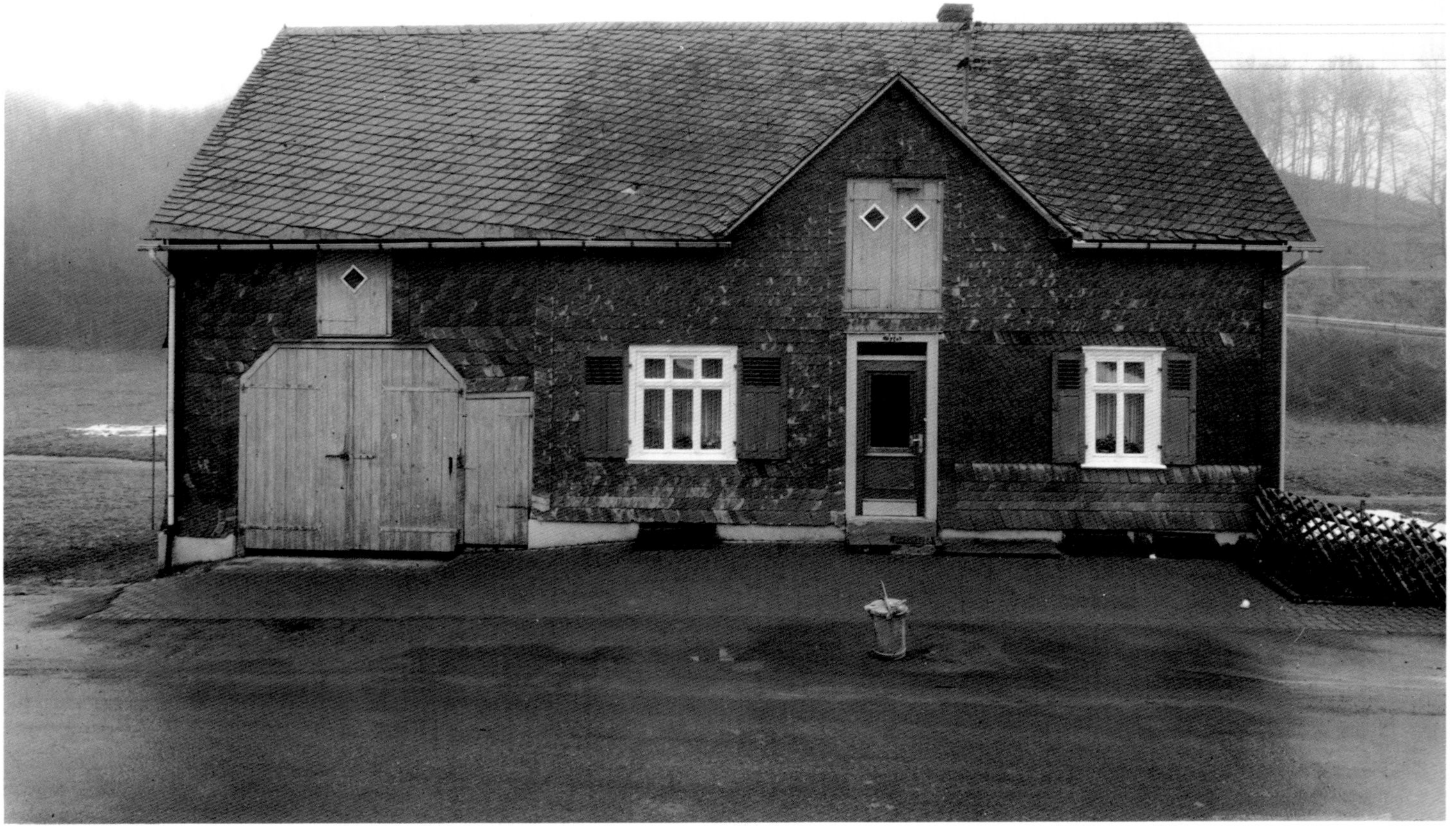

209
Heuslingstraße 348, Oberheuslingen, 1968.

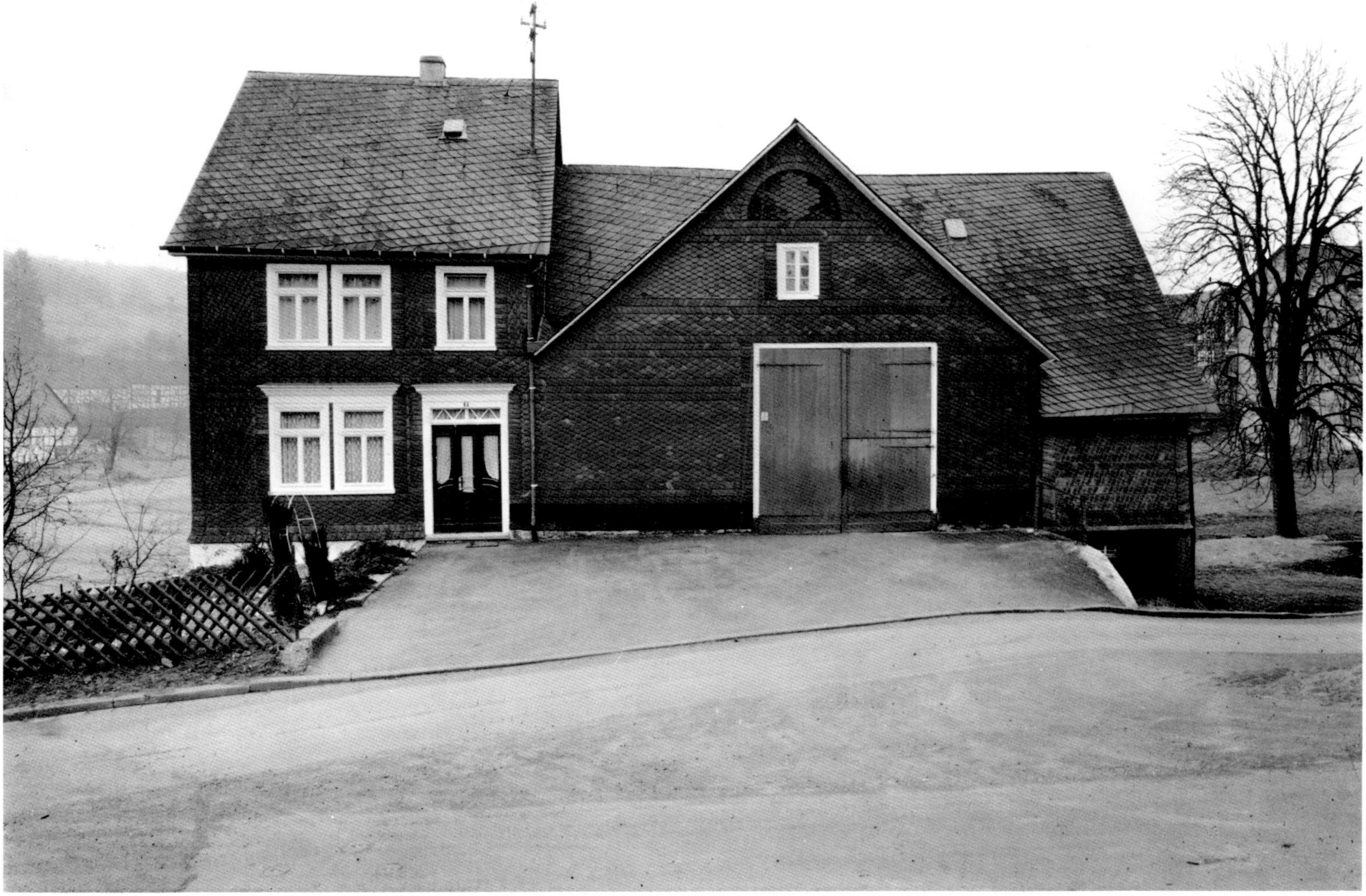

210
Eiserner Weg 9, Wilden, 1962.

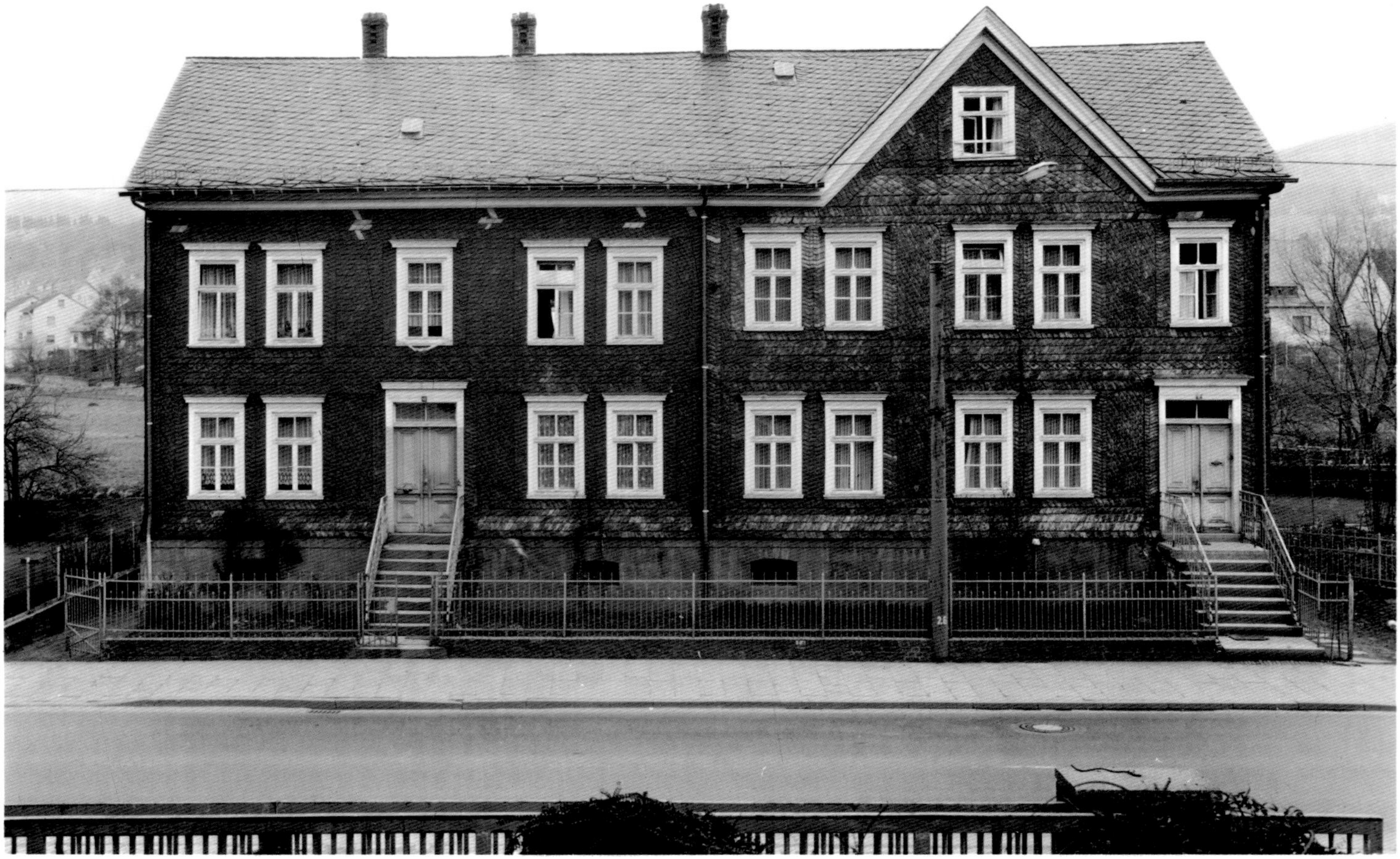

211
Siegtalstraße 40, Eiserfeld, 1971.

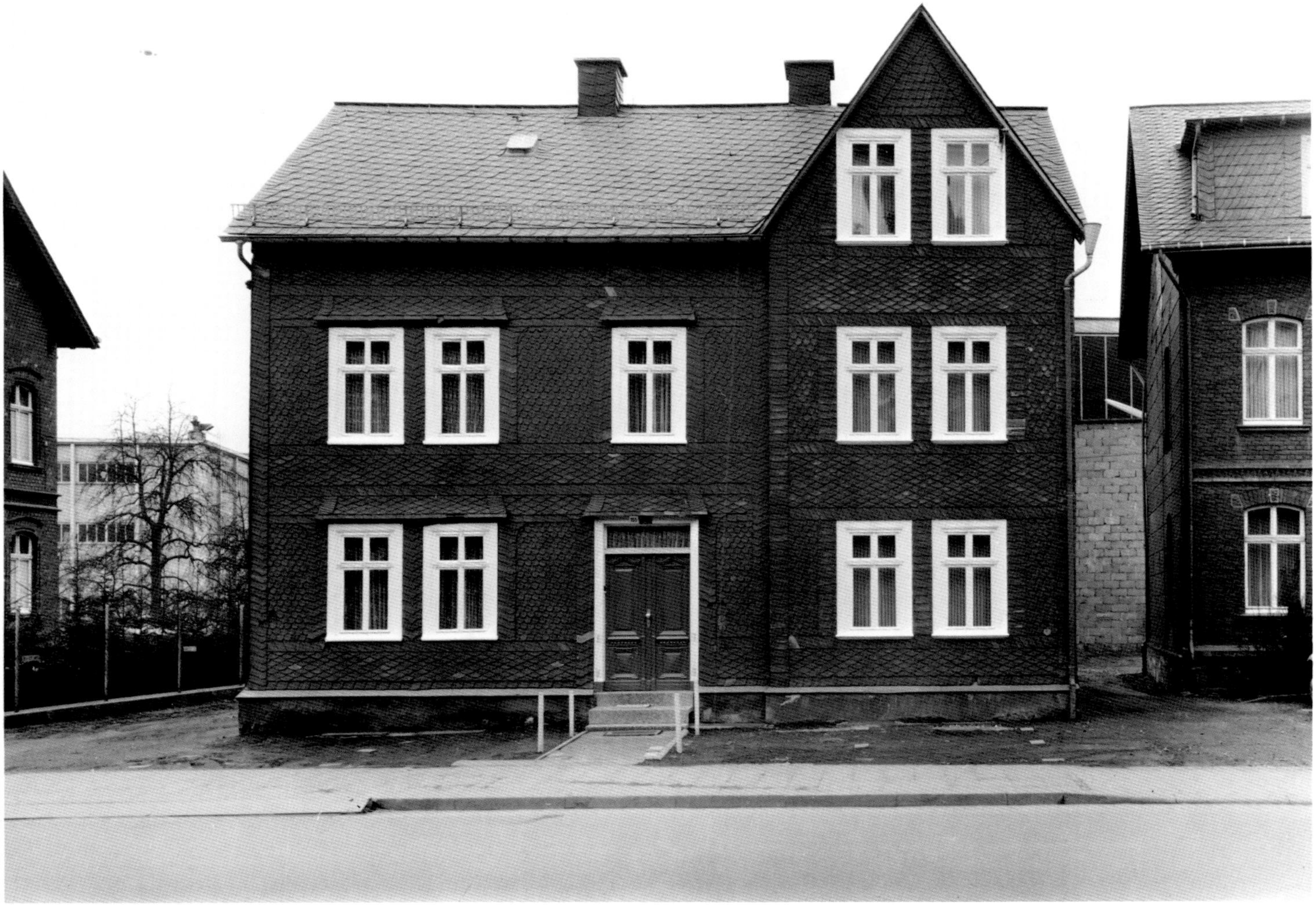

212
Bahnhofstraße 155, Eiserfeld, 1971.

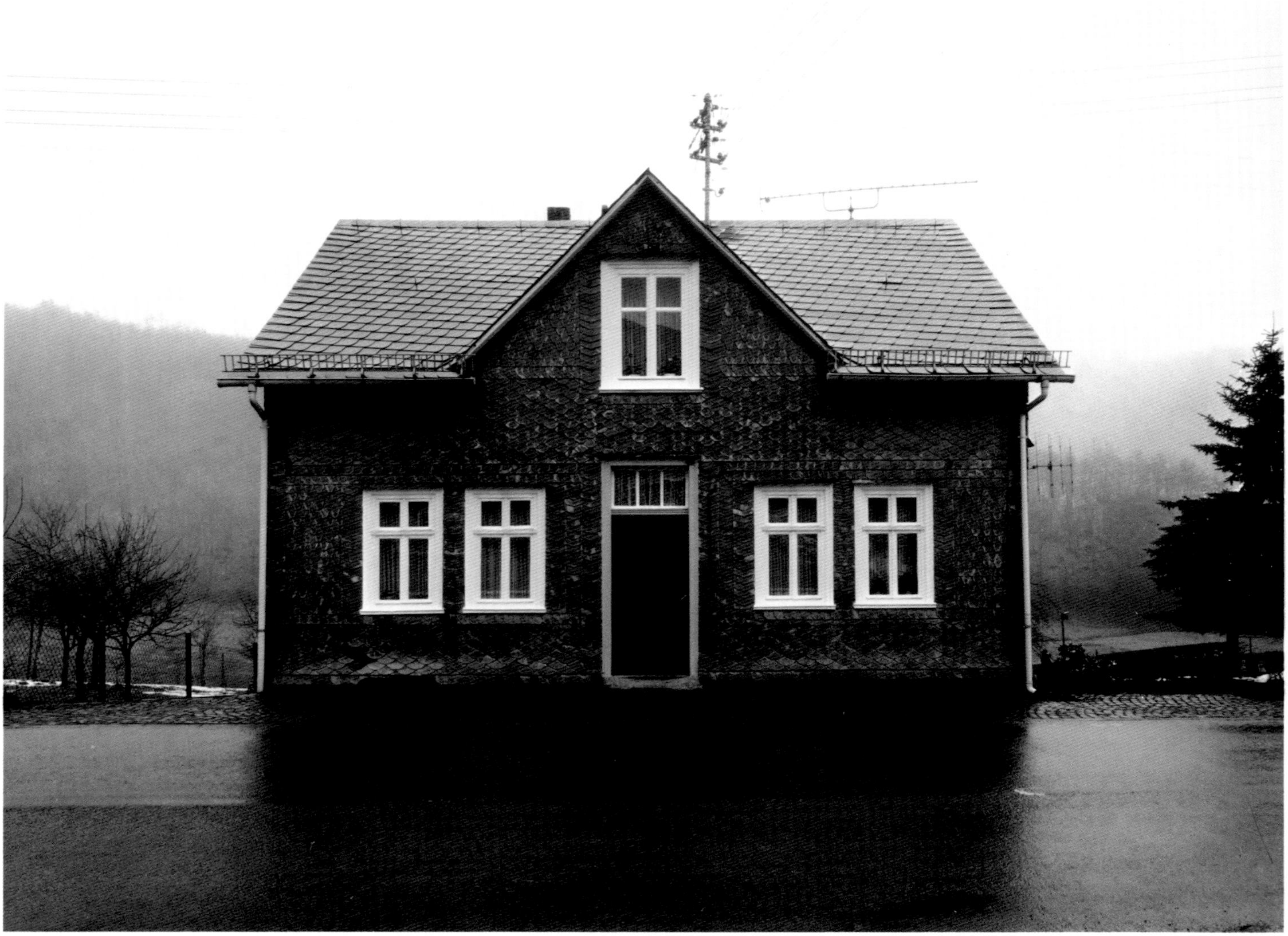

213
Dirlenbacher Straße 68, Niederndorf, 1968.

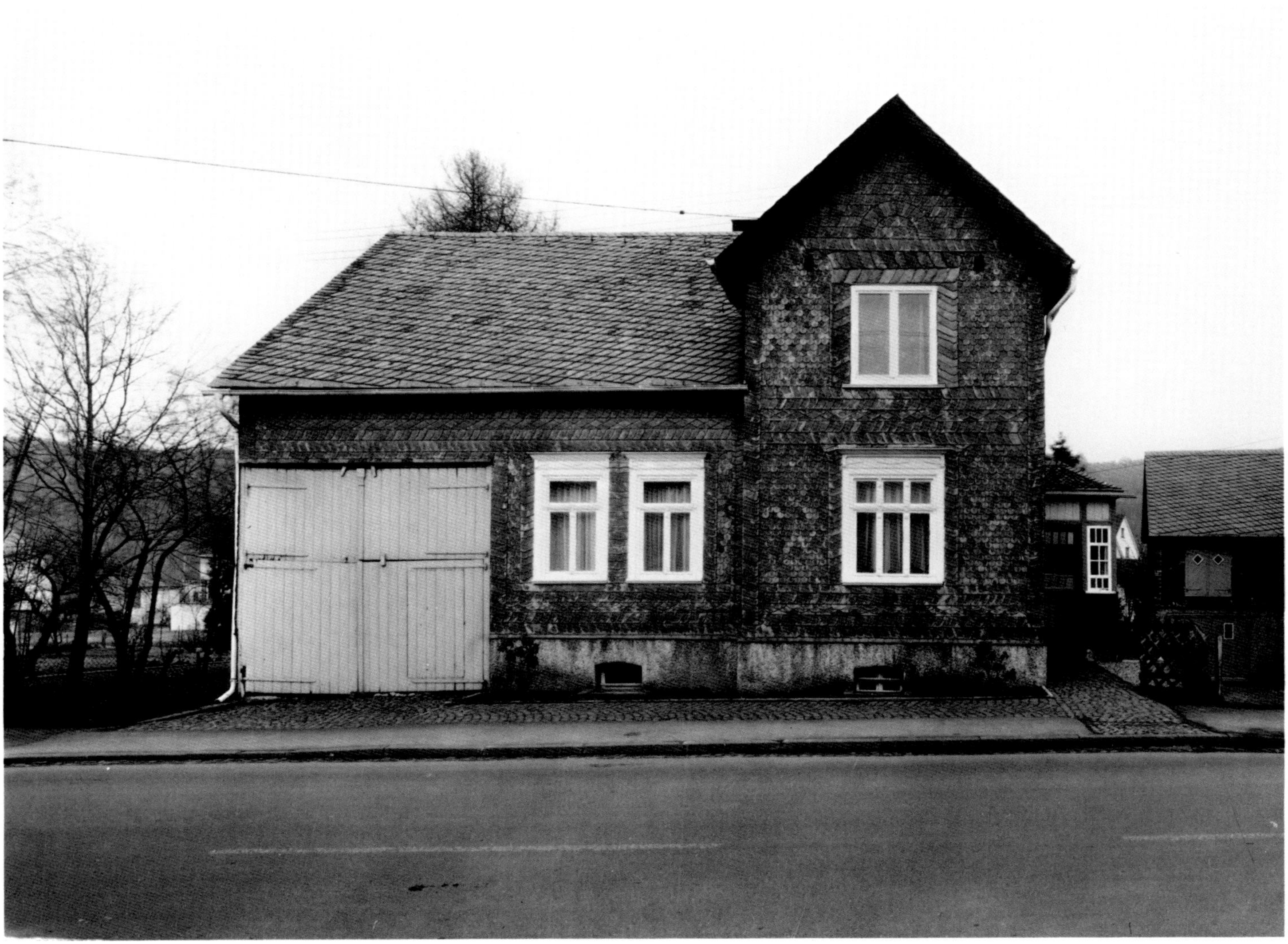

214
Freier Grund Straße 20, Wahlbach, 1971.

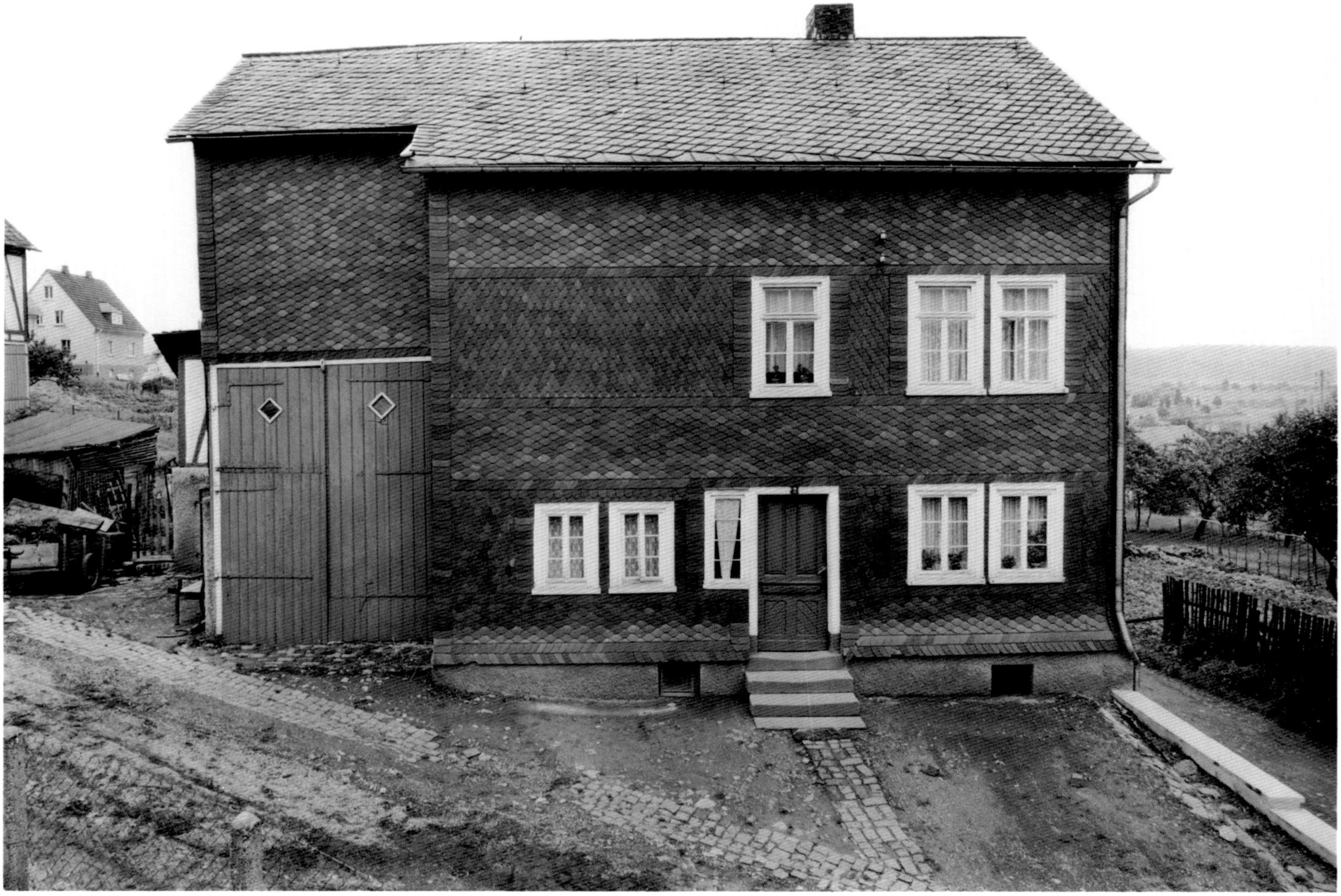

215
Albert-Schweitzer-Straße 2, Wilnsdorf, 1960.

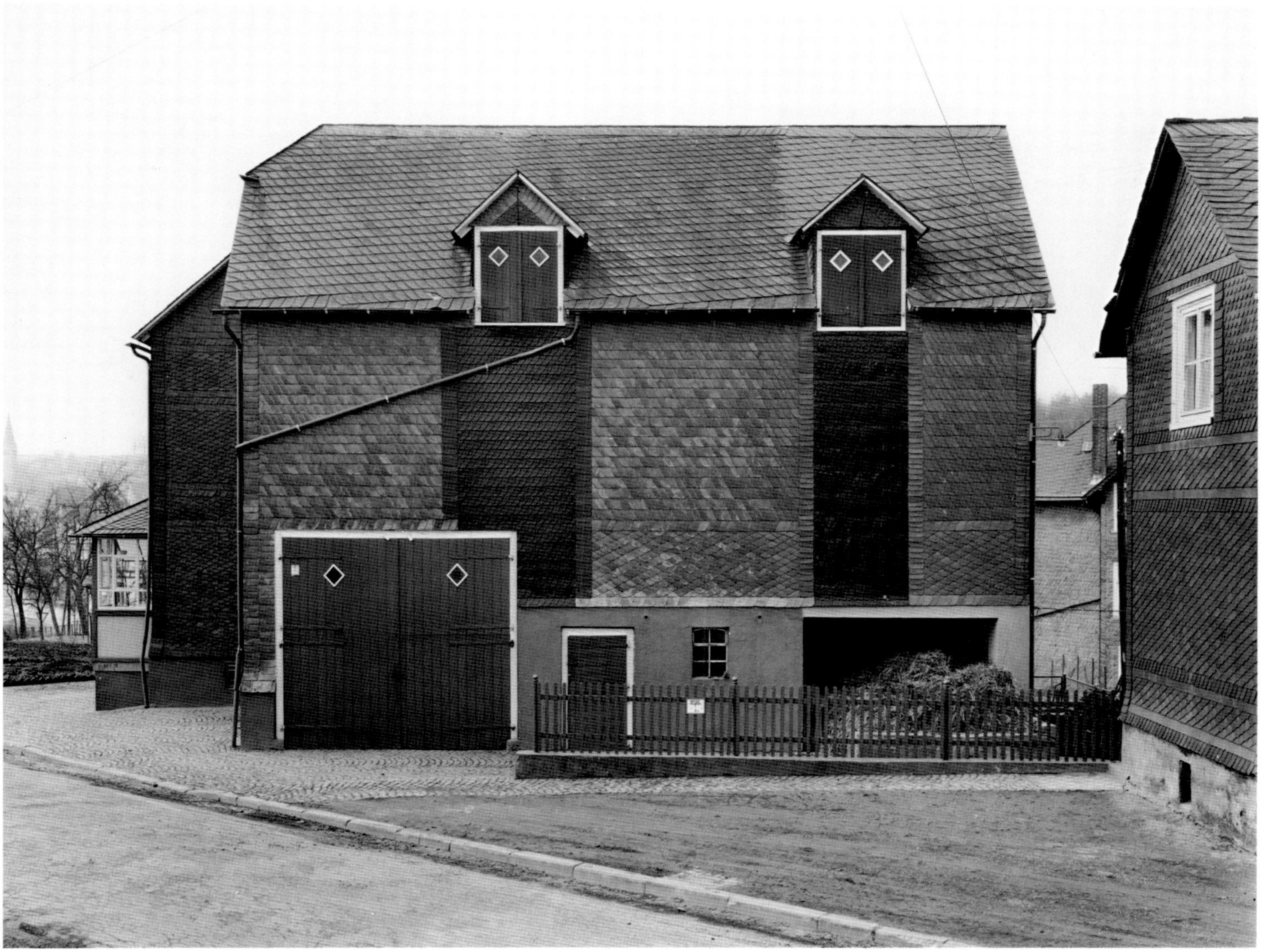

216
Weißtalstraße 1, Wilnsdorf, 1962.

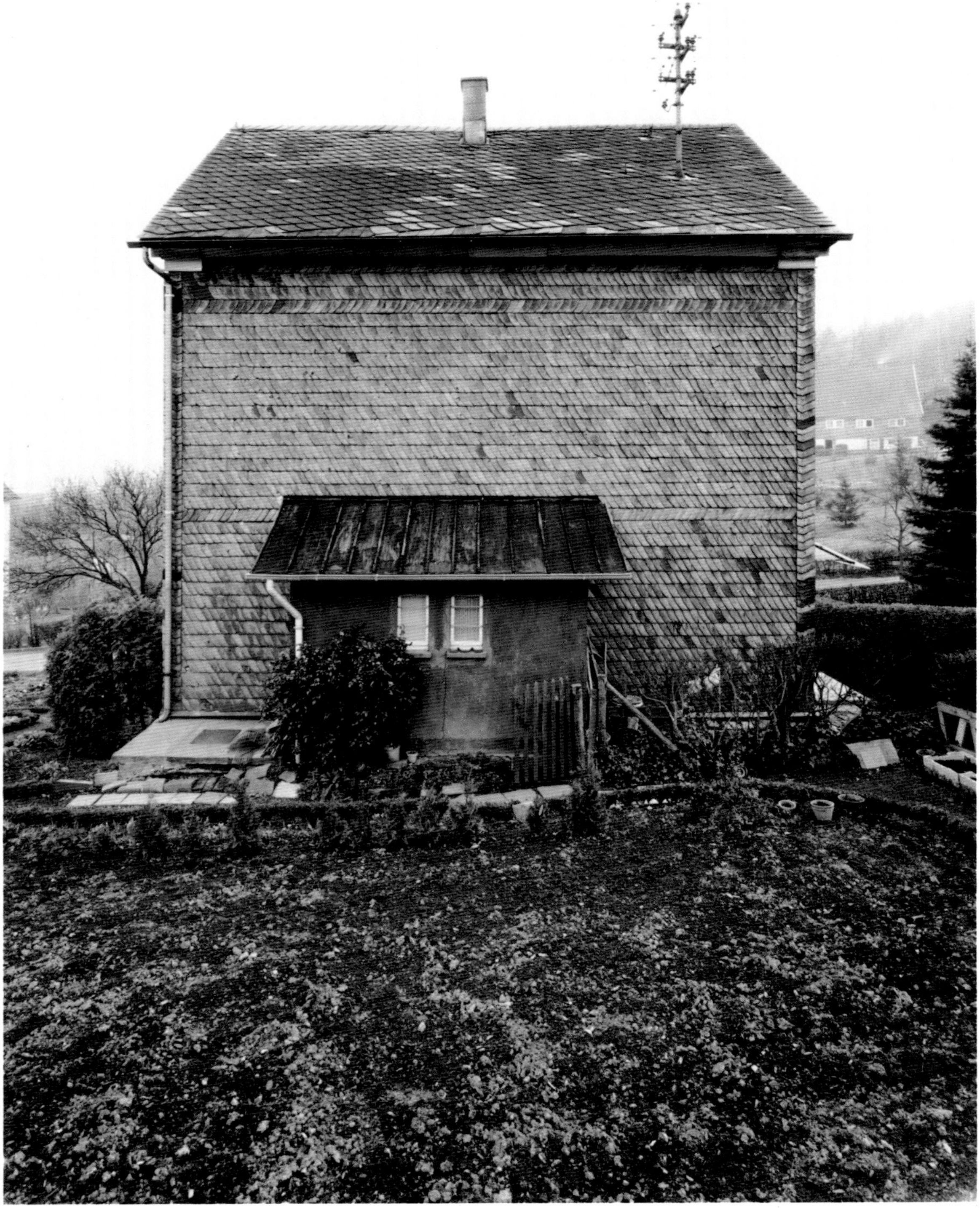

217
Abendröthe 3, Birlenbach, 1972.

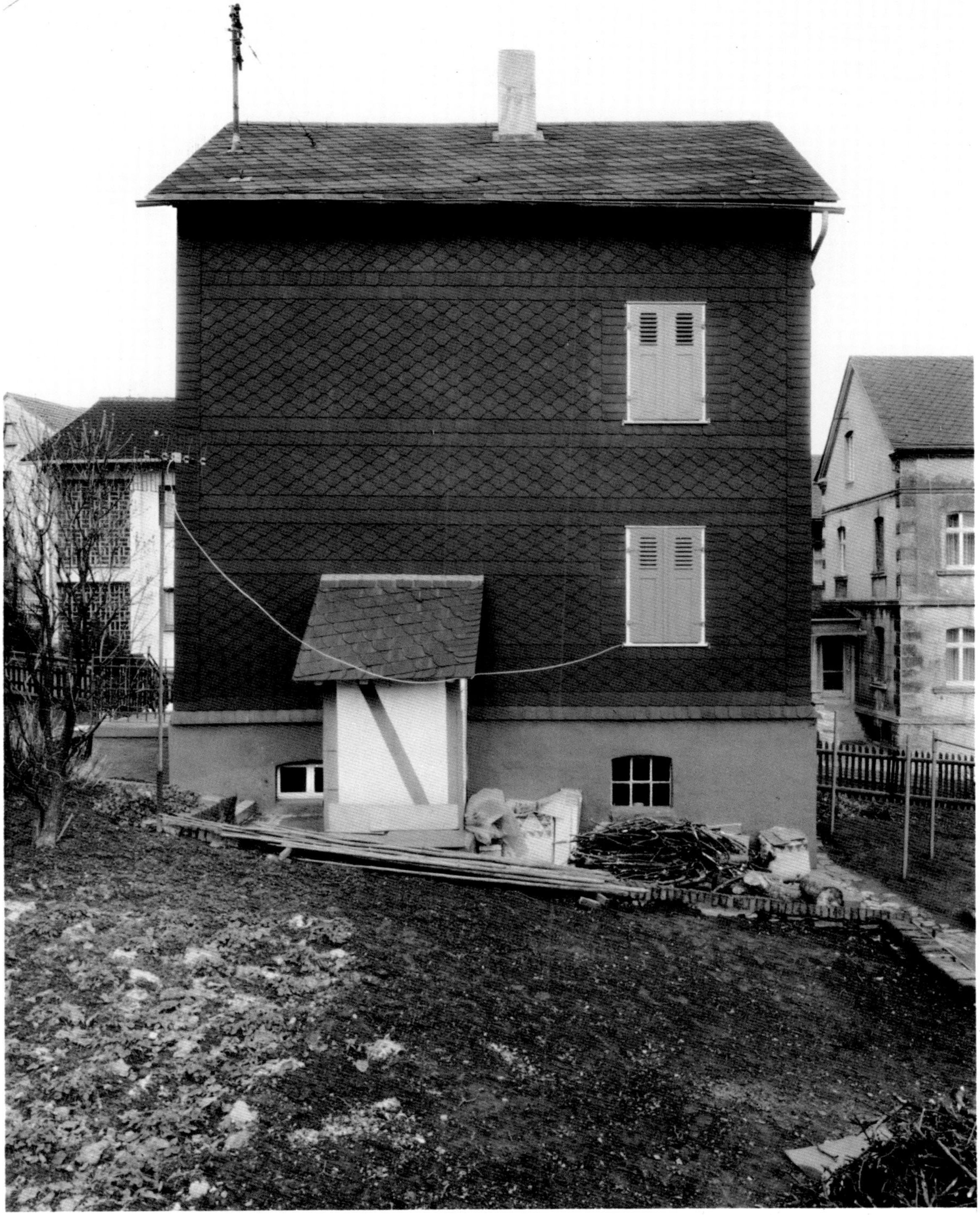

218
Karlstraße 4, Niederschelderhütte, 1973.

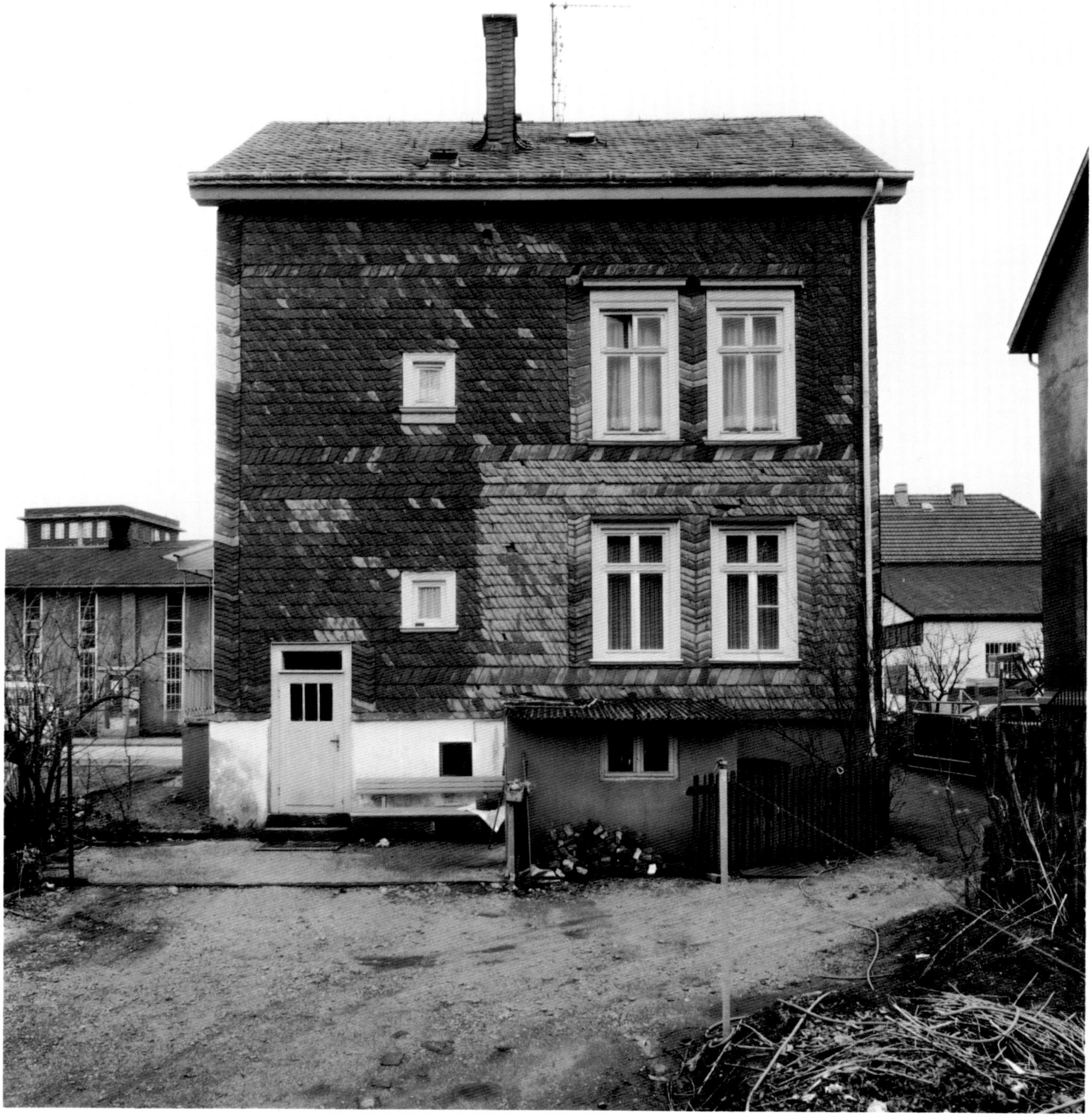

219

Sieghütter Hauptweg 61, Siegen, 1969.

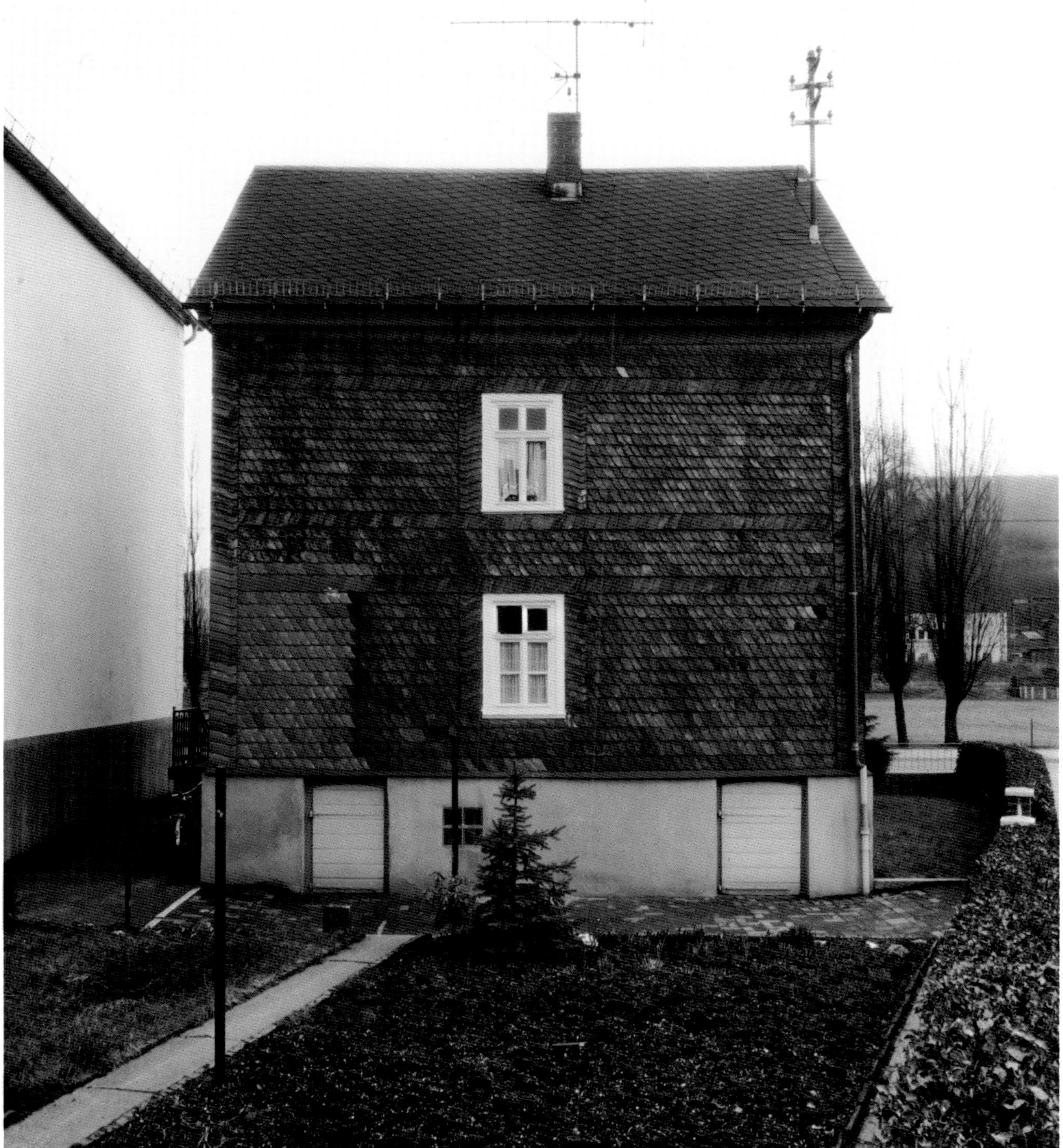

220
Geisweider Straße 127, Geisweid, 1968.

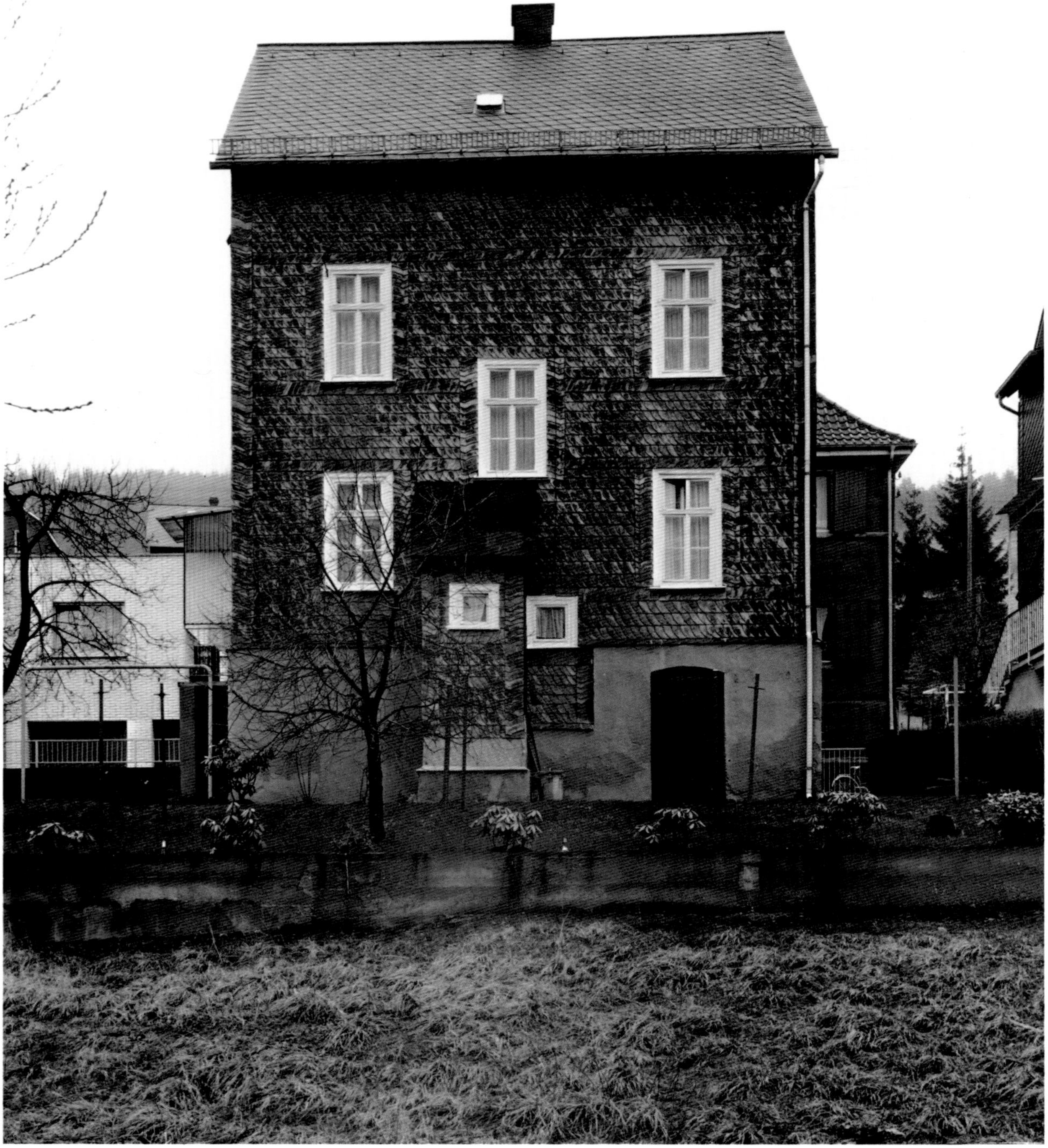

221
Hüttenstraße 43, Eiserfeld, 1972.

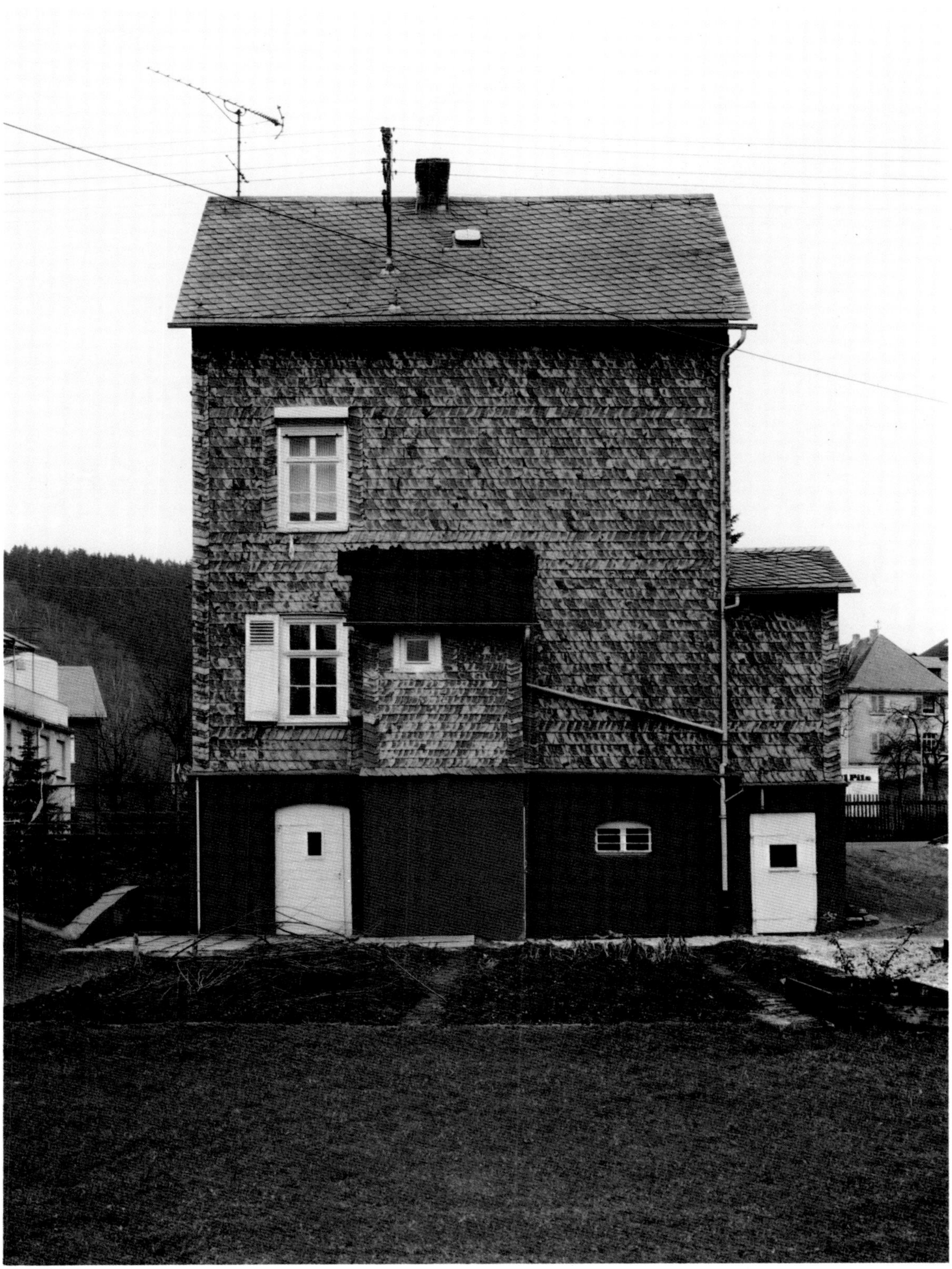

222
Eiserntalstraße 138, Eisern, 1971.

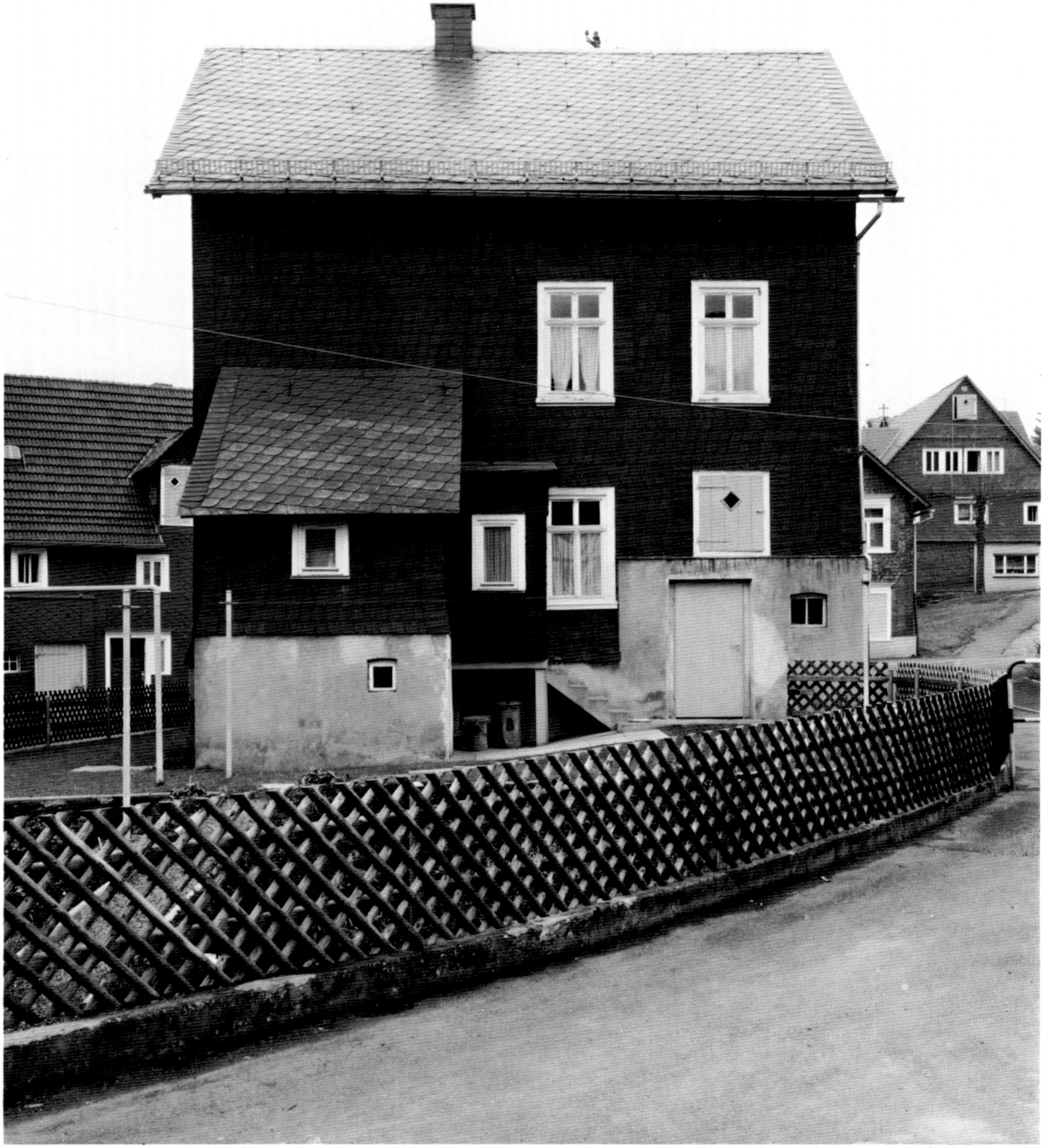

223
Eiserntalstraße 116, Eisern, 1971.

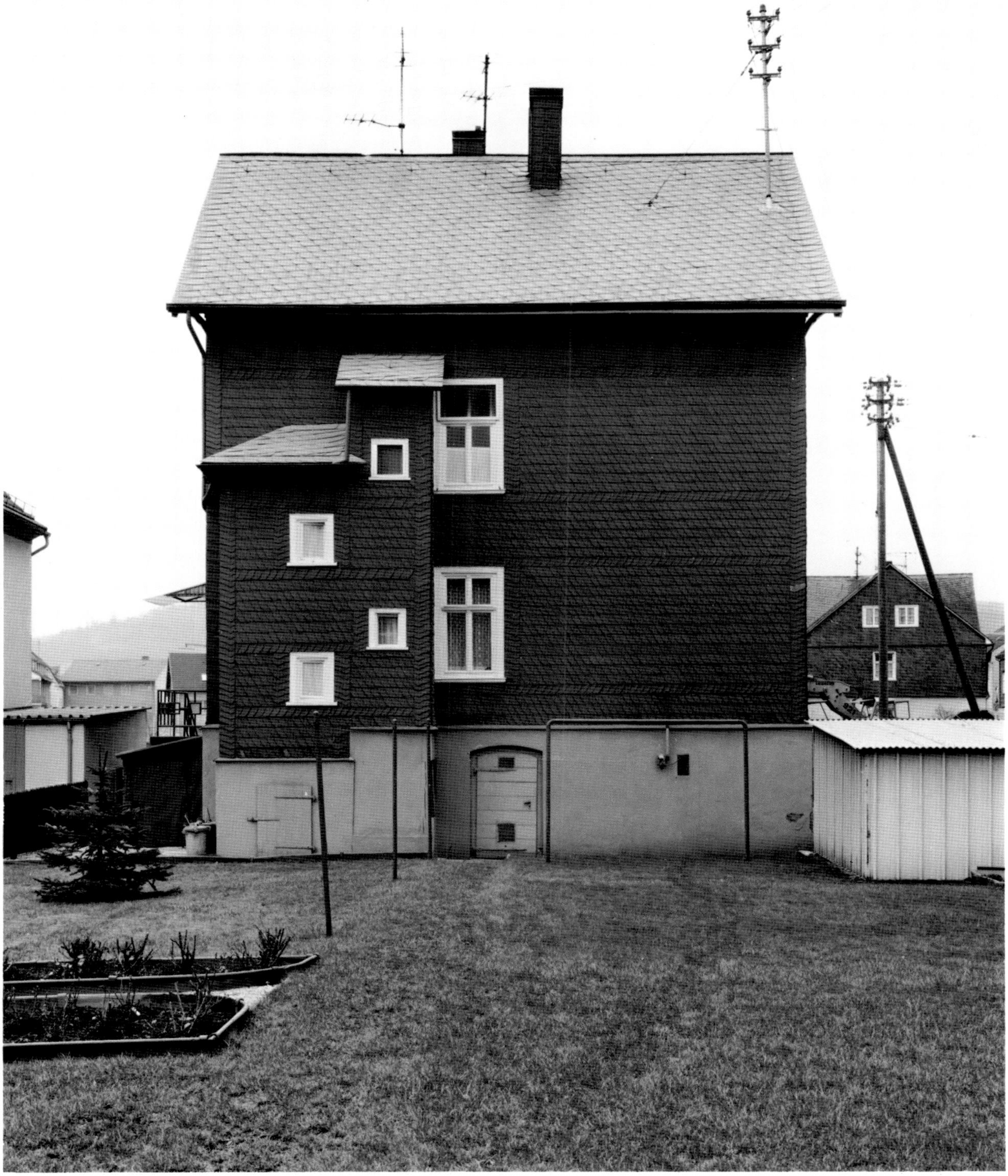

224
Philippstraße 2, Geisweid, 1973.

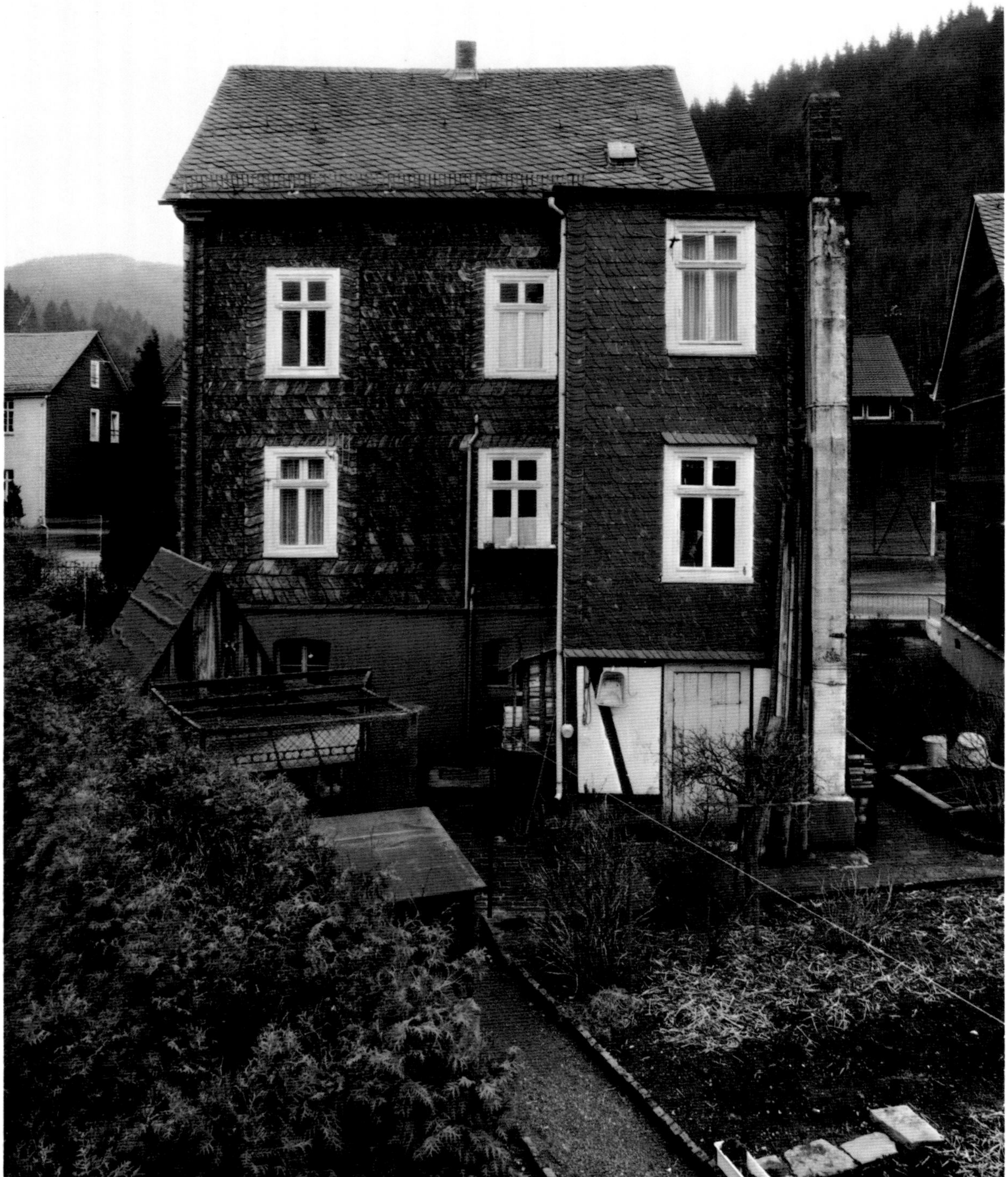

225
Siegtalstraße 36, Eiserfeld, 1971.

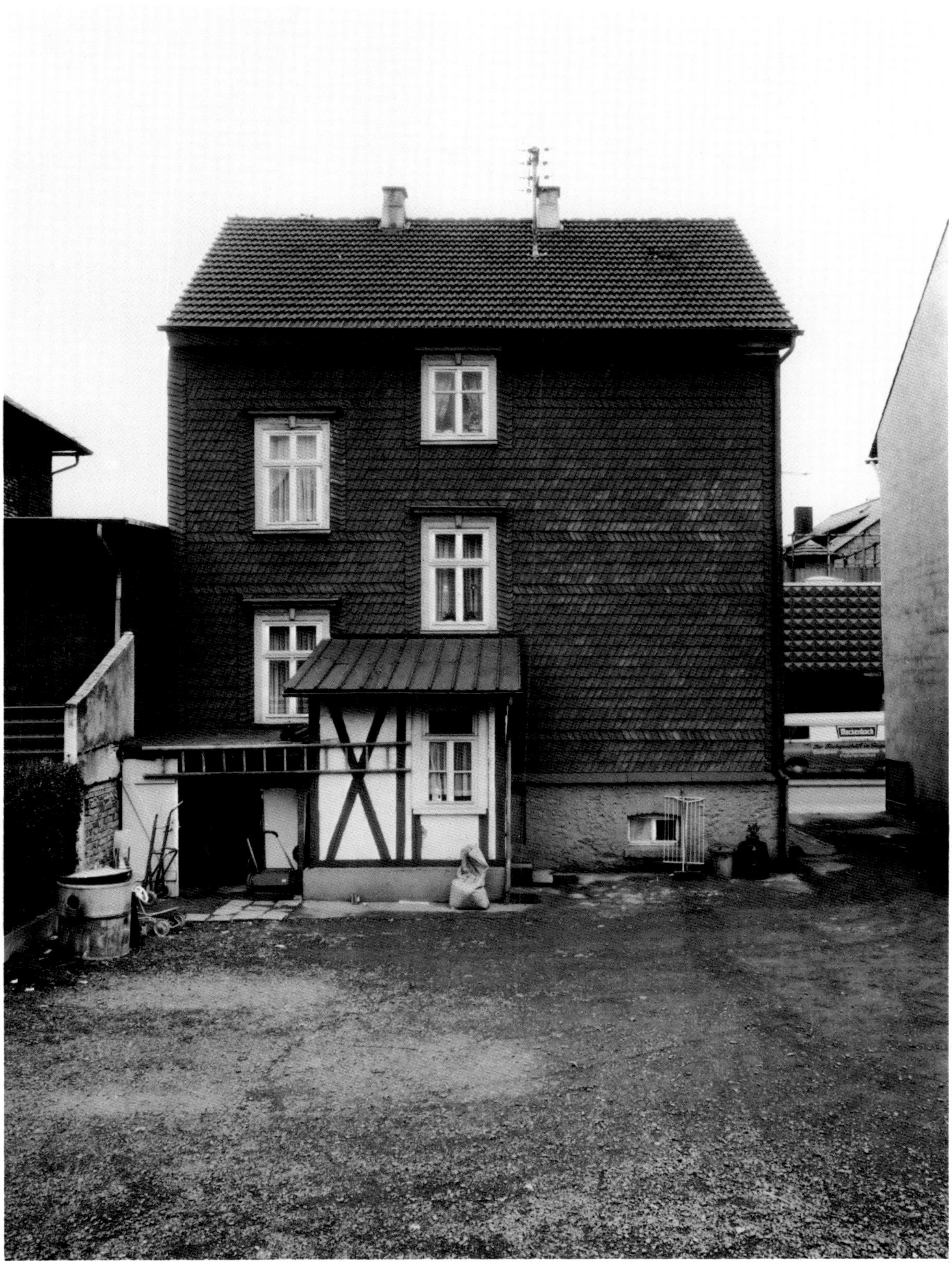

226
Marktstraße 32, Geisweid, 1972.

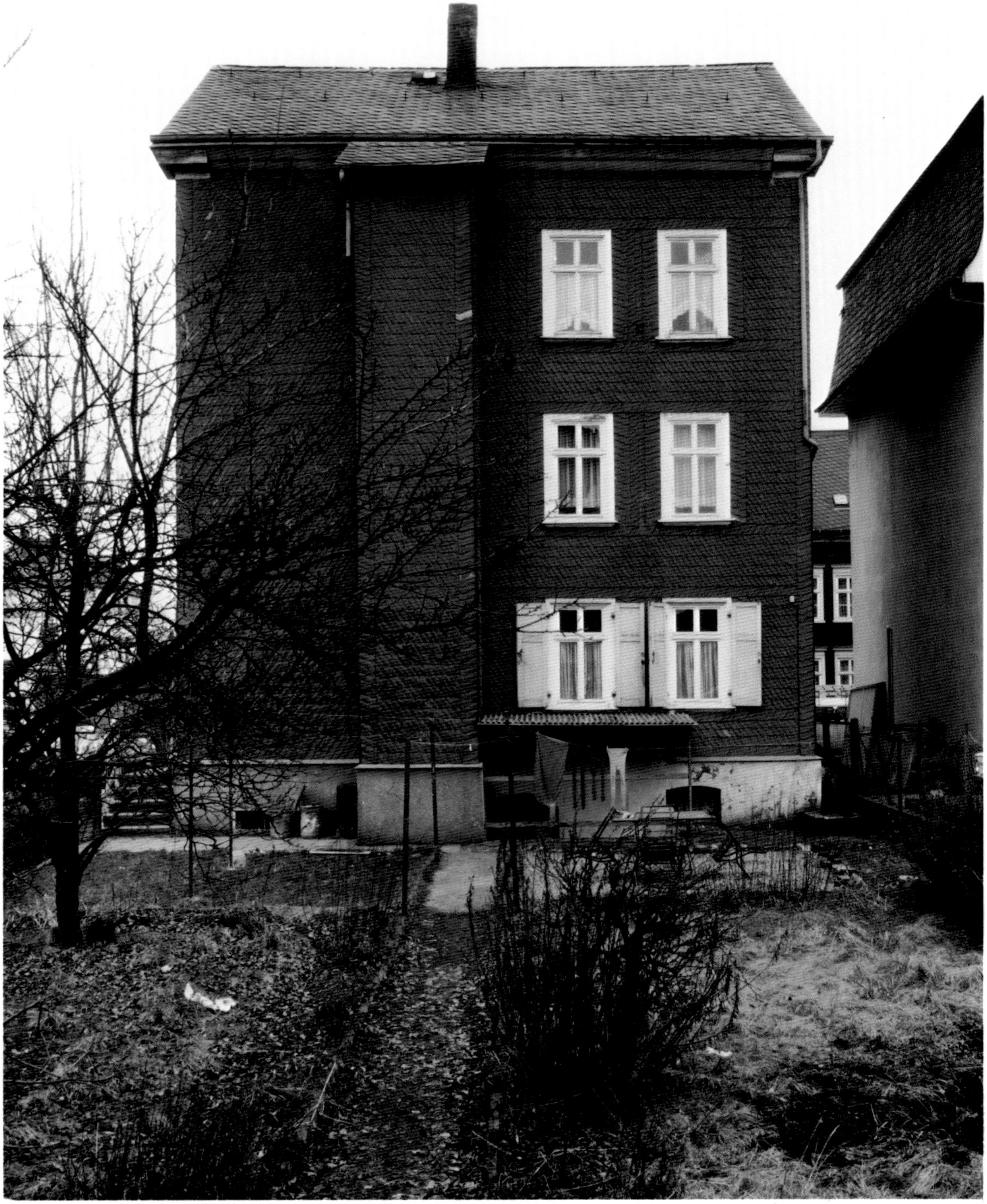

227
Arndtstraße 6, Siegen, 1972.

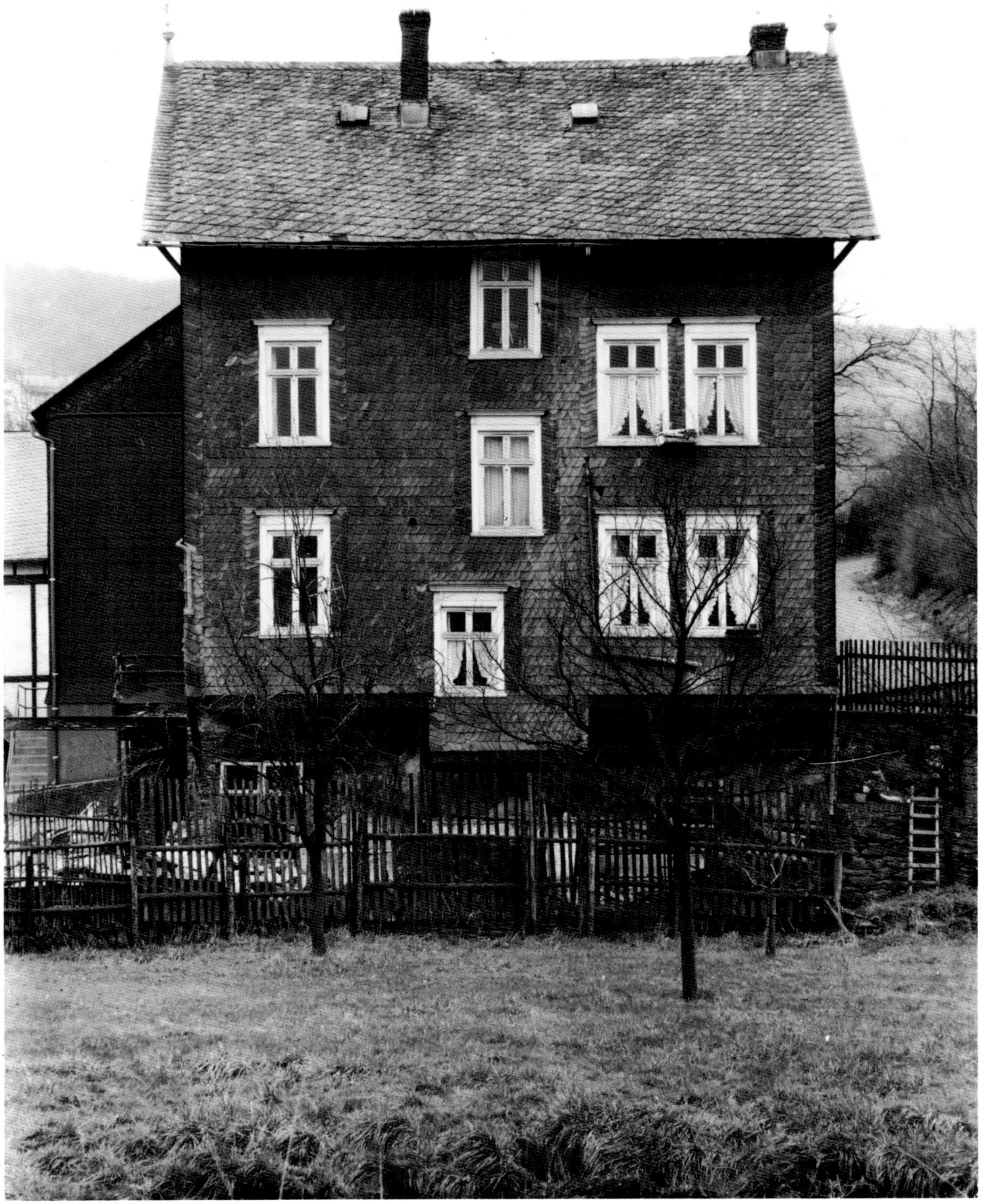

228

Waldstraße 119, Niederschelderhütte, 1961.

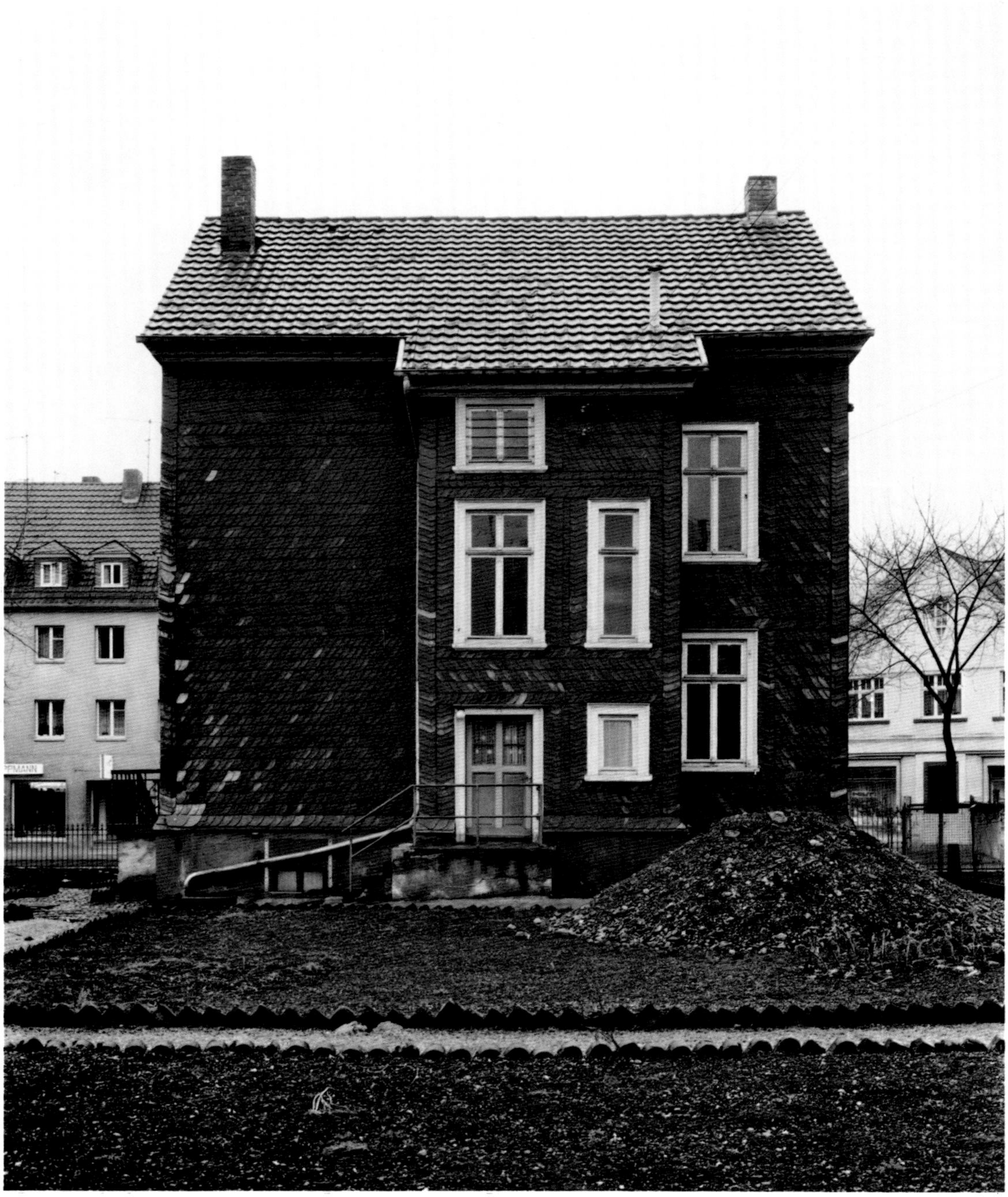

229
Weidenauer Straße 119, Weidenau, 1970.

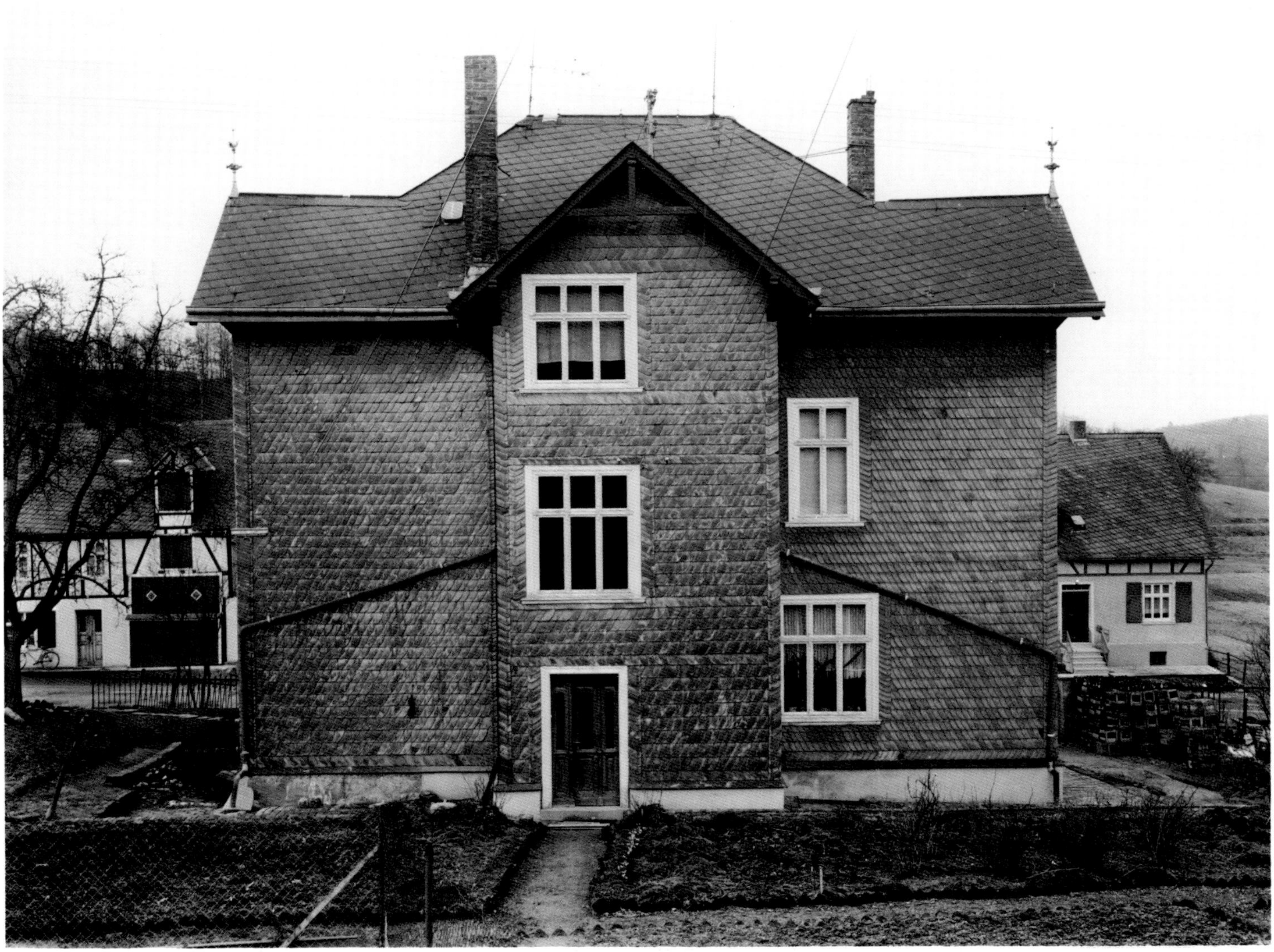

230
Hagener Straße 26, Wilnsdorf, 1962.

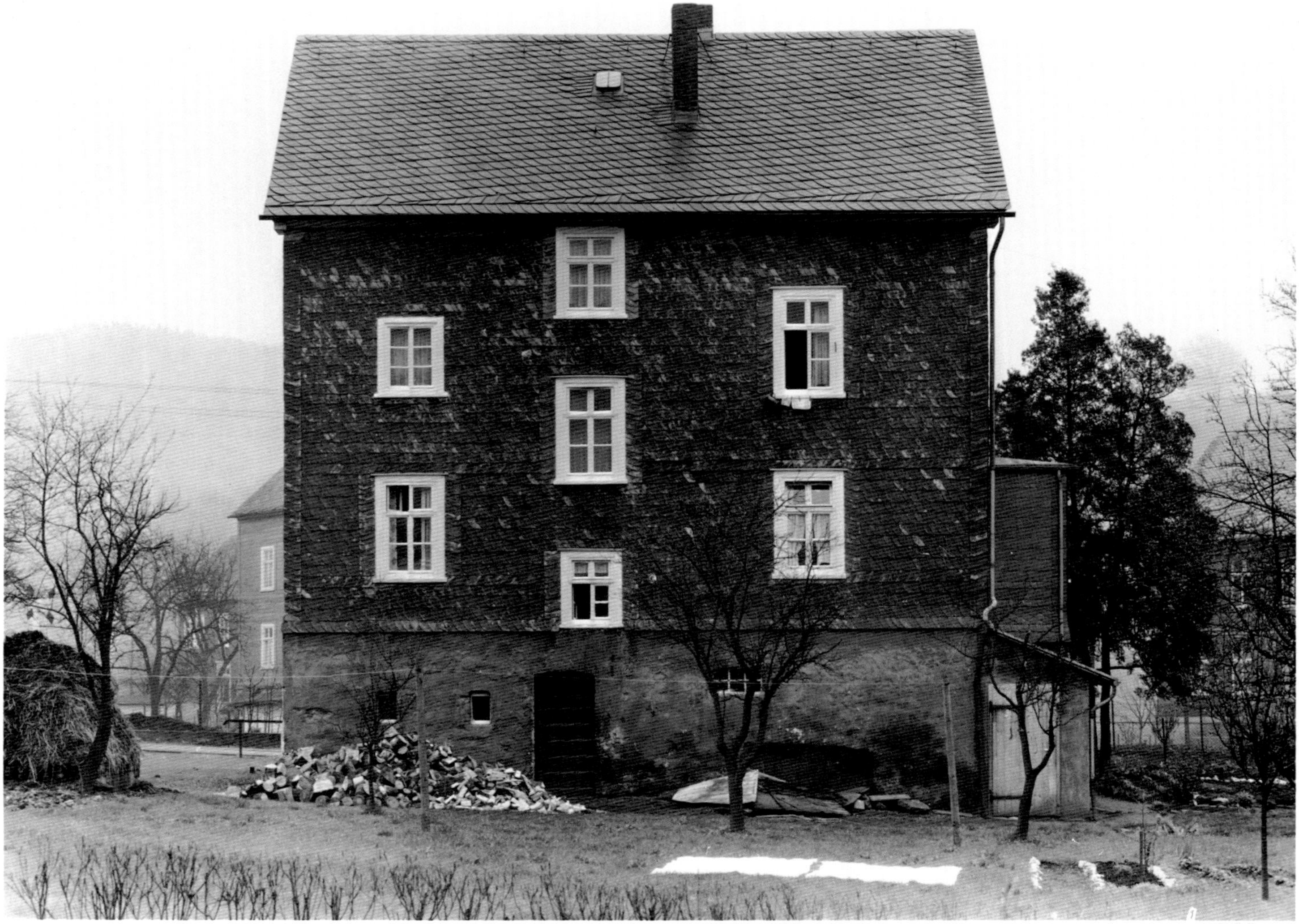

231
Rensdorfstraße 5, Salchendorf, 1961.

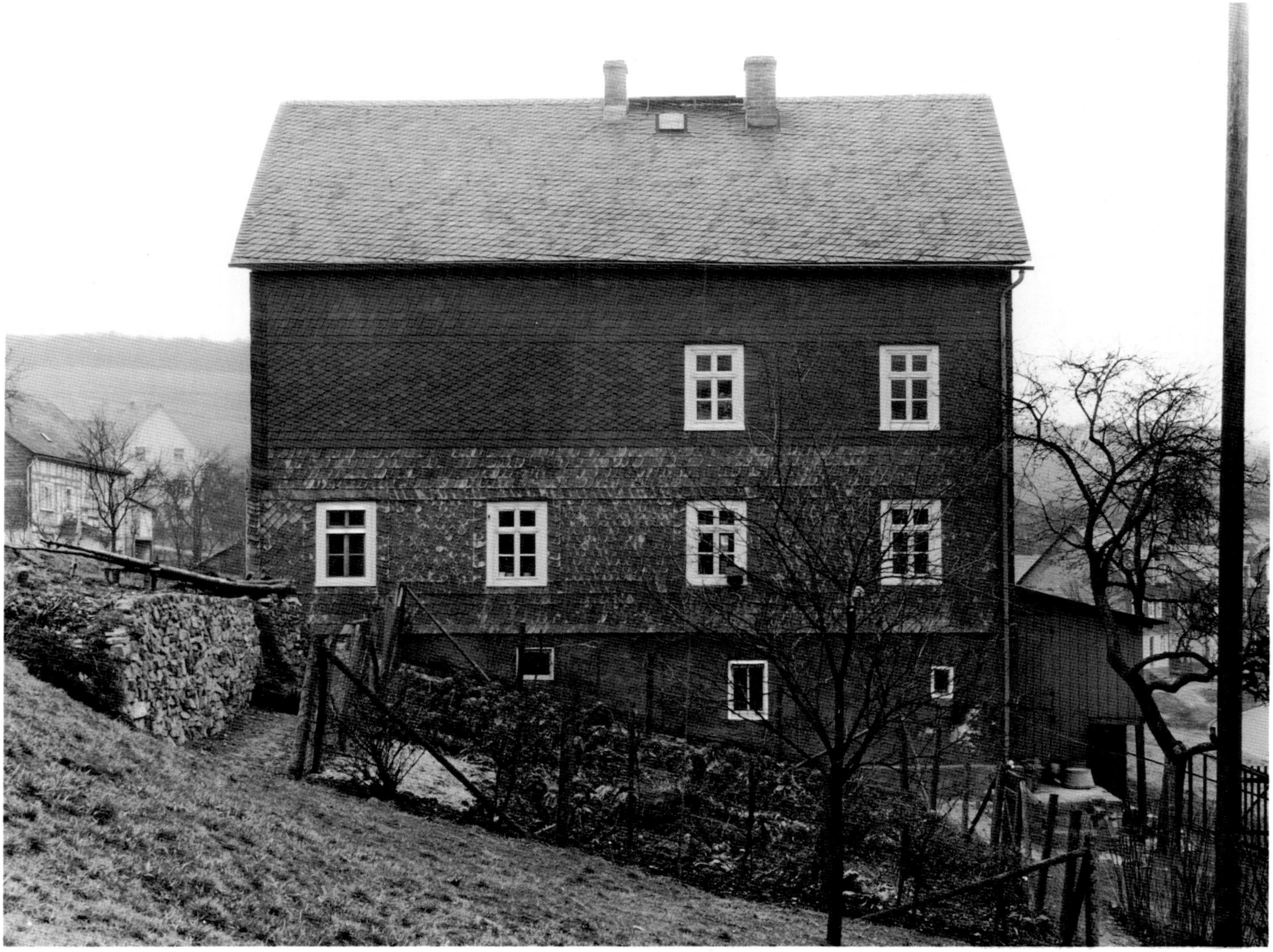

232
Feldstraße 5, Flammersbach, 1960.

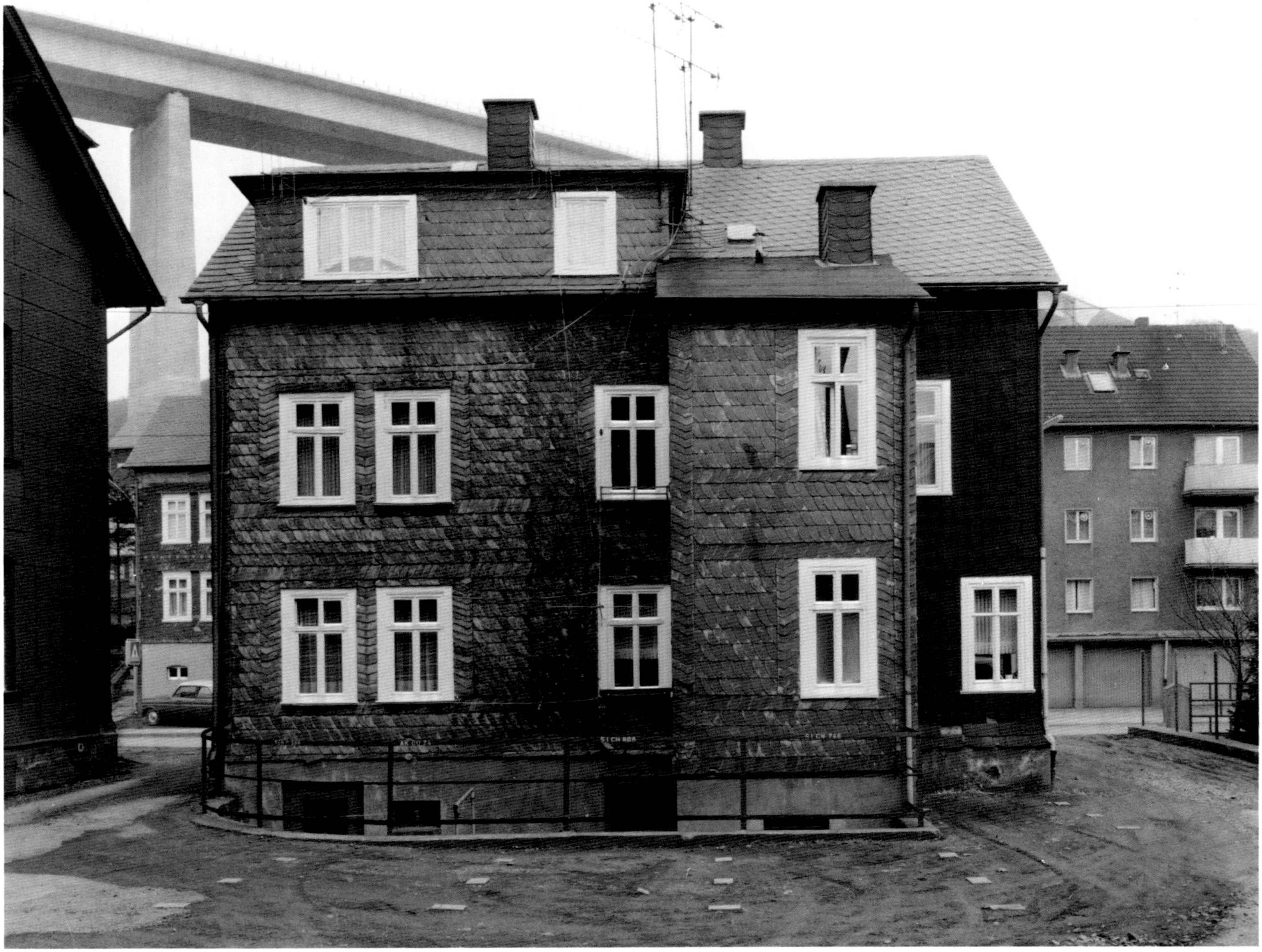

233
Bahnhofstraße 155, Eiserfeld, 1971.

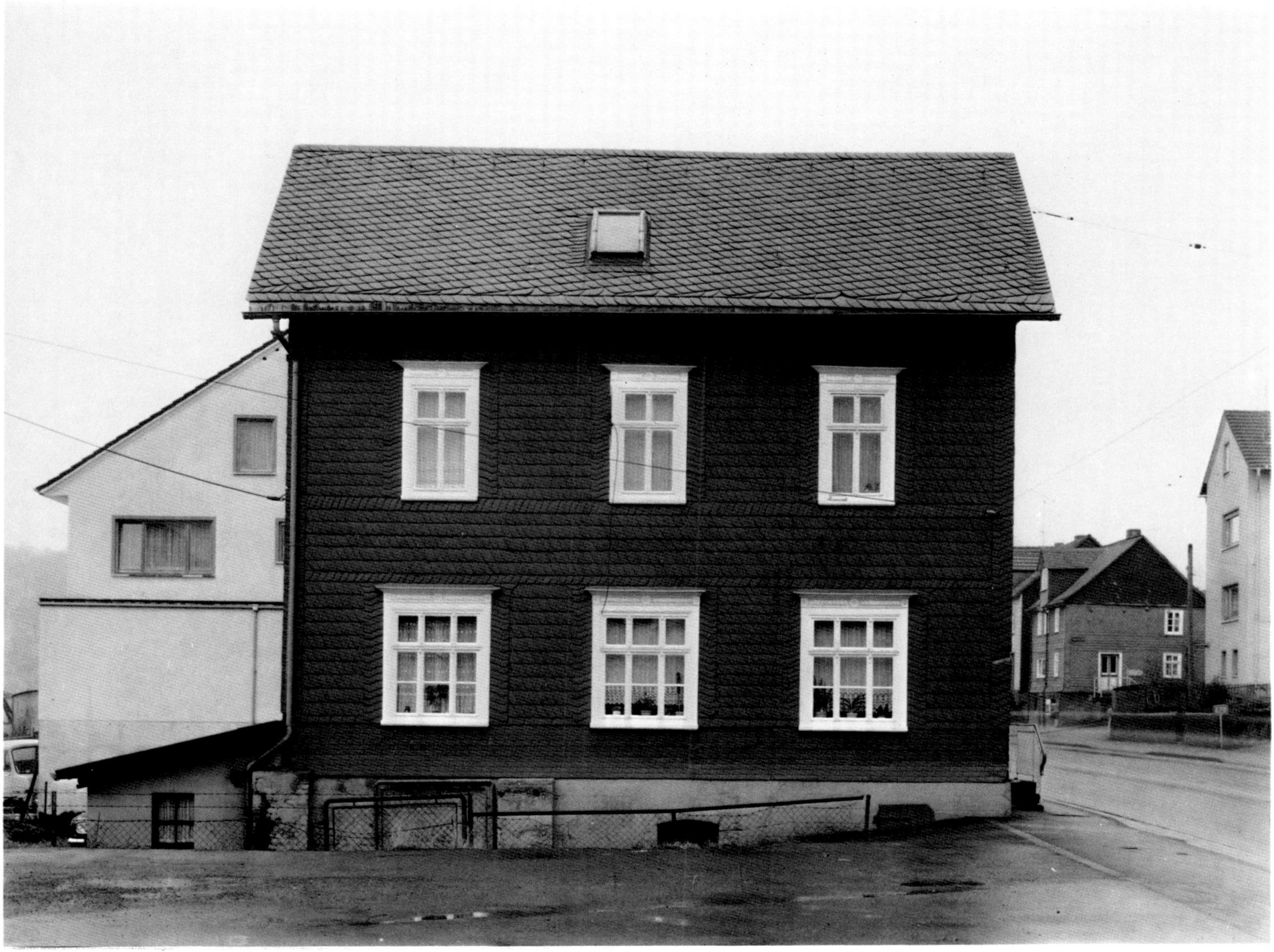

234
Siegtalstraße 164, Niederschelden, 1968.

V.
ECKANSICHTEN
CORNER VIEWS

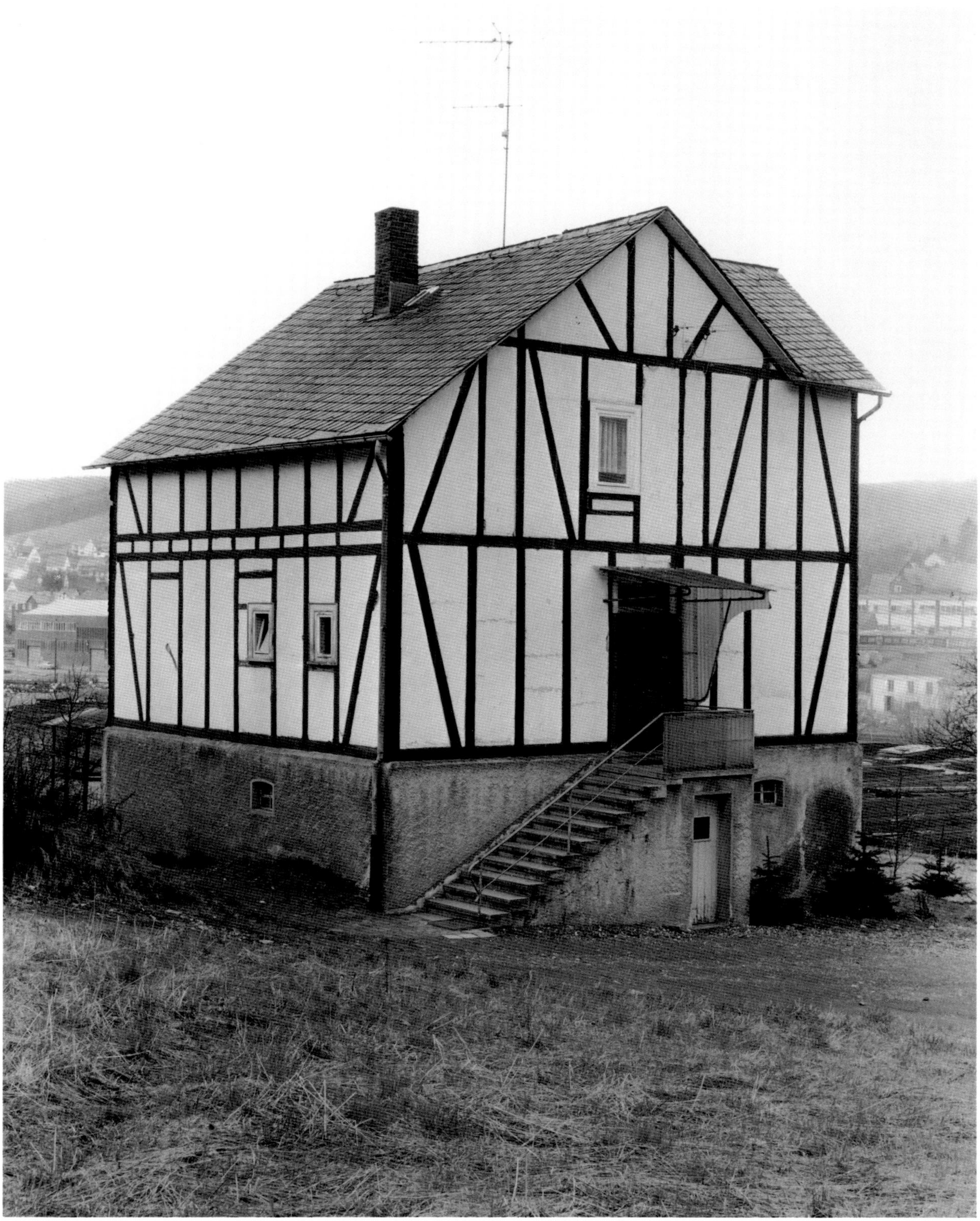

235
Fritz-Schäfer-Straße 24, Salchendorf, 1971.

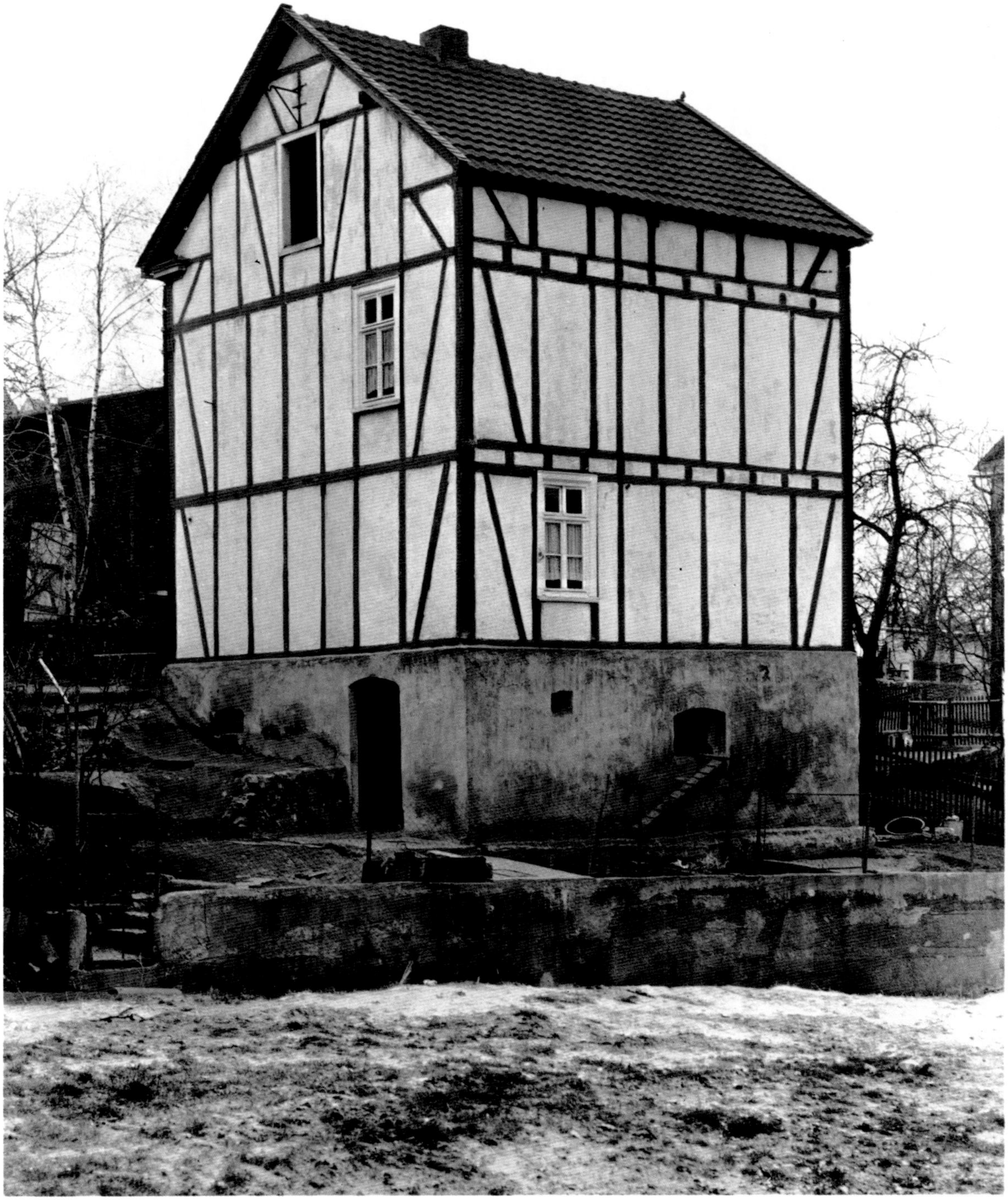

236

Siegener Straße 67, Gosenbach, 1960.

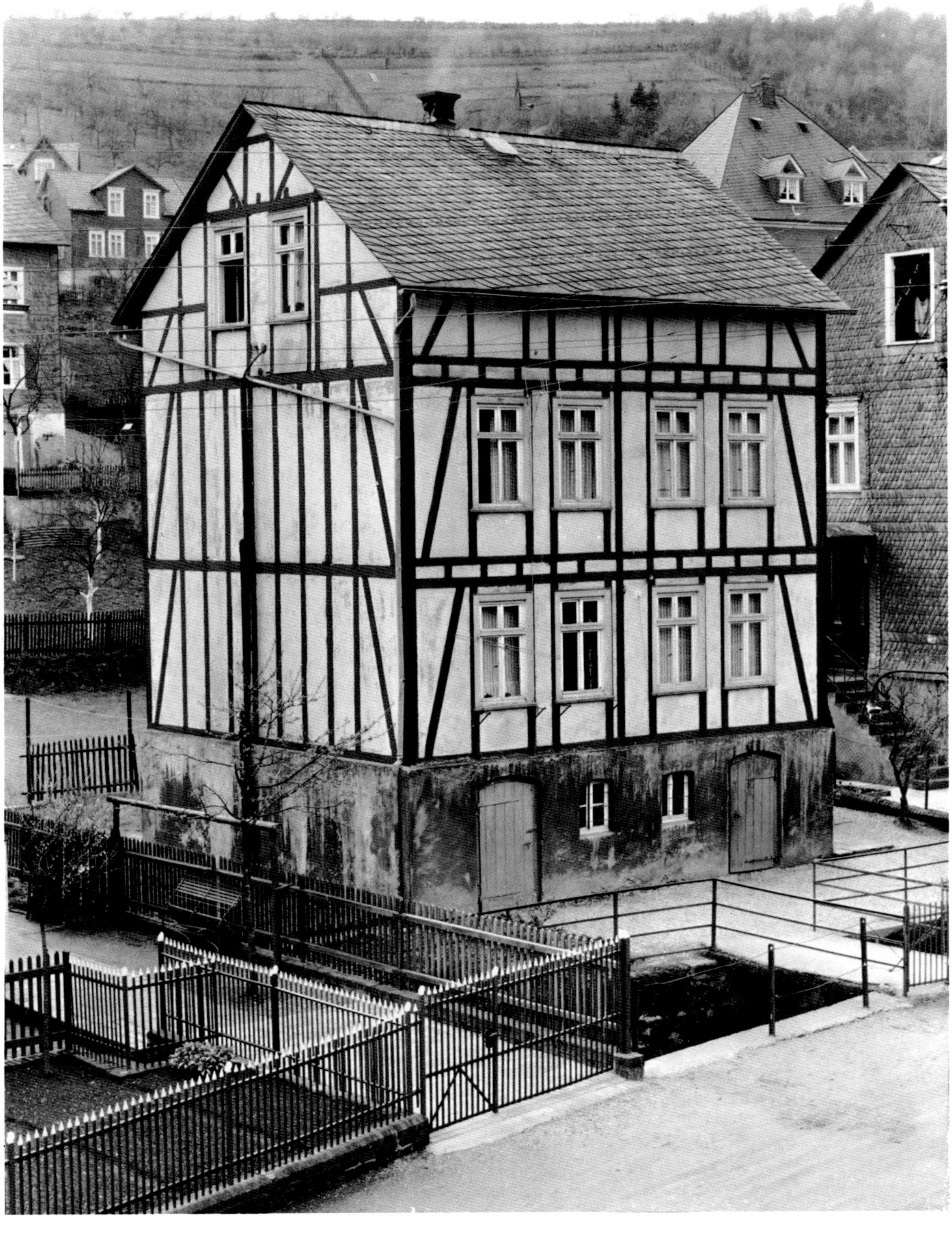

237
Am Gosenbach 15, Niederschelderhütte, 1960.

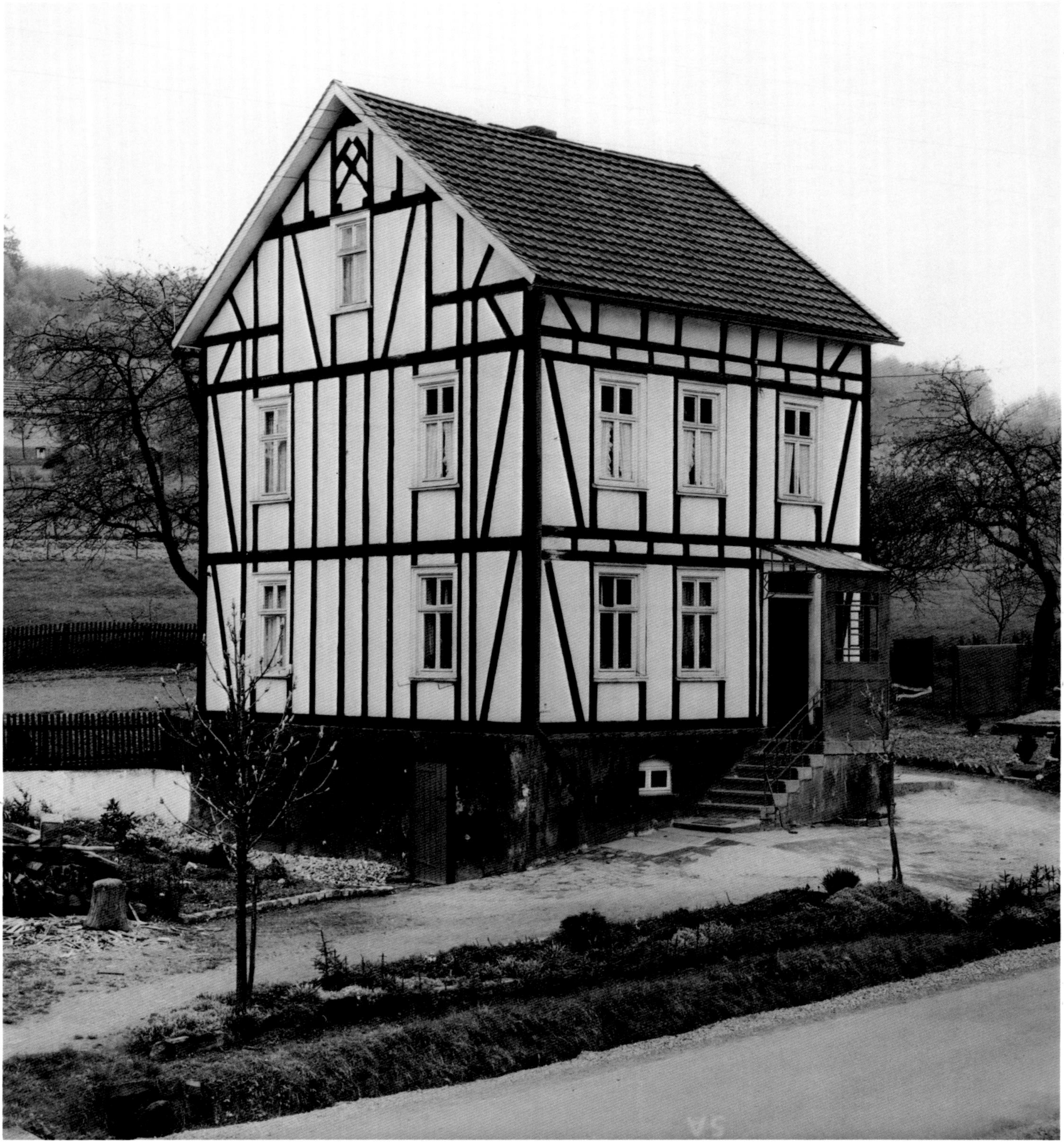

238
Friedenshortstraße 9, Freudenberg, 1960.

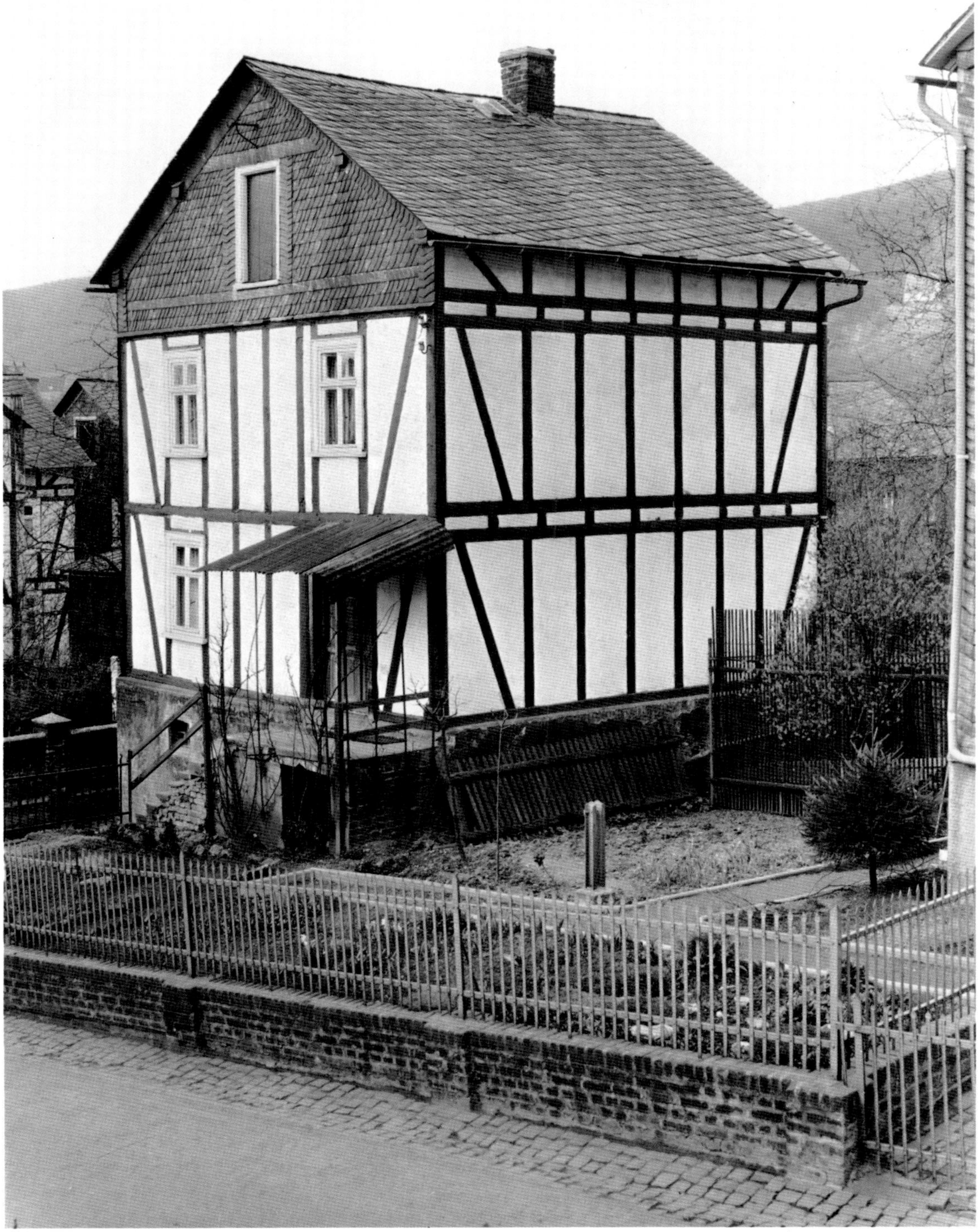

239
Bühlstraße 152, Niederschelden, 1960.

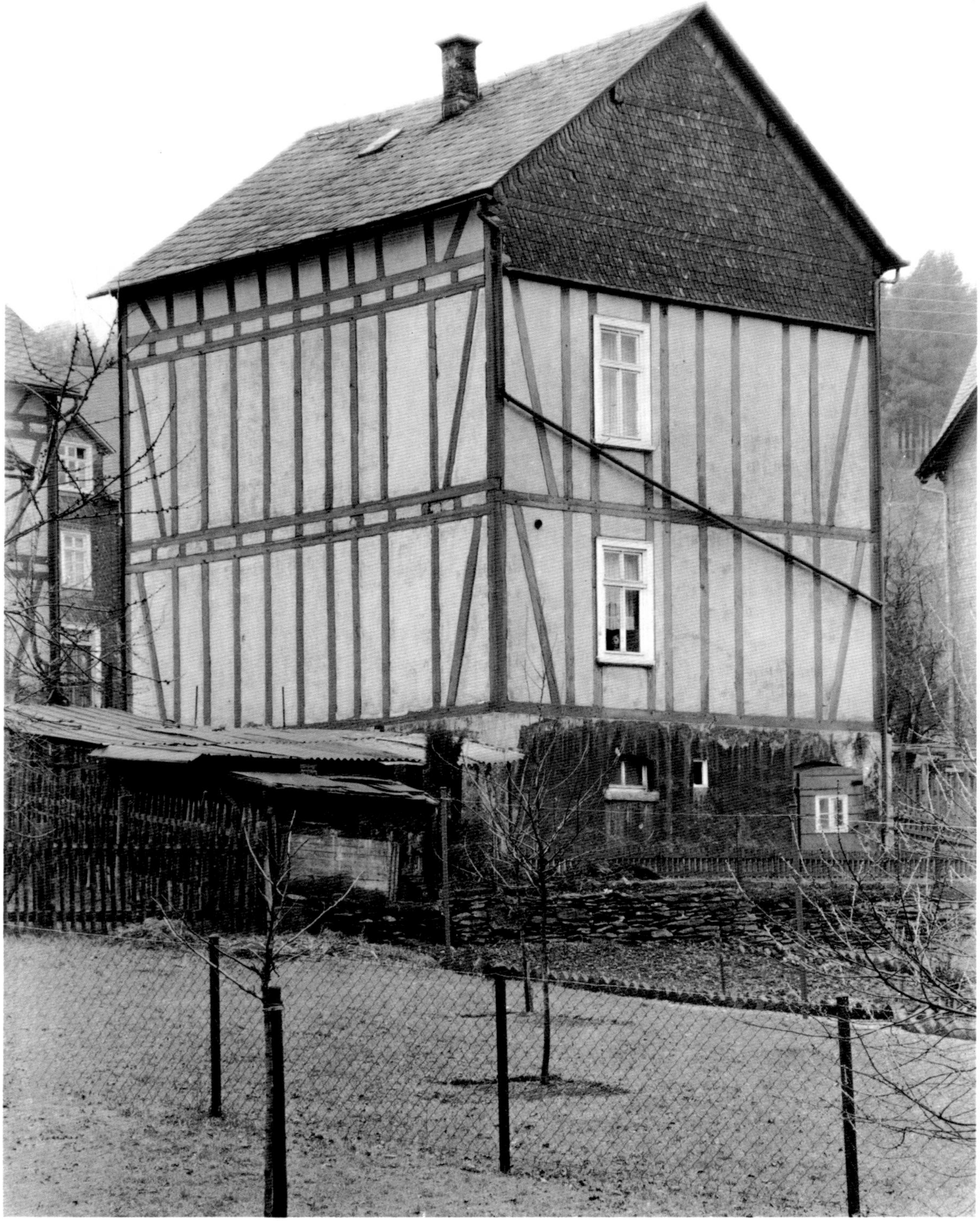

240
Querstraße 2, Eiserfeld, 1959.

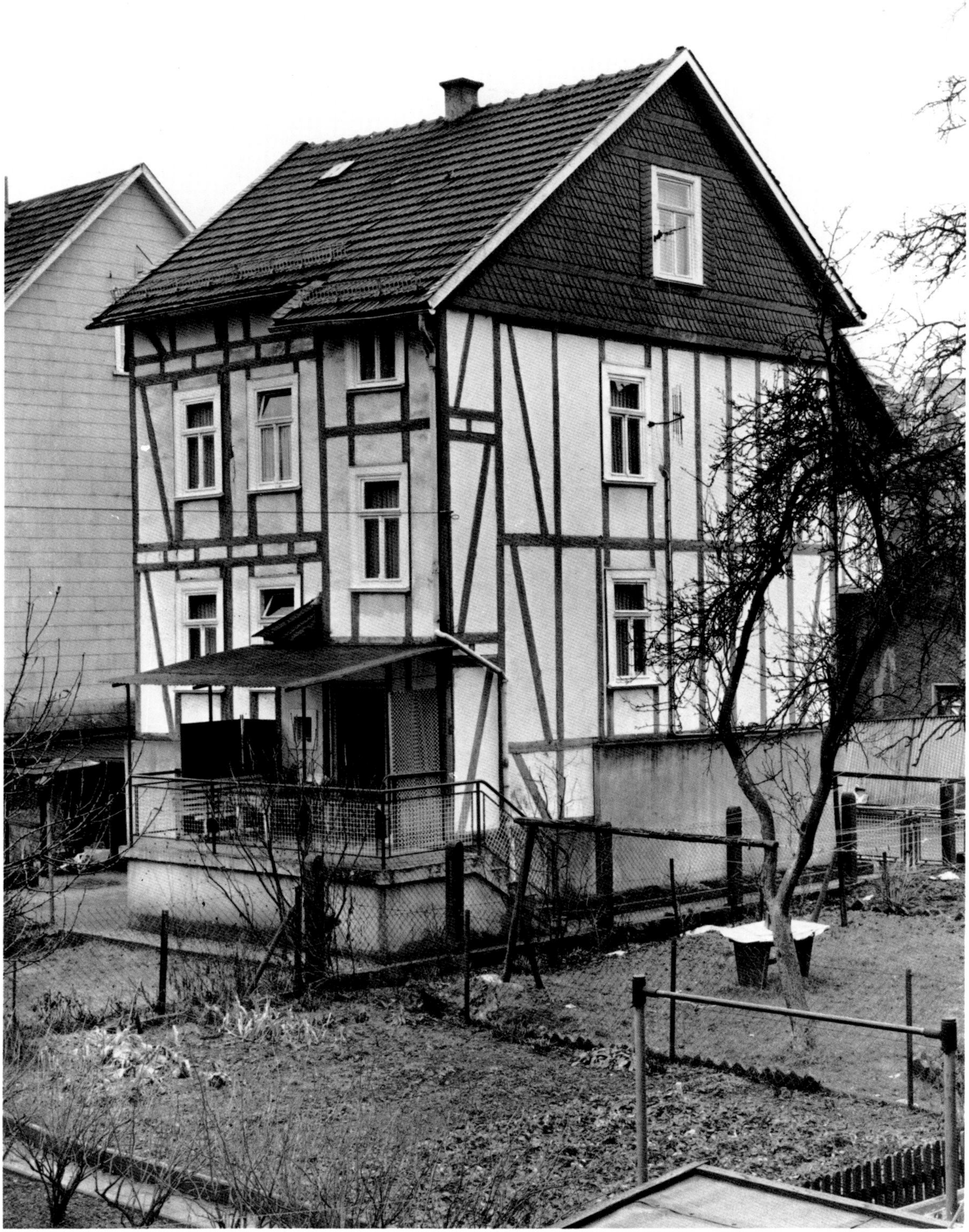

241
Johannesstraße 5, Niederschelden, 1972.

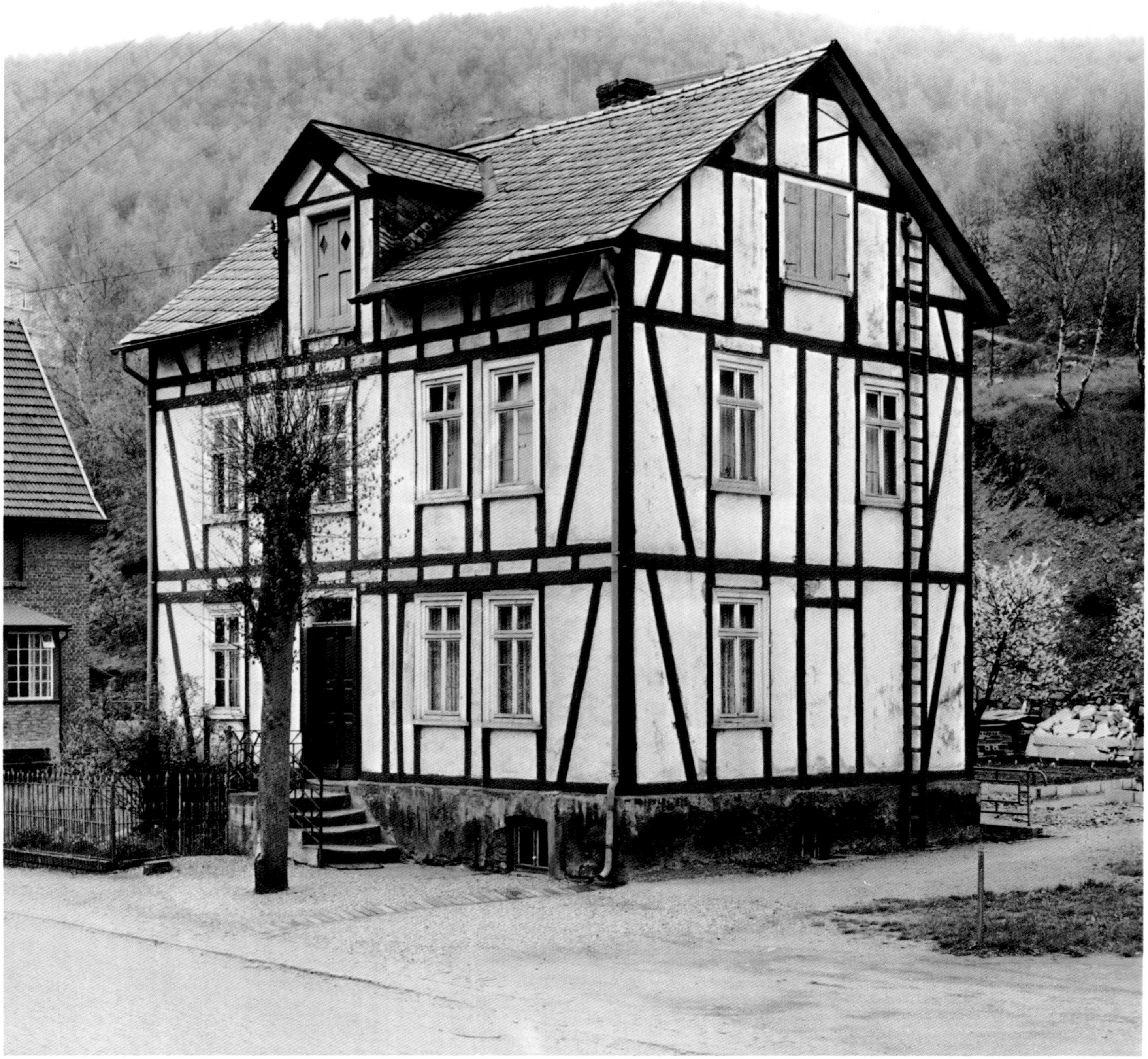

242
Auf der Hütte 45, Gosenbach, 1961.

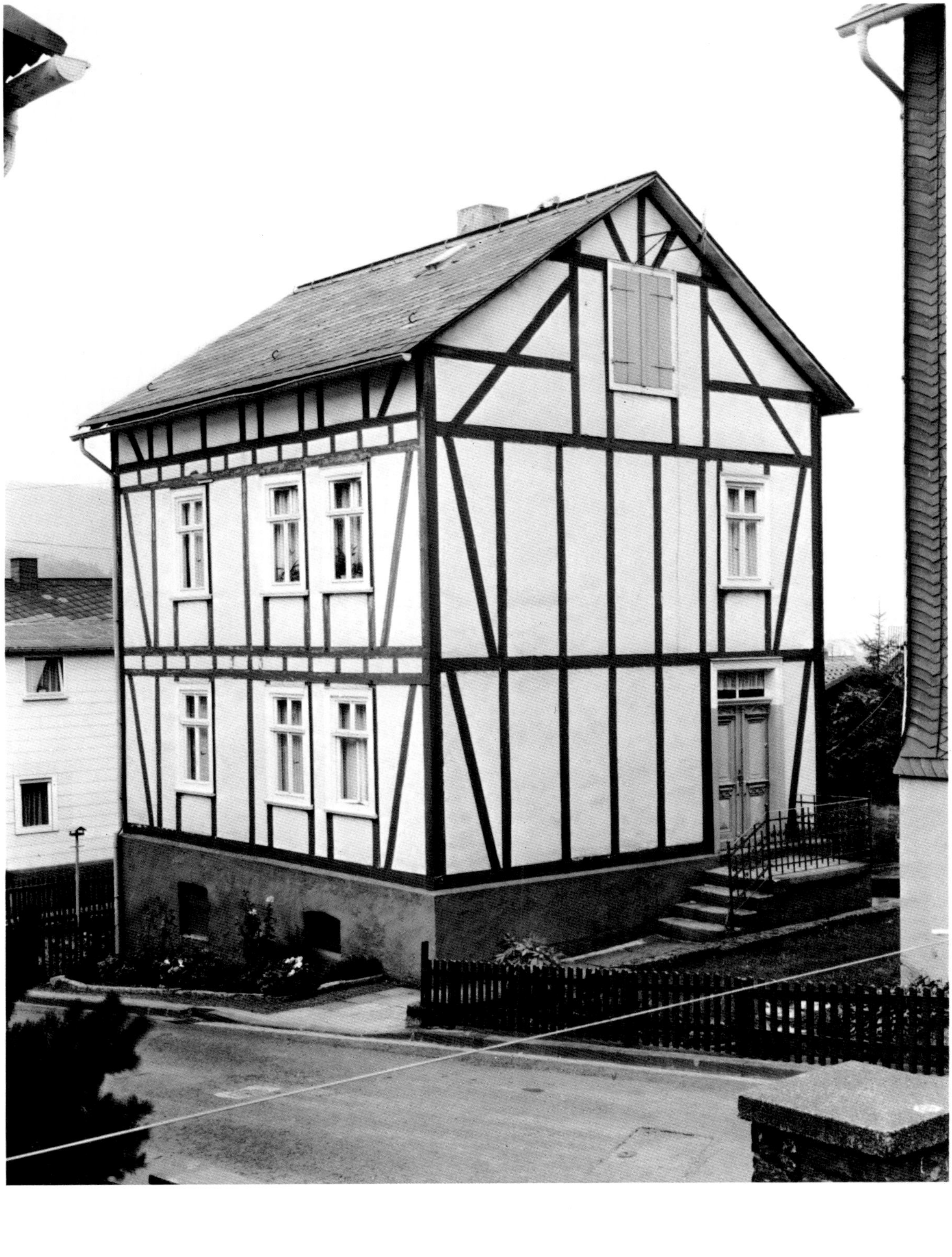

243
Karlstraße 4, Niederschelderhütte, 1976.

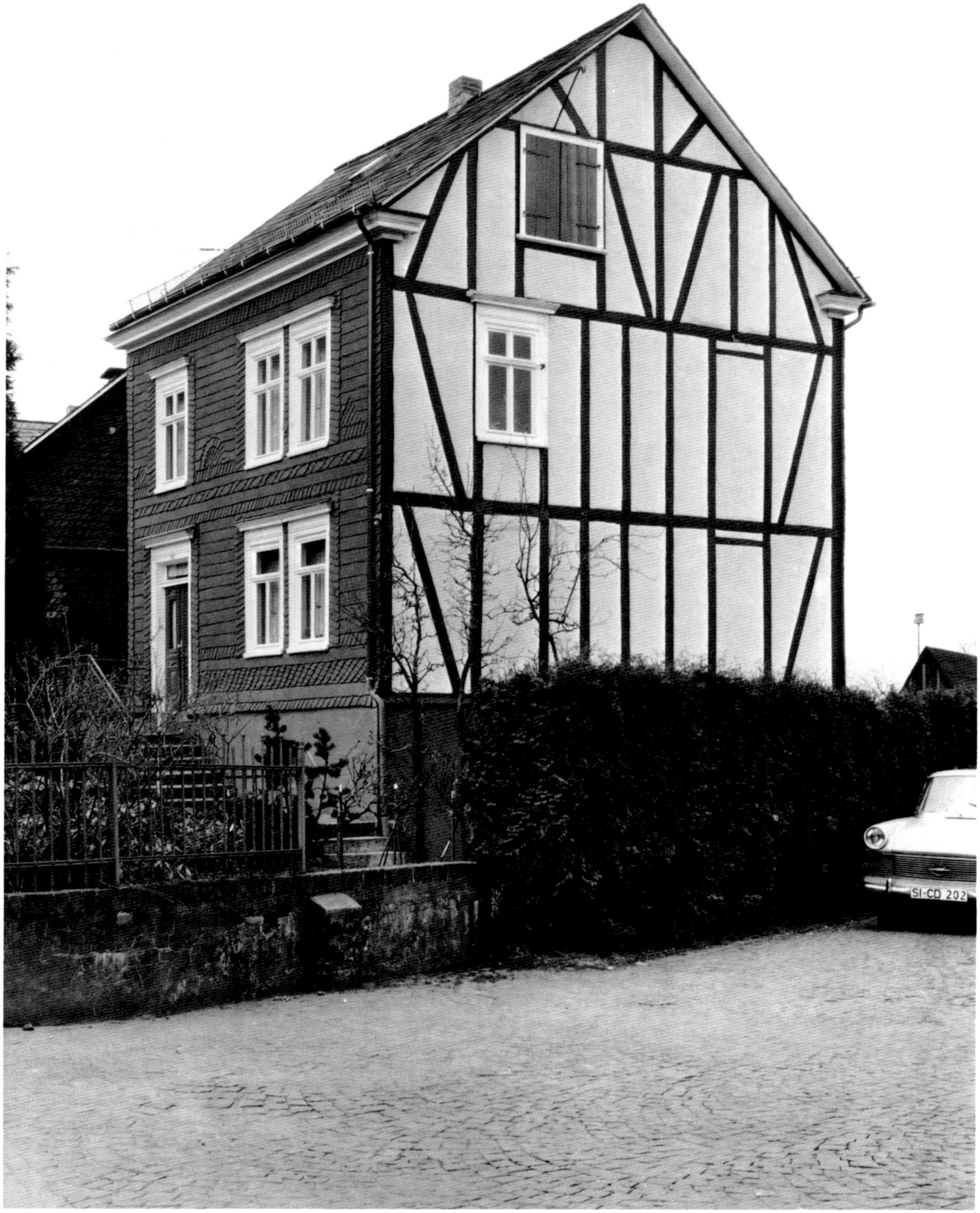

244
Siegtalstraße 36, Eiserfeld, 1971.

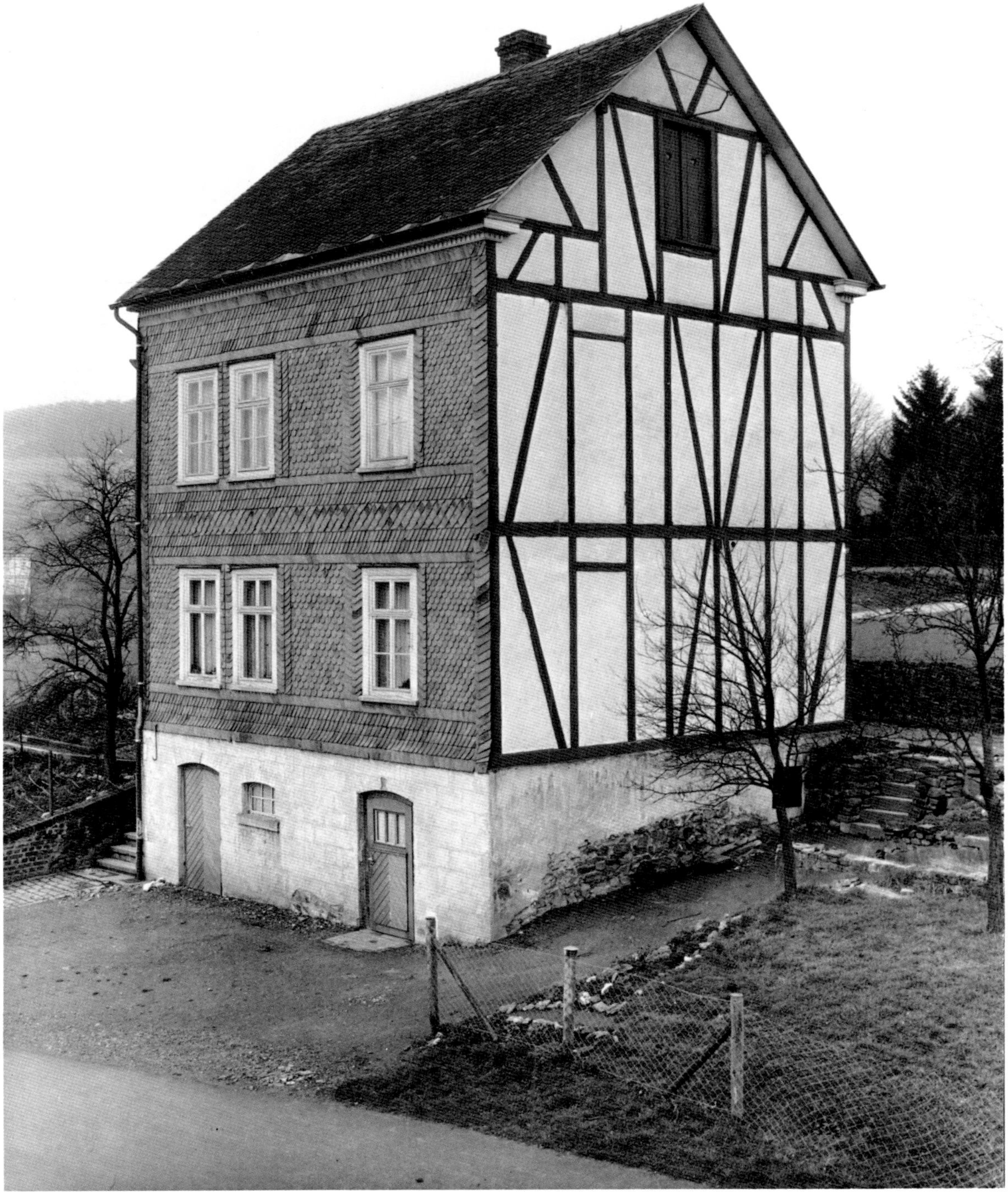

245
Rensdorfstraße 13, Salchendorf, 1960.

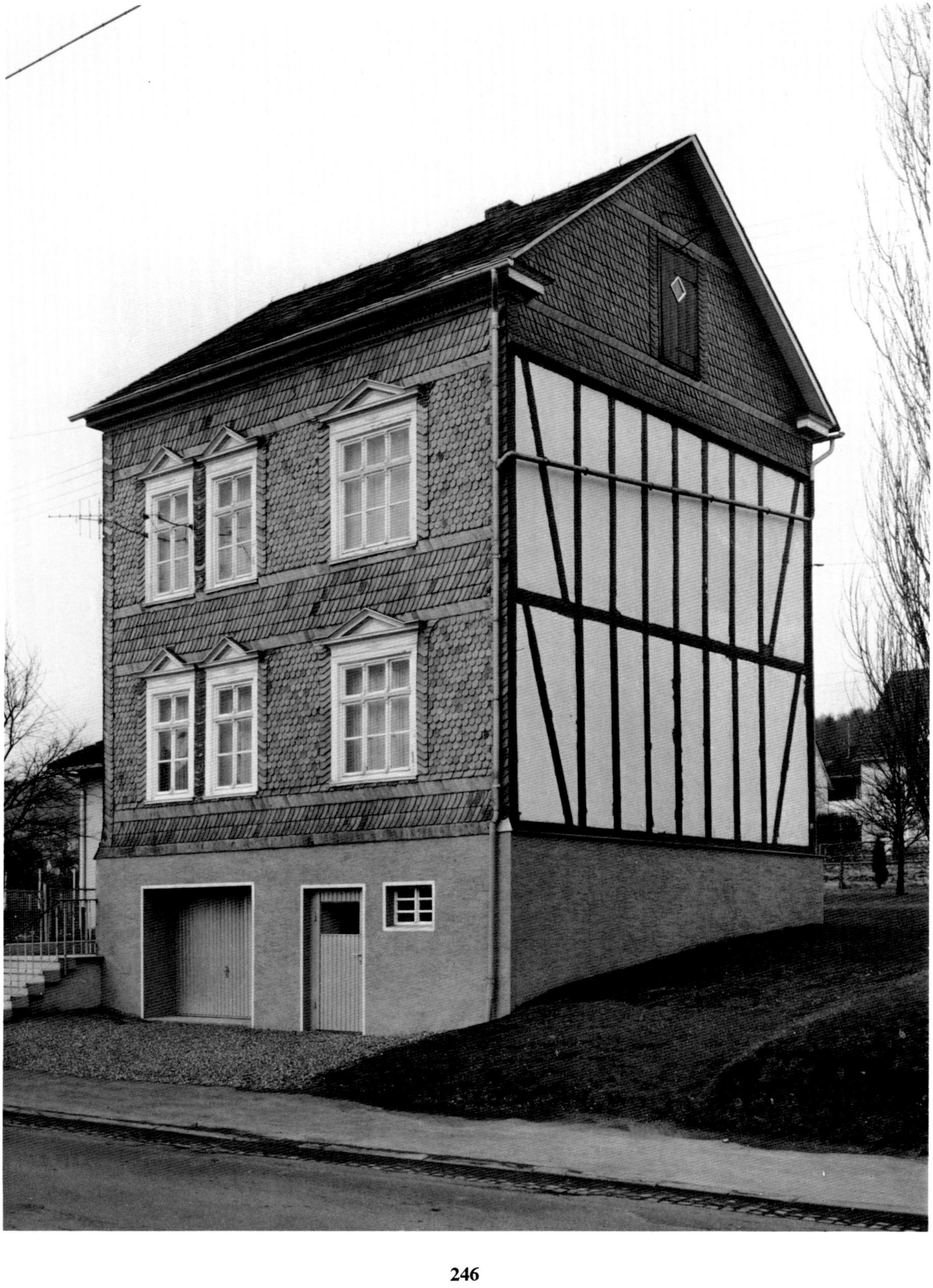

246

Wildener Straße 25, Salchendorf, 1971.

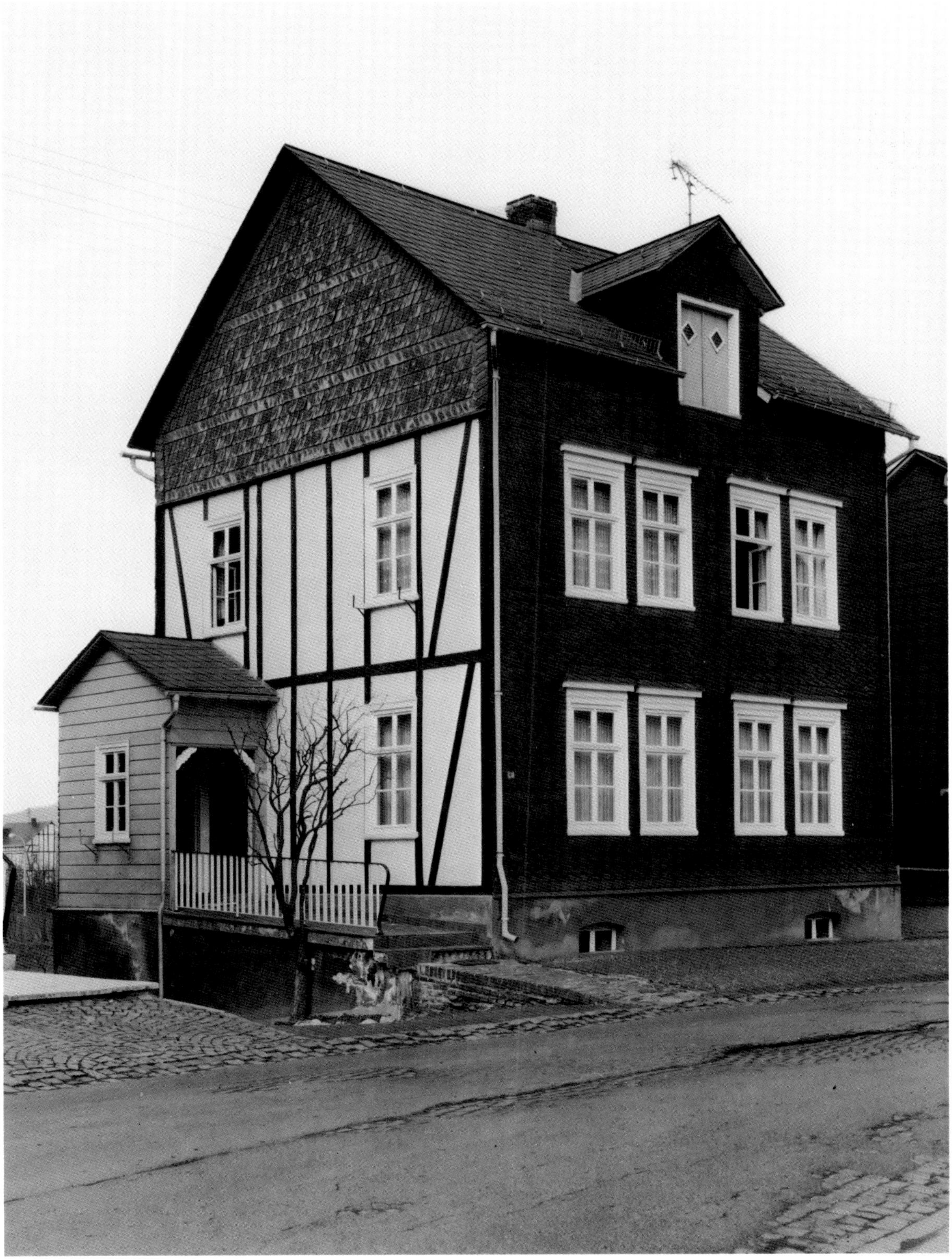

247
Eiserntalstraße 138, Eisern, 1969.

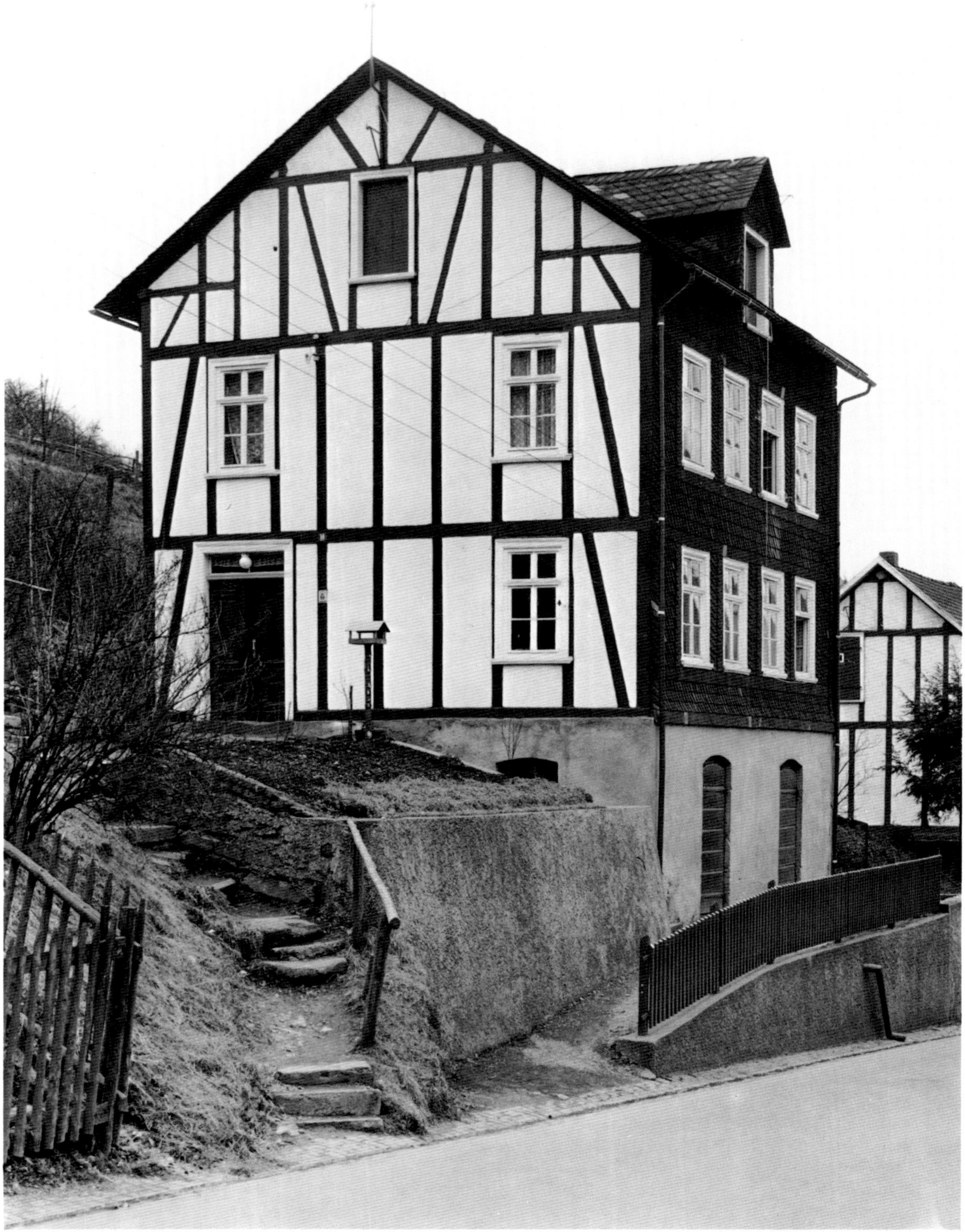

248

Siegener Straße 10, Gosenbach, 1961.

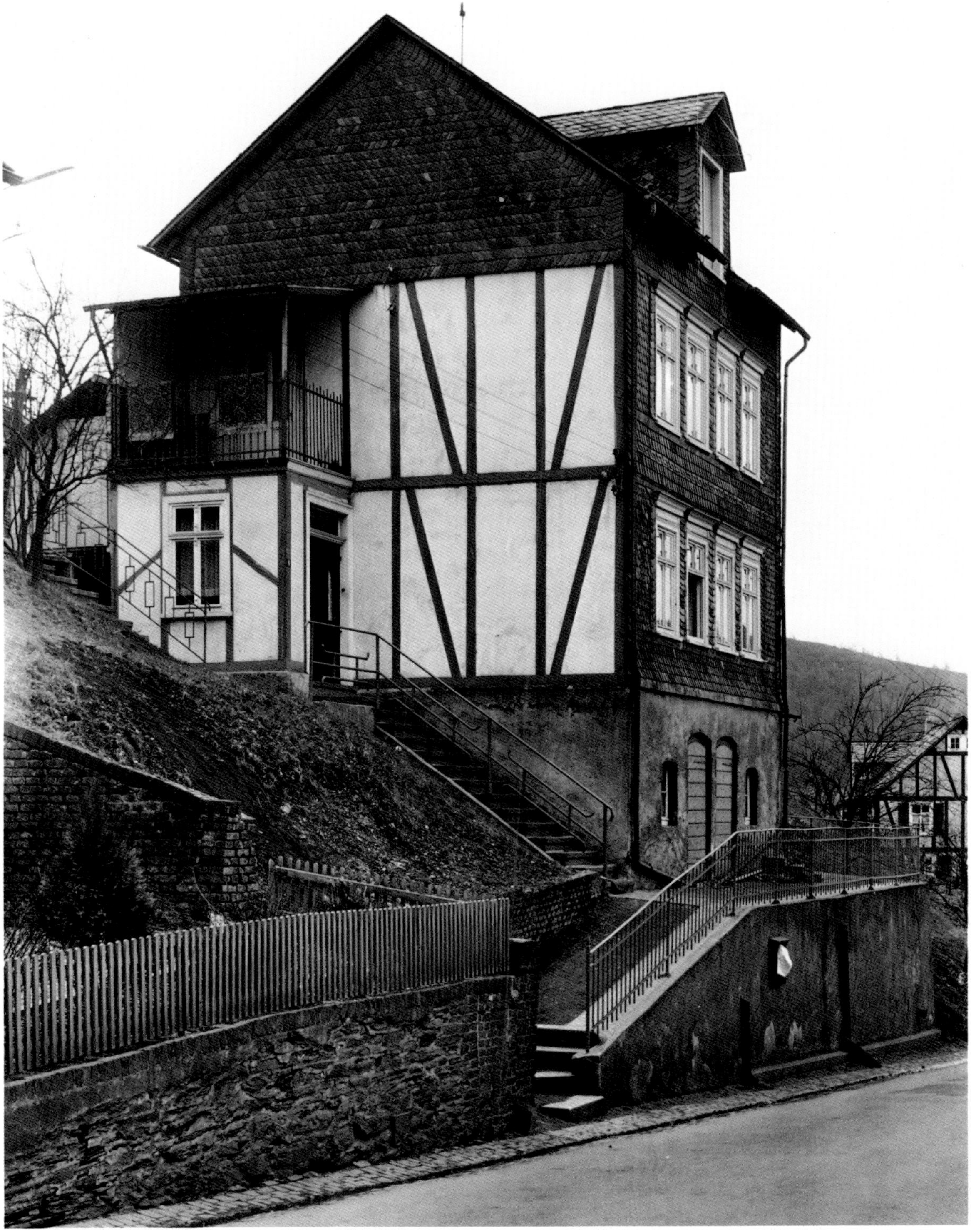

249
Siegener Straße 6, Gosenbach, 1961.

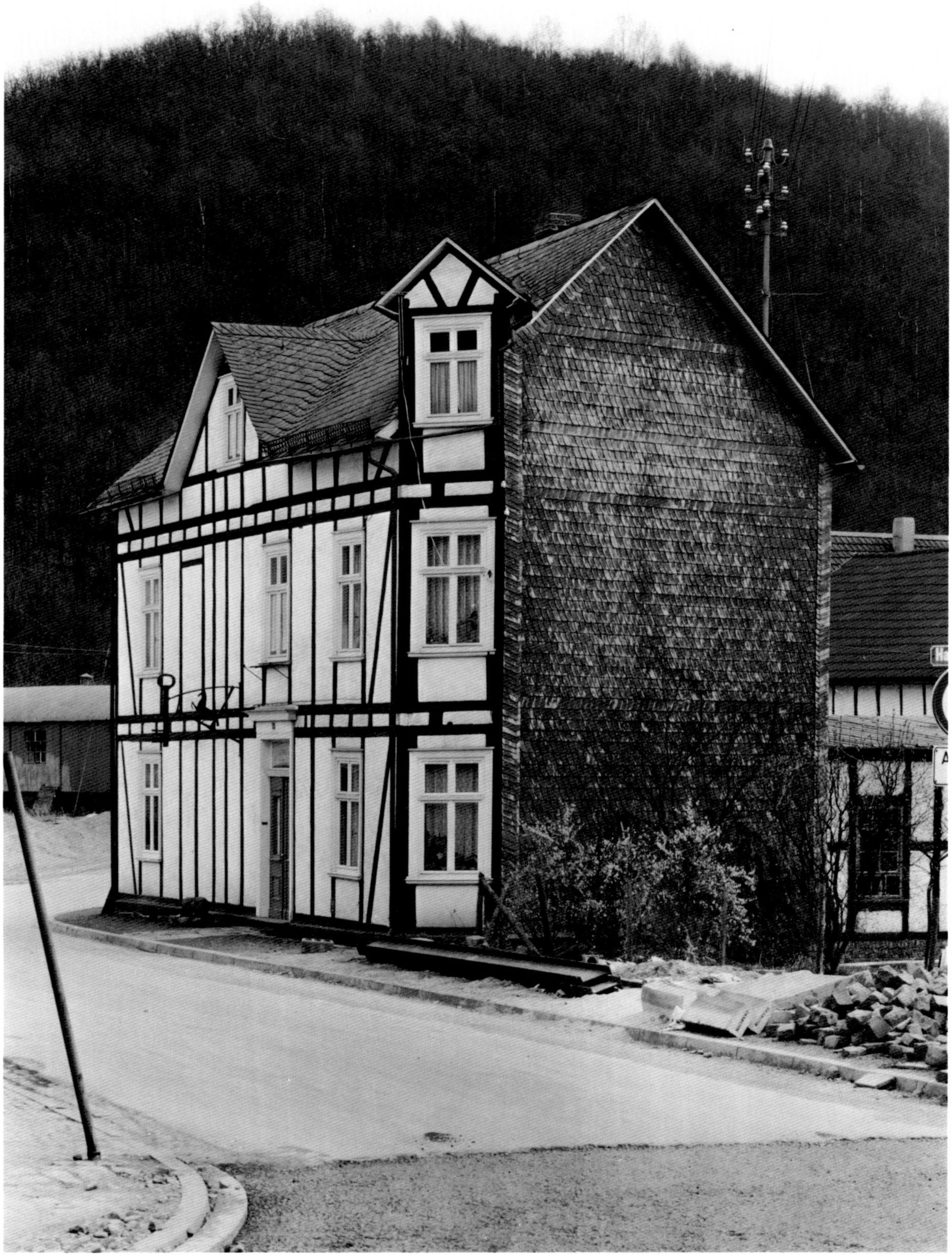

250
Am Silberstern 4, Freudenberg, 1961.

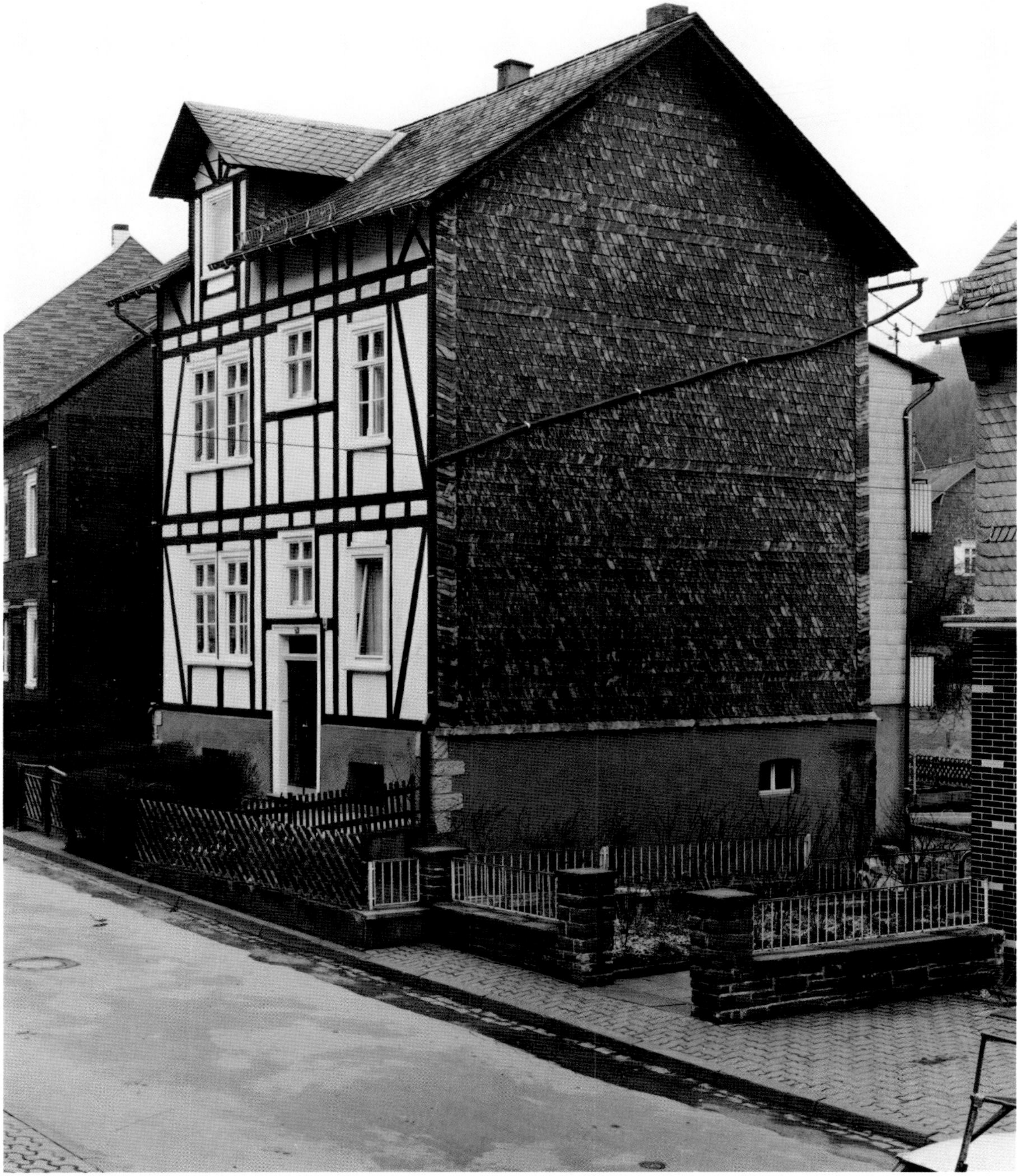

251
Schulstraße 24, Eisern, 1971.

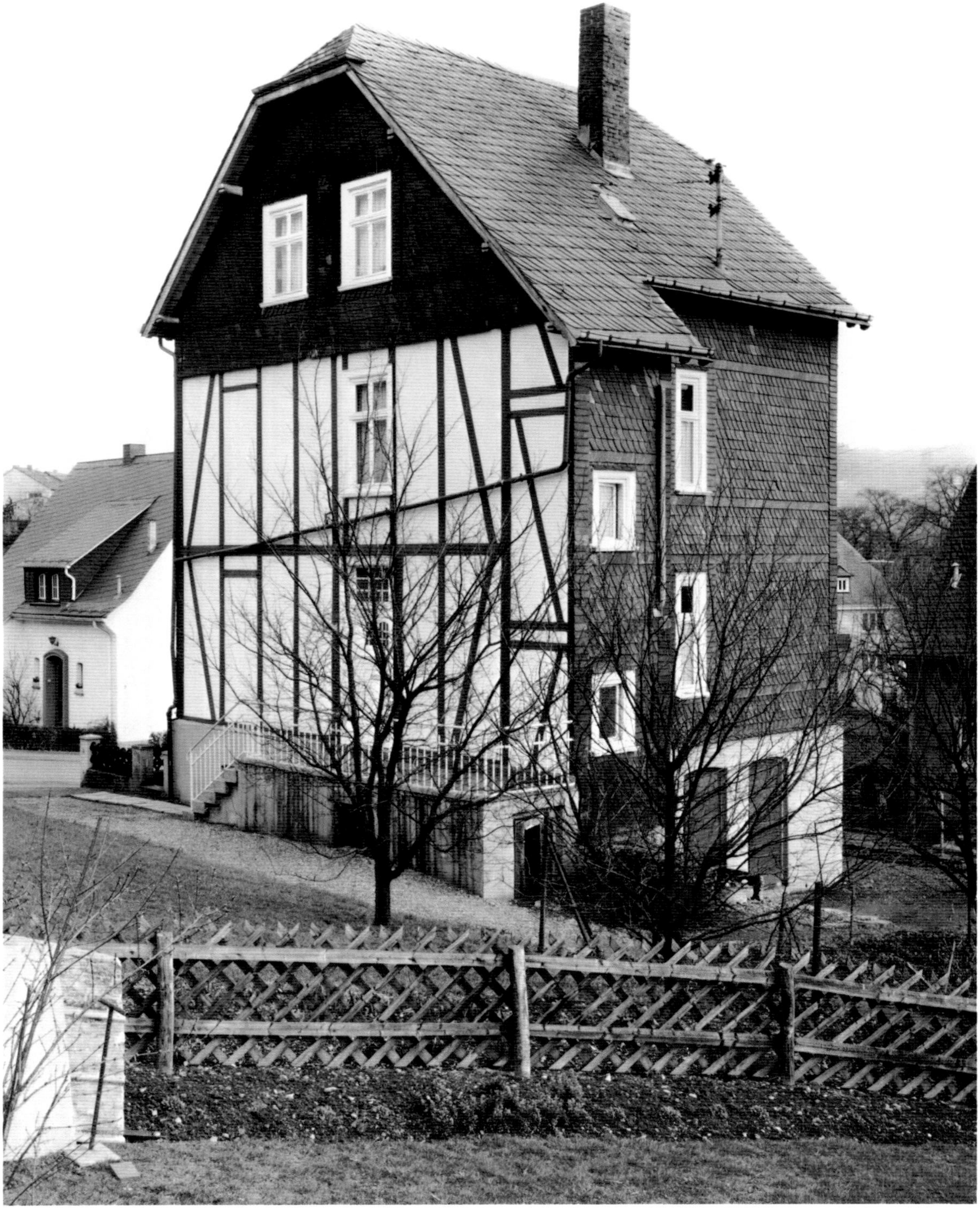

252
Schloßblick 17, Kaan-Marienborn, 1972.

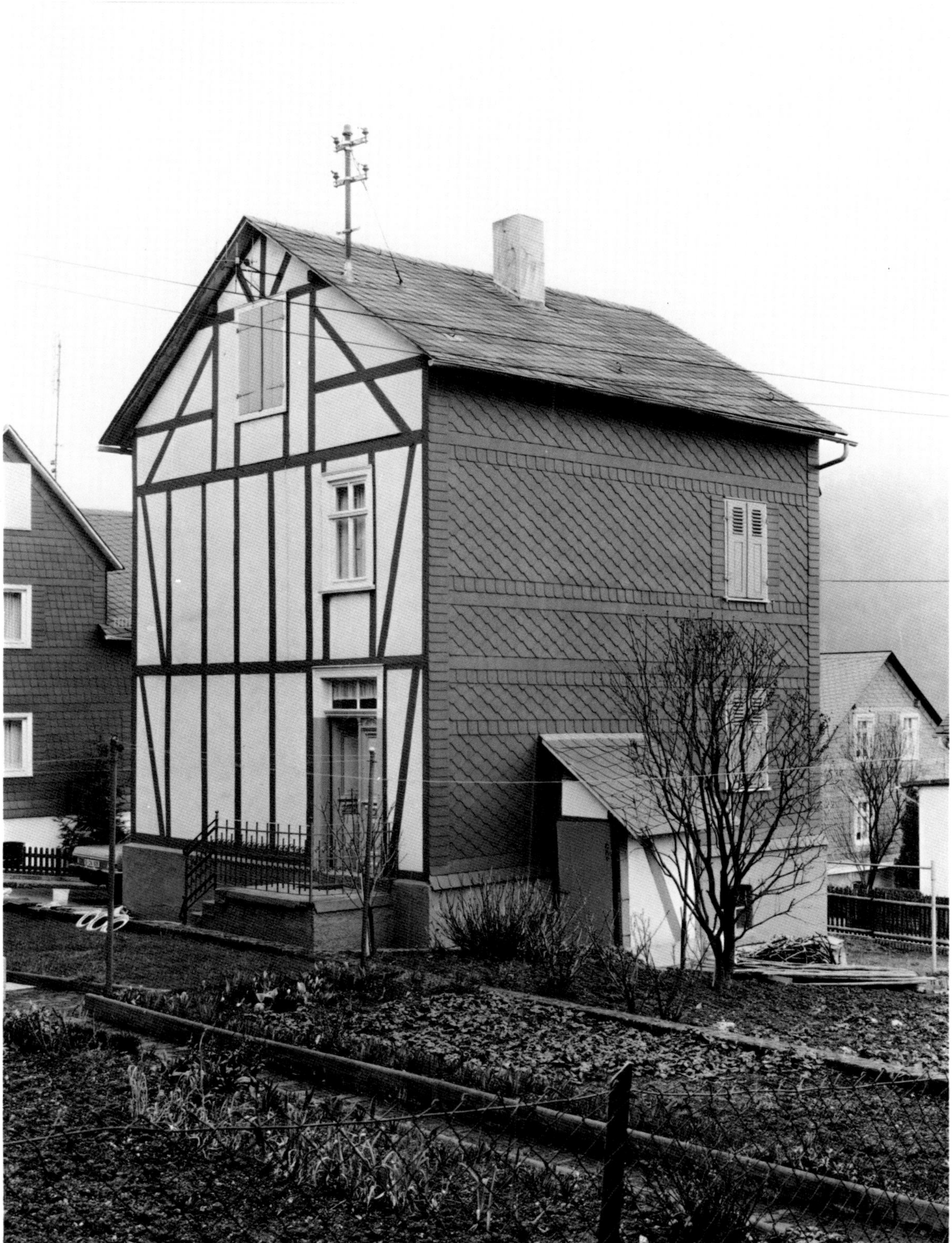

253

Karlstraße 4, Niederschelderhütte, 1973.

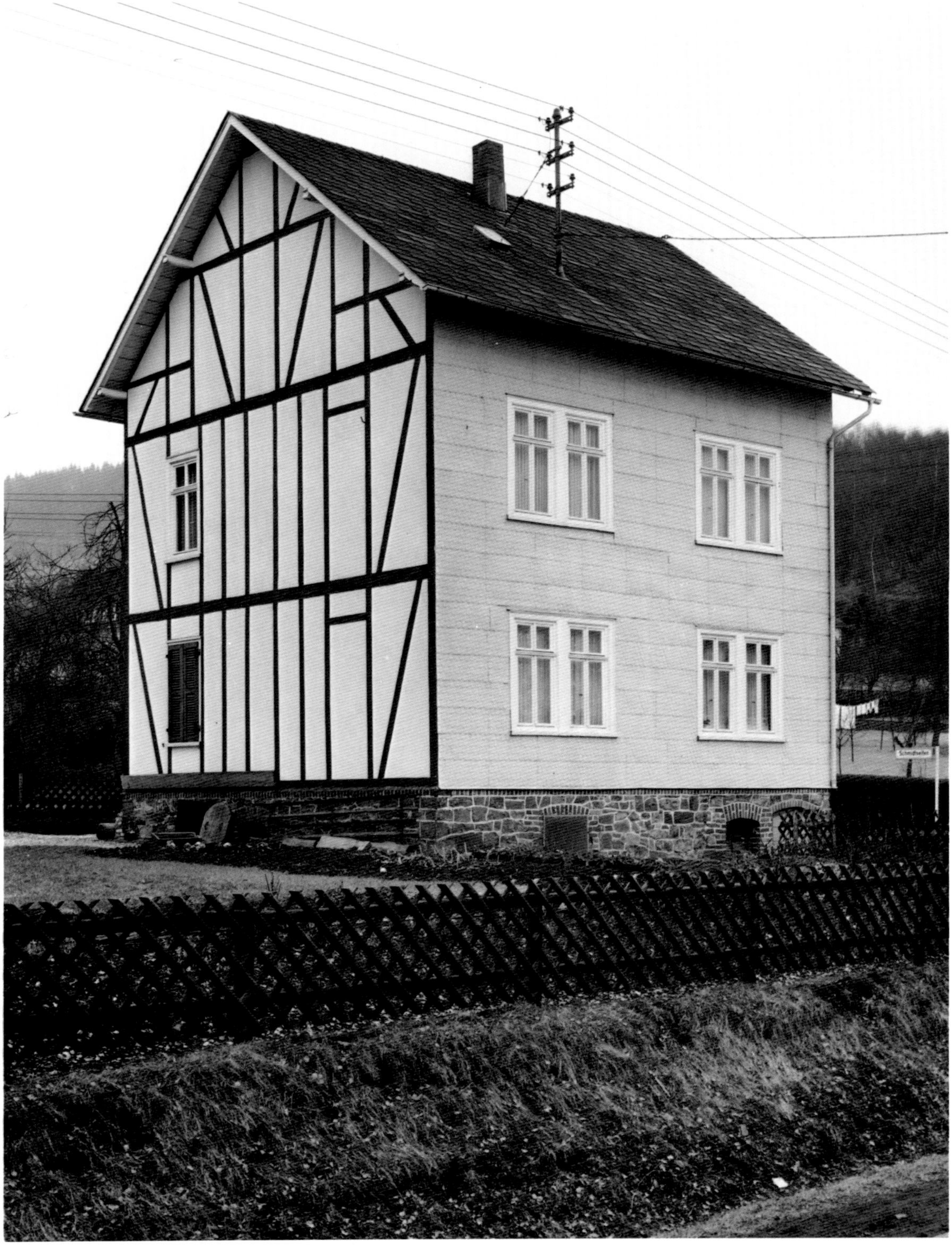

254
Hillnhütter Straße 62, Dahlbruch, 1971.

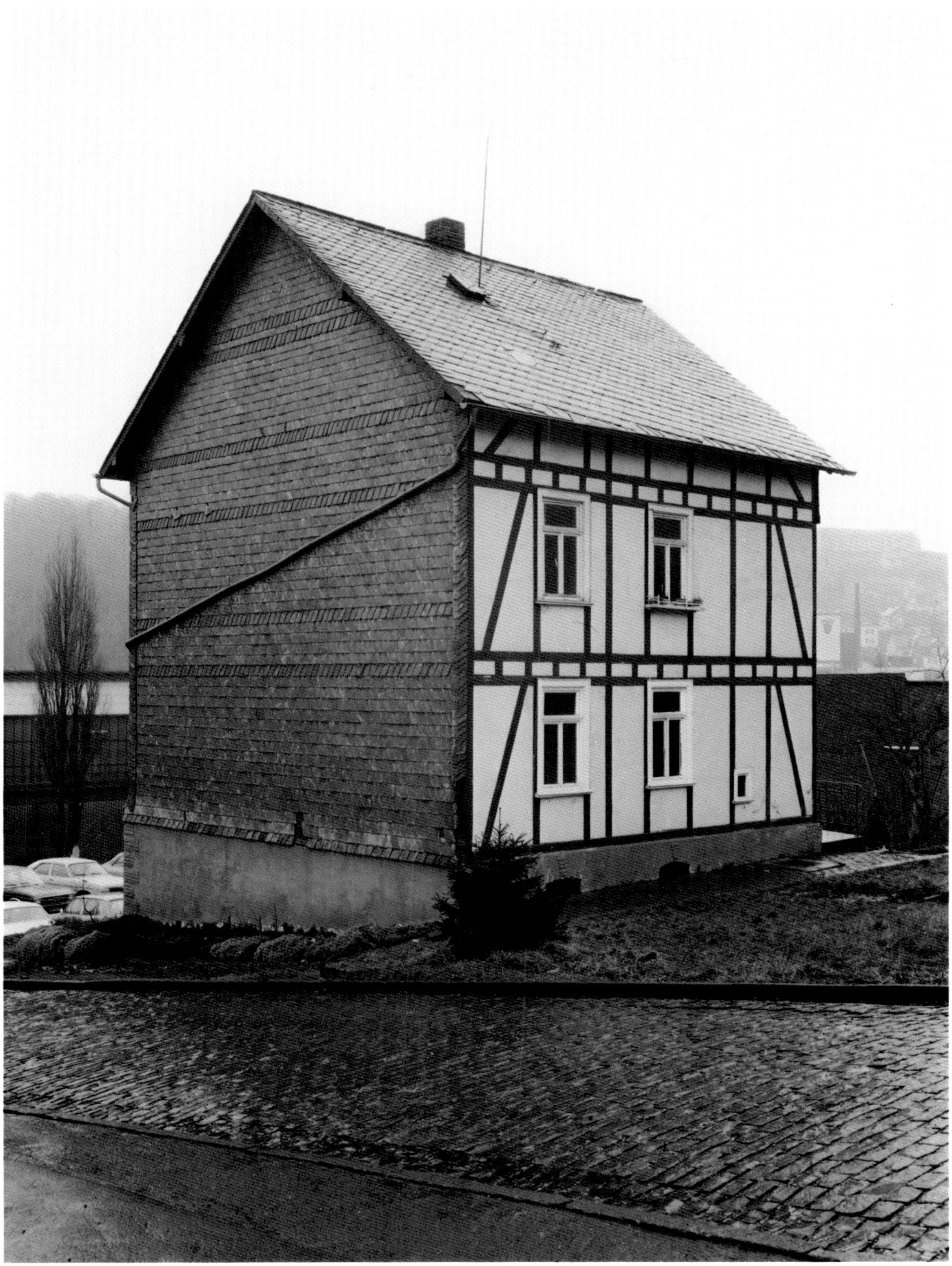

255
Hauptstraße 3, Birken, 1971.

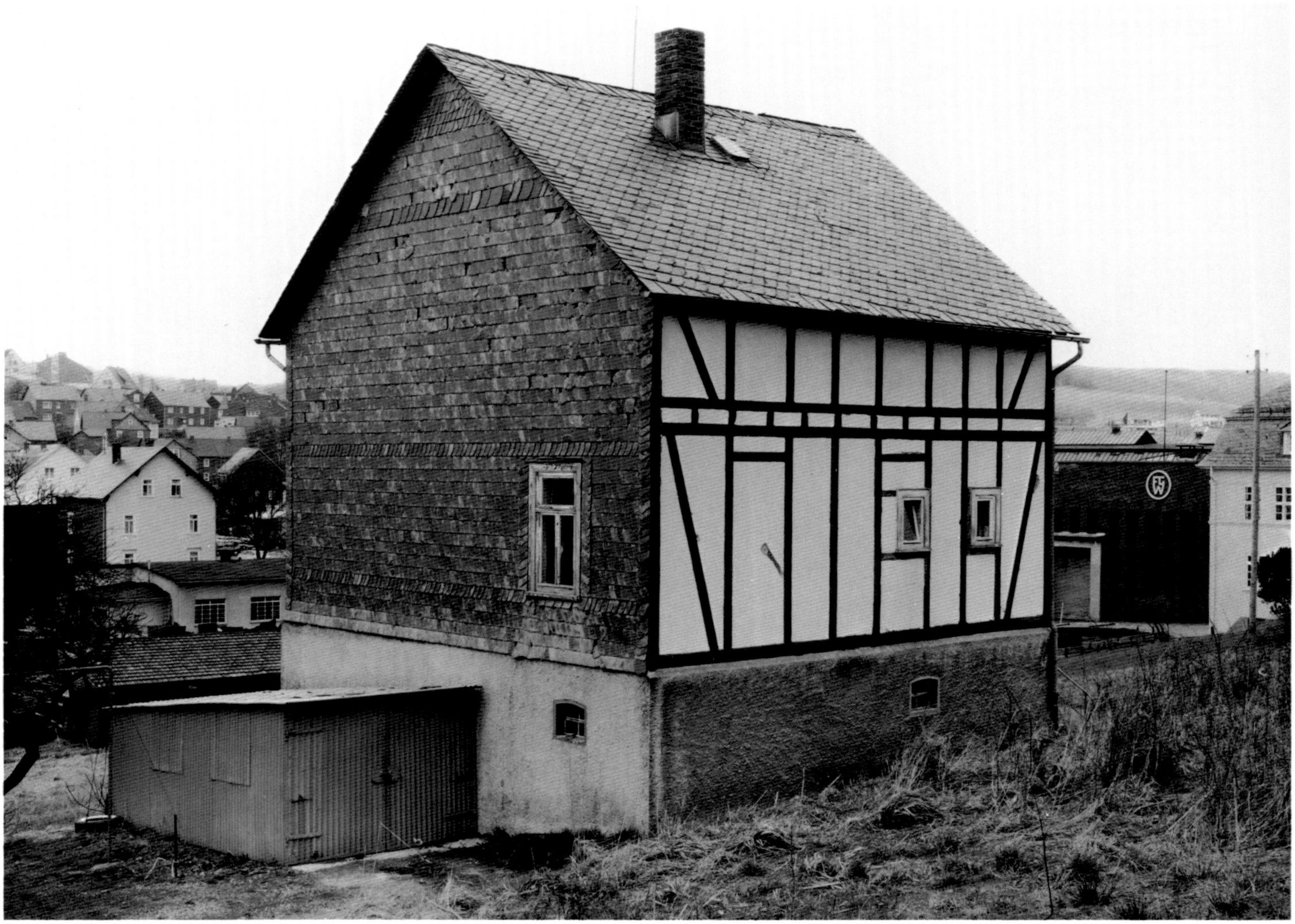

256

Fritz-Schäfer-Straße 24, Salchendorf, 1971.

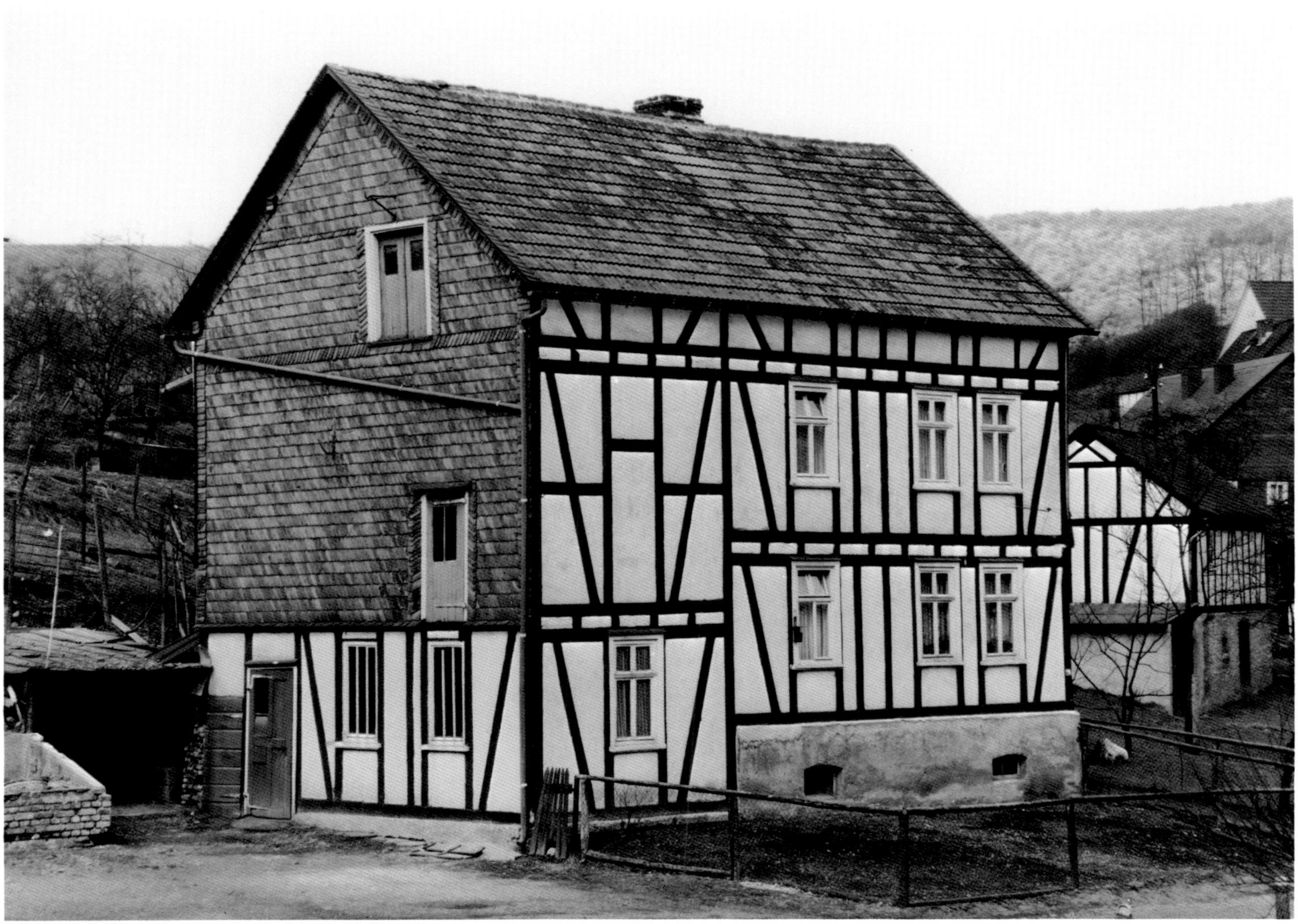

257
Achenbacher Straße 298, Achenbach, 1960.

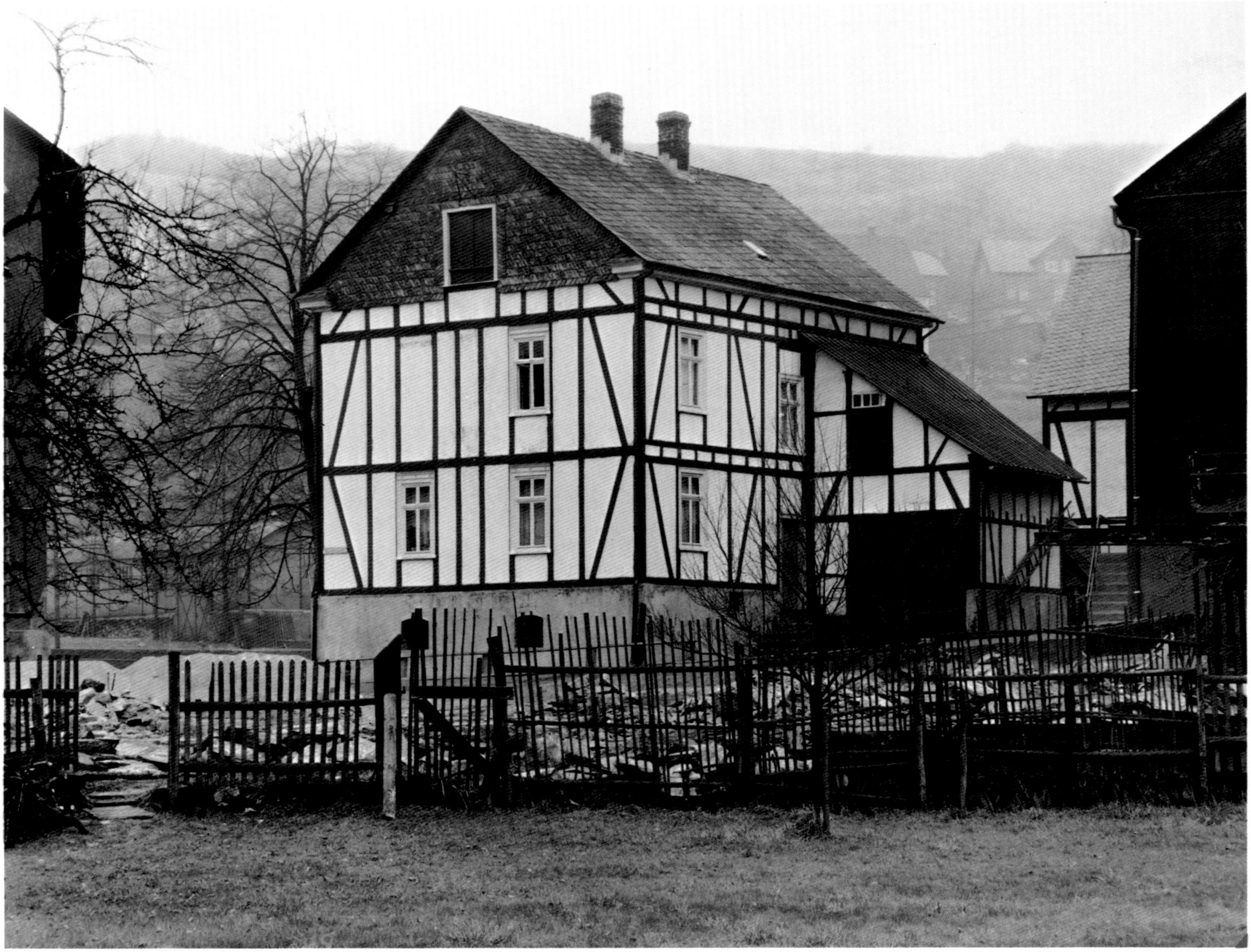

258
Kirchberg 3, Niederschelderhütte, 1960.

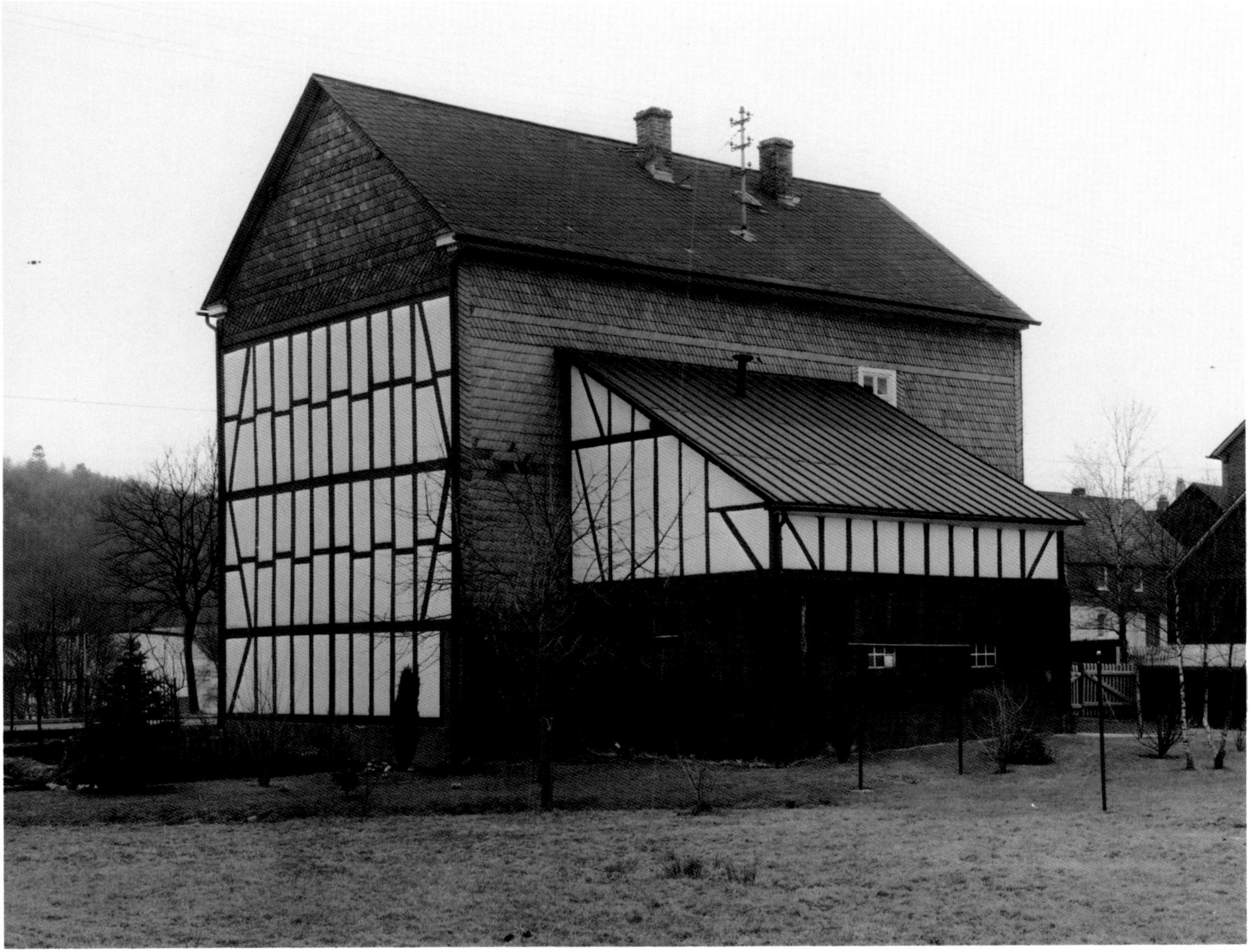

259
Wildener Straße 7, Salchendorf, 1961.

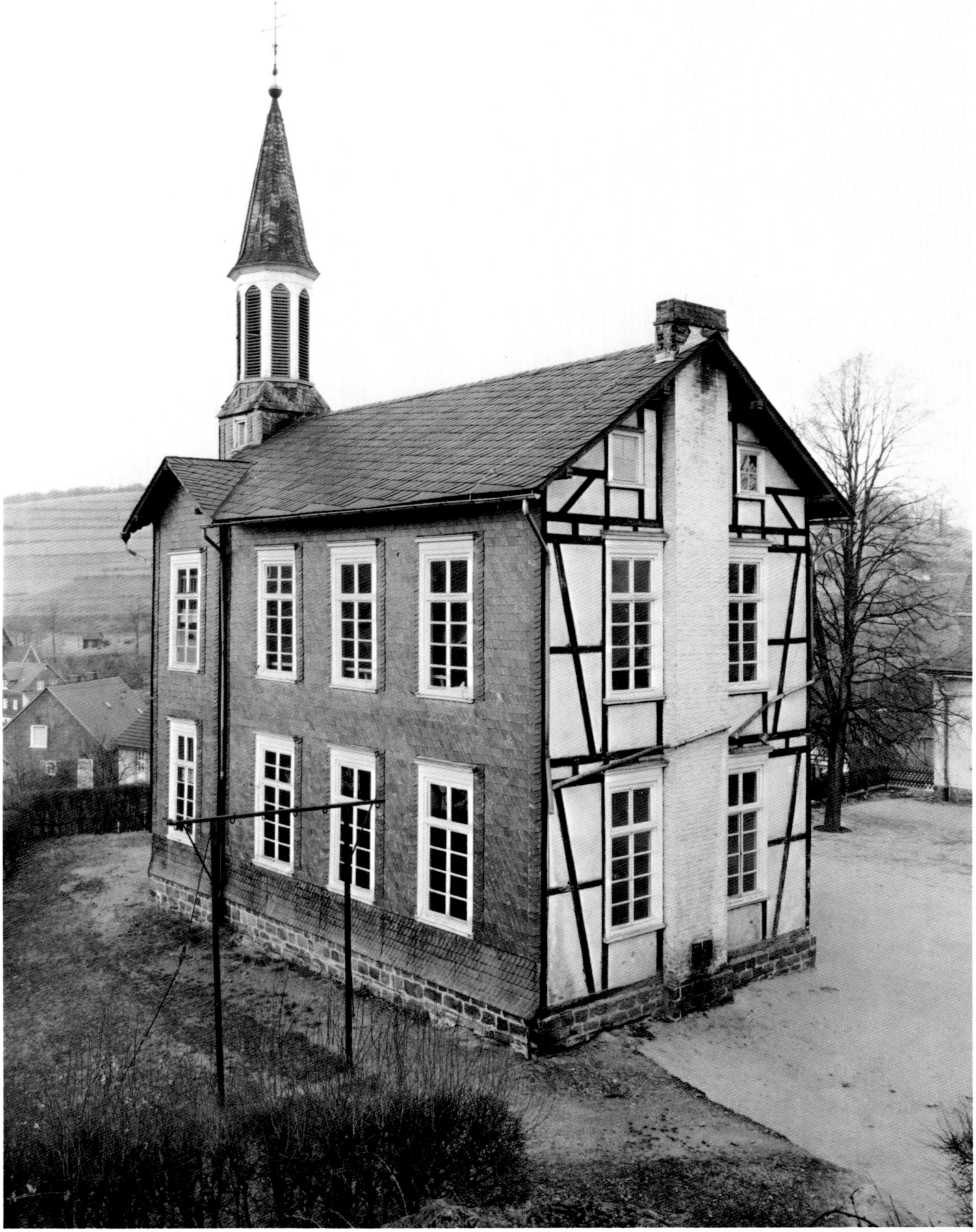

260
Schulplatz 6, Niederndorf, 1964.

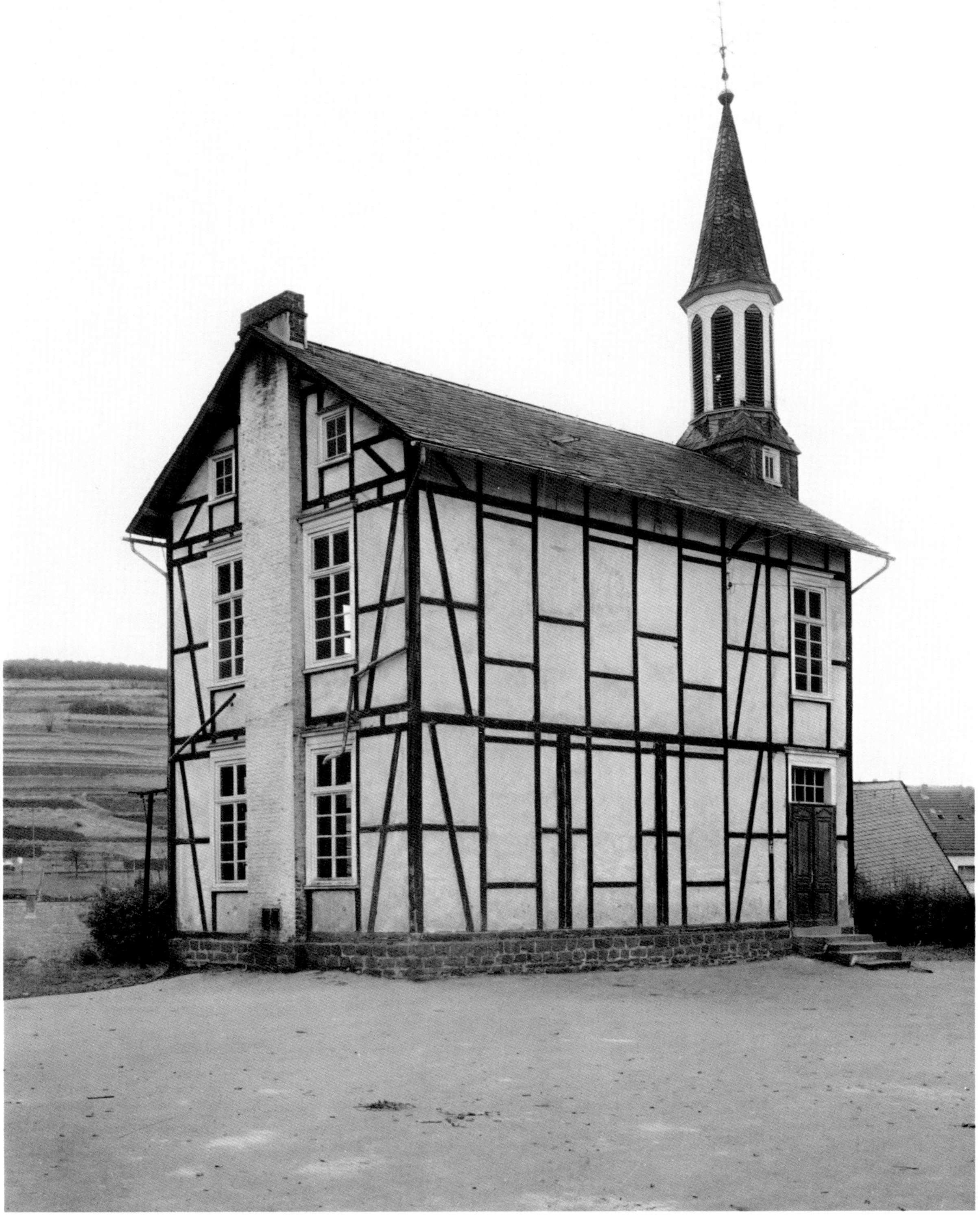

261

Schulplatz 6, Niederndorf, 1964.

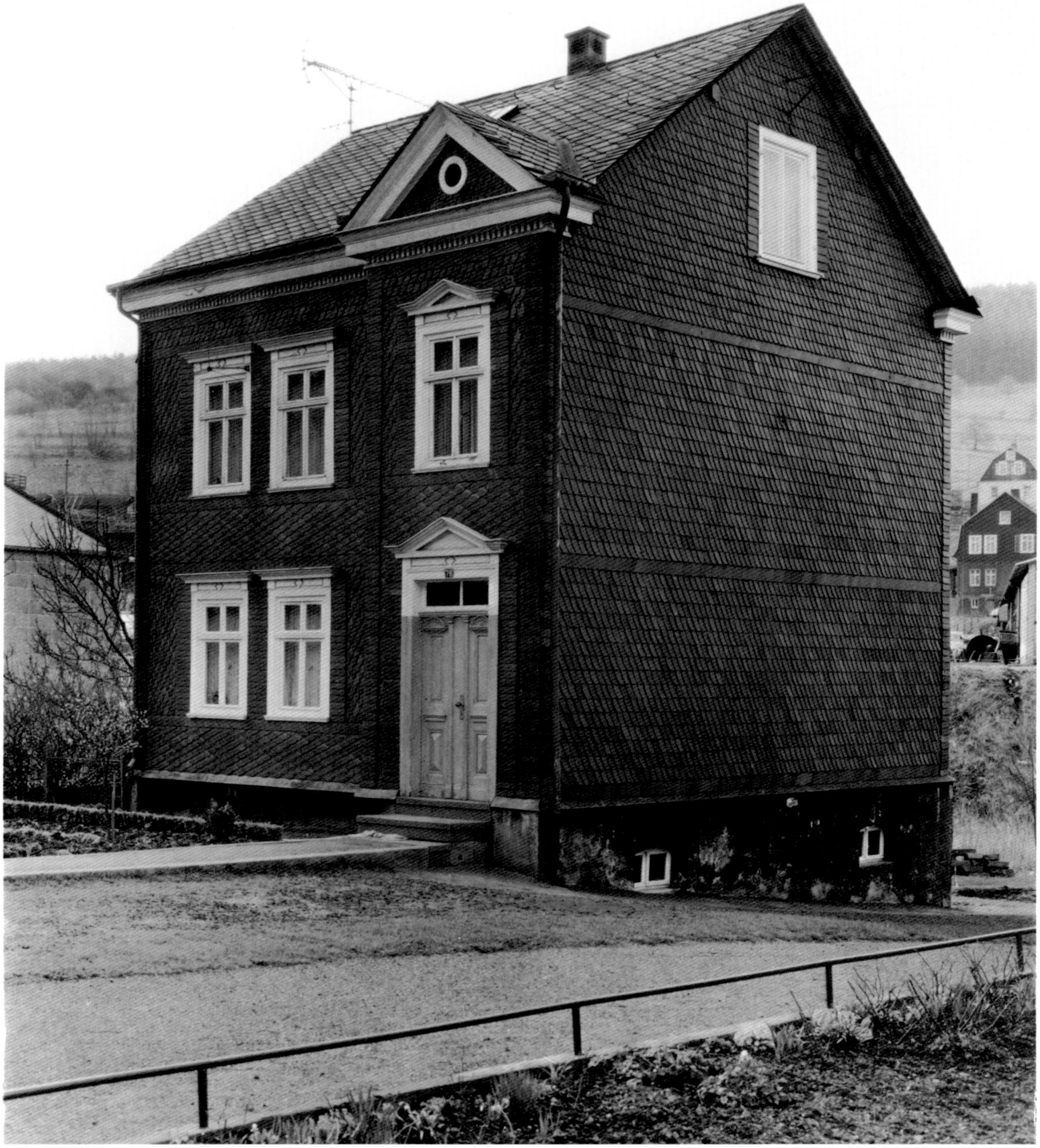

262
Eisernstraße 158, Eiserfeld, 1971.

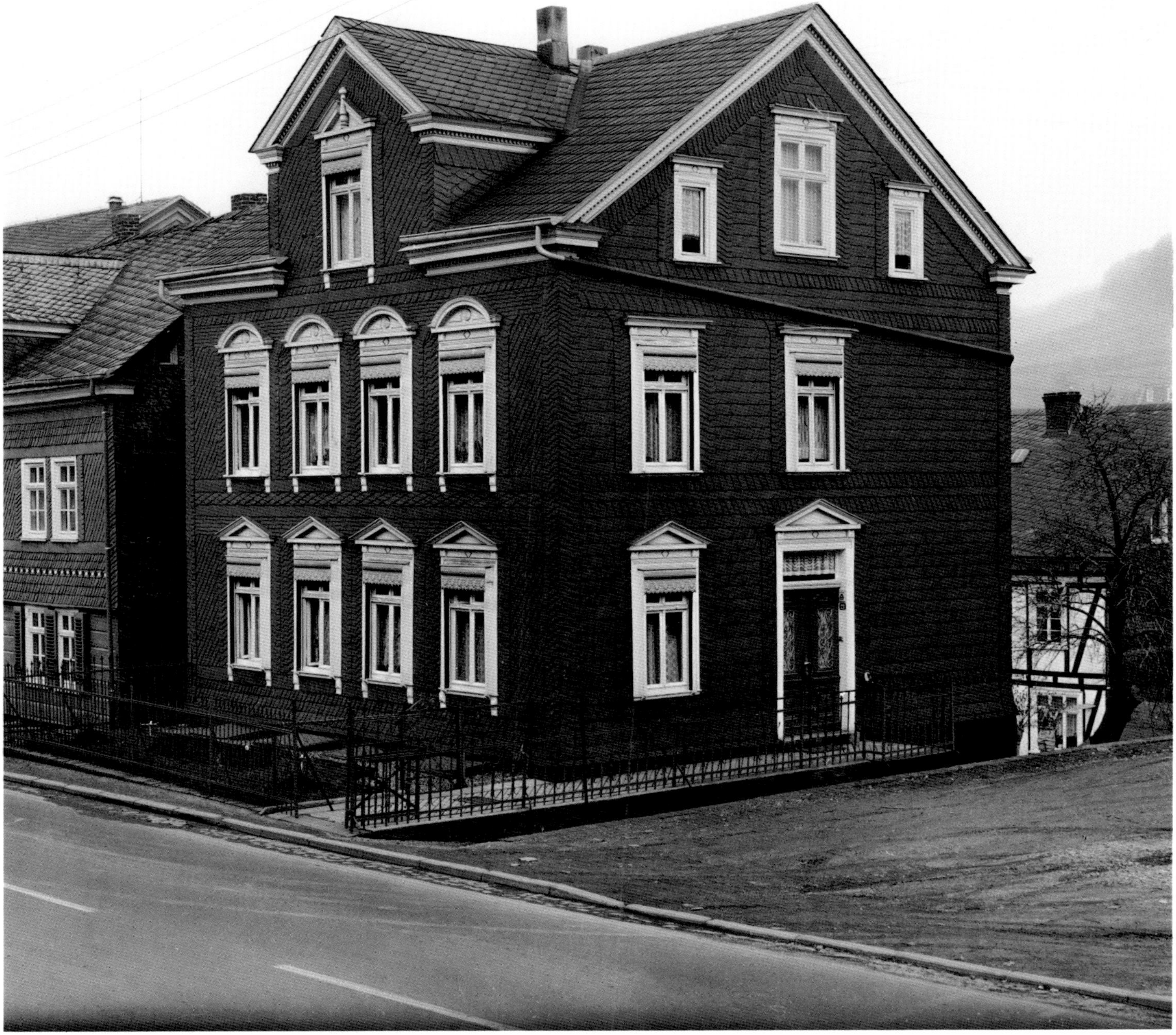

263
Freiengründerstraße 21, Eiserfeld, 1960.

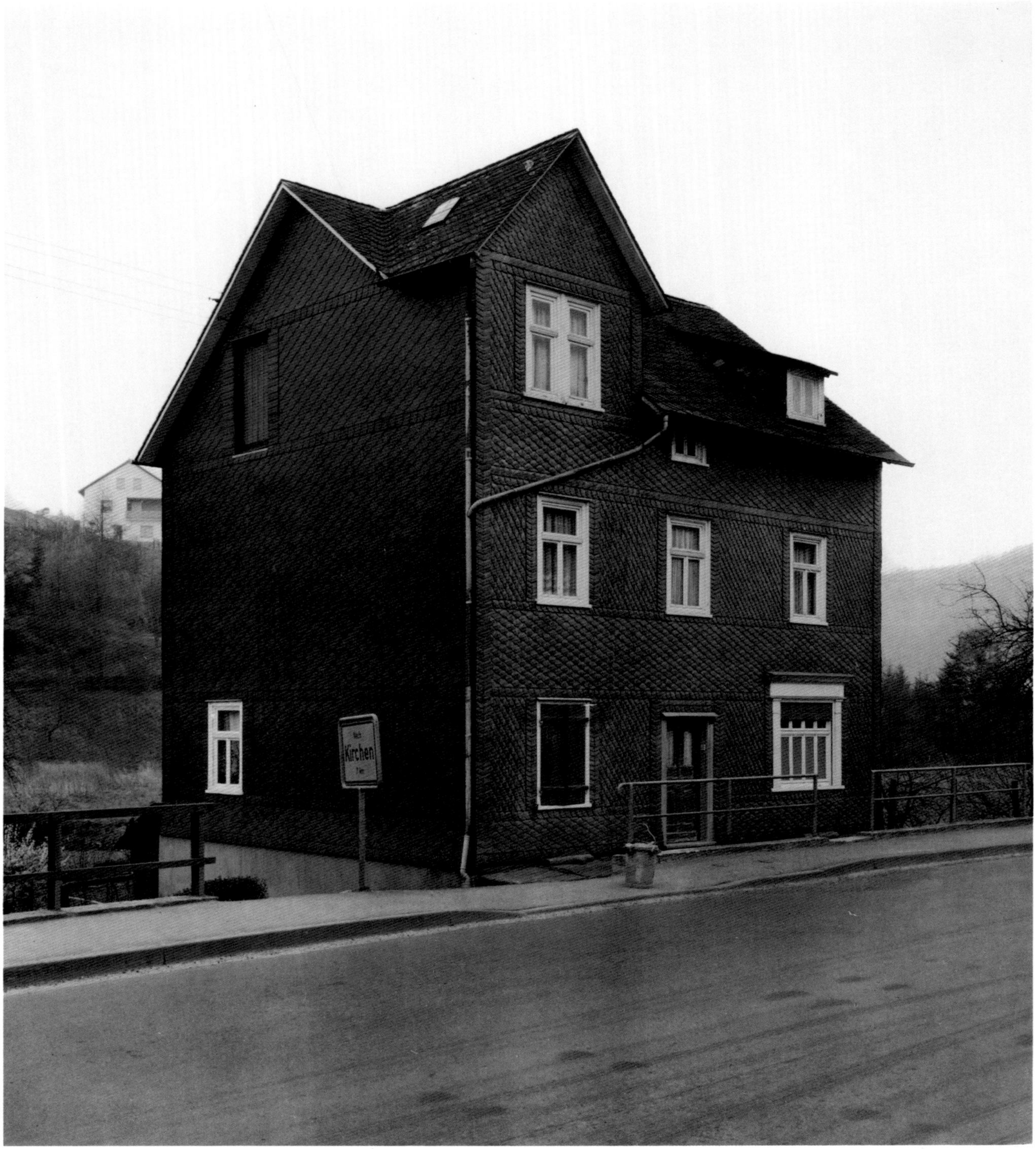

264

Konrad-Adenauer-Straße 1, Niederfischbach, 1971.

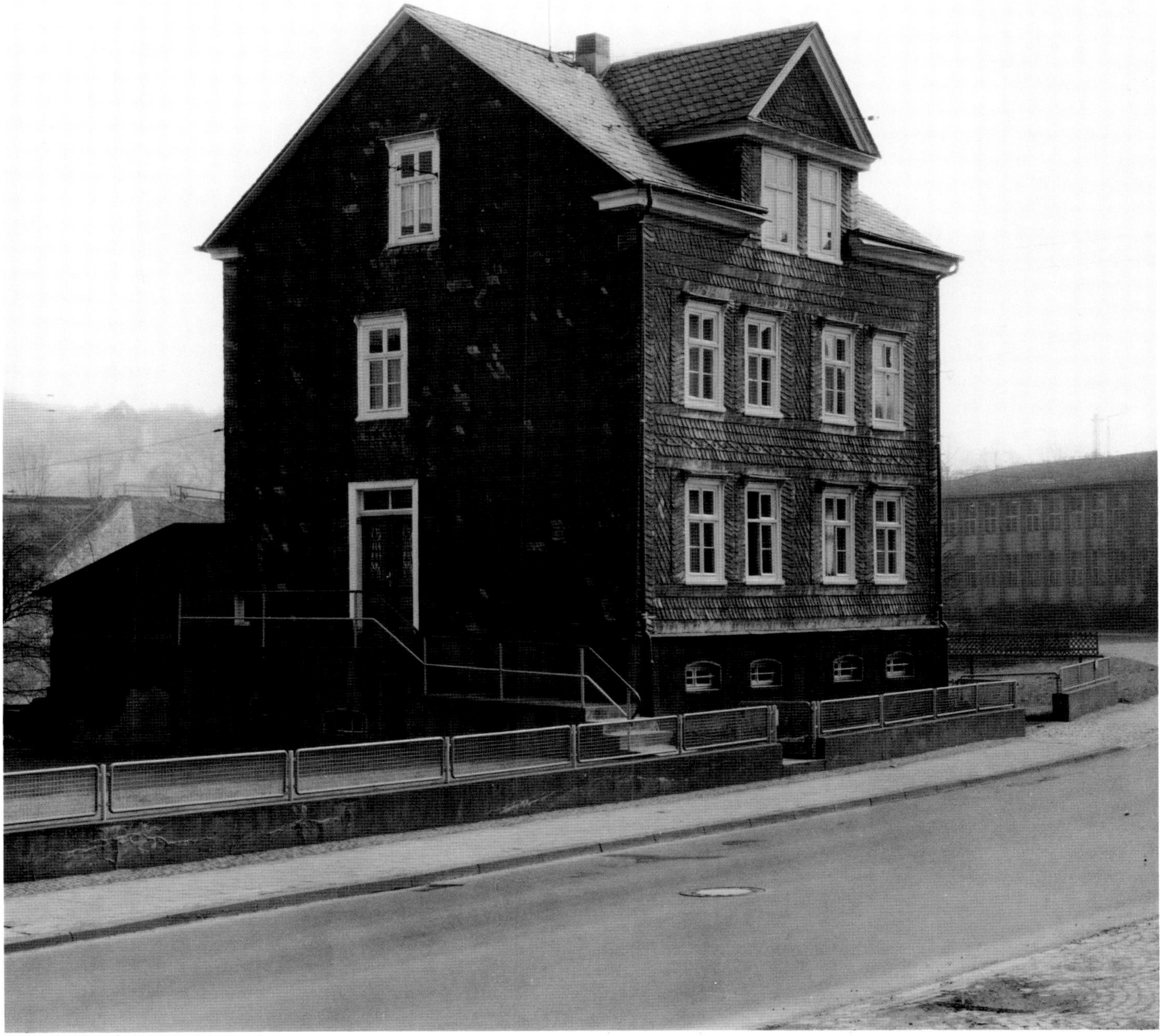

265
Hauptstraße 25, Kaan-Marienborn, 1971.

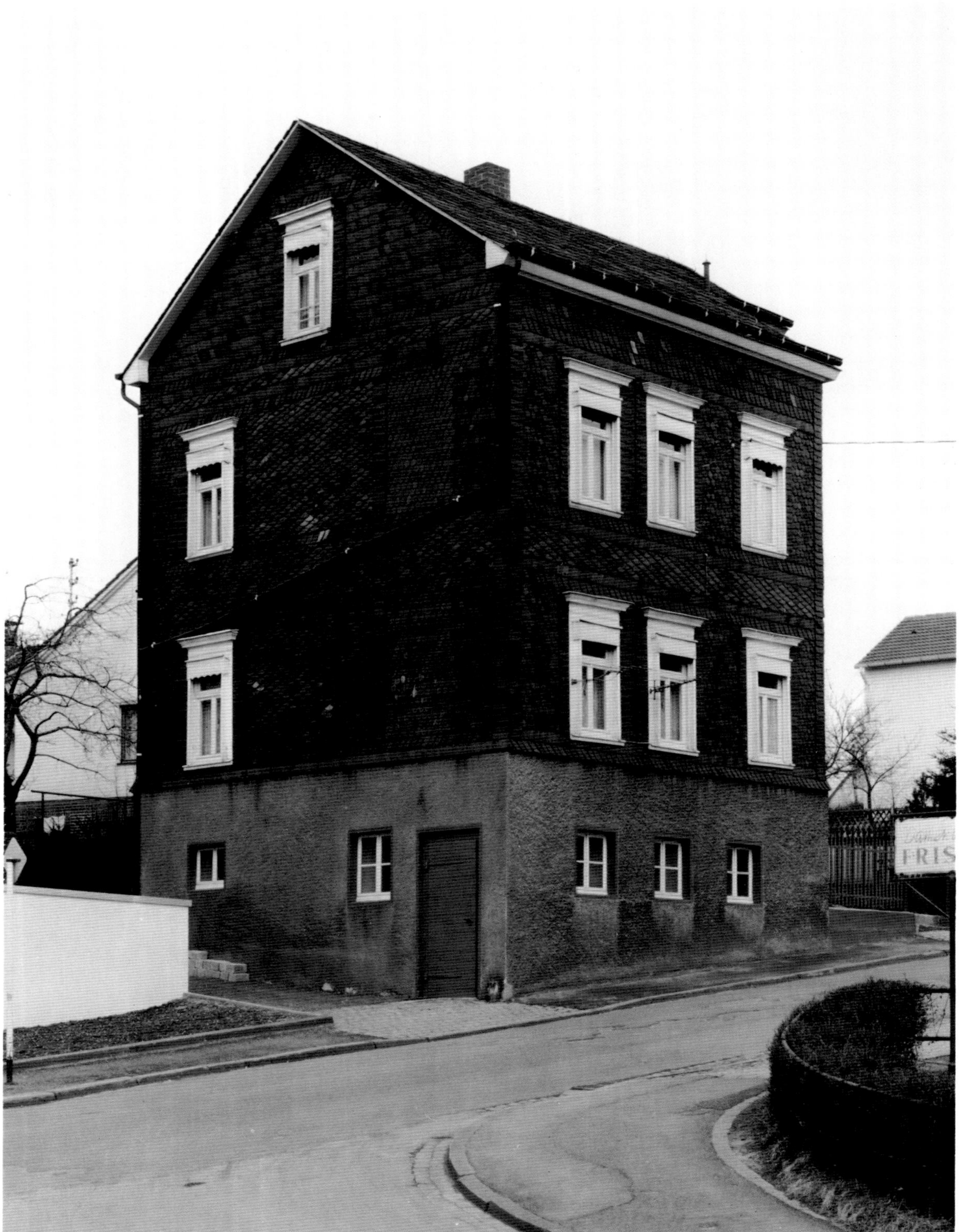

266

Försterstraße 12, Weidenau, 1970.

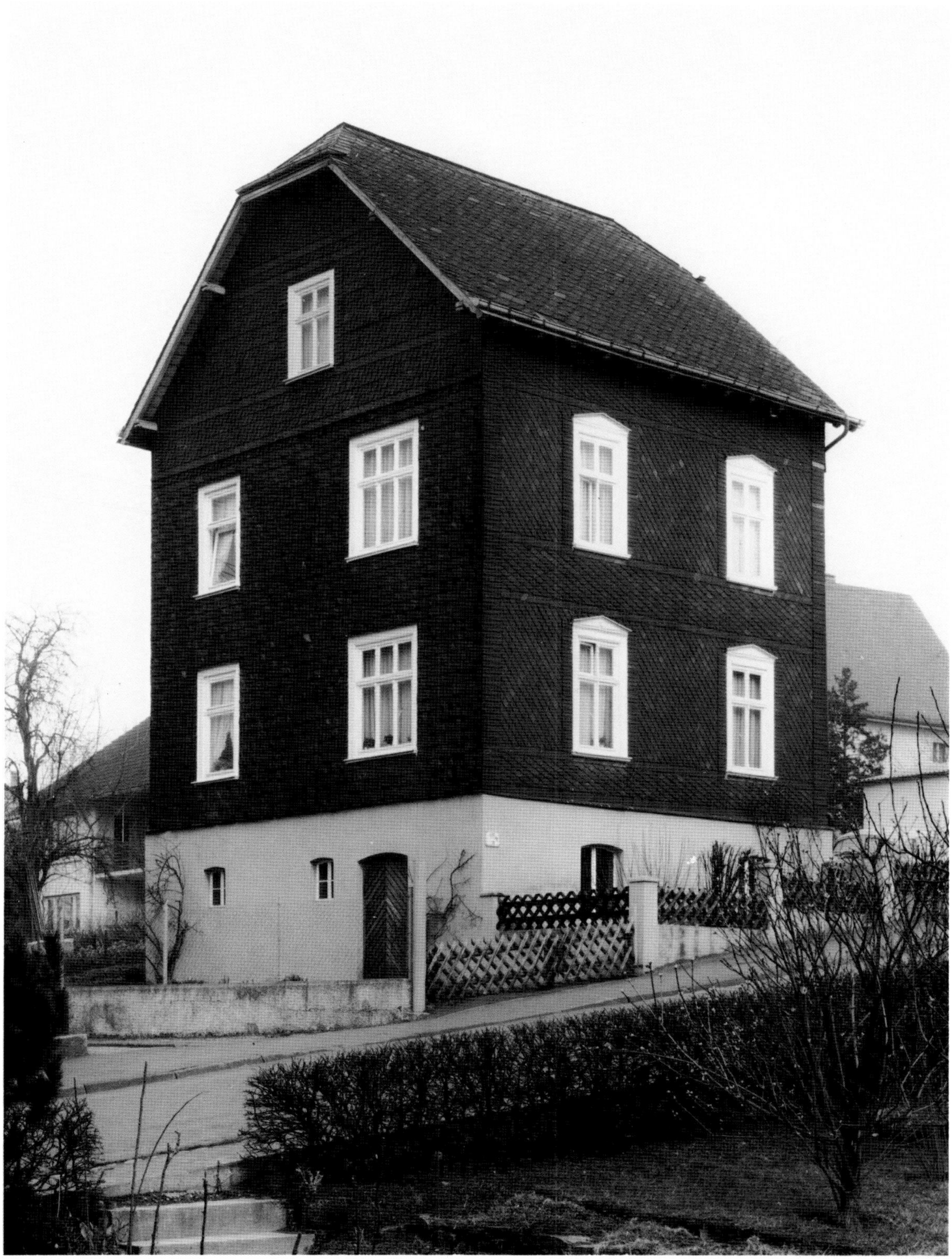

267
Schloßblick 17, Kaan-Marienborn, 1972.

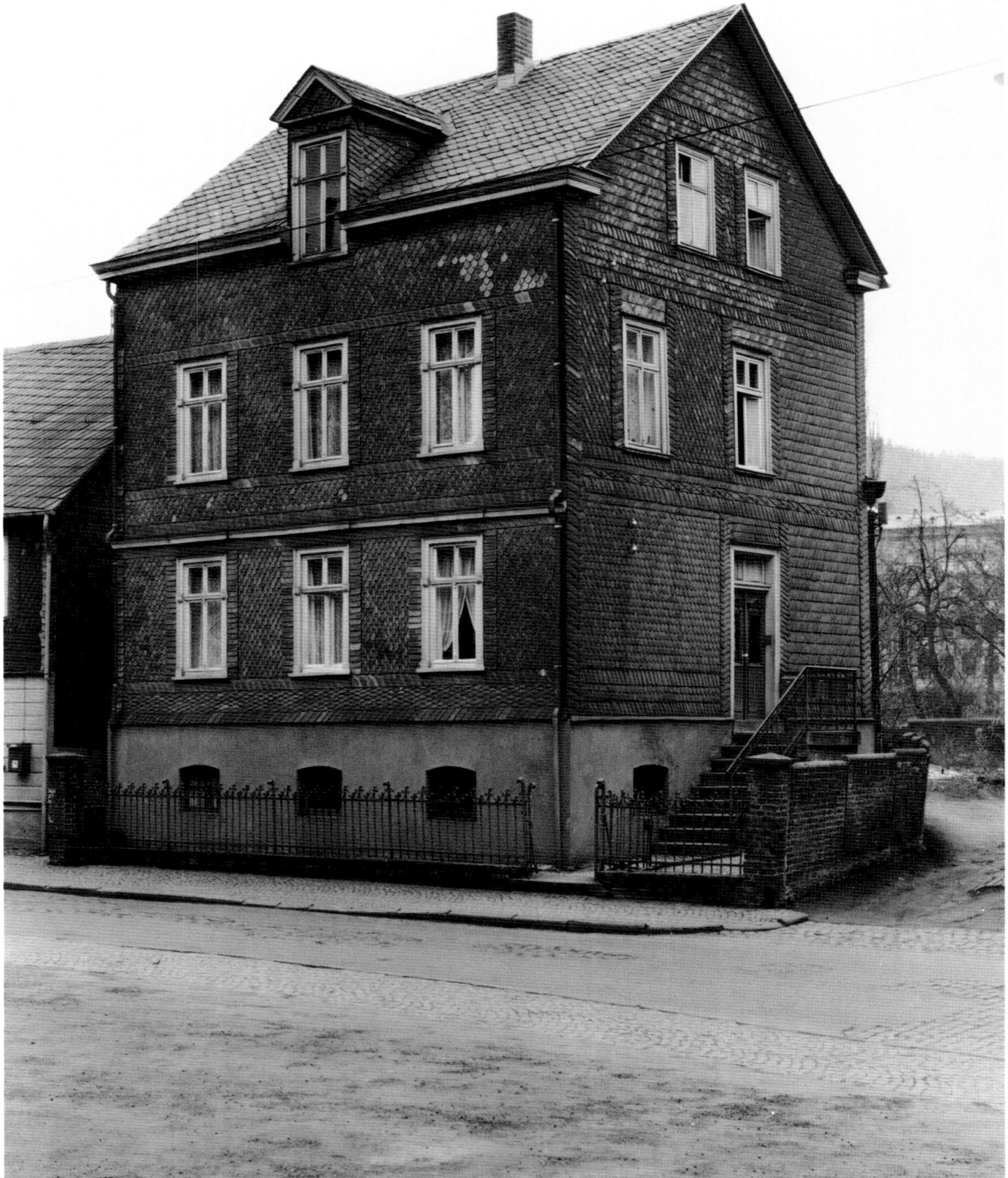

268
Kirchweg 5, Siegen, 1959.

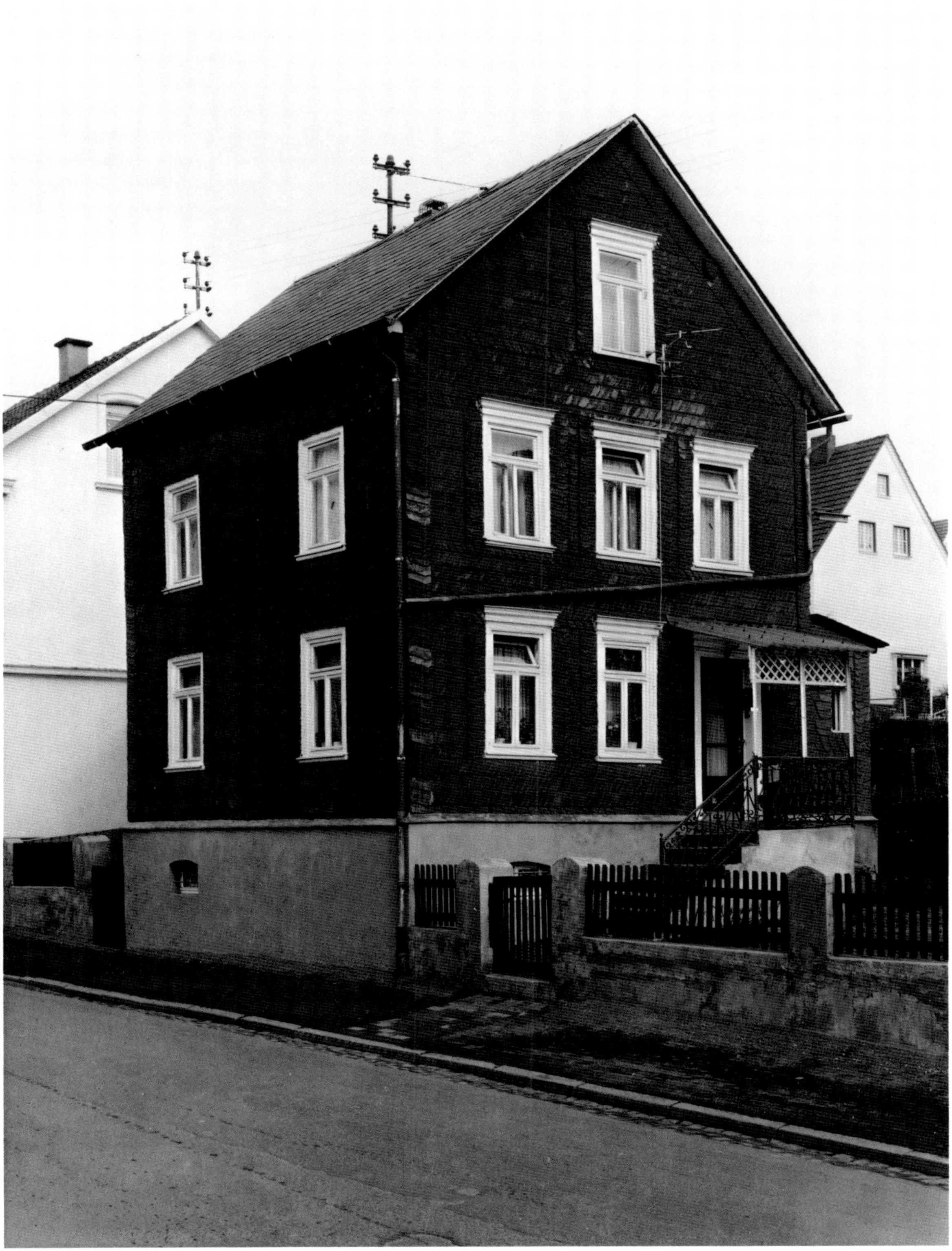

269
Untere Rolandstraße 3, Weidenau, 1968.

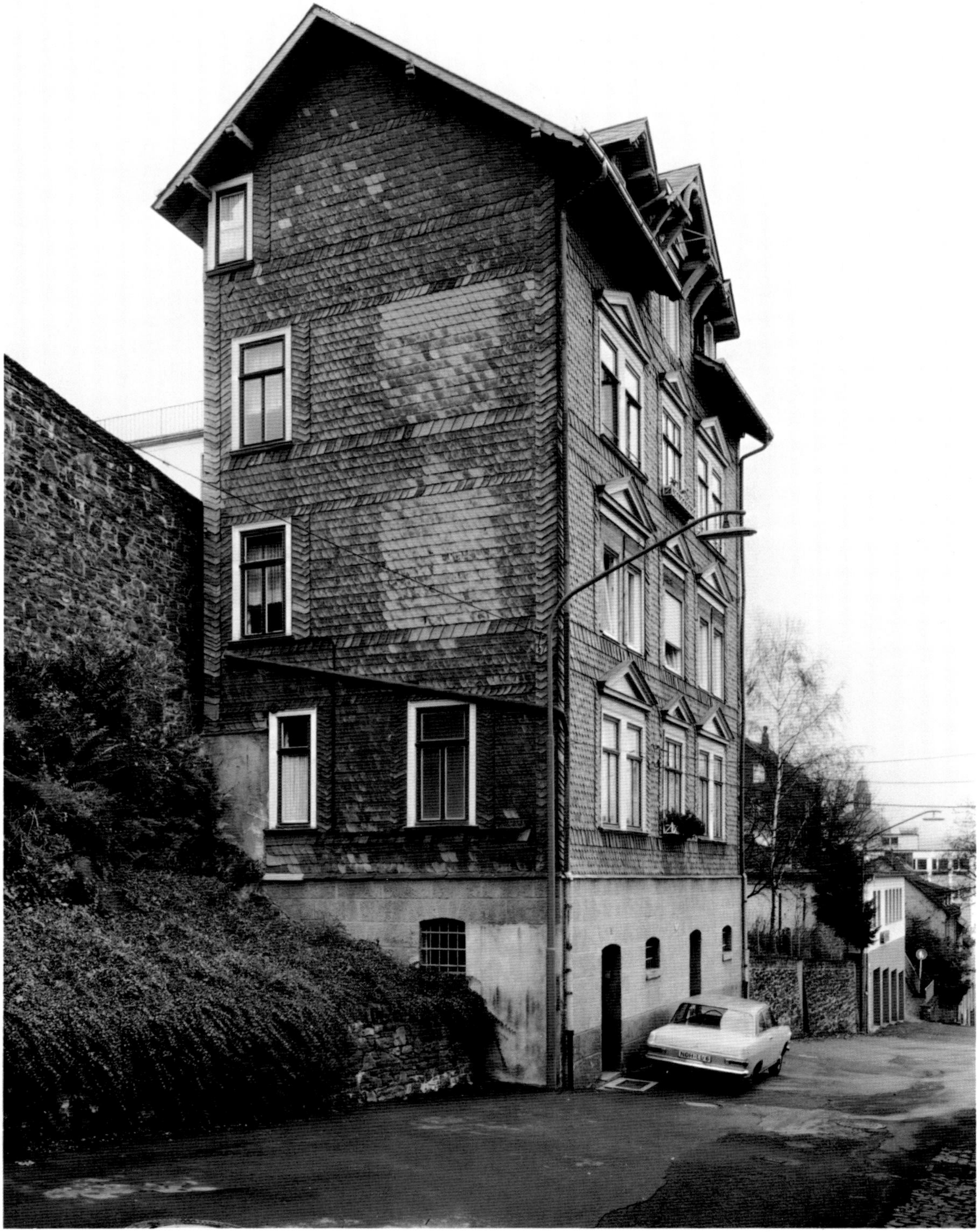

270
Siegbergstraße 34, Siegen, 1975.

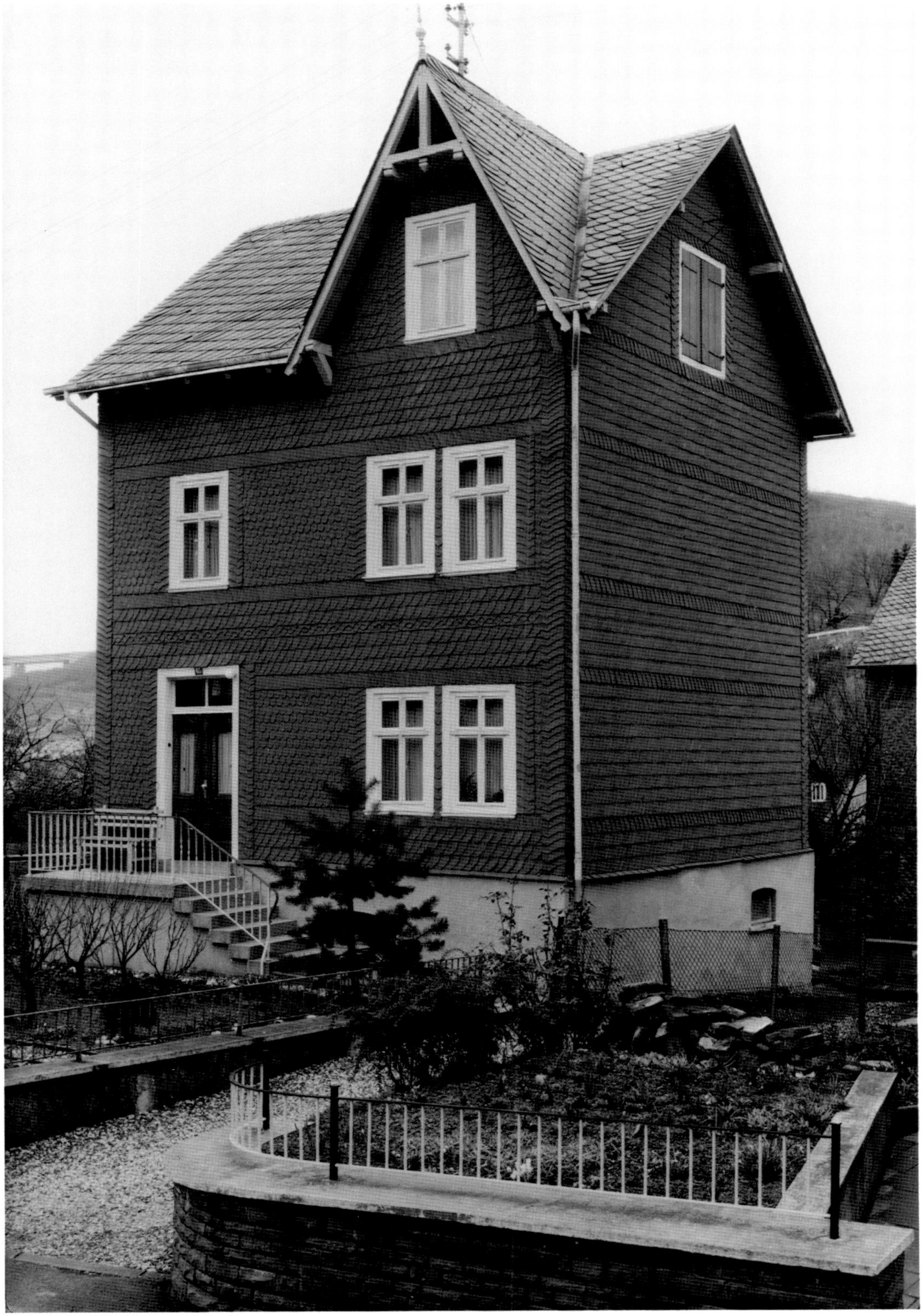

271

Lindenstraße 69, Eiserfeld, 1971.

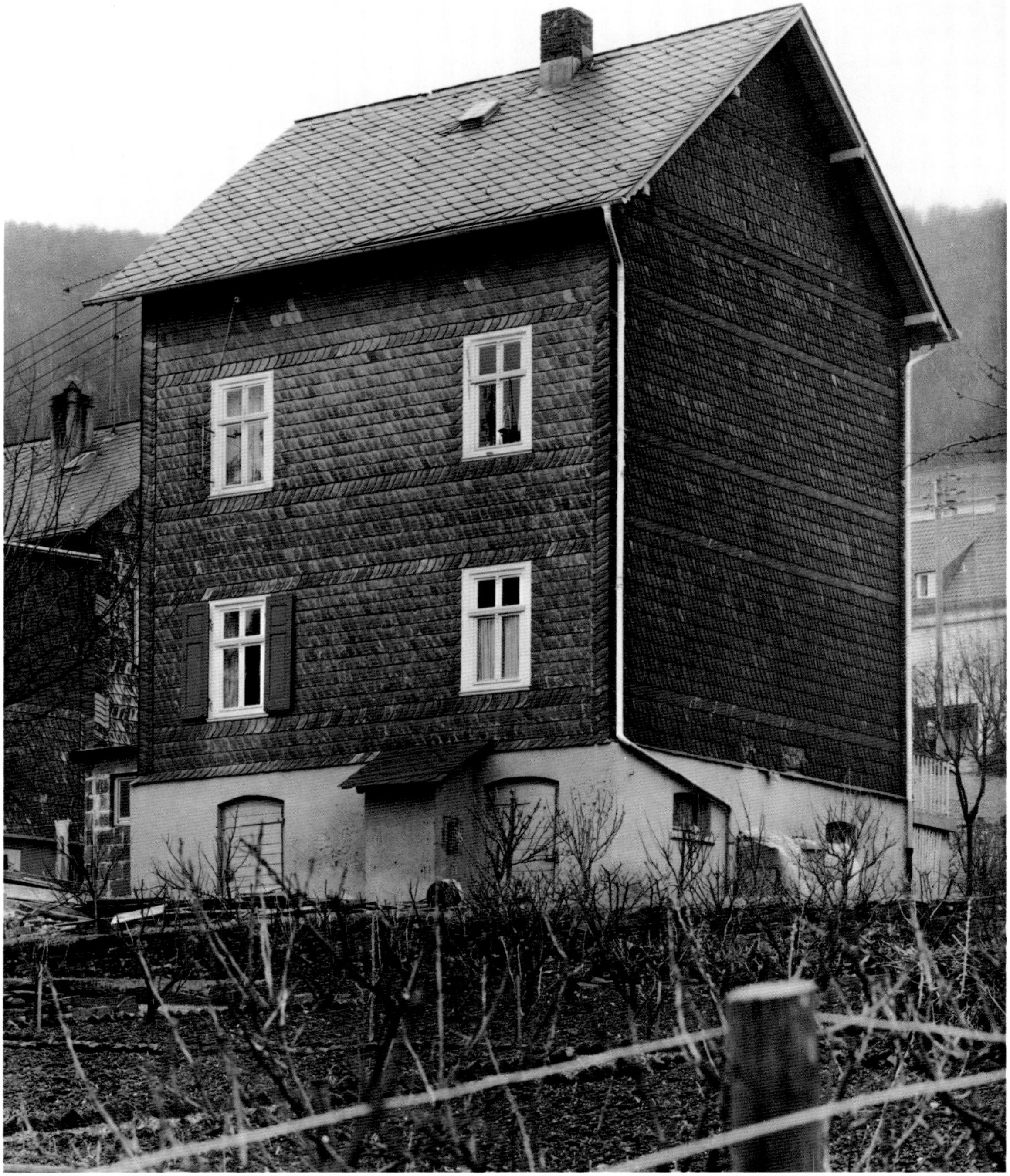

272
Lindenstraße 69, Eiserfeld, 1971.

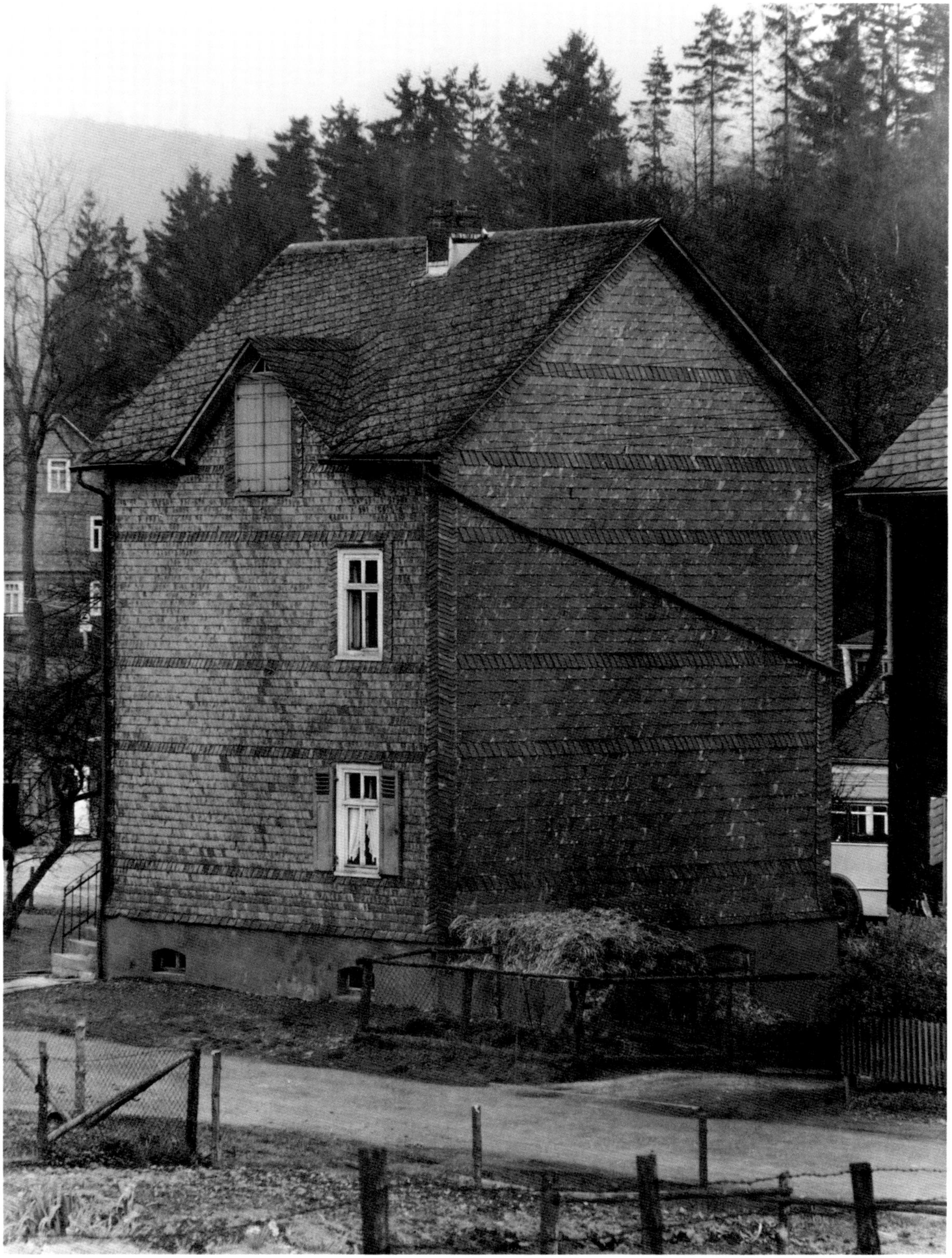

273

Triftstraße 48, Büschergrund, 1960.

VI.
ABWICKLUNGEN EINZELNER HÄUSER
HOUSES FROM DIFFERENT VIEWS

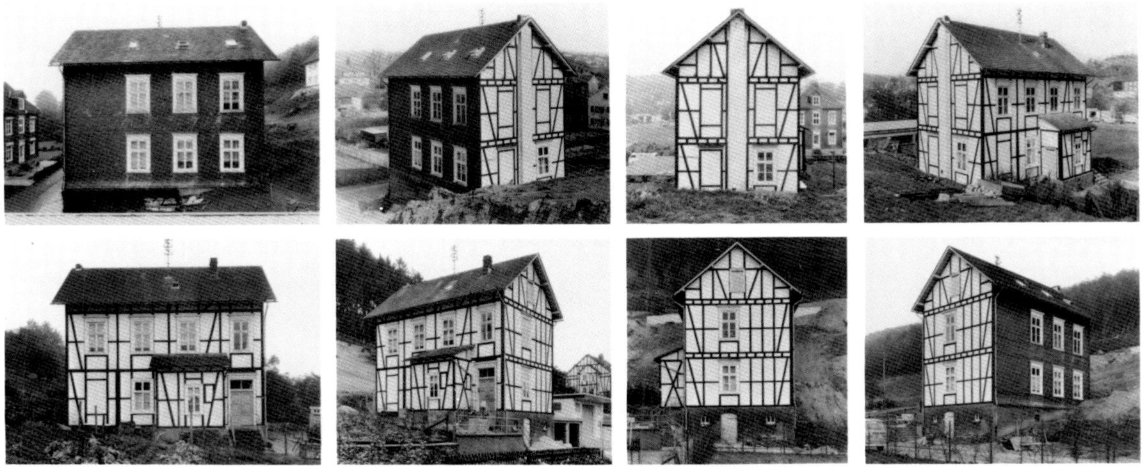

274
Oststraße 16, Freudenberg, 1971.

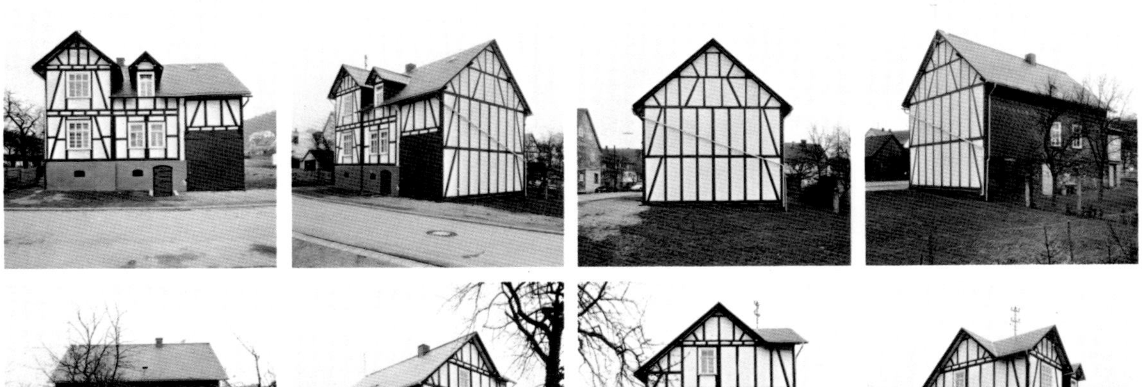

275
Tränkestraße 3, Haiger-Seelbach, 1972.

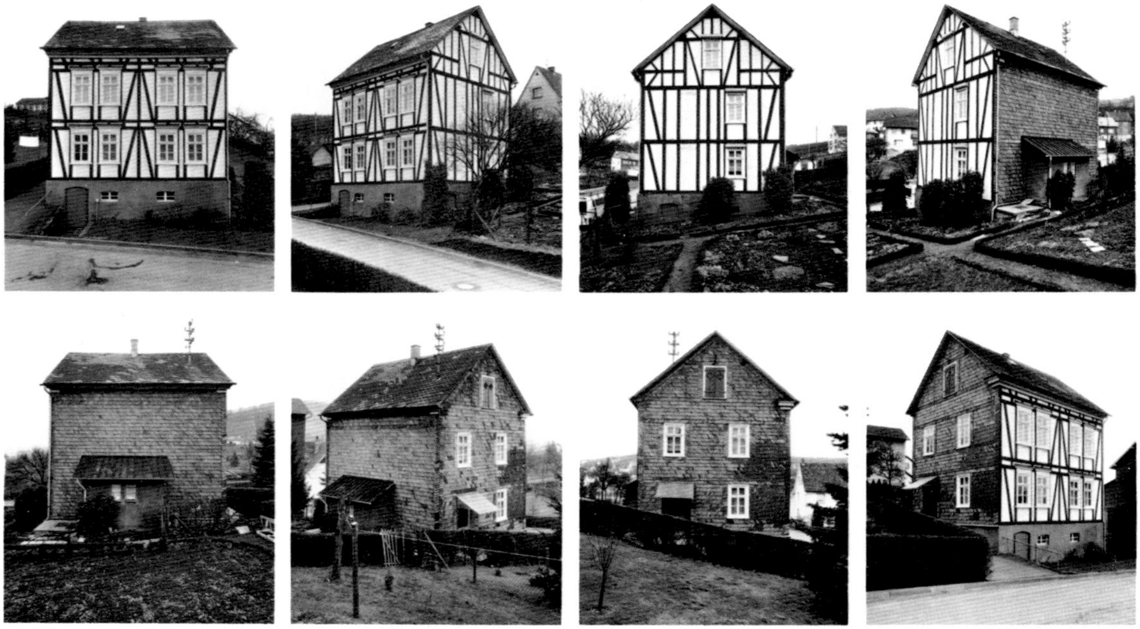

276
Abendröthe 3, Birlenbach, 1972.

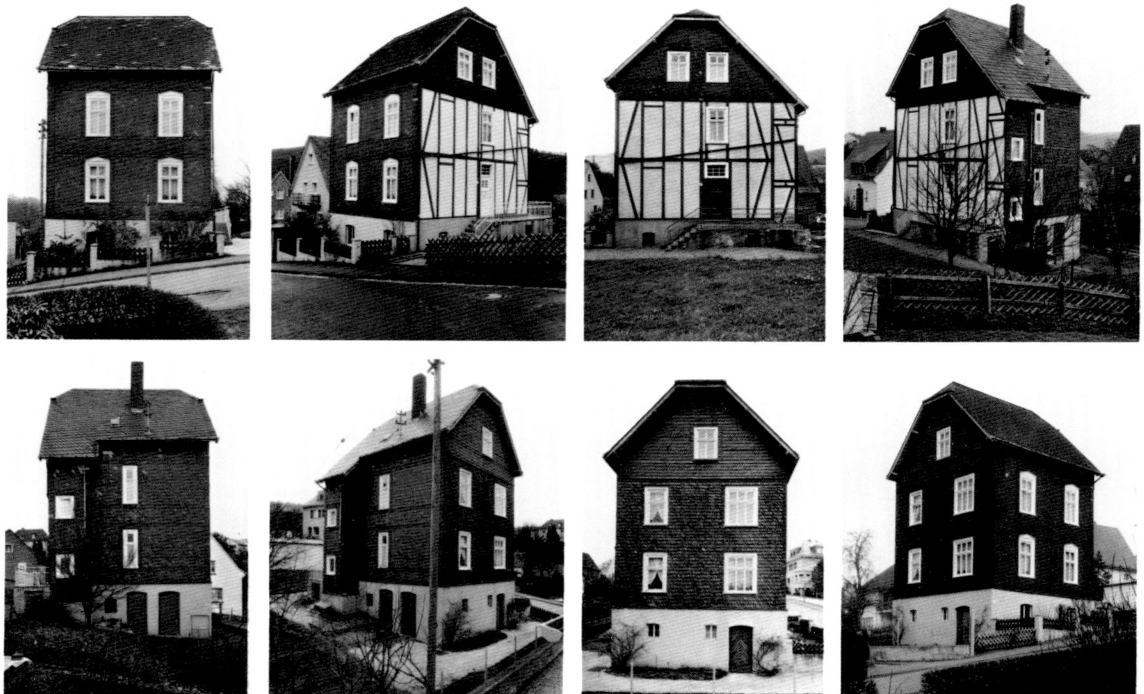

277
Schloßblick 17, Kaan-Marienborn, 1962, 1971.

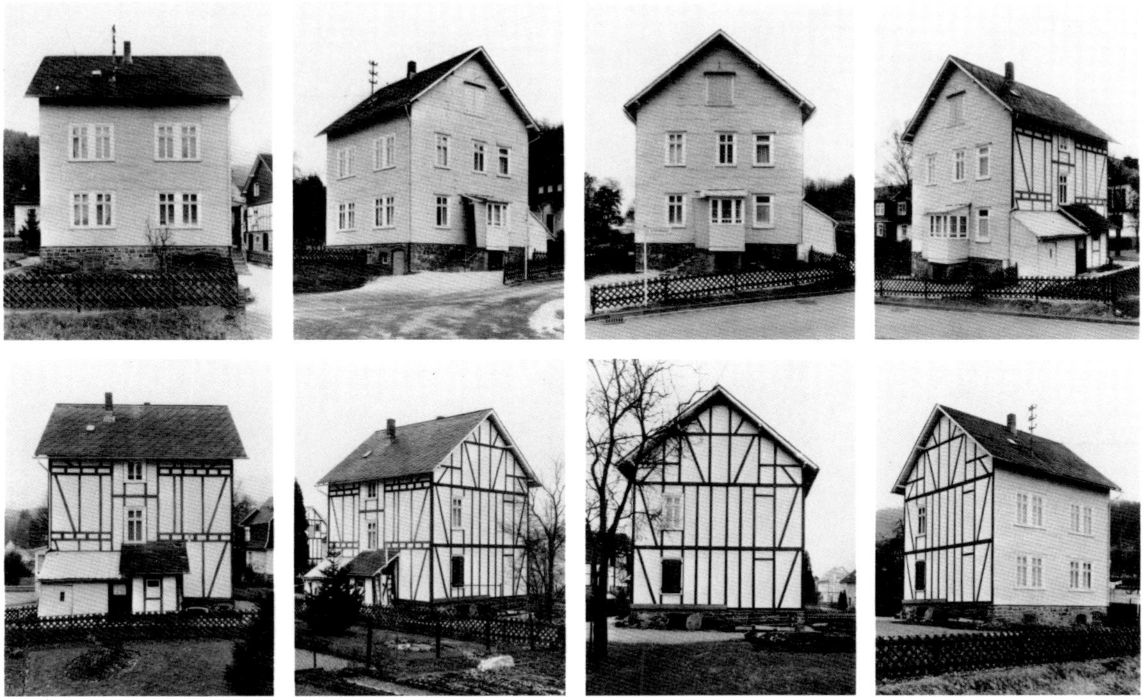

278
Hillnhütter Straße 62, Dahlbruch, 1971.

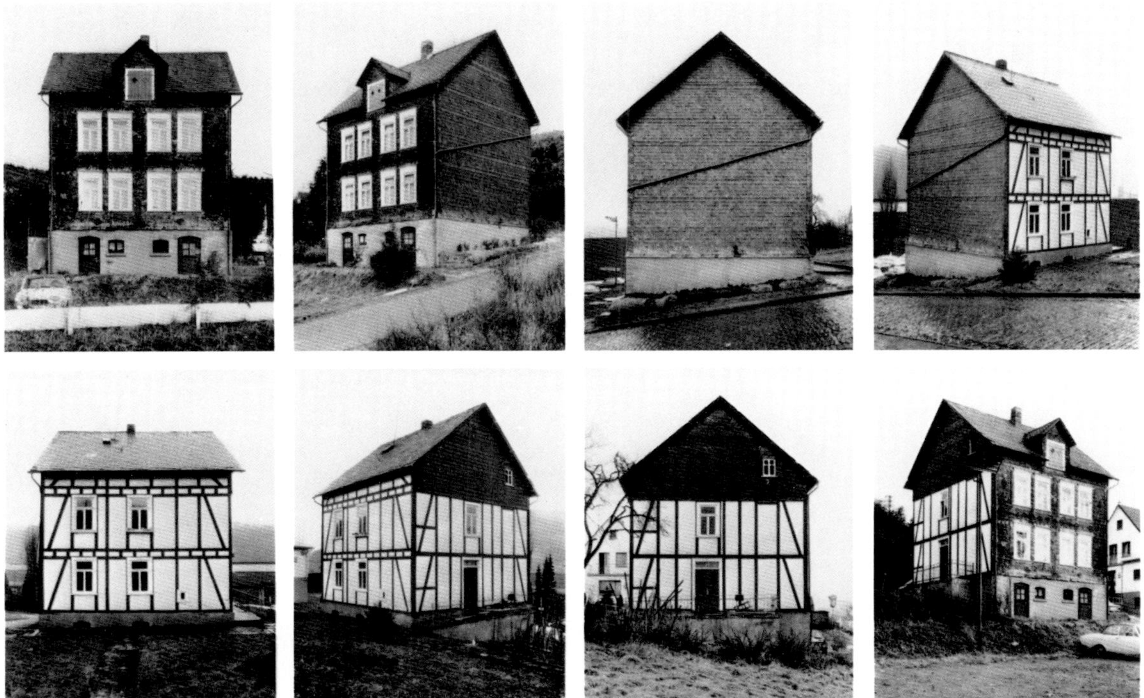

279
Hauptstraße 3, Birken, 1971.

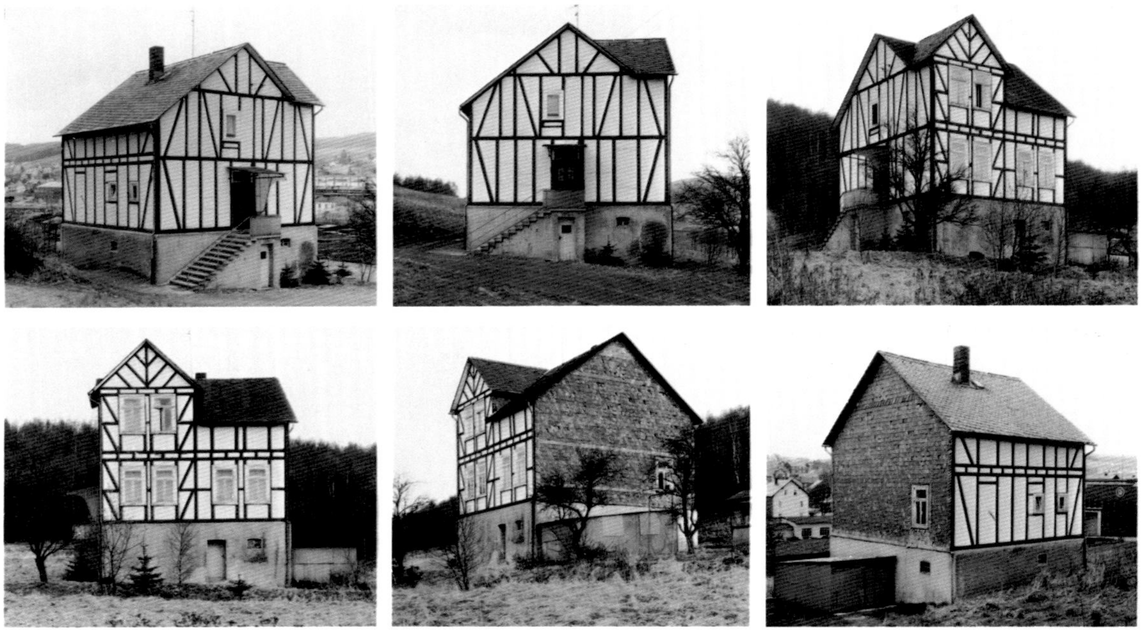

280
Fritz-Schäfer-Straße 24, Salchendorf, 1971.

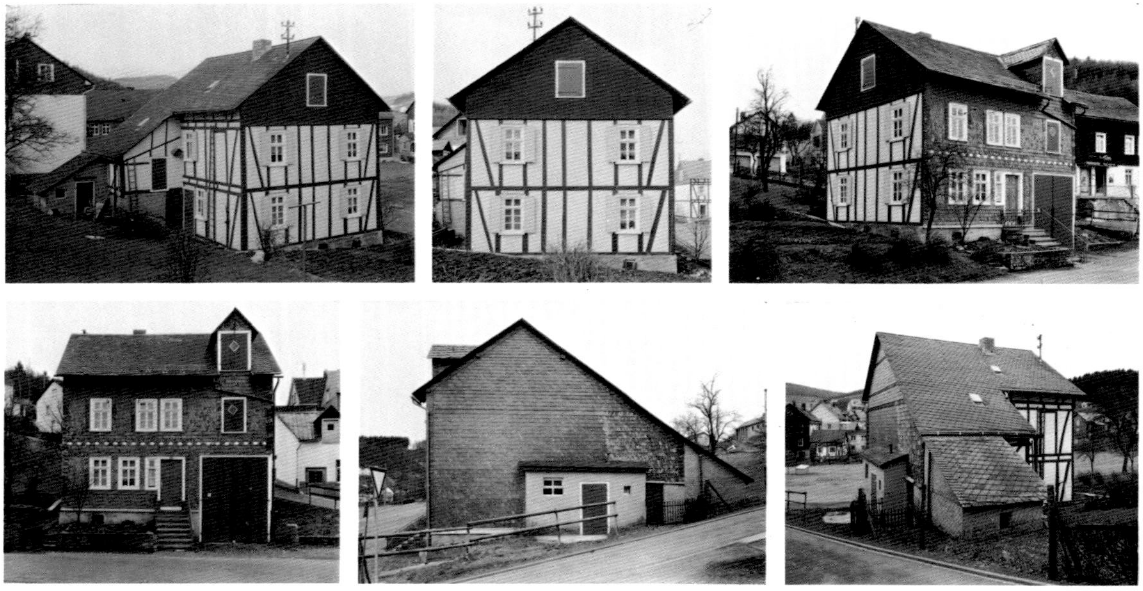

281
Eiserntalstraße 150, Eisern, 1970.

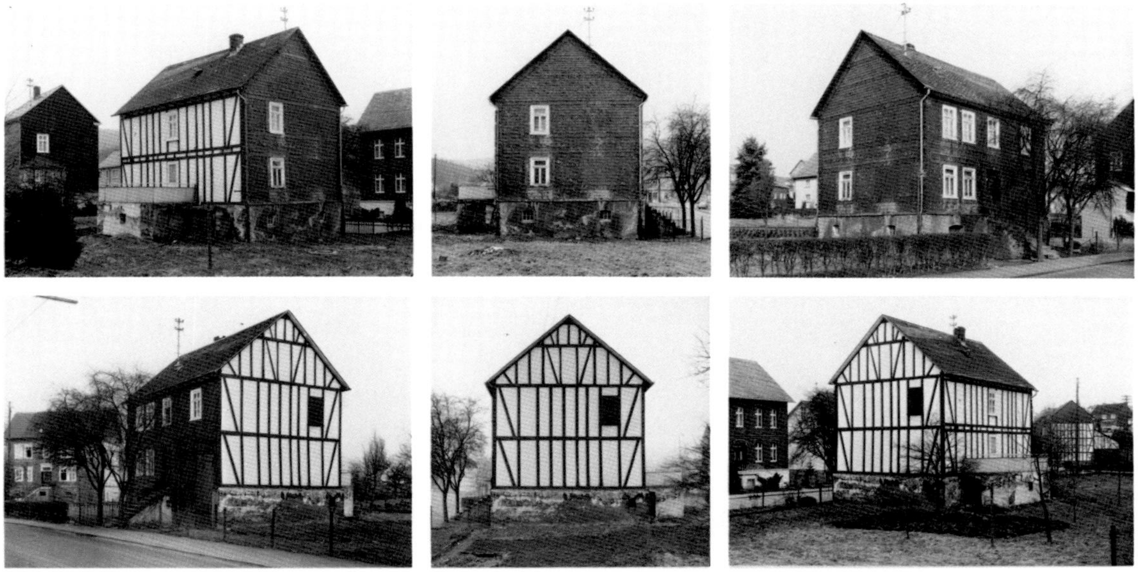

282
Wildener Straße 11, Salchendorf, 1961.

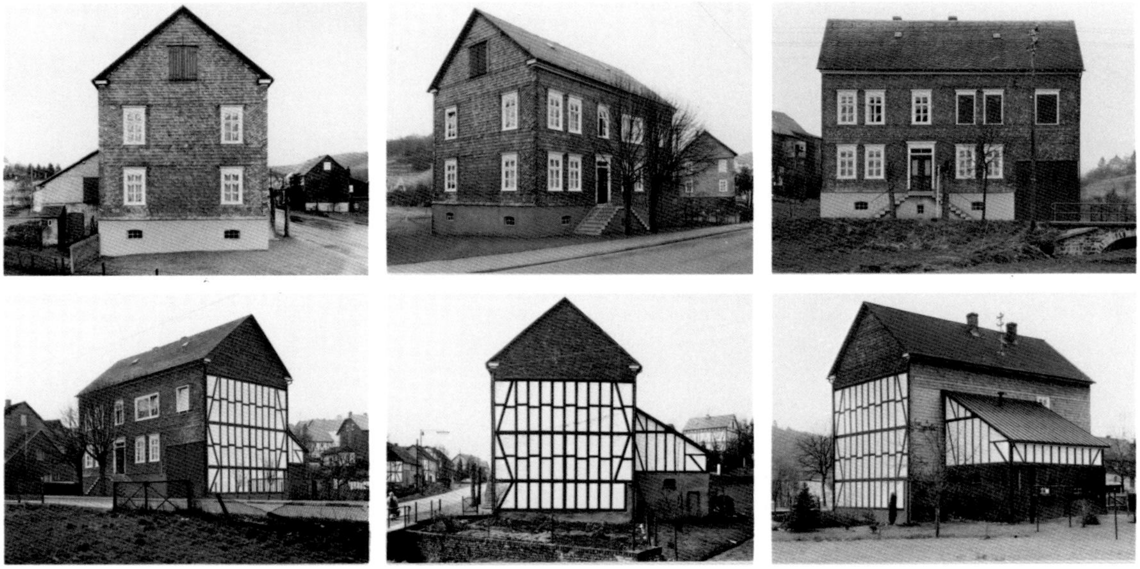

283
Wildener Straße 7, Salchendorf, 1961.

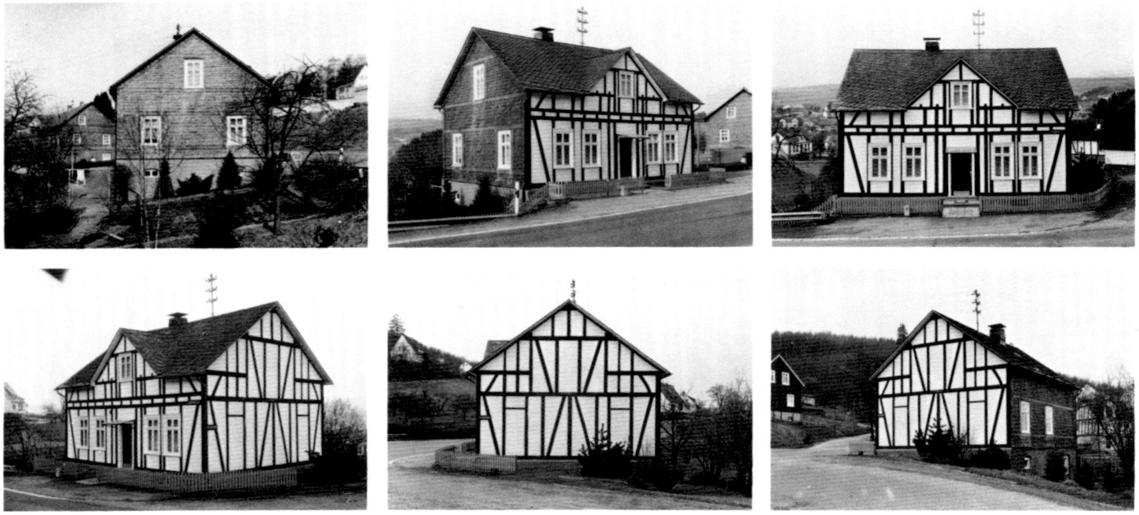

284
Siegener Straße 167, Büschergrund, 1966.

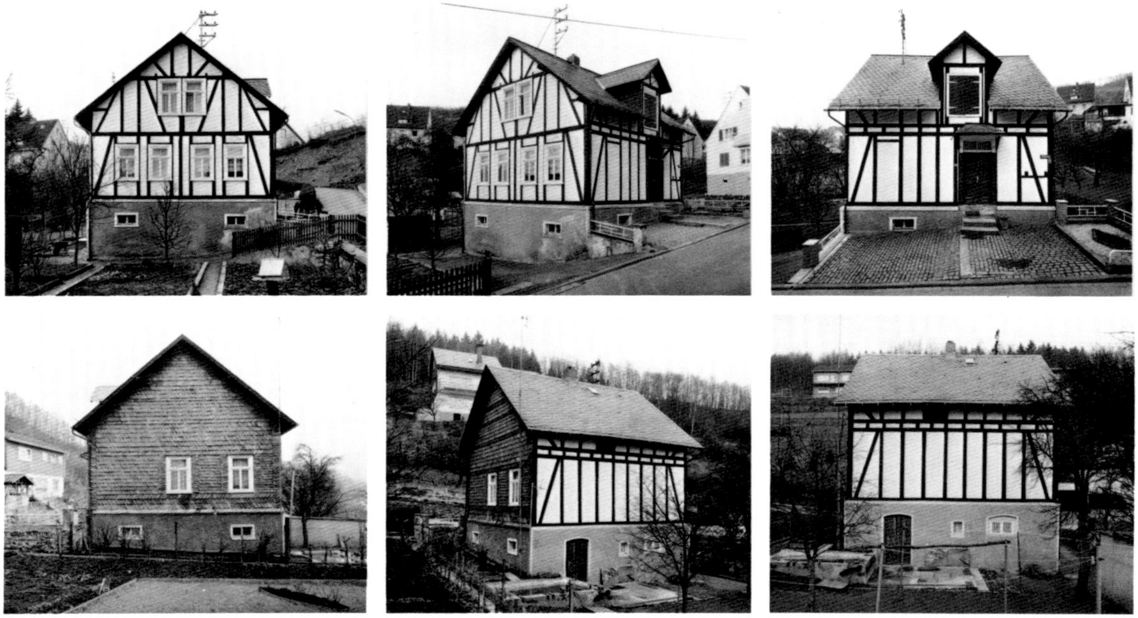

285
Maiweg 23, Gosenbach, 1967.

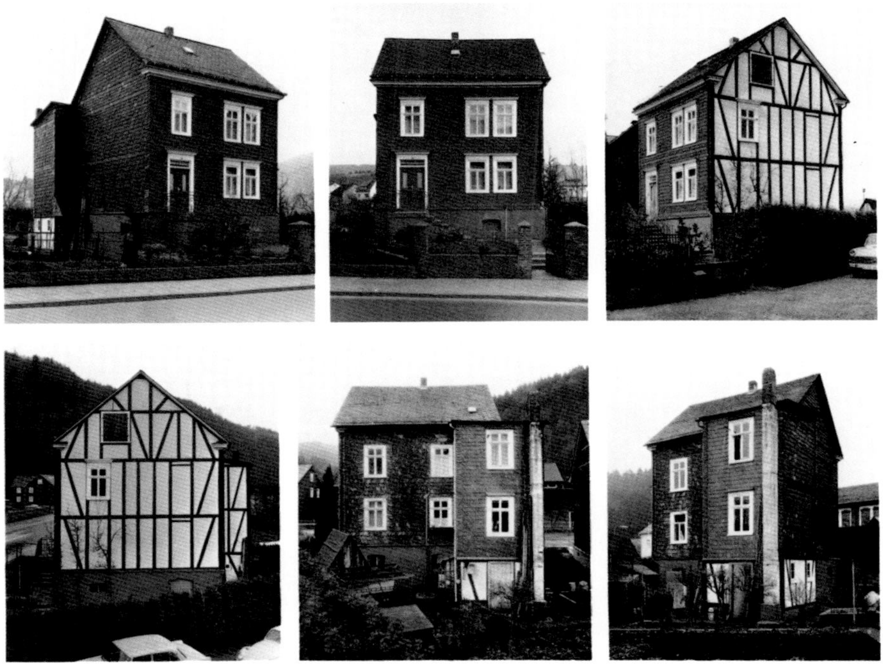

286
Siegtalstraße 36, Eiserfeld, 1971.

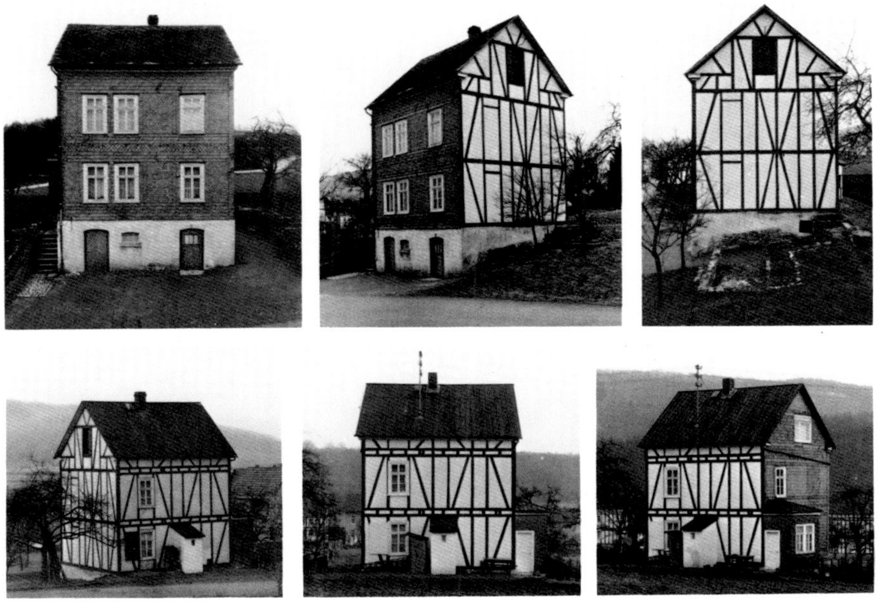

287
Rensdorfstraße 13, Salchendorf, 1960.

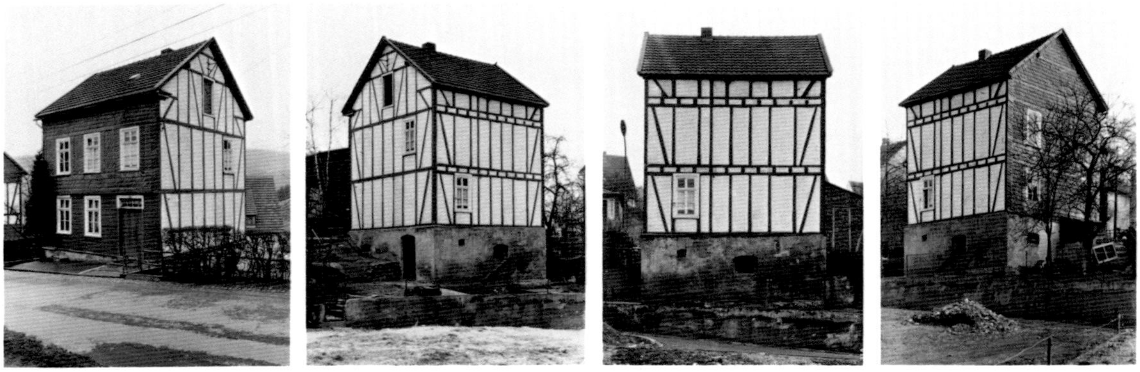

288
Siegener Straße 67, Gosenbach, 1960.

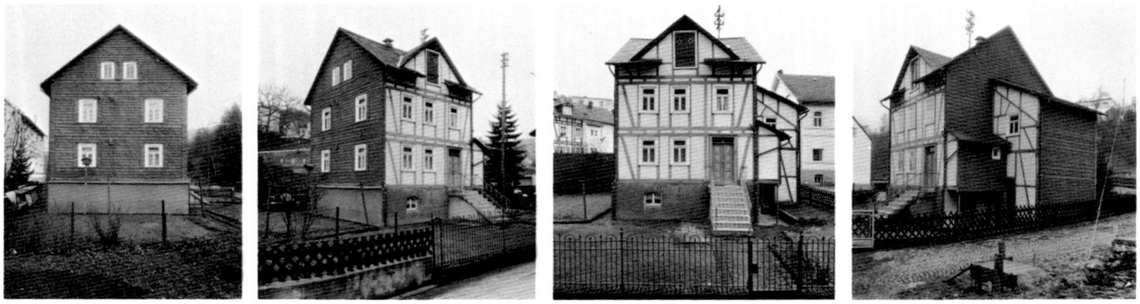

289
Am Gosenbach 3, Niederschelderhütte, 1972.

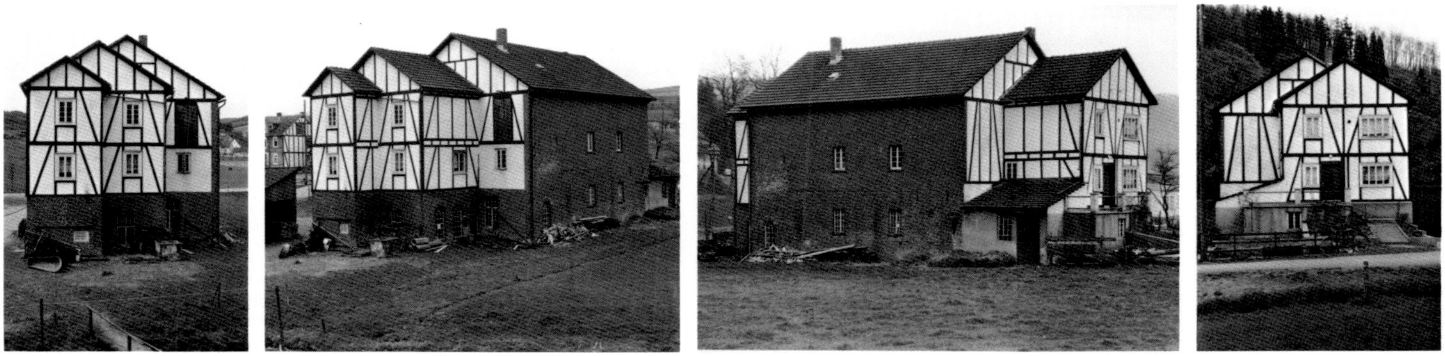

290
Triftstraße 58, Büschergrund, 1959.

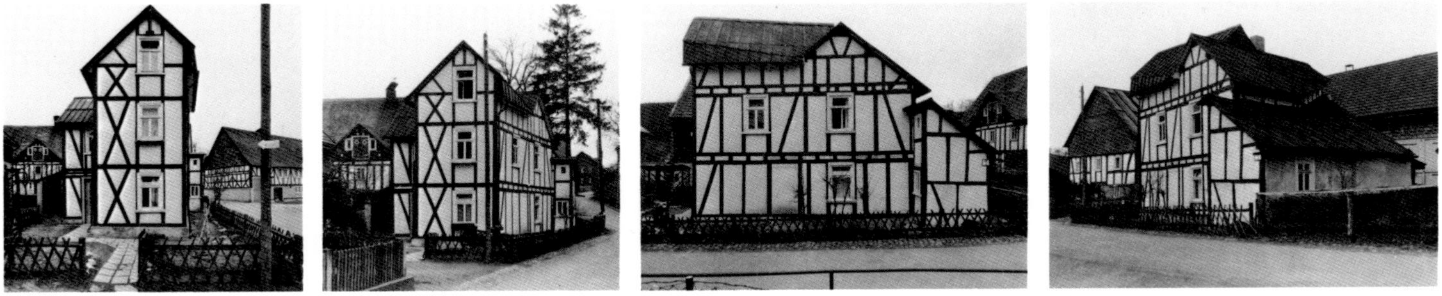

291
Wickersbacher Weg 7, Trupbach, 1960.

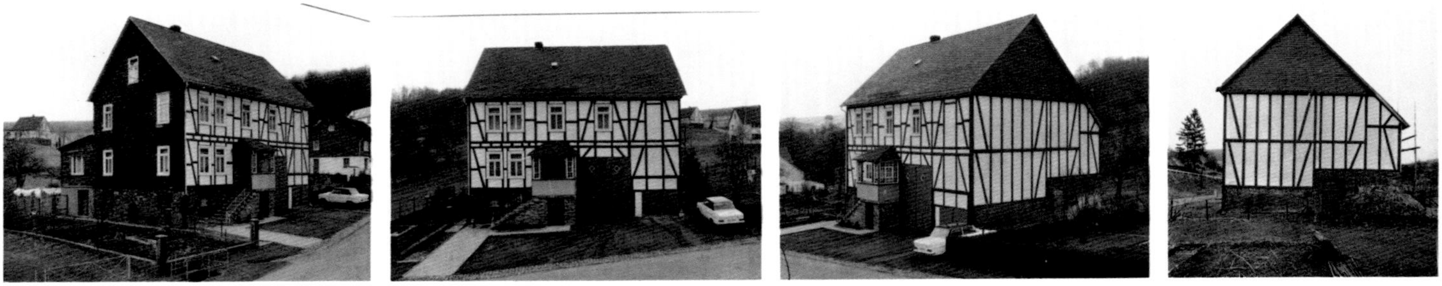

292
Hambachwaldstraße 9, Gilsbach, 1962, 1971.

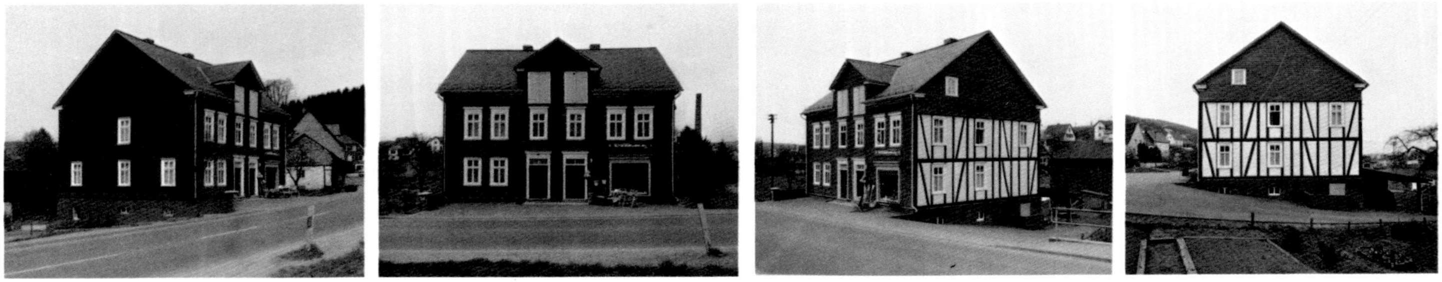

293
Olper Straße 15, Büschergrund, 1970.

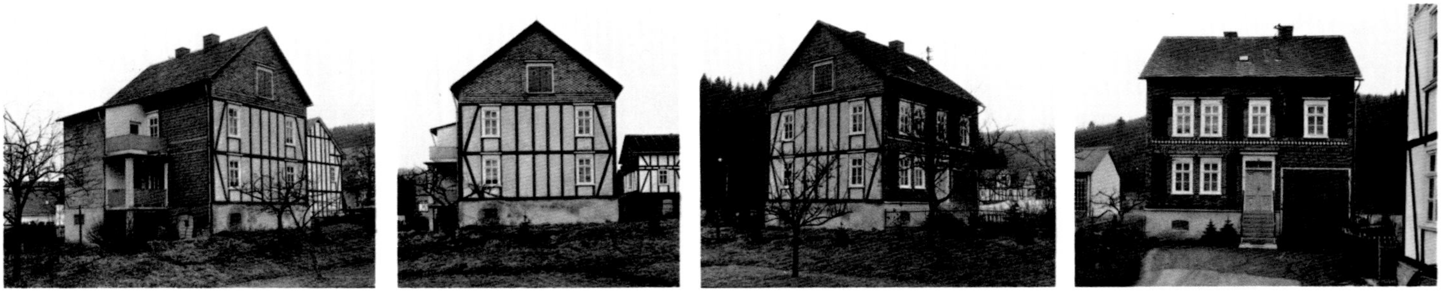

294
In der Bitze 3, Eisern, 1971.

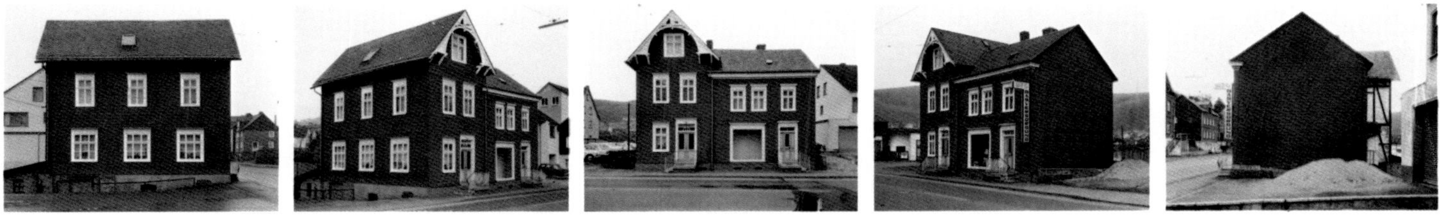

295
Siegtalstraße 164, Niederschelden, 1968, 1971.

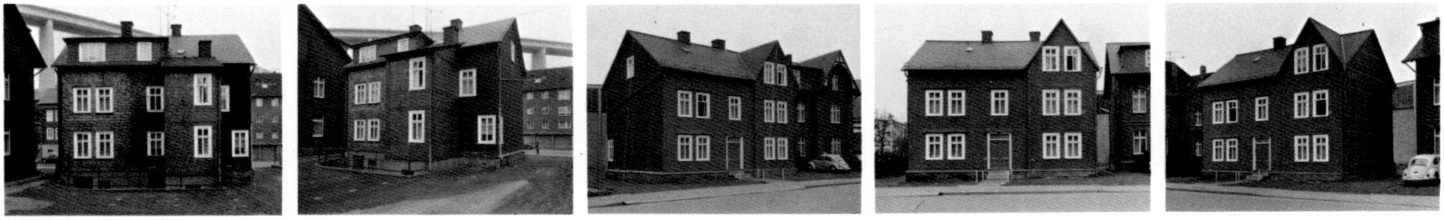

296
Bahnhofstraße 155, Eiserfeld, 1971.

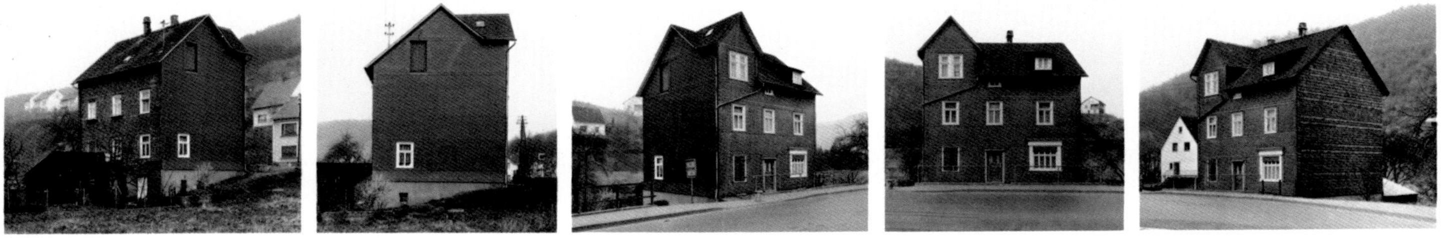

297
Konrad-Adenauer-Straße 1, Niederfischbach, 1971.

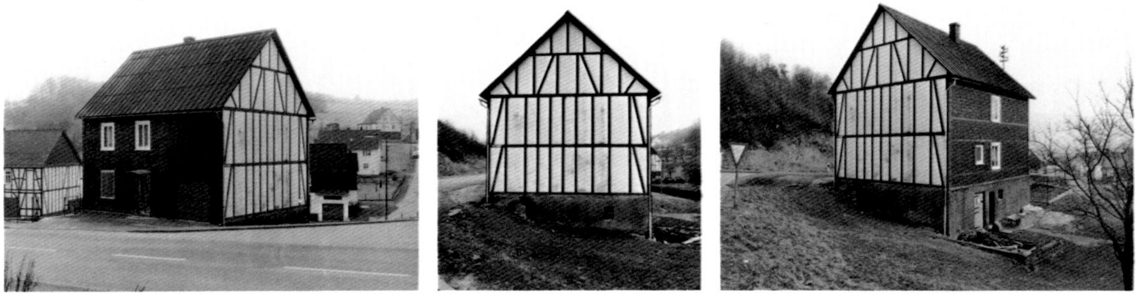

298
Wilnsdorfer Straße 65, Gilsbach, 1970.

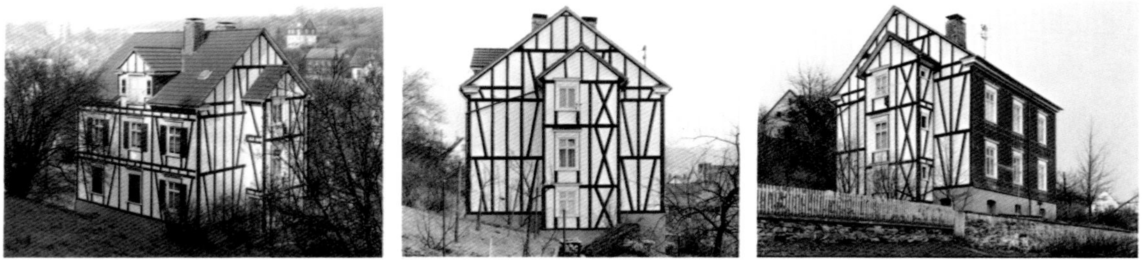

299
Oststraße 10, Freudenberg, 1968.

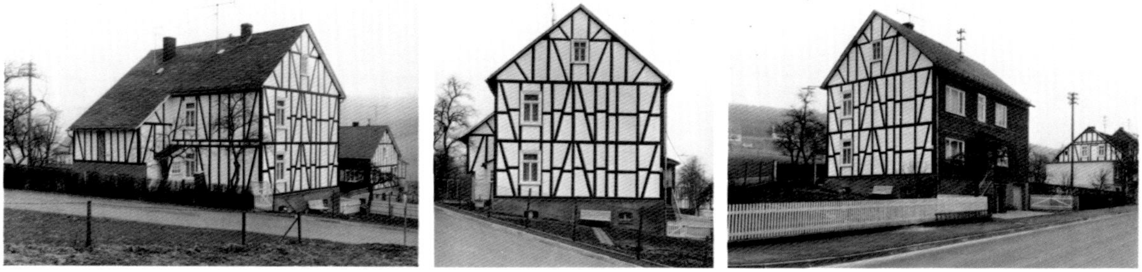

300
Wilnsdorfer Straße 26, Gilsbach, 1972.

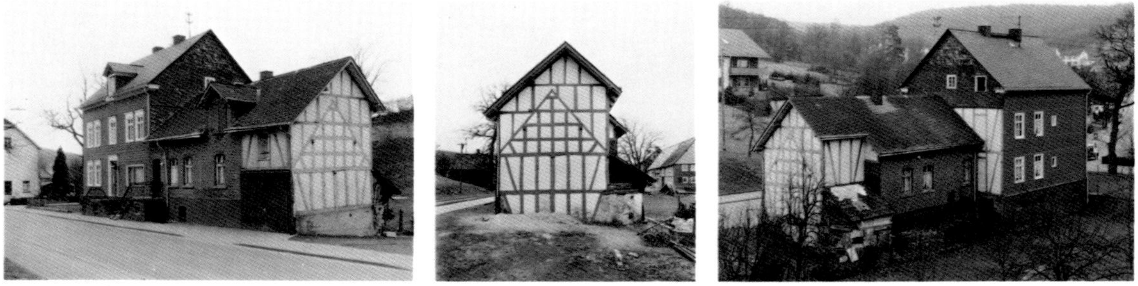

301
Obere Dorfstraße 21, Bürbach, 1962, 1971.

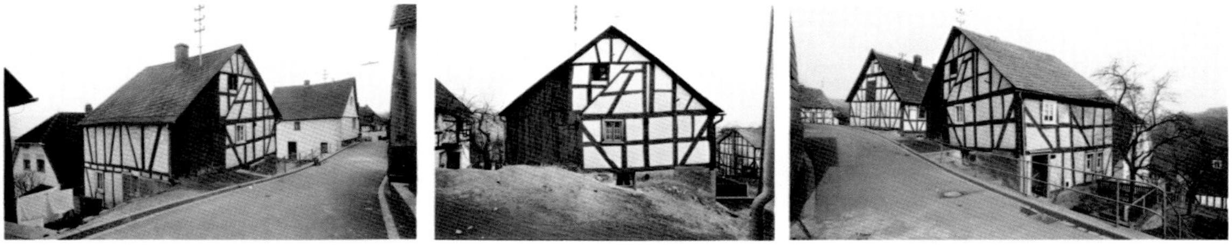

302
Bogenstraße 8, Freusburg, 1962, 1971.

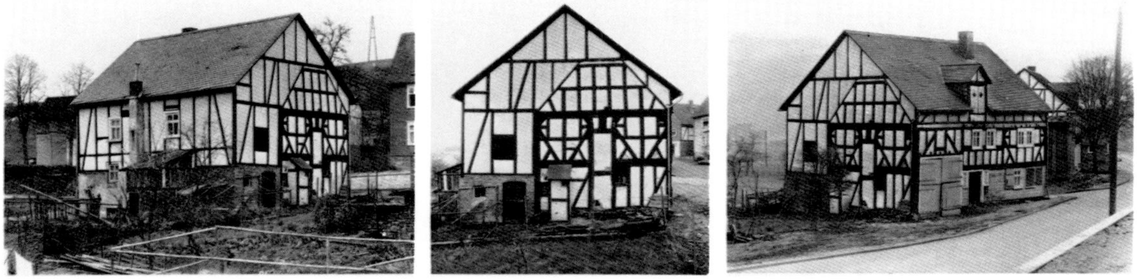

303
Hauptstraße 36, Flammersbach, 1960.

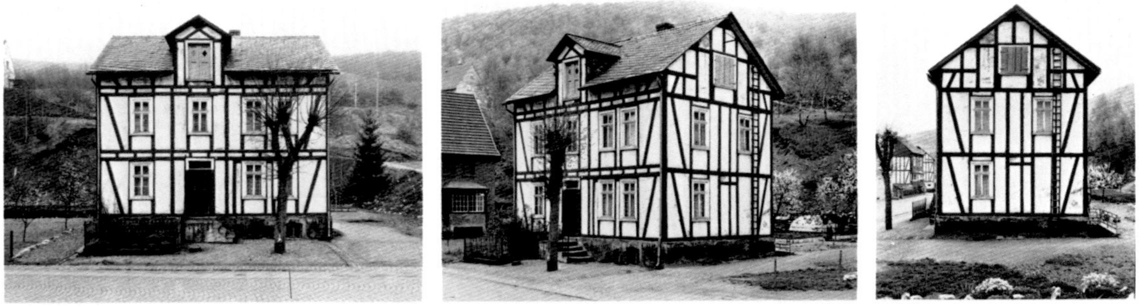

304
Auf der Hütte 45, Gosenbach, 1961.

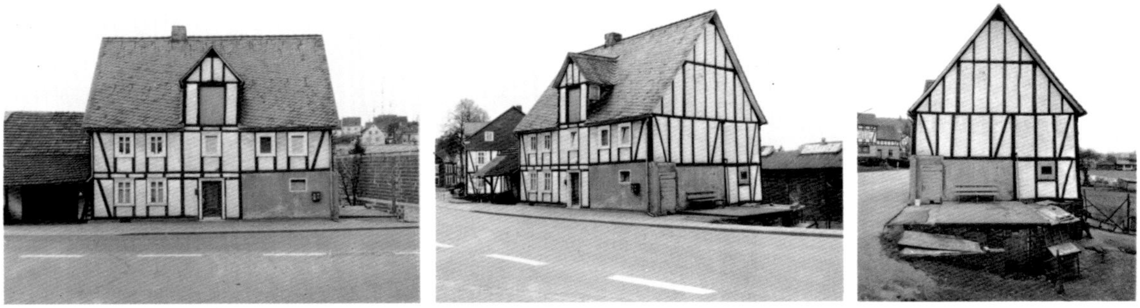

305
Olper Straße 19, Büschergrund, 1970.

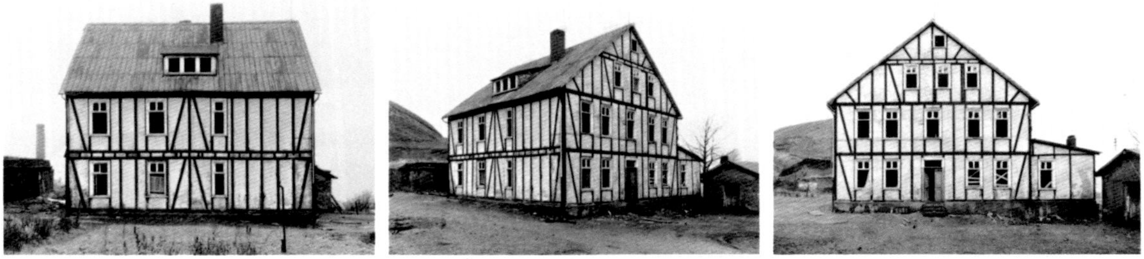

306
Friedhofstraße 11, Niederschelden, 1970.

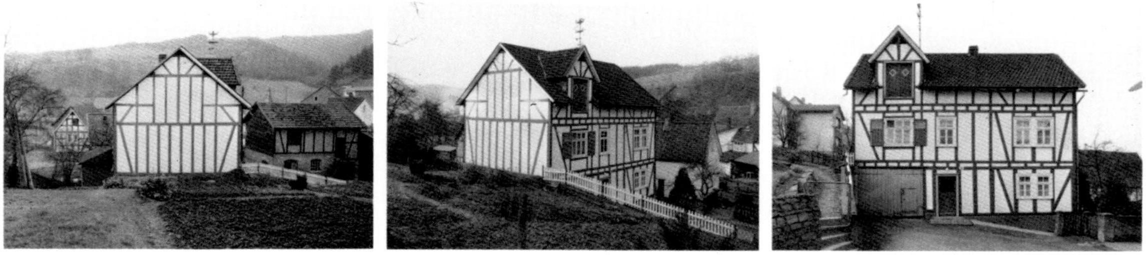

307
Bergstraße 11, Niederfischbach, 1971.

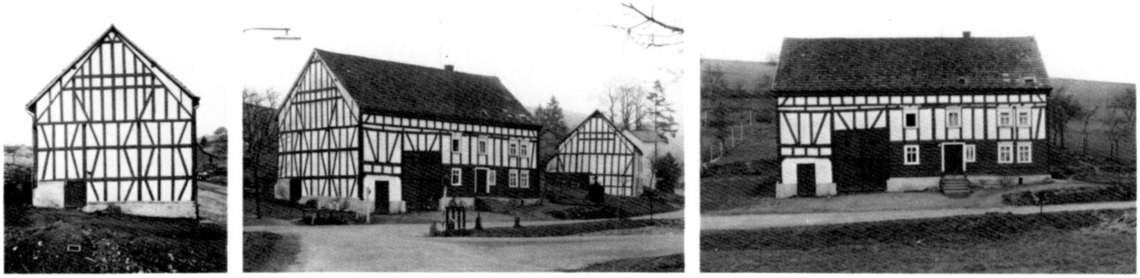

308
Oberdielfer Straße 18, Oberdielfen, 1962.

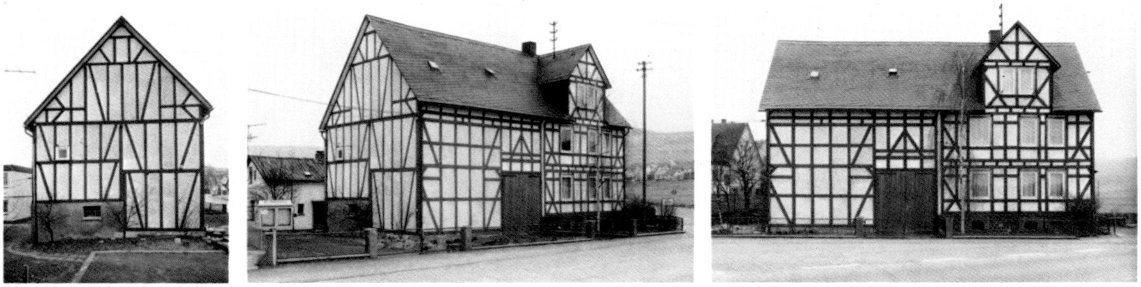

309
Haigerer Straße 2, Allendorf, 1972.

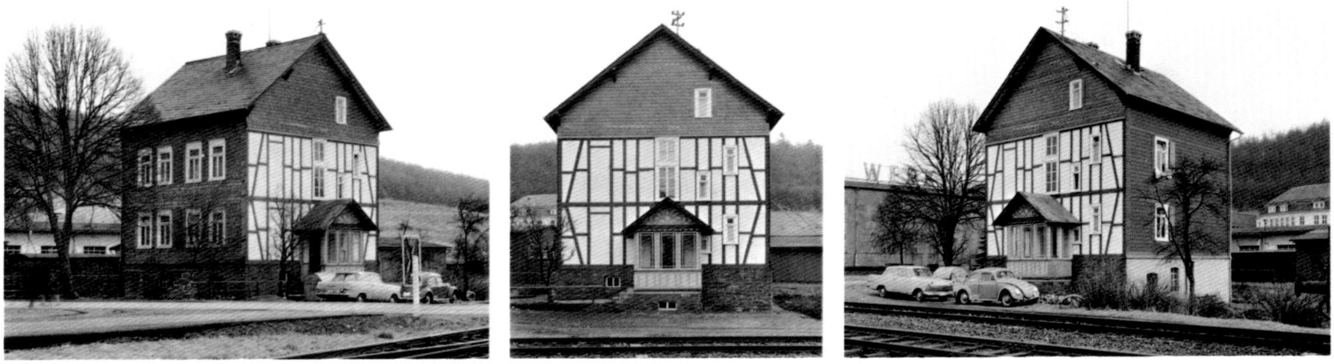

310

Fritz-Schäfer-Straße 22, Salchendorf, 1964, 1972.

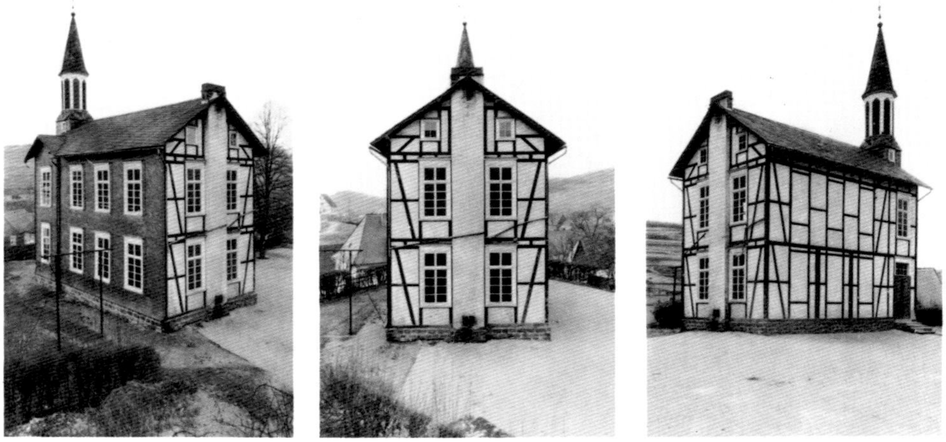

311

Schulplatz 6, Niederndorf, 1964.

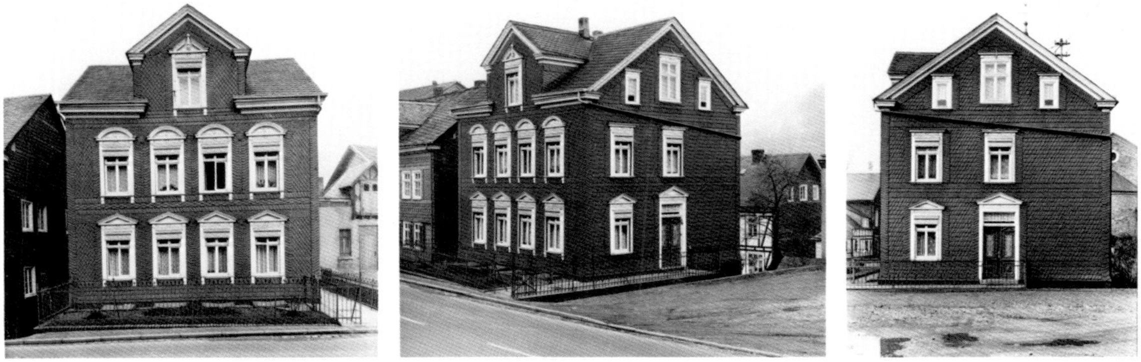

312
Freiengründerstraße 21, Eiserfeld, 1960.

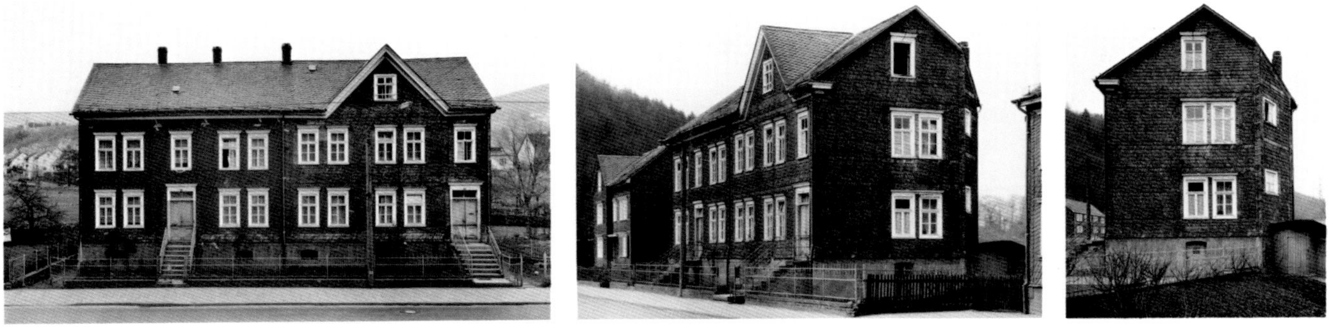

313
Siegtalstraße 40, Eiserfeld, 1971.

VII.
STRASSEN- UND ORTSANSICHTEN
GROUPS OF HOUSES

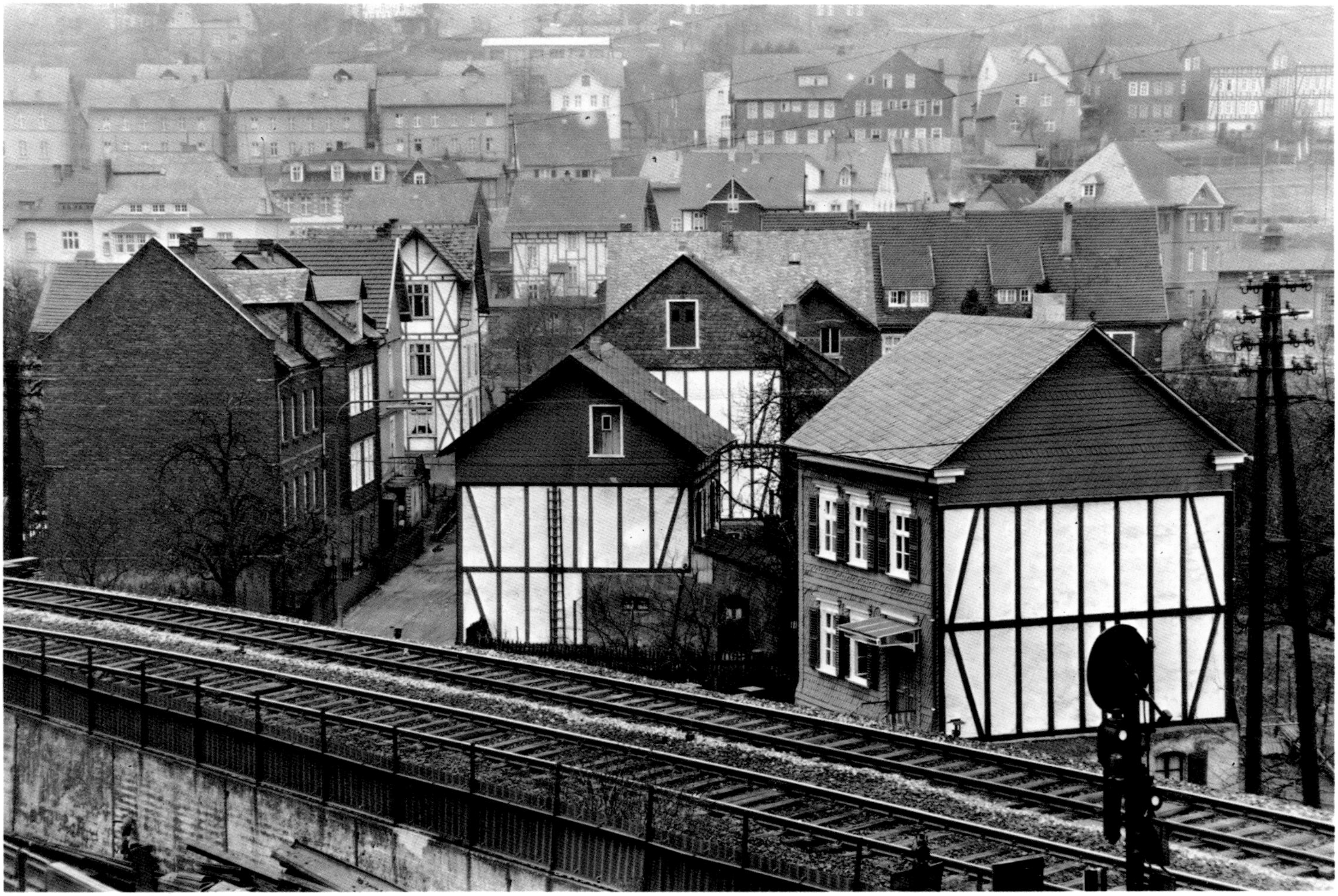

314
Johannesstraße, Niederschelden, 1960.

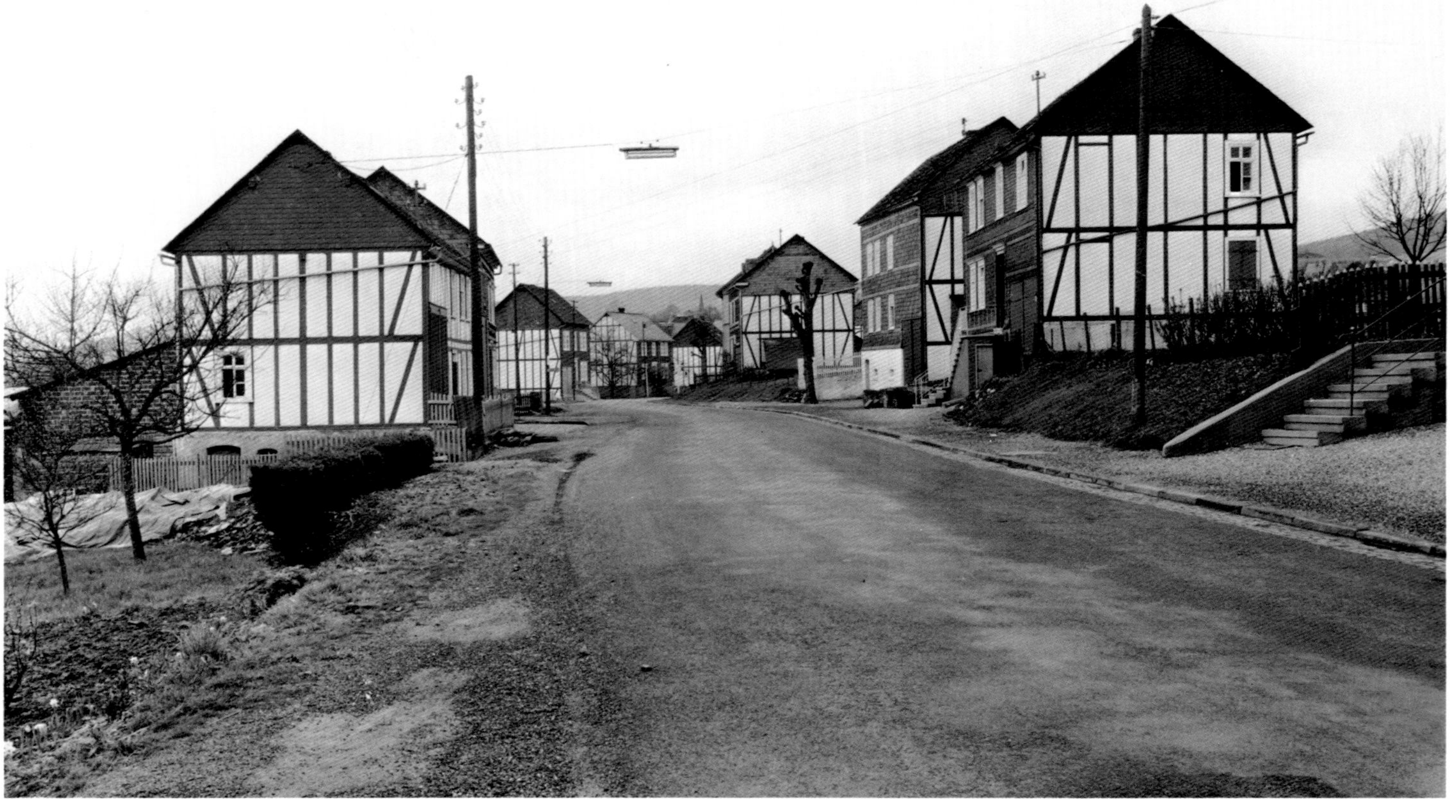

315
Wildener Straße, Salchendorf, 1961.

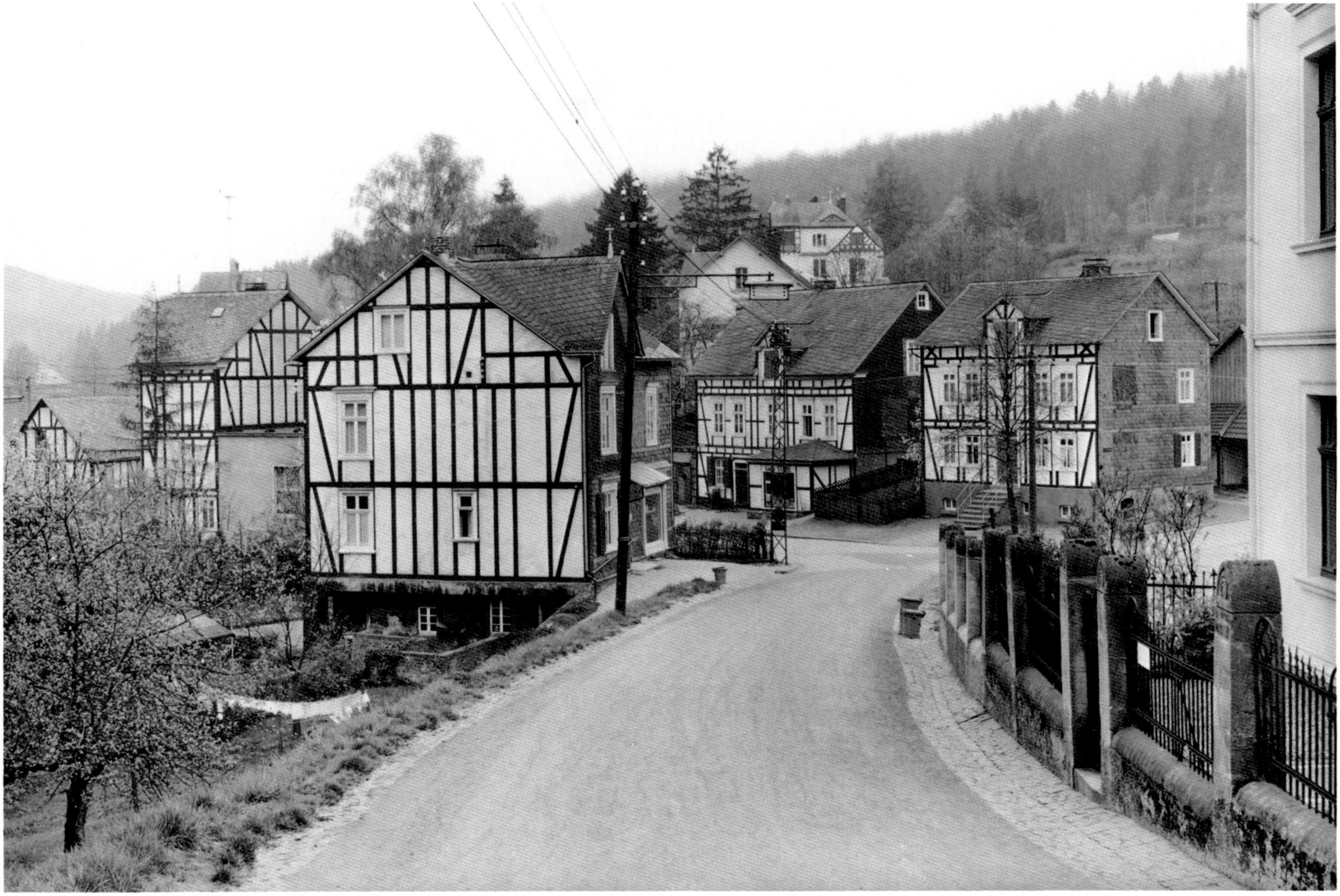

316
Neuer Weg, Freudenberg, 1961.

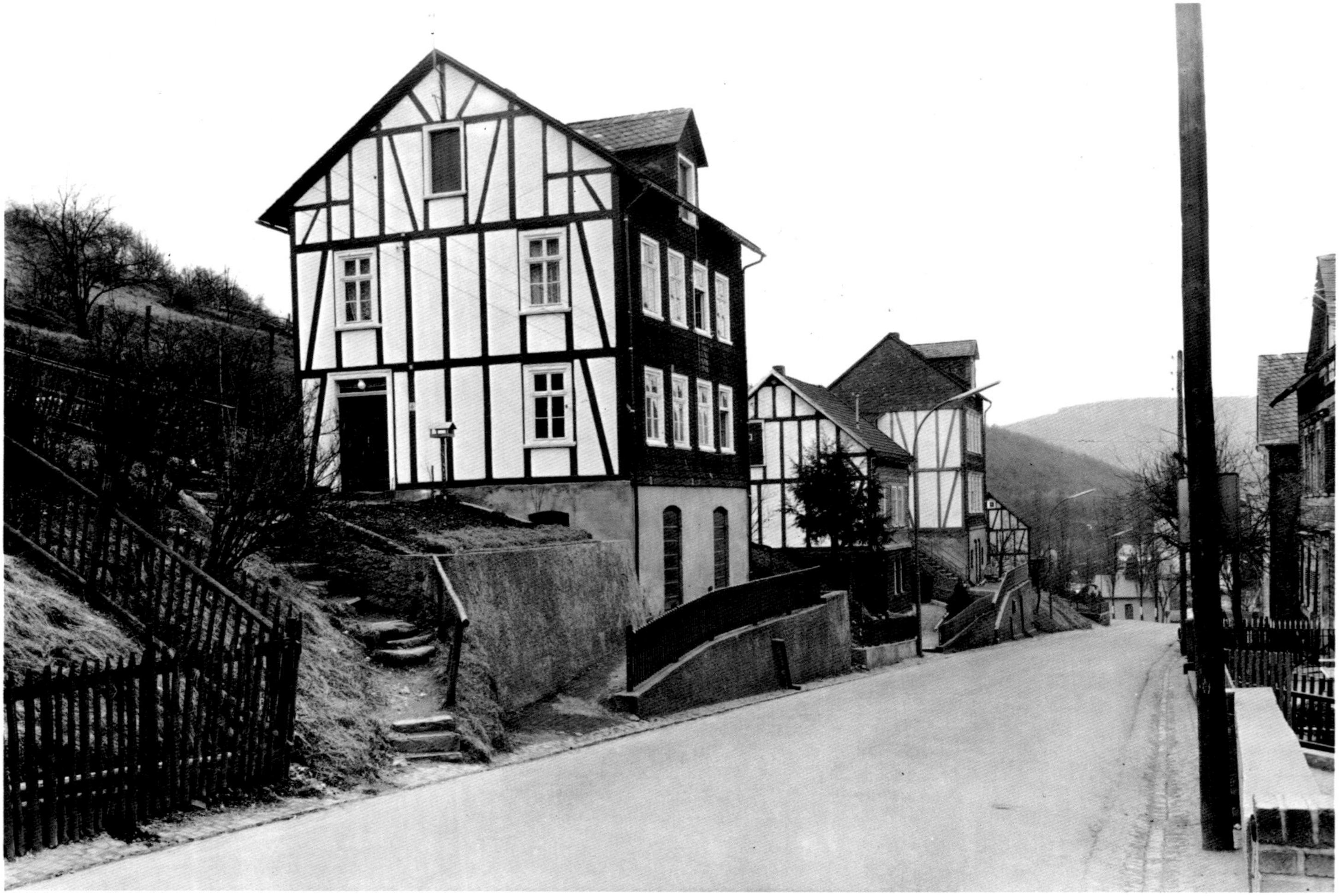

317
Siegener Straße, Gosenbach, 1960.

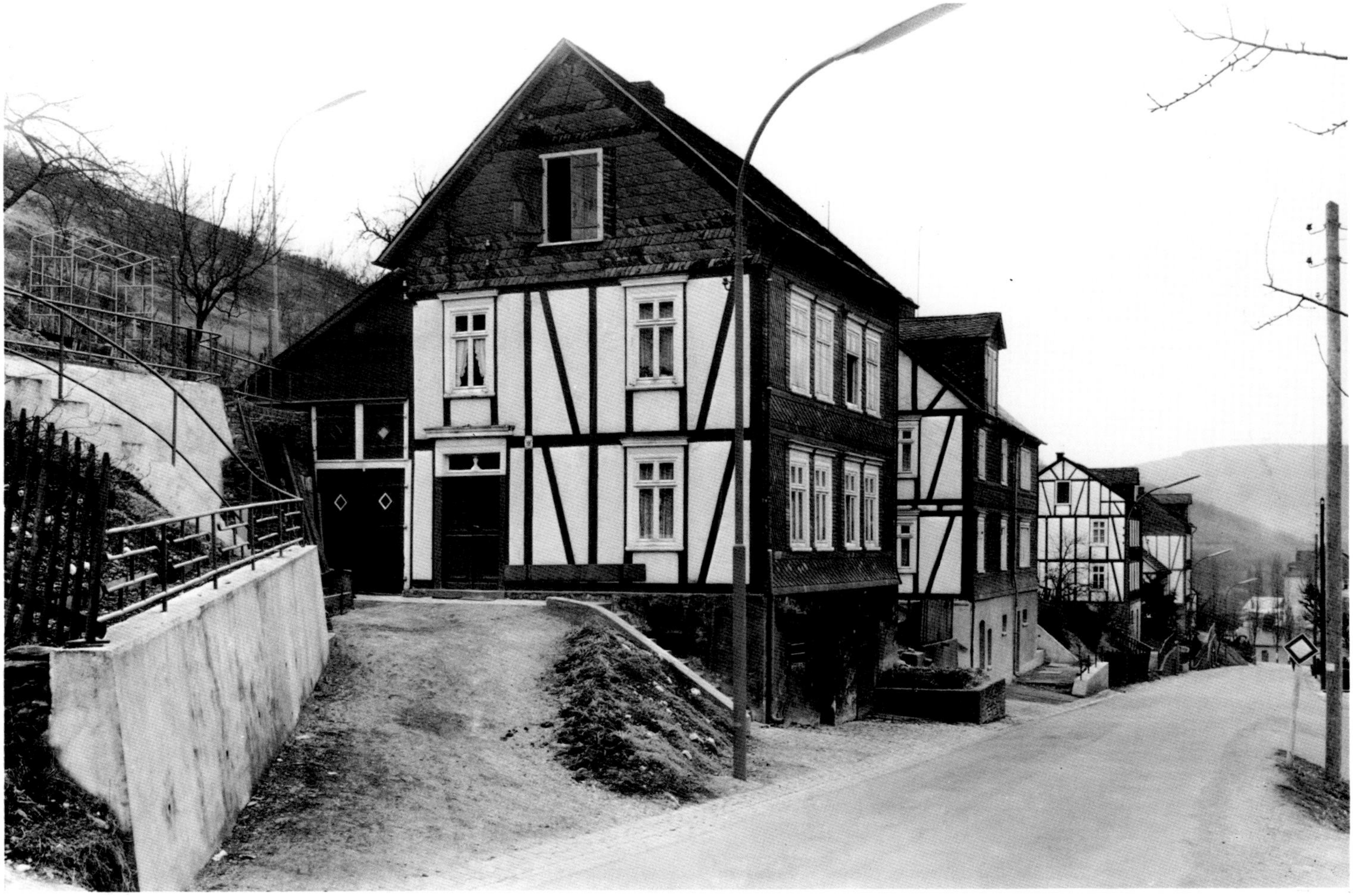

318
Siegener Straße, Gosenbach, 1960.

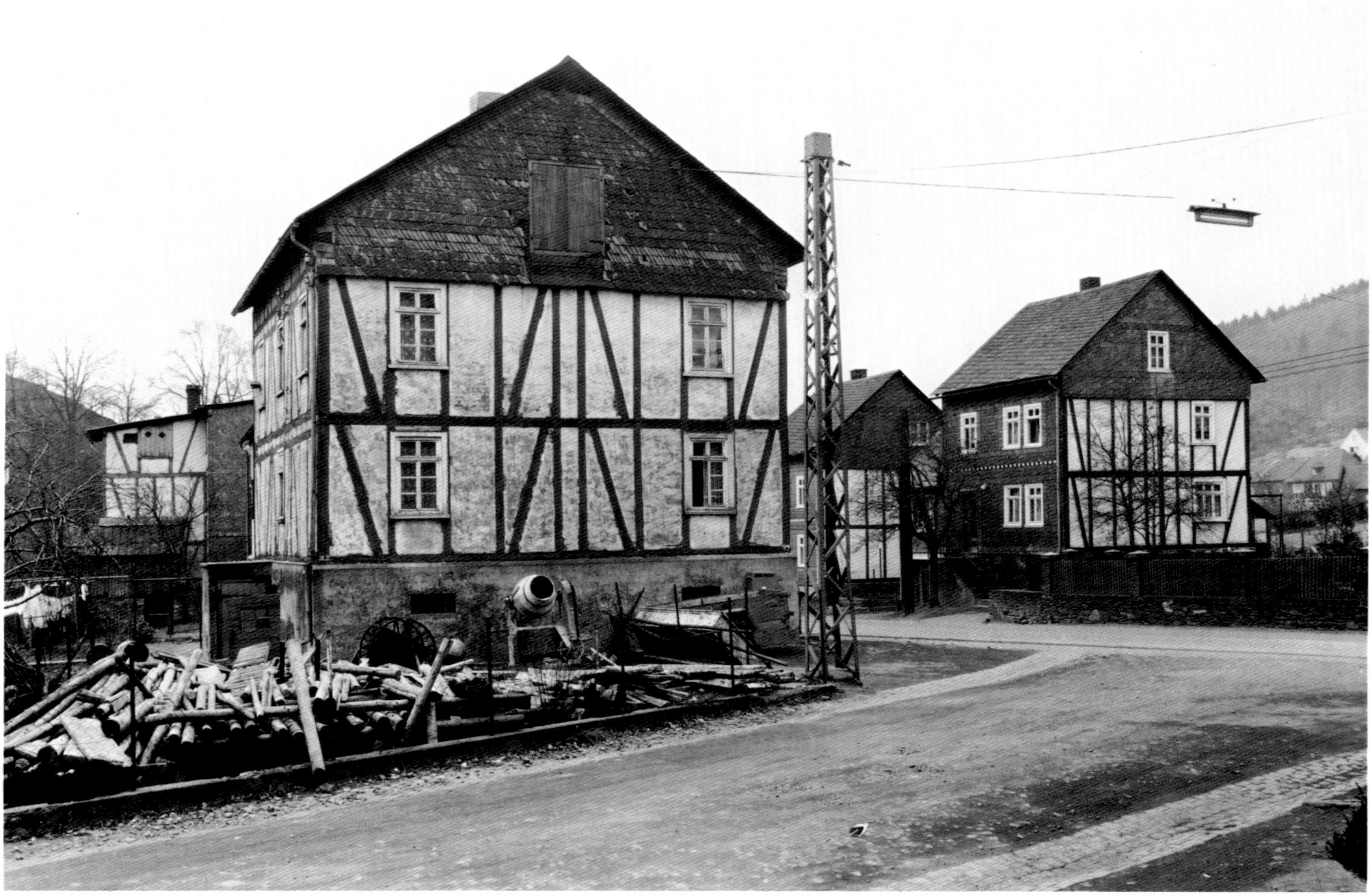

319
Hüttenstraße/Eisernstraße, Eiserfeld, 1960.

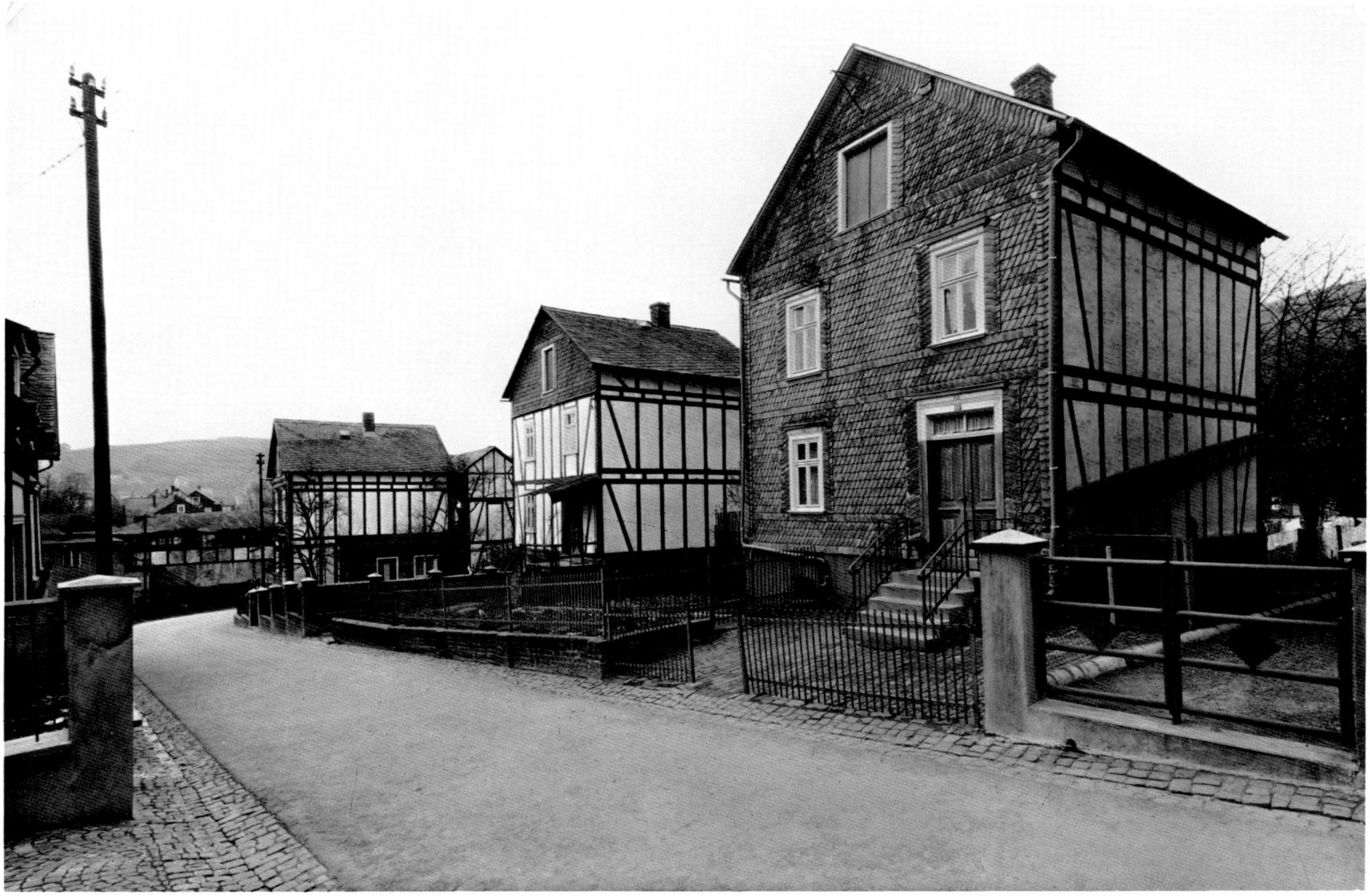

320
Bühlstraße, Niederschelden, 1960.

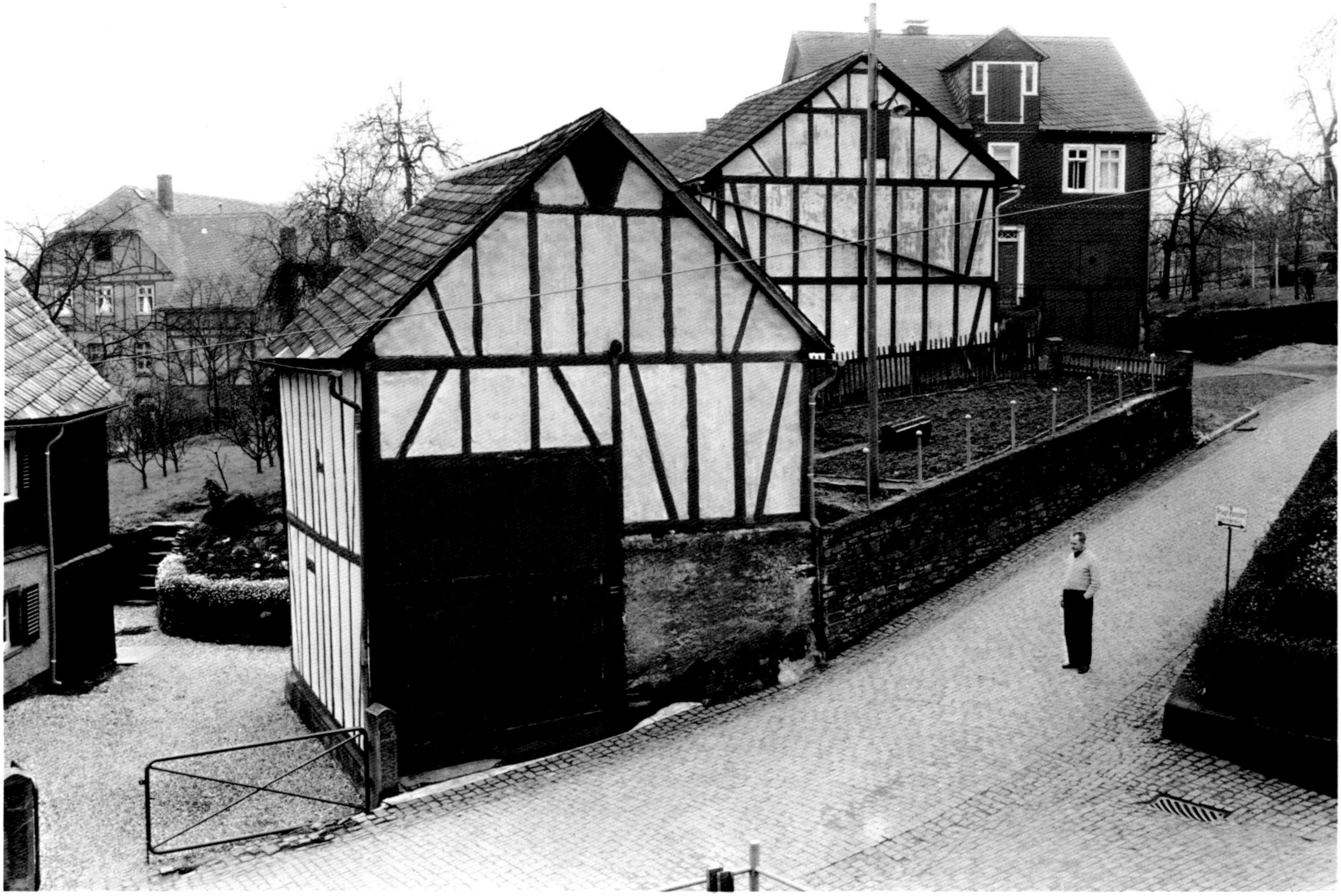

321
Hohlweg, Mudersbach, 1961.

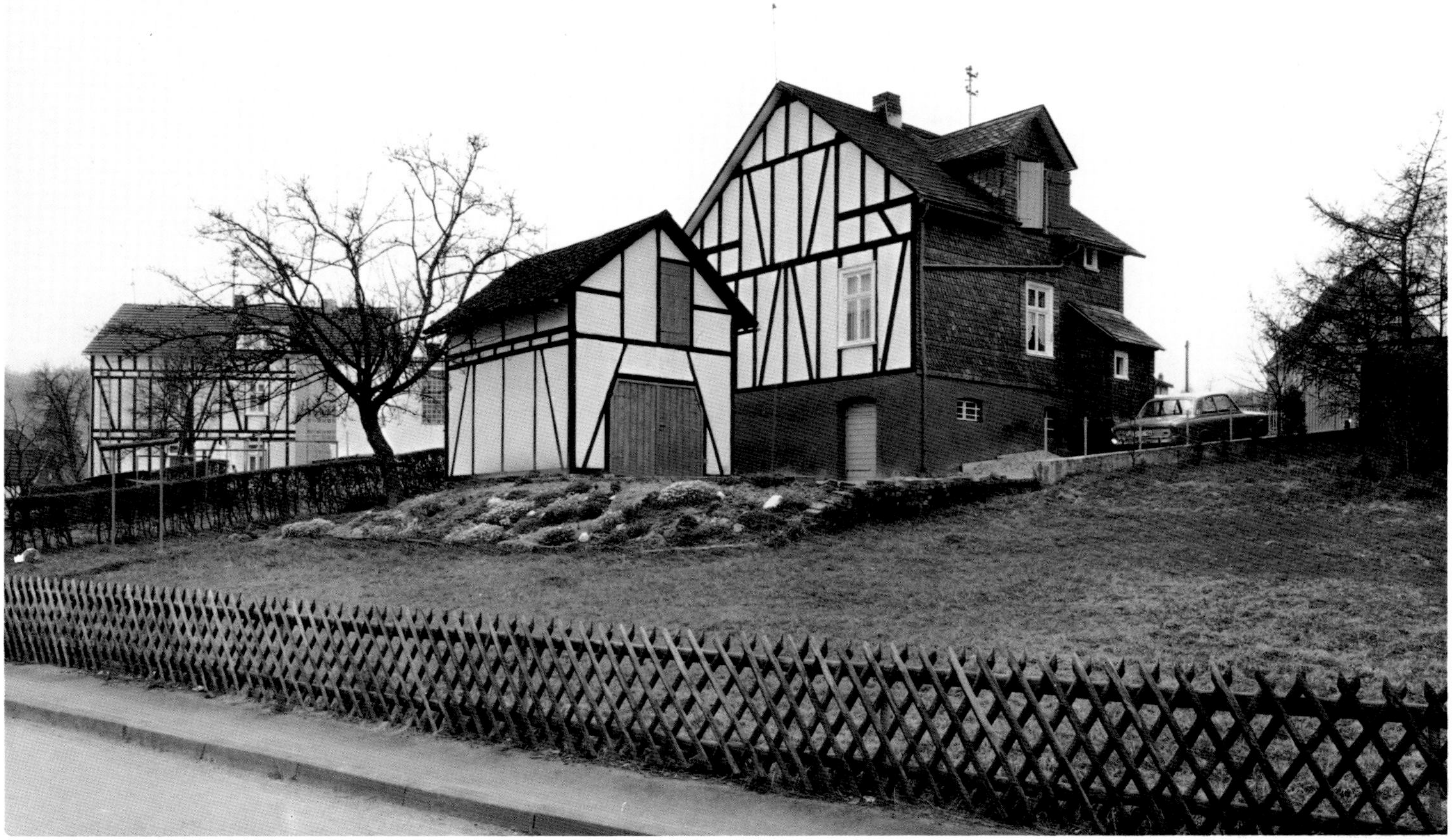

322
Eichstattweg, Freudenberg, 1962.

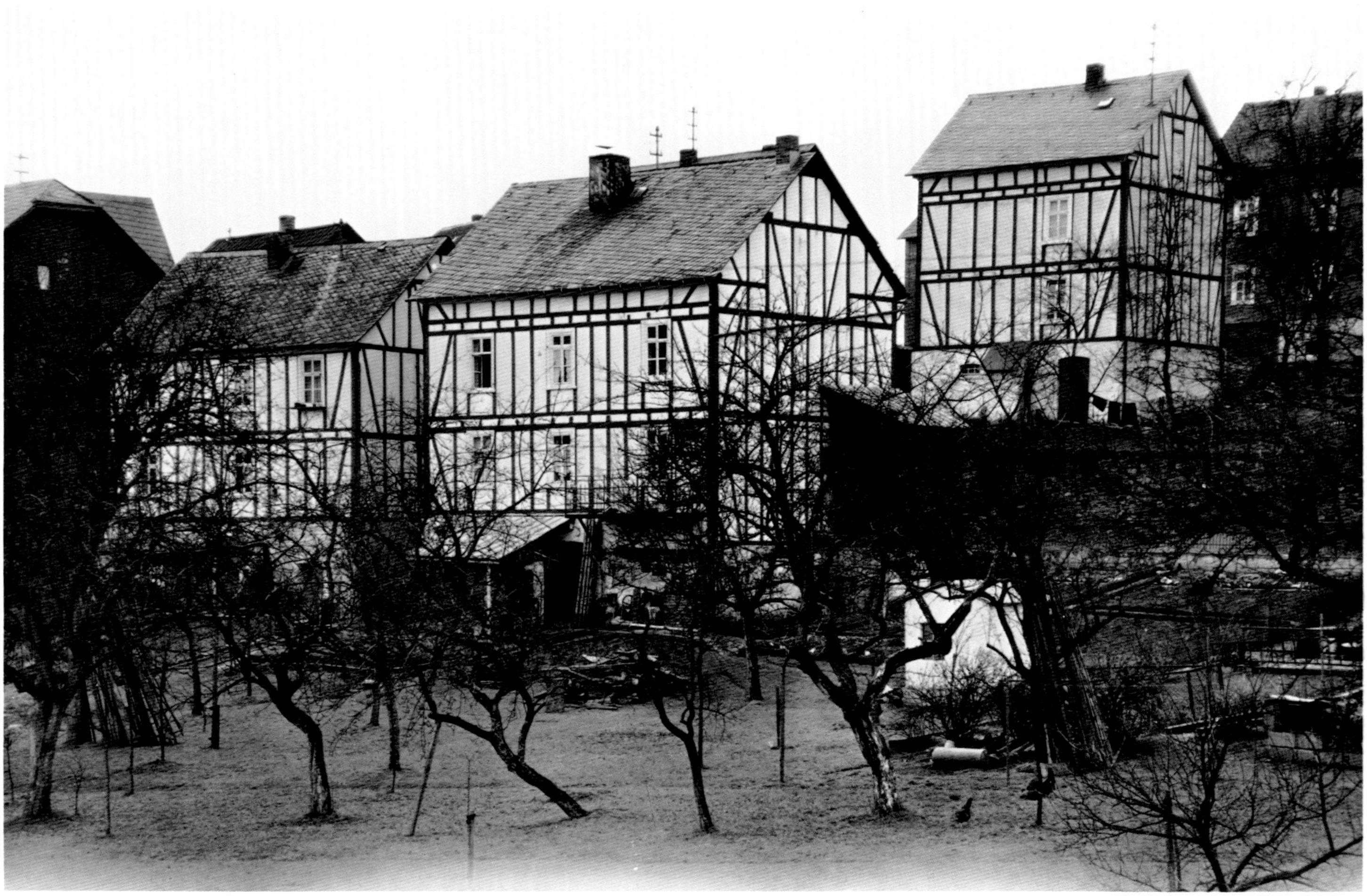

323
Arbachstraße, Salchendorf, 1959.

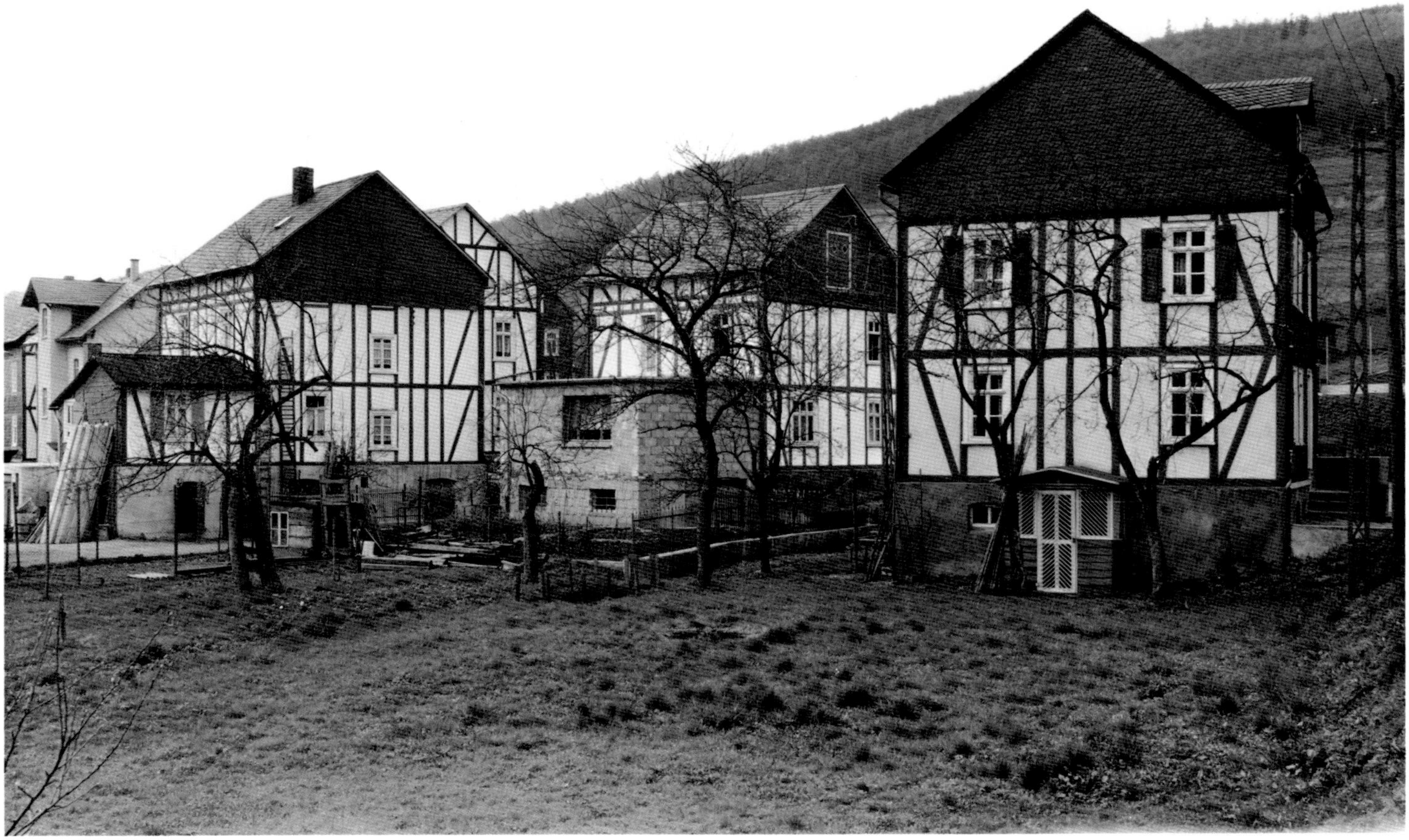

324
Eiserntalstraße, Eisern, 1960.

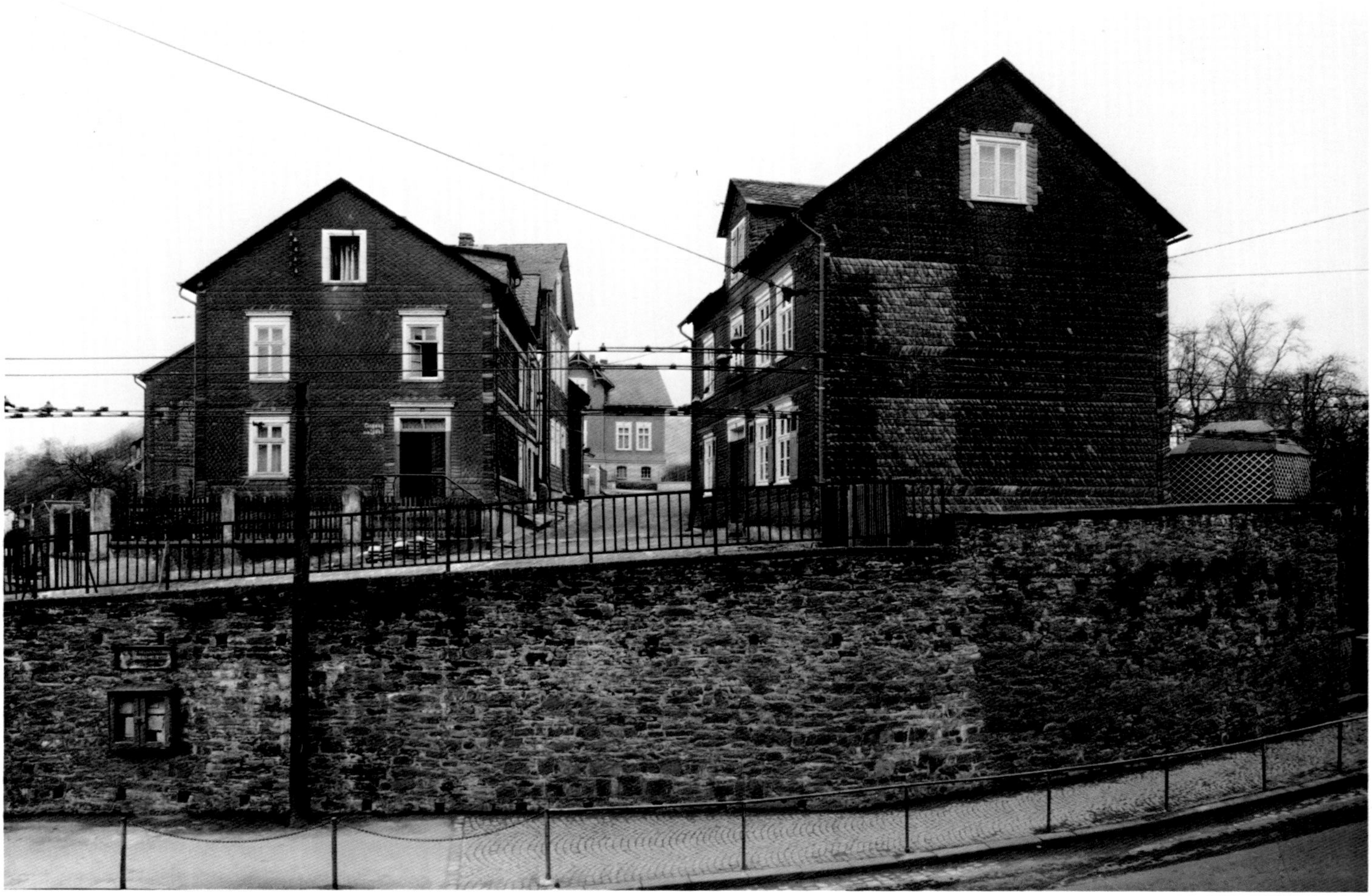

325

Höhstraße, Niederschelden, 1961.

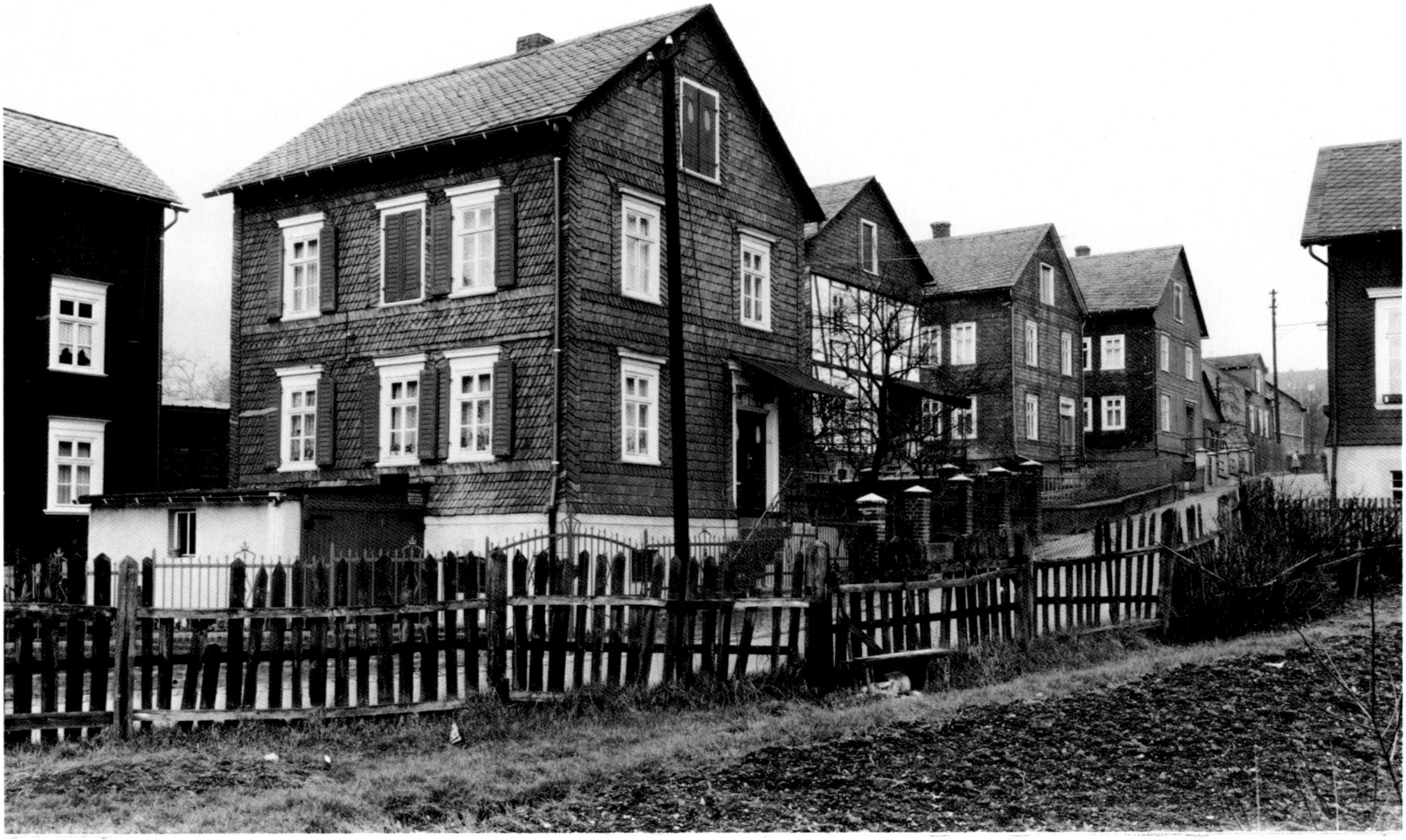

326
Bühlstraße, Niederschelden, 1960.

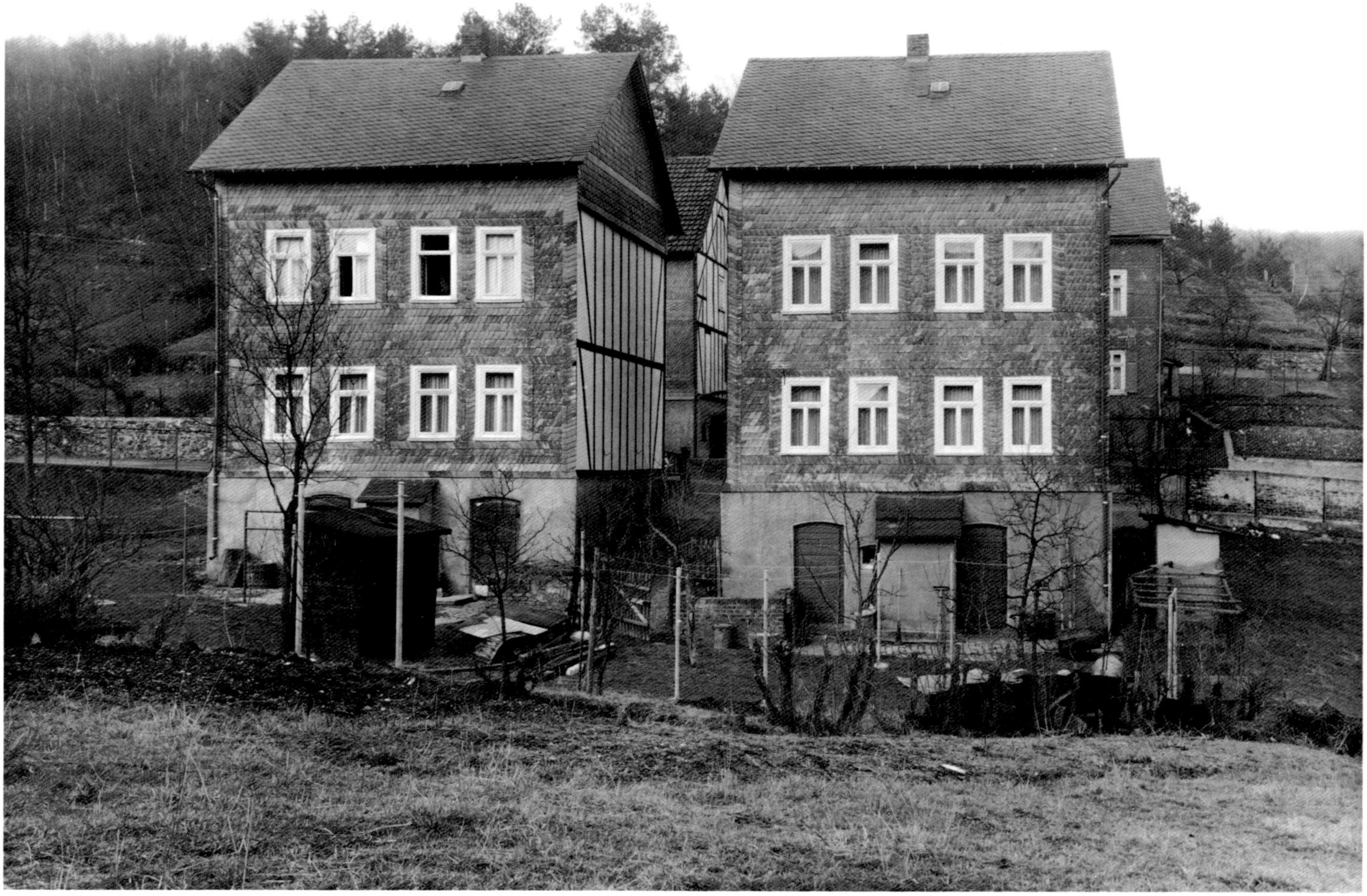

327
Maiweg, Gosenbach, 1960.

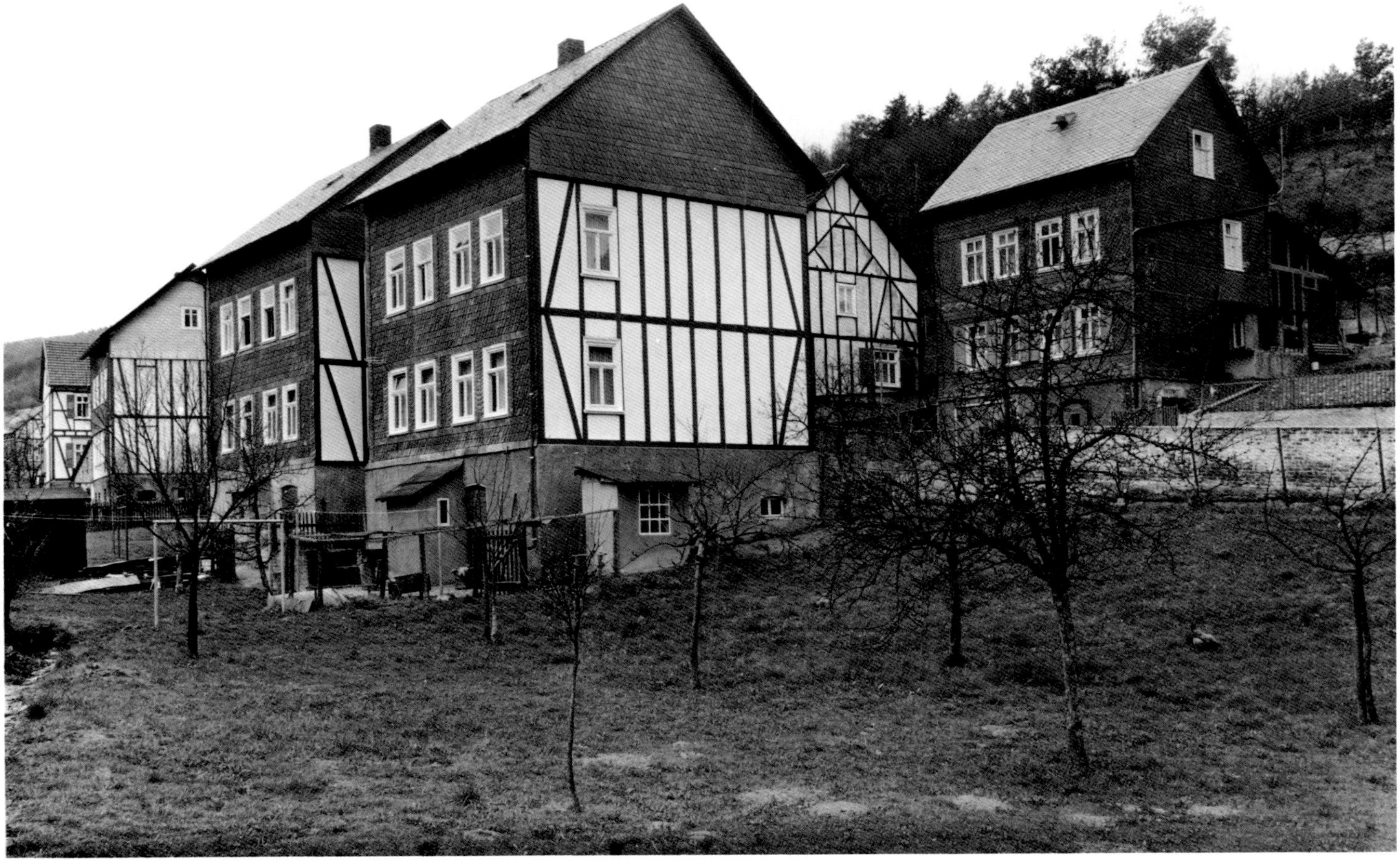

328
Maiweg, Gosenbach, 1960.

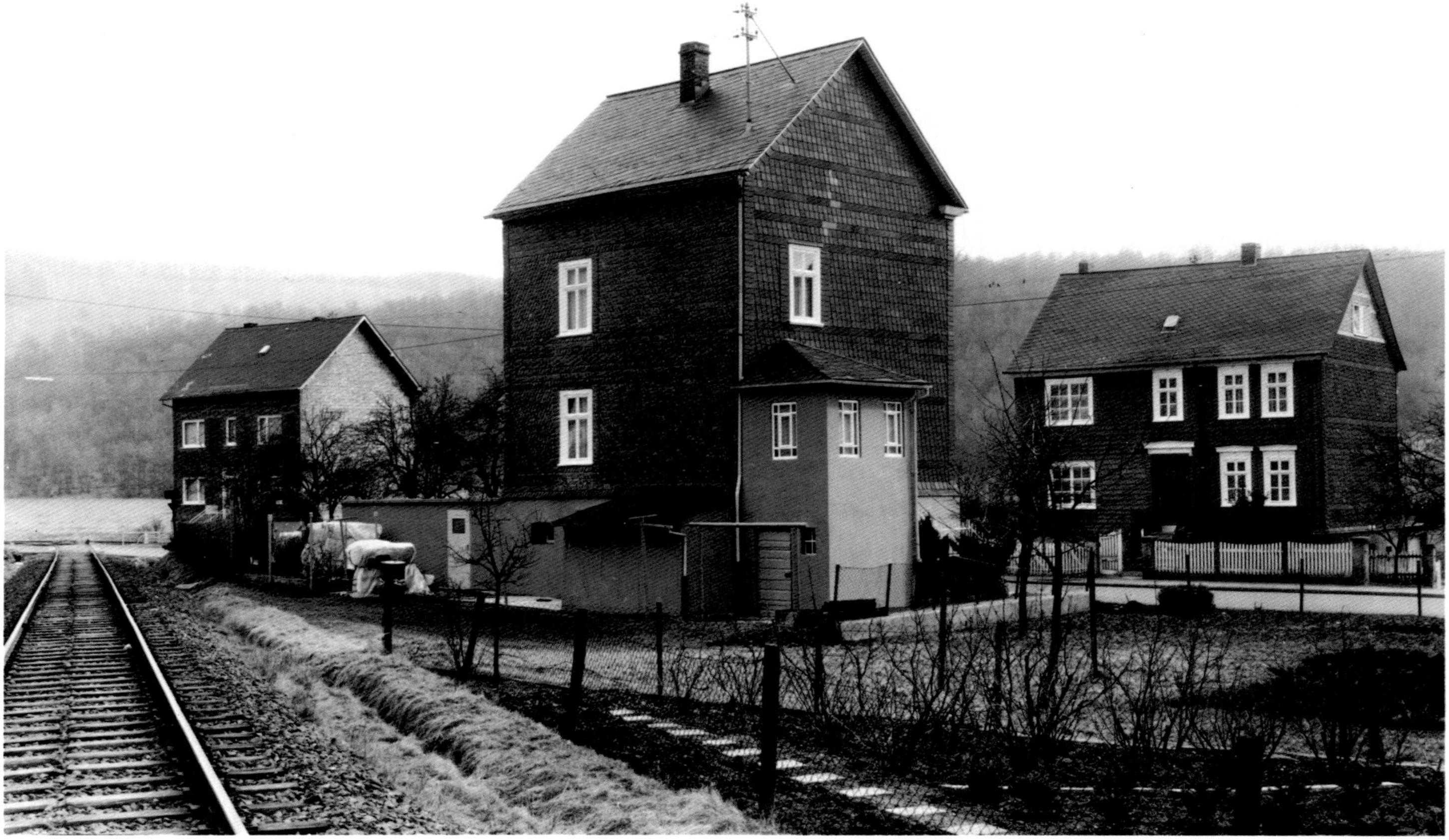

329
Wildener Straße, Salchendorf, 1970.

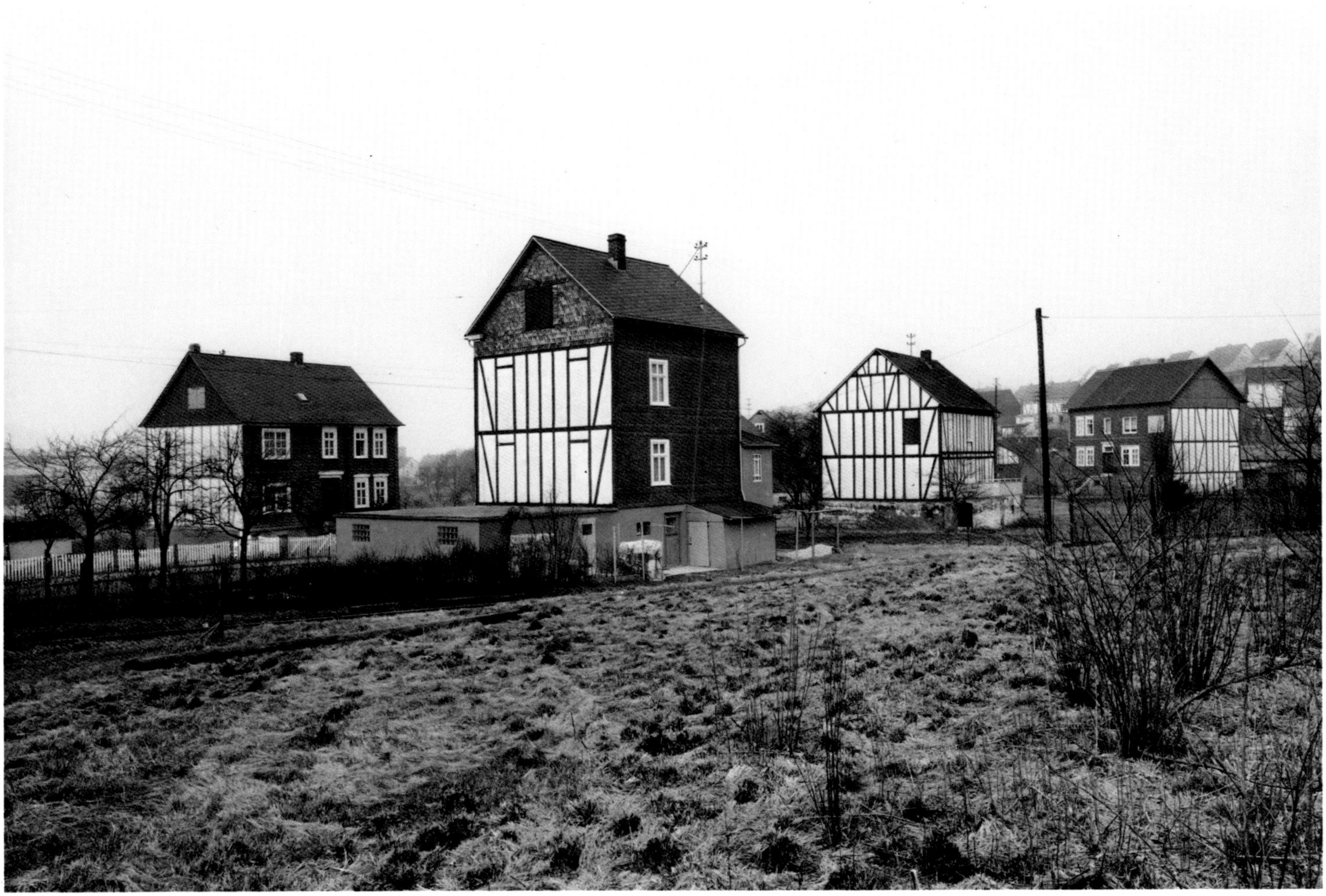

330
Wildener Straße, Salchendorf, 1970.

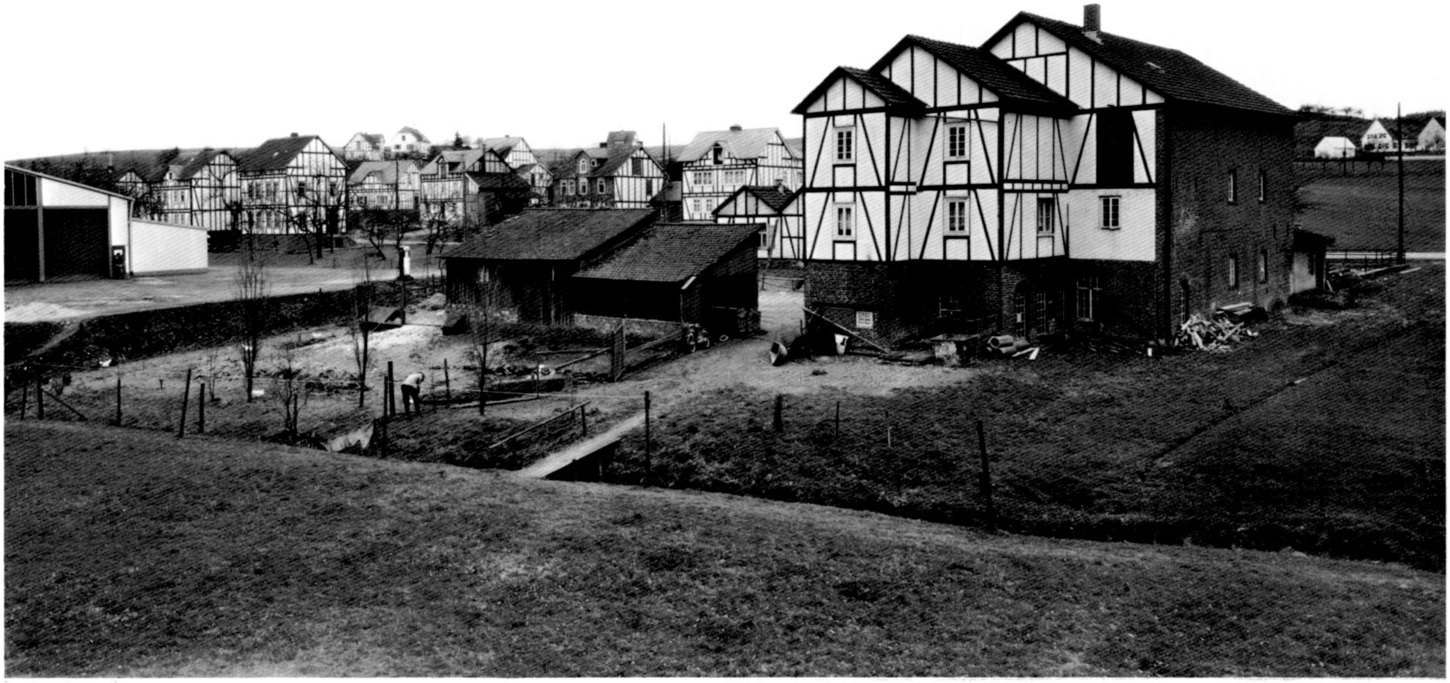

331
Triftstraße, Büschergrund, 1959.

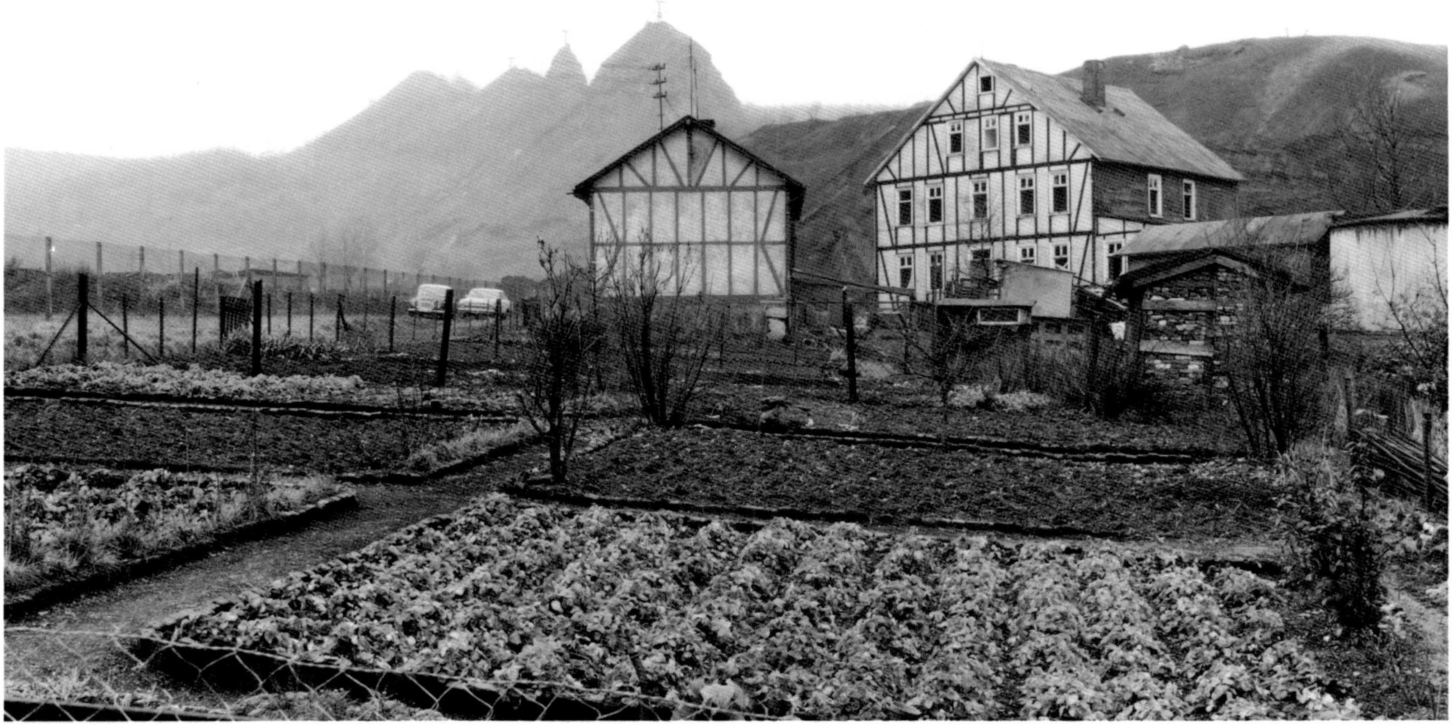

332
Friedhofstraße, Niederschelden, 1970.

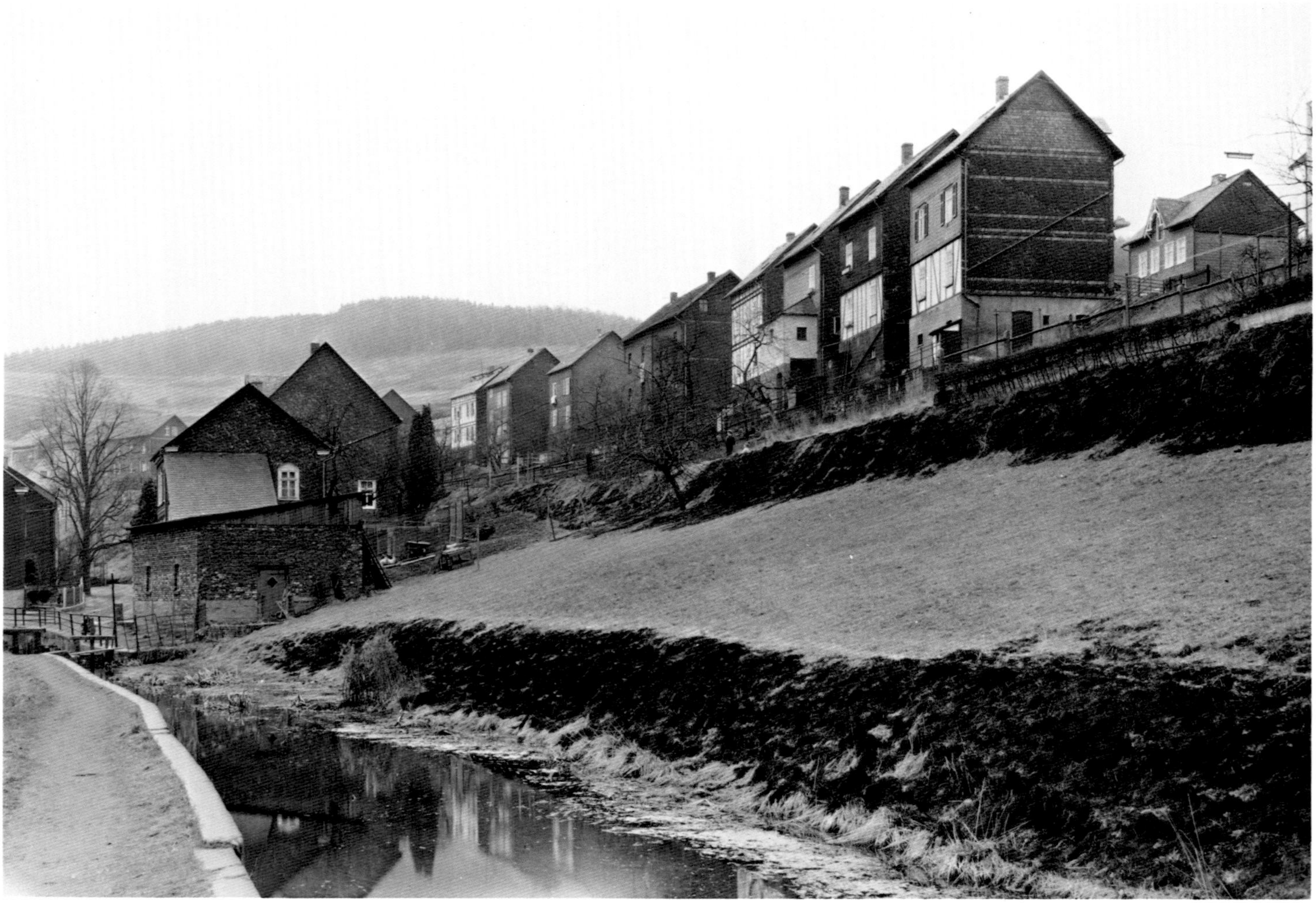

333
Freiengründerstraße, Eiserfeld, 1960.

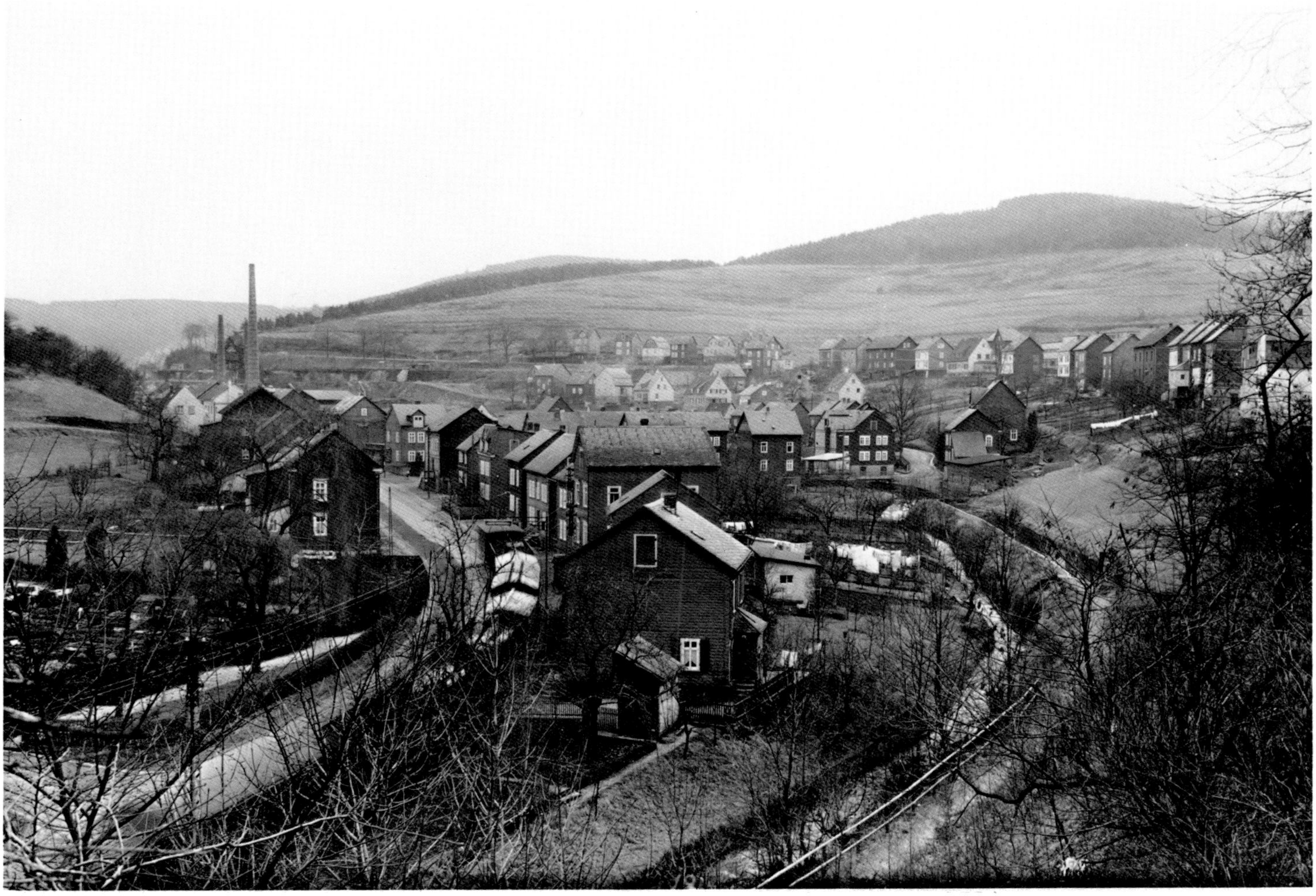

334
Eisernstraße, Eiserfeld, 1960.

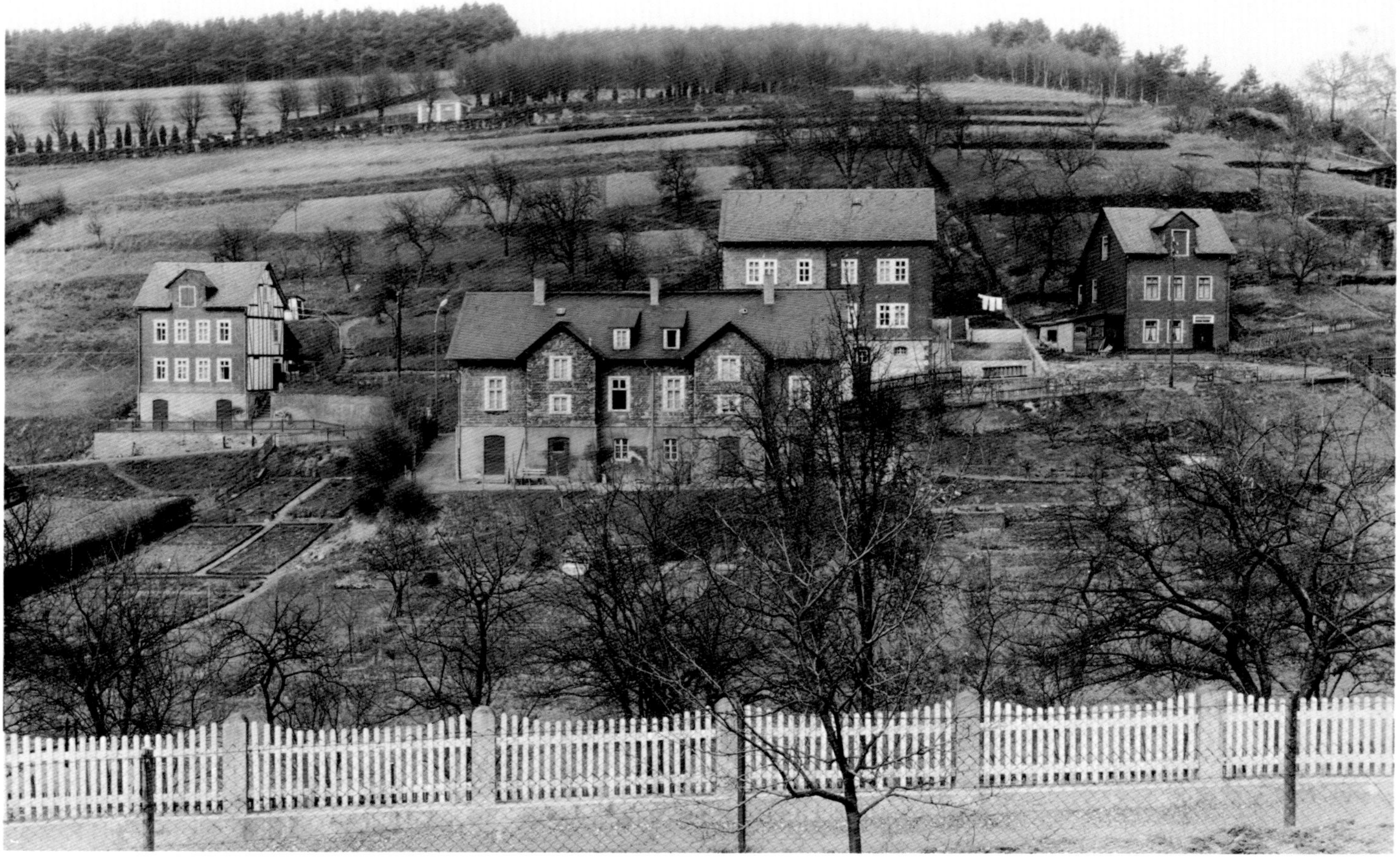

335
Friedhofstraße, Gosenbach, 1960.

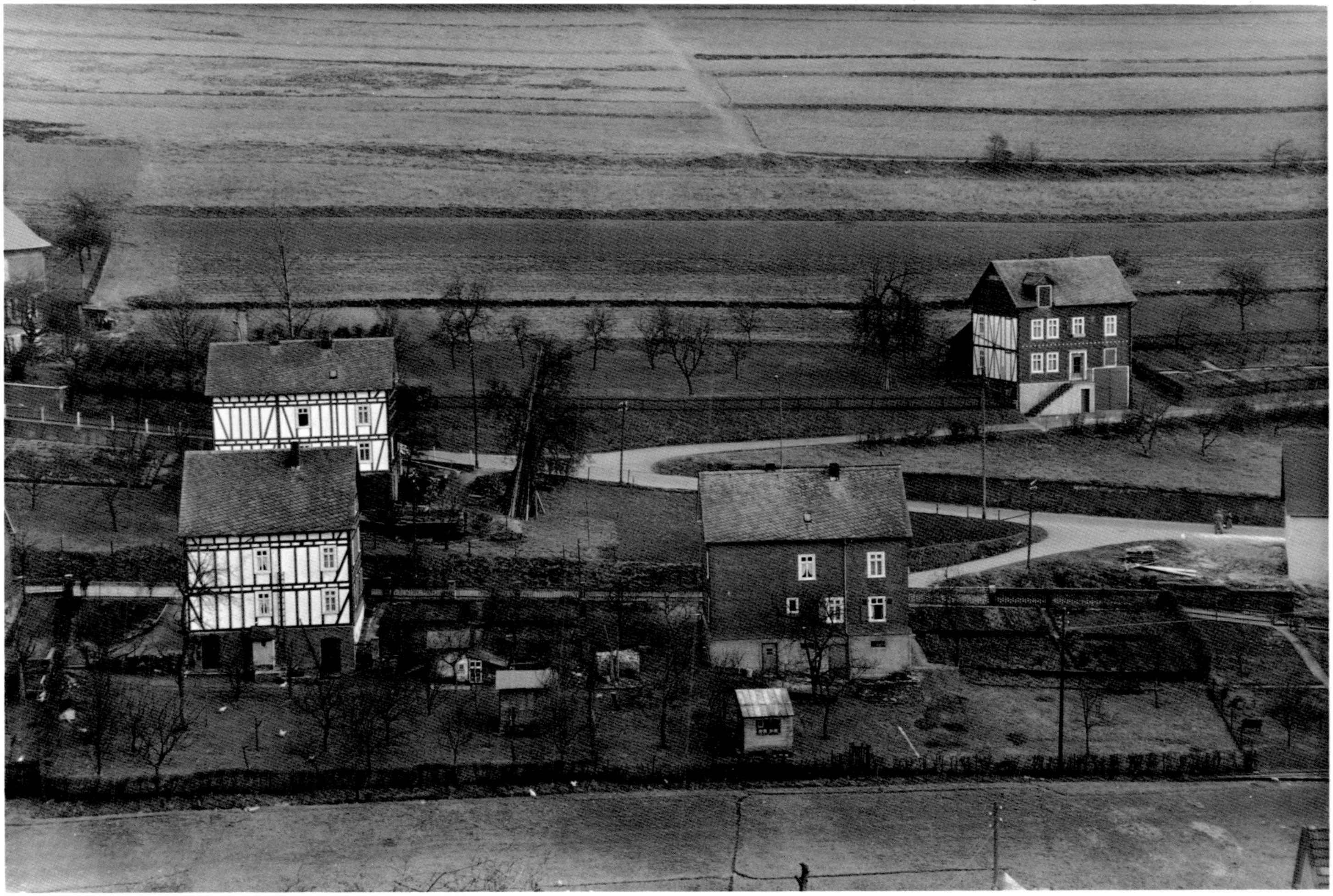

336
Siegener Straße, Gosenbach, 1960.

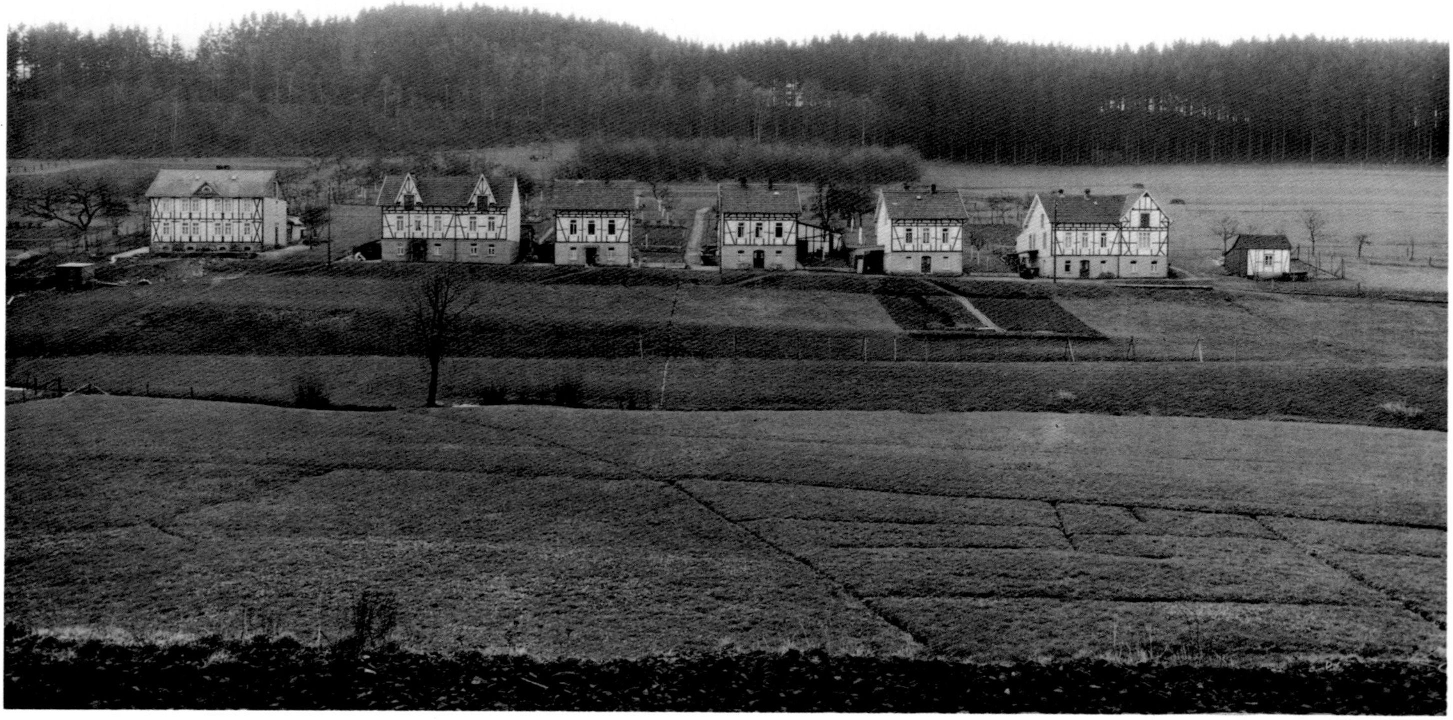

337
Sterzenbacher Straße, Hilchenbach, 1961.

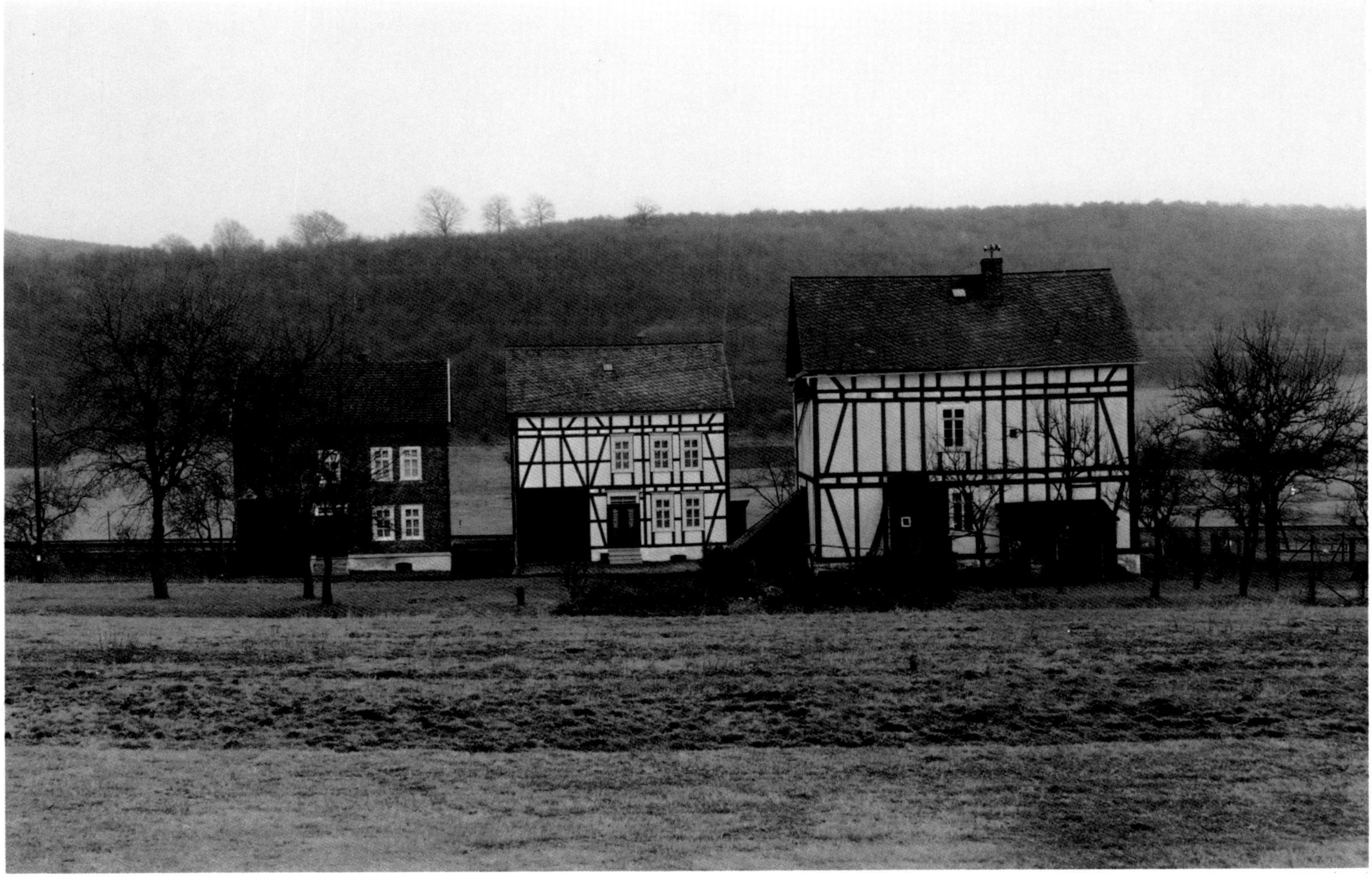

338
Wildener Straße, Salchendorf, 1960.

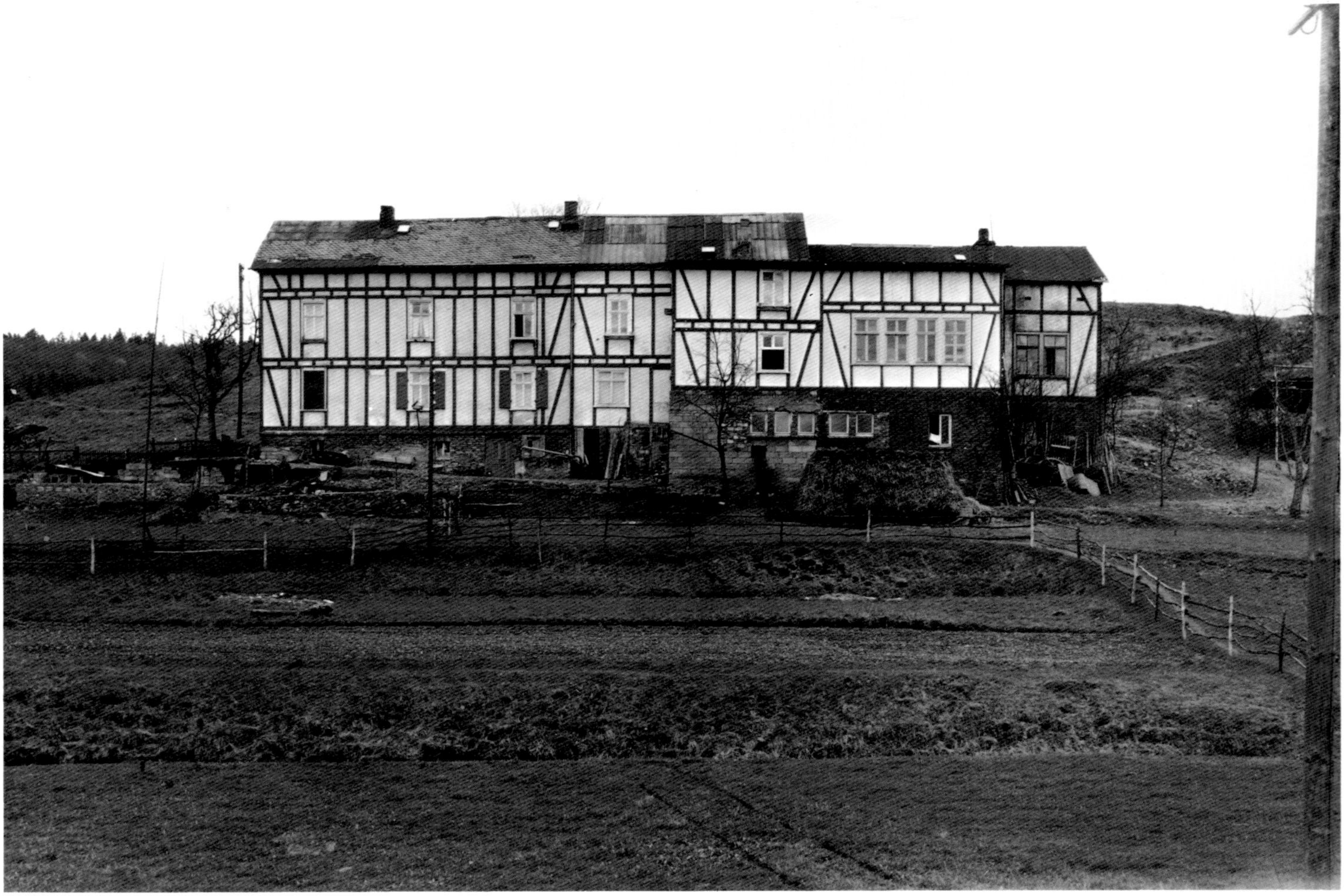

339
Am Wurmberg, Trupbach, 1959.

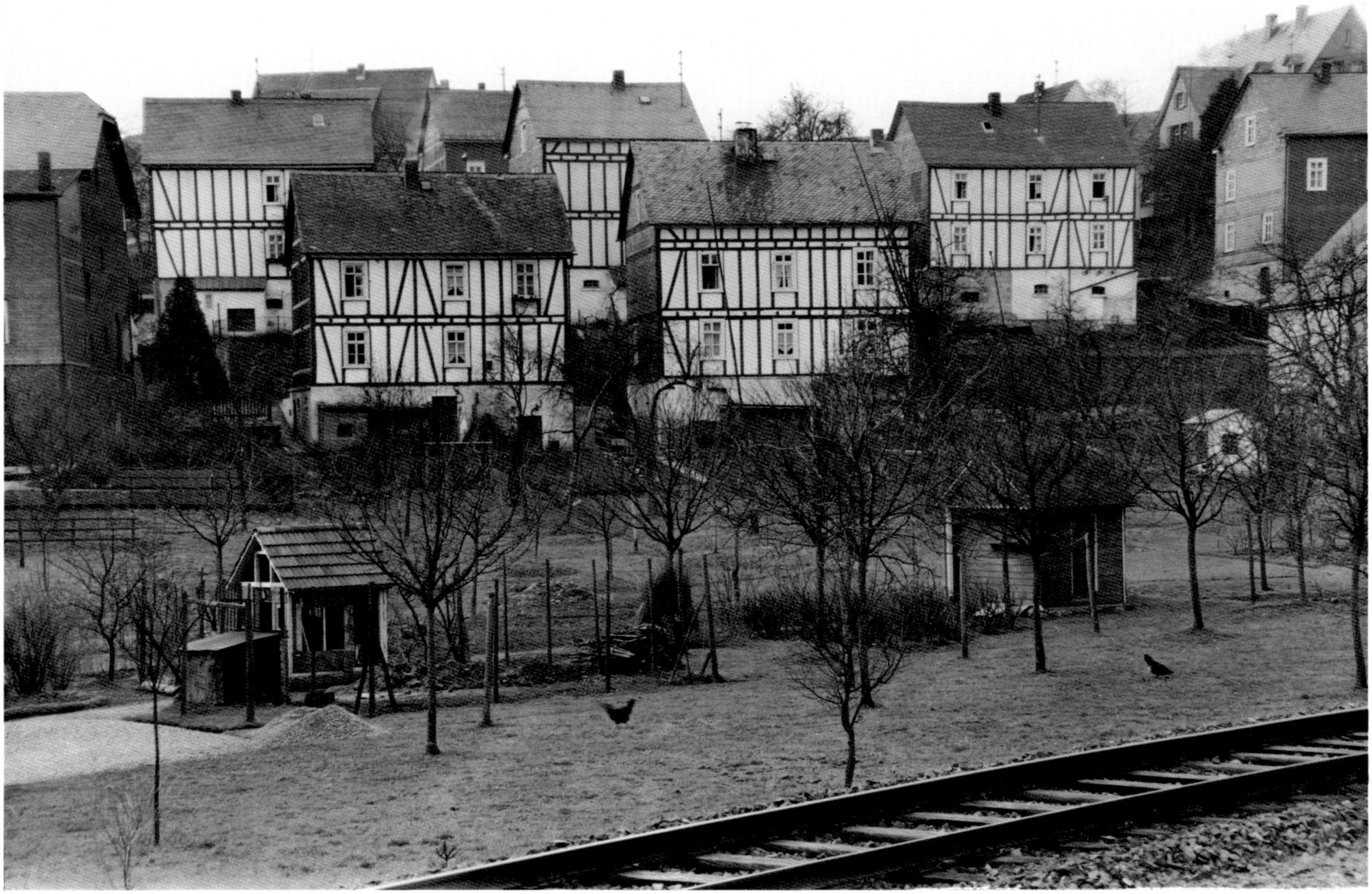

340
Kölner Straße/Arbachstraße, Salchendorf, 1959.

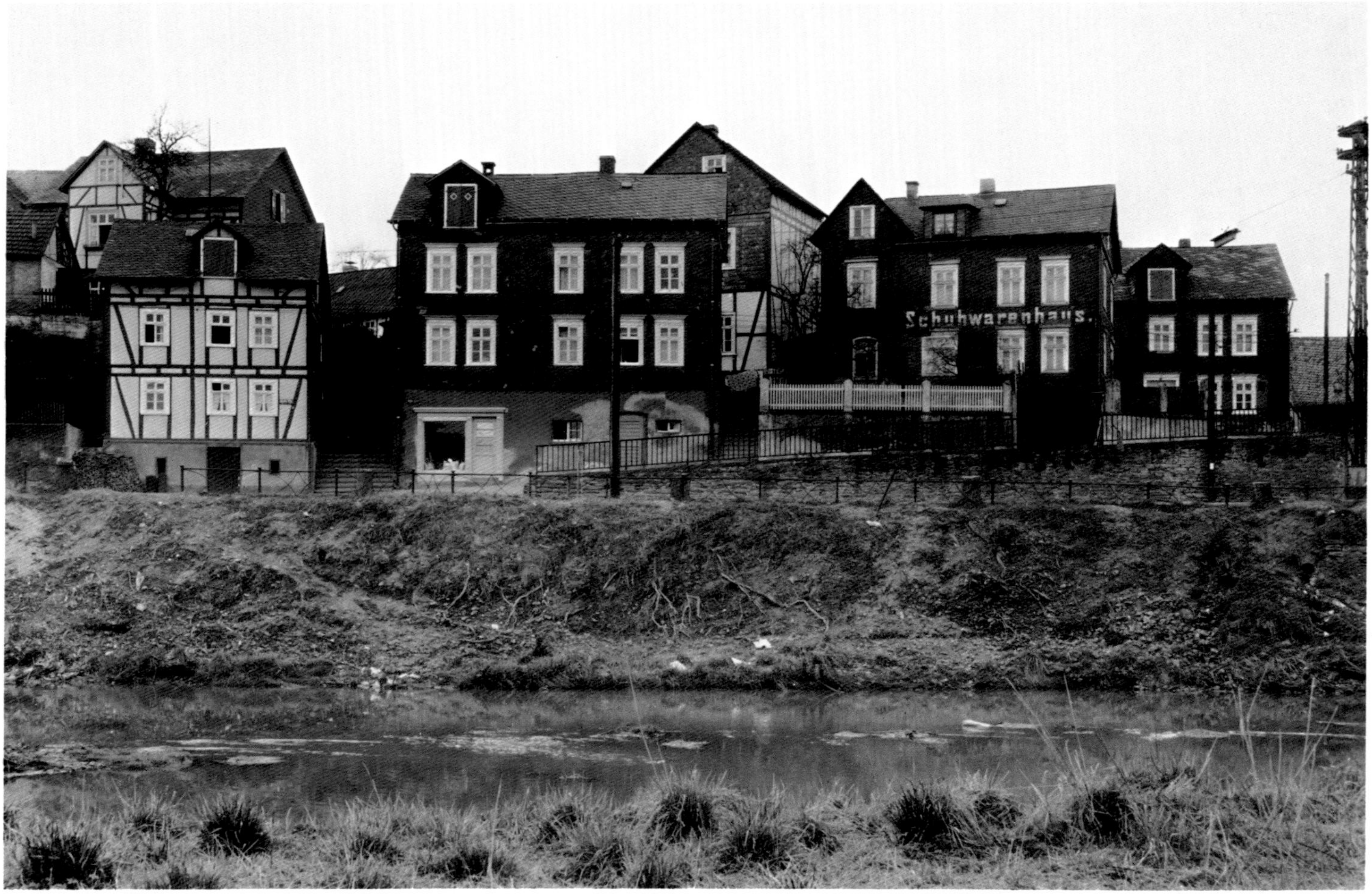

341
Siegtalstraße, Niederschelden, 1961.

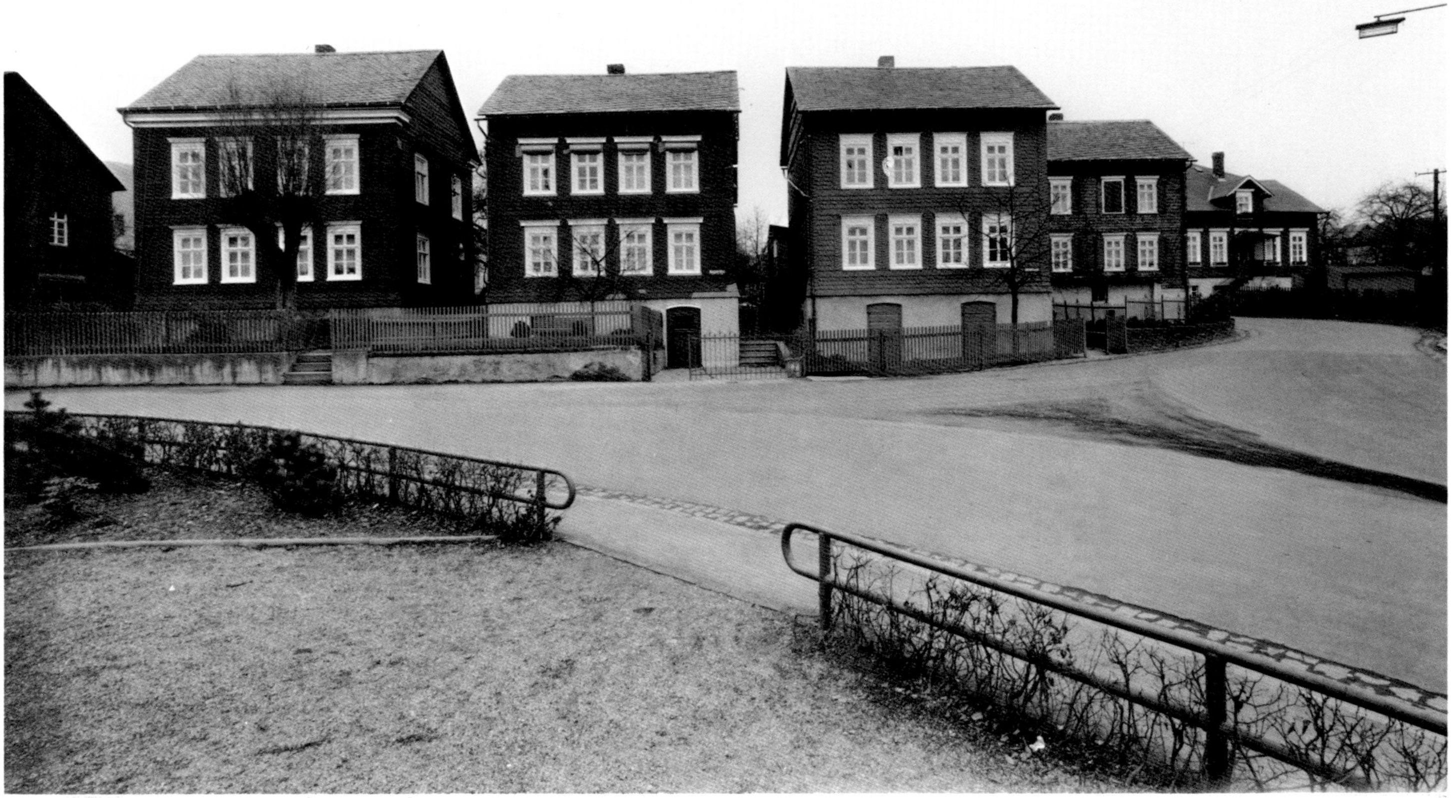

342
Bühlstraße, Niederschelden, 1960.

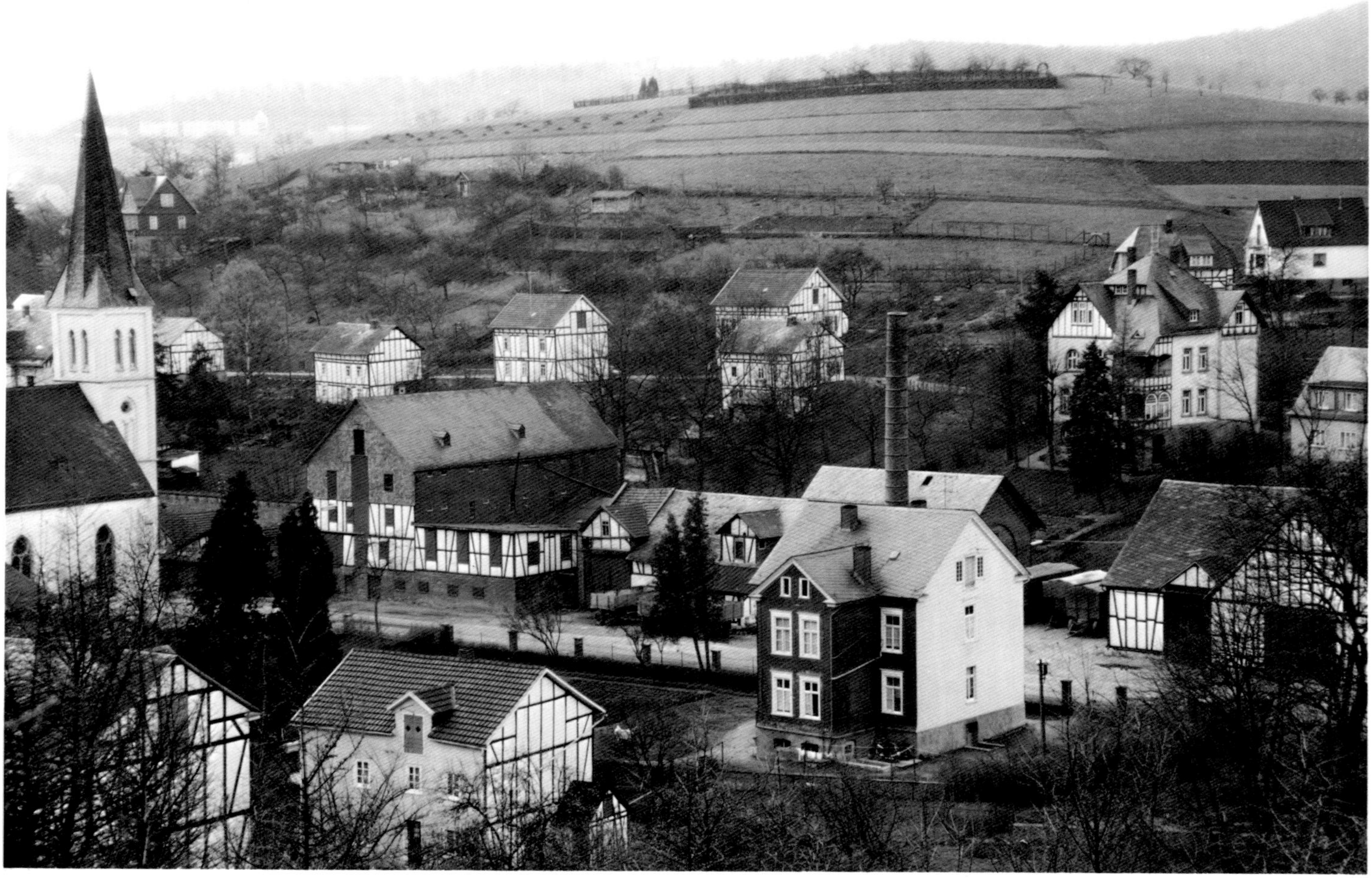

343
Bahnhofstraße, Freudenberg, 1961.

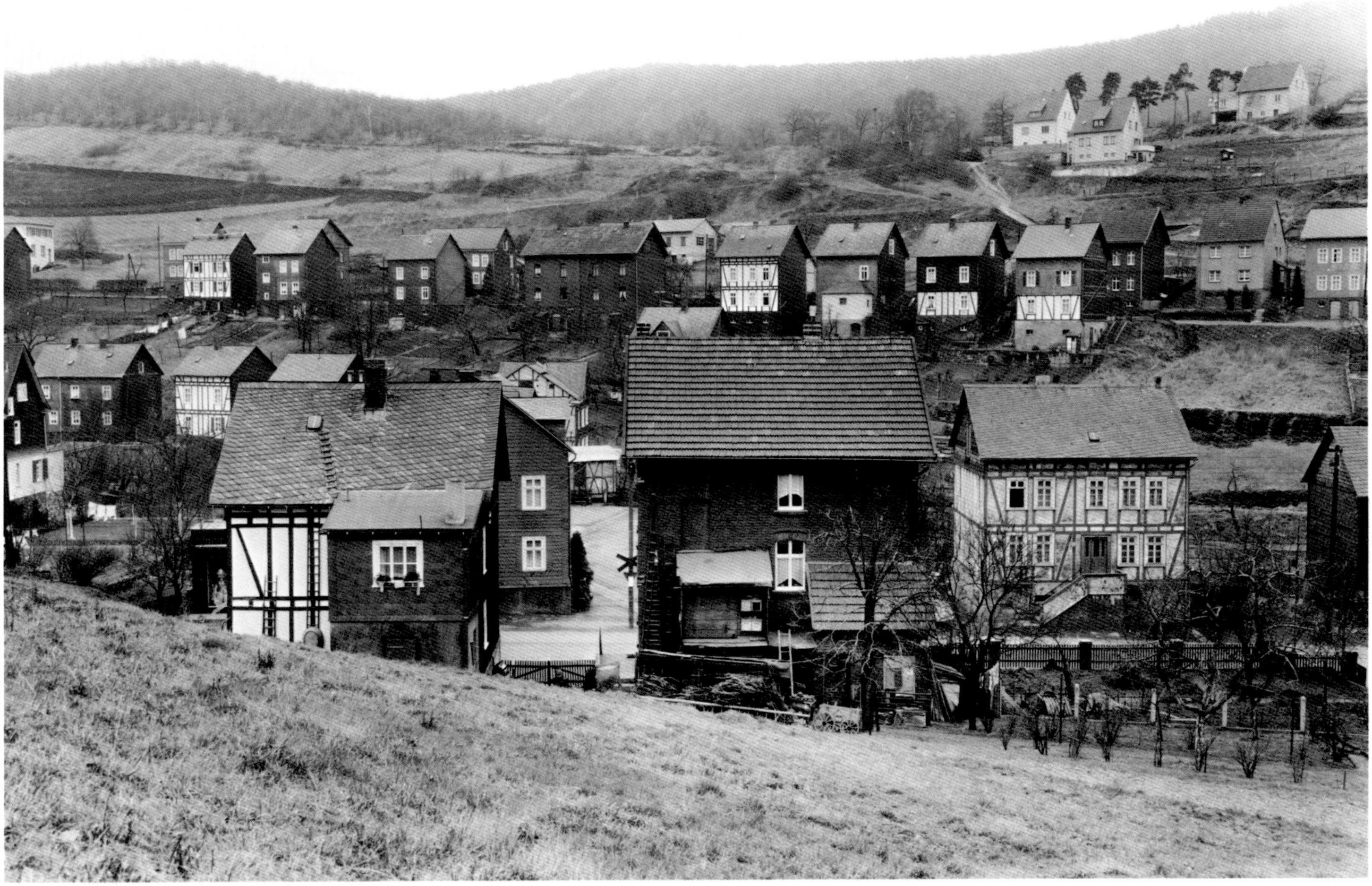

344
Eisernstraße/Freiengründerstraße, Eiserfeld, 1960.

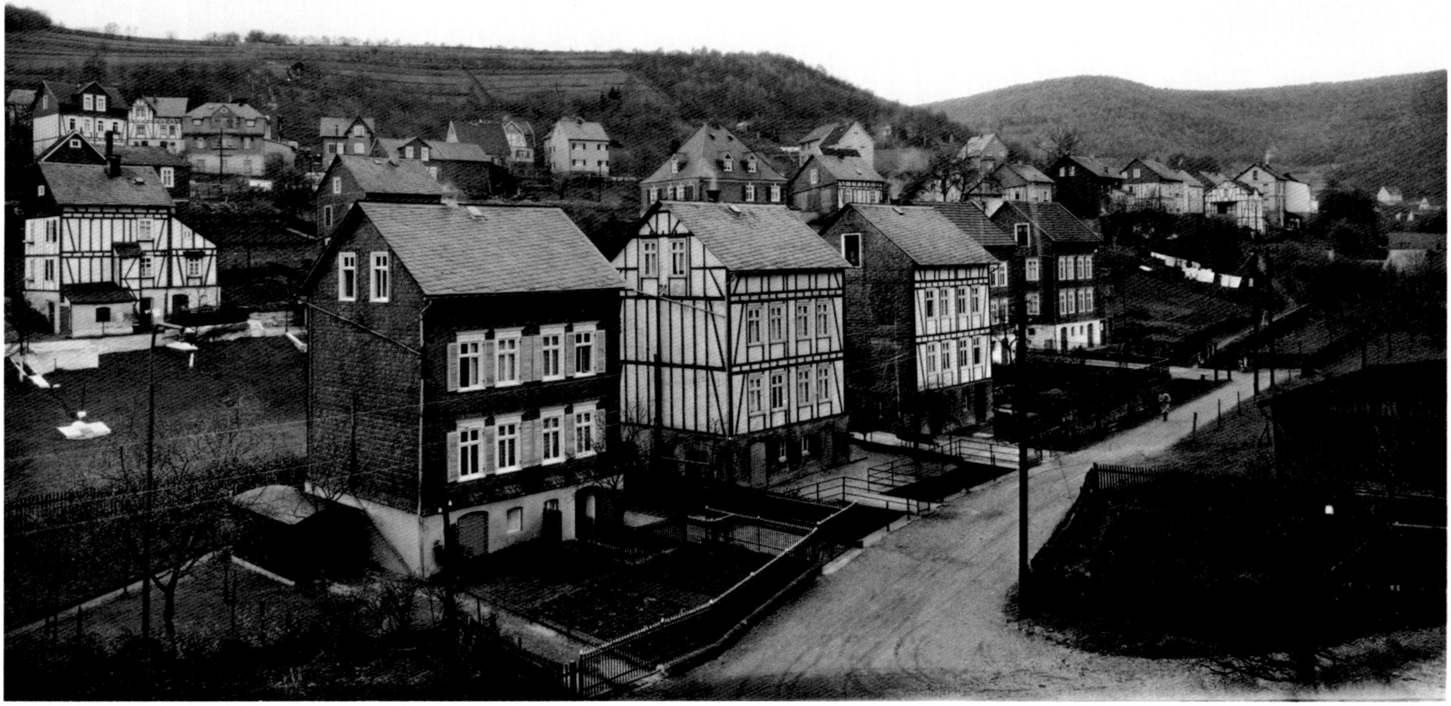

345
Am Gosenbach, Niederschelderhütte, 1961.

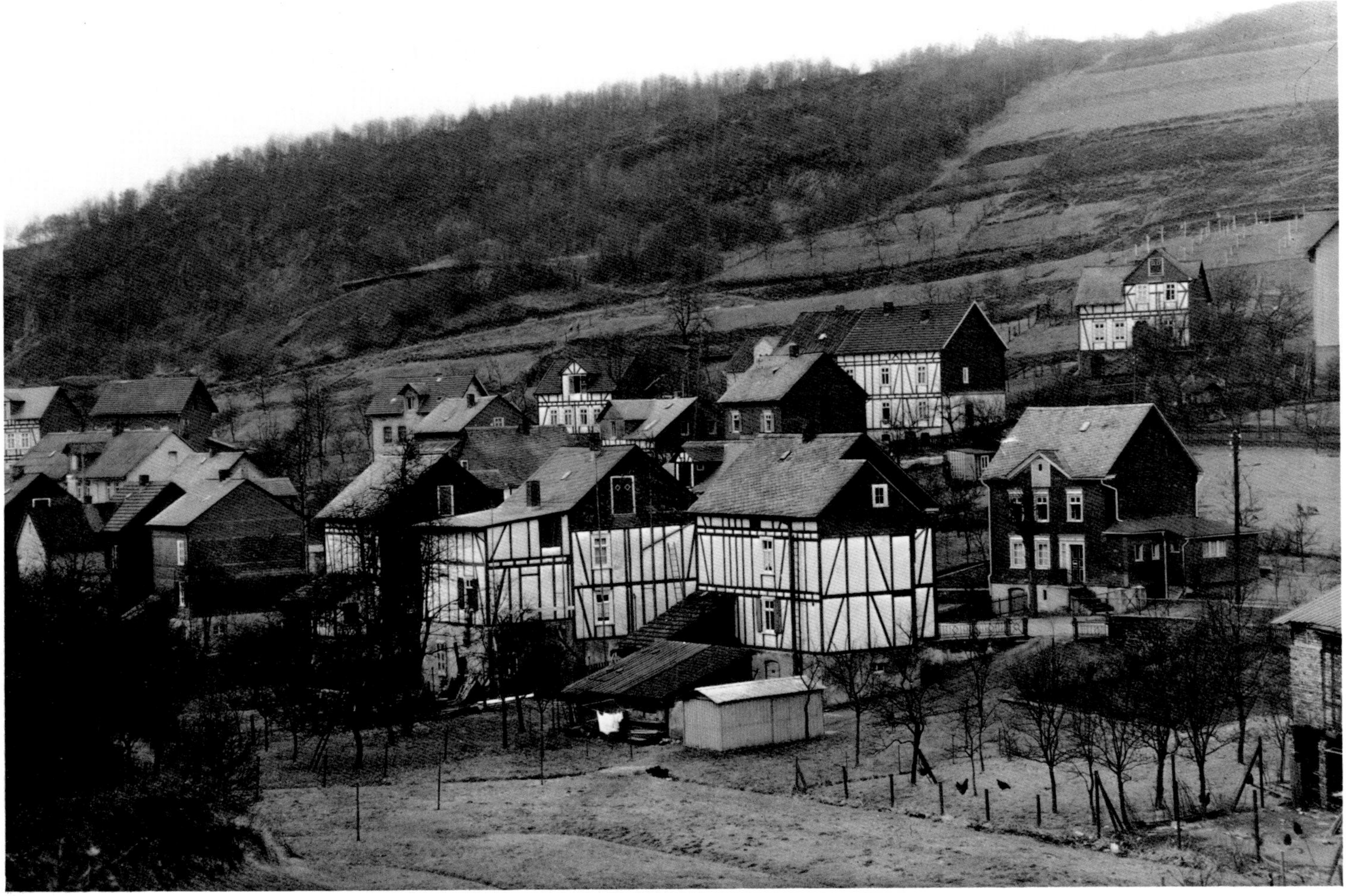

346

Kampenstraße, Gosenbach, 1960.

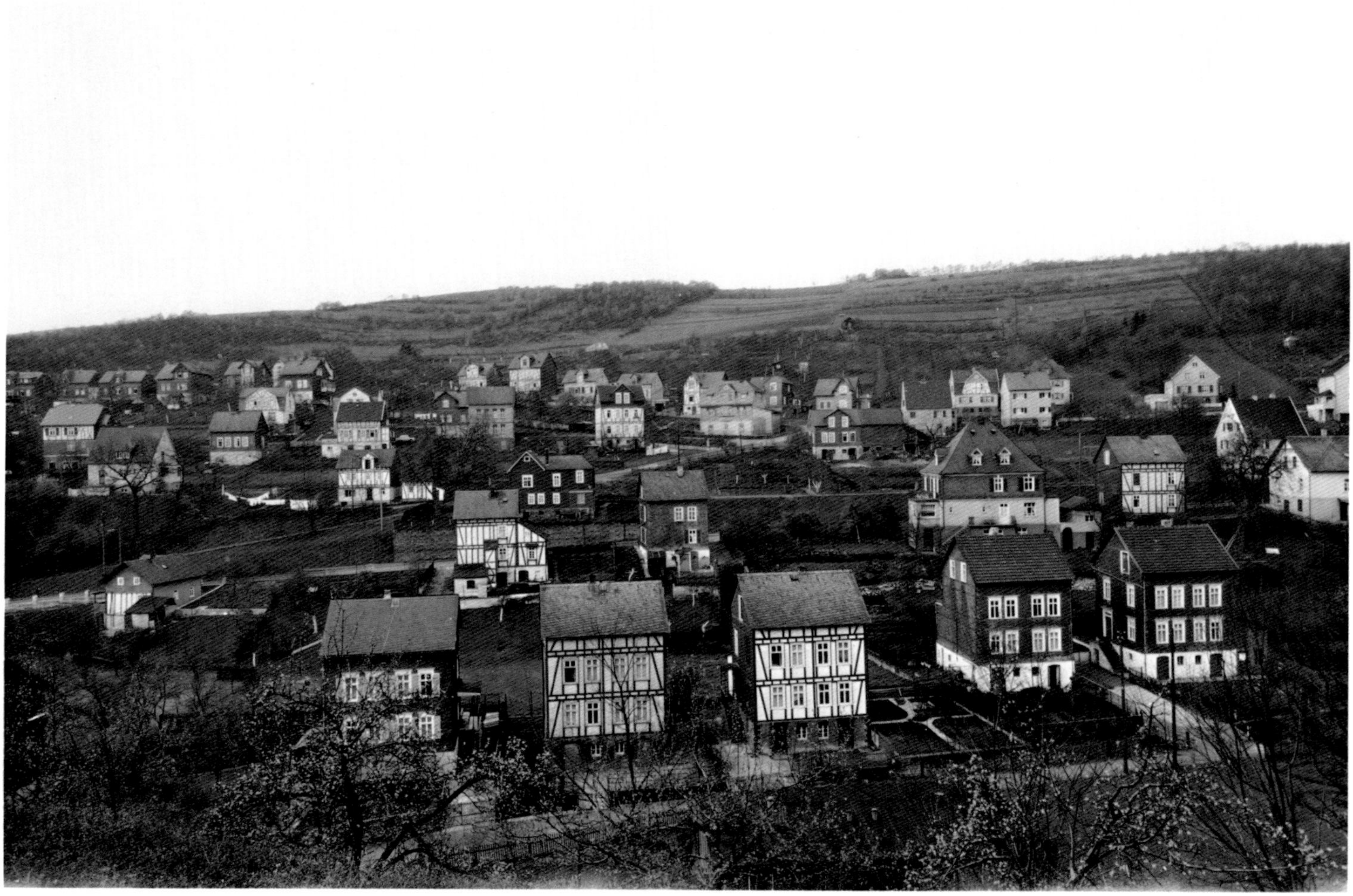

347
Am Gosenbach, Niederschelderhütte, 1961.

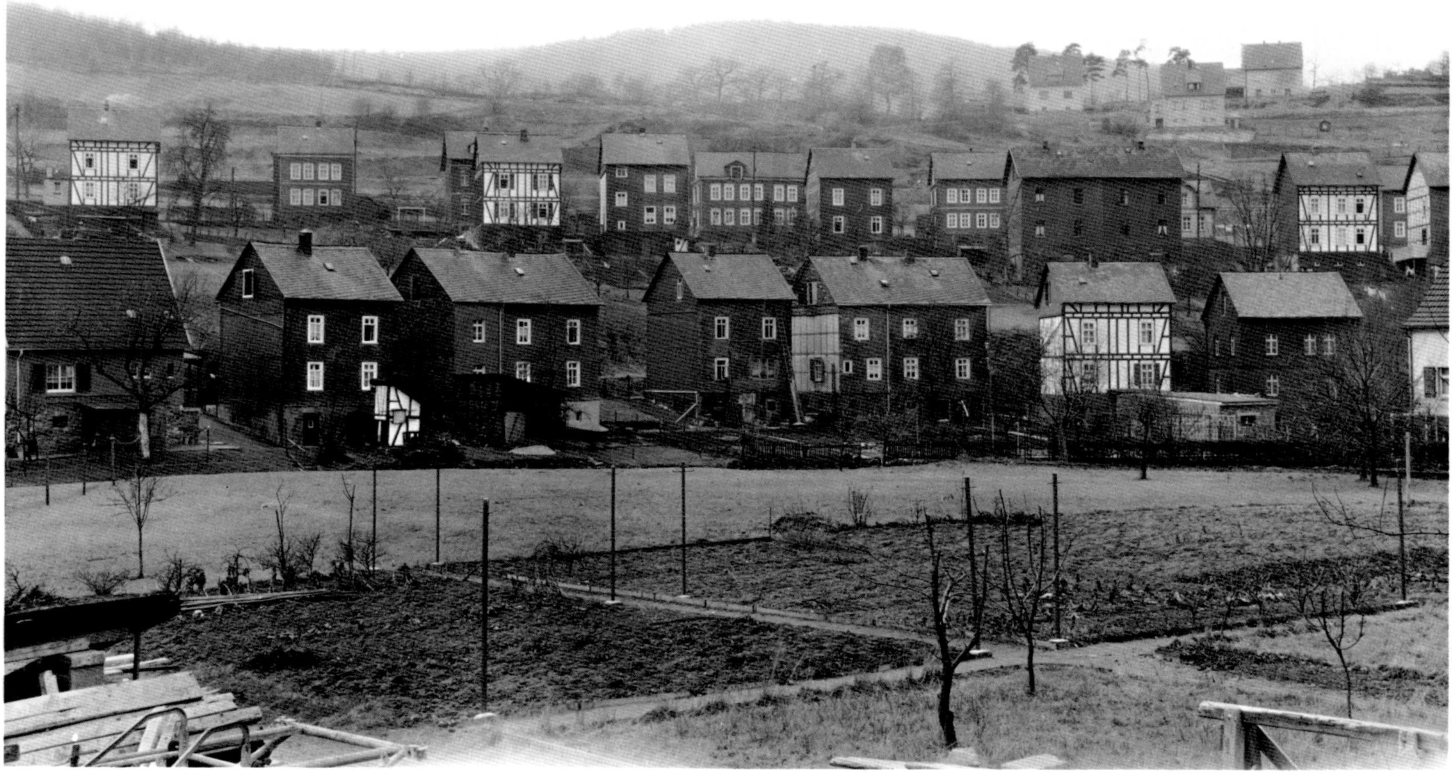

348
Hüttenstraße/Freiengründerstraße, Eiserfeld, 1960.

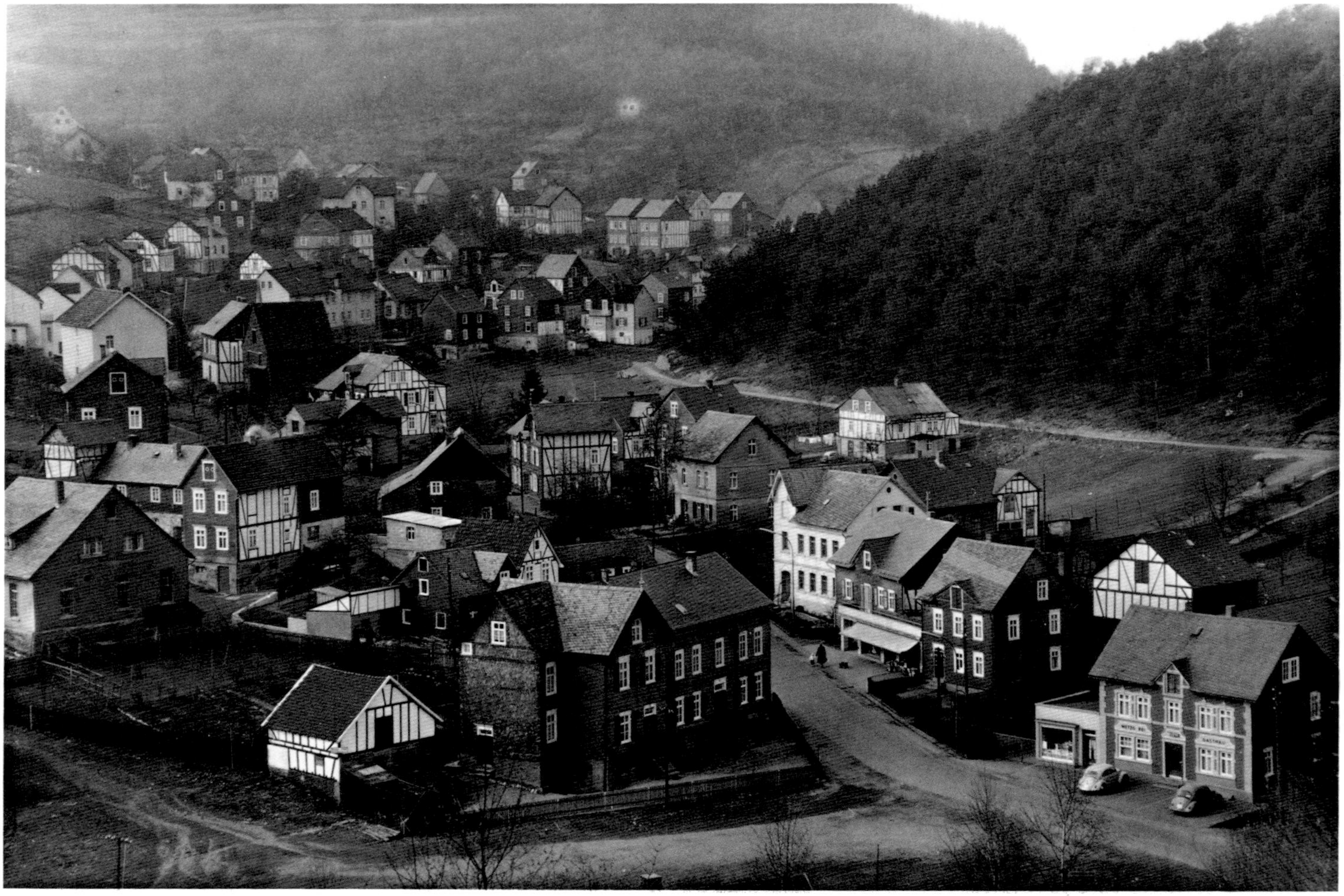

349

Gosenbach, 1961.

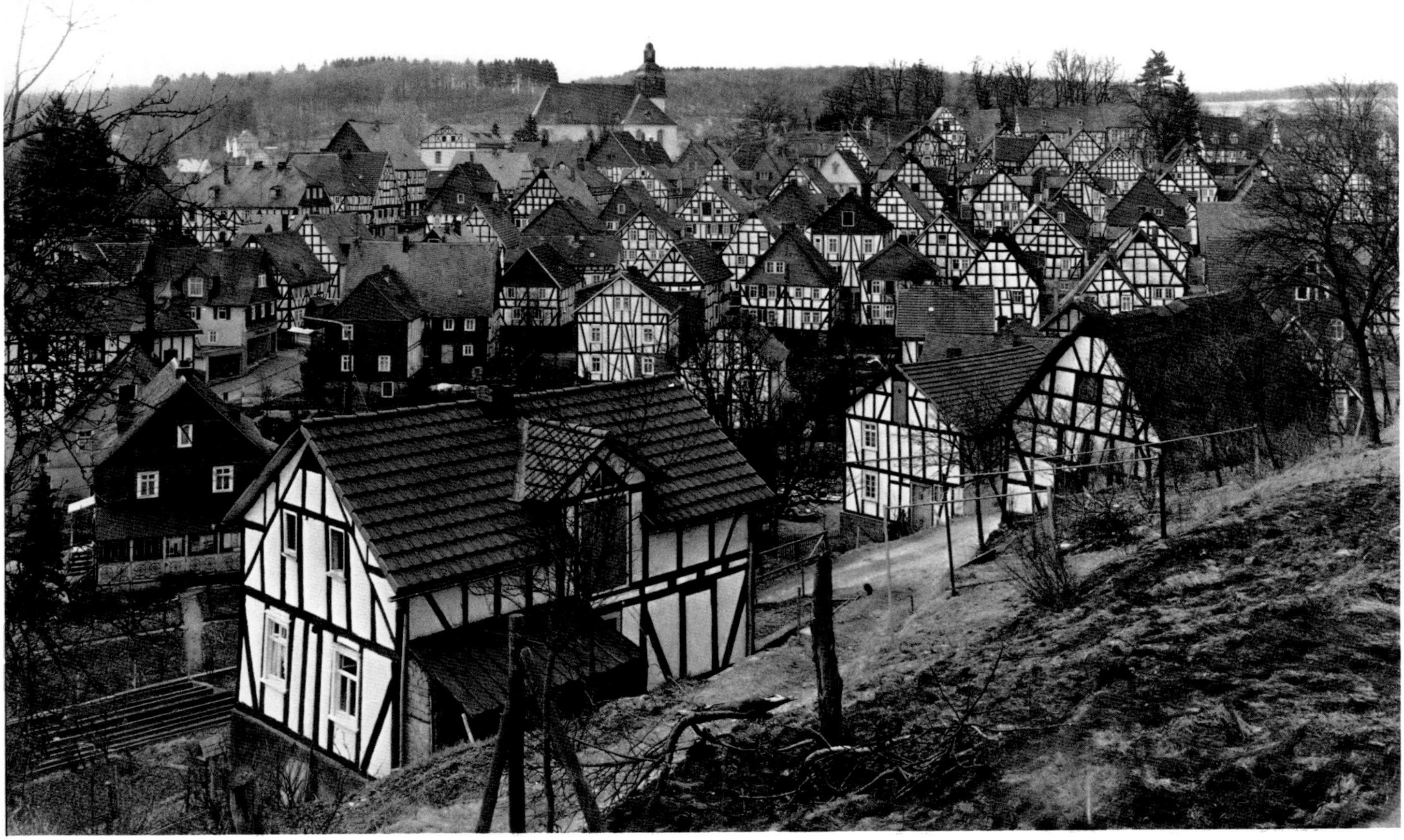

350
Freudenberg, 1962.